Silent Conflict

Silent Conflict

A Hidden History of Early Soviet-Western Relations

Michael Jabara Carley

ROWMAN & LITTLEFIELD
Lanham • Boulder • New York • Toronto • Plymouth, UK

Published by Rowman & Littlefield
4501 Forbes Boulevard, Suite 200, Lanham, Maryland 20706
www.rowman.com

10 Thornbury Road, Plymouth PL6 7PP, United Kingdom

British Library Cataloguing in Publication Information Available

Library of Congress Cataloging-in-Publication Data

Carley, Michael Jabara, 1945–, author.
  Silent conflict : a hidden history of early Soviet-Western relations / Michael Jabara
Carley.
      pages ; cm
  Includes bibliographical references and index.
  ISBN 978-1-4422-2585-5 (cloth : alk. paper) — ISBN 978-1-4422-2586-2 (electronic)
  1. Soviet Union—Foreign relations—Europe, Western—History. 2. Europe,
Western—Foreign relations—Soviet Union—History. 3. Soviet Union—Foreign
relations—1917–1945—History. I. Title.
  D34.S65C37 2014
  327.4704—dc23

                                                                    2013044395

∞™ The paper used in this publication meets the minimum requirements of
American National Standard for Information Sciences—Permanence of Paper
for Printed Library Materials, ANSI/NISO Z39.48-1992.

Printed in the United States of America

Contents

Figures

~

Preface

It is not easy to study the history of Soviet foreign policy or Soviet relations with the West. Until the beginning of the 1990s the Soviet archives were closed tight. After the collapse and dismemberment of the Soviet Union in 1991, the archives gradually opened, but only partially. Sometimes papers were opened only to be closed again. Russian archivists had tens of thousands of *papki*, or files, in their care and, not always knowing what was in them, were reluctant to open them to researchers. These include, inter alia, the important party archives for the inter-war years at *Rossiiskii gosudarstvennyi arkhiv sotsial'no-politicheskoi istorii* (RGASPI) and the diplomatic papers of the *Arkhiv vneshnei politiki Rossiiskoi Federatsii* (AVPRF), the archives of the Russian foreign ministry. In AVPRF there were and are all sorts of difficulties. Researchers have no access to inventories, so it's like playing poker when asking archivists for files. Sometimes the files are rich, and you win, and sometimes not, and you lose. Computers were forbidden for a number of years, and photocopies were so costly as to make a new arrival gasp for air. You got used to the impediments and learned to function around them. The excitement of new discoveries and uncharted ground made you forget the numerous irritations.

The APRF, or presidential archives, contains the papers sent to I. V. Stalin's secretariat. These remain closed, but rich collections from the APRF files are being published.[1] If researchers do not have full access to the Soviet archives, they have sufficient access now to create a new narrative and draw fresh conclusions about the various questions and challenges which faced Soviet policy makers during the formative years of the Soviet Union in the

1920s. The following account draws to a close in early 1930 on the eve of the long run-up to the Second World War and to the eventual formation of the Grand Alliance against the Axis powers.

As readers will quickly notice, this book is rooted in Soviet archival sources. It gives direct voice to the Soviet leaders and officials who made the Russian Revolution and who directed the early Soviet Union. Readers will no doubt recognize familiar names like Lenin, Trotskii, and Stalin. But there are other actors in this narrative, not so well known, who played important roles in the history which you are about to read. Their names are Chicherin, Dovgalevskii, Ioffe, Krasin, Karakhan, Krestinskii, Litvinov, Maiskii, Rakovskii, and Stomoniakov, among others.

These diplomats were among the first generation of Soviet representatives to face "the West" and to establish a Soviet place in the world. They came mostly from the middle-class elite of tsarist Russia. Rarely workers or peasants, they were highly educated in the law, history, philosophy, economics, and medicine. They were multi-lingual, well read, erudite. Sometimes they had obtained a formal university education; sometimes it was informal, obtained as they served time in tsarist jails. Not a few escaped incarceration or Siberian exile and spent long periods in Europe before revolution broke out in 1917. They looked and dressed like members of the bourgeoisie whence they came, with wool jackets and trousers and silk ties. They did not carry grenades in their pockets or pistols in their belts. Nor did they look like western caricatures of the filthy Bolshevik anarchist, armed with smoking bomb and long, blood-drenched knife. These diplomats were dedicated to the Soviet state which they had helped to construct. They were courageous men, and occasionally women, who had often risked their lives during the revolution and following civil war. They knew that if the revolution failed, there would be no mercy shown to them. It was win or die.

The Soviet dramatis personae of this narrative will speak directly to you, the reader, from the papers, memoranda, letters, and reports they left behind and which have been preserved in the Russian archives, many in remarkably fresh condition, as though they might have been written only recently. They will not speak to you secondhand through intermediaries.

By intermediaries I mean their counterparts in Western Europe and the United States. Until the 1990s historians had necessarily to depend on western sources and archives to write their histories of Soviet foreign relations. Even now, some historians still write about the Soviet Union and its international relations without reading the Russian sources.[2]

Because scholars did not have access to Soviet archives, they depended on the judgments and prejudices of western officials, French, British, and American, for example, who hated the Bolsheviks and all their works. Naturally, historians tended to view their Soviet interlocutors through an anti-communist prism which distorted Soviet motives and objectives. Historians often picked up the prejudices of their historical characters from the West, even defending them or presenting their views as fact.

This situation led to errors or misperceptions in the analysis of Soviet foreign policy even by the best scholars and journalists in the field. Louis Fischer, an American journalist, who interviewed a number of Soviet diplomats during the 1920s, said they were divided between pro-German or pro-British and pro-French factions.[3] This is untrue. As readers will discover, Soviet diplomats were neither pro-German nor pro-British, for example; they were pro-Soviet, and they viewed relations with the western states according to their calculations of Russian national interests.

The late, distinguished British historian E. H. Carr rejected out of hand a "bureaucratic politics" model where Soviet foreign policy was subject to intra-governmental rivalries. According to Carr, there were no divergences of policy. Everything was decided in the Politburo, or Soviet cabinet. The NKID, or Commissariat for Foreign Affairs, had no policies or influence of its own. There was no split between NKID "moderates" and Communist Party "hotheads." Public quarreling in the Soviet press between the moderates and the hotheads was mere propaganda to confuse the West. "Not too much should be made of their differences," writes British historian Zara Steiner.[4] These assumptions are also in error.

The late American historian Adam B. Ulam, an energetic defender of a Cold War analysis of Soviet policy, held to a similar view. It was a myth to suppose that Soviet diplomats could "change the ideological content of Soviet policy." There was no contention between the NKID and the Comintern or Communist International, controlled from Moscow. They were strands of the same Soviet foreign policy laid down by the Politburo. With a single exception, according to Ulam, there were no independent-minded Soviet diplomats during the inter-war years. The Soviet worldview was "surrealistic," seeing the capitalist states as determined upon the destruction of the USSR.[5] Not true either, as readers will soon discover. In hindsight, Ulam's views can be seen as ideologically motivated caricatures of a more complicated reality.

British historian Robert Service attempts to update Ulam: "If [Stalin] is judged by his own speeches and articles, [he] rejected any suggestion that Soviet foreign policy was based on the selfish pragmatism of the USSR as a single state." The key rider here is whether Stalin's public statements actually reflected the real directions of Soviet foreign policy. He would not have been the first politician, or the last, to use speech in order to conceal his thoughts. According to Service, and there is no reason to doubt him, Stalin was, inter alia, a past master of subterfuge and dissimulation.[6]

Over-simplifications about the Soviet Union were commonplace in the Cold War environment after 1945, but before it too. Most western historians consider the Cold War to have begun after World War II, but in fact, the great ideological struggle between the West and Soviet Russia began in 1917, the day after the Bolshevik seizure of power in Petrograd, the Russian capital. The Red Scare and containment were first phenomena of 1918–1919, not 1946–1947. In the beginning, the conflict was not a "cold war" at all; it was flaming hot. The Bolsheviks promoted world socialist revolution, stupefying and infuriating western leaders. The Allied powers responded by waging open war against Soviet Russia. The Soviet perception of a hostile capitalist world was not in the least "surrealistic." The western powers were determined upon the destruction of Soviet authority; they lacked only the means to carry out their intentions.

When Allied military intervention and a bloody civil war guttered out in 1921, the Bolsheviks had won, though the West was little reconciled to their victory. When overt means of aggression against Soviet Russia failed, less risky, covert means were adopted. Western anti-communism was also put to other uses. British Tories and their French counterparts in the *Bloc national* raised the Red scarecrow at home to win elections. In the USSR, on the other hand, Soviet propagandists used the "war scare," fear of a new western intervention, to repress dissent and rally popular support.

In 1926 Maksim M. Litvinov, deputy commissar for foreign affairs and an important character in this narrative, referred to Soviet-American relations as a covert, "silent conflict" (*molchalivyi spor*). This characterization also applied to France and Britain, though often the Soviet-western confrontation was neither covert nor silent. The antagonists trumpeted their anger and their hostility like rutting bulls, in the press, on radio, in speeches in Parliament or in Soviet assemblies in Moscow. "Silent conflict" nevertheless seems a suitable title for this book and underscores its major themes.

In this atmosphere of intense animosity, the history of the USSR became not simply a narrative to be read for its intrinsic values; it became a potent cultural weapon in the United States and Western Europe with which to strike at the Soviet Union. During the inter-war years, Soviet leaders were represented as conniving, deceitful, purblind, paranoid ideologues with whom it was impossible to deal. Needless to say, in the West there were no anti-Red ideologues; they were honest-dealing diplomats and politicians up against incorrigible, "lying," dangerous "Orientals." Capitalism had no "universalistic and messianic pretensions." It held to "live and let live" and to non-interventionism in the internal affairs of other states, a European concept established by the Peace of Westphalia in 1649. According to George F. Kennan, one of the epigones of U.S. Cold War ideas, the Bolsheviks challenged this Westphalian principle by asserting "the universality of their own ideological pretensions."[7] The Bolsheviks were the "wolves," and westerners, the "lambs." If this allegory sounds to readers like pot calling kettle black, it is a good guess and a frequent occurrence in the pages of this book. It does after all seem far-fetched for foreign interventionists and colonial powers to invoke Westphalian principles. "Do as I say, not as I do" might better describe their conduct. It was not "live and let live."

Stalin was little different than Hitler, according to the western meme; the Nazi-Soviet non-aggression pact in 1939 was a "betrayal" of the West. In early 1940 the British government intended to publish a "Blue Book," a collection of Foreign Office documents, on the failed negotiations with the USSR in 1939 for an alliance against Nazi Germany. The objective was to demonstrate Soviet duplicity, to show that Moscow was "a wolf in sheep's clothing," as the Soviet *polpred* or ambassador in London put it at the time. Germany and the USSR were really "allies," or if they were not yet "formally" allies, they soon would be. Here again is the image of the Soviet "wolf," but the British government was unsure of its ground and never published that Blue Book.[8]

Other opportunities would arise. In 1948 the United States did publish a collection of documents to demonstrate Soviet culpability in the origins of World War II. No gratitude was thus shown to the Soviet peoples who had almost single-handedly destroyed the armies of Nazi Germany. In rebuttal the USSR published its own collection of papers demonstrating Anglo-French responsibility for the failure of collective security against Hitler.[9] It was tit for tat. Western historians routinely write about the Nazi-Soviet "alliance," which was no alliance at all but rather a short-term, loveless arrangement of convenience—well, unless the circle dance of two scorpions with tails raised high to strike can be called an alliance.

In 2009 the Organization for Security and Co-operation in Europe passed a resolution "equating the roles of the USSR and Nazi Germany in starting World War II." The main idea was to blacken the government of Russia, and in particular its president, Vladimir V. Putin, portrayed in the western press as a Soviet throwback, with hammers and sickles in his eyes. The resolution was scurrilous, politically motivated rubbish. Nothing could be further from the facts, as I have sought to demonstrate in numerous publications.[10]

I am not the only historian to challenge what may be called western consensus ideas. There are others who participate in this still-uphill endeavor. In 1979 Teddy J. Uldricks published an essay in which he attempted to challenge some of the existing Cold War stereotypes about an ideologically driven, one-dimensional foreign policy. V. A. Shishkin has written a number of books on the 1920s where he shows how Soviet diplomacy pursued traditional interests of the Russian state. G. N. Sevost'ianov took the same approach in examining Soviet-American relations. On the eve of the opening of the Soviet archives, in the early 1990s, Jon Jacobson looked at the state of the field and reported on the movement away from the over-simplifications of the past. Gabriel Gorodetsky, Jonathan Haslam, and Geoffrey Roberts have produced revisionist work for the 1930s and beyond, notably in regard to Soviet-German relations and Stalin's foreign policy.[11]

Was Stalin a radical ideologue or a ruthless practitioner of realpolitik? Was Soviet foreign policy driven by pragmatism or ideology? It depends on the historian. Ulam of the Cold War generation had no difficulty offering a reply. Later historians have not been so sure. "This is a tricky topic," according to Service, who avoids giving a definitive answer. Roberts splits the apple in two, holding "that the Soviets did not abandon their revolutionary ambitions, but reformulated them in a synthesis of Realism and ideology that projected the gradual growth of Soviet power [after 1945] alongside communist advances in the states of the capitalist and developing worlds."[12] "The Soviets" of course did not speak with one voice in the 1920s, or later on.

There is a third leg to this "tricky topic," I would suggest, and that is Bolshevik party politics. Foreign policy could not escape the fierce Soviet political debates of the 1920s, nor could it always be determined on its merits. The phenomenon of politics trumping policy affected the USSR as much as it did the leading western powers.

As readers come to know Soviet diplomats and leaders, they will also encounter their counterparts in the west, in Germany, France, Britain, and the United States. For if this book is based solidly in Soviet sources, it is also rooted in western archives. Each side has its say, if you like, without the other's interpretative filters. When Soviet and western diplomats spoke to each other, they sometimes kept records, which are interesting, and frequently perplexing, to compare. Often their messages to each other were misunderstood or lost completely because of confusion or personal agendas and biases.

This story gets "curiouser and curiouser," you may think. But the narrative here is by no means fiction, although at times readers may think it is. Nor is it a cultural weapon, though it is a historical study which endeavors to set some matters straight and to resolve long-unanswered questions about the formative years in the development of Soviet foreign policy.

Notes

1. E.g., A. V. Korotkov et al. (eds.), *Moskva-Tokio: Politika i diplomatiia Kremlia, 1921–1931*, 2 vols. (Moscow, 2007); S. V. Kudryashov et al., *SSSR-Germaniia, 1933-1941* (Moscow, 2009); V. I. Vasil'ev et al. (eds.), *Moskva-Vashington: Politika i diplomatiia Kremlia, 1921–1941*,

3 vols. (Moscow, 2009); and V. I. Vasil'ev et al., *Moskva-Berlin: Politika i diplomatiia Kremlia, 1920–1941*, 3 vols. (Moscow, 2011).

2. E.g., Keith Neilson, *Britain, Soviet Russia and the Collapse of the Versailles Order, 1919–1939* (Cambridge, 2006); and Fraser J. Harbutt, *Yalta 1945: Europe and America at the Crossroads* (Cambridge, 2010).

3. Louis Fischer, *The Soviets in World Affairs: A History of Relations between the Soviet Union and the Rest of the World, 1917–1929* (New York, 1960), p. xii; and Gabriel Gorodetsky, *The Precarious Truce: Anglo-Soviet Relations, 1924–1927* (Cambridge, 1977), p. 266.

4. E. H. Carr, *Socialism in One Country, 1924–1926*, 3 vols. (Harmondsworth, 1972), III, pp. 17–18; Gorodetsky, *Precarious Truce*, p. xi; and Zara Steiner, *The Lights That Failed: European International History, 1919–1933* (Oxford, 2005), pp. 154–55.

5. Adam Ulam, *Expansion and Coexistence: The History of Soviet Foreign Policy, 1917–1967* (New York, 1968), pp. 131, 142.

6. Robert Service, *Stalin: A Biography* (Cambridge, MA, 2004), pp. 380–81.

7. George F. Kennan, *Russia and the West under Lenin and Stalin* (New York, 1960), p. 180.

8. Ivan M. Maiskii, *Dnevnik diplomata*, 3 vols. (Moscow, 2006–2009), entries of 8 Jan., 2 and 21 Feb. 1940, II, pp. 102, 118, 126.

9. Geoffrey C. Roberts, "Stalin, the Pact with Nazi Germany, and the Origins of Postwar Soviet Diplomatic Historiography," *Journal of Cold War Studies*, vol. 4, no. 4 (Fall 2002), pp. 93–103; and Teddy J. Uldricks, "War, Politics and Memory: Russian Historians Reevaluate the Origins of World War II," *History & Memory*, vol. 21, no. 2 (Fall/Winter 2009), pp. 60–82.

10. E.g., M. J. Carley, *1939: The Alliance That Never Was and the Coming of World War II* (Chicago, 1999); idem, "Caught in a Cleft-Stick: Soviet Diplomacy and the Spanish Civil War," in Gaynor Johnson (ed.), *The International Context of the Spanish Civil War* (Cambridge, UK, 2009), pp. 151–80; and idem, "'Only the USSR Has . . . Clean Hands': The Soviet Perspective on the Failure of Collective Security and the Collapse of Czechoslovakia, 1934–1938," *Diplomacy & Statecraft* (UK), part 1, vol. 21, no. 2 (June 2010), pp. 202–25; part 2, vol. 21, no. 3 (Sept. 2010), pp. 368–96.

11. E.g., T. J. Uldricks, "Russia and Europe: Diplomacy, Revolution, and Economic Development in the 1920s," *International History Review*, vol. 1, no. 1 (Jan. 1979), pp. 55–83; V. A. Shishkin, *Stanovlenie vneshnei politiki poslerevoliutsionnoi Rossii (1917–1930 gody) i kapitalisticheskii mir* (St. Petersburg, 2002); G. N. Sevost'ianov, *Moskva-Vashington: Na puti k priznaniiu, 1918–1933* (Moscow, 2004); Jon Jacobson, *When the Soviet Union Entered World Politics* (Berkeley, 1994); Jonathan Haslam, *The Soviet Union and the Struggle for Collective Security in Europe, 1933–39* (New York, 1984); Geoffrey C. Roberts, *The Soviet Union and the Origins of the Second World War: Russo-German Relations and the Road to War, 1933–1941* (London, 1995); idem, *Stalin's Wars: From World War to Cold War, 1939–1953* (New Haven, 2006); and Gabriel Gorodetsky, *Grand Delusion: Stalin and the German Invasion of Russia* (New Haven, 1999).

12. Service, *Stalin*, p. 381; and Roberts' review essay of Jonathan Haslam, *Russia's Cold War: From the October Revolution to the Fall of the Wall*, in *International Affairs*, vol. 87, no. 6 (2011), pp. 1475–84.

~

Acknowledgments

This book has been a long time in gestation. It was first conceived in discussions with a friend and colleague, Richard K. Debo, more than twenty years ago.

"Let's do a book together," he proposed, on the formative years of Soviet foreign policy making. "It's too big for one person to take on, but in a partnership, we could do it."

We wanted to cover Soviet relations with the major western powers, Germany, France, Britain, and the United States. It was an ambitious project.

I remember my hesitation, wondering whether such a large undertaking was feasible. But not for long. *Tope*, I said, let's do it.

We applied for research assistance to the Social Sciences and Humanities Research Council of Canada in Ottawa (SSHRC) and obtained two generous three-year grants. I would like to underline this point, for without SSHRC funding, it would have been impossible to accomplish the archival research upon which this book rests.

I set off on a number of trips to Paris, London, Washington, and Moscow; and Richard went to Bonn and London. We wrote a first article together published in 1997 in *French Historical Studies*.[1]

Then tragedy struck. Richard seemed to drift away. He was diagnosed with Huntington's disease. Our partnership was dissolved.

We had nevertheless done much research and had exchanged research notes. So I have many of his from German sources and from London, which I stored away in boxes, along with my own, for I was then working on the 1930s.

Three and a half years ago, I pulled out the notes and photocopies with the intention of writing an introductory chapter on the 1920s for a book on the origins and formation of the World War II Grand Alliance. As I dug deeper into my boxes, I embarked on a voyage of discovery which has led to the writing of this book. Not with Richard, unfortunately, but let's say dedicated to his accomplishments as a historian.

Better late than never, eh, Richard? I dare to hope readers will agree. Свершилось!, as Russians would say, it's done.

I first met Richard in Paris in the early 1970s. He was my senior, already a professor at Simon Fraser University in Burnaby, British Columbia; I was an unproven graduate student doing doctoral research. We immediately got on well together, talked a lot about our mutual interests, and joked about the eccentricities and foibles of our historical characters. He had a good sense of humor and a raucous laugh which sometimes drew curious, perplexed looks from bystanders. Richard never noticed. We struck up a long correspondence, exchanged publications. Some people said we were like older and younger brothers. I don't know about that, but he was for a time a mentor. He has suffered a cruel fate, but I remember how he was in his best days, and the memories still make me smile.

As for the book on the Grand Alliance, I have started the manuscript and now see it as the sequel to the present study. I hope eventually to cover the entire period of Soviet relations with the West until the end of 1941.

In the meantime I should like to recognize those who have helped me to complete the present work. First of all, I would be remiss if I did not acknowledge the long-suffering patience of my spouse, Irina Borisovna, who has put up with my endless seasons of writing—not always without complaint, she might add.

I note also that the *Faculté des arts et des sciences* at the *Université de Montréal* has supported my research endeavors while I have labored as chair of the Department of History.

My thanks to Geoffrey Roberts and Zara Steiner who read earlier drafts of the manuscript. They made very useful suggestions for revisions even if I did not always follow them. Thanks are also due to Stephen Schuker, who carefully read the proofs, and to Sergei Valer'evich Kudryashov, who has helped me in many different ways to gain a better understanding of Soviet foreign policy making. My Russian bookseller, Leonid V. Mejibovski, from Esterum Books in Frankfurt, Germany, supplies me with Russian-language books and with the various collections of Soviet documents found in the selected bibliography. I would also like to acknowledge the help of my research assistants, Daria Vladimirovna Dyakonova, Louis Fortier, Arthur de Robert, and Marie-Christine Boucher.

The *Arkhiv vneshnei politiki Rossiiskoi Federatstii* (AVPRF) in Moscow provided me with photographs of some of the Soviet diplomats which are published herein with its permission. I thank the AVPRF, its chiefs, archivists, and clerks, for their kindness toward me over the years in spite of inevitable stresses and strains arising from my persistent, stubborn quest for deeper access to Soviet files. Other photographs and illustrations were obtained from the Granger Collection and Art Resource in New York; the *Bundesarchiv*; the German foreign office archives; *Rodina*, Moscow; the *Bibliothèque de documentation internationale contemporaine*, Nanterre; and the *Bibliothèque nationale de France*.

The David Low cartoons are published with permission of Solo Syndication in London and provided by the British Cartoon Archive at the University of Kent in the UK.

Writing is a solitary occupation, accomplished alone. But the research depends not only on one's own labors, but on those of others, archivists in particular, who preserve, catalog, and protect the historical papers on which researchers depend. Along my life's path, I have met many of these often anonymous but dedicated civil servants and preservationists of our heritage, not only in Moscow, but in France, the United Kingdom, and the United States. I take this occasion to recognize and thank them all.

MJC
Université de Montréal
November 2013

Note

1. "Always in Need of Credit: The USSR and Franco-German Economic Co-operation, 1926–1929," *French Historical Studies*, vol. 20, no. 3 (Summer 1997), pp. 315–56.

Biographical Notes

Stanley Baldwin, British prime minister, 1922–1924; 1924–1929.

Louis Barthou, head of the French delegation at the conference of Rapallo, 1922; minister of justice, 1922–1924.

Philippe Berthelot, secretary general of the French foreign ministry, 1920–1922; 1925–1932.

*Ian Antonovich Berzin, Soviet deputy *torgpred* and *polpred* in London, 1921–1925.

Frederick Edwin Smith, Lord Birkenhead, Conservative "Die-Hard"; Secretary of State for India, 1924–1929.

Jean-Jacques Bizot, official, *Mouvement general des fonds*, French ministry of finances, 1926–1927.

Meyer Bloomfield, U.S. go-between with NKID, 1922–1923.

*Dmitrii Vasil'evich Bogomolov, Soviet counselor in London, 1925–1927; chargé d'affaires in London, 1929–1933.

*Mikhail Markovich Borodin, Comintern agent in China, 1923–1927.

Henry Noel Brailsford, Labour journalist, author; editor of the *New Leader*, International Labour Party, 1922–1926.

Aristide Briand, French premier, 1921–1922, 1925–1926; foreign minister, 1925–1932.

Ulrich Graf von Brockdorff-Rantzau, German ambassador in Moscow, 1922–1928.

*Saul Grigor'evich Bron, director, Amtorg, New York, 1927–1929.

*Nikolai Ivanovich Bukharin, head of Comintern, 1926–1929; member, Politburo, 1924–1929.

Maurice Bunau-Varilla, owner of the Paris right-wing daily, *Le Matin*, 1920s.

Austen Chamberlain, British Foreign Secretary, 1924–1929.

Chiang Kai-shek, general, eventually leader, Guomintang, 1920s.

Georgii Vasil'evich Chicherin, Soviet commissar for foreign affairs, 1918–1930.

*Semen Borisovich Chlenov, professor of international law, secretary general of the Soviet delegation to the Franco-Soviet conference, 1926–1927.

Winston S. Churchill, Conservative "Die-Hard"; Secretary of State for War, 1919–1921; Secretary of State for the Colonies, 1921–1922; Chancellor of the Exchequer, 1924–1929.

Walter Citrine, general secretary, British Trade Union Congress, 1926–1946.

Georges Clemenceau, French premier, 1917–1920.

W. P. Coates, Hands off Russia, Soviet go-between, 1920s.

Laurence Collier, Far Eastern Department, 1924–1925; Northern Department, Foreign Office, 1926–1932.

Calvin Coolidge, U.S. president, 1923–1929.

Sir Eyre Crowe, permanent undersecretary, Foreign Office, 1920–1925.

Julius Curtius, German minister of foreign affairs, 1929–1931.

George Nathaniel Curzon, 1st Marquess Curzon of Kedleston, Foreign Secretary, 1919–1924.

Hugh Dalton, Parliamentary undersecretary of state, Foreign Office, 1929–1932.

Herbert von Dirksen, head, East European desk, Auswärtiges Amt, 1928; German ambassador in Moscow, 1928–1933.

Valerian Savel'evich Dovgalevskii, Soviet *polpred* in Paris, 1928–1934.

William Norman Ewer, British journalist, London *Daily Herald*; paid Soviet go-between, 1920s.

Feng Yuxiang, Chinese warlord, 1920s.

Aimé de Fleuriau, French ambassador in London, 1924–1933.

Ferdinand Foch, *maréchal*, commander in chief, Allied armies on the Western Front, 1918.

*Iakov Stanislavovich Ganetskii, member of the NKID *kollegiia*, 1921–1923; of NKVT *kollegiia*, 1920–1929; Soviet delegate in trade negotiations with Germany, 1924–1925.

James P. Goodrich, former governor of Indiana; U.S. go-between with NKID; president, National City Bank, Indianapolis, 1920s.

John D. Gregory, head of the Russian Department, 1923–1925; assistant permanent undersecretary of state, Foreign Office, 1925–1928.

Warren G. Harding, U.S. president, 1921–1923.

Arthur Henderson, Foreign Secretary, 1929–1932.

Jean Herbette, journalist at *Le Temps*, 1918–1924; French ambassador in Moscow, 1925–1931.

Édouard Herriot, député, 1919–1940; leader of the Radical Party, 1919–1936; French premier and foreign minister, 1924–1925, 1932; many times cabinet minister, 1926–1936.

Sir Samuel Hoare, Secretary of State for Air, 1924–1929.

Robert M. Hodgson, chargé d'affaires, British embassy in Moscow, 1924–1927.

Herbert Hoover, U.S. Secretary of Commerce, 1922–1929; president, 1929–1933.

Alanson B. Houghton, U.S. ambassador in London, 1925–1929.

Charles Evans Hughes, U.S. Secretary of State, 1921–1925.

Adol'f Abramovich Ioffe, Soviet *polpred* in Beijing, 1922–1923.

William Joynson-Hicks (Jix), Conservative "Die-Hard"; Home Secretary, 1924–1929.

*Lev Mikhailovich Kamenev, member, Politburo, 1919–1926; acting chairman, Sovnarkom, 1923–1924.

*Lev Mikhailovich Karakhan, Soviet *polpred* in Warsaw, 1920–1921; head, Eastern Department, NKID, 1922–1923; member, NKID *kollegiia*, 1922–1923; Soviet *polpred* in Beijing, 1923–1926; deputy commissar, NKID, 1926–1934.

Robert F. Kelley, chief, Division of East European Affairs, U.S. Department of State, 1926–1937.

Frank B. Kellogg, U.S. ambassador in London, 1923–1925; Secretary of State, 1925–1929.

Aleksandr Fedorovich Kerenskii, briefly head of the Provisional Government, 1917.

*Nikolai Klement'evich Klyshko, Soviet deputy *torgpred* in London, 1921–1923.

Kominternovskii, Comrade, fictional character, advocate of Comintern policies and *bête noire* of Comrade Narkomindel'cheskii (see below).

Leonid Borisovich Krasin, Soviet commissar for external trade, 1920–1925, Soviet *polpred* in Paris, 1924–1925; in London, 1925–1926.

*Nikolai Nikolaevich Krestinskii, Soviet commissar for finances, 1919–1921; member, Politburo, 1919–1921; *polpred* in Berlin, 1922–1930.

Eirik Labonne, secretary general, French delegation to Franco-Soviet conference, 1926–1927.

Robert Lansing, U.S. Secretary of State, 1915–1920.

Reginald A. Leeper, Central Department, 1920; Northern Department, Foreign Office, 1921–1923.

Alexis Léger, *sous-directeur d'Asie*, 1925–1927; *sous-directeur des Affaires politiques*, Quai d'Orsay, 1927–1929; *directeur des Affaires politiques*, 1929–1932.

Vladimir Il'ich Lenin, leader of the Bolshevik party, member, Politburo, 1919–1924, chairman of the Soviet of peoples' commissars (Sovnarkom), 1917–1924.

Ronald C. Lindsay, assistant permanent undersecretary of state, 1921–1924; permanent undersecretary, Foreign Office, 1928–1930.

Maksim Maksimovich Litvinov, deputy commissar for foreign affairs, 1920–1929; commissar for foreign affairs, 1930–1939.

David Lloyd George, British prime minister, 1916–1922.

Ramsay MacDonald, British prime minister, 1924, 1929–1935.

Ivan Mikhailovich Maiskii, Soviet counselor, Soviet embassy in London, 1925–1927.

Anastas Ivanovich Mikoian, commissar for external and internal trade, 1926–1930.

Alexandre Millerand, French premier, 1920; president, 1920–1924.

Charles E. Mitchell, "Sunshine Charley," president, National City Bank, New York, 1921–1929.

Viacheslav Mikhailovich Molotov, secretary, Politburo, 1921–1930; member, Politburo, 1926–1957.

Anatole de Monzie, French cabinet minister, 1920s; head of French delegation to the Franco-Soviet conference, 1926–1927.

George A. Mounsey, head, Northern Department, 1925–1926; head, Far Eastern Department, 1926–1929; assistant permanent undersecretary, Foreign Office, 1929–1939.

Benito Mussolini, head of the Italian government and prime minister, 1922–1943.

Narkomindel'cheskii, Comrade, fictional character, advocating a pragmatic Soviet foreign policy.

Vladimir Grigor'evich Orlov, aka Vladislav Orbanskii, or Orlitsky (Orletskii), White Russian in Berlin, counterfeiter of Soviet documents, 1920s.

Edmond Ovey, British ambassador in Moscow, 1929–1934.

Paul Painlevé, French premier, 1925; minister of war, 1925–1929.

C. M. Palairet, British chargé d'affaires in Beijing, 1925–1926; head, Northern Department, Foreign Office, 1926–1928.

Emmanuel Peretti de la Rocca, *directeur des Affaires politiques*, Quai d'Orsay, 1920–1924.

William Peters, counselor, British embassy in Moscow, 1924–1927.

Eric Phipps, chargé d'affaires, British embassy in Paris, 1922–1928.

*Georgii Leonidovich Piatakov, deputy head, Supreme Economic Council, 1922–1932.

Józef Piłsudski, generalissimo of Polish armies, 1919–1920; head of state, 1926–1935.

Raymond Poincaré, French premier, 1922–1924, 1926–1929; minister of finances, 1926–1929.

Arthur Ponsonby, Parliamentary undersecretary of state, Foreign Office, 1924.

Pot, Mr., and Comrade Kettle, fictional name-callers and hypocrites with double standards, especially Mr. Pot, frequently encountered in Soviet-western relations during the 1920s, and later on.

*Akeksei Vasil'evich Prigarin, director, Amtorg, New York, 1925–1927.

*Karl Berngardovich Radek, member, IKKI, Comintern, 1920–1924; later, journalist for *Izvestiia*, *Pravda*.

*Khristian Georgievich Rakovskii, Soviet *torgpred*/*polpred* in London, 1923–1925; *polpred* in Paris, 1925–1927.

Henri Rollin, journalist for the Parisian daily *Le Temps*; Soviet go-between, lobbyist, 1920s.

Fedor Aronovich Rotshtein, director of the NKID press bureau, 1920s; member, NKID *kollegiia*, 1923–1930.

*Arkadii Pavlovich Rozengol'ts, Soviet chargé d'affaires in London, 1925–1927.

*Aleksei Ivanovich Rykov, deputy chairman, Sovnarkom, 1921–1925; chairman, Sovnarkom, 1925–1930; member, Politburo, 1922–1930.

Albert Sarraut, Radical politician, French minister of the interior, 1926–1928.

Carl von Schubert, State Secretary, Auswärtiges Amt, 1924–1930.

Horace James Seymour, head, Northern Department, Foreign Office, 1929–1932.

Aron L'vovich Sheinman, head, Gosbank, 1921–1924; commissar for internal trade, 1925; head, Gosbank, and deputy commissar for finances, 1926–1928; de facto head, Amtorg, New York, 1928–1929.

*Boris Evseevich Skvirskii, unofficial Soviet representative in Washington, 1922–1933.

*Gregorii Iakovlevich Sokolnikov, Soviet commissar for finances, 1922–1926; deputy director, Gosplan, 1926–1928; *polpred* in London, 1929–1932.

Iosif Vissarionovich Stalin, general secretary (*gensek*) of the Communist Party of the Soviet Union, 1922–1953; member, Politburo, 1919–1953.

*Boris Spirodonovich Stomoniakov, *torgpred* in Berlin, 1920–1925; member, NKID *kollegiia*, 1926–1934.

William Strang, Northern Department, 1924–1925; Far Eastern Department, Foreign Office, 1927–1929.

Gustav Stresemann, German chancellor, 1923; minister of foreign affairs, 1923–1929.

Sun Yat-sen, Chinese nationalist leader; chairman, Guomintang, 1912–1925.

*Mikhail Pavlovich Tomskii, general secretary, Profintern, 1920–1929; member, Politburo, 1922–1930.

*Lev Davidovich Trotskii, Soviet commissar for foreign affairs, 1917–1918; commissar for war, 1918–1925; member, Politburo, 1919–1926; nemesis of Stalin until his assassination in 1940.

William G. Tyrrell, assistant permanent undersecretary of state, 1918–1925; permanent undersecretary, Foreign Office, 1925–1928; British ambassador in Paris, 1928–1934.

*Iosif Stanislavovich Unshlikht, deputy commissar for war, 1925–1930.

Kliment Efremovich Voroshilov, Soviet commissar for war, 1925–1940; member, Politburo, 1926–1960.

S. P. Waterlow, head, Far Eastern Department, Foreign Office, 1924–1926.

Victor Wellesley, assistant permanent undersecretary of state, 1924–1925; deputy undersecretary, Foreign Office, 1925–1936.

Woodrow Wilson, U.S. president, 1913–1921.

E. Frank Wise, British go-between at the Genoa Conference in 1922; in Anglo-Soviet negotiations for the reestablishment of diplomatic relations, 1929; and Labour MP, 1929–1932.

Wu Peifu, Chinese warlord, 1920s.

Zhang Zuolin, Manchurian warlord, 1920s.

*Grigorii Evseevich Zinoviev, president of the Comintern, 1919–1926; member, Politburo, 1919–1926.

*Perished during the Stalinist purges, 1936–1941.

~

Abbreviations and Acronyms

AFL	American Federation of Labor
Auswärtiges Amt	German ministry of foreign affairs, Berlin
Bolsh/Bolshies (Brit.), Bolos (Amer.), *Bolchos* (Fr.)	Western slang for the Bolsheviks
CCP	Chinese Communist Party
CER	Chinese Eastern Railway, Manchuria
Comintern	Communist (Third) International
Die-Hards	Far-right members of the British Conservative Party
Entente	Bolshevik terminology for the Allied powers, Britain, France, and the United States
FO	Foreign Office, London
gensek	secretary general of the Politburo, I. V. Stalin
Gosbank	Soviet state bank
Gosplan	Soviet state planning committee
GPU	Soviet State Political Directorate, secret police, 1922–1923; later the OGPU
Guomintang	Chinese nationalist party, led by Sun Yat-sen, then by Chiang Kai-shek
HMG	His Majesty's Government
IKKI	Executive Committee of the Communist International
ILP	International Labour Party
Instantsiia	the Politburo, in effect Stalin

kulaks	"rich" or relatively prosperous Russian peasants
May 30th movement	General strike movement provoked by British shooting of unarmed protesters in Shanghai, 30 May 1925
narkom	people's commissar; *zamnarkom*—deputy people's commissar
NEP	New Economic Policy, 1921–1928
NKID (Narkomindel)	People's Commissariat for Foreign Affairs
NKVD	People's Commissariat for Internal Affairs
NKVT (Narkomvneshtorg)	People's Commissariat for External Trade
OGPU	Soviet Joint State Political Directorate (secret police)
poilu	a French soldier
Politburo	Governing body of the Russian Communist Party, the Soviet government, and the Comintern
polpred	Soviet ambassador or plenipotentiary representative
Profintern	Red International of Trade Unions
Quai d'Orsay	French ministry of foreign affairs, Paris
RKP	Russian Communist Party
SIS	British Secret Intelligence Service
Sovnarkom	Council of People's Commissars
Tommy	a British soldier
torgpred	Soviet foreign trade representative
Torgpredstvo	Soviet foreign trade mission
TUC	British Trade Union Council
USSR	Union of Soviet Socialist Republics, established in December 1922
VKP(b)	All-Union Communist Party (Bolsheviks)
vozhd'	also *khoziain*, the boss, i.e., Stalin
VSNKh	Soviet Supreme Economic Council
VTsIK	Soviet All Russian Central Executive Committee, VKP(b)
VTsSPS	Soviet All-Union Council of Trade Unions
Whites, or White Guards	anti-Bolshevik forces during the civil war against the Soviet government

Europe, ca. 1925

~

CHAPTER ONE

How It Began

Revolution, Intervention, Civil War, 1917–1921

In 1917 there occurred a great revolution in Russia. It unfolded in two stages one after the other in March and November of that year, and was followed by a long, bloody civil war, which cost the lives of millions of people and did not sputter out until 1921–1922. Many people believed that, in its breadth and world impact, the Russian Revolution eclipsed the 1789 revolution in France. The French overthrew Louis XVI and sent him to the guillotine. They put an end to the Bourbon monarchy, at least for a while, but they accepted the nascent capitalist world as it was. The revolutionary leaders were mostly bourgeois. Property, wealth, money were left undisturbed unless they belonged to royalists. Even so, the other great European powers, all governed by kings and emperors, took fright because the revolution looked like spreading beyond the borders of France behind the bayonets of French revolutionary armies. To defend their crowns and privileges, the great powers made war against the French revolutionary republic. They encouraged civil war in France, supported the royalist counter-revolution, and earnestly hoped for restoration of the monarchy in France. After the defeat of the upstart but formidable Napoleon Bonaparte, they succeeded temporarily in putting the Bourbons back on the throne.

Much the same occurred in Russia after 1917, except that the hoped-for restoration did not materialize. The revolutionaries who took power in Russia, the Bolsheviks, had great ambitions beyond those of their predecessors in France. They established a government based on workers', soldiers', and peasants' councils, or Soviets. Their new government seized, nationalized, collectivized property, banks, money, the sacred icons of western capitalism,

1

all in the name of the proletarian and peasant masses. And this was only just a beginning, for the Bolsheviks were internationalists; they wanted to make a world socialist revolution.

You can imagine the reaction of the great powers, then preoccupied in the mass slaughter of the First World War. Busy destroying one another, they looked up suddenly to see the evil genie of revolution out of its lamp again. With the exception of France, the kings and emperors of the European belligerent powers were the spiritual descendants of the royalists who attempted to put down the bourgeois revolutionaries of France. Their instincts remained the same: to strike at the revolutionary Soviet government much as their predecessors had struck against revolutionary France after 1789. In a sense the Great War was an immense distraction which impeded the capitalist world from uniting to crush the Russian Revolution. After the Armistice in November 1918, all the powers, defeated and victorious alike, looked to their defenses against the spread of the revolutionary tide seeping out of Russia. Unlike their predecessors, however, the victorious Allies, mainly Britain, France, and the United States, failed to destroy the revolution in Russia, though not for want of trying. They dealt it hard, almost fatal blows and prevented its spread into Europe. It was at this point, in 1921, that Soviet Russia, battered but victorious, and the West, writ large, eyed and circled one another, neither able to strike a fatal blow, but still dreaming of it. By the end of the 1920s, those dreams were less vivid as the peril of each to the other began to fade.

Who Led the Russian Revolution?

The Bolsheviks, who seized power in Russia in November 1917, were theoretical Marxists. They had studied every aspect of the works of Friedrich Engels and Karl Marx, the latter a brilliant and prolific 19th-century German philosopher, historian, and economist. In the 1880s and 1890s, the Bolsheviks called themselves Social Democrats and seemed relatively harmless, though the tsarist secret police, the *Okhrana*, tracked and jailed them. In 1903 the Social Democrats split into Mensheviks and Bolsheviks, soft- and hard-core revolutionaries. They debated Marxist ideas and developed their own for making revolution in Russia, reversing the hated tsarist order. They tried for the first time in 1905, but lacked experience and close organizational ties to Russian workers and peasants. The *Okhrana* of course did what it could to stop them. All the important revolutionary leaders, V. I. Lenin, I. V. Stalin, L. D. Trotskii, and many others, spent time in tsarist jails or in exile. The first revolutionary upheaval of 1905 subsided. Trotskii was then the most prominent leader. Lenin was noticed only for his newspaper commentaries, and Stalin scarcely at all, an obscure Georgian operative active in the Caucasus.

The revolution is dead, Trotskii declared afterward, long live the revolution! 1905 was a dress rehearsal. Fresh opportunities would come, and the next time we will be ready.

Ironically, the Bolsheviks were *not* ready when the next opportunity presented itself in 1917. Even Lenin failed to see it coming, though all of Europe, from Russia and the Ottoman Empire to the Channel ports, had been at war for two and a half years. This was not just any war, but a bloody, senseless massacre beyond the darkest imagination. Government censors on all sides hid the truth with propaganda about glorious victories and heroic, fearless soldiers. In France it was called *bourrage de crâne*—head stuffing, if you like—rubbish to hide the reality of mass slaughter at the front. The truth was that the battlefields were killing grounds cut up by trenches filled with mud, piss, and excrement while rotting corpses and body parts littered the no-man's lands between opposing front lines. The *bourrage de crâne* worked for a while, but it was hard to explain away the long lists of dead, wounded, maimed, and missing. And "victories" produced little movement in the front lines which stretched across Belgium and France in the West.

In 1916 a French soldier whose name was Henri Barbusse published a series of *feuilletons*, or short stories, in the French newspaper *L'Oeuvre*, based on his experiences at the front. The stories were put together in a novel, *Le feu*, published in 1916, which won the prestigious Prix Goncourt and was published in Britain the following year as *Under Fire*. Barbusse's comrades came from all walks of life, bakers, butchers, machinists, schoolteachers, peasants. They have unfamiliar names, Volpatte, Tirette, Barque, Biquet, Tulacque, Cocon, Pépin, but the reader gets to know them and thinks kindly of them. Most perished in the fighting, their bodies pierced by machine-gun bullets or blown apart and half buried by artillery rounds and shrapnel. From men and comrades whom we know, they became frightening *things*, stiff, gutted, bloated, grotesque, from which the survivors averted their eyes. There was no glory in any of the stories of Barbusse or in real life at the front. It is a wonder that the censors passed Barbusse's work; but it would have been pointless to hide the truth.

The soldiers of Barbusse saw themselves as slaves. Herds of cattle, they said, led to slaughter by *chauvins*, super-patriots, and encouraged by comfortable shopkeepers, war profiteers, and lounge lizards who skulked in Paris or London. For them, the war was merely something to read about in the newspapers, comfortably seated in their clubs or bistros. Formidable fellows those *mecs*, those lads at the front, they said to themselves, not thinking of giving

4 ~ Chapter One

up their comforts for rat and crud-filled trenches. But many soldiers who survived the mass slaughter were angry, traumatized dreamers of vengeance.

"*Gare aux trônes!*" one heard from Barbusse's *grognards*; maybe "it's the revolution that's going to start again," others thought. Perhaps we will have to fight some more after the war.

"*Oui, p't'êt'*," said a comrade. "Yes, perhaps, and not against foreigners perhaps?"

"*P't'êt oui*," maybe so. "Two armies fighting each other, is like one army committing suicide," observed another soldier. Men were made to be husbands and fathers, "*des hommes quoi!—pas des bêtes qui se traquent, s'égorgent et s'empestent*," not wild, befouled beasts who stalk and devour one another.

Da konechno, yes, of course, Lenin would have said from his exile in Switzerland in early 1917. This is a war, he declared, between rival imperialist states and colonial empires struggling for dominance. They are governed by powerful capitalist elites, the rich and privileged. They will be the only ones to profit from this war, if any profit there is to be. You soldiers in the trenches, you are workers and peasants who have no interests in common with the elites who govern you and have sent you off to slaughter one another in battle. You are disposable, pawns, cannon fodder, for toffs and big shots. Better to knock off their top hats and stick your bayonets in their guts. Convert the war into a civil war, Lenin said: overthrow the bloody ghouls of capitalism and make the world socialist revolution.

As Barbusse suggested in *Le feu*, such ideas were spreading fast without any help from the Bolsheviks, most of whom were in exile, in tsarist jails, or isolated from one another and the masses they sought to lead. War in the East was equally murderous and had gone badly for Russia, an ally of France and Britain. In 1914 Russia was still an agricultural society; industrialization had only begun in the late 19th century. As a result, Russian industry could not produce the armaments necessary to pursue the war against Germany and its allies. Russian soldiers often had to fight with clubs, since there were not enough rifles; artillerymen had to ration their rounds. Without sufficient guns and without a competent officer corps connected to its men, the Russian army suffered heavy casualties, losing millions in dead, wounded, and missing. By the beginning of 1917 a million soldiers were deserters. Russian troops who remained at the front were like the comrades of Barbusse in France, but worse, or better, depending on your point of view: they were far more willing to turn their arms on a hated tsarist officer corps and a hated government.

Revolution spread on its own in Russia where the empire of the tsars collapsed like a house of cards in March 1917. One of the early Russian revolutionary posters portrayed the helmeted tsar standing on a sledge, whip in hand, with other privileged servitors. The porters, who carried the sledge, were brutalized, emaciated peasants and workers, the skulls and corpses of dead comrades at their feet. "*Tsar, pope, bogach,*" said the epigram: "Tsar, Priest, Rich man." The message was clear. Tsar Nicolas II, the last of the Romanovs, abdicated, though no one was quite sure what government would or should replace him. Of course, the Russian elite knew, and they tried to set up a Provisional Government to continue the war and avert a socialist revolution. A right-wing socialist, Aleksandr F. Kerenskii, eventually rose to lead the new government, which was quickly swept away by rough-necked, unwashed soldiers and by the Bolsheviks, who put themselves at the head of the popular revolutionary movement. Lenin, Trotskii, and their colleagues in exile hurried to get home. "Peace, Land, Bread" became the watchwords of the revolution. In Paris and London the situation looked dangerous. Mutiny and revolution could spread. "Distribute the land in Russia today," said one British general, "and in two years we'll be doing it in England!"[1] The French high command contemplated a separate peace, putting the cost of the war on Russia, before it was too late. In London the British prime minister, David Lloyd George, was of a similar mind.[2]

At the front, French soldiers, the *poilus*, had had enough. After another senseless frontal assault against German trenches in April 1917, the French army broke. The *poilus* mutinied. The high command shot a number of them and reimposed discipline of a sort, though the British army had to take over the brunt of the fighting in the West until the following year. The French mutineers were not as determined as their Russian counterparts, but they frightened their officers. Nothing instilled dread in the officer corps so much as mutinous soldiers, who could turn to mayhem, and worse, to revolution. Their greatest fears were realized too, not in France, but in Russia.

The "October Revolution" and Early Allied Reaction

In November 1917, or October according to the Julian calendar, the Bolsheviks seized power in Petrograd and Moscow. There was little resistance to them, and their authority spread quickly—"by telegraph," someone observed—as news of the Bolshevik takeover spread eastward across Siberia to Vladivostok on the Pacific Ocean. The Bolsheviks were smart enough to win the endorsement of the All-Russian Soviet of workers' and soldiers' deputies, a tumultuous, democratic assembly representing local and municipal Soviets from across Russia.

"Long live the world socialist revolution!" shouted cheering deputies. The Bolsheviks were not interested in making revolution only in Russia; they wanted to spread the revolution to Europe and beyond. But first they had to have an armistice and peace negotiations with Germany and its allies to end the war in the East. Let's be clear, however: the Bolsheviks promoted peace as a step toward revolutionary war; they encouraged soldiers of all armies to fraternize as brothers and to turn their bayonets against kings and presidents to bring down the bourgeois, capitalist order in Europe.

At first, western governments were incredulous, stupefied. Their leaders could scarcely believe the first reports that the Bolsheviks had seized power. How could a gang of coffeehouse extremists and "radicals" seize power in Russia? It's "opéra bouffe," declared the American president, Woodrow Wilson. "It's impossible," was the general reaction in Petrograd and then, "Hah, hah, they won't last." But the Bolsheviks did last, defeating small forces near Petrograd and in Moscow to establish their authority.

In Paris, London, and Washington, governments took stock of the incredible news. They encouraged the Russian commander in chief to refuse orders from the new Soviet government. His soldiers lynched him.

Koshmar!, a nightmare, said the "better Russians," the "patriots," according to the western allies, who swigged champagne and bet fat wads in gambling saloons in a last fling in Petrograd, or who headed south to the Ukraine or the Caucasus to escape Red Guards out looking for them.[3]

Western hostility was only just beginning. In December 1917, the Allies, mainly Britain, France, and the United States, extended the naval blockade of Germany around Russia. The Bolshevik "bacillus" had to be kept from spreading into Europe. It was anarchy and it could "infect" the easily deceived, gullible lower orders, workmen and peasants, immigrants, Africans, American Negroes, whipped up by Jews, coffeehouse radicals, and murderous anarchists who had forgotten their place. All the strong institutions of society would be swept away, the "ignorant and incapable mass of humanity," as Secretary of State Robert Lansing called them, would turn the world on its head.[4] Bolsheviks were of course far from being anarchists, but it was easy to label them as bloody, impudent radicals. The better classes were afraid for their property, their comforts, and their lives. Lansing, who knew a little history of the French Revolution, reckoned the Russian terror would be far worse than the French.[5] He trembled with indignation and fear.

The U.S. government's hostility to the Bolshevik seizure of power was immediate and visceral. Lansing raised the alarm. Funds to the Russian government, no longer an ally, were at once cut off. The State Department was quick to agree to the blockade of Soviet Russia. Nothing should get in or out, especially Bolshevik agents, propaganda, or money for subversion. The radicals would be isolated, starved out. Tsarist officers would get money to organize forces to overthrow the "Bolos," the "Bolsh," the Bolchos. Whatever the language, it was a word spat out with fear and loathing.

The French and British reacted in similar fashion to the Americans. A ruthless French premier, Georges Clemenceau, came to power in November 1917, vowing relentless war against the hated *Boche* invader. He arrested "defeatists" and had some of them shot. You can imagine his reaction to Bolshevik calls for peace negotiations and world socialist revolution, especially with his shaky divisions of frontline soldiers. Western exasperation increased in early 1918 after the Soviet government nationalized banks and industries and annulled the tsarist state debt in which foreign nationals had invested billions. The Bolsheviks actually did what they said they would do; this was something to which western politicians were unaccustomed. It was incredible: property, contracts, money were no longer safe. French and British agents funneled fat bundles of rubles to would-be rebels, tsarist officers, Ukrainian nationalists, and Cossacks, who wanted to break away from Soviet Russia. In Britain, Prime Minister David Lloyd George was less aggressive, more cautious than his counterparts Clemenceau and Wilson, the U.S. president, but his cabinet colleagues reacted violently to the Bolshevik takeover of power.

The Bolsheviks: Friend or Foe?

Then, in January 1918, there was a new, curious development. The Soviet government obtained an armistice with Germany and its allies, but not a general armistice including the western allies. Peace negotiations opened in the German-occupied Polish town of Brest-Litovsk, and the Bolsheviks turned the talks into a propaganda circus, playing to the press and treating Germany as a ham-fisted, fat-bellied Prussian aggressor. The Bolsheviks resisted, insofar as they could resist, against draconian German territorial demands. Russian soldiers had abandoned the trenches, as the Bolsheviks had urged them to do, and so the Soviet government could do little but resort to a show of bravado for the world press, hoping revolution would spread to Germany.

In Paris and London, government officials took notice, for the propaganda made the Germans look bad. In February and March, an unusual idea germinated: perhaps the Allies should help the Bolsheviks to fight the Germans. Here was the prototype concept of the 1941 Grand Alliance against Nazi Germany. Then, as later, the western powers had to put the question: who is the greater threat, Germany or Soviet Russia? In early 1918, the idea of allying with Soviet Russia even against Germany was so heretical, and the general indignation so great at the Bolshevik seizure of power, that pragmatism gained little traction in western capitals. Perhaps surprisingly, Lenin himself, the arch-Bolshevik, was willing to contemplate cooperation, however grudgingly. What "potatoes and guns," he wanted to know—real support, he meant—would the Allies send him?[6] We are not going to stick out our necks only to be left in the lurch. It was the first of many such questions which the Soviet government would put to France and Britain in later years, as the Nazi menace increased during the 1930s.

David Lloyd George

In London, Lloyd George was open to a favorable response to Lenin's query, though his colleagues were scandalized. Rubbing shoulders with Bolsheviks was a heretical idea, but it was not the first time the prime minister had stood out among his colleagues. He is an interesting man, who merits introduction. Lloyd George was born in 1863, the son of an English schoolmaster who died shortly after his birth. His mother took him and his brother to Wales to live with an uncle, a strong-willed man, both shoemaker and Nonconformist minister. Like so many of his contemporaries, David proved to be a good student. He eventually studied law, opening a successful practice before getting interested in politics. In 1890, he won a seat in the House of Commons at age 27 for the Liberal Party, a seat he held until his death in 1945. In early photographs, he appears a handsome gent, confident, with a wry smile, sufficient to ignite fires of interest and passion among the opposite sex. Even after he married, he was said to wench shamelessly. In later photographs he is a diminutive man, with an iconic pince-nez hanging around his neck, often noticed in political cartoons or photographs. His hair and moustache are gone gray—indeed, he often looks in need of a haircut—but his smile is infectious and impish.

Lloyd George, or LG, became a cabinet minister for the first time in 1906, and three years later was named Chancellor of the Exchequer. He won a reputation as a radical, looking to tax land and high incomes to pay for social services, pensions, and the Royal Navy. The House of Lords opposed the Chancellor's bills, but eventually they became law after a long political battle. The "dukes," as he called them, reacted badly to their defeat, accusing him of being a socialist in disguise. Lloyd George took it all in stride.

He became prime minister in 1916, and head of the coalition government of mostly Tories at a time when the war was going badly and about to get worse. Many people saw him as the only political leader who could lead the country to victory. He was as slippery as an eel and as wily as a fox. "Of course, he would not pick your pocket," one colleague noted, "if he knew there was nothing in it." Another contemporary observed that "one could say fifty things of LG that might appear contradictory, and all would be true."

**Figure 1.1.   David Lloyd George, ca. 1918–1919.
Art Archive, Art Resource, NY.**

He proved an effective wartime leader who clashed with his woodenheaded
generals, who were too quick to waste the lives of British soldiers.[7]

In February 1918 the War Cabinet angrily debated the issue of backing
the Bolsheviks. It was not a popular idea. Bolshevism is a menace to "civilization," we should take care, said one minister, not to think that Bolshevism
might only be "catching" in Germany. Ever the radical, Lloyd George left
his colleagues aghast with the idea that HM government should help the
Bolsheviks fight the Germans. "My view," he said, "is that Russia is our most
powerful ally now in Germany."

His colleagues were shocked. "The discussion got rather hot at one time,"
observed the Cabinet secretary; "they were getting to fundamentals, the
rights of property owners, et cetera." "Very amusing," he thought, but not
to others.[8] "Let's make them our Bolsheviks," Lloyd George said outside the
Cabinet room. While the prime minister talked about an alliance with the
Bolsheviks, the Foreign Office offered bulging packets of rubles to anyone
who would oppose the Reds.

The Bolshevik as Foe

In Paris, too, cooperation with the Bolsheviks was mooted. Even the soon-to-be-Allied generalissimo Ferdinand Foch seemed disposed to listen. It made sense because the anti-Bolshevik factions were weak and pro-German. The "better" Russians hoped that the Germans would put down the revolution.[9] On the other hand, in February and March 1918 the Bolsheviks were preparing to fight the Germans. Foch and Lloyd George were among the first "realists" or pragmatists, ready to overlook Bolshevik revolutionary ideas in order to ally with them against the greater German danger.

Would pragmatism prevail? Would the enemy of my enemy become my ally? The concept had a long tradition in France, dating back to the 15th century when French kings allied with Turkish sultans against a common Habsburg enemy. Such an idea would have been well understood among the erudite clerks of the French foreign ministry, the Quay d'Orsay. But there, powerful civil servants were as scandalized as British cabinet ministers by the prospect of an alliance with Reds. They nipped that wild idea in the bud and had no trouble persuading Clemenceau that the Bolsheviks were too dangerous.[10]

In Washington, cooperation with Soviet Russia never got beyond lower-ranking officials, "cranks," according to the State Department. Lansing and Wilson were adamantly opposed to supporting the new Soviet government for *any* reason. The Bolsheviks appealed to the worst elements of society, said Lansing: "to the ignorant and mentally deficient, who by their numbers are urged to become the masters. Here seems to me to lie a very real danger in view of the present social unrest throughout the world." Lansing was just getting wound up: the Bolsheviks are "dangerous—more so than Germany"; they "threatened us with revolution."[11] Wilson felt the need to disguise his anti-Red hostility so as not to "disillusion left-leaning Americans and Europeans." We need to hide our hand, one adviser told Wilson, "to limit the possibility for damage to America's idealistic image." President Wilson, the so-called democratic idealist, was not above deceit "where it related to matters of public policy."[12]

"Any attempt of the Germans to interfere in Russia," said Lloyd George, "would be like an attempt to burgle a plague-house."[13] This was a common western metaphor for Bolshevism; it was a contagious disease, a plague, a virus, a pestilence which threatened world socialist revolution. The idea that the "ignorant" lower orders could become the "masters" terrified western elites. That is the main reason why an alliance with the Bolsheviks to fight the Germans did not get very far. "Out of the question," said Lansing, and Wilson agreed.[14] Early forms of disinformation were used to accuse the

Bolsheviks of being "German agents." One American in Russia, Colonel Raymond Robins, observed that if the Germans bought the Bolsheviks, they had bought "a lemon." In fact, he was talking about the intrepid Trotskii, who was the first Soviet commissar for foreign affairs. He's "a four-kind son of bitch," said Robins, "but the greatest Jew since Christ," and a potentially formidable adversary of Germany.[15] Reasoning of this kind fell on barren ground in Washington. The Bolsheviks are organizing an army for "social revolution," said the French, and the Allies would be crazy to help build up the instrument of their own destruction.[16] The State Department, the Foreign Office, and the Quai d'Orsay were hotbeds of anti-Bolshevism.

In the spring of 1918 the answer to the question, who was the greater enemy, turned out to be the Bolsheviks. They were a greater long-term threat than Germany, as Lansing said openly, even as the German army launched its spring offensives in the west to win the war before the arrival of fresh American divisions shifted the military balance in favor of the western Allies. Of course, the Bolsheviks did not have an army in the spring of 1918, apart from undisciplined Red Guards, and they had to sign the draconian Treaty of Brest-Litovsk in early March 1918. Many Bolsheviks wanted to fight the Germans, but Lenin dismissed the idea as infantile and imposed his will on reluctant colleagues. Not that Lenin took the treaty seriously. When a colleague asked him if he wanted to read its terms, he declined. "I don't mean to read it," he replied, "and I don't mean to fulfil it, except in so far as I'm forced."[17] It was during the Brest-Litovsk negotiations that Lenin established his preeminence as a leader vis-à-vis his fractious colleagues.

Vladimir Il'ich Lenin

Vladimir Il'ich Ul'ianov, alias Lenin, was born in 1870 in Simbirsk, now Ul'ianovsk, on the west bank of the Volga River, in the far reaches of Eastern Europe. His parents were of the wealthy middle class; his father was a superintendent of schools in the Simbirsk region. Ul'ianov was a bright student, obtaining a gold medal on graduating from *gimnaziia*, or high school. Even as a teenager he was known to be aggressive and iconoclastic. At age 16, he denounced God and declared himself an atheist. He took after his older brother Aleksandr who became involved in the revolutionary movement and was hanged in 1887 for plotting to assassinate the tsar. The younger Ul'ianov's future seemed predestined after his brother's execution. There were scores to settle.

He was soon involved in run-ins with the tsarist police, eventually ending up in St. Petersburg where he obtained a degree in law. In the capital he joined the Russian Social Democratic Labour Party; he got involved in the

trade union movement and was eventually jailed. In this he was like contemporaries of his generation. In other ways, however, Ul'ianov was not like
his fellow revolutionaries. He possessed a relentless intellect and an absolute
certainty in the correctness of his own ideas, which soon made him the main
leader of the Bolsheviks after 1903. He was choleric, vociferous, sarcastic in
argument, and he quarreled with just about everyone. But that didn't matter.
He was right and his colleagues were wrong.

If Trotskii became the sword of the revolution, Lenin was its brain and the
driving force behind the Bolshevik seizure of power. In March 1918, by dint
of will, vituperation, and skill in debate, he persuaded or browbeat a majority
of his colleagues into accepting the Brest-Litovsk peace terms, when many
other "Left" Bolsheviks preferred to wage partisan war against the German
army. Lenin ran through all the arguments in favor of such a course and demolished them one by one. They're all pipe dreams and phrase mongering.
Just like getting "boots" and "shells" from the "Anglo-French bourgeoisie."
It's only a trap. We will fight the Germans and they will "plunder" us, and

**Figure 1.2. Vladimir Il'ich Lenin, ca. 1922.
Adoc-photos, Art Resource, NY.**

"Soviet power will be swept away." Lloyd George had just such ideas in mind, making use of the Bolsheviks as a "stalking horse."

"Please do fight, Bolshevik 'allies,'" Lenin mocked. "We shall help you! And the 'Left' (God save us from them) Bolsheviks are walking into the trap by reciting the most revolutionary phrases." Let's not be gulled, he pleaded: "We must fight against the revolutionary phrase, we have to fight it, we absolutely must fight it, so that at some future time people will not say of us the bitter truth that 'the revolutionary phrase about revolutionary war ruined the revolution.'"[18] Brest-Litovsk was an important victory for Lenin, though he proved right for the wrong reasons. Revolution in Europe would not force the withdrawal of the German army from Soviet Russia, but the Armistice in November 1918 did. Lenin's judgment seemed so often vindicated afterward that most of the time he got his way on important matters of policy. "Vote with Il'ich," went a common epigram, "and you won't be wrong." Lenin did not always get his way, nor was he always right, far from it, but all the same everyone knew he was the boss.[19]

In March 1918 Lenin was right about Lloyd George, a shrewd politician, but wrong about Clemenceau and Wilson. Wrong in the sense that provision of "boots" and "shells" to Soviet Russia to fight the Germans was the furthest thought from the French or American mind. Nor did the British Cabinet support the prime minister's pragmatic approach. It was playing with fire and far too dangerous.

In Moscow, early on the morning of 17 March 1918, the resolution to accept the harsh German peace carried in the All-Russian Congress of Soviets by 861 votes for to 261 against. The debate was over. Lenin had won. You have to know when to attack and when to retreat, he said. This is a time to retreat. Is it any wonder that Lenin read and admired Niccolò Machiavelli?[20] Brest-Litovsk was a kind of weak man's version of the Nazi-Soviet non-aggression pact 21 years later. Buy off the Germans and build up your strength to fight another day was, mutatis mutandis, the idea behind both arrangements since the western powers did not want to join with Soviet Russia against a common foe.

Allied Military Intervention

In the meantime, the western Allies decided to "burgle the plague house" themselves. They intervened in Russia to "down the Bolshies," but they promoted it as "reestablishing an Eastern Front" in Russia to fight Germany. This was good propaganda, but it was also a canard. Not even Wilson believed it could be done, but why needlessly provoke the left by revealing the truth of Allied intent?

During the spring and summer of 1918, the Bolsheviks clung to power by the tips of bleeding fingers. The western allies thought it was only a matter of weeks before they collapsed. To help matters along, the Allies subsidized local resistance to Soviet authority. These "Whites" were mixed groups of right-wing socialists, Czechoslovak legionnaires, and tsarist officers and officials. The Czechoslovaks were former Austro-Hungarian POWs organized in Russia to fight for Czechoslovak independence. In the spring of 1918 they were strung out along the Trans-Siberian Railroad, heading east toward Vladivostok, going, so they were led to believe, to fight in France. The French ambassador in Russia, a determined anti-Bolshevik, had other ideas. He paid over 15 million rubles to Czechoslovak agents to encourage a revolt against Soviet authority along the Trans-Siberian. The last payment of 5 million was made ten days before the outbreak of the revolt at the end of May.[21] The French consulate general in Moscow distributed another 12 million to "Russians" or "Russian contingents" between April and August 1918. Twenty-seven million in the cause of the counter-revolution was a small price to pay, beer money, Clemenceau would have argued, to overthrow the Bolsheviks. French agents also financed an anti-Soviet rebellion northeast of Moscow in July 1918. Bulging bundles of rubles were freely distributed to *anyone* who said they would fight the Bolsheviks.[22]

The Soviet government teetered on the brink of destruction, surrounded on all sides in central Russia by the Germans—who did not intend to respect the Brest-Litovsk Treaty any more than Lenin did—and by small, Allied-brokered anti-Bolshevik forces. Ironically, the Germans and Allies briefly made common cause against the Bolsheviks while continuing to exterminate each other on the Western Front.

As 1918 unfolded, British troops moved into the four corners of Russia to overthrow Soviet authority. From the Baltic and Murmansk in the north, to the Caucasus and Central Asia in the south, and to Vladivostok on the Pacific Ocean, British army and naval units supported the enemies of the Soviet state. The British government eventually sent guns, stores, and munitions, worth more than £100 million and sufficient to supply large anti-Bolshevik armies.[23] The United States sent forces to northern Russia and Siberia. Even the French, who had few troops to spare from the Western Front, dispatched small contingents to northern Russia and to Siberia. The Japanese sent the largest forces, some 70,000 men, to Vladivostok and eastern Siberia. Allied troops were small in number, but the Soviets were surrounded and on the brink of collapse. A slight nudge would push the Bolsheviks into hell.

Lev Davidovich Trotskii

The western allies were too optimistic. Trotskii returned from Brest-Litovsk to become commissar for war in March 1918. His remit was to organize and lead the fledgling Red Army, which began to win victories in the summer and autumn of 1918 as the war on the Western Front was drawing to its conclusion. Trotskii was a leader as interesting and extraordinary as Lenin. Readers should get to know him for he became the main opposition leader to Stalin during the 1920s.

Lev Davidovich Bronshtein was born in 1879 in the southern Ukraine. His parents were well-to-do Jewish farmers. His father sent him to Odessa, a bustling port city on the Black Sea, at the age of nine to be educated. He finished his secondary schooling, but the revolution sidetracked his intended university studies in mathematics. He ran afoul of the *Okhrana* for union organizing and spent two years in prison where he studied philosophy and Karl Marx. He was an early member of the Russian Social Democratic Labour Party, escaping to London from exile in Siberia and eventually taking the pseudonym Trotskii. He quarreled with Lenin—who did not?—and flirted with the Mensheviks, not declaring fully for the Bolsheviks until 1917. One joker would say of him that he was "the Bolshevik among the Mensheviks and the Menshevik among the Bolsheviks." A British diplomat called him an "enigmatic personality."[24] Many of his colleagues thought he was an arrogant Johnny-come-lately. Trotskii was many things, but not that. Unlike Lenin and Stalin, he was one of the main leaders of the 1905 revolution, and in November of that year he was elected president of the St. Petersburg Soviet. He was only 26 years old.

After the 1905 revolution collapsed, he was again arrested, jailed, and sent to Siberia. Again he escaped, first to London, then to Vienna. Prior to the war he worked as a journalist, for a time running his own newspaper out of Vienna and then writing for Russian papers. When the revolution broke out in Russia in 1917, he was in New York City. He booked passage home but was arrested in Halifax, Nova Scotia. Held in a POW camp, he talked revolution to German POWs. "He is a man holding extremely strong views and of a most powerful personality," observed one Canadian official: "his personality being such that after only a few days stay here he was by far the most popular man in the whole Camp with the German Prisoners of War, two-thirds of whom are Socialists."[25] Canadian authorities therefore thought it best to get rid of him and sent Trotskii on his way. He became Lenin's chief ally and was elected for the second time as president of the Petrograd Soviet. It was Trotskii who oversaw the Bolshevik seizure of power.

Figure 1.3. Lev Davidovich Trotskii, ca. 1917. Snark, Art Resource, NY.

Trotskii was a remarkable individual: multi-lingual, an erudite man of letters, but also a man of action. Revolutionary agitator and an orator of great power, he became the chief executor of Lenin's strategy for revolution in Russia. Trotskii's name was often hyphenated with Lenin's in and out of Russia; they were the preeminent leaders of the revolution and of the embattled Soviet republic.

Founder of the Red Army, Trotskii was an audacious, relentless soldier. He had the courage not only to stand alone in politics, but also to stand under fire. When conditions were at their worst, he led his Red Army men from the front lines, putting his own life at risk against the enemy. Lev Davidovich is "a man of extraordinary capacity and courage," said one colleague, "and the finest orator [I've] ever listened to . . . his personal courage . . . saved Russia." In battle "he exposed himself recklessly and inspired the troops with new enthusiasm."[26] Trotskii traveled in an armored train, with arms, propaganda, and leather-dressed soldiers, to weak points on the multiple fronts of the civil war. The Whites portrayed Trotskii as the Red Jew, and a devil perched atop a mountain of dead. In Bolshevik propaganda he stood astride Soviet Russia as guardian of the revolution. Where there was danger, Trotskii would be found. Some say his greatcoat was cut by enemy bullets. Soldiers do not ask more from their commanders, and they rallied to him and to the revolution. In the late summer of 1918, the Red Army began to win victories, pushing the White Guards away from the heart of Soviet Russia. The Bolsheviks suddenly sprang from the brink of defeat to the edge of victory, terrifying the West.

The Red Scare

Autumn 1918 marked the beginning of the first Red Scare. On the Western Front, the German armies were beaten: their spring offensives had failed. The increasingly numerous American army had helped to turn the tide of battle. On 11 November 1918 Germany capitulated, and war ended in the west. Lenin declared the Treaty of Brest-Litovsk null and void. The German high command hastened to get its soldiers out of southern Russia before they became infected with the Red bacillus. Austria-Hungary, Germany's most important ally, disintegrated into several new states. Revolution stirred in Berlin and Vienna. Was the West's worst nightmare about to become true?

In October 1918 President Wilson told his cabinet that he was worried about the spread of revolution. "The spirit of the Bolsheviki," he said, "is lurking everywhere." It is "the most hideous and monstrous thing that the human mind has ever conceived," added Secretary of State Lansing, bidding up the rhetoric, a "monster which seeks to devour civilized society and reduces mankind to the state of beasts."[27]

When the Soviet government put out peace feelers in October 1918, the French government rejected them out of hand. Composition with the Bolsheviks was *not* on the western agenda. According to the French foreign minister, "The Bolshevik problem is no longer a purely Russian affair; it is now an international question." "All the civilized countries" should unite to oppose this "anarchic contagion which should be fought in the same way as an epidemic."[28] There again was the metaphor of plague: it had to be snuffed out before it could spread.

Lenin, who noticed, taunted the West. The "Entente" imperialists "are making ready to build a Chinese wall to protect themselves from Bolshevism, like quarantine against the plague." Hah! Lenin boasted, "The bacillus of Bolshevism will pass through the wall and infect the workers of all countries."[29]

The civil war in Russia continued, however, nourished by the western Allies. It was Red Terror against White Terror; quarter was seldom given. Blood flowed copiously on both sides of the struggle. With their hands free of war in the west, the French and British general staffs thought they could make Lenin eat his mocking words. These high hopes were quickly dashed by the realization that their soldiers would fight no more. Grandiose plans for sending 20 Allied divisions to Russia were whittled down to six or eight. While British Tommies were more obedient than the French *poilus*, it was clear that neither gang was keen to fight the Bolsheviks. At the end of 1918 the Red Scare intensified, and so, whittled down or not, Anglo-French forces were sent to the Ukraine and Caucasus to reverse Soviet power.

Les Boches vaincus, voilà les Bolchos. The *Boches* are beaten, now for the "Bolsh"!

The mind was willing, but the body was not. After more than four years in the abattoir, the common soldier had had enough. Neither Tommy nor *poilu* wanted to fight in Russia.

"To Hell with this," they said: "Fuck all of you!"

"What the devil have we got against the Bolsheviks!" If toffs want to fight the Bolsheviks, be my guest, they can go themselves. But not us! We've had enough. "*Vive les Bolcheviks!*," said the *poilus*. "Hands off Russia," declared the British left.

"I know nothing of Bolshevism," commented one Frenchman. "I have neither the leisure nor the means to study it. But my landlord, my boss, and my neighbor—each of whom is more greedy and reactionary than the next—speak badly of it. Therefore it must be doing something worthwhile."[30]

In March 1919 Lloyd George warned Clemenceau in a secret letter, "The whole of Europe is filled with the spirit of revolution. There is a deep sense not only of discontent, but of anger and revolt among the workmen. . . . The whole existing order . . . is questioned by the masses . . . from one end of Europe to the other."[31]

One can imagine Clemenceau's scorn: he would down the Bolsheviks, if he could, whether Lloyd George liked it or not.

The *poilus* will fight if ordered.

No, they wouldn't, not this time. In February and March 1919, French soldiers mutinied only weeks after arriving in the Ukraine. In Odessa, the port city on the Black Sea, young women offered sex to lonely French soldiers and sailors on leave to bring them over to the revolution. The brothels of Odessa, said the commander in chief of French occupation forces, were the most dangerous nests of Red propaganda in all of southern Russia.[32]

In April, it was the turn of sailors of the French Black Sea fleet. They raised the red flag on the battleships *France* and *Jean Bart* to the consternation of their captains. These brutes, officers thought, could take our ships over to the Bolsheviks. This was enough for Paris, and the French hastily withdrew.

"The complete failure of a ridiculous adventure," spat out the French commander in Odessa.[33]

British, American, and Canadian troops were less rebellious, but their commanders knew they had little enthusiasm for overthrowing Soviet power. Anyway, Russia was too big for that.

Defeat in southern Russia did not persuade the French government to abandon its hostility toward Soviet Russia. On the contrary, the French devised a new strategy which came to be known as the *cordon sanitaire*, the erection of a barricade of barbed wire and bayonets from the Baltic to the Black seas. Poland, Romania, and Czechoslovakia were to be armed to block Red expansion to the west. If it sounds to the reader like a policy of containment, it was, more than 25 years before the Americans devised theirs after 1945.

Bolshevism was still "catching." In March 1919, as events were going wrong for the French in southern Russia, a Red government was established in Hungary. There was unrest in varying degrees nearly everywhere in Europe, as Lloyd George noted. Soldiers came home from the war, happy to be alive and intact, but surly and angry at those who had sent them to fight. Many were content to crawl into bed with wives or girlfriends, but others were traumatized, and some ready for revolution. The ghosts of Barque, Biquet, Cocon, Pépin, and their dead comrades cried out for vengeance. Russia is where they got it.

In March 1919, the Soviet government set up the Communist International, or Comintern, to spread the mayhem, or the cause of world revolution, depending on your point of view. The Bolsheviks acted as much from self-defense as out of principle. They were blockaded and surrounded on all sides in a bloody, merciless civil war. Communist propaganda was the only way to take the war against "the Entente" outside the frontiers of Russia and hit them back. The propaganda was dangerous. The *cordon sanitaire* was intended to stop its leaking into the West. Containment appeared to work because unrest in the West quieted down, and the Romanian army snuffed out the revolution in Hungary.

In the autumn of 1919 Clemenceau's center-right coalition exploited the *péril rouge* to crush the socialist opposition in national elections. An iconic election poster portrayed a swarthy, drooling Bolshevik, clenching a knife between broken teeth. One could easily imagine the fetid odor of this unwashed, blood-drenched vampire of the left, stinking of sweat and tobacco, feeding upon the innocent, better classes of the bourgeoisie. The Germans had their poster too: the Bolshevik looks the same: a dirty, foul-smelling workman, carrying a long dagger and a smoking bomb, challenged by a red-clad, blond-haired, winged angel, protecting the innocent. In January 1919 German *freikorps*, or right-wing militias, put down a communist movement in Berlin and lynched its leaders.

The United States too had its anti-Red propaganda: a political cartoon, for example, portrays the gallant U.S. army holding back a great mob of knife- and club-wielding red ghouls, dirty "Wobblies" or syndicalists, demanding Soviet government in America. The so-called Palmer raids targeted union radicals and immigrants. American "Negroes" might be vulnerable to Red propaganda, worried President Wilson, a convinced segregationist, especially those soldiers who had been in France. Equality "had gone to their heads," he thought: they might think they deserved equal rights with whites. Returning home, trained at arms, Negroes "would be our greatest medium in conveying Bolshevism to America." The Ku Klux Klan, Wilson believed, would "protect the southern country from some of the ugliest hazards of a time of revolution." But what about the north? New York Jews, especially on the East Side, were whipping up Bolshevism. Wilson crisscrossed the country in the autumn of 1919: "The poison of disorder, the poison of revolt, the poison of chaos" was loose in America![34] Fear of immigrants and "Wobblies," white racism, anti-Semitism, and "anti-Bolshevikism" were a poisonous brew in the United States. But America was not unique. Winston Churchill, then Secretary of State for War, unfurled his own images of bloody baboons and gorillas. Bolshevism might go to the heads of "colored" peoples in the Empire. Red "propaganda" struck fear into government ministries and security services. In 1919 it would have been hard to imagine the "civilized" West *ever* being reconciled to Soviet Russia.

While the western allies kept Bolshevism bottled up in Russia, they could not strangle it. At the end of 1919, against long odds, the Red Army emerged victorious. The White Guards were reduced to debris streaming toward death or exile. And again something interesting occurred. In France, general staff officers noticed that the Soviet government was growing stronger, reconstituting a Great Russian state. This was "necessary for [the maintenance of] a balance of power in Europe," observed the war ministry's *2ᵉ Bureau*: "By an unexpected turn of events, this Russia of the future might develop from the present efforts of Lenin and Trotskii."[35] At the beginning of 1920, this was a heretical idea indeed. Sensible French staff officers already foresaw a resurgent, revanchist Germany. France needed strong allies, and the newly independent Polish state established in November 1918 could scarcely be an adequate anti-German counterweight. Only Russia could do that, Soviet or otherwise.

So who was the greater threat: the *Bolcho* or the *Boche*? That was the question. In 1920 an open mind about Soviet Russia had limited appeal in Paris: the Quai d'Orsay, like the State Department in Washington, remained intransigent.

Figure 1.4. *"Comment voter contre le communisme?"* French anti-Bolshevik election poster, 1919. *Bibliothèque de documentation internationale contemporaine, Nanterre, France.*

In London, Lloyd George, still the British prime minister, pondered an opening to Moscow, though he was up against heavy opposition. Always the maneuvering, practical politician, Lloyd George worried more about British unemployment and economic recovery than about a revanchist Germany. A post-war recession had struck Europe. "Workmen" were on the dole, a dangerous situation when Russian Bolsheviks offered interesting alternatives to capitalism. Soviet Russia was theoretically the perfect trading partner, having unlimited natural resources to sell and unlimited needs in every sort of manufactured product, from machine tools and locomotives to shoes and shovels. British industry produced them all and needed the orders. Lloyd George bided his time, waiting for the opportune moment. It had not come yet.

The Russo-Polish War

While the Red Army was preoccupied, fighting more dangerous enemies, the new Poland expanded eastward, biting off sizeable portions of Byelorussian and Ukrainian territory. This expansionist Poland was dominated by nationalist leaders who dreamed of restoring their country to great power status in its 1772 frontiers, reaching far into the Russian borderlands to Kiev in the Ukraine. In early 1920 the Poles sent secret envoys to Paris and hinted to the French minister in Warsaw that they wanted to launch a springtime offensive to take Kiev. The minister thought the Poles had lost their minds, but in Paris dreams of eradicating Bolshevism remained strong. The French government therefore feigned not to notice the Polish feelers, with a wink and a nod, while sending bullets and shells to Warsaw, knowing in fact what the Poles had in mind. France was Poland's main arms supplier, and its opinion mattered. Still, the French had to conceal their enthusiasm for the Polish offensive because Lloyd George was against it, thinking the idea the height of folly. The Poles, he said, should take care they didn't get their heads punched. The Polish generalissimo, Józef Piłsudski, could afford to ignore Lloyd George, with the French on side, and he launched his offensive in late April 1920, seizing Kiev in May.

This was very good news indeed, *if* the Poles could hold on to their ill-gotten gains. The Red Army pulled out of Kiev in order better to prepare a counter-offensive, which soon threw back the Poles in headlong retreat toward the west. Kiev was not going to be a Polish city. During the summer the situation looked grim in the west but encouraging in Moscow. At the second Comintern congress in Moscow, a huge map on the wall traced the Red Army's advance. The Soviet counter-offensive reached the outskirts of Warsaw in mid-August 1920. A Red victory seemed near, and the Treaty of

Versailles, built upon a strong Polish counterweight, teetered on the brink of collapse only a year after it had been signed.

Brest-Litovsk is history, soon Versailles will be too!

So the Bolsheviks hoped; even, or especially, the normally more pragmatic Lenin.

Fortunately for the Versailles powers, the Red Army's lines of supply and communication were over-extended and its left flank exposed, thanks to the insubordination of no less than Stalin, the political commissar with the southern wing of the Soviet advance. Piłsudski saw his opening and advanced into the breach, throwing back Soviet forces. The Polish victory came to be known as the "Miracle on the Vistula."

"Miracle" is the right word: it should remind readers of the Duke of Wellington's comment about the Battle of Waterloo against Napoleon in 1815. "It was the nearest-run thing you ever saw in your life." The Red wave toward the West had crested and the Treaty of Versailles was saved—for the time being.

The French hoped to keep the Poles fighting against Soviet Russia along with the Romanians and the debris of a White Guard army in the Crimea. This harebrained scheme soon collapsed, though it indicated the extent to which the Quai d'Orsay remained hostile to the Bolsheviks.[36] The Poles and Soviets eventually came to the sensible conclusion that enough was enough, and they agreed to peace terms in the Treaty of Riga in February 1921. Each side tried to out-swindle the other, but neither entirely succeeded, so that the terms of the treaty were unsatisfactory to both sides.[37] Piłsudski had not won Kiev or the 1772 frontiers, and he gained less territory in the east than he had possessed at the start of his April offensive. On the other hand, Soviet Russia had suffered a calamitous defeat—perhaps avoidable if Stalin had followed orders and covered the Red Army's left flank—and had to concede large territories occupied by majority Byelorussian and Ukrainian populations. It is true that Poland and Russia had fought over these borderlands for seven centuries, but the unsatisfactory treaty remained a thorn in the side of future Soviet-Polish relations. The thorn became a spike in the 1930s when the perennial question arose again of who was the greater enemy, Nazi Germany or the USSR. Would the Polish government know the right response?

Last Faint Hopes

The last faint hopes of the West in the extinction of Bolshevism guttered out in March 1921 when the Red Army put down a rebellion of dissident soldiers and sailors at the Red fortress of Kronstadt near Petrograd. The French and British gave the go-ahead to send supplies to the rebels, but it was too little, too late.[38] For the government in Moscow, the reports of Red Army soldiers killing one another raised a warning signal that the country was on the brink of chaos. The Bolsheviks had to look to economic and social recovery. True, the Bolsheviks had won the civil war, a conflict so violent that it made the American Civil War look like child's play. Eight million people, both soldiers and civilians, had died. The Russian economy was in ruins. War, Allied blockade, foreign intervention, and civil war had reduced industrial production to 10 to 15 percent of pre-war levels—and Russia in 1914 was still a largely agricultural economy. Paper money was worthless and the cities were starving. Peasants refused to sell produce, or even to plant their land, beyond immediate needs, because there was nothing they could buy. They did not give a damn about hungry people in the cities if they could not sell their produce for something of value. The Soviet economy was reduced to primeval levels and to barter exchanges, but there was little enough to barter. Red Army units had to requisition grain to feed the desperate cities, which led to equally desperate peasant resistance. So, yes, the Bolsheviks had won, but really they had lost, for Russia was in ruins. As Marx had observed and Lenin knew, one could not build socialism on ruins. The Bolsheviks turned their minds, however reluctantly, from world revolution to rebuilding their shattered country, or risk losing power.

In a malicious twist of fate, the revolutionaries had to appeal to the capitalist West for trade, credit, and technical expertise to rebuild. Above all, the Soviet government needed to borrow. A "ruthless" practitioner of realpolitik, as his Brest-Litovsk policy demonstrated, Lenin swallowed his pride and enjoined his comrades to do the same. He called it "peaceful coexistence." Go west, he said, not as communists, but as merchants. "Learn to trade" were his orders. The Soviet government launched the New Economic Policy (NEP), which privatized agricultural production and the production and retailing of certain goods, but retained state control of heavy industry.[39] The NEP represented a mixed economy to go with a tightening of political control. How ironic: the Bolsheviks became good businessmen. At the beginning they learned the hard way, by being chiseled, paying too much for shoddy goods, bought from shady "speculators."

It's all right, said Lenin: "I can understand that Communists need time to learn to trade, and I know that those who are learning will be making the crudest of mistakes." We have to rid ourselves of Russian bad habits, and we will.[40]

Lenin was right: Bolshevik traders caught on quickly and gained a reputation for driving a hard bargain, as any good merchant should do. As a British Treasury official eventually remarked, "Credit is Russia's God!"[41] The Soviet government enticed scoundrels first, and then progressively more respectable businesspeople and companies to trade with the USSR. The Bolsheviks scrupulously respected their contracts, and they tempted the West with profitable business. They taunted those who held back with sounds of jingling gold in competitors' pockets. This strategy galled the West, dividing new merchants and old investors, and it divided the former Allies, for no one wanted to be left out of trade in the potentially profitable Russian market.

Western-Soviet commerce was not easy. The Soviet government had annulled the Russian state debt and nationalized private property. Industrialists and investors had lost billions. When Soviet Russia said it wanted to trade and needed credit to do so, western bankers tapped their pens on the table and said nothing doing until you've paid off your debts. Who could blame them? They punished Soviet Russia, as they would any defaulted borrower, by denying credit for foreign trade, or by making it very dear.

Soviet diplomats had their work cut out for them. Their diplomacy was skillful and multi-faceted, and it took place on two planes: political and economic. Beyond trade, the Soviet government wanted diplomatic recognition to enhance the terms and conditions of trade, and also to improve political relations with the West. The Soviet government feared—and not entirely without reason—the formation of a new western anti-communist bloc against it. Trade and better political relations would avert this danger.

Lloyd George, who had been biding his time until the end of the Russo-Polish War, now moved ahead to obtain a trade agreement with the USSR in April 1921. It was a breakthrough for Soviet diplomacy but only the beginning of Soviet efforts to escape from economic and diplomatic isolation. Each side had to make large accommodations. The "Entente" and Soviet Russia had been at war since November 1917; neither had succeeded in gaining the upper hand. The revolution had failed to spread into Europe; the capitalist West had failed to crush it in Russia. It was a standoff, though Moscow was the weaker of the two foes. Would bygones be bygones? Would the foes come to an accommodation, or would the conflict between them continue by other means?

Notes

1. General Sir Alfred Knox, quoted in Lloyd C. Gardner, *Safe for Democracy: The Anglo-American Response to Revolution, 1913–1923* (New York, 1984), p. 148.

2. M. J. Carley, *Revolution and Intervention: The French Government and the Russian Civil War, 1917–1919* (Montréal, 1983), pp. 15–17; and Lloyd C. Gardner, *Safe for Democracy*, pp. 147, 168.

3. David S. Foglesong, *America's Secret War against Bolshevism: U.S. Intervention in the Russian Civil War, 1917–1920* (Chapel Hill, 1995), p. 84; and Carley, *Revolution and Intervention*, pp. 19–21.

4. Gardner, *Safe for Democracy*, p. 157.

5. Donald E. Davis and Eugene P. Trani, *The First Cold War: The Legacy of Woodrow Wilson in U.S.-Soviet Relations* (Columbia, Mo., 2002), pp. 88–89; Foglesong, *America's Secret War*, p. 30; and Gardner, *Safe for Democracy*, pp. 198–99.

6. Richard K. Debo, *Revolution and Survival: The Foreign Policy of Soviet Russia, 1917–1918* (Toronto, 1979), pp. 138–41.

7. Michael Kettle, *The Allies and the Russian Collapse, March 1917–March 1918* (Minneapolis, 1981), pp. 37–38.

8. Gardner, *Safe for Democracy*, pp. 166–67.

9. Carley, *Revolution and Intervention*, pp. 33–44.

10. Ibid., pp. 50–53.

11. Foglesong, *America's Secret War*, p. 66; and Gardner, *Safe for Democracy*, pp. 160–61, 170.

12. Foglesong, *America's Secret War*, pp. 2, 5, 65, 94, 234.

13. Gardner, *Safe for Democracy*, p. 165.

14. Ibid., p. 170.

15. R. H. Bruce Lockhart, *British Agent* (New York, 1933), p. 222.

16. Carley, *Revolution and Intervention*, pp. 39–41.

17. J. W. Wheeler-Bennett, *Brest-Litovsk: The Forgotten Peace, March 1918* (London, 1963), p. 276.

18. "The Revolutionary Phrase," 21 Feb. 1918, V. I. Lenin, *On the Foreign Policy of the Soviet State* (Moscow, 1968), pp. 28–38.

19. Robert C. Tucker, *Stalin as Revolutionary, 1878–1929* (New York, 1974), pp. 50–51.

20. Robert Service, *Lenin: A Biography* (Cambridge, Mass., 2000), p. 376.

21. Carley, *Revolution and Intervention*, p. 213, n. 50; and General Jean Guillaume Lavergne, French military attaché in Moscow, no. 1343, 21 June 1918, *Château de Vincennes, Service historique de l'armée de terre* (hereinafter SHAT), 16N 3185.

22. Carley, *Revolution and Intervention*, pp. 67–71; and "Remise de fonds en Russie et en Roumanie," 1917–1918, SHAT 8N 20.

23. R. H. Ullman, *Anglo-Soviet Relations, 1917–1921*, 3 vols. (Princeton, N.J., 1961–1972), II, pp. 339, 365–68.

24. Sir Robert Hodgson, British chargé d'affaires in Moscow, no. 581, confidential, 13 Aug. 1926, N4052/53/38, National Archives of the United Kingdom, Kew (hereinafter TNA) Foreign Office (hereinafter FO) 371 11780.

25. Internment Operations Office, Ottawa, 10 May 1917, TNA, KV2 503.

26. Sir Basil Thomson, head of Special Branch, Metropolitan Police, "Conversation with M. Krassin," 4 June 1920, KV2 503.

27. Gardner, *Safe for Democracy*, p. 198; David W. McFadden, *Alternative Paths: Soviets and Americans, 1917–1920* (New York, 1993), p. 35.

28. Stéphane Pichon in November 1918, quoted in M. J. Carley, "Episodes from the Early Cold War: Franco-Soviet Relations, 1917–1927," *Europe-Asia Studies*, vol. 52, no. 7 (Nov. 2000), pp. 1275–1305.

29. Robert Wohl, *French Communism in the Making, 1914–1924* (Stanford, 1966), pp. 115–16.

30. Ibid., p. 121.

31. Ibid., p. 116.

32. General Henri M. Berthelot in March 1919, quoted in Carley, *Revolution and Intervention*, p. 145.

33. General Philippe Henri d'Anselme in April 1919, quoted in Carley, *Revolution and Intervention*, p. 176.

34. Foglesong, *America's Secret War*, pp. 31–32, 40–42.

35. M. J. Carley, "The Politics of Anti-Bolshevism: The French Government and the Russo-Polish War, December 1919–May 1920," *Historical Journal*, vol. 19, no. 1 (March 1976), pp. 173–74.

36. M. J. Carley, "Anti-Bolshevism in French Foreign Policy: The Crisis in Poland in 1920," *International History Review*, vol. 2, no. 3 (July 1980), pp. 423–26.

37. Jerzy Borzecki, *The Soviet-Polish Peace of 1921 and the Creation of Interwar Europe* (New Haven, 2008), passim.

38. Carley, "Episodes," p. 1276.

39. Jon Jacobson, *When the Soviet Union Entered World Politics* (Berkeley, Calif., 1994), pp. 19–21.

40. "The International and Domestic Situation of the Soviet Republic," 6 March 1922, Lenin, *Foreign Policy*, pp. 368–79.

41. "Russian Solvency," F. H. Nixon, Export Credits Guarantee Department, 15 Dec. 1931, TNA Treasury (hereinafter T), 160 790/F7438/5.

CHAPTER TWO

∼

"We Must Trade and They Must Trade"

First Attempts at Peaceful Coexistence, 1921–1922

When the western powers contemplated relations with Soviet Russia at the beginning of the 1920s, their first concern was the security of the capitalist order, or the family "spoons." The image comes from Arthur Steel-Maitland, Minister of Labor in the 1924 British Conservative government. As he put it, "until the burglar has given proof of repentance one doesn't hand over the spoons to him for safe keeping."[1] Soviet "repentance" meant in effect renunciation of world revolution before Moscow would get normal political and economic relations. Soviet Russia had given the West a good scare, and the "spoons" had to be protected. "Repentance" was not going to be obtained easily.

Though the Red Scare subsided after the Battle of Warsaw in August 1920, the western powers were not convinced that the Bolsheviks were ready to renounce world revolution, any more than the Bolsheviks were convinced that the West was ready to renounce its hopes in the failure of the revolution in Russia. As it happened, the suspicions of both sides were justified, though the Bolsheviks, being more needy, had to work harder at sorting out the contradictions in their policies toward the West and thus at downplaying world revolution.

Even in 1918 the Bolsheviks looked for ways out of the dilemma of how to keep at bay both the Germans and the Entente. Survival was a month-to-month, or even week-to-week exercise, so that any short-term compromise or surrender, no matter how ugly, was acceptable if it gave the Soviet government time to strengthen itself. In a way, the Bolsheviks were naïve. They thought they could threaten the world capitalist order; encourage angry soldiers to turn their guns against their governments; and abolish property, banks, and foreign debts, but at the same time negotiate with their capitalist enemies. Reality is an ugly thing, Lenin said to his comrades: be ready to crawl in the mud of fetid compromise to protect the revolution in Russia. So it was that Georgi Vasil'evich Chicherin, who succeeded Trotskii as *narkom* or commissar for foreign affairs, tried to convince low-ranking American diplomats in Moscow during the spring and summer of 1918 that the Soviet government was ready for business-like solutions with the West, and particularly with the United States.

Georgii Vasil'evich Chicherin

Chicherin was an apt choice to put over this position to the West. Born in 1872, Georgii Vasil'evich descended from an old family of the Russian nobility and had served for several years in the tsarist diplomatic corps as an archivist and historian. He was highly educated, cultured, and multi-lingual, anything but the archetypical Bolshevik vampire so often represented in western propaganda. Chicherin liked music, especially Mozart, and played his work on piano. In politics, he became a Menshevik after the split in the Social Democratic Party in 1903, quarreling with Lenin before the war. Yes, of course, one might well ask who did *not* quarrel with Lenin before the war. Chicherin left Russia in 1904, missing the first revolution, but getting involved in exile politics. He lived in Germany and France and was in England when the revolution broke out in 1917. Chicherin was what one would now call a workaholic. Ascetic, highly disciplined, with little personal life and no spouse, he hardly fit the caricature of a profligate dandy of the Russian nobility that he had once been. His life was dedicated to the revolution. Instead of dressing elegantly, noted a colleague, he wore workmen's clothing. Having preferred good food and vintage wines, he became a vegetarian and teetotaler. His family had money, and he did not lack for it. Once a spendthrift, he became a pinch-penny, giving his unneeded money to the cause and to the party. Arriving in London after the war broke out, he joined the Communist Club and the British Socialist Party. He was in the thick of the movement, playing a public role in anti-war activities. These began to irritate the British police and he was briefly arrested in 1915. He was arrested again in August 1917 and confined in the notorious Brixton jail.

After the Bolsheviks took power, Trotskii demanded Chicherin's release along with other émigrés, threatening as a reprisal to deny exit visas to British nationals in Russia, including the British ambassador in Petrograd. The threat worked: Chicherin was released and he returned home in January 1918.[2]

Years later, Chicherin remembered the Italian barber who had often provided the back room of his shop in Kentish Town for meetings and then was condemned to six months in prison. A good comrade, Chicherin recalled, and he sent instructions to the *torgpredstvo* in London, the Soviet trade mission, to help him out.[3]

He remembered the British socialists too. When Henry N. Brailsford, a Labour journalist, noted sarcastically that Chicherin's noble lineage went back further than Lord Curzon's, then the British Foreign Secretary, Chicherin commented that the British socialists were "now almost our most malicious enemies."[4] Whether Chicherin held a personal grudge against the British government would not be surprising, but he did not let it affect his policies. He pursued better relations with Britain as with other countries in the national interests of the Soviet Union.

Appointed commissar for foreign affairs in March 1918, Chicherin gave up his workman's blues for unfashionable wool suits. He was not exactly the best-

Figure 2.1. Georgii Vasil'evich Chicherin, ca. 1918–1920. *Arkhiv vneshnei politiki Rossiiskoi Federatsii.* **Moscow (AVPRF), f. 779, d. 2168/1, l.f. Chicherin, G. V., p. 1.**

dressed man in Moscow. The British agent R. H. Bruce Lockhart observed that he had seen Chicherin every day in the same "hideous yellow-brown tweed suit, which he had brought with him from England . . . during the six months of our almost daily contact." Eccentric and bohemian in his ways, Chicherin cared little about personal appearance. In later years, readers will be relieved to know, Chicherin bowed to conventions and had the necessary derby hat, frock coat, and other accoutrements for diplomatic meetings abroad. He gave up the "hideous" tweed suit. He also gave up the teetotaling. In fact, he could hold his drink. He once challenged the Polish ambassador to a series of toasts and downed his first large tumbler of whiskey with a cry of "Long live *Polska!*" The ambassador was the first to lower his glass and declare himself "*hors combat.*"[5]

Chicherin got on well with his staff, who greatly admired him and laughed at his eccentricities. He was a night owl who worked late, often receiving diplomats or journalists past midnight, much to the irritation of the NKID security detail. He worked closely with Lenin, who admired him, though not uncritically. Who did Lenin not criticize at one time or another? Chicherin's relations with Stalin were not as constant or as cordial. There were often clashes over the foreign policy gaffes of Stalin's allies in the Politburo, or Soviet cabinet.

Chicherin had an extraordinary memory but insisted on keeping important papers in his office, where they piled up on his desk, on the sofa, or anywhere there was empty space. Of course, when he needed a document, proximity did not help, and he had to call for a secretary to find it.

"Comrade Chicherin, perhaps it is on your . . . desk," she would say.

Well, yes, but where? Chicherin might reply. The secretary would eventually find the missing report under a pile of papers.

When Chicherin was late to a meeting, a colleague whispered, "He has lost another telegram." And comrades smiled.

His mind, however, was sharpened to a fine point. He worked 16 hours out of every 24, according to Bruce Lockhart, and was "indefatigable and relentless in his attention to his duties." He spoke English, German, and French equally well, and wrote with elegance. One of his stenographers said that she could tell what kind of mood he was in by which language he used for dictation.[6]

British diplomats paid him grudging respect. "He reminds one of a rather amiable and agreeable snake," according to Lord D'Abernon, the British ambassador in Berlin:

> Not devoid of kindly feeling towards the world in general and towards rabbits in particular, provided they surrender their burrows to the State without too much fuss. Like many personages in history accused of wholesale cruelty he is sensitive and humane almost to exaggeration in regard to minor acts of blood-

shed: he will not shoot game as he cannot bear to see an animal killed—and he crosses the street to avoid a butcher's shop. At the same time, the poison fangs are there at the disposal of theoretical conceptions fanatically held.[7]

Chicherin, a hypochondriac, was often in Berlin to see not only German ministers but also his German doctors. The British embassy observed his comings and goings. "The arrival of Tchitcherin [sic] in Berlin can only be compared to the arrival of a film artist," D'Abernon noted: "He is interviewed by every reporter of every journal, sees a good many officials, and nearly all the leading Jews."[8] Well, D'Abernon would have thought, at least Chicherin is not a Jew.

He is "one of the keenest brains in Russia," noted a Foreign Office clerk in 1925: "The brains have however been developed on pre-war German conceptions of foreign affairs, and on 'Weltpolitik' and 'Machtverhältnisse.'"[9] Foreign Office diplomats had a curious attitude, redolent of great powers: they thought Britain operated along different lines than other states. This was of course untrue. Nothing was more in line with *Machtverhältnisse* than Lord Palmerston's epigram that "England has no permanent friends and no permanent enemies, only permanent interests."

Early Soviet Policy

New in his job in the spring of 1918, Chicherin talked to American diplomats in Moscow, trying to avert an open conflict with the United States. Soviet policy intended to treat the United States differently from France or Britain, in the hopes that this apparently more progressive society might be less hostile to the Russian Revolution. The idea was to prevent the West from forming a bloc against Soviet Russia; this remained Soviet policy until World War II.

In 1918 Chicherin's idea was naïve since Lansing was just as determined to overthrow Soviet authority as his counterparts in Paris or London. In his public statements Chicherin liked to recall the American Revolution, believing the United States to be a more democratic society than France or England. Even hardened Bolsheviks, though perhaps not Lenin, could be fooled by appearances. In fact, the United States was not so far removed from black slavery. Jim Crow, the Ku Klux Klan, and lynch law ruled the American South. President Wilson was a segregationist, who envisaged the Klan as a kind of bulwark in "the southern country" against "the ugliest hazards of a time of revolution."[10] American capitalism was just as tightfisted and ruthless as, and perhaps more so than, its European varieties, for there was no strong socialist party in the United States to put a brake on a barely regulated capitalist elite.

Nevertheless, even superficial distinctions were worth exploiting to prevent the consolidation of a western anti-Soviet bloc. Americans thought of themselves as an exceptional society, above all others. The Bolsheviks played to such conceits in order to keep the United States away from an interventionist bloc with France and Britain. It was the "red thread" of Soviet foreign policy in 1918–1919.[11] Chicherin and his Soviet colleagues would talk to shadowy middlemen, profiteers, politicians, and more respectable businessmen, *anyone* who might help to break Soviet Russia's isolation. As R. K. Debo has noted, the Bolsheviks always preferred talking to fighting.[12] It was a sensible position given the precarious state of Soviet affairs.

In 1920 the Soviet government conducted business negotiations in order to improve the atmosphere for political discussions. Diplomatic recognition was the key to better trade relations, and vice versa. It did not matter if contracts resulted from such discussions, for the very fact of talking would improve the political atmosphere. The idea was to keep the former western allies from ganging up again on Soviet Russia in a "common front." In discussions at the Narkomindel, the commissariat for foreign affairs (NKID), Chicherin and his colleagues developed a strategy: exploit the contradictory interests of the western powers; negotiate with them separately; delay any discussions of compensation for debts. This policy is often attributed to Marxist conceptions of "contradictions" between the capitalist or imperialist powers, but divide and rule one's adversaries was and is a classical strategy practiced since the beginning of states and empires. The imperialist or colonial powers were in fact adept at its application.

In applying Soviet strategy, Leonid B. Krasin, a most unusual sort of Bolshevik, stressed the importance of putting off any indemnification for tsarist debts or nationalized foreign property. Every available ruble had to be invested in economic reconstruction and development, for otherwise Soviet Russia could never pay a kopek on the tsarist debt, or if it did, it would have to sacrifice its development and remain in a state of backwardness. Economic development and debt repayment were closely linked. Soviet Russia would need a long period of peace and security to recover and develop its economy; this could only be achieved by "mutual guarantee with all the most powerful capitalist states." Krasin's exegesis was an elaboration of Lenin's concept of "peaceful coexistence" with the West.[13] It is not clear whether the new policy originated in the NKID, or with Krasin or Lenin himself.

Leonid Borisovich Krasin

Krasin, who was charged with obtaining contracts in the West, was well suited to his job. Unlike Chicherin's parents, Krasin's father was a low-ranking government official and his mother of Siberian peasant descent. Leonid Borisovich was born in 1870 in Kurgan, western Siberia, not too far from Cheliabinsk. His father saw to his formal education. Like many others of his generation, Krasin became involved in the revolutionary movement as a university student during the early 1890s. He was a charming, masculine fellow, fond of his female contemporaries, and not particularly concerned over any scandals which that interest might provoke. He passed through the various stages of arrest, imprisonment, and exile, with the difference that he also pursued a career as an engineer. This respectable bourgeois cover camouflaged Krasin's eventual role as bomb maker, arms supplier, and "finance minister" of the Bolshevik party during and after the 1905 Russian Revolution. Nikitich and *Zima* were among his revolutionary pseudonyms. Like Chicherin, indeed like almost everyone, Krasin quarreled with Lenin, and he eventually joined the German manufacturing firm Siemens-Schuckert Electrical Company, returning to Moscow as the company's chief sales representative. Krasin moved easily from the revolutionary underground to the industrial board room. In 1912, the tsarist police even permitted him to take up residence in Moscow. Like many other Bolsheviks, Krasin was multi-

Figure 2.2.   Leonid Borisovich Krasin, ca. 1920s.
AVPRF, f. 787, d. 725/1, kor. no. 13, ch. 2.

lingual, which served him well in doing Siemens' business. When the Great War broke out in August 1914, Krasin supported the Russian war effort and managed an arms manufacturing plant for the tsarist government. After the Bolsheviks took power, Krasin again answered the call to revolution, and he got back his old job of overseeing military procurement for the Red Army. Later, he became commissar for external trade and fireman *par excellence* whenever the Soviet government had to negotiate with the West.[14]

His name turns up frequently in British, American, and French diplomatic papers during the early 1920s. According to one State Department official, Krasin was "a person . . . we could do business with," who was "not at heart a Bolshevik." He might also be an "important factor in an eventual Bolshevik compromise with, or surrender to, capitalism." He was even perceived as someone who could be turned against the Soviet government. There is even an anonymous report in British Secret Intelligence Service files to the effect that Krasin "was at one time an agent of the Czarist police."[15]

Unfortunately for the West, Krasin was no Trojan horse, though the Quai d'Orsay saw him as a *"bon bourgeois."* British officials regarded Krasin as a "moderate," "accredited rather to the City than to the Foreign Office." The Foreign Secretary, Austen Chamberlain, wondered whether the City would be able to resist his "temptations." One Foreign Office official warned against any illusions: Krasin "has always remained a thorough Russian at heart and a fanatical communist by conviction."[16]

He was well regarded by his Soviet colleagues. According to Chicherin, Krasin was "a person of authority for Lenin." Another said that "Lenin counted on no one like he did on Krasin and liked no one as much as he did Krasin." He was "our first Red *kupets*," or trader, observed fellow commissar A. V. Lunarcharskii, and a smooth negotiator, Trotskii also spoke well of him. He had a special "Krasinskii" way of speaking. "Give Russia a chance to keep its word" was his favorite line with western interlocutors. But he battled with the Politburo and with the NKID over concessions to the West. Often at the front lines of conflict, he was prepared to deal to obtain agreement, and sometimes Moscow thought he went too far.[17]

Jingling Bolshevik Gold

Krasin was a good choice to lead early negotiations with the West. Trade was the hook; jingling gold was the bait. Western manufacturers, who had order books to fill, were interested in trade with Soviet Russia, if the appropriate legal guarantees, credits, and trade insurance were available. Their governments hesitated, divided between pragmatists, like Lloyd George, who wanted the trade, and anti-communist ideologues, "Die-Hards" like

Churchill, who still wanted to "down the Bolsh." One French newspaper referred to the Russian market as a "new Eldorado." It was tempting. Who could blame manufacturers who wanted to keep their plants operating and to move into a market where seemingly anything could be sold? The ideologues tended to look down their noses at the businessmen, too eager for contracts, too crass, and not part of the *real* elite. They were "a great bore," said one snobbish Foreign Office clerk.[18] Western historians who debate whether Soviet foreign policy was driven by ideology instead of common sense and realpolitik appear to forget that western policy toward the Soviet Union was also torn between similar impulses.[19]

To entice the West, the Soviet government at first bought with gold and then sold petroleum, timber, grain, and agricultural products to obtain foreign exchange. The ideologues worried that the Soviet government would use its profits for "propaganda." The propaganda was worrisome for governments with restive colonial populations, or impatient "Negroes" in the United States, now with military training, who had to endure Jim Crow and the Ku Klux Klan. Caught between the interests of businessmen who wanted to trade and bankers who wanted to collect unpaid debts, western governments made compromises. Trade was permissible on a cash-only basis, without trade credits or insurance and without government guarantees. The western powers still refused to recognize the Soviet government and so could not offer consular services in Russia to their nationals. They hoped that business on a cash-only basis would break the Soviet treasury and lead to a change in government.

Propaganda remained a serious concern. Even though the danger of revolution in Europe had passed, independent-minded colonial populations were restive, on the move, and often inspired by the success of the revolution in Russia. We forget sometimes that western "democracy" was primarily for people with white faces, who lived comfortably. In April 1919 a British brigadier in Amritsar, India, ordered his troops to fire on a crowd at an open-air meeting. It was a massacre. That same year, the "May 4th movement" launched in China, a western semi-colony, and sought to end western domination. In September 1920, the Comintern sponsored a congress of eastern peoples at Baku in the Caucasus. The congress obtained wide publicity and represented a Soviet commitment to colonized populations. If Europe was less vulnerable to Bolshevik propaganda, Asian populations were ripe for revolt. They represented potential allies against the British, who were expanding into oil-rich areas of the former Ottoman Empire and approaching Soviet southern frontiers. Chicherin worried about a British threat to Soviet security in the Caucasus and Central Asia.

At first Krasin's golden temptations were easy to resist, though not for long. The U.S. government considered it a matter of principle not to trade with Soviet Russia, or at least to keep business on a cash-and-carry basis. The Bolsheviks were good at propaganda, thought Sheldon Whitehouse, a State Department official: they "make various countries think the others are doing 'big bizness' & so enlist general commercial support for resumption of trade."[20] In 1921 Charles E. Hughes, the Secretary of State, and a hard-line anti-communist, laid out the State Department line to his diplomats: there is no basis for Soviet-American trade relations until there are fundamental changes in Soviet Russia regarding "safety of life, the recognition by firm guarantees of private property, the sanctity of contract, and the rights of free labor."[21] Hughes' statement defined American policy during the 1920s, but at the behest of Commerce Secretary Herbert Hoover, it was softened a little so as not to leave all the "bizness" to the British and "to the damage of our citizens."[22] It galled Hoover that there might be a free-for-all between foreign companies for the private property confiscated by Soviet authorities. He proposed to Hughes that an agreement be sought with other governments to discourage "a panic of grabbing." "No honest nation," added Hoover, "could refuse to prevent its citizens from receiving stolen goods."

Well, yes, it could. Although the prospect was galling, Hughes declined to take any immediate action, probably because American businessmen were already in on the "grabbing" in Soviet Russia.[23]

Since the Bolsheviks could not get bank credit and in 1921 had nothing to export, they had to pay gold for their acquisitions. They did not have enough for all they needed, reckoned the State Department, and "the sooner it [the gold] is totally dispersed the better."[24] The Bolsheviks would then become desperate and would see reason or collapse. "Economic failure," one State Department official observed, "has forced the Bolsheviki to adopt many capitalistic methods and has launched them recently upon a general program of compromise with capitalism. This movement is insincere and involuntary . . . but the pressure of acts may make it real." The Bolsheviks held on to power because of the "practical political efficiency of some of their leaders," especially Lenin, but they had never been able to exert complete control over all Russian territories. "Life in some of these regions seems to have reverted to a sort of medieval parochialism."[25] This "Orientalist" view was widely held inside and out of the State Department. It was a matter of "sanity" and of "recognition by Communist Russia of the capitalistic business system of civilized nations." The "right-wing Bolsheviki" or "the more conservative elements in Russia" were leading the way, but who knew how long "the lucid moment" would last?[26] Like the Foreign Office and the Quai d'Orsay, the State Department was a hotbed of anti-Bolshevism: "Each crisis," noted one clerk, "increases disorganization and weakens the prestige of the Soviets. Sooner or later they seem doomed to collapse. Their fall may be announced tomorrow; it may be months off."[27] M. M. Litvinov, *zamnarkom*, or deputy commissar for foreign affairs, observed that the U.S. government was so hostile to Soviet Russia that even the competitive activities in the Far East of arch-rival Japan had not led it to reevaluate its policies.[28]

Soviet Russia did indeed face a grave domestic crisis beginning in the spring of 1921. Famine struck southern Russia as a result of the chaos of foreign intervention and civil war, but also because of severe drought. The Soviet government was in such desperate straits that it accepted international aid, notably from the American Relief Association (ARA). The very anti-communist commerce secretary Hoover headed the operation. The ARA was not above encouraging Russians to emancipate themselves from Bolshevik "tyranny." The Foreign Office, too, saw an opportunity to exploit famine relief "for bringing all the European Powers into line against the Soviet government and besides destroying the pet weapon of the latter—which is to play off one power against the other—would assist us very materially in defeating the pro-Bolsheviks at home."

"An international combine against the Soviet has been impossible so far," noted one Foreign Office official, "but if the French government are prepared to be accommodating now, the thing becomes realisable and we ought to take swift advantage of it." There was even some thought to including Germany in a new anti-Soviet front.[29] The Foreign Office was quite touchy about famine aid, not wanting the Bolsheviks to profit from it politically. Indeed, it would do no harm if the famine brought down the Bolsheviks. According to J. D. Gregory, head of the Foreign Office Northern Department responsible for Russian affairs, Bolshevik collapse "would relieve Europe of a nightmare."[30] Each side knew the other's strategies and did their best to thwart them. It was easier, however, for the Bolsheviks to divide and rule than for the West to unite in an anti-Soviet bloc.

Krasin knew all the arguments against better relations with Soviet Russia, but he persisted. Hughes' opposition was not insurmountable, he said in a published interview. It was inevitable that trade relations would be resumed, and the sooner the better. Everyone would gain: Russian reconstruction would facilitate stability in Europe. He assured his interlocutors that the Soviet government would "keep its word" and respect its contracts with the West. It needs to trade. "Revolutions are not easy things," he added: "All sorts of mistakes will be made and abuses will creep in." When the perennial question of "propaganda" came up, Krasin pointed out that Bolshevik propaganda was a "weapon of self-defense." Indeed, the United States used propaganda as a weapon of war against Soviet Russia. He also reminded the Americans that there was a distinction to be made between the Soviet government and the Comintern.[31] And if rational argument did not work,

Krasin knew how to jingle a bag of Bolshevik gold to get the attention of businessmen who would then pressure their governments to permit trade with Soviet Russia. This approach was so galling because it was so effective in attracting western attention.

The French were just as susceptible to Krasin's strategy and therefore just as irritated as the Americans by Soviet maneuvering. Philippe Berthelot, secretary general of the French foreign ministry, hated the Bolsheviks and all their works. He fumed at Krasin's strategy of jingling gold, and he warned that France would have to be on its guard against Soviet "traps" and "chicanery."[32] *Hélas* for Berthelot, Krasin was not the only one to work on the French. Another of the Soviet "pragmatists" was Maksim Maksimovich Litvinov.

Maksim Maksimovich Litvinov

Litvinov has a prominent role in this narrative, and readers should get to know him. Maksim Maksimovich was born in Bialystok in tsarist Poland in 1876. He was the offspring of an uncharacteristically dysfunctional Jewish middle-class family. His father's surname was Vallakh. Unlike Chicherin and Krasin, Litvinov's formal education was limited to the local secondary school. Being Jewish in tsarist Russia, his chances of entering university were limited. So he went into the Russian army at age 17. There he became an artilleryman and discovered Marx and Engels. Litvinov followed the usual path of a Russian revolutionary, eventually escaping from a tsarist jail to Western Europe. Litvinov sided with Lenin's Bolsheviks after the Social Democratic movement split in 1903, becoming a smuggler, clandestine newspaper publisher, gunrunner, and fence for "expropriated," stolen tsarist rubles taken in bank heists in the Caucasus. He was a kind of Bolshevik "Sundance Kid," an incongruous background for someone who would become a polished, multi-lingual diplomat of the first order and one of the Soviet Union's most important interlocutors with the West. And yes, Litvinov also had his differences with Lenin, who he thought was too dogmatic.

After the failure of the 1905 revolution, like Krasin he drifted away from the revolutionary movement. In 1908 Litvinov ended up in England, eventually taking a job with a London publisher. It was there that he met Ivy Low, a somewhat bohemian English woman from a middle-class family of historians and journalists. Litvinov married her in 1916 and seemed ready to settle into the conventional middle-class life of a regular job and children. But he told Ivy that if revolution ever broke out again in Russia, he would return to it.

And so he did, though not to resume his role as the "Sundance Kid." At age 40, he was putting on weight, needed spectacles, and wore a wrinkled

**Figure 2.3.   Maksim Maksimovich Litvinov,
ca. 1920s. AVPRF, f. 787, d. 687/1, kor. no.
13, ch. 2.**

suit, pockets stuffed with newspapers, not grenades. In short, his days as
"Sundance" were over. Multi-lingual, well read and informed, he became
instead the first Soviet diplomat in England. At the outset his communications with the new government in Russia were sporadic and *en clair*: he
learned of the revolution in Petrograd and his appointment as Soviet representative from the newspapers. In June 1918 Chicherin wanted to send
Litvinov to the United States where he might be more useful in stopping
the Allied intervention. The State Department did not want him, and he
stayed in London where he was later arrested and eventually exchanged for
British diplomats in Moscow.[33]

His main interlocutor in the British government was R. A. Leeper, then
a junior Foreign Office clerk. Leeper left a handwritten recollection of
Litvinov 15 years later when the then commissar for foreign affairs came
to London.

> In 1918 I was in almost daily contact with him for many months at a time when
> he was being subjected to innumerable annoyances & indignities. I had then
> found him, apart from occasional explosions, good-tempered & reasonable. He

was in fact as frank & natural as the circumstances permitted. Fifteen years have passed. . . . I had been told by journalists . . . that if I met him again I should find him very much changed with a hard crust of cynicism which he employs as a weapon of self-defence in dealing with foreigners. . . . I found nothing of the sort. Away from the atmosphere of Moscow he was exactly the same in his manner as formerly, affable & natural.

Leeper noted that Litvinov "spoke with regret rather than with bitterness" about the difficulties of dealing with the British government. "There were constant setbacks," Litvinov said.

His main desire had always been to establish satisfactory working relations with us. He had married an English wife, he had lived longer in this country than in any other outside Russia, & he had in consequence a greater regard for it. Yet in conducting official relations with the British Government he was confronted with much greater difficulties than with any other Government. . . . Nowhere were the press & Parliament so vindictive against Russia. . . . He could only conclude that there were powerful influences at work here to prevent any kind of working arrangement between the two Governments.

Litvinov's laments should be taken with a large grain of salt; he sometimes said the same thing about France to sympathetic French diplomats, though, to be sure, there were few of those. Soviet relations with France were most certainly not easier than with Britain. And many Foreign Office officials would have scoffed at Litvinov's complaints, blaming the Soviet government for all the difficulties. Leeper's account is nevertheless a sympathetic introduction to Litvinov, who, along with Chicherin, directed the effort for better relations with Britain in the 1920s, and for the formation of a grand alliance against Nazi Germany in the 1930s.[34]

Other British officials had a less kindly view of Litvinov. One official who saw him in 1922 said he was "a horrible looking brute with a fat sensual clean-shaven puffy face, and very thick lips," who made "the most preposterous claims on behalf of Russia."[35] In 1924 the Foreign Office tried to keep Litvinov out of Britain when the Soviet government wanted to send him to London for negotiations, his anti-war activities having not been forgotten. The Foreign Office clerks need not have worried; Litvinov's days as anti-war propagandist were long over. As deputy commissar and then commissar for foreign affairs, he strongly disapproved of propaganda activities organized out of Soviet embassies and trade missions. In diplomacy, exchanges should be conducted in private and in secret. Litvinov preferred candidness and realism to polemics. "Litvinov is a hard looking man," according to one unsigned French report, "but is frank and honest in his negotiations. He does not hide his ideas. He talks about them directly, but keeps his word and one can come to agreement with him. He has a practical mind and likes realities."[36]

Litvinov did *not* like making speeches that obliged him to communicate in a polemical, party language quite different from the secret language of realpolitik in the NKID. This latter discourse was not always appreciated by his Soviet audiences, who were more easily inspired by defiance toward the capitalist West and visions of world revolution. In the Soviet Communist Party, one French diplomat observed, no one had a greater disdain for public posturing than Litvinov. He preferred his office to the podium, and he worked long hours there, nearly as long as those of his titular boss Georgii Vasil'evich. In his normal routine Litvinov left the NKID at 4 p.m. for supper at his flat with his spouse and children, then returned to work late into the night. The former gunrunner and money launderer was now a skilled diplomat of the Soviet Union.[37]

His relations with Chicherin were complex, "complicated" according to one historian. Litvinov being deputy commissar, Chicherin was his titular superior, but they often appeared to act as co-commissars—or as sibling rivals.

Figure 2.4. Georgii V. Chicherin and Maksim M. Litvinov, 10 April 1922, Genoa. Photographer: Walter Gireke. Ullstein Bild, Granger Collection, NY.

Litvinov knew of course who was boss in the end. On strategy and basic ob-jectives, they rarely disagreed; on tactics, however, they were often at odds, as if instinctively, being rivals for the attention of Stalin and the Politburo. One joker in the NKID noted that if Litvinov was *for* something, Chicherin would be *against* it, and vice versa.[38] Readers will soon encounter examples of such behavior. Historians and contemporaries have often observed that Chicherin was pro-German, and Litvinov pro-British. This is untrue; they were both pro-Soviet. The primacy of the interests of the Soviet state was their shared preoccupation.

In the 1930s Litvinov had no serious rival inside the NKID; but elsewhere in Moscow, in the Politburo, wolves prowled, especially when the Stalinist purges began in 1936. Litvinov kept a loaded revolver under his pillow and slept in his street clothes. If the secret police came in the middle of the night, he did not want to be arrested in pajamas. According to V. M. Molotov, Sta-lin's right arm during the 1930s, "Litvinov remained among the living only by chance."[39] Molotov and Litvinov were not friends. Nevertheless, Stalin appeared to retain a certain respect for Litvinov even at the worst of times. He was one of the few "Old Bolsheviks" to survive the purges.

In early 1919 Litvinov was in Norway launching peace feelers toward the Allied heads of government, then in Paris for the peace conference to settle the war with Germany. His message was clear: "Russia needs for her economic reconstruction and development all the technical skill, experience and material support which can be obtained from other countries." And then there was the already habitual Soviet hook to attract Allied interest: "Should an understanding with the Allies be arrived at, the Soviet government would be willing to reconsider some of its decrees affecting the financial obliga-tions of Russia toward other countries." The one Soviet condition for these concessions was that the Allies stop "all direct or indirect military operations against Soviet Russia, all direct or indirect material assistance to Russian or other forces operating against the Soviet Government, and also every kind of economic warfare and boycott."[40] In early 1919 at the height of the Red Scare in Europe, with Churchill, Clemenceau, and others determined to crush the Soviets, Litvinov's offers went unanswered.

"Wearing Down" the French

In 1920 Litvinov returned to the charge, this time with the French. In March Litvinov told a French intermediary that the Soviet government wanted trade relations and would "pay its debts" when war with Poland had ended. Just as importantly, Litvinov stressed that France, unlike Britain, should have an interest in a strong Russian state.[41] This was special bait for France which was already worried about a revanchist Germany. Both baits were tempting, but would the French bite?

Not at first, but in 1921–1922, the circumstances were changing. Soviet trade prospects became more attractive after the launching of the New Economic Policy. The Russian market was a "gold mine," noted the French paper *L'Information*: "Are we going to be the only ones to miss out?" In Berlin, Soviet diplomats observed that the centrist Radical Party had started to press for an end to the *cordon sanitaire*. "The Russian question" was moving to the forefront of French attention because of intensifying fears of German *revanche*. But France faced a dilemma. We don't want to recognize the Soviet government, said Aristide Briand, then the French premier, but we would not mind trading with Russia. And here, noted a Soviet observer in Berlin, "is the basic problem to which Briand is seeking a way out."[42]

The Soviet government also faced a dilemma. It wanted better economic and political relations with France, but recognized that being in a hurry would be self defeating because the French would play harder to get. The Soviet solution was a policy of *Ermattungsstrategie*, of wearing the French down and of isolating and ignoring them. Soviet officials could read the French and British press. In July 1921 the *Manchester Guardian* noted, "Recently the French press has discovered that, besides the danger of going into Russia, there was [also another] danger, that of being kept out of it." It was the intensifying sound of Krasin's jingling gold which the French could not ignore. Officials in the Quai d'Orsay understood the strategy: get businessmen "to bite" at attractive contract offers, but link them to the establishment of diplomatic relations. This was a dupe's game, thought the French, and they were not going to play . . . well, anyway, not at first.[43]

The Comintern

Apart from maneuvering around the West's sticky principles of sanctity of property and debts, the Soviet government also had to do something about the Comintern, a thorn in the side of insecure colonial empires and of Jim Crow America with its "uppity" Negroes and militant union "Wobblies." At the outset, when the Soviet government was fighting for survival against Allied military intervention, it did not matter whether the Soviet government and Comintern as institutions were indistinguishable. In 1919, propaganda was dangerous for the West; after 1921 it was a nuisance for Soviet diplomacy. Even in 1920 the NKID recognized the importance of keeping its diplomats away from propaganda and foreign communists. In 1921 the Politburo started to disentangle NKID establishments from those of the Comintern. At first this was like trying to unravel the Gordian knot.

Stay out of "illegal" work or be careful not to get caught at it were some of the first directives. Frictions developed over money and interference in one another's backyard.[44] Chicherin informed the trade mission in London that the Comintern was being disentangled from government agencies. It would have its own apparatus and resources, and more foreign communists would be added to the Comintern leadership.[45] The NKID wanted Comintern agents out of its establishments abroad; the Comintern wanted to retain the right to keep one "under the roof" of all NKID embassies. Lenin suggested, rather casually considering Anglo-French irritation, that Chicherin and Comintern boss, Grigorii E. Zinoviev, meet periodically to discuss differences and that the Politburo then "consider the matter 'closed.'" Work it out yourselves was the Politburo's directive.[46]

These fine distinctions were not appreciated in the West. All directives to the NKID and the Comintern came from the same source: Lenin, later Stalin, and *Instantsiia*, the Politburo. Krasin liked to point out that the Comintern was a weapon of defense against the Allies when they waged war against the Soviet republic surrounding it with "a starvation blockade." If the Allies were ready to negotiate with Soviet Russia, Moscow would be ready to stop the hostile propaganda on a reciprocal basis.[47] Krasin had a point, but the Soviet government was going to have to do a lot better than that to satisfy susceptible western diplomats. Even the deputy Soviet trade representative in London, Ian A. Berzin, advised that Moscow had to do more to get separation between the Comintern and the Soviet government. And Berzin was a former Comintern official. It would help, he suggested in a case of understatement, if Lenin and Trotskii left the Comintern executive committee.[48] Perhaps unbeknownst to Berzin, Chicherin had already proposed the idea to Lenin, who rejected it out of hand.[49] The Gordian knot was not going to be so easily unraveled.

"We shall always have trouble over the connection with [the Comintern] and the Soviet Government. The latter will always, when charged, say that it is a separate institution," observed Gregory at the Foreign Office in April 1921. "The Soviet government, the Russian CP and the Third International," said another clerk, not quite correctly, "are a trinity in unity." Gregory assured the Home Office that the Foreign Office was "keeping a close watch" on Soviet activities.[50] So were the Secret Intelligence Service (SIS) and the Colonial and India Offices.

"Not Enough Snap"!

The British government did not like the Bolsheviks stirring up trouble in the Empire, though occasionally Foreign Office officials retained a sense of humor when dealing with the Soviet trade mission in London. Two bundles of printed "propaganda" somehow ended up at the British Museum, where the SIS picked them up. Gregory wrote to the trade mission to ask if he could assist in the redirection of the parcels. N. K. Klyshko, then deputy *torgpred*, acknowledged receipt of "the case of literature which was detained by the Director Intelligence" and thanked Gregory for his "trouble."[51]

British humor was the exception to the rule when it came to Bolshevik propaganda. But who could tell what was real and what was a forgery? When the Stockholm embassy reported on an apparent Comintern communication to the International Union of the Unemployed, Leeper minuted that there was "not enough snap" in the report to make it worth publicizing. When SIS forwarded another report from Stockholm about a clandestine draft for £35,000 made out to Klyshko, Foreign Secretary Lord Curzon wanted clarification.

"What does this mean?" he asked. "What is the evidence? Can we act on it?"

"I am sorry," responded Gregory. "I fear I failed to explain adequately. . . . The SIS are rather fond of making positive statements of this kind, and I have asked that, in every case . . . they [should] have the actual evidence: otherwise they are practically worthless—and dangerous."

"I am very glad that you brought the oversight to my notice," replied Malcolm Woollcombe from SIS, "for it was obviously wrong that the report should have been circulated without a comment of this sort. . . . We . . . have a good deal of stuff to deal with and slips such as this occasionally occur, though we do our level best to avoid them." For emphasis, Curzon underlined Woollcombe's first lines in blue pencil.[52]

The Orlov "Factory"

The French and British intelligence services certainly did have a lot of propaganda and clandestine money to track. The trouble was they had a hard time telling real from counterfeit "propaganda." Forging Soviet documents during the inter-war years was a lucrative business. There was even a professional organization of counterfeiters in Berlin run by Vladimir Grigor'evich Orlov, a White Russian, aka Vladislav Orbanskii, or Orlitsky (Orletskii), according to French military intelligence and the Soviet Cheka, the secret police. Orlov originally worked for the anti-Bolshevik Volunteer Army, and after its defeat ended up in Berlin, where, again according to French military intelligence, he set up an *agence de "Fausses Informations."* Orlov soon established an important network across Europe with links to various European intelligence services, including the French

2ᵉ Bureau. Soviet intelligence named his organization the "White International," which included anyone who dreamed of a tsarist restoration. According to one Soviet report, Orlov was obtaining financial support from at least ten countries, including France, Britain, and the United States. He also worked part time for the German police and had close ties with the German general staff, but he got his start in the hire of British intelligence agents who helped him set up his agency or "factory."[53]

Orlov became an entrepreneur of forged Soviet documents, based mostly on information in the Soviet press or on rumors circulating in European capitals. French military intelligence reckoned that the Soviet authorities knew about Orlov's activities but did not take them too seriously. In fact, Chicherin kept a file on Orlov, as well he might, since apparently the latter plotted his assassination in 1922. Litvinov did not know much about Orlov beyond what was in Chicherin's dossiers. The forgeries were good enough to fool the British and French police, though the wish being father to the thought, this did not take much doing. Hating the Bolsheviks, the French especially were takers for all Orlov could sell. Even *Soviet* intelligence bought some of his "documents," though unlike the French they were not so easily duped. On the other hand, the German police were takers of large quantities of Orlov's "intelligence," sometimes true, sometimes not.[54]

In 1929 Orlov and an accomplice ran afoul of their German patrons. They tried to sell counterfeit documents to an American journalist, H. R. Knickerbocker, which demonstrated that two U.S. senators, William Borah and George William Norris, had accepted Soviet bribes. Knickerbocker, indignant at being hoaxed, instigated the proceedings. The trial proved to be a carnival of the absurd, revealing "a lively activity between Russian émigrés acting as anti-Soviet spies and the *Reichskommissariat* for Public Order." Various émigré groups were "apparently so keen that they did not hesitate to spy on each other in order to prove themselves invaluable to the German authorities." Not only were the counterfeiters making a living from their forgeries, but the trial revealed that they were also in the pay of the German police, thus profiting coming and going. As the U.S. embassy in Berlin reported, "The trial has shown that the demand by the German authorities for anti-Soviet documents and material on subversive Communist activities at home was greater than the actual supply. This led to a flood of forged documents some of which, cleverly done, were able to influence international policy." In fact, Orlov was reputed to be the author of the so-called Zinoviev letter, "which was responsible in large measure for the defeat of the Labor [sic] Party in the 1924 election in England." But this is getting ahead of the story.

The British embassy in Berlin also reported on the trial, noting "that Orlov produced documents of all kinds as required and that in certain cases

German departments utilized Orlov's services for purpose of obtaining information about other German Government departments." Newspaper syndicates and "information" bureaus also "paid considerable sums for worthless information and forged documents." The chief witness for the prosecution, a Baltic Russian named Sievert, was the butt of jokes in the press and an embarrassment to the German government. He caused a "sensation" when he failed to finish his testimony, claiming illness and producing "a medical certificate to the effect that the excitement of cross-examination had brought about a nervous breakdown and that his memory had lapsed." The prosecutor let his chief witness off the hook, and German government departments breathed a sigh of relief, especially the Reich ministry of the interior, which was Orlov's "most credulous and generous patron."

The trial embarrassed German authorities who tried to limit court revelations as much as possible. After all the attention in the media, Orlov and his accomplice got only four months in jail and were immediately released from custody for time served. They were then rearrested pending expulsion as undesirable aliens.[55] From the German point of view, the sooner the matter was forgotten, the better. The NKID however was not amused by the Berlin carnival.

Propaganda, Real or Forged?

The Orlov trial took place in spring of 1929, but the Foreign Office was suspicious of its sources long before that. Curzon thought the Foreign Office ought to be careful so as not to be caught plumping forgeries "and then experience the humiliation of being knocked over." The Foreign Office was reading Krasin's cables to Moscow and knew that he was contemplating a lawsuit against two London papers for publishing counterfeit documents.[56] In September 1921, however, Curzon issued a formal complaint to Chicherin, though much of the indictment was based on faulty or erroneous information. Curzon's note flopped, but Chicherin was riled. What is this new policy, he asked Krasin. Is a new intervention being planned or is it blackmail? The Soviet pendulum swung easily from optimism about the future to worries about a new western assault. What's the issue, Chicherin wanted to know, debts or the Comintern?[57] Well, it was both and everything else too: Soviet Russia angered the West just as much as the West angered Soviet Russia.

In 1922, the Foreign Office kept up its monitoring of alleged Soviet activities. Afghanistan, Persia, Central Asia, and India were key areas of British interest, but it was "damned hard" to assemble evidence. The idea was to be patient and build up an airtight case, not using "pop-gun tactics against an organization worthy at least of field artillery." The Foreign Office compiled a long report on Bolshevik activities, based mostly on SIS reports. This was the work of Leeper, Litvinov's former London go-between, who was keen to expose Bolshevik propaganda activities. He would come a long way when in the late 1930s he became a staunch advocate of closer relations with the USSR. While the Foreign Office was busy compiling evidence, so was the Home Office, which thought it had built a solid case against the Soviet trade delegation.[58]

Curzon was particularly keen on this file and made inquiries about its progress. Unfortunately, it was the same old problem. As Gregory explained, "This has hung fire partly because of the monumental length of Sir W. Childs' indictment . . . and, partly, I suspect, owing to his inability properly to substantiate all his charges." Sir Wyndham Childs was an assistant commissioner of Scotland Yard, always keen to nail Bolshevik propagandists. Curzon was glum in response: "I anticipated no other result."[59]

Robert Vansittart, then Curzon's private secretary, was equally gloomy: taking up "propaganda" complaints with Moscow was futile; Curzon had "already tackled Chicherin hard on this subject."

> His [Curzon's] account of it shows that Chicherin is a hopeless person to talk to . . . as indeed are all Bolsheviks. They simply cannot and will not stop this kind of thing, for it is of their essence and they must go on with it or perish. This has always been the case in every movement of this kind. Representations are useless, & even if they produced an admission or a promise, it wd. be disregarded.[60]

The India Office was even more sensitive about propaganda, giving the impression of being ready to pounce, half cocked, on any bit of evidence incriminating the Soviet government. Clerks in the Foreign Office had constantly to advise patience until a proper case could be built. "If we are to cut at the Third International," observed one clerk, "it will have to be a first class affair, and for this our material is hardly good enough."[61]

British government agencies, like those elsewhere in the West, abhorred Soviet "propaganda" and meddling in their domestic affairs. The position was understandable but also paradoxical. It took a short memory to forget that France, Britain, and the United States had intervened in Soviet affairs from the first day of the October Revolution. Propaganda, money, guns, troops were all employed to overthrow Soviet authority. After overt Allied military intervention failed, covert means continued to be used to compel the Bolsheviks to see reason and embrace capitalism. Great powers of course do not recognize that turnabout is fair play. But Lenin knew the principle and was loath to go too far in making concessions to the West even though some would be necessary.

Breaking Out of "Splendid Isolation":
The Genoa Conference, April–May 1922

"Propaganda" and meddling did not prevent Soviet negotiations with the West. In October 1921 Chicherin proposed an international conference to discuss the claims and counter-claims of the western powers and Soviet Russia.[62] In 1922 there followed the conferences at Genoa and The Hague. The Soviet government was looking for trade and diplomatic recognition. Oddly, "propaganda" did not come up. France and Britain wanted Soviet recognition of tsarist debts and the restitution or indemnification of nationalized private property. Ambitious plans were mooted for foreign economic development of Soviet Russia, as though it were to become a new western semi-colony, like China. These issues were discussed in meetings between the French and British in particular, in London and Cannes, in December 1921 and January 1922. At Cannes the French and British governments invited Moscow authorities to send a delegation to Genoa, based on a resolution which required Soviet recognition of debt obligations and property rights in exchange for diplomatic recognition.[63]

In preparation for the Genoa negotiations, Krasin offered his view on Soviet policy. The "Entente" had made war on Soviet Russia and set up a blockade to starve us out, he observed, and Russia therefore had no obligations toward the Entente or its nationals because of the existing state of war. The upcoming Genoa Conference should be viewed as a conference to conclude peace and approve the various conditions associated with it. Negotiations had to start from the "peculiar situation" that neither side had achieved "decisive victory." The war had stalemated.

> Soviet Russia has beaten off all military attacks, but stands on the brink of ruin because of exhaustion and hunger, inability to restore independent agricultural production, industry, and transportation.
>
> Capitalist Europe has coped with an incipient proletarian uprising, but suffers from its inability to reestablish a normal circulation of manufactured goods, from an industrial and commercial crisis, unemployment, and a catastrophic currency situation.
>
> Russia is nevertheless the weaker country and a continuation of the struggle would lead to huge sacrifices, with the loss of much of the life forces of the people.
>
> The capitalist countries can live for some time on accumulated resources and then at the last minute count on the help of America, interested in the preservation of the foundations of the capitalist system in Europe.
>
> From the point of view of the Soviet delegation, it would be utopian to conduct negotiations based on an imminent victory of the proletariat. This

would only be appropriate if [General Semen] Budenny stood on the Rhine, or at least in Berlin.

The Soviet delegation must clearly understand that it cannot impose its will on Europe and is obliged to look for compromises, agreements for an extended period. Possible surprises in European developments do not count because they defy calculation.

Our task will be to lose as little as possible and to regain as much as possible from that which has been taken from us.

The "big questions," Krasin correctly noted, were going to be the restoration of property and recognition of debts. No agreement would be possible if the Soviet delegation stood on "proletarian" principle. Krasin was making the case for another Brest-Litovsk at Genoa.

> Just as at home we were forced to retreat to the position of state capitalism, so in the upcoming negotiation with Europe on the conditions of peace we will have to stand not so much on the position of the communist revolution, but on the ground of European principles of private property and "international law" even if subject to the maximum qualifications and limitations.[64]

Krasin's report went on for six tightly spaced pages, but it came down to the reality that the Europeans and Americans had the upper hand and that Soviet Russia was going to have to conclude another longer-term Brest-Litovsk in order to reconstruct and develop Soviet society and its economy. Soviet representatives, like Krasin, in direct contact with their western counterparts, were willing to concede more than their colleagues in Moscow who were not faced directly with the hard positions of western negotiators.

Chicherin proposed patience:

> There is some kind of orgy of harebrained schemes swirling around an agreement with us; so that this agreement is seen as our suffocation. If we will not rush forward and get ahead of ourselves, we will gain much more than if we project impatience. In the present case one can say: slow and steady wins the race.

An improving economic situation meant that the Soviet government would not have to accept "dictated" terms.[65]

Lenin would not go as far as Krasin, whom he accused of "signs of panic." We should not be afraid of a breakdown of negotiations; if they collapse, there will be other opportunities for discussions with the West more advantageous to us. When Lloyd George suggested publicly that the conference could break down without prior Soviet consent to western conditions on debts and property, Lenin laughed. This is a French idea, he replied, but not even the British press agree with it. Lloyd George is bluffing.[66]

The business-like Litvinov had already anticipated Lenin's views. In early February he informed Krasin in London that the Soviet government would not accept prior conditions and asked him to make this known to Lloyd George through a British go-between, E. Frank Wise. When the Politburo endorsed this position, Litvinov sent another cable to Krasin asking him to leak the Soviet position to the British press, again through Wise.[67]

"Arch-Bolshevik" was how Curzon described Wise. If he had dared, Curzon might also have said the same of Lloyd George, for whom Wise worked. Most Conservative members of Lloyd George's cabinet were little interested in the Genoa initiative, or opposed it altogether. Churchill, then Secretary of State for the Colonies, was never at a loss for words when it came to the Bolsheviks. It's "out of the question," he said in a Cabinet meeting, to recognize "a band of dastardly criminals." What held the Conservatives in line was the fear of a party split or the breakup of the government.[68]

The Tories might have worried less. Litvinov, who drafted the policy guidelines for the Genoa negotiations, was pessimistic and reserved. Even in the event of agreement, diplomatic recognition could well be delayed. Hopes for big government loans are an "illusion." No government, not even the American, has the resources or would dare to hint to their electors or to their parliaments that they contemplated loans for Russia. Even bank credits, supposing the extension of diplomatic recognition, are unlikely to be on a large scale or to produce immediate results for the Soviet economy.

Even if we could obtain agreement, Litvinov concluded, the gains would be "very limited." In the eventuality of a rupture of negotiations, no "catastrophes" were likely. The delegation therefore needed to establish its tactics and define the "limits of its concessions" in order to divert the "odium" of rupture to the other side and namely to the creditors of Russia.

"The conference will be thwarted by France," Litvinov concluded, "and a separate agreement with her, impossible unless we want to become its vassal and a second Poland. In European questions, let's focus on England, going for an agreement with the necessary compensation even on Eastern questions."

What Litvinov meant by "eastern questions" was Soviet policy in Asia, where Britain and Russia had often clashed in the past. Eastern leaders were not advocates of national liberation, Litvinov went on to point out: on the contrary, "they are ready to sell themselves and the interests of their countries and that is all the same to us." It frees our hands to help "revolutionary democratic" movements insofar as there are any in the East.[69] In the meantime, "eastern questions" might be used as concessions to obtain agreement with Britain.

On 28 February the Politburo endorsed Litvinov's ideas. The Genoa Conference was thus written off, or nearly so, even before it began, and a backup strategy was prepared for bilateral negotiations with Britain, including concessions to it in the East.[70] Chicherin was optimistic, in fact dithyrambic, in his praise of trade and cooperation with the West. We want to establish "friendly relations if possible with all governments." We are not playing one country off against another, but we will undertake bilateral negotiations with any government which wants them. Having so advised Berzin in London, Chicherin emphasized the Soviet desire to improve relations with the British government, echoing the new Politburo line. "We see the indisputable merit of English governmental figures, with Lloyd George at the head; they clearly understand the great importance of economic relations between England and Russia."[71]

What has come over Comrade Chicherin? Lenin might well have asked. Has he suddenly developed holes in his head? We will do business with the devious Lloyd George, but only with our eyes wide open.

Publicly, Lenin had this to say:

We are going to Genoa not as Communists, but as merchants. We must trade, and they [France and Britain] must trade. We want the trade to benefit us; they want it to benefit them. The course of the issue will be determined, if only to a small degree, by the skill of our diplomats.

We can conclude agreements at Genoa, "if the other parties . . . are sufficiently shrewd and not too stubborn," or we can do it "bypassing Genoa."[72]

Commercial agreements were more complicated than Lenin could explain in a speech. Trade functioned on credit provided by banks and covered by insurance. But where was the banker who would willingly loan to a defaulted, defiant client, and not a small one at that? Billions in Russian debt were lost. The tsar's debts or not, the Soviet government was held responsible for them and would have to pay. It was not just a question of paying off bad debts, but of accepting, according to the State Department, "civilized" principles of capitalism.

Secretary of State Hughes thought the capitalist West had the Soviet government by the throat, but he underestimated his Bolshevik adversaries by a long way. We should concede as little as possible, Krasin said, in exchange for as much as possible. This was also the position in Moscow, except that the Politburo, and Lenin in particular, were as tightfisted as *kulaks*, or "rich" peasants, when it came to concessions to the West. If trade agreements benefit us, said Lenin, all well and good, but we are not interested in discussing or accepting capitalist "principles." They have their "principles," Trotskii liked to say, and we have ours.

The probable failure of the Genoa negotiations got Litvinov thinking of other possible bilateral agreements. Britain was one idea; Germany was another. In May 1921 the Soviet government signed a trade agreement in Berlin. In October 1921 Litvinov broached with Chicherin the idea of a defensive alliance with Germany. With no peace in sight with the Entente and with Poland likely to remain a "sword of Damocles" hanging over our heads, would it not be a good idea, he asked sarcastically, to think about breaking out of our "splendid isolation"? "Needless to say that an alliance [with Germany] would significantly raise our prestige in international politics, would frighten France, and force it to seek a rapprochement with us." Of course, we would have to keep the negotiations secret, so that Germany did not try to use them as a "trump" to obtain concessions from France.[73] Here Litvinov was thinking in terms of realpolitik, more in line with Machiavelli than with Marx and Engels.

As planning for Genoa continued, Germany remained on Litvinov's mind. On 10 March 1922, just ten days after the Politburo approved his Genoa guidelines, he submitted a proposal to the Politburo "to create a strong point in Germany." Discussions had already started in Berlin, Litvinov reported, but the time seemed right to press ahead. An agreement with Germany would strengthen our hand at Genoa and would also remove the danger of a "new economic blockade." The NKID *kollegiia*, or cabinet, had discussed this initiative and, along with Krasin and others, unanimously supported it. Litvinov proposed terms for the agreement with Germany which were approved by the Politburo and pursued in Berlin as the Genoa Conference approached.[74] Here was Litvinov recommending the opening to Germany, and Chicherin to Britain, just the opposite of what historians have long believed.[75]

"Swallowing a Camel and Straining at a Gnat"

The Genoa Conference opened on 10 April 1922; it was attended by the Allied and European powers, 34 countries in all, including Japan but not the United States. The Italian government as conference host presided over the plenary sessions. Deliberations were to focus on the big issues of European security and economic reconstruction, but for the Soviet delegation it was really about their desiderata, diplomatic recognition and trade and credit for the economic rebuilding of the devastated Soviet economy. The Soviet negotiating position was what it would always be during the 1920s: Moscow would make concessions on debts on a de facto basis in exchange for loans or commercial credits and diplomatic recognition.

Raymond Poincaré, the French premier and foreign minister, was determined to hold Soviet Russia to the Cannes resolution and thus to formal recognition of debts and property rights, but he was little interested in offering recognition or credits in return. In fact, Poincaré appeared more interested in picking a fight than in coming to terms with the Soviet delegation. Lloyd George contemplated diplomatic recognition and trade and investment in Soviet Russia in exchange for large Soviet concessions on debts and compensation or restitution of private property nationalized during the revolution. The prime minister was a not a free rider, however, and was constrained by divisions in his coalition government. Conservative colleagues were not nearly so anxious to compose with Moscow and certainly not at the risk of a break with France. Even so, there was tension between Lloyd George and Poincaré. In press leaks each accused the other of attempting to wreck the Anglo-French entente which had already shattered long before. When Lloyd George launched just such a sally, Poincaré riposted with a quotation from the Bible: before looking for a mote in the eye of France, the British prime minister should pull the beam from his own eye.[76] Much could go wrong at Genoa and did.

Apart from the all-European and Russian issues, the Genoa Conference was also about Germany's reparations to the Allied powers, and especially to France. The German government did not want to pay reparations any more than the Soviet government wished to discharge the tsar's foreign debts. These circumstances, and the common standing of Germany and Soviet Russia as pariahs, the one defeated in war, the other a social and political deviant according to the West, had the potential to upset Anglo-French calculations.

Poincaré did not go to Genoa, not wanting to leave Paris. Instead, he sent his justice minister and deputy premier, Louis Barthou, an experienced politician who was caught between Poincaré's hard line and Lloyd George's more subtle positions. Lenin sent Chicherin, Litvinov, and Krasin as the principal Soviet delegates. Chicherin did most of the talking at the plenary sessions and sparred at length with Lloyd George over war debts and gigantic Soviet "counter-claims" for the Allied intervention during the civil war. Each demonstrated his erudition with references to the history of the French Revolution and the English Civil War. It was a good show for those who watched.

According to Barthou, Chicherin and Krasin seemed ready to deal, or at least wanted to avoid a rupture of the conference. Litvinov was the hardliner. One British observer thought Lloyd George had the better of the exchanges, though he reckoned Chicherin "no mean Parliamentarian."[77]

After listening to the debates between Chicherin and Lloyd George, Barthou was not so sure about Chicherin. This is a man who can talk for hours without relent. "He wields irony," Barthou advised Poincaré, "with the insolence of an outcast grand seigneur, and Lloyd George had to endure

Figure 2.3. Members of the Soviet delegation at the Genoa Conference. Left to right, unknown man, Ian Ernestovich Rudzutak, Georgii V. Chicherin, Khristian Georgievich Rakovskii, Leonid B. Krasin, Maksim M. Litvinov, Nikolai Nikolaevich Krestinskii, April 1922. *Agence Meurisse,* Paris. *Bibliothèque nationale de France.*

. . . his [Chicherin's] jagged edges during a veritable indictment of Britain's responsibilities for the war . . . and the expeditions which it supported against Russia."

Barthou's evaluations of his Soviet counterparts were mixed with scorn and admiration. "Litvinov is of another race and another world."

> Round-faced, a gold pince-nez hiding furtive eyes, he speaks little as if he were embarrassed to be here . . . but numbers, statistics give him an audacity which he does not have in words. He is the one who established the account of 50 billion gold rubles owed by the Allies to Soviet Russia. He does not enter into explanations where he would undoubtedly lose himself and he even agrees, with the clumsiness of a Germanic laugh, not like Chicherin's [more ironic] smile, that they could settle for something less than the demanded sum. This rude partisan provokes all the same a physical aversion and a mistrust which puts him out of the negotiations. But one guesses that he is in the action and that one has to reckon with his audacity.

Barthou also assessed the other Soviet delegate, the Red *kupets.* "Krasin, alone, gives the impression of a businessman come to do business."

> This tight lipped, hard-eyed engineer knows what he wants, but he is not the master of what he wants, being the captive of his accomplices and also of a

regime where his abilities are only used by turning them to other purposes. When Chicherin discourses . . . he [Krasin] looks out an open window, and one senses his impatience as a man of action, disgusted by this empty talk . . . [about the French Revolution] which will not give to Russia the means of its restoration.

Through all of the debates Barthou observed that Lloyd George handled himself well, but that he was ill at ease with the skilled parries of his Soviet interlocutors from whom it was impossible to extract any concrete commitments.

"My belief," Barthou wrote, "is that there is nothing to do, and that they [Chicherin et al.] will do nothing, or nearly nothing.

If negotiations continue, we will find ourselves on each question confronted by the same evasions. . . . The Russians will promise perhaps, but will they give? Some papers, and nothing more. It's not enough. . . . I do not yet see the hour of Russia's restoration from outside and, left to itself, it can only conclude by perishing . . . in anarchy.[78]

After five days of discussions Barthou reckoned that the Genoa Conference would accomplish nothing with the Russians.

There were other observers of the Genoa scene, of course, but perhaps none so unique as Count Miklós Bánffy de Losoncz, the Hungarian foreign minister. Bánffy was of noble descent like many other European diplomats of that period—including Commissar Chicherin. He was a man of many talents: a politician who eventually gave up politics to become an important theatre entrepreneur and a playwright and novelist. Bánffy also had a further talent pertinent to this narrative; he was a very good sketch artist. Over the pseudonym Ben Myll, he made caricatures of many of the diplomats at Genoa, among them important players in the high-stakes game between Soviet Russia and the West.

Barthou was right to see that the Genoa negotiations were headed toward failure, but he did not anticipate the dagger that would deal the fateful blow. On 16 April Germany and Soviet Russia signed the Treaty of Rapallo, along the lines of agreement proposed by Litvinov in March. It was a simple contract which provided for diplomatic recognition, the opening up of trade relations, and the renunciation of mutual claims for pre-war debts and post-war reparations. Suddenly the two outcasts had broken out of their isolation.

The news was unexpected, and the British and French governments were taken by surprise. Incensed, Poincaré said the Rapallo Treaty was an act of defiance, planned in advance and containing secret clauses. Right in the first instance, wrong in the second, he directed Barthou to organize a collective Allied protest. If that did not work, he should threaten French withdrawal from the conference. There were reports in the American press that Lloyd

Figure 2.6. Sketch of Louis Barthou, by Miklós Bánffy, pseudonym Ben Myll, 1922.

George had prior knowledge of the Rapallo Treaty, though Poincaré, in spite of his ire, would not go that far.[79]

On 18 April Lloyd George convoked a plenary meeting, excluding German and Soviet representatives, to approve and issue a joint comminatory letter to the German delegation. Barthou concurred, though he would have preferred "a more energetic and brutal document."[80] On the following day the German chancellor and the foreign minister were summoned to a meeting with Lloyd George to renounce the treaty with Russia. The prime minister treated the German leaders like naughty children.

"The misunderstanding . . . had been a very unfortunate one," said the mournful Lloyd George, "and he wanted to discuss the matter informally . . . to see what could be done." The Russo-German treaty has set everything back. M. Barthou is threatening to leave Genoa.

I had "no idea," Lloyd George went on lugubriously, that you were contemplating "this disastrous step." Perhaps by "bold" action you "might put the matter right. Everyone made a mistake now and again. It was inevitable in politics." You had "meant the best" no doubt, but realizing your error, would not the German government "take a bold step" and withdraw the treaty?

The Germans were polite in response. They had come to the conference with high hopes of some relief from Versailles Treaty impositions. Germany

Figure 2.7. Sketch of David Lloyd George, by Miklós Bánffy, pseudonym Ben Myll, 1922.

is "dying"; the Rhineland is occupied. France threatens us, said the Germans, though they did not mention how the German army had sacked the occupied French territories leaving only ruins and desert as it retreated at the end of the war.

We tried to obtain a meeting with you to talk things over, said the German foreign minister, but you refused to see us. The German government had concluded that no relief was in sight and they had therefore to come to their "own arrangement with Russia."

It's "no use to take this line," Lloyd George replied: you could have warned us that you were making "a separate agreement with the Russians." You made the agreement even before the conference began. But it's pointless discussing the past. "That did not help the future."

On this point the Germans agreed. What we have done, we have done. However, they were also clear that they "could not undo the Treaty with Russia." The conversation continued for yet a while along these lines, but without movement on either side.[81]

The next day, 20 April, Lloyd George met "the Russians" to see if any agreement could be salvaged. They had their tails up; they knew they were now in a stronger position. Lloyd George could not help but upbraid them for Rapallo.

I am "sorry," he said, that you could not see your way "to letting the Germans off their Treaty." The French are "delighted"; they hope that it will "not be withdrawn." I don't wish to "dwell on the subject," Lloyd George added, but could you "see [your] way to getting the Treaty out of the road of the Conference?"

Having cleared his mind on that subject, Lloyd George turned to the main points of a treaty with Soviet Russia, debts and property rights. There was no question of "writing off" war debts; they could only be "written down." On nationalized property, "all we asked," said Lloyd George, "was for compensation if restitution was impossible." There are only three countries who could "raise credits," Britain, Belgium, and France, but not unless the property issue is settled. "It was a question of principle."

It's a point of principle for us also, replied Chicherin, on which our people are "deeply set." Could the prime minister not find "a formula leaving the question for future settlement"?

There's no future, replied Lloyd George, unless the point of principle is agreed to. It's "a very difficult point," but you "Russians must get over it." You are "really swallowing a camel and straining at a gnat."

Figure 2.8. Sketch of Georgii V. Chicherin, by Miklós Bánffy, pseudonym Ben Myll, 1922.

In fact, the contrary was true. Chicherin commented that he had very definite instructions on the point at issue.

I am "equally bound—hand and foot," Lloyd George said.[82]

So was Barthou who received a cable from Poincaré telling him not to make any concessions to the Soviet delegates even at the risk of a breakup of negotiations. Public opinion would prefer a rupture "to any sort of capitulation."[83] Poincaré sounded like Lenin.

Lloyd George must have had trouble deciding who was more difficult, Poincaré or Chicherin. He tried to soften up Chicherin over lunch, but there was nothing doing. "He was polite," LG said to a colleague, "but always official and diplomatic. . . . You never get any human touch with him."

Molodets, well done, Comrade Chicherin, Lenin might have commented, had he been privy to LG's comments.

With the exception of Krasin, Lloyd George observed, the Bolsheviks "are impossible people."

Konechno, of course we are, Lenin would have said, and we keep an eye on Comrade Krasin.

"Very clever" they are, LG added, "but entirely concerned in ideas and arguments. They don't seem to have any real desire to achieve anything definite."[84]

Au contraire, Lenin would have retorted, "we want to trade," but in *our* interests, not according to *your* "principles."

Chicherin's written reply to Lloyd George was clever in that it appeared to agree to most of the Anglo-French principles on debts and private property but, as Barthou correctly noted, conditioned them on Soviet desiderata, inter alia, on recognition and important western credits for Soviet reconstruction. Moreover, while Chicherin indicated that the Soviet government was willing to *consider* restitution of the *use* of property nationalized during the revolution, it was not willing to restore it to previous owners or to pay compensation in the event that restitution was not possible.[85]

An indignant Poincaré categorically rejected the Soviet position on the owners' "use" of their nationalized property or any of Chicherin's other proposals. Understanding the Soviet strategy, Barthou declined to accept a link between Soviet debt recognition and western diplomatic recognition.[86] Moreover, while Lloyd George had indicated that three European countries were in a position, or willing to extend credit to Soviet Russia, in fact only one, Britain, had the financial resources to do so. In his February note for the Politburo, Litvinov was right to observe that Europe, not to mention the United States, was facing budget deficits and had little credit to spare for Moscow. But quite apart from this difficulty, Poincaré or Hughes would never accept an agreement with the Soviet government that did not include unconditional submission to all western demands. Tsarist debts and Soviet neediness were useful levers to force compliance with western precepts of capitalism.

Litvinov sent a long cable to Moscow reporting on what had happened on 20 April. Matters, he wrote, had taken a turn for the worse. He correctly observed that Lloyd George was in too weak a position to break with France, although the prime minister appeared to have gotten Barthou "in tow," which was only partially true. "There is not the least doubt that both Lloyd George and [Carlo] Schanzer [the Italian foreign minister] are attempting by every possible means to reach agreement with us and are ready to make the maximum concessions." Unfortunately, Litvinov added, we have had to resort to "semi-official" discussions, through the go-between Wise. The trouble with go-betweens was that they risked getting the message wrong. Would Lloyd George really go the limit on concessions to Moscow? Even the prime minister's cabinet colleagues were not sure what he was going to do.

Litvinov explained that he had tried to get agreement on a formula putting off the difficult questions, but both Lloyd George and Barthou had rejected it. According to Wise, Lloyd George had changed his mind and seemed open to the Soviet formula linking debt recognition to the extension of "sufficient credit." Actual payments on the tsarist debt would be subject to a moratorium and put off into "the more or less distant future" after the conclusion of credit agreements. Still unresolved was the issue of

Figure 2.9. Sketch of Maksim M. Litvinov, by Miklós Bánffy, pseudonym Ben Myll, 1922.

nationalized property, which was likely to be the main "stumbling block." We are still a long way from agreement, concluded Litvinov, even if Lloyd George does accept our latest propositions.

Litvinov then turned to the Rapallo agreement which had provoked a "far greater storm" than anticipated. The French delegates had "packed and then unpacked" their bags. Lloyd George was even more "outraged," threatening the Germans and demanding that they renounce the treaty. In the end however the treaty had caused the "Allies," as Litvinov put it, to become more flexible with us.

"The Germans took all the lumps." They behaved in "the most cowardly fashion . . . [wanting] to hide behind our backs. Yesterday, they begged us to annul the treaty, but we steadfastly refused."[87]

In Moscow Lenin appeared to believe that Chicherin's reply to Lloyd George on 20 April was too clever by half, opening the door to undesirable compromises. He accused his main delegates of "succumbing to" Lloyd George's "deceit." If this was true, Barthou at least did not notice, reporting to Poincaré that "the Russians were using their habitual negotiating tactics."[88] Krasin appears to have been willing to make compromises— "absurdities" Lenin called them—though he (Lenin) may have been blowing off steam, as he sometimes did. Litvinov's report might have caused anxieties in Moscow, since it suggested slippage in the Soviet position. Once the Rapallo agreement had been secured, Lenin thought only of a "breakup" of the conference. For him, the "question of restoring the capitalists' property" was a good justification for doing so.[89] This result would have suited Poincaré. Indeed, Lenin's relationship with his delegation was similar to Poincaré's with Barthou, both watching carefully for slippage going the wrong way. If Lenin was willing to risk a conference breakup, so was Poincaré.

"You must understand," Poincaré told the Italian ambassador in Paris, "that we are at the limits of our patience."[90] What galled Poincaré, among so many Soviet provocations, was the idea that the Soviet war debt would be written down and in effect never paid, while French debts to Britain and the United States remained on the books and had to be paid.[91] Of course, the French government was no keener to pay its war debts than the Bolsheviks were to discharge those of the tsar. Still, it was hard for France, as creditor, to stand on bankers' principles which it did not intend to respect regarding Anglo-American war debts. The French never did work out that inconsistency; they chose simply to ignore it.

The Genoa Conference dragged on well into May, but its fate had already been sealed in April. No agreement was concluded with Soviet Russia either at Genoa or at a second conference of "experts" held in The Hague in June and July. Secretary of State Hughes thought the Genoa Conference was a mistake: the Bolsheviks had come "to such a pass" that with a little more pressure, they would have had to agree "to anything that did not involve public repudiation of the doctrines of Communism even though it involved complete practical abandonment of communistic organization."[92] Curzon was disgusted with Lloyd George's maneuvers "to scrape something out of Genoa," but Austen Chamberlain, then Conservative House leader, thought that the prime minister was lucky to get away from Genoa as well as he did.[93]

The Hague conference of experts ran up against the same sticking points, the gnat, which Soviet diplomats refused to swallow. During the autumn of 1922 the Soviet leadership hardened its position on negotiations with the West.

"We prefer to wait," said Chicherin, "than to make concessions. And wait we can." The Soviet international position was stronger, and at home the New Economic Policy was beginning to work, whatever its unpalatable features. No Bolsheviks really liked the NEP, Chicherin not less than his colleagues. He summed up the objectives of Soviet policy as twofold: "the strengthening of our position in Europe as a great power . . . and the strengthening of our position in Turkey."[94]

Soviet "Eastern Policy"

In its search for a way out of "splendid isolation," the Soviet government began to develop an "eastern policy" which was essentially a search for allies in Turkey, Afghanistan, Persia, and China. These were all places where Britain had imperial interests, and Chicherin recognized that Soviet policy could put them at odds with London, with which the NKID also wanted to improve relations. In September 1922 Turkey and Britain appeared on the brink of war. The so-called Chanak crisis was settled without fighting, but in the aftermath Lloyd George resigned as prime minister, leading to the formation of a Tory government under Andrew Bonar Law. Chicherin did not like to see the "western powers" threatening Turkey, even though the British and French governments fell out over the crisis. Turkey was "guardian of the Straits" protecting Soviet security in the Black Sea, and the NKID opposed any British control of them. From the point of view of the "real interests of the Soviet republic," Chicherin observed, Turkey must retain full sovereignty over its territory. In taking this position, the Soviet government would have "to reckon on antagonism between us and England on the eastern question. Of course, diplomacy consists of compromises and it is in our own interests to soften the sharp corners and to look for such compromises with England also."[95]

The NKID would pursue policies based on an evaluation of Soviet interests, Chicherin noted, and not according to the bad temper of Curzon or

Gregory. Otherwise, Soviet policy would be reduced to the level of Sweden or Denmark, always licking the butts (*podlazhivat'sia*) of British ministers. Chicherin was often unsure of what was riling the British. Was it the family spoons or propaganda?[96] Like other Bolsheviks, Chicherin remained oddly naïve: *everything* about Soviet Russia riled British and western elites.

Secretary of State Hughes or Poincaré would have gasped at the idea of treating Soviet Russia like a great power. Prospects for agreement were therefore remote, especially after the departure of Lloyd George. If Hughes had his say, the Bolos were going to eat their proletarian ideals one by one and accept with a splintery wooden spoon the nasty porridge of capitalist "principles," or else there would be no deals.

Notes

1. Arthur Steel-Maitland to Austen Chamberlain, Foreign Secretary, 27 Dec. 1927, TNA, FO 800 261, fol. 716.

2. T. E. O'Connor, *Diplomacy and Revolution: G. V. Chicherin and Soviet Foreign Affairs, 1918–1930* (Ames, Iowa, 1988), pp. 3–46.

3. Chicherin to Kh. G. Rakovskii, Soviet *torgpred* in London, no. 22, 18 Nov. 1923, *Arkhiv vneshnei politiki Rossiiskoi Federatsii*, Moscow (hereinafter AVPRF), *fond* 069, *opis'* 7, *papka* 7, *delo* 8, *list* 8 (hereinafter f., o., p., d., l(l).).

4. Chicherin to Nikolai K. Klyshko, counselor, *torgpredstvo* in London, no. 3, 18 March 1923, AVPRF, f. 069, o. 7, p. 7, d. 8, ll. 2–3.

5. Jules Laroche, French ambassador in Warsaw, no. 10, 11 Jan. 1929, *Ministère des Affaires étrangères*, Paris (hereinafter MAÉ), Russie/1113, fol. 100.

6. Bruce Lockhart, *British Agent*, pp. 218–19; and O'Connor, *Chicherin*, pp. 50–55.

7. Excerpt from Edgar Vincent Lord D'Abernon's diary, Berlin, private and confidential, 15 Aug. 1922, India Office (now located at the British Library), London, Curzon Papers, F.112/204.

8. Excerpt from D'Abernon's diary, Berlin, private and confidential, 11 Feb. 1923, Curzon Papers, F.112/205.

9. Minute by Hugh Ledward, Northern Department, Foreign Office, 4 June 1925, N3153/102/38, FO 371 11016.

10. Foglesong, *America's Secret War*, p. 31.

11. M. M. Litvinov, member of the Narkomindel (NKID) *kollegiia*, to L. K. Martens, Soviet representative in New York, 27 May 1919, *Sovetsko-Amerikanskie otnosheniia, Gody nepriznaniia, 1918–1926, Dokumenty* (hereinafter SAO, *Gody nepriznaniia*), Moscow, 2002, pp. 99–102.

12. R. K. Debo, *Survival and Consolidation: The Foreign Policy of Soviet Russia, 1918–1921* (Montréal, 1992), p. 404.

13. Excerpt from a record of meeting at the NKID in 1920 (but not otherwise dated), including Chicherin, Litvinov, Krasin, and others, SAO, *Gody nepriznaniia, 1918–1926*, pp. 170–71.

14. T. E. O'Connor, *The Engineer of the Revolution: L. B. Krasin and the Bolsheviks, 1870–1926* (Boulder, Colo., 1992), passim; and Adam B. Ulam, *Stalin: The Man and His Era* (New York, 1973), pp. 59–63.

15. DeWitt C. Poole, head, Russian division, Department of State, to Charles E. Hughes, Secretary of State, 15 Dec. 1921, National Archives, Washington, D.C., Record Group 59,

microfilm series 316 (hereinafter NA RG M-), 861.00/9433, reel 50; Poole to Hughes, 11 Apr. 1922, 861.51/1461, M-316, reel 121; and untitled, unsigned report, 18 Oct. 1928, TNA KV2 574.

16. Memorandum by J. D. Gregory, head, Northern Department, 5 Apr. 1923, N3198/3198/38, FO 371 9365; Austen Chamberlain to Winston Churchill, Chancellor of the Exchequer, confidential, 5 Nov. 1925, FO 800 258, ff. 655–66; Robert Lord Crewe, British ambassador in Paris, to Chamberlain, confidential, 29 Nov. 1925, ibid., ff. 793–95, reporting the view of the secretary general of the Quai d'Orsay, Philippe Berthelot; and "Russia," by Gregory, 24 Oct. 1926, N4818/387/38, FO 371 11787.

17. Semen S. Khromov, *Leonid Krasin: Neizvestnye stranitsy biografii, 1920–1926gg.* (Moscow, 2001), pp. 124–25.

18. Minute by Owen O'Malley, Foreign Office, 24 Oct. 1923, N8234/209/38, FO 371 9353.

19. E.g., M. J. Carley, "Behind Stalin's Moustache: Pragmatism in Early Soviet Foreign Policy, 1917–1941," *Diplomacy & Statecraft*, vol. 12, no. 3 (Sept. 2001), pp. 159–174, in response to Keith Neilson, "Stalin's Moustache: The Soviet Union and the Coming of the War," *Diplomacy & Statecraft*, vol. 12, no. 2 (June 2001), pp. 197–208.

20. Whitehouse's handwritten note, 14 Dec. 1920, on United States Steel Products Company to Department of State, 9 Dec. 1920, 661.1115/212, NA RG59, box 6150.

21. Hughes to Charles A. Albrecht, U.S. consul, Reval, 25 Mar. 1921, 661.1115/275a, NA RG59, box 6151.

22. Hoover to Hughes, 16 Mar. 1921, 661.1115/264, NA RG59, box 6150.

23. Hoover to Hughes, 15 May 1922, 861.01/464, NA RG59, M-316, reel 71; and Hughes to Hoover, 23 May 1922, ibid.

24. Poole to F. M. Dearing, Assistant Secretary of State, 5 May 1921, 661.1115/333, NA RG59, box 6151.

25. Poole to Hughes, 20 Sept. 1921, 861.01/406, NA RG59, M-316, reel 71.

26. Evan E. Young, U.S. minister at Riga, no. 90 strictly confidential, 1 June 1922, reporting the views of Meyer Bloomfield in Moscow, 861.01/446, NA RG59 M-316, reel 71; and Frank B. Kellogg, U.S. ambassador in London, no. 646, 8 Aug. 1924, 741.61/86, NA RG59 M-582, reel 5.

27. Memorandum for the Secretary of State, Arthur Bullard, 11 March 1921, 861.01/438, NA RG59 M-316, reel 71.

28. Excerpt from Information Bulletin, secret, not for publication, Litvinov, June 1921, SAO, *Gody nepriznaniia 1918–1926*, pp. 181–82.

29. David S. Foglesong, *The American Mission and the "Evil Empire"* (Cambridge, UK, 2007), p. 61; Gregory's minute, 12 Sept. 1921, N10365/8614/38, FO 371 6923; Gregory's minute, 12 Sept. 1921, N10364/4/38, FO 371 6851; and MAÉ note, *Sous-direction d'Europe*, 23 Dec. 1921, MAÉ Grande-Bretagne/61, ff. 220–23.

30. Gregory's minute, 12 Sept. 1921, N10365/8614/38, FO 371 6923.

31. "Soviet to Persist in US Trade Plea," an interview with Krasin, *Washington Post*, 1 April 1921, R-6000-US, NA RG59 M-333, reel 4; and E. L. Dresel, U.S. commissioner in Berlin, no. 1048, 4 June 1921, enclosing a record of a private meeting with Krasin, 861.01/313, NA RG59, M-316, reel 71.

32. "Declaration of the official representative of the RSFSR in Great Britain, L. B. Krasin, on trade relations between the RSFSR and France," Sept. 1921, *Dokumenty vneshnei politiki SSSR* (hereinafter *DVP*), 24 vols. (Moscow, 1958–), IV, pp. 384–85; Berthelot's minute on Krasin to P. Maréchal (French businessman), Kr/5592, 6 June 1921, MAÉ Russie/78, fol. 79; and Aristide Briand, French premier, to Fernand Couget, French minister in Prague, no. 506, 4 Oct. 1921, MAÉ Russie/348, fol. 127.

33. H. D. Phillips, *Between the Revolution and the West: A Political Biography of Maxim M. Litvinov* (Boulder, Colo., 1992), pp. 1–29; and McFadden, *Alternative Paths*, pp. 132–33.

34. Leeper's untitled, handwritten minute, 17 June 1933, N4812/5/38, FO 371 17241.

35. Maurice Hankey, secretary to the Cabinet, to Austen Chamberlain, then Conservative House leader, personal and secret, 16 April 1922, Curzon Papers, F.112/225A.

36. Note, Moscow, not signed (ns), 3 June 1926, MAÉ Russie/1113, f. 23.

37. Jean Herbette, French ambassador in Moscow, no. 139, 22 Feb. 1927, MAÉ Grande-Bretagne/65, ff. 14–21.

38. O'Connor, *Chicherin*, pp. 57–58.

39. Jonathan Haslam, "Litvinov, Stalin and the Road Not Taken," in Gabriel Gorodetsky (ed.), *Soviet Foreign Policy, 1917–1991: A Retrospective* (London, 1994), pp. 55–62; and Albert Resis (ed.), *Molotov Remembers, Inside Kremlin Politics, Conversations with Felix Chuev* (Chicago, 1993), p. 69.

40. Litvinov (Stockholm) to Ludwig Meyer, a Norwegian intermediary in Christiania, Norway, letter in English, 10 Jan. 1919, *Rossiiskii gosudarstvennyi arkhiv sotsial'no-politicheskoi istorii*, Moscow (hereinafter RGASPI), f. 359, o. 1, d. 13, ll. 30–31.

41. M. A. Mikhailov, agent of the French trading firm SOCIFROS (Copenhagen), to SOCIFROS, Paris, 2 March 1920, MAÉ Russie/69, ff. 83–91; and Henri Martin, French minister in Copenhagen, nos. 109–12, 13 March 1920, ibid., ff. 106–9.

42. "France's Russian Policy," Soviet diplomatic agent in Berlin, ns, nd (but summer 1921), AVPRF, f. 04, o. 42, p. 259, d. 53579, ll. 16–26.

43. Ibid.; "Note de M. [Fernand] Grenard pour le directeur des Affaires politiques," 22 July 1922, MAÉ Russie/582, ff. 256–60; and "Note sur les relations commerciales entre la Russie soviétique et les citoyens français," *Sous-direction d'Europe*, 25 Aug. 1921, MAÉ, ancienne série C—*Relations commerciales* (hereinafter RC), 1920–1940, Russie/2044 (files not paginated). This collection has now been integrated into other archival series, but I cite from the original classification system.

44. Chicherin to Martens, 16 Jan. 1920, SAO, *Gody nepriznaniia, 1918–1926*, pp. 125–26; and excerpts from Politburo protocols nos. 21 and 27, 14 May 1921, G. M. Adebekov, et al., *Politbiuro TsK RKP(b)-VKP(b) i Komintern, 1919–1943, Dokumenty* (hereinafter *Politbiuro i Komintern*), Moscow, 2004, pp. 74–76.

45. Chicherin to Ian Antonovich Berzin, deputy *torgpred* of the Soviet trade mission in London, no. 15, 8 July 1921, AVPRF, f. 069, o. 5, p. 4, d. 3, ll. 3–5.

46. Excerpts from Politburo protocols nos. 55 and 60, 25 Aug. 1921 and 14 Sept. 1921, *Politbiuro i Komintern*, pp. 92–94, 99–100.

47. Krasin to Richard W. Child, U.S. ambassador in Rome, 7 June 1922, SAO, *Gody nepriznaniia, 1918–1926*, pp. 229–31.

48. Berzin to Litvinov, no. 9, 1 Jan. 1922, AVPRF, f. 04, o. 4, p. 21, d. 305, ll. 1–6.

49. Lenin to Chicherin, 16 Oct. 1921, *Lenin: Foreign Policy*, p. 348.

50. Gregory's minute, 5 April 1921, N3914/1/38, FO 371 6843; and P. M. Roberts' minute, 1 April 1921, N4007/1/38, ibid.; and Gregory to Thomson, head, Directorate of Intelligence, Home Office, 15 April 1921, N4557/1/38, FO 371 6844.

51. Gregory's minute, 3 Sept. 1921, N10271/1/38, FO 371 6845; and Klyshko to Gregory, 15 Sept. 1921, ibid.

52. Leeper's minute, 29 Sept. 1921, N10868/1/38, FO 371 6845; Curzon to Sir Eyre Crowe, permanent undersecretary, nd, N10941/1/38, ibid.; Gregory's minute, 26 Sept. 1921, ibid.; and Major Malcolm Woollcombe, head, Political Section, SIS, to Gregory, 23 Sept. 1921, ibid.

53. "Renseignement a.s. de l'Organisation Orlov," no. 1648/S.C.R. 2/11, 19 March 1928, MAÉ Russie/1113, ff. 51–57; Cheka report, no. 1512/NR, very secret, 20 Sept. 1921; Summary on "White International," ns, Jan. 1922; Cheka report, no 842, very secret, 21 Jan. 1922, *Russkaia voennaia emigratsiia 20x–40-x godov XX veka: Dokumenty i materialy*, 6 vols. (to date), Moscow, 1998–2013, I, bk. 2, pp. 87–89, 150–55, 481–85; and Report from the Constantinople resident of the GPU, S. D. Triandafilov, April–May 1923, ibid., II, pp. 180–86.

54. *Russkaia voennaia emigratsiia*, I, bk. 1, p. 48; Litvinov to Chicherin, no. 3195, secret, 19 March 1927, AVPRF, f. 05, o. 6, p. 21, d. 89, l. 19; and Keith Jeffery, *The Secret History of MI6* (New York, 2010), pp. 181–87.

55. Jacob G. Schurman, U.S. ambassador in Berlin, no. 4725, 15 July 1929, 811.44 Borah, Wm E, NA RG59, box 7554; and Harold Nicolson, counselor, British embassy in Berlin, no. 536, 24 July 1929, N3449/1668/38, FO 371 14048.

56. Curzon's minute, 8 June 1921, N6428/36/38, FO 371 6863; and Crowe's minute, 8 June 1921, ibid.

57. Chicherin to Krasin, no. 6, 2 Oct. 1921, AVPRF, f. 069, o. 5, p. 4, d. 2, ll. 12–13; and Chicherin to Krasin, no. 9, 16 Oct. 1921, ibid., ll. 14–15.

58. Minute by Sir Ronald Charles Lindsay, assistant undersecretary of state, 19 Jan. 1922, N479/123/38, FO 371 8170; and "Anti-British Activities of the Soviet Government," by Leeper, 11 Oct. 1922, N9302/123/38, ibid.

59. Gregory's minute, 2 March 1923, N3053/44/38, FO 371 9334; and Curzon's minutes, nd, ibid.

60. Vansittart to Crowe, 9 Jan. 1923, N336/44/38, FO 371 9333.

61. William Strang's minute, 28 Sept. 1923, N7700/44/38, FO 371 9334.

62. Chicherin's note to the governments of Britain, France, etc., 28 Oct. 1921, *DVP*, IV, pp. 445–48.

63. Cannes resolution, 6 Jan. 1922, *Documents on British Foreign Policy, 1919–1939* (hereinafter *DBFP*), 1st series, 27 vols. (London, 1947–), XIX, pp. 35–36.

64. Krasin to Chicherin, no. LK/6379, by courier, 19 Jan. 1922, AVPRF, f. 04, o. 4, p. 21, d. 304, ll. 14–19.

65. Chicherin to Berzin, no. 22, 4 Jan. 1922, AVPRF, f. 04, o. 4, p. 21, d. 303, l. 1.

66. Lenin to Chicherin, 7 Feb. 1922, Lenin, *Collected Works* (hereinafter *CW*), XLV, pp. 463–64; and Lenin to Chicherin, 15 Feb. 1922, ibid., pp. 469–70.

67. Litvinov to Krasin (London), no. 90, 2 Feb. 1922, RGASPI, f. 359, o. 1, d. 3, l. 6; Litvinov to Krasin, no. 110, 10 Feb. 1922, ibid., l. 7.

68. Curzon to Austen Chamberlain, private and confidential, 13 May 1922, Curzon Papers, F.112/223; Chamberlain to Curzon, 24 March 1922, ibid.; and TNA, Cabinet, 21(22), secret, 28 March 1922.

69. "To the Politburo," very secret, Litvinov, 18 Feb. 1922, RGASPI, f. 359, o. 1, d. 3, ll. 8–13.

70. Lenin's draft resolution for the Politburo, approved on 28 Feb. 1922, Lenin, CW, XLII, pp. 401–4.

71. Chicherin to Berzin, no. 25, 6 March 1922, AVPRF, f. 04, o. 4, p. 21, d. 303, ll. 26–27.

72. "From the Political Report of the Central Committee . . . ," 27 March 1922, *Lenin: Foreign Policy*, pp. 380–83.

73. Litvinov (Revel) to Chicherin, 22 Oct. 1921, RGASPI, f. 359, o. 1, d. 3, ll. 9–12.

74. Litvinov to Trotskii, and Politburo, no. 306, secret, 10 March 1922, RGASPI, f. 359, o. 1, d. 3, ll. 15–16.

75. E.g., Fischer, *Soviets*, p. xii.

76. Poincaré to Barthou, nos. 186–87, 27 April 1922, MAÉ B—*Conférence de la paix, Conférence de Gênes, télégrammes de Paris à Gênes*, carton 183.

77. Barthou to Poincaré, nos. 70–73, 14 April 1922, MAÉ Y—*Conférences politiques, conférence de Gênes/29*, ff. 110–13; and Maurice Hankey to Austen Chamberlain, 16 April 1922, Curzon Papers, F.112/225A.

78. Barthou to Poincaré, 16 April 1922, MAÉ Gênes/29, ff. 186–95.

79. Poincaré to Barthou, nos. 58 and 63, 18 April 1922, MAÉ Gênes/30, ff. 30–32, 35.

80. "British Secretary's Notes of a Meeting . . . ," 18 April 1922, *DBFP*, 1st, XIX, pp. 431–45.

81. "British Secretary's Notes of a Meeting . . . ," 19 April 1922, *DBFP*, 1st, XIX, pp. 452–63.

82. "Conversation held at the at the Villa d'Albertis . . . ," 20 April 1922, *DBFP*, 1st, XIX, pp. 474–78.

83. Poincaré to Barthou, no. 101, 21 April 1922, MAÉ Gênes/30, fol. 200.

84. George Riddell, *Lord Riddell's Intimate Diary of the Peace Conference and After, 1918–1923* (London, 1933), p. 370.

85. Chicherin to Lloyd George, 20 April 1922, *DBFP*, 1st, XIX, pp. 477–78.

86. Poincaré to Barthou, no. 103, 21 April 1922, MAÉ B—*Conférence de Gênes*, carton 183; Poincaré to Barthou, no. 121, 22 April 1922, MAÉ Gênes/31, fol. 18; and "Second meeting of the Sub-Commission . . . ," 21 April 1922, *DBFP*, 1st, XIX, pp. 487–91.

87. Litvinov to NKID *kollegiia*, no. 187, 20 April 1922, RGASPI, f. 359, o. 1, d. 3, ll. 29–30.

88. Barthou to Poincaré, nos. 200–202, 24 April 1922, MAÉ Gênes/31, ff. 63–64.

89. Lenin to Stalin, L. B. Kamenev, Trotskii, 19 April 1922, Lenin, CW, XLV, p. 532; Lenin to Politburo, 24 April 1922, ibid., pp. 533–34; and Lenin to Politburo, 2 May 1922, ibid., pp. 537–38.

90. Poincaré to Barthou, nos. 122–24, 23 April 1922, B—*Conférence de Gênes*, carton 183.

91. Poincaré to Barthou, no. 103, 21 April 1922, B—*Conférence de Gênes*, carton 183.

92. Sir Auckland Geddes, British ambassador in Washington, to British delegation, Genoa, no. 1, 17 May 1922, FO 371 8192.

93. Curzon to Chamberlain, private and confidential, 13 May 1922, Curzon Papers, F.112/223; and Chamberlain to Curzon, private and confidential, 15 May 1922, Curzon Papers, F.112/227B.

94. Chicherin to Berzin, no. 270/i, 25 Sept. 1922, AVPRF, f. 04, o. 4, p. 21, d. 303, ll. 70–75.

95. Chicherin to Berzin, no. 1, 16 Oct. 1922, AVPRF, f. 04, o. 4, p. 21, d. 303, ll. 42–43.

96. Chicherin to Krasin, no. 5-i, 24 June 1921, AVPRF, f. 069, o. 5, p. 4, d. 2, ll. 8–10.

CHAPTER THREE

~

Which Way Soviet Policy?

Confusion and Incoherence, 1922–1923

Soviet foreign policy in Europe, Chicherin or Litvinov would have empha-sized, was not limited to seeking better relations with Germany. Britain and France also figured largely in Soviet calculations. Chicherin was relatively optimistic about Anglo-Soviet relations, and Litvinov, though perhaps more skeptical, also favored exploring the possibilities in spite of accusations in Moscow that he was too sympathetic to Britain. Evidently it was not just later historians who thought he was an Anglophile. The resignation of the pragmatic Lloyd George in the autumn of 1922 seemed to dim the prospects in London. Lord Curzon, still Foreign Secretary, had more room to pursue an anti-Soviet policy after Lloyd George's departure.

George Nathaniel Lord Curzon

If there was joking about whose noble lineage went back further, Curzon's or Chicherin's, it was certain that Curzon's family could trace their lines back to Norman ancestors. George Nathaniel was born in 1859 in the place where his forebears had lived since the 12th century. That was going back a long way, though Chicherin's family, as the *narkom* sometimes pointed out, traced its roots to imperial Rome. Like most members of the British elite, Curzon was well educated at Balliol College, Oxford. He did not appear quite as haughty as some of his contemporaries, Austen Chamberlain, for example. His hair was receding and swept back, his eyebrows slightly arched, his ex-pression not unkindly, though he looks stone-faced in later photographs. He gained a reputation early on for a strong personality. Most people did not feel

**Figure 3.1.   George Nathaniel Lord Curzon,
ca. 1921. Granger Collection, NY.**

neutral about him, least of all Chicherin with whom he was sometimes compared. Many of Curzon's contemporaries found him insufferable. "Knowledge
of human nature" was not one of his strong points. "He does not understand
the ordinary man," a cabinet colleague noted, "and most men are ordinary."[1]
Curzon was viceroy of India at the turn of the century, before he was 40.
There he acquired a strong mistrust of Russia, reciprocated of course by the
tsarist government and later by Chicherin. Turkey, Afghanistan, and Persia
were Anglo-Russian borderlands and stakes in the Great Game, that is, the
imperialist rivalries of the European powers prior to World War I.

A cabinet minister since 1915, Curzon became Foreign Secretary four
years later. He possessed a Tory's loathing of the Bolsheviks which he shared
with Churchill. He was not as expressive as Churchill in his anti-Bolshevik
philippics, but his hatred was equally intense. Curzon often clashed with
Lloyd George who pursued a more pragmatic line toward Soviet Russia. The
prime minister did not much like Curzon, but kept him in the Cabinet as
a concession to the Tories. "He has plenty of brains," LG observed, "but is
feeble in a crisis." After the 1918 Armistice, Curzon resisted efforts to pull
British troops out of Russia and Persia. In 1921 he was unenthusiastic about
the Anglo-Soviet trade agreement, calling Chicherin a "colossal and finished

. . . liar." His exchanges with Chicherin, he declared, were like a "fusillade," which "might go on til the dark-haired among us become grey, the grey-haired white, and white bald."[2] Curzon was frustrated that the Foreign Office and all the intelligence agencies of the British government could sometimes not tell the difference between bogus and genuine Bolshevik propaganda. He had an aristocrat's contempt for the Bolsheviks, but with Chicherin, it was personal, feelings which the *narkom* generously reciprocated. If Lloyd George and Chicherin dueled at Genoa, it was Curzon and Chicherin who clashed at the Lausanne Conference which began in November 1922 to determine the status of the Turkish straits, entryway into the Black Sea. A good show, according to Ernest Hemingway, who reported for the western press.

> It was this daily, bitter struggle between the British Empire and the future Russian Empire with Curzon, a tall, cold, icicle of a man holding the whip hand with the British fleet, and Chicherin fighting, fighting, with arguments, historical instances, facts, statistics and impassioned pleas and finally, seeing it was hopeless, simply talking for history, registering his objections for future generations to read, that made the Lausanne Conference so interesting.[3]

Litvinov considered Curzon's policy not only anti-Bolshevik, but also anti-Russian, a traditional 19th-century "Beaconsfield" line. Nevertheless, Britain had good reasons for seeking better relations with Soviet Russia, according to Litvinov, and it remained to be seen whether pragmatism or the "social antipathy," the anti-Bolshevism, of Curzon and the Tories would prevail.

Soviet Policy Options

Litvinov saw two important options for Soviet policy, if London proved to be a dead end. One option was France. The French were making overtures, though Litvinov wondered whether accepting them was a good idea. A turn to the French would mean getting so entangled in their orbit that escape from it would be difficult.

The second option was in the East. Our Eastern Department (*Otdel Vostoka*) was getting impatient, observed Litvinov, and putting on pressure for a change in Soviet policy. Because of hopes for improved relations with Britain, the Eastern department has been reduced to "almost complete inactivity." However, they have "already long ago developed very interesting and ingenious multi-year plans for action," always approved higher up. We cannot delay these plans indefinitely, or pursue them halfheartedly, on the fond hope of an improvement of relations with London. So in the spring of 1923 Litvinov proposed to send V. V. Vorovskii, another talented Soviet diplomat, to London to determine if British policy had been fixed to an anti-

Soviet, anti-Russian line. Go to London, he said, without *"fil'stva ili fobstva,"* without preconceived ideas, and see what you can find out.[4] This idea was cut short by Vorovskii's assassination in May 1923 by a White Russian in Lausanne. Litvinov would have to turn to other channels of communication to explore the possibilities in London. Already the consummate political realist, Litvinov was alert for diplomatic openings, keeping options open, as Soviet policy almost always did during the inter-war years. The main objective was to break out of "splendid isolation," as Litvinov had put it in 1921.

The French were also struggling to think more pragmatically, frightened as they were by the Rapallo Treaty. Nineteen twenty-two was not only the year of the Genoa Conference and Rapallo, but also of the Washington Naval Conference. The Anglo-Saxon powers ganged up on France to force it to accept unpalatable limitations on naval building. If the French were not careful, *they* could find themselves isolated.[5] By the end of 1922, the Russian connection therefore began to look more attractive in Paris, as Litvinov duly noticed.

Édouard Herriot

Édouard Herriot, leader of the Radical Party, along with his younger colleague Édouard Daladier, traveled to Soviet Russia in September–October 1922 in a much-publicized visit.[6] Herriot was one of the first and most important proponents of a Franco-Soviet rapprochement—his *idée fixe* to which he held fast throughout the inter-war years. This was unlike Daladier, who was premier and war minister in the late 1930s and often opposed a Franco-Soviet alliance against Nazi Germany. In fact, French advocates of a Soviet rapprochement were rare on the branch; the Soviet ambassador in Paris in the late 1930s called them "white crows."

Herriot was an unusual advocate of good relations with the USSR. He was born in 1872, the son of an army officer. In 1905, scarcely into his thirties, he became the mayor of Lyon, a post he held for the rest of his life with the exception of the German occupation during World War II. He was head of the centrist Radical Party during the inter-war years until replaced by Daladier, and he was three times premier of France. In the 1930s he presided over the Chamber of Deputies. Paradoxically, he was a *bon bourgeois*, of large girth, who loved to eat and drink, not the sort who, one might imagine, would want to consort with hardened revolutionaries like the Bolsheviks. But he knew his history, and he knew that the kings of France had made an alliance with the Turkish sultans against a common Habsburg enemy. He could read a map too, and he knew that the Franco-Russian alliance, which had forced

Figure 3.2. Édouard Herriot, ca. 1924. *Agence Meurisse. Bibliothèque nationale de France.*

Germany to fight on two fronts, was crucial at the beginning of the Great War in preventing the German high command from throwing all its armies against France. The enemy of my enemy is my friend, and France needed allies against what Herriot saw as the continuing menace of Germany. It was not without a certain irony that in 1945 Herriot, without the girth, was liberated by the Red Army from a Nazi prison in Berlin.

His principal weakness, like that of most of his contemporaries in French politics, was that he could not form a stable electoral coalition to take and hold power on the center-left. In the 1920s it was the *Cartel des gauches*, an electoral alliance with the French socialists; in the 1930s it was the *Front populaire*, a political alliance with the socialists and communists to face the rising menace of Nazism. With some notable exceptions the French right opposed close ties with the Soviet Union, and the center-left was never strong enough or resolved enough to forge an alliance with Moscow even at the height of the Nazi threat to Europe. So when it came to better Franco-Soviet relations, Herriot often seemed indecisive, though this was usually induced by the fragility of his political alliances.

In October 1922 Soviet officials warmly welcomed Herriot to Moscow. He met at length with Chicherin, Krasin, and various NKID officials. Herriot was blunt in these discussions:

> The position of France is lamentable. As a result of the war, we find ourselves cheated on all sides. What a paradox—our country is portrayed as implacable and predatory at a time when it has demonstrated in reality the maximum moderation. England on two accounts twisted Germany's neck: it seized its [Germany's] colonies and seized and sank [sic] its fleet and is now content. Then it rearranged its jacket and smiled. . . . And France, France was returned Alsace-Lorraine, it exploits the Saar coal mines, and only wants to be paid for the ruins created by the war. . . . [France] showed the maximum moderation. It was too magnanimous to its enemy. The price of this magnanimity is that we are hated by everyone and Germany does not pay us. The reparations question will be resolved very simply. It will have two stages. First stage: Germany is too weak and cannot pay; second phase: Germany is too strong and will not pay. I am absolutely persuaded that in 15 years Germany will fall upon us again.[7]

Herriot's foresight was startling and only a little off target—barely two years. Soviet officials were interested in improved relations with France, as they were with all countries. In a familiar refrain heard during the inter-war years—whenever a Franco-Soviet rapprochement was broached—Lev M. Karakhan, then head of the eastern bureau in the NKID, observed that France and Soviet Russia had no opposing foreign policy interests and ought to improve relations. Herriot and Daladier agreed, but noted that two obstacles stood in the way: the Soviet repudiation of tsarist bonds and the absence of rights to private property. Karakhan thought solutions could be found to these problems. In what was already a familiar refrain, he noted that if the Soviet government was to satisfy French claims, it would require trade credits in exchange.[8]

On his return to France, Herriot wrote to Chicherin, marking his determination to bring about an improvement in Franco-Soviet relations. I have met opposition, he wrote, but I shall be persistent and "I will succeed."[9] Herriot also reported to the premier, Poincaré, and to President Alexandre Millerand, asking for a reconsideration of French policy toward Soviet Russia. Let's drop the "political theories," the anti-communism, which served no French political or economic interest.[10] In hindsight, readers will certainly recognize that Herriot had a good idea. The Germans were bothered by the apparent French warming up to Moscow. According to the NKID chief of protocol, the Herriot visit "obviously disturbed them greatly." He recorded bumping into a drunken German diplomat at a Petrograd café. "When I came up to say hello, he told me how sad he was that we had started to flirt with France."[11] Everyone played the game: who loves me, who loves me not.

Rocambolesque in Early Franco-Soviet Relations

The Soviet government was willing to encourage the French, modifying its policy of *Ermattungsstrategie* and offering "allowances" (*dovol'stviia*) to French newspapers with the objective of promoting diplomatic and economic relations with France. It was hard-earned foreign exchange, a sure indication of the NKID's serious intent. The semi-official Paris daily *Le Temps* received the largest sum, 520,000 francs, between August 1922 and January 1923. Individual journalists benefited, and Radical politicians too. The conservative Paris daily, *Le Petit Parisien*, published a series of articles by Herriot on his trip to Russia, his travel expenses having been picked by the Soviet treasury. *Le Temps* journalist Henri Rollin was also on the Soviet payroll. Even Poincaré noticed his more favorable articles on Soviet Russia: Rollin had become "a convinced adherent" of Moscow. The Foreign Office thought Rollin was "a member of the French secret police."

Did Poincaré know? It is hard to say.

Perhaps Rollin was a double agent. In 1928 a French police report characterized him as an "*intrigant*" and a paid go-between in Franco-Soviet trade deals. The French police even noticed that Rollin's wife liked to cheat when he was away on business.[12] There was nothing like a sex scandal for the police to keep in reserve, although they were commonplace in France.

The Soviet press campaign was hard going, according to the NKID report on expenditures: "The campaign provoked a bitter struggle in journalistic circles and intrigues against participating newspapers, which demanded constant, intense effort for the maintenance of gains made in their positions." It is no secret to historians that the French press accepted bribes, but *Le Temps* is a little surprising. It was the semi-official mouthpiece of the Quai d'Orsay, and one of the standard-bearers of French anti-communism. No wonder the Soviet government had to pay so much to acquire its services, such as they were. And still the NKID complained that "inadequate resources" prevented it from achieving a "fundamental change in the political direction of the right wing press in relation to Russia."[13]

Because of French hostility, the NKID had to improvise, often using unsavory, opportunistic, even glamorous go-betweens. These included one Semen Nikolaevich Rekhtzammer. An obscure figure, known to the French police as a Soviet "agent," but perhaps simply a paid lobbyist who had connections with the once and future Premier Paul Painlevé, with exiled Russian bankers, and with French journalists.[14] Another name that turns up in Soviet diplomatic correspondence is *Sénateur* Anatole de Monzie, who organized a group of parliamentary colleagues to lobby for diplomatic relations with the Soviet Union. He first met Chicherin in 1920 and then twice thereafter, always exploring the possibilities of a Franco-Soviet rapprochement. Monzie went to Moscow in the summer of 1923 to talk to Chicherin and other Soviet officials. More dubious Soviet intermediaries were former anti-Bolsheviks like Dimitrii Navashin, assassinated in 1937 by the French fascist Cagoule.[15] Soviet lobbyists even ventured into the political salons of Paris, which was known to support French recognition of the Soviet Union. Here they could meet with Painlevé, Herriot, and Briand. Other visitors had ties to Poincaré, who opposed political discussions with Soviet officials.[16] The French wife of the Soviet trade representative was a well-known actress with connections in the world of Paris politics, and she too was an agent of better Franco-Soviet relations.[17]

The ways of Soviet diplomacy were necessarily imaginative, and they exasperated French officials who knew in spite of themselves that there were compelling arguments in favor of better Franco-Soviet relations.[18] *Ces bandits de bolcheviks*, these damned Bolsheviks, swore one French diplomat; it was not a pleasure to deal with them. But what choice do we have? The Soviet Union is growing stronger: we have to have Russia with us, not against us.[19]

France was increasingly at daggers drawn with Germany over reparations. The Germans would not pay, and the French tried to collect by sending troops into the industrialized Ruhr valley in January 1923. As with the Anglo-Saxon collusion against France at the Washington Naval Conference, the Ruhr crisis encouraged some French politicians to think geopolitically and to adopt Herriot's position on Soviet Russia. The British ambassador in Paris, Robert Lord Crewe, noticed: "Although France has excellent reasons for disliking the present régime in Russia, she has still better reasons for disliking and mistrusting Germany."[20] The "obvious policy for the French to pursue would be to try to separate Russia and Germany," observed the prolix Foreign Office clerk Mr. Leeper; the French "have always regarded Russia merely as a force to be used against Germany."[21]

Apart from the politicians, some civil servants in the Quai d'Orsay got behind Herriot's idea. The Ruhr crisis made it imperative "to resume a policy of entente with Russia as soon as possible," said Emmanuel Peretti de la Rocca, political director at the Quai d'Orsay. Not known for his softness on communism, Peretti went to see Marshal Foch, who had, in the spring of 1918, favored cooperation with the Bolsheviks against Germany. But not then, and Foch sent Peretti away. The political director persisted: "An alliance with the Russian people is necessary to France," he said: "We need a point of support in Europe which only the Russian land mass can offer us and with which we have no conflict of interest."[22] This is just what Karakhan had said to Herriot.

Peretti promoted this view throughout 1923, but Millerand was unmovable. In answer to French merchants who wanted to trade in Russia, he remarked, you are "building on sand." In October 1923, Peretti learned that the president had "not changed his mind." And in December, when Peretti wanted to pursue informal contacts with Soviet trade representatives, Millerand said no.[23] Poincaré was more flexible. In fact, his fear of Germany and his intense irritation with the British inclined him to consider a Soviet rapprochement. France had to "placate Russia in order to prevent her from making a closer alliance with Germany." According to one British report, Poincaré, angry with Curzon, declared that "Britain was a far greater threat to France than Germany and the only way to deal with both was to reach agreement with Russia."[24] Angry or not with London, Poincaré was restrained by Millerand and by his own anti-Soviet animosity.

Such were the arguments heard in the corridors of power and in public debates as national elections approached in the spring of 1924 between Herriot's *Cartel des gauches* and Millerand's *Bloc national*. Even in 1922, Herriot reckoned that public debate on resumption of Franco-Soviet relations would be useful in winning political power. A rapprochement, leading to a debt settlement and increased trade, would win broad voter support.[25] Millerand's advisers calculated that improved Franco-Soviet relations could help the *Cartel* by gaining French communist votes. But the Poincaré government was not above making small concessions to bondholders to counter the *Cartel's* strategy. The Soviet government hoped for a breakthrough after the 1924 elections, or so the Quai d'Orsay believed.[26] For France, it was not a bad position to be in with the Anglo-Saxon powers standing across its policies. Needy as France was for allies, one might have expected the Quai d'Orsay to show greater interest in Soviet inquiries.

Raymond Poincaré

Not Poincaré. Born in Lorraine in 1860, he studied law at the *Université de Paris* and was first elected to the Chamber of Deputies in 1887. In French politics he stood to the center-right. Prior to the war, he was several times a cabinet minister before becoming premier for the first time in 1912. The following year he became president of the Republic. He was a French nationalist: Germany was the main enemy, having annexed the French provinces of Alsace and Lorraine after the Franco-Prussian war of 1870–1871. For Poincaré, these were unredeemed territories. As president, he supported the increase of mandatory military service to three years and reinforced the Franco-Russian alliance, concluded in 1894, the better to hold Germany in the vice of two fronts, should there be war.

Figure 3.3. Raymond Poincaré, ca. 1910.
Universal Images Group, Art Resource, NY.

After war broke out in August 1914, he encouraged French unity, a *union sacrée*, against the Hun invaders. The unity lasted for a while until the war's horrors undermined it. From the left he gained the moniker of "*Poincaré-la-guerre*," a warmonger drenched in blood. After the Armistice, Poincaré called for harsh measures against Germany, but was not in a position to impose them. In 1920 his term as president of the Republic ended, though he returned to power as premier and foreign minister in January 1922. Poincaré made the decision to send French troops into the Ruhr in order to force recalcitrant Germany to pay reparations.

Poincaré had trouble getting along with his main interlocutors whether French or British. He quarreled with Clemenceau when the latter was premier, and with Millerand after he became president. Poincaré also got on badly with the British, but here the feelings were mutual. Of course, the British were always impatient with the French. "The whole nation," according to Charles Hardinge, the British ambassador in Paris, has got "a swollen head." But Poincaré was the worst of the lot. He is "a dirty dog, a man of mean character."[27]

"A friend of mine," Lord Hardinge quipped, "who knows Poincaré well, told me that Poincaré is under the impression that I like him very much.

Either Poincaré is very dense or I am full of duplicity for I have seldom come across, in my diplomatic career, an official whom I dislike more."[28]

Was it just Hardinge who did not get on with Poincaré? His successor Lord Crewe reported that almost no one did. "The extreme dislike of Poincaré . . . is shared . . . by a great many of his compatriots. Most of those who have to deal with him would describe him as a *mauvais caractère*, and I doubt if anybody in the official world is really attached to him. Still, there he is, and there is no present prospect of his being politically shaken."[29]

There he was indeed. Premiers were rarely popular in France, and most did not last long in office. Poincaré was more prudent and cautious than his stiff-necked, reserved persona suggested—except when it came to Soviet Russia. If he hated Lord Curzon and hated the Germans, he hated the Bolsheviks even more. Poincaré could not bring himself to pursue an opening to Moscow, though he permitted Peretti to talk about one in the Quai d'Orsay.

Complications over the Ruhr Occupation

While the Ruhr crisis disposed at least some people in France to consider an opening to Moscow, it had the opposite effect in the Soviet Union, where the Politburo, and no less than Trotskii, still commissar for war, saw the French occupation of the Ruhr as dangerous, especially if Poland intervened against Germany, thus destabilizing a fragile balance of power in Eastern Europe. The security of Russia itself could be threatened. But Trotskii also evoked other motives for intervening on the side of Germany. "The German bourgeois republic is not our friend. But the German people are now the object of unprecedented villainous oppression and enslavement." We cannot stand by in these circumstances, especially when "Soviet Russia is always on the side of the oppressed against the oppressor." And if Germany is "enslaved," Soviet Russia would find itself face to face with "victorious European imperialism."[30]

Trotskii was only giving a lead to the Soviet press, but his language was too much for Chicherin who wrote to Stalin. Clearly he was alarmed by the sudden turn in Politburo thinking and sought to discourage an over-reaction to the Ruhr crisis that would alienate France and spoil overtures from Herriot and other French contacts. Nor did Chicherin like the idea that Soviet support would be offered as a sort of Good Samaritan's *beau geste* without obtaining satisfaction for outstanding Soviet economic issues with the German government.

To reinforce his point, he quoted Stalin's own words: "We have thought enough about foreign interests; it is time that we thought about our own interests." And he quoted Stalin on another occasion: "Must the Red Army pay for everything, get everyone out of a mess?"

"We have *interests*," Chicherin emphasized, like the security of the Black Sea coasts. "Either the Red Army sorts everything out [for others] or we defend our interests by *diplomatic combinations* [Chicherin's emphasis], by the correct international relations. But in that case it's time to say good-bye to the policies by proclamation of 1919 and to verbal excess." Chicherin attacked Trotskii's proposals to throw support behind Germany. "Are we a government," he asked, "or are we chairing a meeting [of comrades]?" Why are we suddenly getting involved in a quarrel to support Germany? What is the quid pro quo for our action? And what damage will our action cause to our diplomacy in other areas, for example, in pursuit of a rapprochement with France?[31]

Decisions were taken quickly in Moscow, and the Politburo approved the dispatch of a "special commission" to Berlin to discuss technical issues of military cooperation and mutual defense. The commission's mandate was nevertheless limited, as if the Politburo had to some degree heeded the NKID's warnings.[32] If so, it was not without irritation, for Stalin replied sharply to Chicherin. He must not have liked Chicherin's citing back to him his own words of caution about Soviet policy, and he defended the Politburo's decisions to support Germany.

"I think," he wrote, that Chicherin's letters . . . are the fruit of a sad misunderstanding. There is no agreement, no hint of an agreement with France, or will there be, I think, in the near future." France is supporting Romania and Poland with hundreds of millions in credits. Here are French agreements, added Stalin, which are "not with Russia, but against Russia."

So, asked Stalin, "what can Comrade Chicherin put up against these credits besides his conversations with some Frenchmen about more than doubtful things, which the Politburo has already once assessed?"

"In my opinion," Stalin went on, "Comrade Chicherin did not understand the essence of the present crisis in Europe, which could lead to a pan-European war; he missed the main subject and unfortunately he was confused by swindling promises of French blackmailers."[33]

In February there were meetings in Berlin and Moscow to discuss technical issues of military cooperation. In the meantime, French and German tempers calmed and steps were taken away from the brink. The German government opposed passive, not military resistance to the French occupation. The Ruhr crisis thus only briefly interrupted Franco-Soviet peace feelers. In the short term, however, these initiatives produced no positive results.

Litvinov was riled and wanted reprisals against the French because of trade difficulties. "There is not a single country in the world where we do not run up against the resistance of France to our interests," Litvinov remarked.

"Its anti-Soviet activities are manifest literally everywhere and on every occasion." Chicherin was less concerned and thought the problems with France were only a new, passing phase. Litvinov remained unconvinced: it is an "old, continuous, unrelenting" policy of hostility.

> From the time of the Genoa Conference, French government policy has not changed one iota. With us there are flirtations and caressing words from various people without authority; we wait for the charity of French intermediaries, a few Radicals, and the tone of the French press changes only in a measure equal to the amount of our subsidies, but Poincaré during all this time has not given us even one single smile and his position toward us remains unrelentingly hostile.

Litvinov sounded like Stalin. Let's send a message to Paris was Litvinov's strategy: issue press releases, withdraw Soviet trade agents from France, and hold up contracts with French firms. With elections coming, we can give some levers to "our friends" to pressure the French government.[34]

Sour Grapes in London

While the French argued among themselves about relations with Moscow, the American and British governments maintained their anti-Soviet hostility. They had the Channel or "the pond" to protect them from German *revanche*, and so Russia was less important to them as a geopolitical factor in Europe.

In fact, the Foreign Office became impatient with the French interest in better Soviet relations. Curzon was abusive: it was the French who had long held to an intransigent policy and "treated recognition almost as a political crime." Sir William Tyrrell, an assistant undersecretary, said that French waffling was due to "Soviet gold spent on French journalists."[35] True perhaps, but everyone knew, Tyrrell included, that the French press was for sale, so even the Foreign Office did not expect Soviet agents to do anything less than pay. What rankled was that the French were "flirting with Moscow" and ready to pursue "a separate policy," heading off in the opposite direction from London.[36] Once the Foreign Office decided to get tough on Moscow, it expected France to follow suit. This too became a recurring pattern in Anglo-French relations during the inter-war years. "It is very important," Gregory noted, that the French "should not choose the moment when we are contemplating the reduction or eventual suppression of our mission [in Moscow] to send one of their own and step into the place which we have vacated. . . . We should, if possible, work together with regard to Russia." Gregory's idea behind a rupture with Moscow was to bring down the Soviets. "The only real way to stop propaganda is to overthrow the Soviet Government and we seem as far off being able to do that as ever."[37]

Still, for the Foreign Office there were domestic issues to consider, as there often were during the inter-war years. What would the Liberal and Labour parties think about a rupture with Moscow? The assistant undersecretary, Ronald Lindsay, doubted whether a rupture would have any effect "on the stability of the present odious regime in Russia especially if the action contemplated were to be opposed by the Liberal and Labour parties."[38] A row in the House of Commons could be anticipated, and who knew how it would turn out? While the Foreign Office thought about neutralizing the Parliamentary opposition, Litvinov thought to mobilize it to counter British government hostility.

Litvinov was convinced that even if Moscow agreed to some solution of the debts question, a "rapprochement with Curzon [would be] completely impossible." Nor did he ignore the issue of propaganda: Litvinov joked that given the "sporting inclinations of the English," we should offer a prize to the individual or charitable organization which could produce "objective evidence" of "propaganda from the Soviet government and its organs in England or its colonies." The trouble is, Litvinov noted, that "our opponents" and other "pillars of English society" consider any utterance of the Soviet government to be propaganda. Try drumming these distinctions into the heads of the Englishmen whom you meet, Litvinov instructed Berzin in London.[39] Naturally, Litvinov was referring to the Soviet government and not to the Comintern, for which the former did not answer. Berzin was aware of the distinction, but no one in the British government took it seriously, as he was well aware. However, the Foreign Office also knew just how hard it was to tell the difference between real and bogus "propaganda."

The Curzon Ultimatum

Without Lloyd George's restraining hand, Curzon picked a fight with Moscow in May 1923, provoked by the Soviet seizure of a British trawler fishing inside territorial waters claimed by the Soviet Union near Murmansk in the Barents Sea. Curzon sent an ultimatum to Moscow, summoning the Soviet government to stop all anti-British propaganda within ten days or face a rupture of relations. The British trawler was only a pretext, but Curzon did not forget to demand an indemnity even though Soviet authorities had released the trawler on 7 May, the day before Curzon's ultimatum was delivered in Moscow. The NKID was well aware of British intentions.

"Bourgeois Europe and America from the very first day of the communist government have not ceased to repeat that Carthage must be destroyed, that the hub of communism must be wiped out." After the failure of armed intervention, Litvinov wrote to Berzin, the West hoped that the "internal degeneration of Soviet power" would be accelerated by a rapprochement with the West and the establishment of the NEP. Lloyd George was the most important proponent of this idea, but he was not alone. The British still pursued a traditional policy of weakening Russia, and Curzon was "especially irritated" by Soviet activities in the East. Fearing a resumption of the maritime blockade, the Soviet government would make some concessions, he said, but there was no question of yielding to the ultimatum. At the same time, Litvinov instructed Berzin to conduct a publicity campaign in London to counter the "lies and distortions" in the British press. Increased sums were also allotted to finance the "Hands off Russia" movement.[40]

Later in the year, the Politburo approved subsidies for the Labour Party leaders through the Comintern and British Communist Party, including Ramsay MacDonald. We do not think, Litvinov advised, that they would divulge this information since it would harm the Labour Party itself. "However we have to keep in mind the usual inattentiveness of foreigners to secrecy, and therefore we are afraid that sooner or later this would become public or at least become known to English intelligence. This could have more serious consequences for us than for the Labour Party." Nevertheless, Soviet "higher authorities" approved £10,000 for a new Labour electoral campaign, a modest sum, though the NKID was against it.[41] Soviet representatives in Britain maintained close relations with the British left, Labour, trade unionists, and communists. W. P. Coates, the head of Hands off Russia, asked the NKID for increased support to maintain an office in London. The British journalist William Norman Ewer was also a source of information on British politics. One of his reports is marked "completely secret" in NKID files.[42] The networks, both open and clandestine, that Soviet diplomats developed in the 1920s would become useful in the 1930s when the Soviet government attempted to build an anti-Nazi alliance.

In the meantime, the Soviet fireman Krasin was sent to London to calm down the British. He succeeded so well that Litvinov and Chicherin accused him of making too many concessions: the Politburo reckoned that Krasin should be put on a short leash. Chicherin lectured him:

Our public humiliation in the East suggests to all eastern peoples that in face of England we are helpless, and this means that they will all cross over to the side of England. English domination in Afghanistan means the loss by us of any security at Tashkent. Central Asia will be under constant threat, and anti-Soviet intrigues could spread as far as Kazan and Ufa. . . . English domination in Afghanistan beats us in our most vulnerable place. English domination in

Persia will mean the acquisition by them of concessions near the Caspian Sea and the creation of a perpetual threat to Baku which with a nod from London can be wiped out by English airplanes.

Such an eventuality, concluded Chicherin, would mean "the destruction of the most elemental security of our Republic."[43]

Litvinov also weighed in, not liking Krasin's "polemical phrases that supposedly in Moscow we want a rupture when in fact we are not ready to surrender everything." The Eastern peoples will no longer count on us and will thus yield to British pressures. If you cannot see that, Litvinov added, you cannot understand "realpolitik." We have gone as far as we are going to go.[44]

How ironic that the NKID had discouraged a too aggressive policy against British interests in the East and that Curzon's *beau geste* may have loosened these restraints. In any case, Chicherin saw the "eastern question" in terms of Soviet national interests and not primarily in terms of revolutionary objectives, though these might be employed to protect those interests. Independent governments in Kabul and Teheran could keep the British away from Soviet southern frontiers. The problem was that London had restive colonial populations, especially in India, and the very existence of the Soviet Union could inspire them. In the aftermath of the Curzon crisis, Litvinov and Chicherin jointly signed a dispatch to Khristian G. Rakovskii, the new *torgpred* in London, which explained that Soviet policy "was based on the encouragement of self-determination, independence . . . and on friendly relations with democratic movements. We have nowhere created any revolutionary committees." Indeed, had it not been for the presence of Curzon in the Foreign Office, they added, we might have had better luck in concluding a general agreement with the British government.[45] This was a very unMarxist analysis, attributing Soviet troubles in London to the personality of Curzon. Nevertheless, both Chicherin and Litvinov remained committed to better relations with Britain.

The United States "Is Not Proposing to Barter Away Its Principles"

We left the narrative of Soviet-American relations in the spring of 1922 at the end of the Genoa Conference. The State Department remained just as hostile to Moscow as the Foreign Office, but like the proverbial "Yankee trader," it kept one eye cocked on business in Russia so as not to let it go to competitors. After the failure of the Genoa and The Hague conferences, Commerce Secretary Hoover, who had earlier recommended against "grabbing," now recommended an exploration of Russian trade possibilities.

Secretary of State Hughes agreed, thinking there might be an opening for U.S. businessmen to gain an advantage over their European competitors. As he put it to President Warren Harding in July 1922, "this is our opportunity to take a forward step, and I should like to take advantage of it at once." His idea was to organize an American expert commission to inquire into the Soviet economy and possible business opportunities. The ultimate objective was still to oblige the Soviet government to embrace capitalism, "to meet the conditions essential to be taken into the family of nations," as Harding saw it.[46]

To discuss the possibilities, Harding summoned Meyer Bloomfield, a friend and Boston lawyer, who had recently visited Moscow. Bloomfield was positive and Harding approved the Hughes initiative. Bloomfield would go back to Moscow to continue discussions with Soviet officials.[47] In pursuit of this objective, American diplomats in Europe met with Krasin, Chicherin, and Litvinov during the summer and autumn of 1922. Bloomfield was however the most important American go-between, and he returned to Moscow in the autumn. "The Right wing Bolsheviki have chosen the road of sanity," Bloomfield wrote, "but it remains to be seen how long the lucid moment will last. If forced by internal conditions they will travel the entire road returning to capitalism step by step."[48]

Hughes' idea of an expert commission died quickly when the Soviet government proposed reciprocity, that is, the dispatch of Soviet "trade delegates" to the United States. In relations with Soviet Russia, American proposals were asymmetrical. Hughes had in mind a take-it-or-leave-it offer to Moscow: no "bartering" and definitely no reciprocity. If Moscow did not like our proposition, Hughes reckoned, we can "wait awhile." The Soviet authorities would likely come around.[49] This sounded like Lenin and Chicherin: the Soviet government could *also* "wait awhile" for better offers.

Bloomfield still went ahead with his trip to Europe and met Litvinov in mid-October 1922 in Berlin. Bloomfield's account is short on details, but he described a meeting of four hours. "How can we set up good relations with America?" Litvinov asked. Bloomfield replied in a condescending way that Soviet diplomacy had blundered in proposing reciprocal missions, that American "officials are concerned only with the welfare of the Russian people," and so on. Litvinov appears to have reacted politely to Bloomfield's condescension, at least according to the American's account. Two weeks later Litvinov sent a message to Stalin reporting briefly on these discussions, noting that the technical mission was dead, but that the U.S. government apparently wished to establish some form of "unofficial relations" without taking any initiative. Litvinov suggested the establishment of a Soviet "information bureau" in the United States to facilitate contacts with American companies. Nothing came from this initiative either, although the Politburo approved of Litvinov's further "unofficial discussions" with Bloomfield.[50] These continued, and Bloomfield returned to the United States with new proposals still based on reciprocal missions.

Shortly after Bloomfield's departure from Moscow, and independent of his activities, an ARA official met Lenin, suggesting off his own bat a letter to Hoover inviting him to Russia. Lenin responded positively, but not Chicherin who discouraged the proposal, inter alia, for being certain to cause a sensation in the press.[51] There were limits to how far Moscow would go in seeking better relations with the United States.

After Bloomfield returned home, he went to Washington to report to Hughes. "The spirit in Russia just now," Bloomfield observed, "despite the bad financial and industrial outlook is proud and intensely nationalistic."

> Soviet officials are not only sensitive—they are on the "lookout for insults." They have made a fetish of this spirit. No matter what is proposed to them, the first point they think of is—"are we being regarded and treated as equals" . . . . They are ardent defenders of their failures and mistakes, as well as achievements. There is an auto-intoxication in their attitude, in their thinking, and a feeling that all their troubles will be over after one good harvest.[52]

The Bolsheviks had not yet come down to Earth, according to Bloomfield. Chicherin leaked the Soviet proposals to the press at the end of December 1922, embarrassing Bloomfield and irritating Hughes. But the former persisted. "There are some sane elements that have access to Lenin," he reported, "and their attitude gives hope. There is something to work with." A "disappointed" Hughes did not agree.[53]

The impasse continued. "It was a matter of principle with America," said one visitor to Moscow. "No American banker will loan Russia any money while that action [the Soviet repudiation of the Russian national debt] stands and . . . all hope of any recognition by America or the resumption of trade relations between the two countries was utterly impossible unless Russia receded from her position." The Soviet government stood its ground nevertheless. Krasin responded: "While Russia desires the rapid return to normal intercourse with all powers . . . the [Soviet] government is further than ever from a disposition to buy recognition . . . at a price damning Russia to an intolerable burden of debts."[54]

When demands for diplomatic recognition were raised in the U.S. Senate in the spring of 1923, State Department officials reverted to form. Hughes issued a public statement dismissing the possibility of recognition until the Soviet government recognized its "international obligations," that is, agreed to pay the Russian state debt and ceased its "revolutionary propaganda."[55]

The Soviet government was quick to reply: American business interest in trade with the Soviet Union will eventually force the U.S. government to change its tune. "We, therefore, would advise Mr. Hughes to pass from the methods of a capitalistic agitator to the serious proposals of a capitalistic business man." Commerce Secretary Hoover was also intransigent: "He was completely disgusted with the Bolsheviks and did not believe that a practical government could ever be worked out under their leadership. He said that it was his feeling that Russia would probably go through a process of further disintegration, with local potentates setting themselves up at various points; after which there might be reintegration."[56]

Still, the Soviet government persisted. The Hughes statement and a subsequent public letter by Hoover touched off an interesting exchange in Moscow. It appears to have been provoked by the analyses of a clerk in the Soviet embassy in Berlin, who thought the recent American statements should not be taken too tragically. There was increasing American interest in Soviet trade which would eventually result in a change in policy. The U.S. government was moving from principled intransigence to hard economic demands for trade, and this represented a step forward. Trotskii weighed in based on a report from a Soviet agent in Washington, thinking that the atmosphere was perhaps improving and that the time might be right to send representatives to the United States to look for contracts.[57]

Chicherin was skeptical. The Washington report was a "single swallow," and who knew if this one was real or if others would follow. Our "comrades abroad are everywhere inclined to go beyond the bounds of their responsibilities."

"And in America," Chicherin observed, "where there is no ambassador (*polpred*) to establish order, it is one hundred times worse. All kinds of 'representatives,' sometimes doubtful, play the important people, quarrel with one another, causing unbelievable chaos and doing great harm to us."

When we send people abroad, they must have precise instructions and be told in no uncertain terms not to exceed them. "But this is not enough. At the outset here we must decide whether we have serious business in mind, for it would be better not to begin than to provoke disappointment." It was just this "economic disappointment" which was everywhere at the base of unfavorable opinion toward us. "I would say even more, we need to improve greatly our trade and industrial apparatus . . . because often 'economic disappointment' is the result of . . . our failings." We need to decide what business we want and whether we have something serious to offer to the Americans.

"Foreign capitalists reason thus, in Russia there is big risk, for such risk we can only go for high profits." If we cannot offer the high profits, then foreign capitalists will not come here. If we go to America with only "something absurd, absolutely unprofitable for the Americans, we can only discredit ourselves."[58]

Litvinov was also skeptical, noting "the absolutely hostile attitude to us from [U.S.] governmental circles." There was no point in sending a spur-of-the-moment delegation to Washington. And reinforcing Chicherin's arguments, Litvinov reemphasized that going to America without serious business proposals would be pointless and self-defeating. It is disappointment with our inability to buy that is causing renewed hostility and calls for a rupture of contacts and a new blockade. Our dithering gives fresh arguments to our adversaries.[59]

In October 1923 Litvinov complained that the NKID did not have a seat in various economic agencies and was only present at Politburo meetings for the discussion of strictly foreign policy issues. We are badly informed on internal economic conditions, he said, which nevertheless have an impact on foreign policy and foreign trade. About internal party affairs, all Litvinov knew came from rumors and "corridor discussions."[60]

Soviet discussions continued about relations with the United States, but without results. In July 1923 Hughes issued an open letter hostile to the Soviet government. Chicherin noticed and felt obliged to reply.[61] In December, however, Chicherin appealed for better relations to Calvin Coolidge, who had succeeded Harding after his sudden death in August 1923.[62] Hughes rejected the Soviet démarche out of hand. His position resembled Poincaré's.

> There would seem to be at this time no reason for negotiations. The American Government . . . is not proposing to barter away its principles. If the Soviet authorities are ready to restore the confiscated property of American citizens or make effective compensation, they can do so. If the Soviet authorities are ready to repeal their decree repudiating Russia's obligations to this country and appropriately recognize them, they can do so. It requires no conference or negotiations to accomplish these results which can and should be achieved at Moscow as evidence of good faith. . . . Most serious is the continued propaganda to overthrow the institutions of this country. This government can enter into no negotiations until these efforts directed from Moscow are abandoned.[63]

It was still the policy of capitalist porridge to be fed to Moscow with a splintery wooden spoon, like it or not. Both sides claimed to have their principles, and for the time being, principles held sway over pragmatism.

Lenin's Regrets

While the debates about relations with the West continued in Moscow, Lenin's firm hand slipped from the controls of state. He suffered a series of strokes beginning in late May 1922 which in the following March rendered him incapable of further political activity. A conflict over leadership then erupted between Stalin and Trotskii in which Stalin quickly took the upper hand. Stalin and Trotskii did not like each other, to say the least, and had already clashed many times in the past. In Lenin's last months of relative activity and lucidity at the end of 1922 and the beginning of 1923, he was aware of the developing party conflict and recorded ideas which he intended as working notes and as a warning to his colleagues.

Lenin envisaged changes in the organization of the government. His notes became known as the "testament" because Lenin did not live long enough to see the changes through. He considered Stalin and Trotskii to be the two most capable leaders in the Politburo, and he foresaw that relations between them might eventually lead to "a split" in the party.

"Comrade Stalin . . . has unlimited authority concentrated in his hands," Lenin observed, "and I am not sure whether he will always be capable of using that authority with sufficient caution."

> Comrade Trotskii, on the other hand . . . is distinguished not only by outstanding ability. He is personally perhaps the most capable man in the present C.C. [Bolshevik Central Committee], but he has displayed excessive self-assurance and shown excessive preoccupation with the purely administrative side of the work.

These two powerful men, Lenin foresaw, could turn against one another and "split" the party, perhaps undoing the Soviet state and the October Revolution.

Ten days later Lenin added a postscript.

> Stalin is too rude and this defect, although quite tolerable in our midst and in dealing among us Communists, becomes intolerable in a secretary general [of the party]. That is why I suggest that the comrades think about a way of removing Stalin from that post and appointing another man in his stead who in all other respects differs from Comrade Stalin in having only one advantage, namely, that of being more tolerant, more loyal, more polite and more considerate to the comrades, less capricious, etc. This circumstance may appear to be a negligible detail. But I think that from the standpoint of safeguards against a split and from the standpoint of what I wrote above about the relationship between Stalin and Trotskii it is not a [minor] detail, but it is a detail which can assume decisive importance.[64]

It was indeed. On 10 March 1923 Lenin suffered a devastating stroke which paralyzed half his body and rendered him incapable of speaking. On 21 January

1924 he died, having left unsettled the great issues of government which he had identified but could not resolve.

Even the Die-Hard Churchill noted in an epitaph the importance of Lenin's passing:

> Lenin's intellect failed at the moment when its destructive force was exhausted, and when sovereign remedial functions were its quest. He alone could have led Russia into the enchanted quagmire; he alone could have found the way back to the causeway. He saw; he turned; he perished. The strong illuminant that guided him was cut off at the moment when he had turned resolutely for home. The Russian people were left floundering in the bog. Their worst misfortune was his birth: their next worst, his death.[65]

The Bolsheviks and the Soviet peoples were now on their own. But Stalin breathed easier for he knew that Lenin had wanted to remove him as general secretary.

Iosif Vissarionovich Stalin

In the leadership conflict that erupted as Lenin slipped toward death, Stalin held the upper hand. That he did so might at first glance seem unexpected. In 1917 Stalin was relatively unknown outside revolutionary circles; his role in the Bolshevik seizure of power was secondary to that of Lenin and Trotskii. Everyone considered them to be the two foremost Bolshevik leaders. Stalin was named *narkom* for nationalities in the first Soviet government and was also a member of the first Politburo, or the then party executive committee. The nationalities commissariat was an appropriate place for Stalin, for he was Georgian and had been active in the revolutionary movement in the Caucasus.

Iosif Vissarionovich Dzhugashvili was born in Gori, Georgia, in 1879. His father was a cobbler, his mother a peasant's daughter. Both were the offspring of serfs. The young Dzhugashvili grew up poor, unlike many of his Bolshevik colleagues who came from well-off bourgeois families. Poverty often breeds violence and sorrow, and the Dzhugashvilis were not spared either. Their first three children died not long after birth. The father, Vissarion, was a drunk and often beat his wife Ekaterina in front of their only surviving son. One of Stalin's early biographers, the late Issac Deutscher, reckoned that the father could not have been all bad. He and his wife sent their son to the local church school to be educated. Perhaps the father, who died in 1890, wanted more for his son than he had had. At age 15, Iosif Vissarionovich obtained a scholarship to go to a seminary in Tiflis where he was a good student. Like

Lenin and Trotskii, he ran into trouble however, as a rebellious teenager, and did not graduate. The revolutionary movement intercepted him.

If Litvinov was a money launderer and gunrunner, Dzhugashvili became a rougher Georgian variant: underground *capo* of a gang of armed robbers, itinerant propagandist, union organizer, all in the cause of the revolution in the Caucasus. He soon ran afoul of the police in Baku and did time in tsarist jails. Like Trotskii, he escaped from Siberian exile only to be sent back again. His pseudonyms, among others, were Koba and Ivanovich before he settled on Stalin, *stal'* being the Russian word for steel.

When the revolution broke out in March 1917 Stalin was still in Siberia, but he and other Bolshevik exiles quickly made their way back to Petrograd. During 1917 Stalin rose to prominence, becoming a member of the inner circle of Bolshevik leaders. During the civil war, he was in the south at Tsaritsyn, later called Stalingrad, on the west bank of the Volga. It was here that many of the first clashes with Trotskii took place, with an impatient Lenin in the middle, calming hot tempers.

Stalin was a pedestrian orator, theorist, and pamphleteer. Trotskii called his language "soporific." But Stalin was a smart, capable organizer, a talent

**Figure 3.4. Iosif Vissarionovich Stalin, ca. 1920s.
DeA Picture Library, Art Resource, NY.**

which Lenin noticed and appreciated. In all of these activities, he nevertheless found time to attack Trotskii, attacks which Lenin either ignored or
diverted. In the summer of 1920 during the war against Poland, Stalin's hostility to Trotskii and his insubordination left open the Red Army's southern
flank, which Piłsudski stove in to prevent the fall of Warsaw. Here was a consequence of Stalin's grudge against Trotskii. Bad tempered, moody, vengeful,
pathologically intolerant of dissent, Stalin never forgot or forgave political
opposition. Like the Die-Hards, he was a good hater. Once dirty, always dirty
was his view of adversaries. He could bide his time, wait for years, before
exacting vengeance on oppositionists, or on anyone who looked the wrong
way at him. "The greatest delight is to mark one's enemy," Stalin once said,
"prepare everything, avenge oneself thoroughly, and then go to sleep." His
indiscreet remarks quickly spread inside the party elite, though it is doubtful
his comrades could ever have imagined the lengths to which he would go in
pursuit of his "enemies."

Stalin's "mistake" during the summer counter-offensive against Poland did
not do long-term damage to his reputation. In April 1922 Lenin sponsored
Stalin for the post of general secretary, or *gensek*, of the Communist Party,
less than two months before Lenin's first stroke. Stalin thus obtained control
of government appointments and began to place his allies in key positions.
Trotskii said the choice of Stalin as *gensek* went against Lenin's better judgment. It was not long before Lenin regretted his decision, but by then it was
too late.[66] Ironically, both Stalin and Trotskii rose to positions of great power
with Lenin's support. Only one could survive without it.

Fiasco in Germany

Without Lenin in control, everything became more difficult. During the
summer of 1923 the French occupation of the Ruhr continued and therefore
still irritated London and worried Moscow. Ironically, both governments
feared French continental dominance, though needlessly. France was too
weak for that. At the same time German political instability caused by the
Ruhr crisis aroused hopes in Moscow of communist revolution, which the
Politburo through the Comintern attempted to encourage. No sooner had
the brief war scare of January–February 1923 simmered down than Moscow
moved from supporting the German government against France and Poland
to supporting a communist movement against that selfsame government.

Slippage on the German issue had already aroused Litvinov's ire and led
him to write to Zinoviev, still the Comintern boss, with copies to Stalin,
Trotskii, and Chicherin. It was right in the midst of the Anglo-Soviet crisis
in May–June 1923, provoked by the Curzon ultimatum. The Comintern

had sent agents into the Ruhr region, and the German ambassador, Ulrich Graf von Brockdorff-Rantzau, went to see Litvinov to complain. The German government knew of the arrival of these individuals who had entered Germany illegally. The ambassador suspected that Karl Radek, a Bolshevik member of the Comintern IKKI, was even directing the German Communist Party. The German government, Rantzau commented sarcastically, thought that there were two tendencies in Moscow: one, the Narkomindel'cheskii, which aimed at the gradual ruin of Germany, and two, the Kominternovskii, which calculated that the time was ripe for "decisive action" to facilitate a German revolution. These circumstances, Rantzau went on, made it difficult for him to work for German-Soviet rapprochement. Political elements in Germany who prefer a rapprochement with Britain could take the upper hand. People wonder what value there is in the Rapallo Treaty if it produces no important economic benefits and only leads to the arrival in Germany of unwanted guests. Like the British, Rantzau was aware of the French interest in better Soviet relations and also worried about it.

In reply, Litvinov denied everything: the allegations about Soviet agents in Germany were a "police fantasy," or about the Soviet Union aiming at German ruin, "stupid and absurd in the extreme." Of course, the Soviet government did not conceal its willingness to conclude agreements with all countries, and it would not refuse trade negotiations with France. But no negotiations with France or Britain would influence "our general political line which is the continuation and development of the Rapallo Treaty." According to Litvinov, the German ambassador appeared satisfied with this explanation.

Litvinov was not so sure about the German "police fantasies," which prompted him to write Zinoviev, forwarding his record of meeting with Rantzau. He asked for clarification of German accusations, and then he gave Zinoviev a brief lesson in realpolitik. Germany, he noted, was getting ready to retreat from Rapallo in the event of an Anglo-Soviet rupture so as to please Britain. It was not the time for communist propaganda and interference in German internal affairs. "The present moment requires us to observe exceptional caution, and I do not doubt," added Litvinov sarcastically, "that you will take the necessary measures so that we do not put any weapons into the hands of our enemies in Germany."[67]

Litvinov's warning had no effect on Zinoviev or the Politburo, which became involved in planning a German revolutionary uprising during the summer and autumn of 1923. Germany was in political and economic turmoil, and it seemed like revolution might erupt at any time. German passive resistance against the French occupation of the Ruhr led to economic chaos, destroyed the value of the mark, and put millions of people into desperate straits. On 9 August the Politburo called members back to Moscow from holidays to discuss German developments. With Lenin dying, without his exigent realism as a guide, and with Trotskii and Stalin already maneuvering for power, would either of them, or anyone else, dare to stand for non-involvement in the German unrest? Zinoviev and Politburo ally Lev M. Kamenev sided with Stalin against Trotskii to make sure he did not succeed Lenin. Under the circumstances, no one was going to speak for prudence for fear of being accused of abandoning the German revolution, on which many Bolsheviks had placed their hopes since 1918.

On 21 August the Politburo approved a credit of 1 million gold marks for the Profintern, the Red International of Trade Unions, as well as factory collections, for distribution in Germany. When the German chancellor and foreign minister, Gustav Stresemann, complained that this money was being used to overthrow the German government, Chicherin replied blithely that it was for relief work among unemployed German workers. He was too clever by half, for the Bolsheviks were also supplying guns and got caught at it. Even the Soviet naval attaché, a French communist who went by the name of V. Petrov, appeared to be involved in the gunrunning.[68] Stresemann, naturally, was incredulous.

With revolution apparently about to erupt, no one in Moscow—well, with the exception perhaps of Litvinov and Chicherin—seemed to care what Stresemann thought. "The German proletariat," reckoned the Politburo, "stands at the threshold of the decisive battles for power."[69] The coming German revolution was big news in the press and at party meetings. In Russian cities, walls were plastered with posters urging young people to learn German, the better to serve the world revolution. The NKID could not resist these pressures. The planned uprising, based on miscalculations, divided counsels, and Soviet meddling, was aborted at the last minute after German communist leaders reckoned that they could not pull it off. Orders canceling the uprising did not reach a few militia units in Hamburg, which rose and were quickly crushed. "It is a bad look-out for a revolution which cannot conquer by its own power," Trotskii noted just prior to the fiasco.[70] This was a wise observation, and the Politburo should have let German communists make their own revolution in their own time, if they could. But that was easier said than done.

Recriminations were quick to follow. As Litvinov had done, Chicherin reproached Zinoviev for imprudent comments in the press about Germany.[71] The German government was furious, and the German ambassador so informed Chicherin with a long indictment of Soviet meddling. Chicherin was already well informed. The Soviet naval attaché's alleged gunrunning was only the tip of the iceberg: Radek's involvement was uncovered among other items on a long list which Chicherin thoughtfully forwarded to Zinoviev, with copies to Politburo members. The German ambassador pointed out that making distinctions between the Soviet government and the Comintern was a waste of time. In Germany, public opinion recognized no difference between party and government; they were one and the same, united by the same people and directed by the same policies. They not "only supported, but by every possible means incited the revolutionary movement in Germany against the German government." No government, however weak, could tolerate such a situation, which, Rantzau pointed out, was entirely inconsistent with the Rapallo Treaty. "If the Soviet government does not in some way openly disassociate itself from these activities, the situation will become critical. Already in Germany public opinion is at present deeply alarmed by Russian involvement in German affairs." The present situation is impossible and cannot continue. Rantzau went on and on, and Chicherin did not abridge the ambassador's long monologue in his report to the Politburo. If the Soviet government did not act, Rantzau continued, and these could have been the *narkom*'s words, German opinion will "turn against Russia which could even facilitate that [anti-Soviet] crusade which he and we both feared." According to Rantzau's report, Chicherin agreed completely. "It seems to me extremely important," Chicherin wrote in quite an understatement, "to discuss . . . the general question of our relations with the German government."[72]

Chicherin followed up with a letter to Stalin hammering home the point that changes were essential if Soviet-German relations were not to be ruined. Rantzau had been to see him *again* to stress that these relations were in serious danger. German "right-wing circles" had learned about the Soviet naval attaché Petrov, whose real name was Garnier: he was a French communist *and naval officer* (it is not clear whether he was then still a serving officer). If he was, French intelligence had done very well indeed to place him in the Soviet embassy in Berlin. As Chicherin pointed out to Stalin, Monsieur Garnier, aka Petrov, had been involved in "the most secret questions between us and the German war ministry and intelligence services." The whole business was a scandal in that we, as Chicherin put it, had involved a French naval officer in the most secret sort of business with the German government. "If this became known in a wider world," Chicherin concluded, again indulging in understatement, "it could provoke a real storm."[73] As it turned out, Petrov was recalled without hubbub, but Soviet foreign policy in Germany was a shambles, flip-flopping from supporting the German government during the winter to plotting to overthrow it in the summer and autumn. Did anyone in Moscow remember Rapallo? Rantzau wondered. We'll have to wait, he observed, and see if Chicherin can win a "trial of strength" against the Comintern.[74]

There was a continuing anti-French angle to NKID calculations about Germany. Chicherin and Litvinov speculated on a French occupation of Berlin, even pushing up to the Vistula, should revolution break out. "We consider this a serious threat and a preface to an attack on us." Rakovskii was instructed to suggest to his British interlocutors "very cautiously, for we would not want to be seen breaking up the Entente, that Russia might in some way come in handy for England in the struggle against a new Napoleonic empire." So trade with France was one thing, but the danger of French "hegemony in Europe" put ideas of a Franco-Soviet rapprochement temporarily on hold. Prospects of German revolution, it seems, confused even the NKID. Would the spread of communism in Central Europe, Litvinov wondered, be considered "a lesser evil" in London than French hegemony? We have only skimpy information on likely Anglo-French reactions to "future events." Better information would have persuaded Litvinov that in the choice of lesser evils, Britain would *never* opt for the Soviet Union.[75] In the game of who loves me, who loves me not, Moscow was rarely if ever considered an attractive choice, at least not until 1941, and even then there were many naysayers.

In London Rakovskii signaled that the French franc was coming under pressure in foreign exchange markets and falling in value against the U.S. dollar and sterling. The idea that France could send troops to the Vistula must have soon seemed foolish. The French exerted successful control over the Ruhr mines, but Poincaré would go no further, mindful of British and U.S. opposition. Rakovskii saw a silver lining in the economic chaos in Germany, the weakening French franc, and an industrial "standstill" in Britain. Opening our order books, he noted, would "undoubtedly exert pressure on all sides." Rakovskii was preaching to the choir: Litvinov had already sent him a shopping list of orders for British goods.[76]

Notes

1. Riddell, *Diary*, p. 389.

2. Riddell, *Diary*, p. 387; and R. K. Debo, "G. V. Chicherin: A Historical Perspective," in Gorodetsky, *Soviet Foreign Policy*, pp. 21–30.

3. O'Connor, *Chicherin*, pp. 124–25.

4. Litvinov to Klyshko, no. 554, 13 Dec. 1922, AVPRF, f. 04, o. 4, p. 21, d. 303, ll. 78–79; and Litvinov to Vorovskii, Soviet *polpred* in Rome, no. 2251, secret, 6 April 1923, AVPRF, f. 05, o. 3, p. 1, d. 1, ll. 19–22.

5. Robert J. Young, *An American by Degrees: The Extraordinary Lives of French Ambassador Jules Jusserand* (Montréal, 2009), pp. 165–80.

6. N. N. Krestinskii, Soviet *polpred* in Berlin, to Litvinov, no. 545, 8 May 1922, AVPRF, f. 04, o. 42, p. 259, d. 53620, l. 41.

7. "Report of the director of the department for the Anglo-Saxon and Romance countries to comrade Veinshtein," S. Bronskii, 22 Sept. 1922, AVPRF, f. 04, o. 42, p. 259, d. 53619, ll. 23–25; and Chicherin to Trotskii, commissar for war, 9 Oct. 1922, ibid., l. 45.

8. "Résumé of comrade Karakhan's first conversation with Herriot and Daladier on 20 September 1922," AVPRF, f. 0136, o. 5, p. 102, d. 35, ll. 9–13.

9. Herriot to Chicherin, 26 Oct. 1922, DVP, V, p. 667 (the original in French is in AVPRF, f. 136, o. 5, p. 102, d. 34, l. 51).

10. Herriot (from Moscow) to Poincaré and Millerand, 2 Oct. 1922, AN Papiers Millerand, 470AP/70.

11. "Information, no. 6, journey of Herriot . . . ," ns, but D. T. Florinskii, 12 Oct. 1922, AVPRF, f. 0136, o. 5, p. 102, d. 35, ll. 46–51.

12. "Northern and Western Summary," no. 951, 8 Nov. 1922, N . . . /573/38, FO 371 8184; Crewe, no. 534, 3 March 1923, N2085/62/38, FO 371 9344; and J.C.4, Oct. 1928, MAÉ Russie/1113, ff. 73–79.

13. Untitled report, rigorously secret, ns, nd (but early 1923), AVPRF, f. 04, o. 42, p. 259, d. 53620, ll. 56–58 (cf., "A.s. propagande russe vis-à-vis des milieux dirigeants européens et notamment français," no. 16108 SCR-2/11 [Ministère de la Guerre], 6 Dec. 1922, Archives nationales, Paris [hereinafter AN], F7 13491); and Jean-Noël Jeanneney, L'Argent caché (Paris, 1981), passim.

14. "Juifs russes suspects: Reichzamer [sic]," P. 5432.U., Préfecture de police, 11 Oct. 1921, AN F7 13490; and "Russes bolchevistes: Rechtzammer [sic]," P. 5571.U., Préfecture de police, 21 Nov. 1921, ibid.

15. Krestinskii to Chicherin, no. 1143, 31 Oct. 1922, AVPRF, f. 04, o. 42, p. 259, d. 53620, l. 50; S. I. Bratman-Brodovskii, Soviet counselor in Berlin, to Litvinov, no. 845, 6 June 1923, ibid., ll. 24–26; Litvinov to Krestinskii, no. 641, 19 June 1923, ibid., l. 35; untitled memorandum, 12 June 1923, covered by Krestinskii to Litvinov, no. 912, 20 June 1923, ibid., ll. 37–38; Chicherin to Krestinskii, no. 73, 24 Sept. 1923, Moskva-Berlin, I, pp. 196–97; and M. J. Carley, "From Revolution to Dissolution: The Quai d'Orsay, the Banque Russo-Asiatique, and the Chinese Eastern Railway, 1917–1926," International History Review, vol. 12, no. 4 (Nov. 1990), p. 743.

16. Brodovskii to Litvinov, no. 877, 14 March 1923, AVPRF, f. 04, o. 42, p. 259, d. 53629, ll. 31–32; and "Mme Félix Decori, Navachine, Dimitri . . . ," P/5047, Préfecture de police, 11 Aug. 1923, AN F7 12952.

17. "Chez les Russes . . . ," P. 5921.U., Préfecture de police, 1 March 1922, AN F7 13491.

18. "Note à consulter," unsigned, nd (but Dec. 1923), MAÉ Papiers Millerand/70, ff. 213–17.

19. "La France et les Soviets," P. 9028.U., Préfecture de police, 17 Jan. 1924, AN F7 13493.

20. Crewe, no. 3032, 29 Dec. 1922, N76/62/38, FO 371 9343.

21. Leeper's minute, 13 Feb. 1923, N1339/62/38, FO 371 9343.

22. "France-Russie," Alfred Vignon, Millerand's deputy secretary general, 22 Feb. 1923, MAÉ Papiers Millerand/70, fol. 31; and "De l'opportunité d'une représentation économique officielle en Russie soviétique," MAÉ, 23 Feb. 1923, ibid., ff. 42–49 (Peretti's handwritten minute is on fol. 49).

23. Millerand to Aimé de Fleuriau, French minister in Beijing, 25 April 1923, AN Papiers Millerand, 470AP/69; "Envoi de M. [Paul François] de Chevilly . . . extrait des Izvestia . . . ," 27 Aug. 1923, MAÉ Russie/82, fol. 87; "Conversation avec Peretti, Russie," Vignon, 10 Oct. 1923, MAÉ Papiers Millerand/70, fol. 144; "Conversation avec Peretti, France-Soviets," Vignon, 22 Dec. 1923, ibid., fol. 197; and "France-Soviets," Vignon, 29 Dec. 1923, ibid., ff. 210–12.

24. Crewe, no. 223, 22 Feb. 1923, N1765/62/38, FO 371 9343; and Sir Edward Grigg, Lloyd George's private secretary, to Crowe, permanent undersecretary, Foreign Office, 7 Oct. 1922, N9208/573/38, FO 371 8184.

25. Joseph Wielowieyski, Polish counselor in Paris, to Jules Laroche, *directeur politique adjoint*, Quai d'Orsay, which covered a note, *strictement confidentiel*, 6 Oct. 1922, MAÉ Russie/350, ff. 37–38; "Note pour le Président du Conseil," *sous-direction d'Europe*, unsigned, 3 Dec. 1923, MAÉ Russie/424, ff. 146–47; and "Le paiement des rentes russes et la responsabilité du Bloc National," Armand Charpentier, *Ère Nouvelle*, 27 Feb. 1924, ibid., f. 162.

26. "Note à consulter," unsigned, nd (but Dec. 1923), MAÉ Papiers Millerand/70, ff. 213–17; and Note by Jacques Seydoux, *sous-directeur des Relations commerciales*, 19 Jan. 1924, MAÉ RC Russie/2090.

27. Charles Lord Hardinge to Curzon, 6 Nov. 1921, India Office, Curzon Papers, F.112/200A; and Hardinge to Curzon, 8 April 1922, Curzon Papers, F.112/200.

28. Hardinge to Curzon, 1 Nov. 1922, Curzon Papers, F.112/200B.

29. Crewe to Curzon, 9 May 1923, Curzon Papers, F.112/201A.

30. Trotskii to N. I. Bukharin, editor of *Pravda*, et al., no. 35/T, very secret, 18 Jan. 1923, *Moskva-Berlin: Politika i diplomatiia Kremlia, 1920–1941* (hereinafter *Moskva-Berlin*), I, pp. 97–98.

31. Chicherin to Stalin, very secret, 19 Jan. 1923, *Moskva-Berlin*, I, pp. 100–101.

32. Politburo resolution, no copies, original to be returned to file, 25 Jan. 1923, *Moskva-Berlin*, I, pp. 102–3.

33. Stalin to Politburo and Chicherin, rigorously secret, 29 Jan. 1923, *Moskva-Berlin*, I, p. 109.

34. Litvinov to Stalin, no. 899, 4 Dec. 1923, RGASPI, f. 359, o. 1, d. 8, ll. 58–63; and Chicherin to Kh. G. Rakovskii, Soviet *torgpred* in London, no. 29, 13 Dec. 1923, AVPRF, f. 04, o. 4, p. 23, d. 327, ll. 185–86.

35. Curzon's minute, 27 Feb. 1923, N1823/62/38, FO 371 9344; and Tyrrell's minute, 1 March 1923, N2028/62/38, ibid.

36. Gregory's minute, 13 Feb. 1923, N1339/62/38, FO 371 9343.

37. Gregory's minute, 12 Jan. 1923, N298/44/38, FO 371 9333.

38. Minutes by Lindsay and Crowe, 5 April 1923, N228/3198/38, FO 371 9365.

39. Litvinov to Berzin, no. 365, secret, personal, 6 April 1923, AVPRF, f. 04, o. 4, p. 23, d. 326, ll. 64–66; and Litvinov to Berzin, no. 384, secret, 11 April 1923, ibid., ll. 68–75.

40. Litvinov to Berzin, no. 505, 10 May 1923, AVPRF, f. 04, o. 4, p. 23, d. 326, ll. 106–8; Litvinov to Berzin, no. 515, 14 May 1923, ibid., ll. 109–13; and Litvinov to Berzin, no. 532, 18 May 1923, ibid., ll. 114–16.

41. Litvinov to Rakovskii (London), no. 879, secret, 23 Nov. 1923, AVPRF, f. 04, o. 4, p. 23, d. 327, l. 157.

42. Coates to F. A. Rothstein, NKID press office, 9 June 1923 (in English), AVPRF, f. 069, o. 7, p. 7, d. 13, ll. 60–67; and "Report from Ewer," very secret, nd (but June 1923 and in English), ibid., ll. 102–6.

43. Excerpt from protocol no. 9, 31 May 1923, G. Adibekov et al. (eds.), *Politbiuro TsK RKP(b)-VKP(b) i Evropa, Resheniia 'Osoboi papki', 1923–1939* (hereinafter *Politbiuro Osoboi papki*) (Moscow, 2001), pp. 17–19; and Chicherin to Krasin, not numbered, 3 June 1923, AVPRF, f. 04, o. 4, p. 23, d. 326, l. 122.

44. Litvinov to Krasin, not numbered, very secret, 4 June 1923, AVPRF, f. 04, o. 4, p. 23, d. 326, ll. 142–44; and Litvinov to Berzin, no. 595, very secret, 4 June 1923, ibid., ll. 130–35.

45. Chicherin/Litvinov to Rakovskii, no. 13, secret, 15 Oct. 1923, AVPRF, f. 04, o. 4, p. 23, d. 327, ll. 100–102.

46. Hoover to Hughes, 14 July 1922, 861.50Am3/25, NA RG59, M-316, reel 109; Hughes to Harding, confidential, 22 July 1922, 861.50Am3/A, ibid.; and Harding to Hughes, 23 June 1922, 861.01/459, NA RG59, M-316, reel 71.

47. Poole to Hughes, 20 June 1922, 861.00/9781, NA RG59, M-316, reel 51, Harding to Hughes, 24 July 1922, 861.50Am3/1, NA RG59, M-316, reel 109; Hughes to Harding, 26 July 1922, ibid.; Hughes to Harding, 31 July 1922, 861.50Am3/2, ibid.; and Harding to Hughes, 31 July 1922, 861.50Am3/3, ibid.

48. Young (Riga), no. 90, strictly confidential, 1 June 1922, 861.01/446, NA RG59, M-316, reel 71; and Poole to Hughes, 11 July 1922, 861.01/511, ibid.

49. Hughes to Harding, 21 Aug. 1922, 861.50Am3/1, NA RG59, M-316, reel 109.

50. Poole to Hughes, 31 Oct. 1922, 711.64/64, NA RG59, M-333, reel 2; Litvinov to Stalin, no. 472, 31 Oct. 1922, Moskva-Vashington: Politika i diplomatiia Kremlia, 1921–1941 (hereinafter Moskva-Vashington), 3 vols. (Moscow, 2009), I, pp. 68–69; Politburo resolution, no. P35/5-d, rigorously secret, 9 Nov. 1922, ibid., p. 71.

51. Chicherin to Lenin, 22 Nov. 1922, SAO, Gody nepriznaniia, 1918–1926, pp. 241–42.

52. Bloomfield to Hughes, 18 Dec. 1922, 861.50Am3/30, NA RG59, M-316, reel 109.

53. Bloomfield to Hughes, 2 Jan. 1923, 661.1115/130, NA RG59, carton no. 6151; and Bloomfield to Hughes, 9 Jan. 1923, 861.50Am3/31, NA RG59, M-316, reel 109.

54. Memorandum, James P. Goodrich, former governor of Indiana, president of the National City Bank, Indianapolis, nd (but June 1922), 50pp., 861.00/9722, NA RG59, M-316, reel 51; and Young (Riga), 8 Sept. 1923, 861.01, NA RG59, M-316, reel 72.

55. Press release, Department of State, 21 March 1923, Papers Relating to the Foreign Relations of the United States (hereinafter FRUS), 1923, 2 vols. (Washington, D.C., 1938), II, pp. 755–58.

56. Hoover to Hughes, 25 April 1923, 861.01/593, NA RG59, M-316, reel 72; and Poole to Hughes, 4 May 1923, 861.48/2215, RG59, M-316, reel 104.

57. Iu. P. Denike, Soviet embassy, Berlin, "Hughes Speech," 6 April 1923, Moskva-Vashington, I, pp. 86–91; Denike, "Hughes Speech and Hoover Letter," 17 April 1923, ibid., pp. 92–95; and Trotskii to Chicherin and Litvinov, cc. Stalin, 2 June 1923, ibid., p. 97.

58. Chicherin to Trotskii, cc. Stalin, no. 530/ChS, 2 June 1923, Moskva-Vashington, I, pp. 98–99.

59. Litvinov to Trotskii, cc. Stalin, no. 594, very secret, 2 June 1923, Moskva-Vashington, I, p. 100.

60. Litvinov to Rakovskii, no. 811, personal, 29 Oct. 1923, AVPRF, f. 04, o. 4, p. 23, d. 327, l. 123.

61. Hughes to Samuel Gompers, American Federation of Labor, 19 July 1923, FRUS, 1923, II, pp. 760–64; Chicherin to Stalin, 30 July 1923, Moskva-Vashington, I, p. 114; and Chicherin's reply, 5 August 1923, ibid., pp. 115–19.

62. Chicherin to Coolidge, 16 Dec. 1923, 711.61/71, NA RG59, M-333, reel 2.

63. Hughes to Myron S. Herrick, U.S. ambassador in Paris, 18 Dec. 1923, 711.61/71, NA RG59, M-333, reel 2; and Denike to P. L. Lapinskii, NKID, Moscow, 18 Jan. 1924, SAO, Gody nepriznaniia, 1918–1926, pp. 358–63.

64. Moshe Lewin, Lenin's Last Struggle (New York, 1968), pp. 71–86; E. H. Carr, The Interregnum, 1923–1924 (Harmondsworth, 1969), pp. 266–71; Service, Lenin, pp. 464–70; and Lenin, CW, XXXVI, pp. 593–611.

65. W. S. Churchill, The Aftermath (London, 1929), p. 76.

66. Isaac Deutscher, Stalin: A Political Biography (New York, 1949); idem., Trotsky, 3 vols. (New York, 1954–1963); Tucker, Stalin, pp. 173–80, 211; Service, Stalin, pp. 129–49, 284–85; Trotskii, My Life (New York, 1970), p. 553.

67. Litvinov to Zinoviev, no. 597, secret, 5 June 1923, RGASPI, f. 359, o. 1, d. 7, ll. 95, covering "Conversation with Ambassador Count Brockdorff-Rantzau in my office, 4 June 1923," ibid., ll. 96–98 (published in Moskva-Berlin, I, pp. 165–67).

68. Politburo protocol, no. 22, 9 Aug. 1923, Politbiuro i Komintern, p. 164; Politburo resolution, no. P26/8, rigorously secret, 21 Aug. 1923, Moskva-Berlin, I, p. 185; and Chicherin to Brodovskii, 24 Aug. 1923, ibid., pp. 188–89.

69. Politburo protocol, no. 27, 22 Aug. 1923, Politbiuro i Komintern, p. 167.

70. Carr, Interregnum, p. 225.

71. Pierre Broué, Histoire de l'Internationale communiste, 1919–1943 (Paris, 1997), pp. 324–26; Chicherin to Zinoviev, no. 276/ChS, 24 Oct. 1923, Moskva-Berlin, I, pp. 229–30; and Chicherin to Zinoviev, no. 290/s, 29 Oct. 1923, ibid., pp. 231–32.

72. Chicherin to Zinoviev, no. 401/ChS, 3 Dec. 1923, Moskva-Berlin, I, pp. 233–35; and Rantzau, no. 39, secret, 4 Dec. 1923, Akten zur deutschen auswärtigen Politik, 1918–1945 (hereinafter AzDAP), series A (1918–1925), 14 vols. (Baden-Baden and Frankfurt, 1966–1983), IX, pp. 90–91. Brockdorff-Rantzau sometimes signed his telegrams "Rantzau," and for stylistic reasons, I have adopted this formulation and refer to him in the narrative simply as Rantzau.

73. Chicherin to Stalin, 10 Dec. 1923, Moskva-Berlin, I, pp. 235–36.

74. Rantzau, no. 128, secret, 1 Feb. 1924, AzDAP, A, IX, pp. 337–39.

75. Chicherin/Litvinov to Rakovskii, no. 13, 15 Oct. 1923, AVPRF, f. 04, o. 4, p. 23, d. 327, ll. 100–102; and Litvinov to Rakovskii, no. 808, secret, 29 Oct. 1923, AVPRF, f. 069, o. 7, p. 7, d. 14, ll. 80–85.

76. Rakovskii to Chicherin, no. 21, 10 Nov. 1923, AVPRF, f. 069, o. 7, p. 7, d. 4, ll. 106–7; and Litvinov to Rakovskii, no. 796, secret, 22 Oct. 1923, AVPRF, f. 04, o. 4, p. 23, d. 327, ll. 108–9.

CHAPTER FOUR

∼

"Hedged in by Reservations"

Peaceful Coexistence in London and Paris, 1923–1924

With the bursting of Bolshevik hopes for a German revolution, the NKID turned back to more sensible speculations, fueled by British Parliamentary elections in December 1923. The fiasco of Soviet policy in Germany and another in Bulgaria, where the Politburo had also meddled, buttressed NKID arguments to put Soviet foreign policy interests ahead of those of the Comintern. This made Chicherin all the more anxious to improve relations with Britain. Not three months after the end of the confrontation provoked by the Curzon ultimatum, a British trade delegation arrived in Moscow for discussions with Chicherin, Krasin, and other Soviet officials. The Foreign Office did not make much of the visit, but Chicherin did, seeing it as a sign of British interest in improved relations with the Soviet Union, driven by the need for trade. With Germany in a state of chaos, Russia would become more valuable as a trading partner in the world economy. Improved relations with Britain, Chicherin thought, would help get over possible tensions created in the event of revolution in Germany. Here was a sign of Chicherin's paradoxical naïveté, for a little more trade with Britain would not make it easier for London to swallow a German revolution. Contrary to the long-standing historical view of Chicherin as anti-British, he aggressively supported better Anglo-Soviet relations. "For our general international position," wrote Chicherin, "I consider the development of these relations one of the most important factors."[1]

How quickly circumstances changed. Only six months earlier the NKID had been dealing with Curzon's ultimatum. In November 1923 the forthcoming British elections looked like they might bring a change of government and the departure of Curzon. Even the anti-Bolshevik Gregory seemed to change his tune—well, depending on whose records you believe. In the Foreign Office, he made a record of conversation with Soviet counselor Berzin in which he reported having taken a hard line on the usual complaints about propaganda. All his colleagues approved the position: Curzon was convinced "of the essential unfriendliness of the Soviet Government." Berzin also made a record of the same conversation in which the propaganda issue was indeed discussed. But at the end of the conversation Berzin noted that Gregory was conciliatory: the City had more confidence in the Soviet, and "in his opinion" the British government was moving toward diplomatic recognition, only "in England he says everything goes slowly." There was no hint of any of this in Gregory's record. Senior colleagues might not have approved. Even when British and Soviet officials were talking directly, the right messages did not always or even often get through. Curzon saw the "essential unfriendliness of the Soviet government," while the NKID made better relations with Britain one of its highest priorities.[2]

Gregory remained conciliatory. In another conversation with Berzin in early December, he speculated that there would be changes in the composition of the government even if the Tories won, and that prospects were good for improved relations. Berzin was skeptical, but Gregory replied that he, Berzin, did not attribute enough importance to the role of personality, a hint at the possible departure of Curzon. Rakovskii interpreted Gregory's remarks to indicate that there were two parties in the Foreign Office: one for agreement, the other against. According to one British source, Gregory was worried about keeping his job if there was a change of government, and "dissatisfied" with Curzon's policies, along with others at the Foreign Office.[3] Rakovskii's interpretation could only have been true if Foreign Office officials were saying and writing the contrary of what they actually thought.

On 6 December 1923 the general election took place: the Conservatives lost 86 seats, and Labour and the Liberal Party made big gains. Labour thus formed a minority government in January 1924. Curzon was out and Ramsay McDonald in as prime minister and Secretary of State for Foreign Affairs. The issue of diplomatic recognition was immediately discussed by the new government and granted on 1 February 1924. Plans were made for a conference to settle outstanding issues concerning compensation for nationalized property and debts, among others, which had theretofore hindered an improvement of relations.

The Soviet government was always willing to discuss these issues, but never willing to give ground on recognition of debts and remuneration for nationalized private property without important loans or state-guaranteed trade credits in exchange. The West had tried to recover its debt "by the sword," according to Litvinov: military intervention was provoked mainly by the repudiation of the tsarist debt. Having lost on the battlefield, they are now trying to obtain indemnification through other means. If not for the military intervention, Litvinov observed, "Russia would have been in a better position not only to recognize its debts, but also to pay them." He recalled an exchange with Lloyd George at the end of the Genoa Conference. Lloyd George had observed that it was not very nice (*nekrasivo*) to refuse to repay debts. "We replied," Litvinov noted, "that it was even more unkind to demand repayment of a debt after having broken into our home, smashed all the crockery and furniture and left us as beggars."[4] Western policy remained that the Soviet Union should be made to embrace capitalist "civilization," as a preface to overthrowing the Bolsheviks, or at least to watching them fade away. As naïve as the Bolsheviks sometimes appeared to be with regard to the West, they were no longer coffeehouse socialists. They had been tested in a war against "the Entente" and their White Guard allies, and they had won. They were not going to surrender by diplomacy what they had won in a bloody civil war.

"Like the Goat without Either Wool or Milk"

In the meantime, the "eastern question" was becoming an important priority in Soviet foreign policy. Curzon's ultimatum appears to have lessened Soviet restraint in challenging British eastern interests, which in many instances were precarious. Britain would have had its problems with India, for example, whether the Bolshevik revolution had succeeded or not. The Amritsar massacre was more damaging to the British raj than any Bolshevik propaganda, real or imagined. But further east in the western semi-colony of China, unrest was boiling over. A great national movement was on the march, which made Indian turbulence look like child's play. It was driven by outrage over foreign domination and the misery of rack-rented peasants and workers ruthlessly exploited by foreign bosses in the so-called treaty ports. This movement took on great force after 1919, inspired in part by the Russian Revolution. A small but dynamic communist party began to organize, while the more established Guomintang Party of Chinese leader Sun Yat-sen took the lead in the nationalist movement. Britain had important commercial interests in China which this revolutionary, nationalist, and anti-foreign movement threatened to destroy. So the British tended to see the Bolsheviks behind every Chinese bush even when they were few and far between.

Soviet "eastern policy" of course did not simply mean Comintern activities in Asia. It also meant the strengthening of security on Soviet southern frontiers in the contested borderlands, where British and Russian interests had traditionally clashed. Chicherin was sensitive to Soviet vulnerability in the south and quick to round on his ambassadors if they were insufficiently attentive to Soviet interests there. When Rakovskii suggested that the Soviet Union should avoid irritating the British in Persia, Chicherin retorted that the Soviet Union had to defend its own national interests. Rakovskii wanted to maintain the "clarity" of Soviet revolutionary principles, and Chicherin, Soviet security. Rakovskii thought for example that the Red Army should leave the Persian port city of Enzeli; Chicherin replied that it would stay for the time being.

"It so happens," Chicherin wrote, "that our security and the brotherhood of nations are not compatible." Resting on our principles, "the English" would gain the upper hand in Central Asia. In the East, "the primitive Muslim masses" are easy targets for the British or the emir's agents with pockets full of "English gold," instead of turning to our "comrades." Enzeli, added Chicherin, was a lever to assure Soviet security in the southern Caspian Sea. The security of the fishery and nearby Baku were vital. "Do you prefer the brotherhood of nations," Chicherin asked Rakovskii, "or the protection of our oil resources for . . . industry?" And then Chicherin quoted another Soviet diplomat, Adol'f A. Ioffe, who had written in 1918 that "revolution is revolution, but gasoline is gasoline." We shall stay in Enzeli, added Chicherin, as long as the English have garrisons in southern Persia. We don't need to explain this state of affairs on an absolutely principled basis. "In reality, our whole policy has completely different content and objectives than that of the English. But into this policy of principle cuts a wedge, and a very important wedge, which are the requirements of our security." We have given up the old tsarist concessions in Persia, "but we must not forget the real requirements of our security." In talking "principles," Chicherin did not want to be put into a situation where the Persian government, bought by "English gold," which was always a possibility, sided with the English to force the withdrawal of the "Russian barbarians" from the north, while the English garrisons in the south remained.[5] Basically, Chicherin's foreign policy was based on the protection of Soviet national interests, seeking trade-offs in negotiations with other states, like Britain.

This was not the first dispatch that Chicherin sent to Rakovskii reminding him of the importance of Soviet security around the Caspian Sea. In Afghanistan too, Chicherin feared that British propaganda and "English gold" would convince the Afghan mullahs to side with the British, having lost faith in Soviet policy. If Curzon had complained about the activities of Soviet diplomats in Afghanistan, Chicherin turned the tables on the MacDonald government, objecting to the presence of British troops in Kandahar and Jalalabad. A new government, led by the reforming emir

Amanullah Khan, had been established in 1919. The emir wanted to modernize what *narkom* characterized as a medieval society. The mullahs had been pushed aside, Chicherin observed, but modernization without foreign help was difficult. Afghans, who were accustomed to torture and flogging, did not like being taxed to support the infrastructure of a modern state. For Chicherin, "the ideas of the English-Indian administration are entirely clear: a reversion back to the Middle Ages and to an English protectorate." This was attractive to the Afghan ruling elite as long as "English subsidies" flowed. Amanullah Khan was faced with a dilemma. The British were close by and we are far away, observed Chicherin: we are "like the goat without either wool or milk." Amanullah's policies went against "Anglo-Indian imperialism," but this did not prevent him from outfoxing the English when he was in difficulty and from disarming his most dangerous enemies. His policies were understandable, observed Chicherin, and "we should not take them too tragically." The presence of British garrisons in eastern Afghanistan should be discussed with the MacDonald government.[6] Chicherin kept a sharp eye on Persia and Afghanistan; his prime concern was Soviet security. Revolution is revolution, and security is security, he often repeated to Rakovskii. Revolution was then, security is now.

Khristian Georgievich Rakovskii

Rakovskii played an important role in Soviet relations with Britain and France in the 1920s. Readers should therefore get acquainted with him. He was born in Kotel, in central Bulgaria, in 1873. His parents were wealthy and his father well educated and progressive in his political ideas. Rakovskii's uncle, Georgi Sava Rakovskii, was the "patriarch" of the Bulgarian revolutionary movement in the mid-19th century. As befitted a son of the *grande bourgeoisie*, Rakovskii was multi-lingual and well educated, studying medicine and law in Switzerland and France. Like many of his contemporaries, Rakovskii was more attracted to Marxism than to conventional studies. In Geneva he met many of the leaders of Russian Marxism, P. B. Axelrod, G. V. Plekhanov, V. I. Zasulich, and others. Swept up by the development of Marxist revolutionary ideas, Rakovskii became involved in the socialist student movement, the Second International, and eventually in the revolutionary movements in Russia, Romania, Bulgaria, and even in France. He crisscrossed Europe, making contact with many European socialist leaders. He was a socialist internationalist in the true sense of the word.

When the Bolsheviks seized power in Petrograd in November 1917, Rakovskii offered his services to the new Soviet government. In 1919 Lenin named Rakovskii head of the Ukrainian Soviet government, a post he

Figure 4.1. Khristian G. Rakovskii, Genoa, ca. 1922. AVPRF, f. 779, d. 992, l.f. Arutiunian, A. A., p. 1, konv. 37.

held until 1923. He took Trotskii's side in the emerging leadership struggle against Stalin, and the latter had him removed from his post in the Ukraine and "exiled" to London as Soviet *torgpred*. Ironically, the revolutionary internationalist became one of the main Soviet advocates of a rapprochement with Britain and France. He ran up against the hard realities of dealing with the anti-communist West and thus like Krasin argued for Soviet concessions, which he thought could obtain agreement in Paris or London.

He was not always well perceived by his western interlocutors. Philippe Berthelot, the secretary general of the Quai d'Orsay, found him to be *épouvantable*, frightful, with the face of a "*voyou*," or no-account, and "in effect a bad man."[7] The British ambassador in Paris, Lord Crewe, was less harsh and had correct relations with Rakovskii. "I imagine he is rather like Napoleon III described by the Queen of Holland: '*Tellement rusé qu'il ne faut pas croire le contraire de ce qu'il dit.*'" Crewe thought the embassy staff should treat their Soviet counterparts correctly, for example, inviting them to the annual embassy garden party, "which is attended by most people in Paris who are not actually in the hands of the police."[8] In his dispatches to Moscow, Rakovskii seemed straightforward enough and not at all so cunning that one dare not believe the opposite of what he said. He was sometimes too optimistic about achieving agreement in the West, giving the impression in Moscow that he was naïve. In photographs Rakovskii hardly looks like the "bad man" of Berthelot's description; indeed, he appears rather gentle and bourgeois in a sometimes wrinkled three-piece wool suit, balding and a little overweight in later years. Few of the Bolsheviks were snappy dressers. When the Home Office wanted to ban Soviet diplomats from Britain in 1927, Foreign Secretary Chamberlain sought to make an exception for him.[9]

Rakovskii could switch from the secret language of diplomacy to Bolshevik public polemics as easily as he changed his socks. The juxtaposition between these two forms of discourse is striking. The latter language he used in defense of Trotskii in the conflict against Stalin. Rakovskii was eventually sent into internal exile until he recanted his support of Trotskii, for which the latter forgave him. After all, what choice did he have? He was later given government posts, but in 1937 he was arrested, like so many other Bolsheviks during the purges, and put in the dock in the last of the show trials. It was a mark of the respect he had earned in France that the Quai d'Orsay—Berthelot had died in 1934—thought to intercede on Rakovskii's behalf to save him, though of course any intercession would simply have made matters worse.[10] He was sentenced to 20 years' hard labor, but was shot after the German invasion in 1941 with other Bolsheviks who had until then escaped execution.

Opening Soviet Positions in London, 1924

There were many discussions in the Politburo about the new situation in London and upcoming negotiations there. Chicherin, Litvinov, and Rakovskii all submitted position papers. Somewhat implausibly, Rakovskii was optimistic about the prospects of successful negotiations. He did not ignore the conflicts of interest between Britain and the Soviet Union, but he calculated that the industrial crisis, widespread unemployment, and impoverishment would take the aggressiveness out of "international imperialism" and make it less of a threat. The time was right for a resolution of basic issues and a long period of "peaceful coexistence." Curzon had said that he was glad to be leaving the Foreign Office, so Rakovskii had heard, because recognition of the Soviet Union was unavoidable, and he did not want to be responsible for it. Curzon would not have been pleased by what occurred after his departure, but his discontents were cut short by his death in March 1925.

Rakovskii reckoned on British hostility toward France to enhance the possibilities of an Anglo-Soviet rapprochement. Arthur Ponsonby, the Parliamentary undersecretary of state, told Rakovskii that his greatest concern was France and its aggressive policy in the Ruhr. "We don't care a pin about France," Ponsonby added, which must have been music to Rakovskii's ears and reinforced his view of a common interest in resisting "French imperialism."[11] Even Berzin, still in London, must have thought Rakovskii too optimistic by half, for he reported that MacDonald's foreign policy gave every sign of moving along the same lines as that of his predecessors.[12] This should not have been a surprise to any well-versed Marxist. If you put on the robes of Mammon and wear his crown, you must serve Mammon.

In Moscow Chicherin worried that the British and Anglophile press would use the upcoming negotiations to suggest to the Afghan and other eastern national movements that the Soviet Union would sell them out to obtain an agreement with Britain. Such a risk, he warned, "is very perilous for our world policy." We must keep this danger to the fore and fight against it.[13]

Litvinov's most important policy statement came in late February, barely a month after Lenin's death, in response to Stalin's call for an "immediate discussion of the basic problems of our foreign policy." The *gensek* was already preoccupied with foreign policy issues. Trotskii was isolated by the troika of Stalin, Zinoviev, and Kamenev and quickly losing ground. According to Litvinov, British recognition, and that of other European countries, notably Italy, Sweden, and Norway, changed everything and marked the beginning of "a new period in our diplomatic activities." Until now, we have sought diplomatic recognition and "legalization" of the Soviet government. But recognition, Litvinov wrote, is just a means to other objectives.

"I leave aside our long-term and final goals, the attainment of which is closely dependent on the further development of the revolutionary communist movement in the West." Having got that sticky issue out of the way in a single sentence, Litvinov then turned to "the near-term tasks arising from the interests of the security and defense of the Soviet republics." He noted the security danger in the Caucasus but quickly moved on, perhaps because of Chicherin's preoccupation with it, to the security threat from the Baltic area, which in the event of war with the West could become a *place d'armes* for an attack on Petrograd and even on Moscow. "Our diplomacy cannot lose sight of this danger for a single minute, and we must with our entire energy attempt to neutralize the consequences of the movement to the east of our Baltic frontiers."

Turning to Western Europe, Litvinov thought France the most natural Soviet ally because it would not fear the strengthening of Soviet power. On the contrary, France would support the reinforcement of the Soviet Union if it saw Moscow as a potential ally. This was in fact the view of Herriot and Painlevé. Unfortunately, the present circumstances did not favor an agreement with Paris except on crushing terms and with little economic advantage, so Litvinov argued for a focus on London. If achieved, then Moscow might obtain better French terms. Britain could offer greater economic assistance, and Soviet security in the Caucasus and Baltic might also be improved through negotiations. It would be "very difficult" to reconcile Soviet "eastern policy" with a British rapprochement, but Litvinov did not see overwhelming obstacles in the way of an accommodation. We ought not to let England approach our borders anywhere, but "at the same time we ought not to organize propaganda against it for the sake of propaganda there where such propaganda cannot be useful either in itself, or for the eastern peoples. There is not a small area of international interests where we can be useful to England, not disturbing its interests and not sacrificing our principles."[14]

Chicherin must have been irked by Litvinov's report because of Stalin's "special" reference to it during a meeting of the Politburo. After all, Chicherin was commissar and Litvinov deputy commissar, but it was Litvinov's ideas getting Stalin's attention. In reading Chicherin's rejoinder, one has the impression that he and his deputy were not all that far apart. Both were irritated with Rakovskii, but for different reasons. Litvinov thought Rakovskii suffered from "excessive optimism" and that he was too willing to concede debt to London, thus ignoring NKID instructions.[15] Chicherin thought Rakovskii made too much of Franco-German hostility. The main quarrel was between France and Britain. He did not like talk of siding with one coalition against another. Litvinov did not propose such a strategy, but Chicherin thought there were better chances of agreement with France than his zamnarkom allowed. Litvinov was not opposed to a French rapprochement, but he thought it might be easier to achieve by concentrating first on London. In fact, both Litvinov and Chicherin were highly suspicious of the western powers, including the United States, but both were wrong to think that any agreement was possible in either London or Paris. And Chicherin made too much of Anglo-French differences, he himself rightly noting that the fall of the franc would lead to a French withdrawal from the Ruhr, thus removing a serious point of contention between Paris and London.[16] If Chicherin had thought about his earlier ideas, he would have remembered that in the last analysis France and Britain would always stand together against the Soviet Union. But he appears to have wanted to twit his deputy and therefore saw differences where only nuances existed. Here was a case of Litvinov saying one thing and Chicherin the other. In any case, they *both* agreed that whatever happened, good relations with Berlin had to be maintained. "Everything else," as Litvinov noted in his report, "is music of the future."

"Hedged in by Reservations"

There were many obstacles in the way of an Anglo-Soviet agreement. The London and Moscow newspapers did not hide their mutual animosity. Rakovskii acknowledged that "the question of propaganda" rankled, which was perhaps understating the case. Zinoviev, who was not known for his discretion, was a favorite subject for quotation in the British press. Some of his less flattering comments were directed at MacDonald, who "crawled on all fours before the British bourgeoisie," and whom the Soviet government supported like "a rope supports a hanged man." If Zinoviev frequently slipped his moorings, so did the British press, with "violent abuse" against Moscow. The Tories were keen advocates of the "Red Peril," or "the Bolsh Bogey," according to the iconic British political cartoonist David Low. In one of his 1923 cartoons, "the Bolsh Bogey," a rickety scarecrow, was laid to rest in a shallow grave before Churchill, among others, and "the Tory press," all crying crocodile tears. Even Lloyd George is among the mourners. "Do not weep friends," said Low, "we can always dig him up again."[17] Low was righter than he knew and did not have to wait long for the resurrection, in fact barely a year. Even the Foreign Office thought matters were getting out of hand and signaled "privately" to the press to calm its rhetoric.[18] Such entreaties were vain.

Litvinov complained that the London embassy was not doing enough to counterbalance adverse public opinion and was being too cautious in maintaining contact with Labour Party leaders. Berzin replied that he kept "very close ties with all the leaders of the trade union movement, the Labour Party and even the Communist Party," even inviting members of the Communist leadership to his flat.[19] Well, perhaps that was going too far, but you could not blame Berzin; it was all uphill work in London.

Foreign Office officials like those in the State Department and Quai d'Orsay were antagonistic to the Soviet government. The Reds would always try to chisel: their "policy . . . is directed towards making other countries fight one another rather than fighting them."[20] This view of the USSR persisted until 1941. Of course, a cynic might see pot calling kettle black, for such policy could easily be attributed to the British themselves. Occasionally, a Foreign Office clerk noticed that the British government was not always on "good ground" when it came to accusing Moscow, "unless like Lockit you can fall on Rakovskii's neck and cry 'Brother Peachum we were both in the wrong.'"[21]

This was only banter between government clerks. Higher up there were no doubters. "The Russians are by nature discursive, disputatious & unbusinesslike," noted the assistant undersecretary Sir Victor Wellesley. "They are past masters in the art of obscuring main issues to suit their own ends."[22] A Northern Department clerk observed that

Figure 4.2. David Low cartoon, LSE6965, "The Bolsh Bogey," _The Star_, 28 June 1923. British Cartoon Archive (Templeton Library, University of Kent, Canterbury, England).

> Soviet leaders—both Jews & Russians—seldom react in the same way as leaders of Western peoples. . . . Differences arise primarily from a complete abnormality which is common to all Russians and nearly all Slavs. In so far as the abnormality is specifically Bolshevik it lies more in the inherited instinctive disposition of the Jew that "every man's hand is against him," than in the Russian disposition of hatred of the oppressed for the oppressor. . . . It is, generally speaking among the Jews that the extremists are found, whereas the evolutionaries [sic] are more often Russians.

The author of these lines, Mr. Maxse, could not tell the difference between a Jew and a gentile, but few cared. MacDonald, the Labour prime minister, summed up the general feeling: "I am not satisfied that Soviet government is playing straight."[23] Even for the leader of the Labour Party, "playing straight" meant accepting capitalism or at least paying the tsar's debts. Hypocrisy is

**Figure 4.3. Ramsay MacDonald, ca. 1924.
Granger Collection, NY.**

always blind: the former Allies did not want to pay *their* debts to the United States. It was the Bolshevik denunciation of capitalism that rankled.

The Foreign Office was not unaware of the objectives of Soviet foreign policy. Occasionally a clerk left some common sense in the files. William Strang, then a junior official in the Northern Department and a future permanent undersecretary, recorded that the Soviet government had often observed that it would be "impossible to decide what is propaganda and what is legitimate protection of interests until our relations in the East are defined."[24] Although Soviet messages rarely penetrated through Foreign Office biases, Strang got this one right.

An accommodation with Britain was Chicherin's first priority, though the NKID would not push for a general agreement if the British government did not want it. Chicherin talked to the British chargé d'affaires in Moscow, R. M. Hodgson, who also correctly conveyed the Soviet message to London. But this was going too fast for the minority Labour government. Prior to becoming prime minister, MacDonald had expressed interest in an informal general understanding, but not "a sealed and signed agreement," and Chicherin had got that message. "From the first moment I advanced the idea [of a "general political agreement with England"], but MacDonald until now has rejected it."[25]

Henry N. Brailsford, editor of the weekly *New Leader*, sometimes talked to Rakovskii about Labour politics. The Labour Party, according to Brailsford, was not united: "There was little disposition to fight hard. The attacks of the bourgeois press had made a deep impression on the weaker members of the Labour Party. . . . The result was that all the determination of the I.L.P. [International Labour Party] was required in order to stimulate the Party to a resolute defence of Russia." And MacDonald was a ditherer: "The spirit of contradiction is the main feature" of the prime minister's mind. "I should not be surprised if he will be against something one day," Brailsford told Rakovskii, "and on another, say that he is against what he said the day before."[26] Chicherin had his own opinion, which was a little more charitable: MacDonald was caught between two conflicting motivations: on the one hand, "he wants to please higher ups," that is, the British elite; on the other, he could not afford to ignore his voters and the trade unions.[27] MacDonald's situation was thus much like Herriot's, which made him look indecisive when he was in fact maneuvering from a position of weakness.

Anglo-Soviet negotiations were not easy and dragged out through the spring and well into summer. Similar to previous negotiations in the West, the big issues were debts, credits, and "propaganda." The latter question was never really discussed. As at Genoa, negotiations focused on the perennial dispute over debts and credits. In fact, Gregory drew a link from Genoa and The Hague to the London negotiations: the Foreign Office still sought an agreement on "pre-war debts and property."[28] The Soviet side was only willing to discuss debts in conjunction with commercial credits or a government loan; the British were interested in debts settlement without the loan, although in August at the last minute the Labour government agreed to the principle of a loan.

In Washington the State Department kept an eye cocked on the negotiations. Secretary of State Hughes was unimpressed with the change in British policy and recognition of the Soviet government. He signaled to U.S. diplomatic posts that there would be no change in American policy as a result of British recognition.[29] The U.S. ambassador in London, and Hughes' eventual successor, Frank B. Kellogg, kept in touch with the Foreign Office. If Gregory was reasonably optimistic when he talked to Rakovskii in December 1923, he took a different line with the American embassy. "Gregory . . . told me confidentially last night that the Foreign Office considers the demands of the Soviet delegation impossible of acceptance and indicated that unless their attitude changes no favorable result could come from the conference."

According to British "public opinion," Soviet demands were "quite unacceptable." Suppose, said Kellogg, "Smith borrows £100. Smith defaults. He subsequently offers to repay Jones if the latter will reduce the amount owed, cancel the interest due and lend him a further sum out of which to repay the reduced debt." This was a disingenuous representation of the Soviet position, but you could not tell that to Kellogg or the State Department. In fact, Kellogg reported that no London bank "will consider a loan to the Soviets upon any security so far offered."[30]

Even when an Anglo-Soviet agreement in principle on debt repayment and a guaranteed loan was concluded at the last minute, on 8 August, Kellogg remained skeptical. The agreements were "so hedged in by reservations and are conditional upon performance by the Soviet Government which may, or may not, amount to anything." Kellogg added that "if performance does eventuate, it is in part a recognition by Communist Russia of the capitalistic business system of civilized nations which may encourage the more conservative elements in Russia and gradually bring that country to a point where normal relations can be resumed."[31]

Take your capitalist porridge with a splintery wooden spoon, and like it, remained the position in Washington and London, Labour government or not. As Hughes put it, "the United States is not a harsh creditor, but indulgence and proper arrangements are one thing and repudiation another."[32] Perhaps Hughes meant to remove the splinters from the ladle, though this is doubtful, but Moscow would still have to swallow the sour capitalist soup.

The "Zinoviev Letter"

Irony often characterized western-Soviet relations during the inter-war years, and Anglo-Soviet negotiations in 1924 were no exception. Both the Soviet and minority Labour governments seemed ready to come to terms, at least up to a point. Ponsonby, the Parliamentary undersecretary, was more committed to an agreement than MacDonald, who quickly absorbed the Foreign Office culture of hostility and suspicion toward Moscow if indeed he did not already possess it when he became prime minister. Not that the Soviet side was less suspicious. Rakovskii accused the City of "requir[ing] . . . that we should renounce our existence as a socialist state."[33] This assertion was quite true not only of the City but of financial institutions and governments in France and the United States. However, Ponsonby and trade unionists within the Labour Party were determined to get an agreement in spite of MacDonald's reticence and to "reverse" Tory government policy.[34] Even on the tough issue of "propaganda," there were grounds for agreement. The Soviet government was willing to discuss this thorny issue, and the India and Home offices wanted a new understanding with Moscow. But MacDonald opposed discussions at the London conference "because the Soviet Government would at once say (as they have said before) that it is impossible to decide what is propaganda and what is legitimate protection of interests until our relations in the East are defined." Chicherin's message had thus gotten through.

But then what about the Comintern? "The crux of the whole matter," MacDonald commented, "is the relations between the Soviet Government & the Third International. That must be settled but this is most inopportune moment for raising it. If we did we should be rebuffed."[35]

Hence, there was no serious discussion of "eastern questions" or the Comintern, and the more limited Anglo-Soviet accord on debts and credit was an orphan, and a lonely one at that. It had to be ratified in the House of Commons, where the Labour minority government needed the support of the Liberals, who opposed a loan to Moscow. On 8 October 1924 the Labour government fell on another minor issue, the case of one John Ross Campbell, a well-known Scottish communist, who published incendiary articles encouraging British soldiers and sailors to join the revolutionary socialist movement. He was arrested and charged under a law of 1797, then released after it was observed that Campbell was saying nothing new. Labour MPs

Figure 4.4.   David Low cartoon, LSE7168, "The Shadow Show," *The Star*, 2 October 1924. British Cartoon Archive.

had said or written much the same thing in the past. It was all rather embarrassing, and the Tories, already worked up to a fever pitch, had a field day. Like hounds after the fox, they smelled blood, but so could cartoonist David Low who poured ridicule on the Die-Hards. In early October Low published a cartoon showing the large shadow of a scarecrow against a wall, labeled "communist influence scare." It was projected by a spotlight, the "stunt machine," in front of which the "Tory press" dangled a small stick figure named Campbell.[36] The Tories were only just getting started, and Low also. In the flurry of Tory anti-communist gesticulations, the Anglo-Soviet treaty fell by the wayside and was not debated in the House of Commons. Elections were called for 29 October.

Even before the fall of the Labour government, there was considerable pessimism in Moscow about the prospects of ratification. "At the present time we cannot yet count on solid, long-term agreements with the bourgeois West," observed Litvinov. "Our policy must still be built upon a system of respites, that is, temporary agreements." Rejection of the Anglo-Soviet treaty in Parliament would nevertheless be a serious setback, and so "we have to do everything that depends on us to prevent failure." Litvinov was vague about concrete measures. He noted that there had been articles in the Soviet press against the treaty, and these should be explained in London, inter alia, as a reaction to a hostile campaign in the British press.[37] It was not helpful, he noted later, that the Soviet press was shouting from the rooftops that the Soviet government had "won a great victory" and that MacDonald had "capitulated." This was only grist for the opposition mills in London. Litvinov also reiterated that there could be no deal on debts without the loan guaranteed by the British government. As the election approached, Litvinov got carried away in instructions to Rakovskii: "It is necessary to exaggerate somewhat in the given circumstances the conditions which will be created by a Conservative victory. You should focus on the inevitability of serious complications, wars in Europe and Asia and so on. We need to help the Labour Party frighten voters with prospects of war."[38] These ideas were scarcely among Litvinov's best, though he was not wrong about the dim prospects for Anglo-Soviet relations if the Tories won the elections.

The election campaign was hot with Tory anti-communist rhetoric, a smoke and light show often ridiculed by cartoonist Low. In one such cartoon published in mid-October, entitled "Much Ado about Next to Nothing," readers can find the familiar themes of the post-1945 period: "Mothers! Communism will tear your little ones from your sides," "Communism will burn your home . . . will abolish the marriage tie . . . baths, umbrellas, motor cars, sausage rolls." In another cartoon, featuring the "Die-Hard" Churchill, he leads a motley squad of clown-like soldiers under the

Figure 4.5.   David Low cartoon, LSE7178, "Much Ado about Next to Nothing," *The Star*, 14 October 1924. British Cartoon Archive.

Figure 4.6.   David Low cartoon, LSE7170, "The Recruiting Parade," *The Star*, 7 October 1924. British Cartoon Archive.

banner of a two-headed donkey called "Anti-Sosh." "The recruiting parade," concluded Low, was directed at gullible Liberals.[39]

The campaign heat was so intense that Ponsonby asked Rakovskii if the Moscow press could call off its attacks on the Labour government, upon which the Tories were merrily feeding.

Soviet "public opinion and government circles," replied Rakovskii, had reason to believe that MacDonald was playing a "duplicitous" role toward Moscow.

Ponsonby rejoined that since the fate of the Anglo-Soviet treaty was in play, it might be "expedient" for the Soviet press to direct its fire against the Tories and Liberals. Rakovskii endorsed this idea.

He advised Moscow that he was being careful not to get involved in the election campaign, *but* was forwarding "the necessary materials and arguments to Labour speakers" through the intermediary of W. P. Coates' "Hands off Russia" lobby group. This meant of course that Rakovskii *was* getting involved covertly in the campaign. There was a chance, he thought, that the Labour government might survive the elections with a slightly increased number of seats.[40] This was Rakovskii's appraisal on 17 October, 12 days before the election, and 7 days before the ground went out from underneath the feet of the Labour government.

What happened? On 2 October the SIS station in Riga forwarded to London the English text of an apparent letter, dated 15 September, from Comintern boss Zinoviev to the British Communist Party. The alleged directive, signed among others by Zinoviev, urged the British Communist Party to rally support for the Anglo-Soviet draft treaty as a prelude to eventual revolutionary activities and infiltration of British armed forces. SIS sent a copy of the "letter" to the Foreign Office, the War Office, and elsewhere on 9 October, the day after the defeat of the government in the House of Commons. "The authenticity of the document," SIS reported, "is undoubted."[41]

"Undoubted" was a familiar SIS line, often open to doubt. Readers will remember that the Foreign Office had a difficult time making out real from forged Soviet "propaganda." And of course this particular letter was not the first to come into SIS hands. A Zinoviev letter arrived at the Foreign Office in August 1923, only a few months after the Curzon ultimatum, addressed to the German communist Heinrich Brandler. This letter had a Berlin origin, prompting Strang, a Northern Department clerk, to minute that "these Berlin documents do not . . . usually inspire confidence."[42] Considering the copious forgeries of the Orlov factory, it was the least Strang could have said. Nothing came of that particular "letter," or of others that followed, due to Foreign Office skepticism, and so readers might well ask why the "Zinoviev letter" of October 1924 would have been treated any differently than previous such productions?

Initially it wasn't. Strang again opened the discussion on the new document: "Anglo-Soviet relations are unfortunately an issue in domestic politics in this country and this fact on occasions—of which the present is one—renders it difficult for the department to advise." So the election campaign, already under way and hot with Tory anti-communist gases, constrained Foreign Office options. Basically there were two, according to Strang: publication or "representations to Moscow." He did not think publication would "do any harm."

"We are assured," he added, "that the letter is of undoubted authenticity."

Gregory was skeptical: "I very much doubt the wisdom of publication. The authenticity of the document would at once be denied." He of course had experience in such matters. In Curzon's day, Foreign Office protests to Moscow had flopped because the evidence on which they were based was bogus, as the NKID had joyfully pointed out. But the old saw, "once bitten, twice shy," did not work in this case.

The permanent undersecretary, Sir Eyre Crowe, intervened: "We have now heard definitely (on absolutely reliable authority) that the Russian letter was received and discussed at a recent meeting of the Central Committee of the Communist Party of Great Britain." As it turned out, this information was incorrect.[43]

Crowe was for immediate action. "It is quite true—and we have always felt—that we get nothing out of the Soviet government, by any remonstrances, simply because these quite shameless liars merely deny everything, however clearly established."

MacDonald remained cautious. "We must be sure that the document is authentic." If it were authentic, he would approve a public protest to Moscow, but it had, as he stressed, to carry "conviction & guilt."

"If not," he added, "it will do harm."[44] The prime minister was more guarded than Crowe, but surprisingly the Foreign Office sought no further evidence of the authenticity of the "Zinoviev letter" in response to MacDonald's cautionary minute.[45] Crowe rushed to judgment with his boss out of the office campaigning for reelection. Why was the document so uncritically treated by the Foreign Office in comparison with previously intercepted Comintern "correspondence"? Perhaps the crucial point of difference was that an election was under way.

A protest letter was drafted and hurried to completion. MacDonald, in the country campaigning, did not approve the final version. Crowe took the responsibility upon himself, to the prime minister's subsequent exasperation.

Figure 4.7. David Low cartoon, LSE7180, "Behind the Smokescreen," *The Star*, 25 October 1924. British Cartoon Archive.

The permanent undersecretary protested his honest intentions, later accepted by MacDonald, but questions remained.

During the afternoon of Friday, 24 October, Gregory, as directed by Crowe, signed and sent the protest to Rakovskii, though not without trying to dissuade the permanent undersecretary from doing so.[46] The following day the story broke in the London papers, the Conservative *Daily Mail* in the van. Cartoonist Low ridiculed the "Tory anti-Bolsh" campaign as a dense cloud of smoke concealing more important issues.[47] He was certainly correct, but a storm had nonetheless been unleashed. And what splendid timing, it was four days before the election.

Rakovskii tried to forestall the worst, quickly writing to the Foreign Office and meeting with journalists to say "the letter" was a forgery, even before he received confirmation from the NKID. The "situation was extremely urgent and I had to act with great speed," explained Rakovskii: there was even a reporter waiting for me when I returned to my flat at the end of the day. The enemy can strike quickly and had pulled off a great stroke against us. Because of "raging political passions," Zinoviev's "letter" had gone off "like a bomb." All the press is talking about it. Many papers are asking why I have not been expelled from the country through the nearest port. Rakovskii could only guess about the origins of the forgery and on the role of MacDonald and

Gregory in publicizing it. "We have done everything to go on the offensive and discredit our enemies," reported Rakovskii, but with the elections only days away, it is difficult to say whether we can influence public opinion.[48]

In Moscow that same day, 25 October, Chicherin informed the Politburo of what had happened. He was not sure what to make of the news. "Strange," he wrote to the Politburo, "that MacDonald would strike at his own party by underlining the role of the Comintern and in general Moscow in domestic British affairs. Perhaps it is a sharp turn to the right by the leadership clique, frightened by the unexpected growth of intensified class sentiments. We will have to wait for an explanation from Rakovskii." The British note is serious business, Chicherin warned, and we will have to treat it carefully.[49]

Events unfolded rapidly, like bolts of lightning, Rakovskii must have thought, as he cabled for instructions. Chicherin speculated that the press campaign was intended not only to defeat the Labour Party, but to stop French diplomatic recognition of the Soviet Union which was then imminent. Gregory, Chicherin added, had signed the note in order to rehabilitate himself with the Tories.[50] This was just guessing, and wrongly, since Gregory had discouraged publication. At the same time, Chicherin sent a line to Zinoviev asking for a denial. "All England," he wrote sarcastically, "is waiting for telegrams from you regarding the latest incident."[51] On the following day, Litvinov wrote the denial, cabling Rakovskii to confirm that "the letter" was indeed a forgery and to provide him with a text to send to the Foreign Office asking for independent, third-party arbitration.[52]

Upon receipt of Litvinov's cable, Rakovskii did as instructed, handing his note to Gregory, who returned it to him on the pretext that it cast doubt on Foreign Office integrity. Rakovskii denied throwing any stones, though he was, and returned the note once again to Gregory. "We obviously cannot go on with this game of bandying about the Soviet note," Gregory then minuted, and he suggested that it be "destroyed."[53] Rakovskii also thought that the "game of bandying" could not go on, but in the end Gregory gave up first. The Soviet note was not destroyed and can still be found in the files at the National Archives in Kew.

The British embassy in Moscow reported that the Foreign Office letter to Rakovskii had set off a "bombshell . . . followed by feverish activity in high Soviet circles." Litvinov distributed his written reply to the press in Moscow even before it reached London. "There is an uncertain tone in attacks on authenticity of letter," the British counselor in Moscow William Peters advised, "possibly due to knowledge that it is impossible in view of published views of leading figures in Communist International to assert that no such letter could have been dispatched. At best, this particular one may not have been sent."[54] "The letter" was beside the point, one influential British journalist told Rakovskii. Bogus or not, it was the activities of the Comintern which rankled and had to stop if Moscow wanted good relations with Britain.[55]

The German ambassador made similar comments to Chicherin, knowing that Berlin had protested, inter alia, against an earlier Zinoviev letter addressed to the German Communist Party, which was published in *Pravda* in late April 1924. In Paris Herriot was also skeptical. Almost everyone, Rakovskii would say of the French, wanted to talk about "the so-called Zinoviev letter."[56] It was a serious blow to Soviet hopes for better relations with the West.

In London, Rakovskii had no chance to turn around British public opinion, though he tried. Even the British Communist Party got into the act denying that it had ever received Zinoviev's letter and challenging the Foreign Office to hand over a photographic copy of it. To no avail, Mac-Donald ordered that to "these gentlemen" no response should be made. Red Scare, the wicked genie whose twin was Revolution, was out of the lamp again. "These last four nights," Rakovskii wrote to Litvinov, "I've had hardly any sleep." He saw Gregory, who seemed rather bewildered by the sudden crisis, implying that he was pushed aside in the affair and that he was obliged to answer to higher authority, meaning Crowe. "I am tired of my job," he told Rakovskii. "I'd like to take off somewhere in America." The last four months of work to get a treaty had been "for nothing."[57] These were remarkably candid comments, though Gregory left no record of them in the Foreign Office files. It was not the first time that Gregory said one thing to his Soviet interlocutors and quite another to his Foreign Office colleagues. The Tories won a big majority of seats in the elections, and the Labour government resigned. Labour's electoral defeat did not however put an end to interrogations about the "Zinoviev letter."

Who Did It?

According to the French ambassador in London, Auguste de Beaupoil de Saint-Aulaire, a Foreign Office "agent" in Riga had copied the "letter" and sent it to London. "Because of an indiscretion, a member of the Conservative Party was made privy to it; this is why the *Daily Mail* was able to circulate copies to the offices of the main newspapers in London." We now know of course that someone with Tory loyalties did obtain the "letter" from SIS or another government source, and did send it to the *Daily Mail* with the obvious intention of gaining electoral advantage. Not even the Foreign Office knew until 27 October that the "letter" had come from Riga. Saint-Aulaire's information was thus very current and very confidential.[58]

British intelligence services decrypted Saint-Aulaire's cable, though it was no fortuitous bit of windfall over which they stumbled.[59] The so-called

Government Code and Cypher School developed the most extraordinary talent of breaking diplomatic codes, which allowed it to read secret telegrams between, among other places, Washington, Paris, Rome, and Moscow and their embassies in London. The "school," a cover name to hide its code-breaking activities, was established at the end of 1918, at which time it already claimed to have solved fifty-two diplomatic codes.[60] The Foreign Office thereby obtained a great advantage in dealing with other states, reading their secret communications. It was like being able to read the other fellow's mind; friend or foe made no difference to British code breakers.

It is not surprising therefore that other diplomatic cables about the "Zinoviev letter" were also decrypted. One from the Italian embassy in London reported that Parliamentary Undersecretary Ponsonby believed "the letter" might well turn out to be a forgery.[61] Another from the Turkish ambassador confirmed and amplified what Saint-Aulaire had reported to Paris.

> It is now understood, in the matter of Zinoviev's letter, that the officials of the Foreign Office, who are Conservatives, secretly gave a copy of the letter to the "Daily Mail" and fearing that the "Daily Mail" would publish it, had it published by the Foreign Office without the consent of the Prime Minister, and that, although the draft of the note, sent by the Foreign Office to the Russian Delegation and given to the Press, had been seen by the PM the latter had not given orders for its dispatch, while it was signed by the head of a Foreign Office section, a "*fait accompli*" being thus created.
>
> The PM, covertly, and the Colonial Secretary, openly, blamed the FO officials and state that they are not yet satisfied as to the genuineness of the letter.[62]

Who were the sources of these diplomatic leaks, based on so much accurate information? Saint-Aulaire did not name his source, saying only, "according to my information." Rumors began to be reported in the press as early as 27 October that the Conservative Party had obtained the letter before it was released to the press by the Foreign Office. But Saint-Aulaire's information did not come from the press; the detail about the Riga origins of the letter was secret and could only have come from the Foreign Office or SIS. The ambassador had regular contacts with Foreign Office officials, notably Gregory, Tyrrell, and Crowe. Did he obtain his information from one of them? If so, Gregory seems the most likely possibility as head of the Northern Department. Tyrrell was out of London, and Saint-Aulaire got on badly with Crowe. If it was Gregory, he did not inform MacDonald of the "indiscretion" for the prime minister was apparently still in the dark.

Where did the Turkish ambassador obtain his information? He did not say, but could it have come from the same Foreign Office source as Saint-Aulaire?

Perhaps not directly. Zekiai was known to be favorably disposed to the USSR and, having only recently been appointed to London, wanted to get in touch with the well-informed Rakovskii. The latter could have supplied the information which the ambassador sent home.[63]

Other questions arise. The decrypted cables were sent to the Foreign Office and to Scotland Yard. Why was there no immediate investigation into the sources of the leaks? Would SIS have launched an investigation of itself or its friends elsewhere in the government? Readers might reasonably doubt it. What can be said is that many people had definite information about the Tory leak to the press prior to the election on 29 October, except, it seems, the prime minister, who could rely only on rumors and late-breaking press reports. During a 1928 inquiry, MacDonald said that "we knew *afterwards* [emphasis added] that the headquarters of the Conservative Association had the Zinovieff [sic] letter for days before it was published and presumably the *Daily Mail* had it for weeks before it was published."[64] It was very likely the other way around.

What is more, SIS was reading not only French, Italian, and Turkish cables, but also Soviet telegrams to and from Moscow. In these decrypted messages are a number of references to the Zinoviev "forgery." The main themes of the Soviet correspondence are that the "Zinoviev letter" was bogus and that the NKID was uncertain about how to counter the setback to its diplomacy. According to Litvinov, MacDonald was "the victim of intrigues on the part of his own officials." Anglo-Soviet relations had been damaged, wrote Rakovskii, by "outside, ill-disposed, obscure individuals or organizations pursuing their own mercenary political ends."[65] But who knew for certain?

There were so many unanswered questions. This is why MacDonald asked Rakovskii to come to see him on 2 November, two days before he resigned as prime minister. Rakovskii took Berzin with him, and the latter made a long record of the conversation which went on for nearly two hours. The prime minister wanted to know about the origins of the "letter" and why he should think it a forgery. Rakovskii drew attention to obvious tip-offs in the text of the letter itself and to various forgeries of the past, but could not persuade MacDonald to disregard the view of his officials. He and Berzin nevertheless gained the impression that MacDonald believed the "letter" to be a forgery. The prime minister said that he did not know how the *Daily Mail* had obtained it—perhaps he did not want to say—but he rejected Rakovskii's suggestion that Foreign Office officials, Tories "almost without exception," had floated the document. MacDonald opined that the letter was "fabricated" to scuttle the draft treaty rather than to influence the election, because SIS had obtained it before the dissolution of the House of Commons. Rumors of its existence, he said, began to circulate in London as early as 6 October.

Rakovskii also reported rumors originating in Quai d'Orsay circles that "the document" had Polish origins. It's a guess, he noted, but worth investigating. According to Berzin, MacDonald, who gave the impression of being ill or at least completely exhausted, vented his spleen about the dirty Tory election campaign. "He was so naïve," wrote Berzin, "that he absolutely did not fore-see the possibility of such [electoral] techniques."[66] Closer to home, Stalin would soon teach Berzin and other comrades a thing or two about "naïveté."

After the resignation of the Labour government on 4 November, Ra-kovskii had a long conversation with former Labour Secretary of State for Air, Christopher Birdwood Lord Thomson, who was far more forthcoming than the prime minister had been a week earlier. MacDonald had "obvi-ously" lost control of his ministry, according to Thomson, and for this reason even the Labour Party had to cover up the affair "in order to save MacDonald" and avoid exposing his "two-faced and stupid policy." A simple minister could be sacrificed, Thomson explained, but not a prime minister. That put Labour in a bind. Thomson was well informed about how the let-ter to Rakovskii had been drafted, but he thought Gregory and not Crowe was the main guilty party in the Foreign Office. The Parliamentary under-secretary Ponsonby knew nothing, according to Thomson, even though he was in London during the week before the crisis broke. Apparently some "sleuth" in Moscow (*syshchik*), some agent, had obtained the letter. When the Cabinet demanded to know the agent's identity, the Foreign Office, meaning Crowe, refused to divulge it "on the pretext that if the Bolsheviks discovered it, they would kill him." Whether he was killed or not, Thom-son continued, was of "little interest, but we need to know who composed this document." The former cabinet minister related all this information to the Soviet *polpred* as if it were dinner table conversation that would go no further, and certainly not to Moscow. Thomson went on to say that he did not think British intelligence was involved, "though to which agency the putative sleuth belongs remained unclear." Hence a member of the Labour cabinet purported not to know about SIS involvement in the acquisition of "the letter." Rakovskii wrote that

> personally he [Thomson] assumes [*schitaet*] that the letter fell into the hands of the press through Admiral Hall. This is a well-known Conservative boss, former head of counter-intelligence during the war, who maintained ties with military and naval ministries; since a copy of this letter was circulated by the FO to these establishments, probably through these channels it fell into his hands.

Rakovskii was describing Admiral Sir William Reginald "Blinker" Hall, former director of naval intelligence and Tory MP defeated in 1923, who regained a seat in Parliament on 29 October. "In all probability," Rakovskii continued, "the forgery was done here in London."[67] Who can say even now if this was true or not? Obviously Lord Thomson had some details wrong, but if he was right about the source of the leak to the press, who then passed "the letter" to Hall?[68]

Rakovskii was well informed about the process by which the Foreign Office prepared its reply to the Soviet government. From pressman Brailsford, Rakovskii learned, for example, that Gregory had opposed the publication of "the letter" and the Foreign Office note to Moscow and had spoken by telephone to Crowe about it and been overruled. MacDonald had been available all day that Friday, 24 October, at a hotel in Wales and could easily have been contacted for his approval of Crowe's proposed actions. Rakovskii was dumbfounded that the prime minister had been left uninformed when he could so easily have been contacted by telephone. And on and on, he went about the implausible tale of the prime minister's exclusion from the decision taken by Crowe to publish the Foreign Office note to Moscow to which MacDonald had not given his final approval. Rakovskii still cast doubt on Gregory as the chief culprit, but on that point he appears to have been mistaken.[69]

With all the information that Rakovskii was able to send to Moscow, the NKID and the Politburo knew almost as much as the Foreign Office about the Zinoviev scandal. There was one question about which Moscow was still in the dark, and that was who had written "the letter" and put it into circulation. Rakovskii's well-informed contacts in London could only guess, for SIS apparently was not talking about it. So Moscow speculated. Two of the potential culprits were adventurers and confidence men, Ignatius Timothy Trebitsch Lincoln and Aleksandr Feofilovich Gumanskii. Trebitsch Lincoln was a completely implausible, rocambolesque character who was briefly a British MP, had ties to German fascists, and ended up a Buddhist abbot in Shanghai who stripped his initiates of their possessions and bedded his nuns. More importantly, he worked for German and Japanese intelligence. Gumanskii was a more conventional adventurer, a White Guard émigré with ties to British intelligence and the document counterfeiter Orlov in Berlin. Chicherin was uncertain who the perpetrator was. He still thought Gregory might be implicated, but he also identified Trebitsch Lincoln and "Berlin," meaning the Orlov factory, as possible leads to follow up.[70] These were indeed the "ill-disposed, obscure individuals" to whom Rakovskii referred in his telegrams to Moscow.

The new Conservative government undertook an inquiry after the elections, but the Tories were investigating themselves. Ironically, the Labour and Conservative parties appear to have been complicit in the cover-up since each had something to hide. As Thomson said to Rakovskii, Mac-Donald had to be protected while Tories worried that their electoral victory would be tainted by proofs that the Zinoviev letter was a forgery. SIS insisted that the "letter" was genuine—of course it had to, for its reputation was at stake—and the Foreign Office held to this line through thick and thin long afterward. "We cannot not believe in our Foreign Office," one journalist told Rakovskii. "We have the best detectives in the world."[71] Why the Foreign Office held to its line, knowing full well the unreliability of previous SIS sources and of the evidence to hand can only be a matter for speculation.

MacDonald left a persuasive explanation of Crowe's actions in his diaries:

He [Crowe] was apparently hot. He had no intention of being disloyal, indeed quite the opposite, but his own mind destroyed his discretion and blinded him to the obvious care he should have exercised. I favoured publication; he decided that I meant at once and before Rakovsky replied. I asked for care in establishing authenticity; he was satisfied and that was enough.[72]

Did Crowe commit the "indiscretion," as Saint-Aulaire put it, or was he merely complicit, knowing the leaker's identity and not advising the prime minister? It is impossible to say, and most historians have acquitted him, but even by MacDonald's own account, the permanent undersecretary rushed the handling of the file. Lord Thomson was wrong to exonerate Crowe and lay the blame on Gregory. Past investigations have focused on Gregory. In Moscow Chicherin suspected him. Crowe was discharged of responsibility or overlooked. But Gregory opposed publication of "the letter," for he feared it might be a forgery, and even if it were not, the Soviet government would claim that it was.

Crowe hated the Bolsheviks and opposed an improvement of relations with them on anything but British terms. He was not involved in the 1924 Anglo-Soviet negotiations—MacDonald did not ask him to participate—and Crowe made no objection, quite the contrary. "The Russian treaty is a ridiculous farce," he wrote to his wife in August 1924, "and a disgrace to this office. However, I have put it formally and repeatedly on record that I entirely disapproved of and protested against the whole proceeding." According to Crowe, the draft treaty rested entirely on Ponsonby. "In the end he will suffer from his idiotic performance," Crowe added. "It may even bring down the government."[73] Did that become Crowe's intention? These are strong words by the senior Foreign Office civil servant and suggest a disposition toward insubordination. After the Zinoviev letter was transmitted to the Foreign Office, Crowe rejected Gregory's advice to hold off publication, which was his prerogative, and initially ignored the prime minister's directive for caution and further verification, which was not his prerogative. Lord Thomson told Rakovskii that MacDonald had lost control of his department. It was a scandal that had to be covered up. For a fortnight Crowe was in effect Foreign Secretary.

In a letter to MacDonald explaining his actions, Crowe was mendacious and presumptuous. "It came upon me like a bolt from the blue that you had not intended the dispatch and publication of the note to Rakowsky." Since several of his officials told Crowe that the prime minister had not signed off on the final draft to the Soviet embassy, the "bolt from the blue" was no bolt at all. But Crowe insisted: "No doubt as to your having approved it had crossed my mind." How could this have been so since "doubt" had crossed the minds of his subordinates? Then Crowe tried to pin the responsibility for the leak to the *Daily Mail* on "some venal informer in the Communist camp here." A permanent undersecretary, so well versed in the literature of the Code and Cipher School and other "most secret" sources, must have known that "venal" British communists had nothing to do with the leak. Was it another deception? "I felt that our only real defence against the treacherous proceedings of the Bolsheviks was publicity," Crowe explained, "and that it did not seem fair to our own people that our knowledge of these Russian machinations should remain concealed." It was not the permanent undersecretary's job to draw these conclusions and act upon them without his minister's, and in this case his prime minister's, consent.[74]

A police investigator, looking for means, motive, and opportunity and at the circumstantial evidence, would have to conclude that Crowe was a primary suspect. He died of cancer the following spring, which meant he gained posthumous sympathy and escaped further scrutiny. To this day, the affair emits the odor of cover-up and widespread collusion to oust Labour, though there should be nothing surprising in that. The Die-Hards knew what they wanted, the defeat of MacDonald and a rupture with Moscow, and they would not burke a fight, or scruple over the means, to get it.

After the elections SIS insisted the Zinoviev letter was genuine based on forged documents, including alleged meetings of the Sovnarkom, the Soviet council of commissars, and the NKID, which apparently never took place, furnished by agents who may never have existed except in the clever minds of Orlov and other document forgers. One can easily imagine their drink-fuelled mirth and backslapping at having hoaxed SIS, though this was not so hard to do, even according to Foreign Office officials. SIS and the Foreign Office ignored the genuine evidence which they did have, that is, the decrypted telegrams between Rakovskii, Litvinov, and Chicherin, who were operating under the belief that "the letter" was a forgery. Who after all would know better than they? Having stooped low to win the election, in apparent collusion with government civil servants, the Tories had to cover up after their return to power. Too many reputations were at stake.

In mid-November Rakovskii reported that the Foreign Office wanted to smother any further polemics over the "Zinoviev letter." They will look for other proofs of Soviet meddling to satisfy doubters of the authenticity of "the letter."[75] On 21 November the Foreign Office informed Rakovskii that the draft Anglo-Soviet treaty would not be submitted to Parliament for approval and further that it regarded the "Zinoviev letter" as genuine. Litvinov considered the shelving of the treaty a foregone conclusion and suggested a short note to the British government regretting the lost opportunity to settle outstanding issues. On the "Zinoviev letter," Litvinov took a stronger line, indicating that the Soviet government should insist on an answer to its demand for an independent investigation. Litvinov must have known he was wasting his time.[76] But he wrote to the NKID *kollegiia* and to the Politburo, echoing Rakovskii's conclusion that the British government was trying to move from the "Zinoviev letter" to the "general issue of Comintern propaganda." "We must," he recommended, "create a counter-diversion and again force the English government back to the dispute over the legitimacy of 'the Zinoviev letter' and our demand for arbitration." We also need to stress that "the Comintern is in reality an organ of propaganda, but that it is completely independent from the Soviet government. We cannot accept protests in regard to activities of this organization which is independent from us." The Tories are testing our toughness, said Litvinov: instructions should be given to the press "to take a very hard, decisive line." We cannot say it in a diplomatic note, but we can say in the press "that we will not expel the Comintern from the USSR, and that we cannot, and we do not have the slightest wish, to influence its activities."

> Who wants to have relations with us, must once and for all come to terms with the fact of the existence of the Comintern on our territory. There is no price which the bourgeoisie can offer to us in its struggle with the Comintern. Who wants to break with us, will always find a pretext, and the existence of the Comintern can of course be such a pretext. The main focus, in my opinion, must be on the attempt by the English government, which has been caught red-handed, to run from accusations against it about the use of forged documents.

In his concluding paragraph, Litvinov returned to a familiar theme, criticizing Soviet press attacks on Germany. "Not yet having established relations with France, not having avoided a serious conflict with England and not having anywhere in Europe even the slightest diplomatic foothold, we cannot permit ourselves a fierce quarrel with Germany." We should ask "Comrade Stalin" to convoke the Politburo to discuss the issue, concluded

Figure 4.8. David Low cartoon, LSE7171, "The New Britannia,"
***The Star*, 11 October 1924. British Cartoon Archive.**

Litvinov, his point being that the USSR could not be at odds with all the European great powers at the same time.[77] "Ask Comrade Stalin" was another indication that he was already *vozhd'*, the boss, and deeply involved in foreign policy issues. Trotskii, still fighting against him, remained a dangerous but fatally wounded foe.

The Soviet optimism of early 1924 about better relations with Britain was thus dashed. The Conservative electoral campaign was invigorated by raising the Red Peril. Die-Hards, like Churchill, were itching for a confrontation with Moscow. The unrelenting Low ridiculed Churchill's ragged anti-Bolshevism, wasteful of lives and money in the past, when as Secretary of State for War he had pressed hard for armed intervention in the Russian civil war. Inadvertently perhaps, Low underlined that the British government knew a thing or two about interference in *Soviet* domestic affairs.

We are in for a long siege, Rakovskii reported to Moscow: even inside Labour the party bosses are working against us. Brailsford "told me that we should not expect honest relations with MacDonald." The Labour Party was little interested in looking for the author of the forged "letter" since MacDonald himself was involved in the scandal. As for the Tories, their electoral win was bigger than expected. Events "have given potential weapons to our enemies to use against us." The Tory victory, and an "epidemic of forged documents," has stirred up "reactionary circles" across Europe.[78] The counterfeiter Orlov was obviously happy; his order book must have been full.

In an anticlimactic gesture, the Home Secretary reiterated in the House of Commons in early December that the "Zinoviev letter" was genuine but that evidence of its authenticity could not be revealed because it would endanger the security of the SIS source in the Soviet Union.

The NKID jumped on this statement and proposed "to pin the British government to the wall" by guaranteeing the safety of the source. The OGPU, the Soviet secret police, bucked at the idea because it would give free rein to "spies." The "mass of lowbrows [massa obyvatelei], held back by fear, would rush to the English mission to become English agents." It was just like the secret police to suspect nearly everybody, but the NKID did not agree, thinking the case exceptional, and had its way. "In the interests of truth," Rakovskii replied to the Foreign Office, the Soviet government would guarantee the safe departure of the source from the USSR.[79] Since the "letter" was bogus, so was the source, and to produce him or her, if it were not the counterfeiter Orlov or one of his colleagues in Berlin or Warsaw, would have embarrassed the Tories. But they had won the election and were savoring victory. They had outsmarted Moscow and beaten Labour in a nice bit of ruthless political gardening. The NKID knew it, and so did Stalin, who took a personal interest in the handling of the replies to London.[80] The affair rankled in Moscow long afterward.

Crowe was feeling righteous when he met Saint-Aulaire in late November to talk over recent events. Propaganda was his main worry. One had only to look around, from the London docks to China, to see its corrosive effects. "We do not want," Crowe said, "that it spreads its ravages into India and into our other possessions."[81]

Time to Get a Move On: French Diplomatic Recognition

The Die-Hards meant to look for trouble in Moscow, and if Litvinov's angry reaction was any indication, the Politburo did not intend to shirk a fight. In the meantime, however, another option opened up for Soviet diplomacy, this one in Paris. We left the story of Soviet relations with France at the beginning of 1924, when the French government was divided on whether or not to open full diplomatic relations with Moscow. As in Britain and the United States, so in France, anti-communist ideology clashed with the realism of state interests. And as in Britain, French national elections gave an opening for improved relations with the USSR. A center-left electoral coalition of the Radical and Socialist parties, the Cartel des gauches, won spring

Parliamentary elections and formed a government in mid-June 1924 under Édouard Herriot. Readers will remember that Herriot had visited Moscow in the autumn of 1922 and revealed his anxieties about a new German menace and the need for better Franco-Soviet relations to counter it. President Millerand, who opposed improved relations with Moscow, was forced to resign and was thus out of the way. As premier and foreign minister, Herriot had a chance to change French policy. However, like the minority Labour government in London, the *Cartel*, which was strong during the electoral campaign, weakened quickly once in power.

Both Chicherin and Litvinov mistrusted the French government, and although Chicherin preferred a less aggressive approach to Paris, he described differences with Litvinov as purely tactical. They perceived two different types of French interest in a rapprochement with the Soviet Union. One was motivated by economic gain or "material profits," as Litvinov put it.[82] The other was driven by geopolitical considerations, in particular the preoccupation with the threat of a resurgent Germany. Herriot of course held to this line, but so did his close collaborator Paul Painlevé, an independent socialist, who was briefly premier during the war and would succeed Herriot in April 1925. Chicherin saw Herriot as a "fierce Germanophobe," Painlevé as more "refined," but "for both of them the fear of German *revanche* is the dominant concern." As Herriot put it to Chicherin, "in all of northern France, cities are composed of wooden shacks [because of wartime destruction], but when I traveled across Germany, I saw museums being built. German capital is unharmed, only hiding; German militarism is unharmed, only hiding. Tomorrow they will again attack France." In 1924, in the aftermath of the French occupation of the Ruhr, Chicherin was not as sympathetic to this line of argument as Litvinov would be ten years later. As for the other type of French interest in better relations with Moscow, driven by profit, Chicherin mentioned Monzie, the center-right *sénateur*, a merchant, who was "little interested" in a future German threat. It would be easier to deal with him, Chicherin noted, than with Herriot and Painlevé, with their concerns about security against Germany.[83] Easier because a French rapprochement based on security concerns could run across the Soviet Rapallo policy.

Nonetheless, Monzie was Herriot's go-between with Rakovskii as the French government discussed recognition. It was time to get a move on. The British electoral campaign, even before the revelation of the "Zinoviev letter," caused doubts in Paris about whether the Labour government would survive, and if it did not, whether Herriot could go ahead with diplomatic recognition. Everywhere Herriot turned, he saw dangers: opposition from the State Department, as hostile as ever to the USSR, or the fall of his ministry in the aftermath of a Tory win in Britain.[84] Hence, in the early hours of 29 October as voting was about to get under way in Britain, French recognition of the Soviet government was announced. The British press accused Paris of wanting to influence election results, but Herriot's haste, if it could be called that, was really motivated by the desire to accomplish recognition before the State Department and a new Tory cabinet in London could gang up on France to block it. The NKID was in a hurry too, for more or less the same reasons.[85]

So the Soviet focus of attention in Europe, apart from Berlin, shifted from London to Paris. "For the achievement of concrete results in our foreign policy," Rakovskii noted, "we cannot boggle at political compromises with capitalist governments." After all, he added, if the French Convention could seek an alliance with the Turkish sultan to protect the revolution, could we do any less?[86]

"No doubt, no doubt," Litvinov or Chicherin might have replied, but were such compromises possible with the French? And if so, at what price?

Rakovskii was the eternal optimist—surprising or perhaps necessary for a revolutionary internationalist—but in Moscow Litvinov and Chicherin were less certain. Nevertheless, the Soviet fireman Krasin, about whom we have heard little since the Curzon crisis, was sent to France to find out and to get Franco-Soviet relations off to a good start. Chicherin wanted him to leave quickly for Paris to head off likely British intrigues.[87] There were limits, however, to what even Krasin could do.

Notes

1. O'Malley's minute, 24 Oct. 1923, N8234/209/38, FO 371 9353; Chicherin to Berzin, not numbered, 22 Aug. 1923, AVPRF, f. 069, o. 7, p. 7, d. 13, ll. 96–98; Chicherin to Berzin, not numbered, 10 Sept. 1923, AVPRF, f. 069, o. 7, p. 7, d. 8, l. 40; Chicherin to Berzin, not numbered, 12 Sept. 1923, AVPRF, f. 04, o. 4, p. 23, d. 327, l. 72; and Chicherin to Berzin, not numbered, 24 Sept. 1923, AVPRF, f. 069, o. 7, p. 7, d. 8, l. 42.

2. Gregory's memorandum, 13 Nov. 1923, N8985/3198/38, FO 371 9370; "Conversation with Gregory," 13 Nov. 1923, Berzin, AVPRF, f. 069, o. 7, p. 7, d. 8, ll. 25–27; and Curzon's minute, 7 Nov. 1923, N8985/3198/38, FO 371 9370.

3. "Conversation of Ia. A. Berzin with Mr. Gregory, 4 December 1923," secret, 5 Dec. 1923, AVPRF, f. 069, o. 7, p. 7, d. 8, ll. 28–30; Rakovskii to Litvinov, no. 35, 5 Dec. 1923, AVPRF, f. 069, o. 7, p. 7, d. 15, ll. 14–18; and Rakovskii to Litvinov, no. 43, 15 Dec. 1923, ibid., ll. 74–83.

4. Litvinov to Berzin, no. 384, secret, 11 April 1923, AVPRF, f. 04, o. 4, p. 23, d. 326, ll. 68–75.

5. Chicherin to Rakovskii, not numbered, 28 Feb. 1924, AVPRF, f. 04, o. 4, p. 27, d. 377 (147), ll. 1–2. For background on Soviet South Asia and Middle Eastern policy, see Jon Jacobson, *Soviet Union*, pp. 66–67 and passim.

6. Chicherin to Rakovskii, no. 40, 11 Jan. 1924, AVPRF, f. 069, o. 8, p. 11, d. 2, ll. 2–3; and Chicherin to Rakovskii, no. 58, 24 April 1924, ibid., ll. 12–13. For background, see Jacobson, *Soviet Union*, pp. 68–77.

7. Crewe to Chamberlain, confidential, 29 Nov. 1925, FO 800 258, ff. 793–95.

8. Crewe to Chamberlain, confidential, 14 Dec. 1925, AC52/237, University of Birmingham, Austen Chamberlain Papers (hereinafter U.Birm., A. Chamberlain Papers).

9. Chamberlain's minute, 5 May 1927, N1633/331/38, FO 371 12597.

10. Yvon Delbos, French foreign minister, to Robert Coulondre, French ambassador in Moscow, no. 139, 4 March 1938, MAÉ *Bureau du chiffre, télégrammes, Moscou, départ, 1938–1 octobre 1939.*

11. Rakovskii to Litvinov, no. 16, 8 Feb. 1924, AVPRF, f. 069, o. 8, p. 12, d. 14, ll. 147–57; and Rakovskii to Litvinov, no. 11, 29 Jan. 1924, ibid., ll. 104–18.

12. Rakovskii to Litvinov, no. 17, 8 Feb. 1924, AVPRF, f. 069, o. 8, p. 12, d. 14, ll. 162–63; and Berzin to Litvinov, not numbered, 7 Feb. 1924, ibid., ll. 243–46.

13. Chicherin to Rakovskii, no. 46, 22 Jan. 1924, AVPRF, f. 069, o. 8, p. 11, d. 2, ll. 4–5.

14. Litvinov to NKID *kollegiia*, not numbered, 25 Feb. 1924, AVPRF, f. 04, o. 4, p. 28, d. 177, ll. 7–15.

15. Litvinov to Stalin, no. 0199, secret, 28 March 1924, AVPRF, f. 04, o. 4, p. 27, d. 157, ll. 55–59.

16. Chicherin to Stalin, no. 53/ChS, very secret, 28 Feb. 1924, AVPRF, f. 04, o. 4, p. 27, d. 157, ll. 21–24.

17. For example, David Low's cartoon, "The Bolsh Bogey," in *The Star* (Liberal evening newspaper, London), 28 June 1923, British Cartoon Archive (http://www.cartoons.ac.uk).

18. Rakovskii to Litvinov, no. 21, 15 Feb. 1924, AVPRF, f. 069, o. 8, p. 12, d. 14, ll. 189–93; Ponsonby to MacDonald, 2 Sept. 1924, N6622/2140/38, FO 371 10495; and Wellesley's minute, 23 Sept. 1924, N7216/2140/38, ibid.

19. Berzin to Litvinov, not numbered, 21 March 1924, AVPRF, f. 069, o. 8, p. 12, d. 14, ll. 269–71.

20. Leeper's minute, 7 Feb. 1923, N1219/674/38, FO 371 9357.

21. A reference to John Gay's 18th-century play "The Beggar's Opera" in W. Monteath, India Office, to P. M. Roberts, Foreign Office, 28 March 1924, N2780/2563/85, FO 371 10511; and "Accusations against His Majesty's Government of Propaganda against the Soviet Government in the East," 20 March 1924, N2563/2563/85, ibid.

22. Wellesley's minute, 10 March 1924, N2030/1822/85, FO 371 10509.

23. Minute by H. F. B. Maxse, Northern Department, N8382/108/38, FO 371 10479; and MacDonald's note, 10 Sept. 1924, N6622/2140/38, FO 371 10495.

24. Strang's minute, 17 June 1924, N4849/3433/85, FO 371 10513.

25. Chicherin to Politburo, no. 181/ChS, 6 March 1924, AVPRF, f. 04, p. 27, d. 157, ll. 26–27; Hodgson, no. 69, 25 Feb. 1924, N2133/1761/38, FO 371 10494; MacDonald to Rakovskii, private (in English), 12 Jan. 1924, AVPRF, f. 069, o. 8, p. 12, d. 14, ll. 64–65; and Chicherin to Politburo, no. 144/ChS, 25 Feb. 1924, AVPRF, f. 04, o. 4, p. 27, d. 157, ll. 1–7.

26. Rakovskii to Litvinov, no. 46, secret, 21 Dec. 1923, enclosing letter in English from Brailsford, AVPRF, f. 069, o. 7, p. 7, d. 15, ll. 97–102; and Rakovskii to Litvinov, no. 3, 11 Jan. 1924, AVPRF, f. 069, o. 8, p. 12, d. 14, ll. 51–56.

27. "Record of conversation . . . with Rantzau," 5 April 1924, *Moskva-Berlin*, I, pp. 248–51.

28. Gregory's memorandum, 28 July 1924, *DBFP*, 1st, XXV, pp. 555–59.

29. Hughes to various U.S. embassies, 23 Feb. 1924, 861.01/744a, NA RG59, M-316, reel 72.

30. Kellogg to Hughes, no. 189, 21 May 1924, 741.61/65, NA RG59, M-582, reel 5; Kellogg, no. 428, 29 May 1924, 741.61/71, ibid.; and Kellogg, no. 436, 3 June 1924, 741.61/75, ibid.

31. Kellogg, no. 646, 8 Aug. 1924, 741.61/86, NA RG59, M-582, reel 5.

32. Hughes to U.S. diplomatic posts in Europe, 23 March 1923, 861.01/575a, NA RG59, M-316, reel 72.

33. Rakovskii to Ponsonby, 29 May 1924, N4642/3028/85, FO 371 10512.

34. Ponsonby's minute, 2 April 1924, N2938/1537/85, FO 371 10507.

35. Minutes by Strang, 17 June 1924; and MacDonald, 21 June 1924, N4849/3433/85, FO 371 10513.

36. Low's cartoon, "The Shadow Show," *The Star*, 2 Oct. 1924, British Cartoon Archive.

37. Litvinov to Berzin, no. 0370, secret, 22 Sept. 1924, AVPRF, f. 04, o. 4, p. 27, d. 147, ll. 29–33.

38. Litvinov to V. M. Molotov, Politburo secretary, cc. to Politburo and NKID *kollegiia*, no. 0426, secret, 13 Oct. 1924, AVPRF, f. 04, o. 4, p. 27, d. 157, ll. 186–87; and Litvinov to Rakovskii, no. 0428, secret, 13 Oct. 1924, AVPRF, f. 04, o. 4, p. 27, d. 147, ll. 38–40.

39. Low's cartoons, "The Recruiting Parade," 7 Oct. 1924; and "Much Ado about Next to Nothing," 14 Oct. 1924, *The Star*, British Cartoon Archive.

40. Rakovskii to Litvinov, no. 2, very secret, 17 Oct. 1924, RGASPI, f. 359, o. 1, d. 6, ll. 262–66.

41. SIS to Gregory and Nevile Bland, Foreign Office, and elsewhere, no. CX/1174, 9 Oct. 1924, N7838G/108/38, FO 371 10478 and KV2 3331.

42. Strang's minute, 27 Aug. 1923, N7194/44/38, FO 371 9334.

43. Gill Bennett, "A Most Extraordinary and Mysterious Business": The Zinoviev Letter of 1924 (London, 1999), pp. 36–38.

44. Minutes by Strang and Gregory, 14 Oct. 1924; by Crowe, nd and 15 Oct. 1924; and by MacDonald, 16 Oct. 1924, N7838G/108/38, FO 371 10478.

45. Bennett, *Zinoviev Letter*, p. 40.

46. Bennett, *Zinoviev Letter*, p. 50.

47. Low's cartoon, "Behind the Smoke Screen," 25 Oct. 1924, *The Star*, British Cartoon Archive.

48. Rakovskii to Litvinov, no. 5, very secret, 25 Oct. 1924, RGASPI, f. 359, o. 1, d. 6, ll. 270–74.

49. Chicherin to Politburo, no. 1324/ChS, 24 Oct. 1924, AVPRF, f. 04, o. 4, p. 31, d. 436, l. 1.

50. Chicherin to Politburo, no. 1326/ChS, 25 Oct. 1925, AVPRF, f. 0136, o. 7, p. 103, d. 67, l. 6.

51. Chicherin to Zinoviev, no. 1331/ChS, 25 Oct. 1925, AVPRF, f. 04, o. 4, p. 31, d. 436, l. 2.

52. Litvinov to Rakovskii, no. 266, immediate, 26 Oct. 1924, RGASPI, f. 359, o. 1, d. 5, l. 142; and Bennett, *Zinoviev Letter*, p. 67.

53. Rakovskii to Gregory, no. CR/8279, 27 Oct. 1924, N8475/108/38, FO 371 10479; and Gregory's minute, 3 Nov. 1924, N8272/108/38, FO 371 10478.

54. Peters, no. 359, 29 Oct. 1924, N8210/108/38, FO 371 10478.

55. Rakovskii to Litvinov, no. 12, secret, 1 Dec. 1924, AVPRF, f. 04, o. 4, p. 31, d. 436, ll. 60–66.

56. "Record of conversation of Chicherin with U. Brockdorff-Rantzau . . . ," 4 Dec. 1924, *Moskva-Berlin*, I, pp. 435–37; "Record of conversation of Chicherin with U. Brockdorff-Rantzau . . . ," no. 432/ChS, very secret, 2 May 1924, ibid., pp. 259–61; and Rakovskii to Litvinov, no. 7, very secret, 9 Nov. 1924, AVPRF, f. 04, o. 4, p. 26, d. 373, ll. 56–72.

57. Albert Inskip, general secretary, Communist Party of Great Britain, 28 Oct. 1924; and MacDonald's minute, 30 Oct. 1924, N8195/108/38, FO 371 10478; and Rakovskii to Litvinov, no. 6, very secret, 29 Oct. 1924, AVPRF, f. 04, o. 4, p. 26, d. 373, ll. 35–42.

58. Saint-Aulaire, nos. 604–6, secret, 28 Oct. 1924, MAÉ Grande-Bretagne/64, ff. 22–24; and Bennett, *Zinoviev Letter*, pp. 44–47, 85.

59. British intercept no. 018378, 31 Oct. 1924, TNA HW12 63.

60. Jeffery, *Secret History of MI6*, pp. 209–10.

61. Gabriele Preziosi, London, to Rome, no. 851, 25 Oct. 1924, intercept no. 018339, most secret, 28 Oct. 1924, HW12 63.

62. Zekiai Salih Bey, London, to Ankara, no. 653, 28 Oct. 1924, intercept no. 018368, most secret, 30 Oct. 1924, HW12 63.

63. Chicherin to Rakovskii, no. 298, 9 Sept. 1924, intercept no. 018218, most secret, 17 Oct. 1924, HW12 63.

64. Jeffery, *Secret History of MI6*, pp. 214–22; and Bennett, *Zinoviev Letter*, pp. 47, 56.

65. Litvinov to Rakovski, no. 360, 27 Oct. 1924, intercept no. 018738, most secret, 27 Nov. 1924, HW12 64; Rakovskii to NKID, nos. 427–29, 26 Nov. 1924, intercept no. 018786, most secret, 2 Dec. 1924, HW12 65; and Bennett, *Zinoviev Letter*, p. 67.

66. Berzin to Litvinov, not numbered, very secret, 5 Nov. 1924, RGASPI, f. 359, o. 1, d. 6, ll. 281–87; Rakovskii to Litvinov, no. 17, secret, 19 Dec. 1924, RGASPI, f. 359, o. 1, d. 5, ll. 147–59; and Bennett, *Zinoviev Letter*, pp. 72–84.

67. Rakovskii to Litvinov, no. 7, very secret, 9 Nov. 1924, AVPRF, f. 04, o. 4, p. 26, d. 373, ll. 56–72.

68. Cf., Christopher Andrew, *Secret Service: The Making of the British Intelligence Community* (London, 1987), p. 437.

69. Rakovskii to Litvinov, no. 12, 1 Dec. 1924, as cited above in n. 55.

70. Chicherin to Litvinov, cc. to NKID *kollegiia*, very secret, 7 Dec. 1924, AVPRF, f. 04, o. 4, p. 31, d. 436, l. 106.

71. Rakovskii to Litvinov, no. 6, 29 Oct. 1924, as cited above in n. 57.

72. Quoted in Bennett, *Zinoviev Letter*, p. 53.

73. Quoting Crowe letters to his wife Clema, 8 and 15 August 1924, in Keith Neilson and Thomas G. Otte, *The Permanent Under-secretary for Foreign Affairs, 1854–1946* (Abingdon, 2009), p. 181.

74. Crowe to MacDonald, private, 25 Oct. 1924, N8105/108/38, FO 371 10478; and Bennett, *Zinoviev Letter*, p. 49.

75. Rakovskii to Litvinov, 16 Nov. 1924, AVPRF, f. 04, o. 4, p. 26, d. 373, ll. 85–88.

76. Litvinov to Rakovskii, no. 0525, secret, 22 Nov. 1924, AVPRF, f. 04, o. 4, p. 27, d. 147, ll. 44–46.

77. Litvinov to NKID *kollegiia* with copies to the Politburo, no. 0524, secret, 22 Nov. 1924, RGASPI, f. 359, o. 1, d. 5, ll. 143–45.

78. Rakovskii to Litvinov, no. 9, very secret, 20 Nov. 1924, RGASPI, f. 359, o. 1, d. 6, ll. 298–301; Rakovskii to Litvinov, no. 10, secret, 27 Nov. 1924, ibid., ll. 309–12; and Rakovskii to Litvinov, no. 13, very secret, 4 Dec. 1924, ibid., ll. 325–28.

79. Chicherin to Politburo et al., no. 1513/ChS, 15 Dec. 1924, AVPRF, f. 04, o. 4, p. 31, d. 436, l. 107; and Rakovskii to Austen Chamberlain, Foreign Secretary, no. CR/9526, 22 Dec. 1924, N9365/108/38, FO 371 10480.

80. Chicherin to Litvinov, cc. NKID *kollegiia*, very urgent, 31 Dec. 1924, AVPRF, f. 04, o. 4, p. 31, d. 436, ll. 110–11; and Litvinov to Chicherin, secret, nd (probably 31 Dec. 1924), ibid., l. 112.

81. Saint-Aulaire, no. 674, 25 Nov. 1924, MAÉ Grande-Bretagne/64, ff. 48–49.

82. Chicherin to Rakovskii, no. 29, 13 Dec. 1923, AVPRF, f. 04, o. 4, p. 23, d. 327, ll. 185–86; and Litvinov to Rakovskii, no. 867, secret, 20 Nov. 1923, ibid., ll. 150–51.

83. Chicherin to Rakovskii, not numbered, 24 March 1924, AVPRF, f. 04, o. 42, p. 261, d. 53670, ll. 1–6; and Chicherin to Politburo, no. 1581/ChS, 31 Dec. 1924, AVPRF, f. 0136, o. 7, p. 103, d. 67, ll. 28–29.

84. Untitled, unsigned memorandum, but a Soviet informant in Paris (probably Rosta correspondent Michel Merle), 9 Oct. 1924, AVPRF, f. 04, o. 42, p. 261, d. 53675, ll. 22–23.

85. Rakovskii to Litvinov, no. 5, very secret, 25 Oct. 1924, AVPRF, f. 04, o. 42, p. 261, d. 53670, ll. 21–25; Saint-Aulaire, no. 611, 30 Oct. 1924 (and Herriot's minute), MAÉ Z-Russie/356, fol. 208; Herriot to Saint-Aulaire, no. 902, 31 Oct. 1924, ibid., fol. 224; and Chicherin to Politburo, no. 1332/ChS, 26 Oct. 1924, AVPRF, f. 0136, o. 7, p. 103, d. 67, l. 7.

86. Rakovskii to Litvinov, with cc. to the NKID *kollegiia*, Politburo, Krasin, not numbered, secret, 21 Nov. 1924, RGASPI, f. 359, o. 1, d. 6, ll. 302–8.

87. Chicherin to Politburo, no. 1423/ChS, 21 Nov. 1924, AVPRF, f. 04, o. 4, p. 27, d. 157, ll. 191–94.

CHAPTER FIVE

∼

"Save the Family Silver"

Fearful Coexistence in Paris and Berlin, 1924–1925

Having failed in London and Washington, the NKID turned its attention to Paris. Unfortunately for Moscow, no sooner had the Herriot government extended recognition than the French right unleashed a fresh anti-communist campaign. If the Tories could take down Labour, the conservative opposition reasoned it could turn out the fragile *Cartel des gauches*. So the Tory victory encouraged the French right, and in December 1924 the Paris right-wing press whipped up anti-communist fears, in spite of continuing Soviet "allowances." The day before Krasin's arrival in Paris there were left-wing street demonstrations which stoked up the anti-communist hysteria. Chicherin warned Krasin to be careful and to make sure his staff kept out of trouble, but it was too much when the opening of the embassy was celebrated by the raising of the red flag and the playing of the *Internationale*. One wonders if French conservatives expected to hear "God Save the Tsar," but even the "serious newspaper" *Le Temps*, Krasin reported, claimed that we did not have the right to raise our flag or play the *Internationale*, then the Soviet national anthem.[1]

Rakovskii gave Litvinov a graphic account of these events: there was a "dreadful tumult" in the press, and the general mood in Paris was "unbelievably panicky." In London before the election, it was "save your purse" from the Bolsh; according to Rakovskii, in Paris it's "save the family silver." If the French bourgeoisie was in a panic, there was also a "great tumult" at the Quai d'Orsay, which Monzie said he had calmed—no doubt to underline his importance to me, Rakovskii observed maliciously. But how long would the calm last? The least incident can set off a panic, and in Herriot first of all.[2]

Figure 5.1.   Leonid B. Krasin's arrival at the Gare du Nord, Paris, December 1924. *Agence Meurisse. Bibliothèque nationale de France.*

Chicherin was full of contempt for the French "petty bourgeoisie" which could panic over a "crust of bread." But he also vented his spleen about Politburo choices of personnel for the Soviet embassy in Paris. "The French ask themselves why people were sent to the Paris embassy who cannot speak French, and naturally they reply—they have come for Comintern work." And then Chicherin made a crack about inviting a French communist orchestra to the embassy to play the *Internationale*.

This seemingly gratuitous comment made Krasin bristle: to refuse to raise our flag above the embassy would have been a "humiliation," and unnecessary too, since the French press would always find a pretext to attack us.[3] These testy exchanges were a sign of frustration over the NKID's lack of control over events, or even the personnel for its embassy in Paris.

In one of their first meetings Herriot was remarkably frank with Krasin: I am being attacked from all sides, by the *Bloc national*, by Italian fascists, and by British Tories. Communist demonstrations in Paris have created a panic and strengthened the right. People with money are buying dollars and sterling and pushing down the value of the franc on exchange markets. A truly difficult situation, Krasin had to admit: "There is no doubt that the main reason behind the campaign against us is the internal struggle against the *Cartel des gauches*. Herriot's recognition of the USSR is being used as one of the main levers in order to topple, if not the *Cartel des gauches*, then at least the present cabinet." Britain is also exerting heavy pressure on the

French government, Krasin observed: "French dependence on England at the present time is already such that scarcely any French cabinet can pursue a policy radically at odds with the English." France was heavily indebted to Britain, and the British treasury only had to threaten to demand payment of French treasury bills to put pressure on Paris to comply with British policy. Krasin saw the English hand in the press campaign against the Soviet embassy in Paris:

> To spend 50 or 100 thousand pounds is a trifle for the Foreign Office, and with money here, you can get the press to do whatever you like. We need to take this into consideration if we want more or less to have any persistent impact on French public opinion. Interviews or communiqués from our press bureau have no effect whatever—for sympathy, one simply has to buy it.

Nor could we rely on Herriot, Krasin added. He was ill and having trouble getting out of his bed. However, his present political "indecisiveness is due not so much to his illness as to the fact that he probably is not quite sure whether to accept open battle with the right, or perhaps move to the side temporarily so that at the appropriate time he may once again serve as premier."[4]

The Soviet embassy was already spending generously on *Le Temps*, and obtaining little "sympathy" for its money. This should not have surprised Krasin or his colleagues in Moscow. They were successful communist revolutionaries who had challenged the capitalism and colonialism of the West. No wonder they could not buy long-term sympathy in Paris. They were apostates who refused to embrace capitalist "civilization." True, they were willing to pursue a policy of peaceful coexistence, but the West was unwilling to do the same—at least not yet. The Soviet Union was the enemy "other," the "Oriental" *Bolcho*, with his long blood-drenched knife in one hand and a smoking bomb in the other. Although it should be emphasized that Krasin in his well-cut suits and homburg hat hardly fit the West's Bolshevik caricatures. Even Chicherin became a better dresser.

Krasin concluded that the suddenly rotten political atmosphere in Paris would not lead to a quick settlement of Franco-Soviet differences. We had better wait awhile before starting negotiations, Monzie told Krasin, until hostile public opinion had quieted down. Herriot was in no rush either, though he publicly denied that there was any communist danger in France. He even told the U.S. ambassador in Paris that he had ordered his secret police chief to pick a fight with local communists "in order to calm public opinion." But my police chief, Herriot quipped, had been unable to find a communist meeting to roust. Herriot added that he would not make the same mistake as the Labour government in London and rush into negotiations with the Soviet Union.[5]

So while Herriot told Krasin that his government was shaky because of communist street demonstrations, he showed a brave face to the Americans and British. The U.S. ambassador in Paris reported a few days later that not everyone shared Herriot's view that French communists were harmless.[6]

When the new British Foreign Secretary Austen Chamberlain paid a visit to Paris in early December 1924, Herriot explained his reasons for French recognition of Moscow: "They were, in the main, his fear that Russia left to herself would combine with Germany. He by no means meant to throw himself into the arms of the Russians." So, unlike his discussions with Chicherin, there was no talk with Chamberlain about German *revanche*, the furthest concern from the British mind. Herriot opined that communism was no "danger to France," except "in certain parts of the banlieu [*sic*] of Paris" and, he added, in Tunis.[7] This conversation took place *before* street demon-

Figure 5.2. Édouard Herriot and Austen Chamberlain, meeting at the Quai d'Orsay, Paris, December 1924. *Agence Meurisse. Bibliothèque nationale de France.*

strations in the capital. Afterward, the French ambassador in London, Aimé de Fleuriau, told the permanent undersecretary, Crowe, that "the French . . . now bitterly regretted their recent recognition of the Soviet government. There had been an outcry all over France against the Soviets and their open instigation of communist revolution in France."[8] Litvinov had a copy of Crowe's report, by the way, which meant that if SIS could decrypt Soviet cables, Soviet intelligence services could also obtain British and French documents.[9] After all, in matters of intelligence, turnabout is fair play.

Fleuriau sent his counselor to the Foreign Office to discuss the possibility of exchanging "information with regard to Bolshevist activities." The British did not mind exchanging intelligence information, but they were reluctant to go further. "Everyone invites us to a new Holy Alliance," noted Chamberlain:

> And I reply to everyone that I or We cannot make war on ideas by material force, but I believe that our respective Scotland Yards, are in touch and exchange information on international crooks, *murderers and other enemies of society* [underlined in the original]. That seems to me all that we can usefully or wisely do. . . . M. Herriot is gravely embarrassed by his Soviet embassy and M. Krassin [*sic*] will knock him over before long if he does not fall first of his own weakness.[10]

Krasin of course had no wish to "knock over" Herriot, though he would indeed fall because of the weakness of the *Cartel*. It was the usual story about an anti-Soviet bloc: a great idea but hard to put into practice. No one wanted to risk war with revolutionary Bolshevism, which could again become "catching." Less dramatically but more practically, when trade was involved, few wanted to interrupt business either.

Krasin failed to give enough credit to Herriot who got up from his bed at the end of January 1925 to speak in the Chamber of Deputies in favor of credits for opening the French embassy in Moscow. He laid out his argument in favor of moving closer to the USSR and bringing it back into European affairs. At the end of debate he won a confidence vote of 364 to 210.

The Foreign Office was doubtful of the argument. "I am inclined," wrote the assistant undersecretary Wellesley, "to question M. Herriot's view 'that it was necessary to bring Russia back within the pale if there is to be any hope of European Peace.' So long as Russia remains in her present state of chaos there is an element of security for western Europe."[11]

Back to Berlin: Could Rapallo Be Saved? 1924–1925

While the NKID worked on its French problem, it was also active in Berlin. It had to be, for when we left the story of Soviet-German relations at the end of 1923, Litvinov and Chicherin were trying to pick up the broken pieces of

Rapallo and regain control over Soviet policy toward Germany. "The sad state of our present relations with Germany," Chicherin observed, "is the direct and in fact inevitable result of what occurred last autumn. The transformation of our former friends into outspoken enemies . . . cannot but be a spreading phenomenon." Nor was Chicherin willing to let go of his ire with Zinoviev, who continued to make trouble for the NKID with his speeches and articles. He was now "the favorite theme of the hostile press abroad but most of all in Germany." So Chicherin asked Krestinskii, the Soviet *polpred* in Berlin, to try to dispel irritation with Zinoviev's undiplomatic comments. Chicherin could not of course say, though likely Krestinskii knew, that Stalin would not do anything against Zinoviev as long as he needed him as an ally against Trotskii. This domestic political situation worked against NKID interests.

Chicherin speculated on how to get beyond the autumn fiasco. The German government was angry with Moscow, but it might also be worried because of British recognition of the USSR and Soviet discussions with the French. These developments could offer an opportunity to defuse the "deeply hostile mood" in Berlin.[12]

In the meantime Chicherin reassured the German ambassador Rantzau: "We continue to stand, as before, on the ground of the Rapallo Treaty and we will, as before, remove all that undermines [*protivorechit*] it." Rantzau was responsive, not without coincidence praising the pragmatists Litvinov and Krasin for their desire to maintain good Soviet-German relations.[13] Krestinskii too became a fireman, Rantzau noting that the ambassador knew how "to maintain good relations with German right-wing circles." Because of him the German government's political line toward the USSR was being sustained. Zinoviev remained the arsonist, continuing to exasperate the German government and business circles. Rantzau remarked sarcastically that Zinoviev's speeches did not give the impression of representing any part of Soviet public opinion but rather appeared to be an attempt to provoke a popular movement in the USSR antagonistic toward Germany. In his recent speeches, Zinoviev "held to an extremely hostile point of view toward foreign capital." In Berlin influential people did not like being treated as a "*quantité négligeable*," and they were getting the impression that all Soviet eyes were on Britain and that Germany did not exist in economic matters.[14] One can only imagine Krasin's alarm had he read this report.

Rantzau knew how to needle on a very sensitive point, for the economic *raison d'être* of Rapallo was trade and investment. Even if the NKID wanted better relations with Britain, it could not neglect Germany. All European relationships were tied together, German, Soviet, British, French, and if the USSR thought it could play Britain off against Germany, the latter could also play Britain off against the USSR.

Ulrich Graf von Brockdorff-Rantzau

Rantzau had an important role in the maintenance of the Rapallo policy. He was born into the German nobility and after taking a degree in law entered the German foreign service. He was a monarchist who then served the Weimar Republic after 1918. During the war, he was German ambassador in Denmark, and in 1917 he played a key role in arranging for Lenin's return to Russia from Switzerland in the so-called sealed train across Germany, not to promote socialism, of course, but to encourage Russian disorganization and withdrawal from the war. In 1918–1919 he became foreign minister just long enough to be saddled with responsibility for obtaining a peace settlement with the Allied powers in Paris. He was quite prepared "to flaunt the danger of Bolshevism" in order to obtain concessions from the victorious Allies. When this strategy did not work, Rantzau opposed the German signature of the Treaty of Versailles and resigned with the government in mid-June 1919.

In the autumn of 1922 Rantzau went to Moscow as German ambassador. He of course had no sympathy for socialism in Russia, but he valued Rapallo for the same reason that Chicherin and Litvinov did, as a counterweight

Figure 5.3. Ulrich Graf von Brockdorff-Rantzau, ca. 1928, Political Archives, Federal Foreign Office, Germany.

against the "Entente." At the reception where Rantzau handed over his diplomatic credentials, Chicherin remarked that the Soviet government had been reluctant to receive a German aristocrat as ambassador. To which Rantzau replied suavely that he knew Chicherin's family could be traced back to the House of Riurik in the ninth century and that therefore he was in no position to criticize. They must have laughed at each other's sallies.

In fact, Rantzau and Chicherin had already met in Berlin in June 1922. Rantzau was slated to go to Moscow as ambassador, and he wanted to sound out Chicherin before agreeing to accept the appointment. He did not intend to become a pawn in anyone's game, especially not Russia's in its relations with "the Entente," nor would he let Germany be used as an instrument of English "colonial penetration" in Soviet Russia. The two saw eye to eye on Soviet-German relations, and over the following years they would get on well together, forming a close personal friendship. They shared interests in history, philosophy, and literature, even if their politics differed. An admiration for Mozart also reinforced their cordial relations. They were both night owls and often conversed long into the early morning hours over brandy, and in the case of Rantzau, cigarettes, for he was a chain smoker, a habit which eventually killed him. Rapallo and their perception of common Soviet-German interests reinforced personal affinities. Chicherin often made long reports of Rantzau's complaints about Soviet policy which he sent to the Politburo in order to hit Zinoviev and others over the head for their repeated political gaffes. Rantzau did the complaining as a proxy for Chicherin, although the *narkom* was by no means reluctant to complain directly. Similarly, Rantzau feared that opponents of Rapallo in Berlin might push the Soviet Union into the embrace of France, though Marianne herself had no such interests. More's the pity, Chicherin must have thought, for he would have greater leverage in Berlin. Rantzau thus worried for nothing. Both men appreciated and practiced realpolitik, and both for the same reason, to rebuild the strength of their respective countries.[15]

Rapallo-Rocambolesque

In April 1924 Chicherin asked the Politburo for authorization to give a press interview on the importance of Rapallo to mark the second anniversary of the treaty. Only two years and Chicherin needed to remind his comrades of Rapallo. Zinoviev was one, and he barged his way back into the limelight with a new article in *Pravda* to recommend the arming of German workers. Stalin would still do nothing about these tempestuous public statements, for the conflict with Trotskii was ongoing.

A shocked Rantzau returned to the charge with Chicherin: "What would you say if members of the German government, or close to it, also spoke in public about [arming] the White Guards movement?" Whatever the Soviet government might say about Zinoviev's comments, the ambassador continued, could not "change the really lamentable impression which these remarks provoked in Berlin." Obviously exasperated, Chicherin sent his record of conversation to the Politburo. Zinoviev was still a member and might have some explaining to do.[16] Rantzau was unsure whether his protest would have any positive result. The situation is not black and white, he noted quite perceptively; the Politburo appeared undecided, or rather caught somewhere between "not being able" and "not wanting" to intervene.[17]

This time, however, Rantzau's protest attracted the Politburo's attention. Poor Zinoviev, acting like the boy who had got his hand caught in the biscuit box, wrote to Stalin to claim his innocence, saying he submitted all texts on international relations to "Chicherin's censorship."

"I of course did *not* [emphasis in original] say that 'the Soviet government, it is us,' and I did not 'reject the separation between the Soviet government and the Comintern.'" One can almost hear the whining.[18]

On 3 May 1924, the very day that Zinoviev protested his innocence, two German police officers with raised revolvers "burst into" the Soviet *torgpredstvo* in Berlin, followed by other police who conducted a search. The Soviet government considered the trade mission to be equivalent to its embassy with full diplomatic immunity.

Krestinskii immediately protested to the foreign minister, Stresemann, who replied that "it all started without him." According to the police, they had been "lured" into the building for a cup of tea by a Soviet clerk whom they had just arrested. There, the arrested clerk freed himself from the police, causing their comrades to enter the building to free them.

Here was another fiasco in German-Soviet relations. Krestinskii denied this German "fictional" account, which sounds rocambolesque even now. It was hard to sort out the truth, but Stresemann promised to get back to Krestinskii. In the meantime protests flew, though Stresemann and other German officials could not be found to hear them. Chicherin saw Rantzau, wanting to know if Germany was now going to side with "the Allies" and abandon Rapallo. On the defensive, the ambassador denied it. He must have cursed the Berlin police, knowing that this new incident had waylaid his protest against Zinoviev. He alerted Stresemann that the police raid could jeopardize German-Soviet relations.[19] Zinoviev was temporarily out of trouble.

The Politburo did not take the matter lightly and demanded to know what had happened. Detecting wider machinations, it guessed that hostile

French and German business circles were behind the incident, hoping to make trouble for the Labour government in London, then conducting economic negotiations with a Soviet delegation. In Soviet-western relations, one could never be sure. As a result, the Politburo stopped all trade and economic negotiations in Berlin. The NKID now had its own bitter complaints to throw back at Rantzau, underlining just how bad Soviet-German relations were in 1924. "Very fragile," was how Stresemann characterized them. Chicherin heard of a new anti-Soviet press campaign being prepared in Berlin and wondered whether the Soviet government should go over to the offensive.[20]

Stresemann reassured Rantzau that there was no change in German policy toward the USSR. The interior minister was responsible for the raid; it had nothing to do with foreign policy. Chicherin's worries about Germany siding with "the Allies" were illogical. "Fantasies," Stresemann said. I am trying to calm things down inside the government, but there is only so much we can do. Zinoviev's declarations and Comintern fishing in troubled German waters did not make the job any easier. For my efforts, Stresemann complained, I have to endure attacks from right-wing circles accusing me of wanting the Cheka (Soviet secret police) for bodyguards and of protecting Bolshevik Jews. Was it worth the trouble? Stresemann must have wondered sometimes, before reckoning that it was. There seem to have been mistakes on both sides, he told Rantzau: it would be "grotesque" if the police raid weakened Soviet-German relations.[21]

Viewed from Moscow, the conflict over the police intrusion into the *torgpredstvo* showed every sign of getting out of hand, even as Stresemann tried to keep a lid on German discontents. According to one Soviet report, anti-Soviet hostility was widespread, ranging from business and banking circles to officials in the Auswärtiges Amt, the German foreign ministry. There was "no doubt" that "reactionary officials . . . were doing everything possible to poison the atmosphere against us in Germany." At daily press conferences journalists received "distorted and often knowingly false information about the conflict." German businessmen boycotted the Soviet trade mission. The news however was not all bad since some German businesspeople and even "political circles" were pushing back against the hostile campaign. B. S. Stomoniakov, the Berlin *torgpred*, tried to calm down bad tempers and made proposals to Moscow to settle the row.[22] The intensity of the German conflict, Chicherin complained, was warping our perspectives. So much so that the Soviet chargé d'affaires in Berlin asked Chicherin facetiously, "If Herriot were to demand compensation for [French] recognition . . . [would we] promise to organize everywhere [street] demonstrations with the slogan 'Vive la France, à bas l'Allemagne'?"[23]

Obviously not, according to Chicherin, for who could trust the French? So the NKID tried to settle the dispute over the Berlin *torgpredstvo* by establishing its extraterritoriality and by steadying Soviet-German relations in general. Stresemann did the same. Discussions dragged out for months and developed into negotiations for a trade agreement. In the meantime, as summer 1924 began, Moscow received information that a "western orientation" was developing in Germany, with a corresponding loss of interest in relations with the USSR.[24] This report was true.

Litvinov stopped off in Berlin on his way back from the London negotiations to see for himself what was going on. It was the old story of who loves me, who loves me not between London, Paris, Berlin, and Moscow. The Anglo-Soviet negotiations were then ongoing—it was June 1924—and Litvinov did not see any immediate danger of a rupture in these talks which might disturb relations with Germany. There was also the prospect of French recognition, which in turn worried the German side. No one wanted to be isolated or left out in the game of European musical chairs. Litvinov knew that Herriot feared Germany more than he feared the USSR. And in Germany the economic situation was "catastrophic" so that the government could not allow its quarrel with Moscow to disturb trade relations.[25] Litvinov advised everyone in Moscow to stay calm.

The Soviet-German conflict dragged on through the summer of 1924 if for no other reason than because it was the holiday period. As serious as the issues were, even Old Bolsheviks went on holiday. Litvinov insisted on getting off on his; the files could wait until autumn. They did, but barely.

In September the OGPU submitted a detailed intelligence report to the Politburo warning of a new British orientation among German right-wing political groups. In the game of European musical chairs, the French and British were not inactive, trying to resolve differences with Germany. These efforts led to the adoption of the Dawes Plan in mid-August 1924 which settled the Ruhr crisis over reparations. In the aftermath of the Dawes agreement, the issue of German entry into the League of Nations was mooted.[26]

Chicherin did not at first appear to take this prospect too tragically. In reply to OGPU alarums, he opined that problems in Germany should not be exaggerated: Rapallo was still Rapallo. Chicherin had thus recovered his poise after the Berlin police raid. "During the conflict with Germany the Politburo always took the basic position that we must value existing relations with Germany and that this line remains in full force." No one said that all Germans were our friends. Foreign policy was not determined by black-and-white assumptions, but rather by taking into consideration "many shades and nuances of reality." We have to remain alert, Chicherin advised, and follow closely all the shifts of German policy.

As we have done and will continue to do so, evaluating the positive as well as the negative sides of the work of German diplomats and businessmen . . . we should continue to make use of the existing contradictory interests of Germany and England . . . but there is no need to reconsider . . . our relations with Germany.[27]

Litvinov worried nevertheless that German entry into the League could be a possible first step toward the creation of "a united front of the western states against the USSR." He informed the Politburo that the NKID was "applying the maximum diplomatic pressure" and launching a press campaign in Germany to strengthen the position of German political circles opposed to League entry.[28]

In November 1924, with hopes of an Anglo-Soviet agreement dashed, trade negotiations went ahead with Germany, even though Zinoviev's articles and speeches continued to irritate the German government. Yet another was published in the German communist paper *Rote Fahne*, and Stresemann complained to Krestinskii.

How can "a Russian official sign such a text?" Stresemann asked incredulously. Can you do something to stop Zinoviev's interference in our internal affairs? Has he not caused you enough problems in Britain, Stresemann asked, making reference to the "Zinoviev letter" and the British elections? The same thing could happen in Germany if our political parties decide to make him an issue.

What could Krestinskii say? So he offered the usual line that Zinoviev was not a member of the government, to which Stresemann retorted that he nevertheless acted like one. In Moscow Rantzau also took up the issue with Chicherin, reiterating Stresemann's concerns.[29]

In December 1924 Rantzau returned to NKID, this time about "an appeal" signed by Stalin, also published in *Rote Fahne*. In fact, according to Chicherin, it was a communication from the Central Committee of the RKP, the Russian Communist Party, addressed to German workers. Chicherin attempted to explain away Stalin's signature, but Rantzau was unrelenting.

These publications are damaging to Soviet-German relations, Rantzau said, and Stresemann has written "a very excited personal letter" to Krestinskii to protest. According to Chicherin,

Rantzau spoke at length to the effect that the situation is becoming worse and worse, that there is no improvement, that we go around and around in circles and after a long time find ourselves at the very point whence we began. The effect of such documents . . . reduces to nothing his efforts and renders completely impossible long-term political relations between Germany and the USSR.

In Berlin I am asked, said Rantzau, what is the use of relations with the USSR? After two years what have you accomplished in Moscow? The ambassador was hard put to reply. Knowing Chicherin well, Rantzau spoke frankly—and Chicherin duly recorded his words: the public gesticulations by Zinoviev and Stalin produce nothing positive and make it impossible to conduct foreign policy. "It is either one or the other, but this duality of policy cannot long continue."

Chicherin replied weakly that "the party cannot but remain the party, and we need to proceed from the facts as they are."

"In that case," Rantzau repeated, "you will perforce be obliged to give up your foreign policy or it will be reduced to nothing because this duality in relation to all governments cannot long continue." Stalin's appeal, for example, is like the bull in the china shop breaking everything so that the proprietor has to start his business all over again. "In Germany I constantly try to explain the difference between the party and the Soviet government," said Rantzau, "but people respond to me, leave us in peace, these formal subtleties mean nothing." And not forgetting the "Zinoviev letter," Rantzau added that the Soviet claim that the "letter" was a forgery did not have much effect on public opinion, since "Zinoviev very often speaks and writes in exactly the same tone."[30] Even Stalin did not escape criticism, though Chicherin made a weak attempt to explain away his signature on the incriminating appeal in *Rote Fahne*.

Chicherin used Rantzau's complaints to criticize the Politburo for the incoherence of Soviet foreign policy. In ordinary circumstances Stalin might have been more responsive to the NKID. But he was not yet ready to move against Zinoviev since the outcome of his struggle against Trotskii was still unclear. First things first, Stalin must have thought: first I'll deal with Trotskii, then I'll settle with Zinoviev. So Chicherin and Litvinov soldiered on doing what they could to protect Rapallo, while party politics appeared to distract attention from its importance.

In Berlin Krestinskii reported on the practical motives behind German protests against the Zinoviev and Stalin publications. These ranged from impressing German conservatives to diverting Anglo-French attention from German violations of military clauses of the Versailles Treaty. Take them with a grain of salt was Krestinskii's message. But he worried nevertheless that the German government might be playing up to the British about readiness to join a united front against the USSR, or worse, might be preparing some of kind of break with Moscow.[31]

At the end of 1924 the Politburo was concerned enough to ask for an NKID report on German-Soviet relations. Written by Litvinov, it was relatively reassuring. Economic relations were unchanged and normal. The

USSR remained the most promising option for the development of German foreign trade. Litvinov was not overly concerned about German protests against Zinoviev and Stalin, agreeing with Krestinskii's speculations. The objective circumstances which had led to the signature of the Rapallo Treaty, Litvinov concluded, remained unchanged. Germany still pursued a policy of *revanche* to avenge its military defeat, still pursued "a radical change in its international position in the more or less distant future," but in the meantime it would make short-term agreements with "the Entente" to loosen "the pressure of the Versailles screws." For those concessions Germany would pay by weakening its ties with the USSR. Moreover, if the Soviet international position weakened, Germany could try to take advantage by "blackmailing" us into making economic concessions. The only future danger, Litvinov concluded, would be "in the case of an extraordinary rise of the communist wave in Europe, when the bourgeoisie would subordinate its particular economic and national interests to the general necessity of crushing the *place d'armes* of revolution and saving the bourgeois order." But Litvinov had been reading Foreign Office papers apparently and did not think this eventuality likely in the near future. "We are too inclined," he commented to one of his ambassadors, "always to see enemies everywhere and to suspect intrigues, from which often we create an unnecessary alarmist mood." Litvinov concluded that the best way to maintain "more or less friendly relations with Germany" was to establish a strong point in either France or Britain. As long as we do not have this point of support, Litvinov concluded, the Politburo needed to avoid unnecessary conflicts with Germany and treat seriously German demands for a trade agreement. On this subject, as Rantzau later reported to Berlin, Litvinov and Chicherin were of one mind.[32]

In spite of Litvinov's assurances to the Politburo, Stresemann remained troubled by Stalin's public appeal in *Rote Fahne* and on 31 December wrote to Krestinskii asking for an explanation. State Secretary Carl von Schubert again took up the question with Krestinskii a week later. We would like written assurances, Schubert said, that Russian and especially Stalin's interference in German internal affairs will cease.

I cannot do that, Krestinskii replied, because the Soviet government (read the NKID) has no influence over party leaders.

Stalin is different, Schubert rejoined, noting in his record of conversation that Krestinskii did not disagree. We consider him to be a member of the Soviet government and we would like written, official assurances.

I can only repeat, Krestinskii said, that the Soviet government will refrain from any interference in German internal affairs. I can also affirm orally that in Moscow they (not identified but surely Litvinov and Chicherin) spoke "very clearly" with Stalin on this topic. I have every hope, Krestinskii continued, that Stalin will no longer address himself to the German population in such a manner. Unfortunately, it's out of the question to put this affirmation in writing "even with a knife to my throat." Please accept my assurances and forego a written reply which will do no good whatever.

It's not so much the correspondence which worries me, Schubert commented, but rather that Stalin reoffends. The Russian government must not interfere in German internal affairs.

I can't be sure, Krestinskii replied, but I consider our discussion as a "gentleman's agreement," which has more value than any paper I could give you.

I'll talk it over with my colleagues was Schubert's response. He discussed with Stresemann, and they decided to let it go at that.[33] What else could they do? Apparently Stalin learned his lesson, for he did not repeat that particular gaffe.

Strange were sometimes the ways of Soviet diplomacy. Krestinskii, the "oppositionist," a Trotskyist, had to step carefully, according to Molotov, for he had no influence on Stalin. The "gentleman's agreement" had limited scope: it did not cover other party leaders in Moscow, who continued, as before, to disturb Soviet-German relations. Stalin would be more careful, but he let his temporary allies continue their verbal gesticulations.

Meanwhile, the Soviet-German trade negotiations continued into the summer of 1925. German negotiators delayed their conclusion because of European security negotiations with France and Britain which began during the winter of that year. These Anglo-French-German discussions eventually led to the Locarno Accords concluded in October establishing security guarantees on French and Belgian frontiers. As part of these agreements the Foreign Office insisted on German entry into the League in order to calm Polish security fears. Stresemann reckoned that Britain wanted to free itself from continental "complications" and prevent a German-Soviet rapprochement. Litvinov feared that Germany would become "an obedient tool of British diplomacy." The NKID thus continued to discourage German entry into the League, for "logically" this would lead to eventual German integration into "an alliance of great powers of the Entente against the USSR." Stresemann was honest about his intentions: he wanted to maintain a "balance between East and West."[34]

Gustav Stresemann

Stresemann played an important role in German foreign policy in the 1920s. Born in 1878, he descended from a lower-middle-class Berlin family. His father was a beer distiller and tavern owner, well off enough to see that his son was educated at gymnasium and the University of Berlin. Stresemann

Figure 5.4. Gustav Stresemann, ca. 1925–1929. *Bundesarchiv* **(Federal Archives of Germany),** *Bild* **146-1989-040-27.**

must have inherited his father's physique, for he was burly and thick necked in appearance and looked as though he could easily handle the beer kegs in the family tavern. He was not tall but stood out in a crowd because of a bald, cannonball head and riveting eyes that seemed to jump out at contemporary photographers. He was said to be the spitting image of a stiff-necked Prussian, though his father was a Berlin innkeeper. In his student days Stresemann was a rowdy fellow who liked drinking and dueling. Later in life he retained a certain *joie de vivre* and sense of humor.

Taking up politics in the years before the war, Stresemann was elected to the Reichstag, the German legislative assembly. During the war Stresemann was a hard-line nationalist and a proponent of German expansionist war aims and unrestricted submarine warfare. The only thing he admired about France was Napoleon. He supported and participated in negotiations with the Soviet government after Brest-Litovsk in March 1918 to obtain economic resources and to secure Germany's eastern frontiers. Only a few months later the German government had to sue for peace. Military defeat and the fall of the monarchy surprised and shocked Stresemann like many other Germans. A center-right nationalist, he wanted to restore Germany's military strength

Figure 5.5. David Low cartoon, LSE7466, "The Good Fairies of 1927," *The Star*, 30 December 1926. British Cartoon Archive.

and place in the world, not exactly the type of politician one would expect to win the Nobel Peace Prize in 1926 along with Austen Chamberlain and Aristide Briand, who was again French foreign minister. Cartoonist David Low portrays the Nobel trio as "the Good Fairies," dressed in tutus with doves perched over their heads.[35] There were officials at the Auswärtiges Amt both enthusiastic and not about the Rapallo orientation. Stresemann sought a balance between them to gain leverage over France and Britain.

Peace prize or not, Stresemann's strategic objectives remained unchanged: he sought to end the Allied occupation of the Rhineland and to obtain more favorable terms for the payment of post-war reparations before seeking their abolition altogether. To achieve these objectives he had to come to terms with Britain and France. Rapallo was a trump in his game. He would give up some closeness with the Soviet Union—although there was precious little of it—in order to obtain Anglo-French concessions. In dealing with Briand and Chamberlain, Stresemann's essential strength came from his effective articulation of the case for treaty revision, supported by most Germans.[36] Briand

Figure 5.6. David Low cartoon, LSE7305, "The Clasp of Friendship (French version)," *The Star*, 8 September 1925. British Cartoon Archive.

of course was no sentimentalist and remained on his guard against Germany; few French citizens did otherwise. Low captures French mistrust in a cartoon where the Nobel trio are shaking hands over the Locarno pact, but Briand keeps his left hand behind his back sheathed in a large boxing glove.[37]

"What Are They Thinking in These Countries?"

In June 1925 Litvinov went to Berlin to talk about Rapallo. Stresemann reckoned that the Entente "no longer existed," that France and Britain were moving apart, that the Italian fascist Benito Mussolini was pursuing an independent policy, and that the USSR had nothing to fear from German entry into the League. "Our main enemy," said Stresemann, meaning Germany *and* the USSR, "is France, not England." We want good relations with the USSR, he added, in spite of communist agitation in Germany and the dubious relationship of the Comintern with the Soviet government.

Apparently ignoring Stresemann's habitual reference to the Comintern, Litvinov responded that differences in Anglo-French interests did not stop France from occupying the Ruhr, and that Britain had not and would not break with France. The strengthening of Germany or France went against British interests; any minor British support for Germany could only be "purchased for the price of submission to British dictates." Nor was Litvinov above waving the French bogey: France and Poland, fearing an Anglo-German rapprochement, would turn to the USSR for support. This might be "a temptation" for us to avoid isolation in Europe. In the back of Litvinov's mind remained anxiety about an anti-Soviet "united front."[38] Each side, German and Soviet, was trying to keep the other honest: Germany with Britain and the USSR with France.

There were limits to how far the Politburo would go in pursuing better relations with Germany. Chicherin proposed an official note of congratulations to Marshal Paul von Hindenburg, the former chief of the German general staff, upon his election as president in the spring of 1925. It was purely a diplomatic formality, according to Chicherin, which in no way would "reinforce fascist prestige." Unconvinced, the Politburo rejected Chicherin's proposal.[39]

Meanwhile, Litvinov complained to Chicherin about the incoherence of the political editorials in *Izvestiia*: in one article saying that France and Britain were in conflict, that France was headed toward a major diplomatic defeat as a result of security negotiations in Geneva, and that Germany should pursue a British orientation. Litvinov had just seen Stresemann and argued against such a policy. It's a good thing, Litvinov observed to Chicherin, that Stresemann was unaware of the *Izvestiia* editorial, for he could have used it against my own arguments and "put me in a very stupid position." And then the following day *Izvestiia* published another editorial contradicting the previous one, emphasizing Anglo-French solidarity and Germany's need to keep a free hand in the east against Poland and so on, just the arguments I used with Stresemann, Litvinov said.

Litvinov reckoned the first article was intended to demonstrate the necessity of a French rapprochement with the USSR. But what was the author thinking? We need to secure our position with Germany *first*; we can worry about France later. It's enough to worry about today's problems; let's cross other bridges when we come to them. Litvinov's key complaint went beyond contradictory editorials in *Izvestiia*.

What are they thinking in these countries about our Central Authorities? Can there be some coordination between editorials from one day to the next? And more importantly, can there be coordination between the Central Authorities, our foreign policy, and the efforts of the NKID? We need to do something so that similar mishaps do not reoccur.[40]

Jean Herbette

While Soviet-German trade negotiations dragged on during the summer of 1925, the NKID focused on relations with France, the more so since German-Soviet relations continued to be strained. With Herriot afraid of an eventual German *revanche* and Germany flirting with Britain, the time was as good as any, in spite of the flare-up of anti-communism in Paris, to explore the possibilities of better Franco-Soviet relations. Herriot's ideas were carried to Moscow by the new French ambassador, Jean Herbette, a well-known journalist and commentator on foreign policy who had written some of the editorials in *Le Temps* in support of a Franco-Soviet rapprochement.

Born in 1878, Jean was the son of a *préfet* and *conseiller d'État*, and thus descended from a family of the French *grande bourgeoisie*. His uncle Jules Herbette was the French ambassador in Berlin during the 1880s and 1890s. He studied in Germany and at the *Université de Paris* and completed a doctorate in the hard sciences. Instead of pursuing a career as a scientist or university researcher, he turned to journalism. During the war he was a journalist at the right-wing daily *Écho de Paris* before moving to the more prestigious "semi-official" *Le Temps* in 1918. He had good political connections including with

Figure 5.7. Jean Herbette, Paris, ca. 1924. *Agence Meurisse. Bibliothèque nationale de France.*

Poincaré. According to the British ambassador in Paris, Herbette was "generally considered to be one of the most moderate and best informed of French journalists." He was someone who believed in recognizing what existed. Herriot named him ambassador in Moscow without any diplomatic experience, no doubt because he supported the policy of recognition. Readers may wonder whether the new envoy received any part of the money paid over to *Le Temps* in Soviet "allowances." Rakovskii was convinced that he did not.[41]

The Moscow post was first offered to Monzie who had larger ambitions in Paris and refused it. Apparently Herbette also wanted to turn it down, but his wife, Jeanne, ambitious for him to enter the diplomatic service, succeeded in persuading him to change his mind. According to gossip in Paris, Jeanne was the "mistress" of Jean's cousin Maurice, French ambassador in Brussels. She was a dancer at the *ballet de l'Opéra*. Jean fell in love with her, promised her marriage, and stole her away from Maurice. Becoming "the subject of a somewhat acrimonious dispute," the two cousins had not spoken to each other since. Well, at least this was the account circulated by the British embassy in Paris.[42]

In London, the permanent undersecretary did not share Lord Crewe's opinion of Herbette and did not approve of his appointment to Moscow. "Although his versatility was well known to me," Crowe informed the French chargé d'affaires, "I could only say that his blatant advocacy of everything anti-British in the columns of the 'Temps' for years had marked him indelibly as an element of definite hostility towards Britain."[43] The Quai d'Orsay normally took this sort of Foreign Office remark with a grain of salt. *Les Anglais* always groused when French diplomats did not do as London thought best.

Franco-Soviet Relations in 1925

Herbette arrived in Moscow in January 1925 and made the rounds of Soviet officials, including Chicherin and Litvinov. The Soviet government, Herbette advised Paris, was anxious for better relations, but concerned by the anti-communist press campaign in Paris, and doubtful of the prospects for improved relations. This assessment accurately reflected the mood of Chicherin, Litvinov, and others in Moscow. The press clamor will pass, Herbette told his interlocutors, but the Soviet government needed to do something about the Comintern which riled French public opinion.

Litvinov commented that the French position was illogical. "On the one hand, you demand a full separation between the Comintern and the Soviet government, which in fact we maintain, and on the other hand, you insist that we intervene, as a government, in the business of foreign communist parties, that we restrain them from demonstrations, and so on." This was true, but also a rhetorical diversion.

Not offended, Herbette also observed that a debts settlement was vital. To which Chicherin replied that no settlement was possible without credits in return.[44] Readers will have heard these lines many times now. Would the outcome in Paris be any different?

Soviet officials were skeptical, but there were also German considerations to keep in mind. Chicherin reckoned that a French trump in Soviet hands would act as "a salutary fear" in Berlin in the form of a possible "Franco-Russian alliance." The Germans, he noted, Rantzau and Stresemann, for example, were very sensitive to this possibility. This observation was quite true: Herbette's arrival in Moscow made Rantzau uncomfortable for he feared that Germany might miss the boat in consolidating its relations with the USSR.[45] The game was still the same. From Moscow to London, everyone played musical chairs; the big question was who was going to be left standing when the music ended.

In response to these early discussions in Moscow, Herriot replied frankly both to Herbette and to Krasin that he was up against opposition on all sides, and that concessions to Moscow would bring down his government.[46] Herbette was more optimistic, as newly arrived ambassadors often are. Peace in Europe could not be assured without breaking up the German-Soviet relationship, consummated in the Rapallo Treaty. To achieve this objective, France had to demonstrate to the USSR that it foresaw a "legitimate" Soviet role in Europe and that it did not seek to exclude Russia from European affairs. "This is exactly my view," Herriot scribbled on Herbette's report.[47]

If Herriot was convinced, it hardly mattered, because he fell from power in April 1925. Herbette kept up the argument with Briand, Herriot's successor as foreign minister, repeatedly making the case that France needed Russia as an eastern counterweight against Germany. If the USSR industrialized and rebuilt on its own, or with the help of France's adversaries, the Soviet government would have no reason to respect French interests in time of crisis. Some Soviet officials feared isolation and wanted "friends," but this situation would not last indefinitely if France failed to respond. Good relations with the USSR, said Herbette, were an important factor in French security on the Rhine border with Germany.[48] In a personal letter to Herriot a few months after the fall of his government, Herbette praised his political courage in recognizing the Soviet government: "You reopened a door through which the destiny of France must pass, or risk mortal peril for its integrity and its independence."[49]

These were prophetic words. Unfortunately, ambassadors can only convey information and offer opinions; they rarely influence policy. In France, as elsewhere, politics trumped an ambassador's common sense. Moreover, like the Foreign Office and the State Department, the Quai d'Orsay was a nest of opposition to better relations with Moscow.

Herbette Is Enthusiastic but Not the Quai d'Orsay

Even before Herriot lost power in April 1925, Quai d'Orsay officials challenged Herbette's policy recommendations. He had been in Moscow less than three months. According to the Quai d'Orsay assessment, overly friendly Franco-Soviet relations would arouse Polish and Romanian anxieties, thus incidentally echoing Stalin's sharp comments to Chicherin two years before.[50] The Soviet Union was not "stable enough" to provide a "serious counterweight" to Germany; for the time being, Poland was the "stronger element of force." Even if the French government ignored Comintern propaganda, these other considerations would impede practical cooperation with the USSR. Moreover, "our relations with England must . . . induce us to maintain a certain reserve in our relations with the Soviet government." The return to power of the Conservatives, their refusal to ratify the Anglo-Soviet treaty, and their concerns about Soviet propaganda, all these considerations dictated prudence. "At a time when we are engaged in difficult negotiations . . . with London on security issues, we risk arousing its mistrust if we give the impression of seeking support in Moscow." France might at times be obliged to pursue policies in contradiction with those of the Foreign Office, but French relations with Moscow should not be one of them. The risk involved would be greater than any gain to be made. France should maintain a reserved attitude toward the Soviet Union, neither overly cordial nor excessively hostile. When Russia regained its power, the French government could then reexamine the situation.[51] It was ever to be so during the inter-war years that France permitted Britain and Poland to be obstacles to better Franco-Soviet relations, even as the USSR developed into a great economic and military power during the 1930s.

When Herbette arrived in Moscow in January 1925, the Soviet government was not prepared to discuss detailed proposals, and Stalin therefore asked for NKID recommendations on relations with France. Here was another sign that Stalin was directing business and was preoccupied with foreign policy, and that the NKID was providing policy advice to the Politburo. Litvinov was dubious about a debts settlement with France. If we recognize the French debt, then we will also have to settle with Britain, the United States, and others. There was no possibility whatsoever of a loan in France as a quid pro quo. Nor was there any likelihood of obtaining one elsewhere. This sounded like Litvinov's reasoning prior to Genoa. The only argument that could therefore be made in support of a debts settlement was that it would remove one of the greatest obstacles to a normalization of relations with the West, reduce anti-Soviet hostility in Western Europe, and *maybe* prepare the ground for loans and credits in the future. When Krasin raised the possibility of a French loan, Litvinov responded irritably that of course the Soviet government wanted foreign loans and would pursue such possibilities even where there was only the slightest chance of success. But let's be realistic and not tilt at windmills, he said: a country (i.e., France) which cannot pay its own debts to Britain and the United States is hardly in a position to loan to the Soviet Union. Can you imagine the scandal in London and Washington?[52]

There was also the problem of the Comintern, to which the recent fiasco in Germany had brought renewed attention. Litvinov directed Krasin to exercise extreme care in embassy relations with French communists, labor unions, even with personal friends.

> Communists of all countries have a tendency . . . to advertise their extraordinary knowledge of our affairs and intentions. You must restrain our French friends from such demonstrations. Everywhere and by every means we earnestly proclaim the absence of ties between the Soviet government and the Comintern, but foreign communists . . . call out from rooftops their intimate proximity to the Soviet government and especially to the Narkomindel.

The French bristle when local communists portray themselves as representatives of the Soviet government. "We have to keep this mind," Litvinov noted, "especially now, when the Comintern has become a 'bull's-eye' for all governments." As if Krasin was unaware: he suggested that it was in Moscow where something needed to be done about the Comintern.[53] NKID problems with the Comintern were not unknown in the West and caught the attention of a Foreign Office clerk: "The Soviet Government is . . . beginning to feel that the Communist International—in so far as it is connected with the Government—is more trouble than it is worth."[54]

Chicherin and Litvinov complained in an unusual jointly signed letter to the Politburo that candidates proposed by the NKID for the Paris embassy had all been rejected. Not one person actually sent to Paris has a clue about diplomacy or NKID protocols. The Paris embassy became a kind of laughing stock as news of its problems spread among Soviet establishments abroad. "Over specialized bunglers" had been sent to France, wrote one Soviet colleague. "From top to bottom," Litvinov confirmed.[55]

The Politburo apparently missed the memoranda from Litvinov and Chicherin about the importance of relations with France, though there were changes of key personnel in Paris in the spring of 1925. As events would demonstrate, it was much easier to change diplomats in the Soviet embassy in Paris than it was to develop a policy toward France or to deal with the Comintern issue. In April 1925 Painlevé succeeded Herriot as premier, but as favorable as Painlevé might have been to better Franco-Soviet relations, he could do no more than Herriot to advance them. The French government, observed Litvinov, continued to pursue a policy of delaying negotiations.[56]

Anatole de Monzie

There were other difficulties. Monzie, the chief French negotiator, and Krasin did not see eye to eye. During the negotiations over recognition, Monzie indicated his distaste for the choice of Krasin as Soviet ambassador. Anyone but him, Monzie pleaded. Krasin reciprocated, complaining repeatedly about Monzie, an oily politician, whose main interest was his own ambitions. He wanted to be president of the Republic, though he might have to settle for finance minister. The man is dangerous, said Krasin, because of his political position and influence and because he could not be bought at any price the Soviet government could afford to pay.[57]

Monzie was in fact not much different from the typical French politician of his generation. Born in 1876 to a family of the French bourgeoisie—his father was a tax collector—he was a good student and well educated, eventually studying law. He practiced briefly and acted on Rakovskii's behalf when the latter applied unsuccessfully for French citizenship in the early 1900s. It was at this time that the two future interlocutors became acquainted. Some said he and Rakovskii were "friends," but it is difficult to imagine Monzie with many friends. Very ambitious, he passed quickly from the law into local then national politics and was elected to the Chamber of Deputies for the first time in 1909. He held to the center-right in French politics, though he moved further right as the inter-war years unfolded. While Monzie had an interest in Franco-Soviet relations in the 1920s, he drifted into appeasement in the 1930s, like many others of his political inclinations, and invested his hopes for French security in fascist Italy. It proved a poor political option.

In 1920 Monzie entered the Senate, and from the mid-1920s until 1940 he was many times a cabinet minister. He took an interest in the reestablishment of French diplomatic relations with the USSR, not so much as a counterweight to Germany but to generate foreign trade for French industry. Monzie met Chicherin three times in the early 1920s, and Herriot made use of him as a go-between with Soviet diplomats in London in the lead-up to French recognition in October 1924.

Krasin and Monzie should have gotten along in view of their common interest in developing Franco-Soviet trade relations, but this did not happen. Litvinov would have to encourage Krasin to overcome his deep aversion for his French counterpart. No one in the NKID had any illusions about Monzie, as Litvinov admitted, but he was influential and could "seriously hurt us" if he chose to do so. We have to deal with him and handle him carefully, Litvinov advised the Politburo: later, we can try to have him replaced by someone more amenable. This would have to be done carefully and secretly, "maintaining outwardly for as long as necessary the friendliest of relations with him and even courting him."[58]

Bear up was the message sent to Krasin; find a way forward. Monzie is a "very cunning and hardened politician and *kupets*," observed Chicherin; he is deliberately aggressive and intimidating. He's on the lookout for big concessions, the profits of which would go to pay off bondholders. When I replied that these profits would not be nearly enough given the huge size of French claims, Monzie was not discouraged. "French bondholders," he replied, "had descended to such a level of despair that a French politician who brought them even a few centimes on the franc would become the most popular man in France." So Chicherin agreed with Krasin's assessment of a "powerful, rising political figure, in big-time politics with big ambitions."

"In my opinion his words are the key to his view of the Russian question," Chicherin noted. Monzie is a representative of the business class. He's not a "pure blooded Radical of the Herriot type"; he's a broker and advocate, not a businessman himself.[59]

Krasin did his best with Monzie, but his frustration mounted: "I am forming the opinion that Monzie is simply not normal." He is talented, but not overburdened with scruples. "No one can understand what he truly wants and what aims he sets for himself." In March 1925 Krasin reported that Monzie was trying to topple Herriot; he expected to be named finance minister (which he obtained in the last week of the Herriot ministry, but lost in the following Painlevé cabinet, having to settle for a less influential post).[60]

One never knew with Monzie. As a government minister in the Painlevé cabinet, he attended the opening of the Soviet pavilion at the exhibition of decorative arts in Paris, but instead of the usual polite remarks, he rounded on the Soviet Union. Afterward, Monzie became "hysterical" when people in the crowd shouted "*Vive les Soviets*" and "*Vive l'ambassadeur des Soviets.*"

"This is a political demonstration," Monzie sputtered.

Krasin tried to reason with "the deranged minister," and just as things began to calm down there was a further provocation when schoolboys began to sing the *Internationale*. It was all "very strange," reported Krasin; even from the French side, "I received apologies and expressions of regret."

Krasin thought there was little chance of getting on better terms with Monzie: he's like a goat from which "we will never get milk." Like many western advocates of better relations with the Soviet Union, Monzie's motives were driven by personal economic gain. "For six months we have been accumulating a rich material on the many-sided interests of Monzie in the

Figure 5.8. Anatole de Monzie, Paris, 1925. *Agence Meurisse. Bibliothèque nationale de France.*

Russian question." Basically it has to be Monzie's way: his plans, his bank, his agents. Isn't it time "to stop fooling around with him?"[61]

Better half an enemy, replied Chicherin, than a whole one. "The question of Monzie is nothing new for us." He's influential and combines hostility and friendliness toward the Soviet Union. This is not ideal, Chicherin admitted, but we can't get rid of him. "Thus, we have always believed that we must follow a careful line, not trusting him, striving to use him as much as possible, even in times of setbacks, and trying to find with him a line of compromise." We have to be "extraordinarily subtle and careful" with Monzie. "In general, black-and-white methods in human relations will only result in losing all our supporters."[62] On this point Chicherin and Litvinov were of one mind.

Although Krasin met with Painlevé, Briand, and others in the new cabinet after the fall of Herriot's government, he made little progress, for the French still did not want to begin serious negotiations. As always, Krasin thought the best way forward was to develop profitable trade links *before* dealing with the debts question. This would lessen anti-communist animosities. Increased "allowances" to the Paris press would also help. Bribe the bastards, was Krasin's view: "We should increase our expenditures five- or tenfold."[63]

Even generous Soviet "allowances" could not stimulate French interest in Moscow, and a frustrated Krasin made little progress. In 1925 French diplomacy was focused on Berlin and security through conciliation of Germany and on the conclusion of the Locarno Accords. This settlement appeared to assure French security on the Rhine, but it worried Krasin who thought it would end French interest in better relations with the USSR.[64] On the other hand, Herbette saw Locarno and worsening Anglo-Soviet relations as a French opportunity, since the Soviet government appeared anxious to conclude political and economic agreements. Anxious up to a point, Herbette said, and he warned against trying to drive too hard a bargain. Moscow would not settle at any price.[65] Aware that he was receiving a skeptical hearing in Paris, Herbette joked at a diplomatic dinner in May 1925 that the Quai d'Orsay considered him to be a Bolshevik.[66] Readers should not worry: he was far from it.

Even before the fall of Herriot, or in spite of him, the Quai d'Orsay civil servants had decided to put Franco-Soviet relations on the back burner. The NKID did not know this, of course, and during the spring and summer of 1925 Litvinov expressed his impatience with the slow pace of Franco-Soviet discussions. He wanted results in order to give the NKID a trump to play in Berlin.[67]

Philippe Berthelot

There were still problems. There were *always* problems in Paris. As readers will remember, Herriot's successor, Painlevé, was favorably disposed to better Franco-Soviet relations. But his government could collapse at any moment, and so caution was the watchword. Briand, as the new foreign minister, brought back with him Philippe Berthelot, who had previously been his right arm at the Quai d'Orsay. Berthelot was an influential civil servant and secretary general in the foreign ministry before his resignation in December 1921 after being publicly linked to a notorious bank scandal. But all scandals came to an end in Paris, especially during the "decadent" inter-war years when they were routine occurrences. In the pages of the French yellow press, old scandals had to give way to new ones, and after all, a man's career should not be forever damaged by mere peccadilloes or transient misfortune. Briand supported Berthelot through thick and thin. When a critic in the Chamber of Deputies pointed out that a British newspaper had called Berthelot "the real minister of foreign affairs," Briand brushed it off. "I am philosophical," he replied placidly. "I've seen far worse than that."[68]

Born in 1866, Berthelot was the son of Marcellin Berthelot, the French chemist and politician who was minister of foreign affairs in 1895–1896. Philippe thus descended from the highest levels of the French *grande bourgeoisie*. Marcellin had big ambitions for his son, who enrolled in the Sorbonne to study literature and law. An *enfant terrible* rather than a brilliant student, Philippe preferred the bistros of the Latin Quarter to his studies at the Sor-

Figure 5.9. Philippe Berthelot, Paris, ca. 1932.
Agence Meurisse. Bibliothèque nationale de France.

bonne. When he took the foreign service exams to enter the Quai d'Orsay, he got a bare pass, thanks to his father's influence, and was sent off to the lowest of low positions in the French embassy in Lisbon. When Marcellin became foreign minister, he promoted his son to a career-track position.

Philippe did not disappoint his father, for he abandoned his youthful extravagances and rose quickly through the ranks to become a dominant influence in the Quai d'Orsay on the eve of World War I. He was the master of all the important ministry files; his handwritten memoranda and marginal notes can be found everywhere in the Quai d'Orsay archives. He was not the foreign minister, but he was the man behind the minister, the *éminence grise*, who directed French foreign policy behind the scenes. Foreign diplomats in Paris saw him as a kind of evil genius and *bête noire*, always working against their respective governments' interests. They would say he was anti-British or anti-Italian, but he would reply with a wry smile that he was merely pro-French.

He made an exception when it came to Soviet Russia. After the Bolshevik seizure of power in November 1917, Berthelot sabotaged the movement to cooperate with the new Soviet government against Germany, and both Krasin and Litvinov worried that he might try again to undermine Franco-Soviet relations. Ironically, Chicherin came to view Berthelot as an "adept Poincaré." Litvinov said that he represented the Anglophile wing in the Quai d'Orsay. Berthelot was no longer the feral anti-Bolshevik he once had been; Krasin found him to be straightforward and friendly. On concrete issues, however, Berthelot made few concessions. How could he? The atmosphere in Paris was still rotten; anti-communism festered. "Reaction in Europe and everywhere" is growing stronger, warned Krasin, and preparing a new offensive.[69]

Aristide Briand

Briand was also friendly with Krasin, but equally difficult to pin down. If Berthelot represented the tenebrous side of French policy, Briand was its brighter face. In the bad cop, good cop routine of French diplomacy, Briand was everyone's friend or nearly so. Born in 1862 and four years older than Berthelot, Briand descended from a family of the *petite bourgeoisie*. His parents owned a café first in a working-class quarter of Nantes on the French Atlantic coast, and then in nearby Saint-Nazaire. His father wanted him to come into the business; his mother wanted him to get an education. His mother won the argument. Briand studied law.

Aristide was a talented student, unlike his amanuensis Berthelot. Like many students of his generation, Briand was attracted to the bohemian lifestyle of the Latin Quarter. He grew an enormous black walrus moustache in the style of the day, which women apparently found highly attractive. Like Lloyd George, he enjoyed the company of the opposite sex and drew their attentions. Too much so, for he took up with a married woman, eventually creating a public scandal, which his political adversaries did not let him forget even 30 years later. Who would have thought that such powerful diplomats and politicians could be rowdies and womanizers during their student days . . . and even after? Briand kept the walrus moustache, which eventually grayed and thinned over time; it was part of his public persona, like Lloyd George's pince-nez. He became stooped with age and dressed carelessly. When Stresemann met him for the first time, he was relieved. Briand reminded him of one of those "bohemians" discoursing late into the night around a Berlin café table with a small circle of friends. So this is the man who represents the great power of France, Stresemann thought, laughing to himself and liking the lack of pretense.

Briand became involved in local, then national politics. In 1902 he first won election to the Chamber of Deputies as a socialist. He was a co-founder of the socialist, then communist paper *L'Humanité* and had close ties with the socialist leader Jean Jaurès, assassinated in 1914 on the eve of the First World War. Briand quickly moved to the political center, however, and became a government minister for the first time in 1906 and *président du conseil*, or premier, in 1909. He was 11 times premier, 20 times a minister, often at the Quai d'Orsay. He held the portfolio of minister of foreign affairs between 1925 and 1932 when he died. In French politics, that was almost an eternity. Briand became the *grand artiste*, the maestro of French foreign policy. During this long period of government activity, he got the reputation as a politician who read nothing but understood everything. He did not read or monitor his files in the way that Berthelot did, which is why he had need of such a collaborator. Berthelot "is irreplaceable," Briand said one day. "He saves me time. In ten minutes he can summarize a situation which others would take three hours to muddle." One critic joked that that Berthelot was Briand's "dictionary."[70]

If Berthelot's hand may be found in all the important Quai d'Orsay files, Briand's is rarely seen. Everyone knew that he had an aversion to paperwork. According to Krasin, Briand confined himself to discussions and listening to reports; he was "a well-intentioned and charming lazybones, who has papers neither in his desk nor on it." He is likeable on a personal level, reported

Figure 5.10. Aristide Briand, ca. 1930. Granger Collection, NY.

Krasin, but I can't "get any sense out of him. It is not that he is antagonistic to the USSR . . . but that he plainly cannot internalize and understand the political importance of a rapprochement between France and the USSR . . . he builds all his policies on the English orientation. Working with Berthelot only strengthens him in this Anglophile direction."[71]

France was not its own boss, Krasin reported: it was nearly bankrupt and the franc under constant pressure on foreign exchange markets. The French government therefore had to make concessions to Britain and the United States. They were hostile to us, Krasin observed, and France would thus avoid any agreements with the USSR which would offend them. Moreover, while Briand sought to smooth out day-to-day difficulties, the clerks at the Quai d'Orsay were "our enemies to the last man."[72] This was a *slight* exaggeration.

Krasin nevertheless lobbied Painlevé, among others, to advance his projects. He proposed to Moscow a debts settlement based on ten centimes to the paper franc, about what the tsarist bonds were worth on the Paris Bourse. Herbette advised Chicherin that Krasin should cultivate relations with Painlevé who "had cursed [Herriot] for his evasiveness on the Russian question." Painlevé was just as evasive, but then so was Moscow: the Politburo favored an active policy toward France but had not yet approved a detailed agenda.[73]

The "Distant Princess"

French government policy drifted between casual interest in Soviet overtures and hostile acts which would have confirmed the worst Soviet suspicions. Chicherin called it the policy of the "distant princess," who would permit the Soviet government to offer her gifts, "but who refuses obstinately to acknowledge them."[74] On 10 July Briand signaled to Herbette that Soviet fears of a "Holy alliance against Bolshevism" were "a morbid exaggeration"; on 31 July Briand authorized discussions with the British government about the formation of an Anglo-Franco-American embargo against Soviet oil exports. No one would be able to obtain "regular and advantageous contracts," reckoned the Quai d'Orsay, without a common oil policy toward the Soviet Union. And the money raised through Soviet oil exports would be used "solely" to fund "dangerous" Bolshevik propaganda. In another tribute to Soviet informants, Krasin heard of these intrigues almost immediately.[75]

On Krasin's offer of ten centimes, matters came to a head at the end of August. Briand called in Krasin to apologize for an incident in which Krasin and his family had been abused by anti-communist hooligans. Krasin ran through his proposals with Briand, who appeared willing to accept them as a basis of discussion. The next day he saw Berthelot, who wanted to slow things down.

Give me some straight answers, Krasin said to Berthelot.

I'll get back to you, Berthelot replied.

Krasin had no illusions. Briand's word had only relative value. One joker said that you could not believe even the *opposite* of what Briand said. Others continued to think that Berthelot was the real minister of foreign affairs. This was not true. Briand handled cabinet politics and his counterparts abroad, and Berthelot almost everything else. It was just as well. Krasin remarked that French ministers held their portfolios so briefly that they regarded themselves as mere visitors to the *palais* where they presided. And they feared "putting their foot in it," looking foolish before public opinion. "One also had to take into account the rivalries between these gentlemen and their willingness to kick the legs out from under one another." They all hedge and leave escape routes to be able to save face. And on this issue where our offer will only be 10 or 15 centimes on the franc, it won't bring special laurels for any government.[76]

On 1 September, Krasin gave Berthelot a formal proposal to settle the debt. It was a low offer and based in large measure on Russian assets in France, including the so-called Brest-Litovsk gold, reparations paid to Germany in 1918 by the Soviet government but sequestered by the Allies after the November Armistice. In exchange, Krasin asked for trade credits. The finance ministry rejected out of hand the Soviet offer, inter alia, on the grounds that it was too low, that credits were impossible, and that the Brest-Litovsk gold was being held as a credit against the Russian war debt.[77] In fact, the French government knew that no credits meant no deal, and that the Brest-Litovsk gold had been divided up under the table between France and Britain. It was a case, as British Treasury officials sometimes admitted, of taking the gold from Russia, and being quick about it, while deceiving former allies in the process, lest Britain "fail to get any part of the spoil." The matter could not stand publicity, as one clerk admitted: "Stone-walling seems . . . the right policy. . . . We have had the gold and used it and possession is 9/10ths (or more) of the law."[78] In other words, we stole the money fair and square.

The finance ministry rebuff was not the only reason for the flat rejection of Krasin's proposal. Berthelot gave as others high politics (*raisons de haute convenance de politique étrangère*) and the need to mitigate the anxieties of "certain powers," unnamed but including Romania and almost certainly Poland. There was an abortive attempt at face saving, an exchange of letters, but even here French officials tried to change the wording *after* Krasin had signed his letters and left Paris. Berthelot invoked high politics as the problem, but really it was low politics, French style, as Krasin had described. I have better things to do with my time, said the Soviet *polpred*, and he went back to Moscow disgusted by the French negotiations.[79]

Litvinov thought the whole business had been a dupe's game. The French government still did not want an agreement; it continued to hold out for its maximum demands, though it asked for new proposals from us. But we are not going any further, he noted, until we have something from the French side. As in London, the Soviet government would not bid against itself. The Soviet chargé d'affaires in Paris, Iakov Kh. Davtian, said that the debts problem needed to be resolved as quickly as possible, and Litvinov agreed. But even then we won't draw France out of a potential anti-Soviet coalition. There was no guarantee the French would not put up other obstacles like the indemnification of dispossessed property owners, the Comintern, or communist "propaganda." We are going to have to put more on the table, Litvinov thought, but in the meantime the Paris delegation should not move too quickly. "We must force the French to abandon their maximum demands and come partway to meeting us." Herbette, who saw Krasin on his return to Moscow, wrote to Berthelot, saying that France was missing an opportunity and that it was time to get a move on.[80]

Soviet "Allowances" for the French Press

The NKID still subsidized the Paris press but obtained little return on its investment. "We consider it necessary," Litvinov told Krasin, "to inform the Politburo about the absolutely unsatisfactory conduct of the big newspaper [i.e., Le Temps]." Its headlines condemn the Soviet Union, but then as if by inattentiveness, there is some more or less kindly notice on a back page. "If it does not change its tune, we will have to cut off our present material relations." Pay them only at the end of the month, Litvinov recommended, and only if they have conducted themselves "decently."[81]

Krasin reported that he had done as Litvinov had instructed, but still the situation was unsatisfactory. The "big newspaper" continued to be antagonistic, "although representatives of the paper, in unabashed naiveté, attempt to convince us that these hostile articles are in truth conditioned by a friendly disposition toward us, because only in this way can the newspaper preserve its authority among its readers, and without such authority even the newspaper's support would be worthless to us." Other newspapers are willing to publish positive articles on page two or three, said Krasin, but without any commitment to changing their lead editorials.[82]

Chicherin, a cautious diplomat, noted that cutting off subsidies might have unexpected consequences. It seemed that Le Temps—no resort here to oblique references—had connections to "very influential politicians, and that from this trough [of Soviet 'allowances'] are served not only asses from the newspaper, but also influential political asses." In other words a decision to cut off payments might have negative consequences far from the precincts of *Le Temps*. Chicherin was looking for reasons to continue the bribes which Litvinov, "not known for his liberality" in such matters, wanted to stop.

According to Krasin, it was wrong to say, as Litvinov had done, that there was hostile comment on page 1 but kinder notices on the back page. *Le Temps* pursued from first page to last a "determined, conscious, well thought out, deeply hostile line toward us." From the day of our arrival in Paris it has been the real leader of the anti-communist press. Of course, from time to time the paper had to publish something from the Quai d'Orsay, but in this case, "it was not from the Quai d'Orsay where originated the reservoir of venom; on the contrary, it was the newspaper's editorial board which had . . . influenced the foreign ministry." As for the other papers, apart from a few outwardly friendly articles they were "without exception tendentious and hostile." I told R., said Krasin—certainly Rollin, the shadowy Soviet go-between—that this situation could not continue. R. shrugged his shoulders, saying he was a mere intermediary.

> I am personally by no means a proponent of stinginess; on the contrary, as you know, I would sooner favor generosity. When the stakes are high, a grudging hand loses, it does not win. But here I am disgusted by the impudence of these gentlemen, who demand tribute for absolutely nothing in return excepting for . . . their very existence. . . . But for that we don't need to pay money.

Krasin suggested further "allowances" on good behavior, but he was pessimistic of success. Litvinov was torn between paying and not. "Not one government pays as generously as we do, but we certainly cannot agree to pay for abuse, as occurred for several months while arrears mounted when the newspaper did nothing but denounce us." In fact, others did pay more generously. Nevertheless, Litvinov agreed a few months later to pay off arrears to "the big newspaper," but only by increasing end-of-month payments, to retain a lever to hold it to a satisfactory editorial line.[83]

There was thus little progress in Paris in 1925 in spite of Soviet interest. Readers will rightly calculate that Moscow must have been serious about Franco-Soviet relations if the Politburo was willing to buy favorable comment in the French press with hard-earned foreign exchange. The Soviet investment was as much for its German as for its French policy. But even Soviet gold could not win over the hard-core anti-communists in Paris.

Notes

1. Krasin to NKID, report no. 4, 17 Dec. 1924, AVPRF, f. 0136, p. 105, d. 104, ll. 26–19.

2. Excerpt from Rakovskii to Litvinov, no. 17, very secret, 19 Dec. 1924, AVPRF, f. 04, o. 42, p. 261, d. 53670, ll. 59–60.

3. Chicherin to Rakovskii, no. 97, 26 Dec. 1924, AVPRF, f. 04, o. 42, p. 261, d. 53678, ll. 36–37; and Krasin to NKID, report no. 9, 1 Jan. 1925, AVPRF, f. 04, o. 42, p. 262, d. 53697, ll. 1–14.

4. Krasin to NKID, report no. 1, secret, 6 Dec. 1924, AVPRF, f. 0136, o. 7, p. 105, d. 104, ll. 8–1; and Krasin, report no. 5, 20 Dec. 1924, ibid., ll. 35–27.

5. Krasin to NKID, no. 05/9, 7 Dec. 1924, AVPRF, f. 0136, o. 7, p. 105, d. 104, ll. 14–9; and Myron Herrick to Hughes, no. 613, 30 Dec. 1924, 751.61/34, NA, M-569, reel 3.

6. Herrick, no. 4733, 7 Jan. 1925, 751.61/36, NA RG59, M-569, reel 3.

7. "Memorandum of conversation between Austen Chamberlain and Herriot . . . ," 5 Dec. 1924, N9233/44/38, FO 371 10471.

8. "Monsieur de Fleuriau, conversation," Crowe, 15 Dec. 1924, N9296/44/38, PRO FO 371 10471.

9. Litvinov to Krasin, no. 0022, secret, 10 Jan. 1925, AVPRF, f. 0136, o. 8, p. 105, d. 95, ll. 5–8; and Litvinov's *dnevnik* (journal), 26 Jan. 1925, ibid., ll. 19–23.

10. Chamberlain's minute, 19 Dec. 1924, N9371/108/38, FO 371 10480.

11. Herriot's comment in the Chamber of Deputies, 28 Jan. 1925, N550/30/38, FO 371 11012; and Wellesley's minute, 11 Feb. 1925, N672/30/38, ibid.

12. Chicherin to Krestinskii, no. 102, 12 Feb. 1924, *Moskva-Berlin*, I, p. 242.

13. Chicherin to Krestinskii, no. 97, 25 Jan. 1924, *Moskva-Berlin*, I, pp. 237–39; and "Record of conversation . . . with Rantzau . . . ," 31 Jan. 1924, ibid., pp. 239–41.

14. "Record of conversation . . . with Rantzau . . . ," 27 March 1924, *Moskva-Berlin*, I, pp. 244–47.

15. Rantzau, no. 131, secret, 23 June 1922, A₂DAP, A,VI, pp. 272–77; O'Connor, *Chicherin*, pp. 94–96; Jacobson, *Soviet Union*, passim; and Lionel Kochan, *Russia and the Weimar Republic* (Cambridge, 1954), pp. 62–63.

16. "Record of conversation of Chicherin with U. Brockdorff-Rantzau . . . ," no. 432/ChS, very secret, 2 May 1924, *Moskva-Berlin*, I, pp. 259–61.

17. Rantzau, no. 54, secret, 2 May 1924, A₂DAP, A, X, pp. 136–37.

18. Zinoviev to Politburo, 3 May 1924, *Moskva-Berlin*, I, p. 264.

19. Krestinskii to Litvinov, Chicherin, no. 473, 3 May 1924, *Moskva-Berlin*, I, pp. 262–63; and Rantzau, no. 59, urgent, 5 May 1924, A₂DAP, A, X, pp. 144–45.

20. Politburo resolution, no. 87/PB/1-s, rigorously secret, special file, 5 May 1924, *Moskva-Berlin*, I, pp. 264–65; Politburo resolution, no. 89 P/1, rigorously secret, 12 May 1924, ibid., pp. 266–67; Stresemann to Carl Severing, Prussian interior minister, no. 65, personal, 6 May 1924, A₂DAP, A, X, pp. 162–63; and Chicherin to Litvinov, no. 526/ChS, ccs. to Stalin et al., 24 May 1924, *Moskva-Berlin*, I, pp. 270–71.

21. Stresemann to Rantzau, no. 71, urgent, 7 May 1924, and no. 73, urgent, 8 May 1924, A₂DAP, A, X, pp. 179–81, 183–84; and Stresemann to Rantzau, no. 79, 13 May 1924, ibid., pp. 196–98.

22. B. S. Stomoniakov to Politburo, no. M31, very secret, 6 June 1924, *Moskva-Berlin*, I, pp. 294–98.

23. Chicherin to Politburo, no. 702/ChS, 19 June 1924, *Moskva-Berlin*, I, pp. 314–17.

24. Stresemann to Rantzau, no. 107, urgent, 27 May 1924, A₂DAP, A, X, pp. 260–62; and Chicherin to Politburo, no. 724/ChS, not later than 27 June 1924, *Moskva-Berlin*, I, p. 327.

25. Litvinov (Berlin) to Chicherin, cc. to Politburo et al., 27 June 1924, *Moskva-Berlin*, I, pp. 330–33.

26. Litvinov to Politburo, no. 0430, secret, 14 Oct. 1924, *Moskva-Berlin*, I, pp. 370–73.

27. Chicherin to Politburo et al., no. 1255/ChS, 6 Oct. 1924, *Moskva-Berlin*, I, pp. 362–66.

28. Litvinov to Politburo, no. 0430, secret, 14 Oct. 1924, *Moskva-Berlin*, I, pp. 370–73.

29. Stresemann's note, no. 129, 29 Oct. 1924, *AzDAP*, A, XI, pp. 317–20; and "Record of conversation . . . with Rantzau," no. 1360/ChS, Chicherin, 3 Nov. 1924, *Moskva-Berlin*, I, pp. 400–403.

30. "Record of conversation . . . with Rantzau," 4 Dec. 1924, *Moskva-Berlin*, I, pp. 435–37.

31. Krestinskii to Litvinov, cc. Chicherin, no. 1371, 16 Dec. 1924, *Moskva-Berlin*, I, pp. 444–46.

32. "Litvinov's theses for a report on economic and political relations of the USSR with Germany," not later than 31 Dec. 1924, *Moskva-Berlin*, I, pp. 448–53; Litvinov to K. K. Iurenev, Soviet *polpred* in Rome, no. 0125, 20 Feb. 1925, AVPRF, f. 082, o. 8, p. 18, d. 2, ll. 9–10; and Rantzau, no. 34, 17 Jan. 1925, and no. 253, very secret, 13 April 1925, *AzDAP*, A, XII, pp. 78–79, 656–57.

33. Schubert to Stresemann, Rantzau, et al., no. 8, 8 Jan. 1925, and Schubert's marginalia, *AzDAP*, A, XII, pp. 18–19.

34. Litvinov to Krestinskii, no. 0266, secret, 8 April 1925, AVPRF, f. 082, o. 8, p. 18, d. 2, ll. 63–70 (with enclosures, published in *Moskva-Berlin*, I, pp. 487–504); Litvinov to Politburo, no. 0352, secret, 13 May 1925, AVPRF, f. 82, o. 8, p. 18, d. 2, ll. 52–54 (and draft memorandum, published in *Moskva-Berlin*, I, pp. 516–70); and "Record of conversation of G. V. Chicherin with the acting German chargé d'affaires . . . ," no. 626/ChS, very secret, 27 May 1925, *Moskva-Berlin*, I, pp. 534–38.

35. "The Good Fairies of 1927," *The Star*, 30 Dec. 1926, British Cartoon Archive.

36. Jon Jacobson, *Locarno Diplomacy: Germany and the West, 1925–1929* (Princeton, N.J., 1972), pp. 71–72.

37. "The Clasp of Friendship (French version)," *The Star*, 8 Sept. 1925, British Cartoon Archive.

38. Litvinov (Berlin) to NKID, nos. 3994–95, very secret, 14 June 1925, *Moskva-Berlin*, I, pp. 541–42; Litvinov (Prague) to Chicherin, nos. 4041, 4043, very secret, 15 June 1925, ibid., p. 543; and Stresemann's note, no. 118, 13 June 1925, *AzDAP*, A, XIII, pp. 319–24.

39. Chicherin to Politburo, no. 509/ChS, 14 May 1925, *Moskva-Berlin*, I, pp. 520–21; and Politburo resolution, no. P63/1-s, rigorously secret, 15 May 1925, ibid., p. 521.

40. Litvinov (Marienbad) to Chicherin, no. 5/M/129/s, secret, 18 June 1925, AVPRF, f. 082, o. 8, p. 18, d. 2, ll. 82–83.

41. Rakovskii to Litvinov, 13 Nov. 1924, AVPRF, f. 04, o. 4, p. 26, d. 373, ll. 78–79.

42. Crewe, no. 2404, 4 Nov. 1924, N . . . /44/38, FO 371 10471; and Charles Mendl, British press attaché in Paris, to Tyrrell, 30 Oct. 1924, FO 800 220, ff. 91–103.

43. "Note by Sir E. Crowe," 5 Nov. 1924, *DBFP*, 1st, XXV, pp. 429–31.

44. Record of conversation between Herbette and Chicherin, 11 Jan. 1925, *DVP*, VIII, pp. 39–45; Herbette, nos. 2–7, 12 Jan. 1925, MAÉ Russie/357, ff. 124–29; and Litvinov's *dnevnik*, 12 Jan. 1925, AVPRF, f. 0136, o. 8, p. 105, d. 96, ll. 8–10.

45. Chicherin to Politburo et al., no. 105/ChS, 29 Jan. 1925, *Moskva-Berlin*, I, pp. 469–70; and Rantzau, no. 10, very urgent, very secret, 8 Jan. 1925, *AzDAP*, A, XII, p. 19, n. 3.

46. Herriot to Herbette, nos. 18–20, 25 Jan. 1925, MAÉ Russie/357, ff. 175–77; Krasin to Narkomindel, 16 March 1925, *DVP*, VIII, pp. 183–86; and Krasin to Narkomindel, 23 March 1925, ibid., pp. 189–91.

47. Herbette, no. 35, 26 March 1925, MAÉ Russie/141, ff. 54–58; and Herbette to Berthelot, secretary general, Quai d'Orsay, 25 Sept. 1925, ibid., ff. 123–28.

48. Herbette, nos. 318–22, 20 April 1925, MAÉ Russie/358, ff. 68–72; and Herbette, nos. 490–94, 29 June 1925, ibid., ff. 103–7.

49. Herbette to Herriot, 24 Oct. 1925, MAÉ Papiers Herriot/16, ff. 65–66.

50. Chap. 3, this volume, n. 31: Stalin to Politburo and Chicherin, rigorously secret, 29 Jan. 1923, *Moskva-Berlin*, I, p. 109.

51. "Note pour M. le Président du conseil," *Sous-direction d'Europe*, 28 March 1925, MAÉ Z-Russie/358, ff. 43–49.

52. Litvinov to Politburo, no. 0026, secret, 12 Jan. 1925, AVPRF, f. 0136, o. 8, p. 105, d. 97, ll. 1–6; Litvinov to Krasin, no. 0621, secret, 27 Dec. 1924, AVPRF, f. 0136, o. 7, p. 105, d. 102, ll. 13–15; and Litvinov to Krasin, no. 0022, secret, 10 Jan. 1925, AVPRF, f. 0136, o. 8, p. 105, d. 95, ll. 5–8.

53. Litvinov to Krasin, no. 0621, secret, 27 Dec. 1924, AVPRF, f. 0136, o. 7, p. 105, d. 102, ll. 13–15; and Krasin to NKID, report no. 9, 1 Jan. 1925, AVPRF, f. 04, o. 42, p. 262, d. 53697, ll. 1–14.

54. Maxse's minute, 9 Feb. 1925, N713/30/38, FO 371 11012.

55. Chicherin/Litvinov to Politburo, no. 0049, secret, 20 Jan. 1925, AVPRF, f. 0136, o. 8, p. 105, d. 97, ll. 8–10; and Litvinov to Politburo, no. 0168, secret, 28 Feb. 1925, ibid., ll. 15–16.

56. Litvinov to Politburo, no. 0367, secret, 18 May 1925, AVPRF, f. 0136, o. 8, p. 105, d. 97, l. 27.

57. B. V. (journalist from *Economicheskaia zhizn*), Paris, to Rakovskii, personal letter, 7 Oct. 1924, AVPRF, f. 0136, p. 103, d. 70, ll. 1–2; and Litvinov to Stalin, no. 0394, secret, 27 May 1925, AVPRF, f. 0136, p. 105, d. 97, l. 29.

58. Litvinov to Politburo, no. 0630, rigorously secret, 31 Dec. 1924, RGASPI, f. 359, o. 1, d. 8, ll. 97–100.

59. Chicherin to Krasin, no. 4, 16 Dec. 1924, AVPRF, o. 42, p. 261, d. 53678, ll. 23–24.

60. Krasin to Narkomindel, report no. 19, 20 March 1925, AVPRF, f. 0136, p. 105, d. 104, ll. 106–2.

61. Krasin to Narkomindel, report no. 31, secret, 6 June 1925, AVPRF, f. 04, o. 42, p. 262, d. 53698, ll. 70–76.

62. Chicherin to Ia. Kh. Davtian, Soviet chargé d'affaires in Paris, no. 1, 12 June 1925, AVPRF, f. 04, o. 42, p. 264, d. 53714, l. 6.

63. Krasin to NKID, no. 05/9, 7 Dec. 1924, AVPRF f. 0136, p. 105, d. 104, ll. 9–14; and Krasin to NKID, report no. 3, secret, 9 Dec. 1924, AVPRF, f. 04, o. 42, p. 261, d. 53676, ll. 18–25.

64. Krasin to NKID, 23 March 1925, *DVP*, VIII, pp. 189–91.

65. Herbette, no. 219, 23 Oct. 1925, MAÉ Russie/358, ff. 178–85.

66. Excerpt from D. T. Florinskii's journal (Florinskii was head of protocol in the NKID), 2 May 1925, AVPRF, f. 0136, p. 105, d. 96, l. 88.

67. Litvinov to Krasin, no. 0272, secret, 11 April 1925, AVPRF, f. 0136, p. 105, d. 95, ll. 56–61.

68. Bernard Oudin, *Aristide Briand. La paix: une idée neuve en Europe* (Paris, 1987), p. 427.

69. Krasin to NKID, report no. 23, 26 April 1925, AVPRF, f. 04, o. 42, p. 262, d. 53698, ll. 1–7; excerpt from Litvinov's *dnevnik*, reporting a meeting with Herbette, 29 April 1925, AVPRF, f. 0136, p. 105, d. 95, ll. 72–74; and Rantzau, no. 543, 7 May 1926, *AzDAP*, B, II, 1, pp. 455–56. Cf., Carley, *Revolution and Intervention*, pp. 33–55.

70. Oudin, *Briand*, pp. 427, 454, 460.

71. Krasin to NKID, report no. 35, very secret, 21 July 1925, AVPRF, f. 04, o. 42, p. 262, d. 53699, ll. 12–15.

72. Krasin to NKID, report no. 16, secret, 21 Feb. 1925, AVPRF, f. 0136, p. 105, d. 104, ll. 80–84; and report no. 26, 17 May 1925, ibid., ll. 150–62.

73. Krasin to NKID, report no. 23, secret, 26 April 1925, AVPRF, f. 0136, p. 105, d. 104, ll. 116–21; and record of a meeting with Herbette, Chicherin, 17 May 1925, AVPRF, f. 0136, p. 105, d. 95, l. 93.

74. Herbette, no. 123, 3 July 1925, MAÉ Russie/358, ff. 118–30.

75. Briand to Herbette, no. 238, and elsewhere, 10 July 1925, MAÉ Russie/358, f. 138; Berthelot to Fleuriau, nos. 1045–53, 31 July 1925, MAÉ RC, *Pétroles de Russie*/100, ff. 100–105; "Note pour M. Berthelot," RC, unsigned, 24 Sept. 1925, with Berthelot's minute, ibid., f. 123; Fleuriau to FO, 2 Aug. 1925, N4491/1247/38, FO 371 11023; Krasin to Narkomindel, report no. 37, very secret, 29 July 1925, AVPRF, f. 0136, p. 105, d. 104, ll. 233–38; and Krasin to NKID, report no. 39, very secret, 30 July 1925, ibid., ll. 252–56.

76. Krasin to NKID, report no. 42, very secret, 13 Aug. 1925, AVPRF, f. 04, o. 42, p. 6, d. 53699, ll. 72–77; Krasin to Litvinov, report no. 43, very secret, 22 Aug. 1925, ibid., ll. 78–84; and Krasin to NKID, report no. 44, very secret, 29 Aug. 1925, ibid., ll. 85–90.

77. Krasin to NKID, report no. 45, very secret, 1 Sept. 1925, AVPRF, f. 04, o. 42, p. 262, d. 53699, ll. 91–97; "Avant-Projet relatif au règlement des dettes remis par M. Krassine à M. Berthelot," 1 Sept. 1925, *Ministère des finances*, Paris (hereafter MF) B32011; "Note pour le Ministre," no. 7395, Clément Moret, *directeur du Mouvement général des fonds*, 2 Sept. 1925, ibid.; and Joseph Caillaux, minister of finances, to Briand, no. 7627, 12 Sept. 1925, ibid.

78. "Chancellor of the Exchequer," B. P. Blackett, 22 Sept. 1920, TNA T 160 777/F815/1; and S. D. Waley's minute, 9 Oct. 1924, T 160 777/F815/3.

79. Krasin to NKID, report no. 45, very secret, 1 Sept. 1925, AVPRF, f. 04, o. 42, p. 262, d. 53699, ll. 91–97; Berthelot's untitled note, 1 Sept. 1925, MAÉ Russie/428, f. 12; René Massigli (Geneva) to MAÉ, Paris, no. 63, 5 Sept. 1925, ibid., f. 29.

80. Litvinov to Davtian, no. 0524, secret, 12 Sept. 1925, AVPRF, f. 0136, p. 105, d. 102, ll. 58–59; Litvinov to Davtian, no. 0543, 19 Sept. 1925, ibid., ll. 60–63; Litvinov to NKID *kollegiia*, no. 0547, very secret, 21 Sept. 1925, AVPRF, f. 0136, p. 105, d. 97, l. 36; and Herbette to Berthelot, personal letter, 12 Sept. 1925, MAÉ Russie/428, ff. 80–82.

81. Litvinov to Krasin, no. 0319, secret, 2 May 1925, AVPRF, f. 136, p. 105, d. 97, ll. 23–24.

82. Krasin to Litvinov, no. 0140, secret, 10 May 1925, AVPRF, f. 136, p. 105, d. 104, ll. 146–48; and Krasin to Narkomindel, report no. 26, secret, 17 May 1925, ibid., ll. 150–62.

83. Chicherin to Krasin, no. 26, very secret, 31 July 1925, AVPRF, f. 04, o. 42, p. 264, d. 53712, ll. 90–92; Krasin to Chicherin and Litvinov, no. 0215, 7 Aug. 1925, AVPRF, f. 136, p. 105, d. 104, ll. 267–71; Litvinov to Davtian, no. 0566, secret, 25 Sept. 1925, AVPRF, f. 04, o. 42, p. 264, d. 53714, ll. 23–24; and Litvinov to Davtian, no. 0598, secret, 3 Oct. 1925, ibid., ll. 25–27.

~

CHAPTER SIX

"Steady! Don't Let Us Get Jumpy"

Revolution in China, 1924–1925

The Comintern "Bull's-Eye"

While the French put off Soviet overtures, the British were more aggressive keeping the Soviet government at arm's length. The Foreign Office reckoned that if it maintained a "policy of reserve" toward the Soviet government, Moscow would have to "come to us, hat in hand, with reasonable propositions."[1] This was also Secretary of State Hughes' policy. In fact, such a policy only reinforced *Soviet* "reserve," though the Foreign Office did not see it.

The Comintern became the main obstacle to progress in London. As Litvinov had noted, it was the "bull's-eye" of western ire. Arguments to the effect that the Soviet government had nothing to do with the Comintern were only technically true and derided in the West. One has to admire Litvinov's tenacity in holding to his line, even though he knew it to be disingenuous, but behind the argument was the message that the West, and the NKID also, would have to live with the Comintern. In Britain someone suggested moving the Comintern out of Moscow to some remote place in Siberia.

I cannot see, Litvinov commented, how the Comintern would be less dangerous if its directives came from Kazan or Ekaterinburg. In any case, "doing away" with it, Chicherin remarked to the British chargé d'affaires in Moscow, is "an impossibility," though "it was gradually losing its virulence." Chicherin proposed that "we should recognise a divorce between the Soviet government and the Communist International." The Foreign Office ridiculed this idea. Echoing the German ambassador Rantzau, Hodgson reckoned that the Soviet government had finally understood that it could not have it both ways.[2] This was true in the NKID, but not in other parts of Moscow.

In the early spring of 1925 the Foreign Office was having trouble finding signs of Comintern mischief. In March one clerk noted that the Foreign Office had made no protests to Moscow since the "Zinoviev letter." But another anti-communist campaign might be in the offing as Parliament reconvened. Gregory did not think the Soviet embassy or trade establishments were involved in spreading propaganda, but there were other ways for the poison to pass.

"We *ought* [emphasis in the original] to do something about this question of Bolshevik agents," noted Gregory, "and yet, though I have discussed it up and down with the Department, we can none of us think of anything that we can do!" Even if we tightened up visa requirements, "a real terrorist" could still get through.[3]

The spring calm in London came before the storm. In the summer of 1925 the French began a colonial war with Rif tribesmen in North Africa, and French communists took the Rif side. In India, the independence movement was gaining momentum. But these were minor issues compared to events in China where an extraordinary national movement was spreading against western spheres of interest, extraterritorial rights, foreign concessions, and treaty ports. Revolution was passing from low to full boil, and British commercial interests were threatened with ruin. If the Comintern meddled in Chinese affairs, it was no more than throwing a small tin of lighter fluid onto a raging inferno.

In May 1925 Chinese discontents blew up in the treaty port of Shanghai. European and Japanese factory owners treated Chinese workers like dangerous beasts of burden. But beasts do not always remain cowed. There had been "trouble" for months in Japanese textiles mills, and on 15 May a Japanese foreman shot dead a Chinese laborer who had dared to raise his head in defiance. This shooting touched off strikes and street demonstrations. Two weeks later the Shanghai municipal police arrested demonstrating student leaders which provoked a protest before the police station where they were being held. On 30 May, Sikh police officers commanded by a British captain fired into the crowd, with the result that nine demonstrators were killed and many others wounded. The incident resembled the Amritsar massacre six years earlier though on a much smaller scale of killing, but the consequences of the Shanghai shootings were greater and more immediate. A strike movement broke out in the foreign concessions and spread across the country, affecting even Canton and Hong Kong farther south. Foreign trade, particularly British, was brought to a standstill. It was a British officer, not a

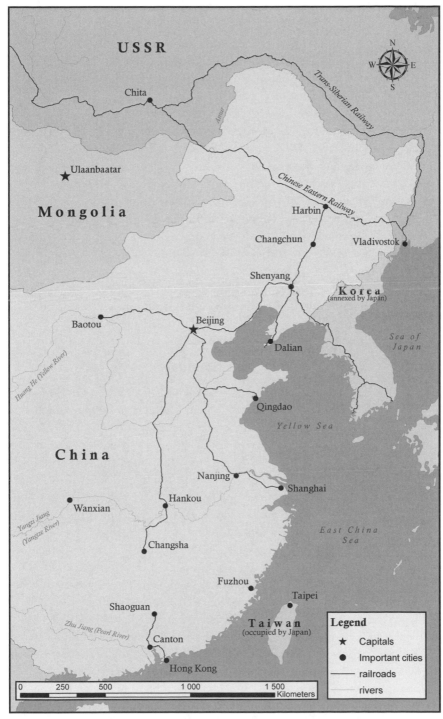

Figure 6.1.   Map of Costal China, Manchuria, Eastern Siberia, ca. 1925.

Comintern agent, who set off this Chinese firestorm. But the Foreign Office was quick to see the hand of Moscow, and of course not for the first time.

Already in 1924 the Foreign Office had thought it noticed Soviet meddling. It was the mirror image of Chicherin's perceptions of British intrigues in Central Asia; each side saw the other's bags of gold in the hands of potential clients. The Soviet delegation in Beijing was up to no good. According to the British minister, Sir James R. Macleay, it had "won over" students "and other noisy and irresponsible elements . . . by flattery, promises and bribes." Now the Soviet government wanted to name Karakhan as *polpred* in Beijing, and Macleay tried to persuade the Chinese foreign minister to refuse the appointment. Karakhan had negotiated the terms of diplomatic recognition with China in May 1924, and Macleay wanted the Beijing government to send him home. His appointment as minister, he told the Chinese, would not be construed as "a very friendly act towards other Powers represented in Peking [sic]."[4] The Soviet government expected as much but was good at turnabout is fair play. If the British could buy off emirs in Central Asia, Karakhan could try his hand in China with warlords and students.

Lev M. Karakhan

Like his NKID colleagues, Karakhan was a sophisticated, erudite diplomat, easily a match for his British counterparts in China. Lev Mikhailovich was born in Tiflis, Georgia, in 1889, but was of Armenian descent. He was thus younger than Chicherin and Litvinov. His father was a lawyer who saw to his son's formal education. In 1904, at age 15, he joined the Russian Social Democratic Labour Party as a Menshevik. Like Lenin and Krestinskii, Karakhan studied law, first in St. Petersburg and then in Tomsk in Siberia where he was sent into exile in 1915. As a law student in the capital he worked in the trade union movement and gravitated toward the Bolsheviks, eventually joining them with Trotskii and others in his group in 1917. He was a member of the Revolution Military Council which directed the Bolshevik seizure of power in November 1917. In the following year, only 29, he went to Brest-Litovsk with Trotskii to negotiate peace with Germany and its allies.

He looked the part of a suave, handsome Armenian with dark swept-back hair and Vandyke moustache and beard. At ease with western diplomats and journalists, Karakhan knew how to present the NKID line on relations with the West. In 1922 a British journalist described him "as an intellectual, good-looking man of the business type who might be a bank manager. He may be the wrong side of 40, is scrupulously neat in personal appearance and has exceptional manners."[5] The reporter seemed almost surprised by Karakhan,

Figure 6.2. Lev Mikhailovich Karakhan and Georgii V. Chicherin, Moscow, ca. 1920s. AVPRF, f. 779, d. 14.017, l.f. Chicherin, G. V., p. 1.

perhaps having been nourished on too many propaganda images of the Bolsh terrorist with his smoking bomb and long dagger.

Karakhan got on relatively well with Stalin during the mid-1920s and in private correspondence sometimes used the familiar *ty* in addressing him. "Hello Karakhan," Stalin wrote in February 1925, "Conqueror of Chinese, Japanese, etc. etc., counter-revolutionaries." Of course with Stalin, who knew how long the good feelings would last? Like Litvinov and Chicherin, Karakhan tended toward pragmatism, though in China, he became swept up in the revolutionary movement. The "ground is so hot" here, he wrote to Stalin, it was easy to get carried away.[6] When Karakhan returned to Moscow from Beijing in the autumn of 1926, he became deputy commissar at the NKID. He had a fatal weakness which led to his execution during the purges; he had been too closely associated with Trotskii. Stalin never forgot such associations.

The Chinese in Beijing, in their weakness, must have thought Karakhan a useful thorn in the foot of the western powers. As in Persia, the Soviet government renounced Russian extraterritorial rights (with the notable exception of the strategic Chinese Eastern Railway in Manchuria). According to Macleay, Karakhan was encouraging Chinese "chauvinism" and especially the "student element against all countries enjoying extra territorial privileges." It was very "disquieting." The Soviet legation risked becoming the "headquarters of anti-foreign propaganda and intrigue." Even more galling, Karakhan could end up as doyen of the diplomatic corps in Beijing.

The Foreign Office did not know what to do. One official proposed a protest to Moscow; another did not see the point. "I agree. It is futile," commented the deputy undersecretary Wellesley.[7]

The Foreign Office worried that the Beijing government of the moment, which controlled very little of China in fact, was falling under Karakhan's influence and was "probably in his pay." A government in Beijing "inspired by the Russians," noted S. P. Waterlow, the head of the Far Eastern Department, could "flout foreign rights and . . . demand the abolition of the [unequal] treaties." It would not do to stand by while Moscow exhorted "China to shake off foreign slavery." We need a plan, Waterlow said, for a "constructive policy." It's "the only remedy for Russian propaganda."[8]

"Steady! Don't Let Us Get Jumpy"

Waterlow was not sure what the "plan" should be, and neither was Foreign Secretary Chamberlain who had just come into office. He wanted to know the U.S. government position on the situation in China, "so pregnant with danger to the rights of all foreign Powers." "Unity of policy and advice" was essential between London, Washington, and Tokyo. We have to keep the Japanese "in our orbit," opined Waterlow. "So long as China is weak and Russia is weak," added another clerk, "in case of emergency the whole position can be cleared up by the despatch of a Division."[9] Now there were words spoken like a true imperialist.

After the May 30th shooting in Shanghai, it would take more than a division to protect foreign "rights" in China. The USSR nevertheless remained a useful scapegoat. The British chargé d'affaires in Beijing, C. M. Palairet, got hold of a letter apparently signed by Karakhan to demonstrate Soviet connivance in the Chinese disturbances.

"Are you sure the evidence is not faked?" the Foreign Office wrote back. The letter may have been genuine, though Waterlow thought it should be kept "for use in an emergency." One could never exclude the "possibility of forgery." The British might brandish Karakhan's letter "as proof of direct Soviet intervention" in China, but more perceptive officials knew their problems were greater than any lighter fluid Moscow could throw on the Chinese inferno.[10]

Palairet reported that police had shot too quickly at demonstrators. Even the "most enlightened Chinese" thought so, a Foreign Office clerk noted. So what was to be done? Nothing for the present. Chamberlain was "uneasy":

one could not be seen to be giving in to "strikes, riots & murders." The international settlement in Shanghai decided to take responsibility for the shooting and to pay an indemnity for the dead Chinese. "The central difficulty," Waterlow noted, "is that responsible and educated Chinese look upon us as murderers, and our own information indicates . . . that there is some justification for this view." There was talk of trying the trigger-happy police captain, but no "British" jury in Shanghai would convict him.

"Steady!" Chamberlain replied. "Don't let us get jumpy."[11]

Austen Chamberlain

Chamberlain's brief note typified his policies as Foreign Secretary. He played an important role in the development of British policy toward the USSR, and therefore readers may like to know him a little better. His father was Joseph Chamberlain, a wealthy industrialist, mayor of Birmingham, member of Parliament, and cabinet minister; his half brother was Neville Chamberlain,

Figure 6.3. Austen Chamberlain, ca. 1920s. Culver Pictures, Art Resource, NY.

also a Tory politician and prime minister at the end of the 1930s. As befitted the son of a wealthy British family, Austen was well educated at Trinity College, Cambridge, and pursued further studies in Paris and Berlin where he mingled with the political elite of those countries. Elected to the House of Commons in 1892, he had already been several times a cabinet minister. Chamberlain was a stalwart of the Conservative Party when it returned to power in November 1924. In photographs he often looks the part of a sour, stiff-necked, monocled Tory patrician.

In the Foreign Office Chamberlain had his hands full with the files on Germany, the USSR, and the revolution in China. With Germany, he pursued a policy of conciliation which led to the conclusion of the Locarno Accords. With the Soviet Union and China, matters were less easy. These two issues were of course related. The Die-Hard trio of Lord Birkenhead, Secretary of State for India; Churchill, Chancellor of the Exchequer; and William Joynson-Hicks, or Jix, Secretary of State for the Home Office, spoiled for a fight with Moscow. Had Lord Curzon lived, he would certainly have made a foursome. These Tories hated the USSR on principle, but were further incensed by the ruin of British interests in China. They thought they could intimidate the Bolsheviks and force them to submit to British conditions. Chamberlain was not so sure, or at least preferred to pursue a more cautious, less confrontational policy. In this he faced opposition not only from the Die-Hards, but also from hard-line officials in the Foreign Office. Some contemporary observers thought the latter were able to manipulate Chamberlain, but the evidence in the Foreign Offices files indicates that he kept his own counsel and his officials under control.

"A Sudden Bolt to Bolshevism"

"Getting jumpy," as Chamberlain put it, was hard to avoid in the spring of 1925. The British position in China looked to be collapsing. Foreign nationals were threatened. In Fujian Province, halfway between Shanghai and Hong Kong, "the enemy has come in like a flood," according to the local American Methodist bishop in Fuzhou. Ten thousand students, "laborers," and "merchants" marched to protest the Shanghai shootings. "Down with imperialism," "Down with Christianity," "Kill the foreign devils," read their placards and banners. "An enemy hath done this," reported the bishop: "One of the most subtle, with the best organized agency of propaganda in the world is here at work. The words on the banners may be the hand of China, but it is the voice of Moscow." The bishop nevertheless was reassuring: "In the long run Christ will win out in China."[12]

The Methodist bishop in Shanghai was a little more nuanced, but not much. The Soviet hand was evident, "pouring vast sums of money into China, taking young Chinese to Moscow to put them through a brief course of training . . . and sending them back to spread their doctrine throughout China." But the Shanghai shooting "was like a match to a gigantic powder box." It was impossible to say what would happen next. Another American missionary in Shanghai, a Presbyterian, called it "a sudden bolt to Bolshevism." The American missionaries sounded like medieval crusaders: "The tactics of the Soviet have placed us where we must fight them, whether by diplomacy or by war. The existence of our Government, our civilization, our religion, and our homes demand it." The American minister at Beijing, John V. A. MacMurray, was just as alarmed. The situation was "more critical" than at any time since the Boxer Rebellion in 1900, a Chinese uprising which had been put down by foreign troops. "The Shanghai incident seems to have awakened instincts and passions hitherto dormant." The Bolos may have had a hand in this "outburst of feeling," but it was "fundamentally" a Chinese movement.[13]

British sources were also alarmed. There's no "use beating about the bush," a *Times* reporter wrote to the Foreign Office: "Things could not possibly have developed in this way if it had not been for Bolshevist propaganda. The whole chaos was without aim or direction until the Bolshevists came in."[14] The strikes spread to Hong Kong where the British governor accused a "Russian agent" of offering to finance the movement. Canton, just north of Hong Kong, was "in the hands of the reds." It looked to Waterlow as though "the Reds" held "all the cards." If the Chinese troubles continued, another clerk noted,

> there will be very few mercantile houses & Banks who could hope to weather the storm. The only assets in China worth fighting for are our vested interests & our commerce. . . . If defensive action is delayed until these are destroyed we should be endeavouring to lock the stable after the horse is stolen.[15]

Trade, not Christ, was what mattered most, in the short run at least, to the Foreign Office clerks.

The French ambassador Fleuriau came in to talk to Waterlow about the Chinese situation. His previous posting had been in Beijing, so he thought he knew a thing or two about handling the Chinese. The best way to deal with the situation, Fleuriau recommended, though without instructions from Paris, was to break off relations with Moscow and run "the Russians" out of China. Then things would calm down. When Waterlow suggested that the

China problem might be bigger than "Russian mischief," Fleuriau "threw plentiful cold water":

"It is impossible to help the Chinese," he said. "We can merely sit tight, and when next we are flouted threaten a bombardment."

Once again, words spoken like a true imperialist, and Litvinov would have laughed had he read this document among those spirited out of Foreign Office files. Perhaps he did.

"Not very helpful," was Waterlow's opinion, "but I did not attempt to traverse M. de Fleuriau's arguments."[16] British gunboats, by the way, were not above bombarding Chinese cities as in August–September 1926 at Wanxian, on the Yangzi, about 2,400 kilometers upstream from Shanghai. Even Waterlow, however, reckoned "the Chinese situation . . . so dangerous" that some action had to be contemplated.

Gregory, just promoted to assistant undersecretary, was asked for his opinion. He was keen: China could be just the "pretext for dealing the Soviet Power a decisive blow." The United States would have to be brought in, of course; "isolated action by us should be ruled out." Gregory ruminated on the possibilities: "It must be a through business. There must be no ultimatum requiring a reply, but a general and summary ejection of Bolshevik agents, official, trade, or otherwise, from every country. Anything short of this would be quite ineffective." And Gregory continued, "We might give such a setback to communism all the world over that it would take an appreciable time to recover." One could dream, naturally, but was the place for it in the Foreign Office?

Gregory's boss, Tyrrell, just promoted to permanent undersecretary, brought him back to earth with a short, handwritten note to the effect that the time was not right for an anti-Bolshevik "crusade."[17]

What galled the Foreign Office was that in Beijing Karakhan denounced western imperialism. He "incites the Chinese government to lawless and forcible rupture of their treaties with this country and other foreign powers."[18] It is a shame that Litvinov did not read this particular minute, for he would certainly have laughed at English hypocrisy, pointing out that Britain and the other western powers had extracted the so called "unequal treaties" at cannon point. The treaty ports, foreign concessions, and extraterritorial rights had been obtained by force. If the Chinese used force to extinguish them, well then, Litvinov might have said, "turnabout is fair play."

In the spring of 1925 Home Secretary Joynson-Hicks and the Secretary of State for India, Lord Birkenhead, made anti-Soviet speeches that aroused Soviet ire. Birkenhead made an inflammatory speech against Bolshevik agitation in China, regretting that a united Europe did not confront the Red "scourge." British officers, Rakovskii reported, "were wont to talk about a move into Russia through an alley bordered by gallows." Even the relatively cautious Waterlow wondered whether "the European civilized powers and especially His Majesty's Government" should "not consider a rupture of relations with Moscow." Waterlow suggested that Birkenhead was playing into Soviet hands, as indeed he appeared to do.[19]

Chicherin made a long reply in *Izvestiia* stating, inter alia, that the Chinese people had a right to determine their own future, but that in any case the Soviet government was ready to negotiate with London or any other government to consolidate international peace. It was not after all the Soviet government that had rejected the Anglo-Soviet treaty of 1924.[20]

"Frankly speeches mainly directed to the domestic situation," commented Chamberlain, "may sometimes greatly increase the difficulties of the Foreign Minister."[21] Here was an ironic comment, for Litvinov and Chicherin would certainly have agreed. As the China situation worsened, from a British point of view, Chamberlain was not as sure that the Foreign Office should be "quite so discouraging" about European cooperation against Bolshevik "propaganda."[22] Anti-communist vituperation was frequent in the British press as was anti-British comment in Moscow. Each side bombarded the other, and when the salvos got too heavy, each side protested. It was Mr. Pot calling Comrade Kettle black and vice versa.

Rakovskii is coming into the Office, minuted Chamberlain at one point: I need evidence of "less than friendly" Soviet conduct toward His Majesty's Government (HMG). Of course, in Moscow the same sort of reaction occurred, and the British press was a treasure trove of anti-Soviet rants. The NKID press service was good at collecting them so that Chicherin always had a ready supply to hand. A reader might be reminded of the children's epigram about "sticks and stones may break my bones, but lies will never hurt me." Of course, the Die-Hard intention was to excite public opinion to prepare for a diplomatic rupture with Moscow, so that "lies" could indeed lead to "sticks and stones." This is why Rakovskii complained to Chamberlain and why Chamberlain sent a letter to Jix in May 1925 asking him to temper his rhetoric.[23] With the China situation deteriorating for the British, Jix paid no attention to Chamberlain's request.

Foreign Office "*Mentalités*"

Naturally, Foreign Office officials did not see themselves as imperialists treating others, in this case the Chinese, like dangerous brutes or spineless compradors. Laurence Collier, then in the Far Eastern Department, thought Britain was being too conciliatory. The Chinese would perceive weakness and "only be encouraged to continue their attacks on us." In the 1930s

Collier became a notable advocate of better Soviet relations; he was one of the few Foreign Office officials who could envisage an anti-Nazi alliance with the Soviet Union. In 1925, however, he held conventional views about dealing with the Bolsheviks, who were "not restrained by our scruples as to telling the truth." They were therefore "likely to win the race for the ear of the Chinese public."

For the Foreign Office, the Bolsh were just not sporting: "It seems extremely unfair," noted Waterlow, "that Russia should at one and the same time have the advantage of trade with us and of being recognized, and be mining our position in the East and our trade with China." According to Collier, China was abnormal, for "even the 'moderate' section [of opinion] would be most immoderate in any other country." The Chinese were "hopelessly invertebrate & unreasonable," according to another clerk. Even with "the best will in the world . . . we may find it impossible to reach any satisfactory agreement" with them. One had to hope that "troubles will simmer down & that the moderate elements will assert their influence."[24] For Collier, the "moderate" to back was the slippery, opportunistic Manchurian warlord, Zhang Zuolin, though Waterlow was dubious about that idea. The Foreign Office sent instructions to their chargé d'affaires in Beijing to convey

> the surprise and pain with which HMG have observed the supine attitude of [the Beijing] government toward the recent anti-British agitations. . . . HMG fail to see how they can give effect to their desire to help the Chinese people so long as the government which represents them is one which not merely does nothing to stop the agitations but even condones and subsidizes them.[25]

This comment would have made a Bolshevik laugh, a point acknowledged in the Foreign Office.

"To Chicherin," one clerk noted, "the psychology of the Englishman who has a strange objection to lying and really does from day to day do the best he can to keep the peace is quite incomprehensible and he consequently believes it to be a sham."[26] Of course, police shootings and naval bombardments were sometimes necessary to "maintain order" among the colonized masses.

Nor were the British above using force. There was another shooting at Canton "almost certainly started by armed men." "The fire was returned by . . . foreign troops . . . and a number of Chinese were killed." The governor general of Hong Kong, Sir Reginald Stubbs, asked for authorization to spend up to 1 million Hong Kong dollars to bankroll an insurrection in Canton: "The sole object of providing the money is to put the forces on the side of law and order in a position to eject the communists from Canton."[27]

Many of the clichés of western imperialism and colonialism can be found in the Foreign Office files: "Extreme Nationalists," "adventurers with Communist leanings," "Russian agents," "insolent" Chinese, "crazy mischief-makers who have in no way at heart the interests of China." "The principles of destructive anarchy" were at work in China, according to the Foreign Office clerks, worked up by "the artificial inspiration of the anti-foreign agitation" and "subversive elements" providing "moral support to the Chinese malcontents against the 'imperialists.'"[28] The British commander in chief, China, recommended an ultimatum to the Canton government that "if normal trading conditions [were] not resumed," the forts south of Canton would be "bombed and destroyed."[29] That was one way to break a strike, and there was nothing like a naval cannonade to teach a lesson to rebellious "natives." With commercial ruin threatening Hong Kong, the British colonists, "indignant at trade losses," were "anxious to take action. . . . They think that strong action on our part would nerve the anti-Bolshevik elements in Canton to overthrow the Communist Government." The Foreign Office preferred a less aggressive approach than that of the Hong Kong governor general, who nevertheless "return[ed] to the charge" in September. Chamberlain, however, thought the idea was "all wrong." He preferred another approach: the British government should not act unilaterally and should not take the initiative of military action.[30] There was still some common sense being exercised in the Foreign Office: "The Soviet government cannot," noted one Foreign Office clerk, "flatter themselves that they are the cause of the disorders, but they are implicated."[31]

Alexis Léger, an upcoming bureaucrat in the French foreign ministry, met Waterlow in London and entirely agreed with British policy objectives, though France could do little to help. It was too busy putting down independence movements in Morocco and Syria to spare warships for China.[32] As readers may recall, Léger was also the poet Saint Jean Perse. We know now that he was better at verse than he was at diplomacy, though in this case his support for British policy better reflected the view from Paris than that of Fleuriau. "We should keep our eyes open," Briand told Chamberlain in July: "The Soviet government had given up the idea of a forcible revolution in Europe. Their policy now was to strike at the Western Powers through their colonies, fomenting communism and disorder." China and Africa had to be watched.[33] Briand was only being prudent with military campaigns under way in Morocco and Syria.

In the summer of 1925 Rakovskii wrote to Litvinov that Britain was running into trouble in China: "The imperialist powers were entering into the realm of colonial complications and difficulties." This was an understatement. Rakovskii voiced no objection to Soviet "eastern policy," but he thought superfluous attacks against Britain in the Moscow press did not strengthen Soviet policy and only provided grist to the mill of antagonists.[34] Echoing Litvinov on gratuitous propaganda, here was an allusion to the residual fear of a western anti-Soviet bloc. The foreign intervention was never far from Soviet minds, as Rakovskii reminded the Foreign Office in the spring of 1925.[35] Litvinov worried about a united front, but only if the French gave up on a separate agreement with us. After reading British documents— well before they were deposited at the National Archives in Kew—Litvinov surmised that western anti-Soviet cooperation would for the time being be limited to police measures, restriction of visas for Soviet citizens, greater surveillance, and restrictions on Soviet financial transactions. Germany had to be drawn "into the orbit of English policies" before an anti-Soviet bloc could be organized. And here Litvinov was determined not to irritate Germany to avoid giving it any more reasons to abandon Rapallo.[36]

Soviet "eastern policy" remained hard to reconcile with policy in Europe. In Berlin, no one cared much about what happened in China, but in London especially and in Paris, it mattered. France and Britain were colonial powers with restive, rebellious populations, and by their lights China was out of control. How were these contradictions to be worked out, or could they be compartmentalized? Rakovskii noted that the Soviet Union had important interests in China which it ought to defend in spite of British attempts to regard any Soviet action there as subversive "propaganda." The Soviet government should not throw in it cards simply to avoid a row with London. This would be "political suicide," according to Rakovskii. Western protests were intended to force Moscow to surrender its interests and renounce its principles. In fact, the Soviet Union had "concrete interests" in China, and also "general principles, which defined Soviet international policies." The Soviet Union shared a 5,000-kilometer frontier with China. The debris of the former White armies had crossed into Manchuria and still represented a threat to Soviet security. But the Soviet Union had also renounced the extraterritorial privileges of tsarist Russia in China, setting it apart from Britain which sought to retain them.[37]

Rakovskii preached to the converted: Chicherin and Litvinov needed no coaching on Soviet policy in China. In fact, Chicherin was thinking precisely along the lines of seeking agreement with London to limit or compartmentalize their conflicts of interest. At least twice in 1925, just as events were blowing up in China, Chicherin proposed to British diplomats the idea of settling disputes in Asia, mentioning Persia and China as examples. "M. Chicherin said that he fully admitted the divergence of principles but there had also been a wide difference of principles in the forties of the last century between a despotic and reactionary Russia and a liberal and progressive England. Nevertheless, the two Governments had understood each other and worked together."

Why not again, Chicherin asked, "leaving all questions of principle in abeyance?"

In reply, one Foreign Office clerk commented that Chicherin's ideas originated in "pre-war German conceptions of . . . 'Weltpolitik' and 'Machtverhältnisse.'" British diplomats understood the principles, so why not negotiate with Chicherin, as they had done with the tsars?[38]

Well, for one thing, Stalin might not have approved. In a speech in July 1925, he warned against a "nationalist" foreign policy replacing that of the October Revolution. This tendency was understandable, Stalin commented, because of "the pressure of the capitalist states." It was hard to hold out against them and not give in to "the course of least resistance." But it was essential to hold out because "nationalism in foreign policy [would] entail . . . isolation and dissolution" of the USSR. And this after all is what western leaders had been saying and anticipating for years: by being obliged to compose with the capitalist world, the Bolsheviks and the Soviet Union would fade away. Hodgson, who reported the speech, noted that the NKID and Soviet Communist Party were at odds over foreign policy, and that Stalin was targeting Chicherin.[39]

In fact, Chicherin *and* Litvinov were fed up with the Comintern and with party "orators" who could not keep their mouths shut. They could not target Stalin, who was too powerful, but they could and did try to bring him around to their point of view. Given the internal political situation in Moscow, Stalin could not go as far as he might like to have done, for he needed to cover his left flank against attacks from Trotskii and others. In January 1925 Trotskii was replaced as commissar for war; it was the beginning of the end for him. With Trotskii defeated, Stalin could build new alliances and free himself of Zinoviev. That break came in the autumn of 1925. The troika of Stalin, Zinoviev, and Kamenev did not last two years.

Ironically, the Foreign Office came to see Stalin as the one to lead toward more Russian, less Soviet policies, and so did not pay much attention to his speech targeting Chicherin. There were no takers at the Foreign Office for Chicherin's ideas, which were "puerile and inacceptable" according to one clerk. The Bolsheviks did not accept the principles of "civilized" behavior. They pursued policies of "wanton mischief making," noted the Labourite MacDonald: "We hold them in contempt." It was not just that the Bolsheviks had made a revolution in Russia, turning "civilization" on its head; it was that they were only a step away from the primitive masses colonized by the West. The Russian character was "brutish," the Russian hold on civilization only "skin deep." The Bolshevik leaders may have come from the café *terrasse* and been educated in the best Russian and European universities, but behind them was "something at once unnatural and unholy." Gregory tried to explain it as some "intangible, indefinable, psychological antagonism." Whether it was "something of the true spirit of Anti-Christ," Gregory could not say. The Comintern only exacerbated mistrust: it could "still be as anti-British and as revolutionary as it likes."[40] Of course, observant Chinese of whatever class, under British guns, knew a thing or two about the "brutishness" of British colonial power. Mr. Pot was again calling Comrade Kettle Black.

Litvinov appears to have been of two minds about "eastern" policy: the NKID had discouraged a too active policy in China, precisely in order to obtain agreement with London. When no agreement was forthcoming, the incentive for restraint dissolved, and in China the Soviet government pursued a more aggressive policy, more in tune with its revolutionary origins and its national interests.

The Origins of Soviet Policy in China

Well then, what about western claims of Soviet involvement in China? Was the Soviet government "pouring vast sums of money into China," as the Methodist bishop in China put it? The first casual exchanges between Sun Yat-sen, leader of the Guomintang, and the Soviet government in Moscow occurred in 1920–1921. In one such letter in August 1921, Sun asked Chicherin to forward his greetings to Lenin.

"Do you know him personally," Chicherin asked Lenin, "since he calls you 'his friend'?"

"I do not know him personally and have not written to dear friend even a single word," Lenin replied sarcastically: "In my opinion we should take pains to be friendly [*liubeznyi*], write on *a more regular* basis and try to send *secretly* our man to Canton [emphasis in original]." Chicherin wanted to be cautious about open relations with Sun in Canton since the NKID was also attempting to establish contact with the government in Beijing.[41] There were so many governments in China, led by quarreling warlords, and so many shifting alliances, it was hard to keep them straight, especially with only a handful of agents in the Far East.

A Soviet agent was duly ordered to Canton in October 1921, but he went no farther than Shanghai. In the meantime, the unofficial Soviet *polpred* in Beijing, A. K. Paikes, entered into contact with the government of the warlord Wu Peifu, who was disposed to improve relations with Soviet Russia. Paikes sought to encourage cooperation between Wu and Sun Yat-sen, though without much success.[42]

**Figure 6.4.   Adol'f Abramovich Ioffe, ca. 1920s.
AVPRF, f. 787, d. 1863/3, kor. no. 24.**

Adol'f A. Ioffe, an experienced Soviet diplomat, arrived in Beijing in August 1922 to negotiate the establishment of formal diplomatic relations. He attempted to promote the same policy: Wu would be the military muscle, and Sun the political brains of a new government to unite China and free it from the unequal treaties. This was not a formula for a Chinese socialist revolution, but a Wu-Sun alliance might become a stick in the wheel of western imperialism. Ioffe was optimistic about his negotiations with Wu and about the overall prospects for success of the anti-capitalist movement. "Without a doubt China is the focus (*uzel*) of international conflict and the most vulnerable spot of international imperialism. . . . Striking a blow against imperialism in its most vulnerable spot might be very important."[43]

Ioffe got a little carried away with the possibilities of cooperation. Working in China was not easy. In July 1922, Sun was driven out of his base in Canton by the local warlord, though Ioffe was not discouraged. Sun advised him about dealing with different warlords and worried about Soviet negotiations with Japan. He did not want China to be the price of agreement with the Japanese, who had vast imperial ambitions and were seeking to expand their privileged position in northern China and Manchuria. Sun was preoccupied with tactics, not the strategy of forming a mass movement.[44]

Ioffe was too, recommending a Soviet loan of $20 million in gold for the Beijing government: "In the East there is much sympathy for us, but no confidence in our strength." A loan would change everything, raising "our prestige." Oppressed peoples will know they can count on us in the struggle against imperialism, wrote Ioffe, "not only in ideological but also in material terms." The Politburo was taken aback by Ioffe's enthusiasm, or was aghast: Karakhan was instructed to "express utter amazement at the recommendations of comrade Ioffe, who would know about the financial situation of the Soviet republics."[45]

Readers will remember Chicherin's comment that Soviet Russia was like the goat without milk or wool, in dire financial straits in the summer of 1922. To propose a loan of $20 million in gold to the Beijing government was unrealistic, to say the least. One sees why Litvinov and Chicherin were more interested in pursuing the possibilities for recognition and further agreement with London: it would be less expensive, potentially more remunerative, and much less hazardous than getting involved in China. What use, after all, was a goat without milk or wool?

The main nationalist party in China was the Guomintang. The Chinese Communist Party was only founded in 1921 by a handful of Chinese intellectuals inspired by the May 4th movement of 1919. At the beginning its members were mainly intellectuals and students, without ties to workers in the cities or peasants in the countryside. So Ioffe focused on Sun and the competing warlords Wu and Zhang Zuolin, attempting to broker cooperation, which was not an easy thing to do. The warlords shifted alliances almost as quickly as they changed their shirts. Everything was calculated on short-term advantages and where the next chest of gold was to be obtained to pay their mercenary armies. Ironically, the Foreign Office also had its eye on Zhang as a potential ally.

Ioffe sent a Dutch Comintern agent in Shanghai, Henk Sneevliet, or Maring, to see Sun. They discussed general principles about Sino-Soviet cooperation and Chinese unity, though Sun did not see much chance of preventing a new war between warlords Zhang and Wu. Sun said he needed an independent, reliable military force that he could control: counting on the warlords for long-term support was unrealistic. Could Soviet Russia supply such an army? Maring's record of conversation was long, but it was short on detail. And of course Maring could not answer Sun's main question.[46]

Ioffe soon came back to earth as he learned about warlord "politics." He was not getting very far with Wu's foreign minister in Beijing. Chinese of this sort, Ioffe noted, were all under the influence of one or another of the imperialist powers; "the latter all play *va banque* against us." And it was the usual story between Sun and the warlords with their ever-shifting alliances. Sun's position was that "revolution" in China could only come through military force, which he did not have. Nor did he have a base of operations, having been expelled from Canton, though he eventually re-established himself there. Soviet Russia was thus left in the same position as Sun, allying temporarily with one warlord against another.[47] Obviously, this strategy did not have much prospect of success or for socialist revolution, but Sun knew political and military strength when he saw it. He was much impressed when Soviet authorities reoccupied Vladivostok in 1922 and the Japanese evacuated their remaining troops there.[48] They would not be so easy to dislodge from China.

In December 1922, Sun renewed his request for Soviet war matériel to support an army of 100,000. At the same time Maring returned to Moscow from China to report on his activities. These were modest: Chinese communists had decided "almost without opposition" to join Sun's Guomintang. A weekly newspaper was started in Shanghai with a print run of 5 to 7,000 copies. Already 12 issues had been published which were attracting the interest of the nationalist movement. Maring recommended linking communist propaganda with that of the nationalist movement, though its objective was also to create an "independent workers' organization." An estimate of expenditures in 1923 for the Chinese Communist Party amounted to 12,000 gold rubles to pay, inter alia, for the activities of 17 "organizers and propagandists."[49] In a country of 500 million people, this was, to say the least, a modest investment. At the end of 1922, 12,000 gold rubles was all the Soviet "goat" could manage, especially with "western" policy still the priority.

In January 1923 the Politburo decided to support Sun's Guomintang, which was essentially Ioffe's recommendation. Comintern agents would take the lead. Ioffe's idea was to back Sun and the warlord Wu, but in the event of a break between these two, to support Sun. Ioffe thought the Guomintang was being transformed into a mass party, and he repeated his belief that China had never been closer to national unity, nor had it faced greater obstacles to that end. He pressed for a stronger Soviet policy.[50]

Ioffe's insistence on a more aggressive policy prompted a reply from Trotskii, indicating that the Politburo supported his general ideas. But Trotskii also noted that the USSR, like China, was a poor country; it did not have the financial resources to make loans, for example, to the Chinese government. Nor would these ever be enough, for the Chinese would need more, and the USSR would not be able to advance the money or entertain any hope of repayment. "That part of sympathy which can be obtained by material handouts is very unstable, for our enemies can give far more handouts." Trotskii also talked more generally about Soviet diplomacy. Before the war, diplomatic relations were clearer; there were more definite lines of policy governed by treaties and traditions. Now, however, circumstances had "radically changed."

> Diplomacy is strongly characterized by maneuver, with one flank of maneuver in London and another in Beijing or Tokyo. This is why now more than ever it is important to have astute policies at the world's most important points of orientation and at the same time have a strong center coordinating maneuvers at the various points of the diplomatic front.

There were some disadvantages to such an approach, Trotskii conceded: "I do not doubt for a minute that at the center we can make not a few mistakes as a consequence of insufficient information . . . especially in the East." But all things considered, these shortcomings were outweighed by the advantages of a "centralized, agile diplomacy."[51]

Did Marx or Engels ever talk about a "centralized, agile diplomacy"? In the West Trotskii is often perceived as a revolutionary *enragé*. In the political opposition against Stalin, he sometimes sounded like one. When he exercised power, he was as sensible and pragmatic as anyone in the NKID. One had to be. Ironically, western anti-communist hostility *imposed* realism on Soviet diplomats, as did Russian backwardness and the need to trade and obtain credit in the West. This was part and parcel of the movement from the café *terrasse* to the Kremlin. One had to face realities. Failure to do so could be dangerous or even fatal.

Ioffe complained that the Politburo did not have confidence in him, tied up his freedom of action "hand and foot," and did not read his dispatches. Chicherin and Litvinov, he thought, were hostile. But this was taking matters too personally; the NKID was attempting to improve relations with Britain, as Litvinov had explained to his diplomats in Europe, and this required Soviet restraint in China.

Litvinov could not keep the brakes on indefinitely. The Politburo moved slowly toward giving assistance to Sun Yat-sen, though not at the risk of provoking Japanese intervention. The Soviet government still kept an eye cocked on Tokyo, as well as on London. So it was tentative support about "possible" financial aid and "technical and military advisers." The Politburo worried that Sun was too preoccupied "with purely military operations at the expense of organization-preparatory work." After the Curzon crisis, the Politburo named the iconic Comintern operative M. M. Borodin as an adviser to Sun. Events in China were going from "bad to worse," according to Trotskii, the Guomintang was hopelessly corrupt and disorganized. Military operations consumed financial resources but had only "episodic" importance. No serious party or propaganda work was being accomplished. Chicherin was of a similar opinion.[52]

A Guomintang delegation came to Moscow in the autumn of 1923 presumably to go to school and learn how to take power in China. A new Soviet *polpred* in Beijing, Karakhan, recommended sending a modest quantity of guns to Sun so he could "hold on," and in early 1924 the Politburo opened its purse to the tune of 500,000 rubles to support him. At the same time the "Eastern Commission" of the Comintern proposed a program for developing the work of the nascent Chinese Communist Party.[53]

The brakes, to which Litvinov had been holding, were slowly coming off Soviet action in the East. "In present-day speeches of senior leaders," Chicherin observed, "they constantly emphasize that the East is just as important if not more important than the West."[54] If he and Litvinov hoped for a different orientation, they could or would not stop the shift in attention to China. The death of Sun Yat-sen in March 1925 appeared to trigger intensified Soviet support for the Guomintang and the Chinese Communist Party.[55]

Even Stalin paid attention. He wrote to Karakhan though he excused himself for responding so slowly. "I've lost any interest in correspondence," he said, which might explain why historians see so few of his directives in the archives. On the main question, however, Stalin advised that "Moscow [would] not skimp, if only the business were for real." The last part of this sentence reveals that Stalin was skeptical of Chinese success. And there were limits. Talking 10 or 20 million rubles was beyond Soviet capabilities. There was no question of throwing in the towel, but we have to be on guard against "fantasy" (*fantazerstvo*). "We have to be revolutionaries—this is without question—but one cannot lose touch with the ground, acting like a fantasist; this is also true." Here were signs of Stalin's realism, having learned perhaps from the German and other fiascos in Europe. Two days later, Chicherin sent a similar message: "In regard to military action, we do not want to be drawn in too far."[56]

Chicherin had picked up the noise of Anglo-French discussions about an anti-Soviet united front. He worried about Germany being drawn in and away from Rapallo. Britain was having trouble not only in China but in other colonies, where its position was being "severely undermined." "For the sake of a diversion, it could jump into an adventure against us like the Curzon ultimatum." So yes, Chicherin noted, we have a line, but a line pursued carefully.[57] This message was delivered to Ioffe, then to Karakhan, from many different sources, from Trotskii to Stalin and Chicherin. We have interests to balance, security and international trade to protect. The imperialists face resistance in their colonies; they could lash out at us suddenly, seeking a scapegoat.

The French and British governments were not too discerning when it came to the USSR. Whether Moscow was in for a penny or a pound, it was a provocation that justified retaliation. Nuances in Soviet policy were seldom observed in western capitals, and only then by clerks and ambassadors whose ideas were not noticed or were overwhelmed by anti-communist domestic politics.

Notes

1. Maxse's minutes, 5 June 1925, N3153/102/38, FO 371 11016; and 12 Dec. 1925, N6905/13/38, FO 371 11009.

2. Hodgson to G. A. Mounsey, head, Northern Department, 23 June 1925, N4077/356/38, FO 371 11020; Litvinov to Rakovskii, no. 0366, secret, 16 May 1925, AVPRF, f. 069, o. 9, p. 20, d. 3, l. 26; and Hodgson to Gregory, 16 March 1925, N1777/114/38, FO 371 11017.

3. Strang's minute, 28 March 1925, N1802/29/38, FO 371 11010; minutes by Maxse, 27 April 1925; and Gregory, 2 May 1925, N2298/29/38, ibid.

4. Macleay, British minister in Beijing, no. 164, confidential, 17 June 1924, F1992/445/10, FO 371 10282.

5. W. Max Muller, British ambassador in Warsaw, to Gregory, 9 Feb. 1922, N1781/646/38, FO 371 8185.

6. Stalin to Karakhan, 19 Feb. 1925; and Karakhan to Stalin, 23 June 1925, A. I. Kartunova and M. L. Titarenko (eds.), *Perepiska I. V. Stalina i G. V. Chicherina s polpredom SSSR v Kitae L. M. Karakhanom: Dokumenty, avgust 1923g.–1926g.* (hereinafter *Perepiska I. V. Stalina i G. V. Chicherina*) (Moscow, 2008), pp. 440–41, 550–53.

7. Macleay, nos. 156–57, 11 June 1924, and minutes, 13 June 1924, F1907/445/10, FO 371 10282.

8. Waterlow's minute, 14 Nov. 1924, F3765/445/10, FO 371 10283.

9. Chamberlain to Sir Esme Howard, British ambassador in Washington, confidential, 11 Nov. 1924, F3701/19/10, FO 371 10245; Waterlow's minute, 7 Nov. 1924, F3720/19/10, ibid.; and F. T. A. Ashton-Gwatkin's minute, 19 Dec. 1924, F4241/445/10, FO 371 10283.

10. Palairet, no. 119, 11 June 1925, F2191G/194/10, green (very secret), FO 371 10942; Foreign Office to Palairet, no. 99, 16 June 1925, ibid.; Waterlow's minute, 12 June 1925, ibid.; and SIS to Bland, Foreign Office, no. C/622, 15 June 1925, F2306/194/10, ibid.

11. Minutes by Waterlow, 24 June 1925, F2504/194/10, FO 371 10943; and by Chamberlain, 22 June, F2420/194/10; and 25 June 1925, F2504/194/10, ibid.

12. Wallace E. Brown, resident bishop, Methodist Episcopal Church, Fuzhou, Fujian, to W. F. McDowell, bishop, Washington, 30 June 1925, 893.00/6500, NA RG59, M-329, reel 45.

13. L. J. Birney to McDowell, 29 June 1925, 893.00/6500, NA RG59, M-329, reel 45; Hugh W. White to Kellogg, Secretary of State, 16 July 1925, 893.00/6530, ibid.; and MacMurray, no 293, strictly confidential, 28 June 1925, 893.00/6453, ibid., reel 44.

14. Harold Williams to Tyrrell, 22 June 1925, F2505/194/10, FO 371 10943.

15. Minutes by Waterlow, 25 June 1925, F2531/194/10, FO 371 10943; and 29 June 1925, F2589/194/10, ibid.; and by G. S. Moss, Far Eastern Department, 29 June 1925, F2622/194/10, ibid.

16. Untitled, handwritten note by Waterlow, 19 June 1925, F2579/194/10, FO 371 10943.

17. Untitled memorandum by Gregory, 21 June 1925; and Tyrrell's handwritten undated minute, F2579/194/10, FO 371 10943.

18. Maxse's minute, 1 April 1925, N1782/102/38, FO 371 11015.

19. Waterlow's minute, 3 July 1925, N3810/102/38 FO 371 11016; and Hodgson to Moun-sey, 23 June 1925, N4077/356/38, FO 371 11020.

20. Chicherin's "interview" in *Izvestiia*, 2 July 1925, G. V. *Chicherin: stat'i i rechi* (Moscow, 1961), pp. 395–400.

21. Chamberlin's minute, 6 July 1925, N3815/102/38, FO 371 11016.

22. Chamberlin's minute, 9 Oct. 1925, N5536/29/38, FO 371 11011.

23. Chamberlain's minute, 1 April 1925, N2290/102/38, FO 371 11015; and Chamberlain to Joynson-Hicks, 5 May 1925, *DBFP*, 1st, XXV, p. 664.

24. Minutes by Collier and B. C. Newton, Far Eastern Department, 22 June 1925, F2420/194/10, FO 371 10942; and Waterlow's minute, 19 June 1925, F2579/194/10, FO 371 10943.

25. Minutes by Collier and Waterlow, 12 June 1925, F2191/194/10, FO 371 10942; and FO to Palairet, no. 109, urgent, 23 June 1925, F2420/194/10, ibid.

26. Minute by Hugh Ledward, Northern Department, 4 June 1925, N3153/102/38, FO 371 11016.

27. Stubbs to Colonial Office, 27 July 1925, F3531/194/10, FO 371 10946.

28. See various documents in files FO 371 10943–49.

29. Commander in chief China to Admiralty, 21 Aug. 1925; and Ashton-Gwatkin's min-ute, 22 Aug. 1925, F4085/194/10, FO 371 10947.

30. Chamberlain's minute, 18 Sept. 1925, F4582/194/10, FO 371 10949; and Strang's min-ute, 29 Sept. 1925, F4748/194/10, ibid.

31. Newton's minute, 4 July 1925, F2951/194/10, FO 371 10944.

32. "Note by Mr. Waterlow," 30 Sept. 1925, F4582/194/10, FO 371 10949.

33. Briand's comments to Chamberlain, 7 June 1925, N3412/29/38, FO 371 11010.

34. Rakovskii to Chicherin, no. 11, very secret, nd (but early July 1925), AVPRF, f. 069, o. 9, p. 20, d. 4, l. 136.

35. Rakovskii to Chamberlain (in English), no. CR/1655, 27 May 1925, AVPRF, f. 069, o. 9, p. 20, d. 4, l. 108.

36. Litvinov to Rakovskii, no. 0525, secret, 22 Nov. 1924, AVPRF, f. 04, o. 4, p. 27, d. 147, ll. 44–46; Litvinov to Rakovskii, no. 0366, secret, 16 May 1925, AVPRF, f. 069, o. 9, p. 20, d. 3, l. 26; Litvinov to Krasin, no. 0619, secret, 24 Dec. 1924, AVPRF, f. 0136, p. 105, d. 102, ll. 11–12; and Litvinov to NKID *kollegiia*, "Draft proposals for French negotiations," 13 April 1925, AVPRF, f. 0136, o. 8, p. 105, d. 95, ll. 64–66.

37. "Memorandum on the Crisis in Anglo-Soviet Relations," Rakovskii, nd (but July 1925), AVPRF, f. 069, o. 9, p. 20, d. 4, ll. 144–50.

38. Williams Peters, counselor, Moscow, no. 347, 22 May 1925; and Ledward's minute, 4 June 1925, N3153/102/38, FO 371 11016; and Muller (Warsaw), no. 467, confidential, 5 Oct. 1925, N5575/102/38, ibid.

39. Hodgson, no. 463, 8 July 1925, *DBFP*, 1st, XXV, pp. 685–89.

40. Maxse's minute, 5 June 1925, N3153/102/38, FO 371 11016; "Account of a Journey to Russia, April–June 1925," Owen St. Clair O'Malley, N4476/652/38, FO 371 11021; Greg-ory's minute, 6 Aug. 1925, ibid.; and MacDonald's minute, 19 Aug. 1924, N6622/2140/38, FO 371 10495.

41. Chicherin to Lenin, 6 Nov. 1921; Lenin to Chicherin, 7 Nov. 1921; and Chicherin to A. K. Paikes, NKID agent in the Far East, Station Manchuria, 7 Dec. 1921, G. Khen'iui, M. L. Titarenko, et al., *VKP(b), Komintern i Natsional'no-revoliutsionnoe dvizhenie v Kitae, dokumenty*, 8 vols. (hereinafter *VKP(b), Komintern v Kitae*), I, pp. 64–66.

42. Paikes to Karakhan, very secret, 4 Aug. 1922, *VKP(b)*, *Komintern v Kitae*, I, p. 93.

43. Ioffe to Karakhan, for Stalin, very secret, 25 and 30 August 1922, *VKP(b)*, *Komintern v Kitae*, I, pp. 102–3, 107.

44. Ioffe to Sun, 22 Aug. 1922, and Sun (Shanghai) to Ioffe, 27 Aug. 1922, *VKP(b)*, *Komintern v Kitae*, I, pp. 98–101, 104–7.

45. Ioffe to Karakhan, for Stalin, very secret, 31 Aug. and 4 Sept. 1922, *VKP(b)*, *Komintern v Kitae*, I, pp. 110–11, 116–18; and excerpt from Politburo protocol, no. 25, 7 Sept. 1922, ibid., p. 118.

46. Maring's record of conversation with Sun, Shanghai, 26 Sept. 1922, *VKP(b)*, *Komintern v Kitae*, I, pp. 126–29.

47. Excerpts from Ioffe to Chicherin, for the Politburo and Stalin, very secret, 17 Oct. 1922, *VKP(b)*, *Komintern v Kitae*, I, pp. 130–32.

48. Sun (Shanghai) to Ioffe, 2 Nov. 1922, *VKP(b)*, *Komintern v Kitae*, I, pp. 134–36.

49. Except from minutes of the presidium of the Comintern executive committee, 29 Dec. 1922; and Estimate of expenditures for the Communist Party in China in 1923, very secret, Dec. 1922, *VKP(b)*, *Komintern v Kitae*, I, pp. 164–70.

50. Excerpt from Politburo protocol, no. 42, 4 Jan. 1923; and Ioffe to Chicherin, et al., no. 7, very secret, 13 Jan. 1923, *VKP(b)*, *Komintern v Kitae*, I, pp. 170–72, 176–83.

51. Trotskii to Ioffe, secret, 20 Jan. 1923; and Trotskii to Politburo/NKID, 20 Jan. 1923, *VKP(b)*, *Komintern v Kitae*, I, pp. 183–85 and 185, n. 1.

52. Excerpt from Politburo protocol, no. 53, 8 March 1923, *VKP(b)*, *Komintern v Kitae*, I, p. 206; excerpt from Politburo protocol no. 21, 2 Aug. 1923, ibid., pp. 239–40; Chicherin to Zinoviev, 1 Nov. 1923, ibid., pp. 277–78; and Trotskii to Chicherin, Stalin, very secret, 2 Nov. 1923, ibid., pp. 278–79.

53. Chicherin to Zinoviev, very secret, 5 Dec. 1923, *VKP(b)*, *Komintern v Kitae*, I, pp. 313–14; excerpt from Politburo protocol, no. 80, 20 March 1924, ibid., pp. 442–43; and "Resolution of the Eastern Commission, IKKI," Moscow, not later than April 1924, ibid., pp. 444–45.

54. Chicherin to Karakhan, no. 58, very secret, 4 Nov. 1924, *Perepiska I. V. Stalina i G. V. Chicherina*, pp. 358–61.

55. Excerpt from Politburo protocol, no. 52, 13 March 1925, *VKP(b)*, *Komintern v Kitae*, I, pp. 527–29.

56. Stalin to Karakhan, 29 May 1925, *Perepiska I. V. Stalina i G. V. Chicherina*, pp. 525–28; and Chicherin to Karakhan, no. 73, personal and very secret, 1 June 1925, ibid., pp. 536–38.

57. Chicherin to Karakhan, no. 76, secret, 23 June 1925, *Perepiska I. V. Stalina i G. V. Chicherina*, pp. 541–43; and Chicherin to Karakhan, no. 78, 7 July 1925, ibid., pp. 560–62.

CHAPTER SEVEN

~

Principles and Reprisals

Hostile Coexistence in London and Washington, 1925–1926

While the Soviet government decided how far to go in supporting the revolutionary movement in China, it did not abandon efforts to avoid the worst with London and to seek agreement with Paris. However, the "Zinoviev letter" and the failure of the Anglo-Soviet draft treaty made the Politburo less disposed to restrain Soviet "eastern" policies. If the Die-Hards thought that talk of avenues lined with gallows meant for Bolsheviks was going to intimidate anyone in Moscow, they miscalculated. With good reason, Chamberlain did not like the public statements of the three main Die-Hards, Birkenhead, Churchill, and Joynson-Hicks. British hostility was evident in the press and in the House of Commons however Chamberlain might like to lower its intensity. Whereas at the beginning of 1925 Litvinov was ready to dismiss the danger of an anti-Soviet bloc, as the year unfolded he was less certain, just as Chamberlain was less adamant about rejecting such possibilities. Any Anglo-Soviet agreement would be impossible, Litvinov reckoned, if there were no loan or commercial credits in exchange for debt recognition and repayment. In any event, the British government would not entertain further discussions until we were "compelled to be more . . . pliable" because of crop failures or the "forever awaited" peasant uprisings. In the meantime Litvinov thought Britain would work toward Soviet isolation from, in particular, France and Germany.[1]

Even Rakovskii was gloomy about better relations with Britain, especially because of events in China. And if the Chinese situation did not give enough ammunition to the Die-Hards, a miners' strike during the summer of 1925 raised new tensions. As usual, Rakovskii reported, everything is being blamed on Moscow. Since the press was a major battlefield, the Soviet embassy put a new comrade in charge of expanding the embassy's contacts with British journalists. This was Ivan M. Maiskii, who eventually became Soviet *polpred* in London in 1932 and played a major role in preparing the way for the Grand Alliance against Nazi Germany. At this point Maiskii's role was modest, though nevertheless an indication that the NKID was trying to get its point of view into the British papers.[2]

Litvinov was unhappy with Soviet press contacts in London, singling out for special scorn journalist W. N. Ewer, who provided "very unreliable information." Either he was being fed disinformation or his connections were poor. Litvinov also railed against the British go-betweens on which the Soviet embassy had to rely: they were self-important people who scurried around like mice, demanding real money, "favors," and contracts of little advantage to us. All the same, they were not so shady as Soviet agents in Paris. Indeed NKID intelligence was good and improving, among other reasons because someone in the Foreign Office or in the British embassy in Moscow was passing documents to Soviet intelligence.[3]

Document stealing and code breaking were an integral part of relations between states, and no one took these activities too tragically. It was one's own fault if security and ciphers were not good enough. Meanwhile, in Moscow the British chargé d'affaires, R. M. Hodgson, attempted to persuade Litvinov that a better environment was developing in London. The NKID was not so sure, Litvinov replied, in referencing recent speeches by Joynson-Hicks and Birkenhead. They were the Birk and Jix Show: no one knew who would outdo the other when it came to the Bolsh Bogey. "We would of course welcome an improvement in relations," Litvinov told Hodgson. "And we would gladly renew negotiations if we believed in the genuine will of the British government to come to terms." Unfortunately, Litvinov did not see it. Nor did Chicherin in Berlin, who held a press conference in October 1925 in the Soviet embassy before 250 newsmen. According to one observer, he was much at his ease with the journalists, regaling them with attacks on British foreign policy. Privately, Litvinov blew hot and cold about Anglo-Soviet relations, sometimes warning against excessive pessimism. Let us try to keep relations with Britain from getting any worse was the NKID position at the end of 1925.[4]

Hodgson, who wanted to persuade Litvinov that the time was right for a step forward, also took the same line with the Foreign Office. When he was in London in December 1925, Hodgson met A. P. Rozengol'ts, the Soviet chargé d'affaires, and Maiskii. He came away from the meeting thinking that the Soviet government was "clearly very anxious to come to terms" and "in a very amenable mood." Indeed, "they might be disposed to come to a more favourable arrangement now than at any other time." The Foreign Office permanent officials reacted skeptically to Hodgson's report, and rightly so, because the mood in Moscow was anything but well disposed to London. The Foreign Office continued to believe that an "attitude of reserve" would force Moscow into concessions. The opposite was true: Soviet policy hardened and became more aggressive, especially in China where the USSR could disturb British interests. Ironically, the Foreign Office maintained the same policy, mutatis mutandis, as that of the NKID: if the Soviet side had "any concrete proposals to submit, likely to lead to the renewal of negotiations on a satisfactory basis, we [HMG] shall of course be happy to consider them." The situation thus remained deadlocked. The NKID was not going to bid against its own previous proposals before a British counter-offer. Like Hodgson, Rozengol'ts tried to push his interlocutors in the right direction, but the Foreign Office would not take any initiative without fresh offers from Moscow. Still it was important to avoid the appearance of intransigence, as Gregory pointed out, because "wild men," that is, trade unionists and Labourites, were "touchy" about "Foreign Office relations with Russia." The idea was not to "throw more of them into the arms of the Bolsheviks and weaken the influence of the Right wing of Labour if and when we come again into conflict with the Soviet Government." This was Gregory's idea, but it was endorsed higher up. The permanent undersecretary Tyrrell, who succeeded Crowe, dead of cancer in April 1925, was in full agreement: we should "deprive the pro-Soviet party . . . of a plausible plea that we oppose nothing but negatives to their overtures." These were political calculations more relevant to the Conservative Party than to Foreign Office civil servants who in principle were supposed to stay out of politics. They did not do so, obviously, and as Berzin had observed in the aftermath of the "Zinoviev letter," the civil servants were "almost without exception" behind the Tories.[5]

In the meantime there were rumors in the press at the end of 1925 about a possible meeting between Chicherin and Chamberlain. Rozengol'ts raised the question with Sir George Mounsey in the Foreign Office, who thought the reports "mistaken." In fact, the rumors appear to have originated with Chamberlain himself, who asked Briand, the French foreign minister, to float the idea to Chicherin when he came to Paris at the end of 1925.[6] Litvinov did not know what to make of Chamberlain's position: some sources said it was "waiting and ignoring the USSR"; others that he was ready to resume negotiations. "We have documentary evidence," commented Litvinov, this language meaning that he had read Foreign Office papers, to the effect that the British were holding to their policy of reserve. And so Litvinov opined that the time was not right to resume negotiations, for they had no chance to succeed. In January 1926 Litvinov conveyed this

Figure 7.1. Austen Chamberlain, ca. 1925. *Bundesarchiv, Bild* **102-04312.**

view to Peters, the British counselor in Moscow, who passed it on to the Foreign Office.[7] In relations between the Soviet Union and the western powers, sometimes the correct messages did get through.

The idea of a Chamberlain-Chicherin meeting was not quite dead. In early February 1926, Walter Citrine, the new general secretary of the British Trade Union Congress (TUC), wrote a confidential letter to Chicherin, offering to act as intermediary to prepare the way for a meeting between Chicherin and Chamberlain and for a renewal of negotiations. Citrine and a TUC delegation had earlier met Chamberlain, and Citrine's letter then followed. Maiskii thought that Chamberlain had made a "clever" move in sowing seeds of doubt in trade unionists' minds about Soviet accusations of British intransigence toward the USSR. Nor did Maiskii like the idea of unreliable trade unionists serving as intermediaries, but he warned that in replying to Citrine the NKID should avoid any impression of bad faith about a renewal of negotiations.[8]

Still a relatively junior Soviet diplomat, Maiskii was hesitant to write so directly to Moscow, but he need not have worried, for Chicherin agreed with him and at once advised the Politburo.

"Naïve British trade unionists," he warned, had been fooled once again by the "nimble bearers of the traditions of the English bourgeoisie." If we do not respond carefully, Chamberlain might produce an even greater impression on them. The Foreign Office idea was not negotiations with Moscow, but rather weakening the "pro-Soviet party" in the House of Commons. Chamberlain wanted to represent himself as the "lamb" and the Soviet government as the "wolf," a preposterous pair of images if ever there was one, Chicherin implied. And Chamberlain needed to know in advance that negotiations would "have a favorable outcome." "A strange approach to negotiations," though not so dissimilar to Litvinov's. "Our sins," Chicherin continued, "are propaganda in the East, help to the anti-British movement in Shanghai, etc., and the establishment in Moscow of a school for eastern revolutionaries. . . . Chamberlain doubts the very possibility of agreement with us because there are links between the Soviet government and the Comintern." Based on such premises, Chicherin concluded, there is not the slightest possibility of agreeing on anything. As for Citrine and his colleagues, Chicherin roared his contempt: "I am sufficiently familiar with English life to know that when trade union leaders become involved in governmental business, they entirely fall into line with the government." We could send some of our own "comrades" to Britain to explain to Citrine and his colleagues what is really going on. This was not a practical idea, though it revealed a commonly held Bolshevik assumption that only Russians knew how to make a revolution.[9] At the time of course this was a demonstrably true statement.

Litvinov was of a similar mind:

> As long as we do not have the possibility or the desire to establish a modus vivendi with Great Britain in the East, we need to recognize that a special meeting and direct talks between foreign ministries of the USSR and Britain . . . are inappropriate and undesirable. Not promising or nearly so any results, a meeting inevitably will arouse suspicions in the East, especially in Turkey. It is possible that Chamberlain had in mind this negative result for us in suggesting a meeting through Briand and Citrine.

Like Chicherin, Litvinov noted that some kind of reply would have to be made to Citrine's letter, but he was just as hostile to trade union involvement in negotiations with the Foreign Office. "Their support of us on the debts question is doubtful, and they [the trade unionists] would certainly support Chamberlain on the issues of propaganda and eastern policy." A Soviet reply would be about appearances: show a willingness to negotiate and defeat the Tory strategy of dividing and co-opting Labour. Like the Foreign Office, Litvinov was more interested in addressing the trade union movement and Labour Party than the British government. Chamberlain wanted to undermine the "pro-Soviet party"; Litvinov wanted to check the Tory strategy. A last point to keep in mind: whereas western and eastern policies had previously been of equal importance, Litvinov acknowledged that Soviet eastern policy now took precedence over relations with Britain.[10] Instead of intimidating Moscow, the Tories had only succeeded in further arousing Soviet hostility and in persuading the Politburo that it had little to lose in pursuing Soviet interests "in the East," particularly in China.

In the meantime appearances mattered, as Litvinov explained to Maiskii in London:

> Concerning Chamberlain's suggestion, passed on by Citrine, we do not expect practical results. However, it is necessary to maneuver so that Citrine and his supporters do not get the impression that we want to avoid a meeting which in their opinion could bring about a settling of Anglo-Soviet relations. We must therefore reply that we entirely agree to the meeting with . . . Chamberlain.

Litvinov added that M. P. Tomskii, head of the Soviet trade union council, would write to his counterpart Citrine "to attempt to explain to him the real character of Chamberlain's démarche."[11]

The Tomskii channel was unnecessary because Maiskii was already developing what would become a remarkable network of contacts in Britain in the 1930s. In 1926 he was in touch with various trade union and Labour leaders, Citrine and Ponsonby among others. According to information from Ponsonby, "everyone is taken up with one fixed idea: with Russia there can now be no relations as long as Russia does not stop its 'propaganda,' by which he means mainly 'propaganda' in the East." Chamberlain had succeeded in sowing seeds of doubt among some Labour leaders. Ponsonby told Maiskii that when he wanted to put a question to Chamberlain in the House about relations with Moscow, colleagues on the benches beside told him to keep quiet: "We have met Chamberlain . . . and we are fully satisfied with his explanations about Russia." One can only imagine Chicherin's utter contempt when he read this report. Even Citrine, according to Maiskii, "had fallen under Chamberlain's influence," but since he was head of the TUC, we have to treat him carefully. So Chicherin kept his scorn private and wrote the required letter to Citrine. But he suggested that Chamberlain should make counter-proposals based on the aborted treaty of 1924, and this he assumed the Tory government would not do.[12]

Citrine did not appreciate the letters from Moscow. He especially did not like receiving a "lecture" from Tomskii about Chamberlain's true intentions. "We don't need pointers from foreigners," he said. Citrine also did not like the reference to the 1924 treaty, as it sounded like a precondition. And it was, but Maiskii replied correctly that if Chamberlain did not like Chicherin's proposal, he could make one of his own.[13] This is what the NKID wanted; it would bargain, and hard, but not against itself. The main point however is that Chamberlain's meeting with Citrine and his colleagues had at least temporarily produced the desired effect, freezing Labour's discontents on Russian policy. Chicherin's scorn was also amply rewarded. Imagine Labour taking up the defense of British imperialism in China.

Nothing seemed to come of the exchange with Citrine, but Maiskii nevertheless thought he noticed a slight thaw in relations in March 1926 and there were the usual discussions with go-betweens on trade proposals, credit, and compensation for bondholders.[14] In late April 1926 a delegation of Tory backbench MPs arrived in Moscow for discussions with Soviet officials. They asked the habitual questions about how to get negotiations moving again. It was also the usual issue about who should take the initiative.[15] Even in London Chamberlain seemed to open up a little about resuming negotiations. There were some papers completed in the Foreign Office about problems with the 1924 treaty and what questions therefore needed to be addressed in a resumption of negotiations. This was in fact what the NKID had long requested.

British General Strike

Then, a sudden crisis erupted. There had been labor troubles building up in the coal-mining industry in Britain since the end of the war. Production was down and management wanted to increase miners' hours and lower their wages. During the summer of 1925 a confrontation loomed between miners and the pit owners, but the Conservative government intervened to avert an immediate crisis and buy time. In the meantime, Soviet and British trade unionists agreed to establish an advisory committee to establish closer relations and to discuss issues of common interest. The intention was to open channels to British trade unionists and to build up support in Britain against Tory anti-Soviet hostility. It proved to be a bad idea.[16]

In April 1926, faced with an ultimatum from pit owners to accept lower wages and a longer workday, the miners were ready for a confrontation. On 22 April the Politburo declared its intention to support the strike and, breaking its own rules, ordered Rozengol'ts and Maiskii to forward advice from the Profintern, the Soviet trade union council, to the TUC to organize an international meeting of unionists in support of the miners.[17] On May Day there were huge demonstrations everywhere in Britain. It was an impressive show of solidarity, but could popular support be mobilized to defeat the pit owners?

The TUC declared a general strike to begin on 4 May. The Politburo reacted immediately, seemingly without debate: it approved an initial contribution of 250,000 rubles for the miners' strike fund, the money coming from the Profintern. Restraint and calm were the watchwords directed to the Soviet press and the Comintern in commenting on the strike. But there were also directives intended for the British Communist Party about moving the strike onto "political rails," calling for the downfall of the Conservative government and the establishment of a real worker's government which would nationalize the coal mines, provide support for the unemployed, and so on.[18] Not exactly a call for Bolshevik revolution, but reminiscent of the forged "Zinoviev letter" and meddling in British domestic affairs. It was just the kind of action to incense the Conservative government.

Knuckling under to fear of or pressure from the government, the strike organizing committee refused to accept Soviet aid. As one historian has put it, this "spectacular refusal" was an affront and a denunciation of the long European tradition of worker solidarity. The trade union leaders—fools, Chicherin must have thought—played into the hands of the Tory government. They were divided between left and right, some hostile to Moscow, and seemed more afraid of rank-and-file militancy than of the failure of the strike. To the relief of the Tories, the strike was called off on 12 May.[19] It was a crushing defeat for the labor movement, but especially for the miners. No wonder Chicherin and other Bolsheviks held the British trade unionists in such utter contempt.

Like puppies with their tails between their legs, the Conservative MPs visiting Moscow hastily returned to London only to be rounded upon by Die-Hards, dismissing them as "foolish children," who ought to make application for entry into the Labour Party. Litvinov noted that the MPs had left so hastily that he had not been able to meet them. They said that they had been much impressed by what they saw and heard during their visit to Moscow. "Naturally, this does not mean," Litvinov added with his usual dry humor, "that they will also repeat the same thing in London." They didn't, of course. The MPs made their excuses to the Foreign Office, not that it did them any good. "All three M.P's [sic] said several times that they quite realized that the coal strike and its developments made it quite impossible for H.M.G. to re-open any kind of negotiations with the Soviet."[20]

The general strike having failed, the miners were left to fend for themselves, eventually being forced back to work by empty pockets and empty cupboards, those anyway whom the pit owners were ready to rehire. Other miners spent years unemployed and living on the edge, though the owners made out all right. The strike and Politburo involvement scuttled any relaxation in Anglo-Soviet relations.

Unchaining of the Die-Hards

The British cabinet met in June to discuss a rupture of relations with Moscow. In spite of the "malignant hostility to the British empire of the Soviet

Government," the Cabinet decided not to break off diplomatic relations. According to one Soviet report, only Churchill and Birkenhead voted for rupture. Increased trade with the Soviet Union and the negative impact of its interruption on unemployment and on the miners' strike led the government to avoid an open break with Moscow. Nor did the Cabinet decide to stop the transmission of Soviet relief funds to striking miners, "since such action could easily be misinterpreted."[21] The Tory government would have been seen to take the side of the pit owners, as indeed it did.

Soviet actions were grist to Die-Hard mills. According to the French ambassador Fleuriau, the Tories were up in arms. Soviet trade unions had contributed £480,000 pounds to the miners' strike fund, which the government could not block because technically the strike was "legal." "There is no doubt," Fleuriau reported, that the Bolsheviks were involved in the crisis. The Home Office had the proof. The Die-Hard trio of Joynson-Hicks, Churchill, and Birkenhead was the most ardent in denouncing Moscow. Nevertheless, Fleuriau advised the Foreign Office against a rupture with Moscow. This was surprising advice coming from Fleuriau, for he hated the Bolsheviks. The Russians, he added, were like the Turks, Chinese, and other "Orientals": the threat of certain execution was much more effective in obtaining compliance than the actual execution itself. Here was an Orientalist remark which was not out of character for the former French minister in Beijing. A quintessential imperialist, Fleuriau knew how to deal with colonial rebellions. Deploy a division of colonial troops and threaten a cannonade. He was not the only one; the secretary general of the Quai d'Orsay, Berthelot, also an old China hand, likened the Soviet Union to the defunct Ottoman Empire. "One must be prepared," Berthelot said, "to deal with modern Russia as the Powers had had to deal with old Turkey, and expect that every question would take six or seven years to settle." It was just this mentality which riled the Bolsheviks, who were determined, as Rakovskii put it, that Russia would not become another China.[22]

There was nothing Litvinov or Chicherin could do in May to restrain the Politburo's support of the British miners, not that they did not deserve help. They certainly ought to have obtained more support from the TUC, upon which Chicherin heaped his unbridled scorn. Even in May, Rozengol'ts was indiscreet enough to say to one of the Tory MPs who had visited Moscow that the Politburo decision to send money to the miners was "folly" and that he had so informed the NKID.[23] As indeed he did. In mid-April he had warned Litvinov of the looming conflict in the British coal industry: "You can anticipate a very sharp campaign arising from our alleged interference in the internal affairs of England."

"I have already written once to you about this," he added to emphasize his point: "The threatening campaign could significantly worsen Anglo-Soviet relations." He asked to be informed of any action by Soviet trade unions to support the strikers. "You can be sure that the press will circulate all kinds of nonsense," and having precise information from Moscow would help to counter it.[24]

Later in the month, Rozengol'ts reported a conversation with Labour Party MP Arthur Henderson, who warned that the Tories were up in arms about Soviet "propaganda." Henderson mentioned that he had been to the Home Office and seen the files of "reliable information" on Soviet activities.[25] Tory co-optation of the "pro-Soviet party" went beyond Chamberlain's efforts with Citrine and other trade unionists.

There was not much Litvinov could do about Rozengol'ts' warnings, except to advise embassy staff against getting involved in the strike. As if Rozengol'ts needed the warning. He informed Litvinov that he knew of only one slip-up where his counselor, D. V. Bogomolov, had spent two days during the strike at the home of the TUC leader, A. A. Purcell, to gather information! Be careful, Litvinov warned. Scotland Yard has probably infiltrated the British Communist Party and the TUC and therefore knows of your conversations with various trade unionists.[26]

What else could Litvinov say? Rozengol'ts explained to one of the contrite Tory visitors to Moscow that the Soviet government, read the NKID, was "much embarrassed" but "powerless against the feeling stirred up [in Moscow] by the Comintern. Chicherin suggested to the French ambassador Herbette that he had had to fight against colleagues who wanted a tougher response to London.[27]

Even Stalin maneuvered, anticipating an attack on his left from Zinoviev who joined Trotskii in opposition to Politburo policy toward the British trade unionist leadership.[28] Stalin moved as politics dictated, tacking right when he defeated the left, and left when he defeated the right. Matters of policy could become secondary considerations. Trotskii noticed and said so publicly: there is a new "tendency" among us "to condemn that which does not conform to the point of view of this or that comrade . . . without taking the trouble to understand the actual situation." The Foreign Office noticed too. It's "misleading," one clerk wrote, "to label Soviet leaders 'extremists' or 'moderates.' Either shade is equally liable to turn redder or whiter for the purpose of scoring over the other."[29]

Wish being father to the thought, Stalin was perceived as a centrist. "He is the general secretary of the party, and, as such, wields immense power," British counselor Peters reported from Moscow, "He rarely appears in public. He never allows himself to be interviewed. He thus gains the reputation of the 'strong, stern, silent man.'" Comrades could tell which way the wind was blowing. When Zinoviev was ousted from his positions of power, "it was a mad rush, helter-skelter, of a herd of terrified Communists whose one idea seems to have been to save their skins."[30]

"How are the mighty fallen and the weapons of war perished!" joked Foreign Office clerk Mr. Maxse: "It is fortunate for people like Zinoviev and Trotsky who suffer the usual ups and downs of revolutionary leadership that the Russians do not execute individuals, else they might have suffered the fate of Danton & Robespierre." This was a wisecrack referring to leaders of the French Revolution who lost their heads in the guillotine, and ironic too as it turned out, for no one in the Foreign Office yet saw the shadow of death lying over Stalin's adversaries. The *gensek* was only "putting his own house in order," remarked another clerk, after a *scène de famille*. Hodgson thought the Soviet Government was moving "in the direction of becoming more of a Russian Government and less of an internatl conspiracy organisation." Gregory was not so sure: "it is notoriously unsafe to prophesy about Russia."[31] This was true of Stalin too.

While the struggle for power continued in Moscow, the NKID had to deal with the consequences of the abortive general strike. Chamberlain made a statement in the House of Commons in June 1926 on "the so-called Russian question," as Chicherin put it. The *narkom* was not sure what to make of the British government's position: was it the first salvo of a new campaign or a gesture to buy off the Die-Hards? We follow the signs very closely, Chicherin told Rozengol'ts, but the information coming from you is so contradictory, we don't know what to think. Chamberlain's ambiguous stance could "go up in smoke." Either the Die-Hards would carry him with them, or they would remove him as Foreign Secretary. Chicherin hoped that economic conditions in Britain and in Europe, among other factors, would restrain British policy.[32] In fact, the debate in the House of Commons was heated: the Die-Hards called for rupture, Labour for the maintenance of diplomatic relations. Fleuriau correctly reported on Chamberlain's restraint, but the debate was so heated that the speaker adjourned the House to keep tempers from getting out of hand.[33]

Unbeknownst to Chicherin, it was economics that restrained the British cabinet. But would this situation last, and would Chamberlain be able to hold out against the Die-Hards? To obtain an answer, Rozengol'ts went to see Chamberlain in mid-July.

The conversation settled nothing, but it clarified Anglo-Soviet differences. The two big obstacles remained debts and the Comintern. On the first issue there was no change in the fundamental differences between Moscow and all the western states, to wit, that the principle of recognition of responsibility for the tsar's debts had to be accepted by Moscow and then negotiations could take place on the particulars of repayment. Rozengol'ts repeated the Soviet position that it would not recognize the debts but would negotiate the terms of mutually acceptable de facto solutions. Krasin had outlined this position long before, and it had not changed.

On the second, then more important issue, Chamberlain considered that the Soviet government and the Comintern were "one and the same." Rozengol'ts insisted that they were two separate organizations but that the Soviet government was not prepared to deny the Comintern a base in the Soviet Union. "I think," responded Chamberlain, "that advice should be given to those people who direct not only the Soviet government but also the Comintern *to control* [underlined in the original] the work of the Comintern abroad." In so doing, Chamberlain alluded to the Politburo, and there he hit the nail on the head. It was quite true that the Politburo was both the cabinet of the government and of the Comintern, even if the Politburo was more attentive in keeping government and Comintern organizations and personnel separate from one another, though it slipped up during the general strike. "I considered it superfluous [*izlishnii*]," reported Rozengol'ts, "to speak with him [Chamberlain] about this point." As well he might have, because how could he deny what was so obvious? Indeed, in his record of conversation, Rozengol'ts underscored the verb "control" regarding the Comintern, suggesting that he wanted to pass on Chamberlain's message to the NKID and beyond.

Readers may admire Chamberlain's honesty in talking to Rozengol'ts. In view of profound differences between our two governments, he said, it was "utterly pointless" to conduct new negotiations. But Chamberlain confirmed the message which he had passed through Briand that he would have been ready to meet with Chicherin in London. He also emphasized his role in trying to avoid the worst from the Die-Hards, mentioning in particular Joynson-Hicks and Birkenhead. "I did and am doing everything possible to avoid a rupture. I will also continue to do everything *that is possible* [underlined in the original] to avoid a rupture."

Rozengol'ts stressed to Chamberlain that Anglo-Soviet relations "were playing an excessively large role in British domestic politics." This remark is interesting not least because his counterpart in Moscow, Hodgson, made the same point to Chamberlain a few months later when he referred to the Die-Hards' "throw the Red bandits out" campaign. Like Rozengol'ts, Hodgson remarked that "the 'Red Bandit' battle-cry" might have some "useful purpose in political warfare at home" but was "detrimental to our essential interests." Put these interests "in terms of pounds sterling," he said.

Did these comments ring a bell in Chamberlain's mind? Apparently so, for he pondered whether to circulate the dispatch to the Cabinet, though conceding it "might provoke opposition." Discretion won the day. "I do not like to 'doctor' the despatch," Chamberlain wrote, "& I doubt whether it wd. be helpful to circulate it exactly as it stands." Prime Minister Stanley Baldwin agreed, and so Hodgson's comments did not leave the Foreign Office.[34] On the Soviet side, Rozengol'ts believed that Anglo-Soviet trade was the foundation for better relations and the primary obstacle to a diplomatic rupture.[35] This was still Krasin's policy.

It is not possible to say whether Chicherin or Litvinov thought to circulate Rozengol'ts' notes to the Politburo. Like Chamberlain, Chicherin concluded that "the center of gravity" had passed to the question of the Comintern, and this issue rendered "completely hopeless" any attempt to conclude a new agreement with London. It remained open however whether he should eventually meet Chamberlain when next he traveled to Western Europe. "On the basic questions," Chicherin wrote, a meeting "will not bring us out of the impasse, for in essence an impasse is where we find ourselves, but it might soften strained relations." At the same time Litvinov agreed to a recommendation from Rozengol'ts that the most active "party workers" be removed from Soviet economic agencies in Britain. This step was intended to avoid giving any pretext for British criticism, particularly by the "ruffian" (khuliganskii) British press, as Chicherin put it.[36]

German diplomats carefully monitored Anglo-Soviet relations, and they reported assiduously on what they heard. Tyrrell explained the situation to the German counselor in London, Albert Dufour-Feronce, whom he bumped into on the street. A long conversation ensued. Tyrrell must have thought a street corner was a good place for a rant, and he unburdened himself with his German counterpart. One wonders what passers-by must have thought.

"It's quite impossible to negotiate with the people in power in Russia," Tyrrell said. "Only idealists of the purest water could even think of succeeding . . . with representatives of the Soviet government."

"Already in 1917," he continued, I "said that the greatest danger for the existence of European civilization would be created as a result of Bolshevism achieving power in Russia."

And I have "a maxim" for dealing with the Bolshevik: always "to do diametrically the opposite of what the Soviet government suggests," and I have "done extraordinarily well by this rule."

The German diplomat gingerly asked if Tyrrell did not think that "the Soviet government was evolving" and whether it might not after all be possible to negotiate with Moscow about debts, for example.

This question caused Tyrrell to hesitate, but only for a moment. If evolution there was to be, it would be long in coming. Nor did he think Moscow would settle the debts; it would be very hard "to repudiate a repudiation."

And Tyrrell quickly remembered the Comintern, which he said had given £800,000 to support the miners' strike, clearly not a worthy cause by his lights. Here he might have been exaggerating since the Cabinet put the Soviet contribution at a rather lower sum. And then he mentioned Soviet activities in China, Persia, and Afghanistan, as if these were places reserved for the British Empire where Russia should have no interest.

Dufour-Feronce also saw Gregory that same day in the Foreign Office, and he again raised the Russia question. Gregory was more open to negotiating with the Soviet government, and he contrasted this position with Tyrrell's. Dufour believed there was a split inside the Foreign Office between Tyrrell, who represented the Tory hard line, and Gregory, who represented the more flexible position of the Conservative "industrial group" in the House of Commons and also that of the Liberal and Labour parties.[37] The only question which the German report did not raise was whether Chamberlain's position—after all it was not primarily Gregory's—could hold up against the Die-Hards.

After his July meeting with Chamberlain, Rozengol'ts went on holidays, as did most other diplomats in Europe, so that Anglo-Soviet relations were allowed to smolder until the autumn. The Foreign Office clerks remained as righteous as ever about the British position toward Moscow. The question of credit for Soviet trade in Britain often came up, though the position remained unchanged. It is "morally wrong for HMG," one clerk thought, "to extend credits to an administration which will not raise a finger to liquidate any of its obligations." Another opined that the "Soviet government have got to learn by experience that repudiation and new credit do not go hand in hand." Yet another clerk commented that Soviet cash balances went to pay for "propaganda." Even Chamberlain could not see the point of credits for Soviet trade "*unless* [emphasis in the original] . . . politics outweigh business."[38]

As the summer of 1926 ended, it was back to business as usual in Anglo-Soviet relations. Litvinov's policy of avoiding the worst was all there was in Moscow, given the continuing impasse. And the NKID still counted on Krasin. There is no doubt that Britain is hostile to us, Litvinov observed to Krasin—on his way to London—but "not all the complaints advanced by our press and by our orators can be proved or substantiated."[39] Try to keep a lid on Anglo-Soviet tensions was Litvinov's main directive. Chicherin sent a list of issues reaching from Poland to Persia, Afghanistan, and Canton, all on a page and a half.[40]

On 11 October 1926 Krasin met Chamberlain. The Soviet fireman said that Moscow attached the greatest importance to "the establishment of more normal relations with Great Britain." In view of the public hostility of the Conservative Party toward the Soviet Union, Krasin was not sure that the British government wanted to renew discussions, but in any case the Soviet

Union was ready to do so. Krasin added that he personally would do all he could to facilitate better relations.

Chamberlain replied in like manner, saying that he did not share the view of certain people who thought the Soviet government could not long survive. He also stressed that the British government did not have any desire to encircle the Soviet Union or organize a united front against it. However, the Soviet Union had failed to reciprocate peaceable British intentions, especially in China. As for the economic issues, the Foreign Secretary explained that the Conservative government would not ask Parliament to guarantee credits for the Soviet Union. It also expected Moscow to recognize its debts with corresponding reductions and advantages in scheduling repayment. Chamberlain again presented his images of the British "lamb" and the Soviet "wolf." Given the circumstances, it was pointless to renew negotiations, for they had no chance to succeed. Basically, he repeated the same positions to Krasin that he had to Rozengol'ts in July.[41]

Hence, the impasse remained, though according to Krasin's record, the meeting was respectful and even cordial insofar as it could be. In fact, both Chamberlain and Krasin shared a common purpose to avert a rupture in relations. Litvinov responded positively. The meeting, he thought, went better than expected and better than with Rozengol'ts during the summer. It was a step forward for Chamberlain to have identified the sticking points in Anglo-Soviet relations. And Litvinov agreed that there should not be further "official" negotiations "without serious chances" of success. We must be patient, Litvinov thought, and sound out the City. Perhaps you should give an interview to the effect that the Soviet government was patiently awaiting an end to the Die-Hard campaign. The sooner the Die-Hards recognized the futility of their campaign, the better were the chances of "a possible agreement."[42]

Krasin kept a busy schedule, meeting with Montagu Norman, head of the Bank of England, and other bankers and businessmen, always trying to advance the idea of business and credit with the Soviet Union. He deplored the "political prejudice" which blocked loans or credits to finance Soviet trade. The Soviet government was going to develop its economy, Krasin said repeatedly, with or without foreign credit and investment. If the Soviet Union had to develop on its own, progress would be slower and more difficult; with foreign capital, the Soviet economy would grow more rapidly, and so would the British economy. Krasin had made these arguments from the beginning, but the bankers were still not willing to advance credit. Bankers' "principles" were behind the financial "blockade," or "semi-blockade," as Krasin sometimes called it, mounted against the Soviet Union.

When his interlocutors suggested that a settlement of the tsarist debts might ease the credit boycott, Krasin shrugged off the problem: "By degrees the creditors will die off and this will automatically extinguish the debts. . . . The heirs will be far easier to deal with than the original creditors." Norman hammered away at the principles violated by the Soviet government. These actions affected "public opinion," though Krasin replied that the Soviet Union had its own public opinion, which would never tolerate paying the tsar's debts. The bankers' blockade was hurting Soviet development, Krasin acknowledged, but it was also hurting western development. That might well be, Norman responded with a shrug of the shoulders, but "the negative mood of public opinion" would not allow "compromise solutions." We will have to wait, Krasin concluded, for a change in public opinion and an end to the banks' "boycott" of Soviet business.[43]

Krasin also met E. Frank Wise, Lloyd George's go-between in Genoa, still pursuing better Anglo-Soviet relations. "We are very interested in an agreement [with Britain]," Krasin said, departing a little from NKID policy, "but in no case should you think that this is something we desperately need. On the contrary, we believe more than ever in our own abilities, and we will in the last resort pursue our economic rebuilding based on our own resources."[44] Krasin said more or less the same thing to Gregory, who concluded that "the Soviet point of view is exactly what it was in 1921: it has not budged an inch."[45] The same could be said of Tory policy: it had "not budged an inch."

Not less interesting, Krasin deplored to a British diplomat, though not to Moscow apparently, the political infighting in Moscow, mentioning Trotskii and Zinoviev in particular, "making fools of themselves by engaging in factional party politics instead of carrying on the work of the country." He thought the various public slogans and programs were "to a large extent, nebulous, fantastic, and imaginary and only camouflage for what were really personal bids for power and position." Krasin regarded party politics as harmful to his plans for Soviet economic development.[46] Stalin, he appeared to think, was more friendly to his ambitions.

Litvinov was not encouraged by Krasin's conversations with British bankers. Taken together with the latest Die-Hard attacks—he mentioned Birkenhead in particular—it was pointless to wait for any British initiative to resume negotiations. If we start discussions with the Americans, Litvinov commented, this might spur action in London. "Our hope is the eventual fall of the Conservative government."[47]

"The Enormous Importance of Improving Relations with America"

While relations with London were going badly, the NKID turned its attention back to the United States. Washington remained an important focus of Soviet interest. Although no important developments occurred in 1924, there was joy in Moscow when Secretary of State Hughes unexpectedly announced his resignation at the beginning of the new year (January 1925). The NKID was relieved, and Soviet public reaction, mocking. "Hughes is the most irreconcilable of irreconcilable enemies of the Soviet Union," Chicherin commented. He would not be missed. Chicherin's press statement went all the way to Stalin for editing, and the Politburo instructed Chicherin to stress that American investment in Soviet concessions would be welcomed. The Soviet government even sought to buy a patent for refining gasoline owned by Frank B. Kellogg, the incoming Secretary of State.[48]

After Hughes' departure there was a flurry of activity in Moscow to get American relations moving forward. The Politburo authorized Krasin to meet Standard Oil representatives and even Commerce Secretary Hoover in Brussels. One NKID official proposed recognition of a Provisional Government (headed briefly by Aleksandr F. Kerenskii) debt to the United States. Chicherin was against it but suggested a discussion in the Politburo.[49] Recognition of the so-called Kerenskii debt was rejected, but the Politburo approved a resolution in favor of a more aggressive public relations campaign in the United States to promote economic and political relations. As Chicherin noted to Karakhan in Beijing, "great attention was being devoted to the enormous importance of improving relations with America." The Soviet embassy in Berlin picked up information or rumors of a more positive American disposition to Soviet recognition. Goodrich, a previous American go-between, again visited Moscow during the summer of 1925, and this too drew NKID's attention. The Politburo would not retract the repudiation of tsarist debts, but would be flexible in finding ways to get the Americans talking.[50]

Litvinov's account of a meeting with Goodrich is similar to one which the latter had with a State Department official after his return to the United States. There were the usual points about the Soviet government needing to recognize the Kerenskii debt, but Goodrich also advised the State Department about his discussions with Soviet officials concerning the Comintern. The available Soviet records make no mention of such discussions, but Goodrich stated

> that the responsible Soviet leaders, in discussing the activities of the Communist International, insisted that they were unable to control this organization, that they could not as yet put an end to its activities, that an attempt to do so at the present time would lead to a split in the Party, and such a split would be fatal to the continuance of the Soviet régime and to the rehabilitation of Russian economic life. Governor Goodrich is apparently convinced that there is a group of Soviet leaders who are persuaded of the futility of propaganda abroad and are sincerely desirous of abandoning the foreign subversive activities of

the Party, but who do not feel that they are strong enough as yet to curb the extremists and are therefore obliged to proceed cautiously.[51]

It is a shame that the State Department report does not name the Soviet officials holding these views, but it could have been anyone from Litvinov and Chicherin to Stalin himself. In the autumn of 1925 Stalin was preparing to crush Zinoviev, though there was still a threat on his left if Zinoviev allied himself with Trotskii. In fact, this is what actually happened in mid-1926, though by then it was too late, for in attacking one another, Trotskii and Zinoviev had weakened themselves. Stalin must have laughed at the ineptness of his opponents, but still he had to be cautious. Nothing could be taken for granted in the tumultuous world of Communist Party politics in Moscow. Of course, the Politburo, dominated by Stalin, continued to involve itself in the business of virtually every communist party in Europe, and this may have been when Stalin developed his unvarnished contempt for foreign communists.

A number of American go-betweens visited Moscow during the summer of 1925, but no official discussions took place. The State Department was quick to accuse the go-betweens of supporting recognition, as it did in the case of Goodrich. They were naïve and susceptible to Bolshevik manipulation in a way that the Department of State could never be. State Department officials were too smart for that. So there was much hubbub in Moscow about Soviet-American relations, but no corresponding excitement in Washington. Kellogg, the new Secretary of State, would only affirm that the American government would issue visas to "bona fide" Soviet representatives looking for business in the United States.[52] It was a way to deflate demands for recognition. American businessmen could trade and the State Department could still refuse to recognize the Soviet government. It was a neat formula, but not new.[53] Trotskii wrote a long interview for publication addressing the American finesse of recognition, mocking a comment by Hoover or Kellogg to the effect that the U.S. government did not support trade with the Soviet Union, but did not prevent it either. It was borrowing from the British, Trotskii commented, but it was also borrowing from the French. Litvinov offered his opinion on Trotskii's text since interviews and public statements were *sometimes* sent to the NKID for vetting.

"Comrade Chicherin finds your interview to be too long," wrote Litvinov. European and "even more so American readers" will only "flick through" it, or not read it at all. The shorter the article, the better the chances were that it would be "read and digested."[54] Litvinov marked his letter secret, but it is hard to know why, unless common sense was secret.

In Moscow it often had to be. In September 1925 Chicherin asked to meet the U.S. ambassador in Berlin who twice declined "on ground of previous engagement." Kellogg approved.[55]

Still, the Soviet government persisted. "Almost every comrade returning from the United States," Litvinov reported in February 1926, "has heard about a significant shift in attitudes in America to the USSR." The shift could be attributed to the strengthening Soviet economy and also, not coincidentally, to important Soviet purchases of American cotton. Trade makes new "friends" in favor of a Soviet-American rapprochement, Litvinov observed, but the most powerful banks and the American Federation of Labor still opposed recognition. The very increases in Soviet-American trade worked against recognition, for "our enemies" say that trade can grow without recognition. So the swing in some sectors of American opinion has not led to a shift in government policy. It might be, Litvinov speculated, that Kellogg did not share the "doctrinal hostility" toward us of Hughes, or that Coolidge had "more friendly intentions," but the State Department was following British policy on "the Russian question" and opposed any initiative to improve relations. Still, Litvinov was willing to explore the possibilities through one of the U.S. embassies in Europe. The options were not encouraging: we are checking with Rakovskii, Litvinov informed Stalin, about the American ambassador in Paris.[56]

In New York, A. V. Prigarin, the head of the Soviet trading company Amtorg, was discouraging about the prospects for better relations. Domestic politics, he reported, were in play. Congressional elections would occur in the autumn of 1926, and congressmen and senators had to hold their tongues about recognition until after the elections to prevent anti-communist groups, and not least the American Federation of Labor, from attacking them.[57] The intrusion of anti-communism into electoral politics was thus by no means limited to France and Britain.

"Silent Conflict"

In 1926 a number of American businessmen visited Moscow. Litvinov took advantage of one such occasion to explain Soviet policy to Samuel Vauclain, president of Baldwin Locomotive Works, and John Hamilton, a vice president of Guarantee Trust Company. It is a "silent conflict" (*molchalivyi spor*) with the U.S. government, Litvinov told them.

> We are not absolutely opposed to the satisfaction of the material claims of America, but we cannot do this without prior negotiations and the elucidation

of the American government position to our counter-claims. We cannot re-
peal the decrees of the revolution; it would not be possible to explain how this
would serve the interests of our people. We are not persuaded that in exchange
for this declaration there will really follow the establishment of normal relations and that new demands will not be presented to us about the removal of
the Comintern and so on, nor any guarantee that we will really obtain credits
and loans in America.

And Litvinov did not stop there. "Our Union has a right to be mistrustful
of the outside world which has never hidden its hostility to the Union or to
the Soviet communist government." This was of course true, as readers will
now know: the "broad masses," said Litvinov, meaning the Politburo, did
not believe that you wanted to help us reestablish our economy out of simple
friendship (*druzheliubiia*) toward us, and so we do not believe "any promises."
What we want, Litvinov went on, is a "prior agreement on mutual obligations, and this can be obtained only by direct negotiations."

The banker Hamilton commented that negotiations would end the moment the Soviet side asked for credits and loans in exchange for recognition
of debts.

Simultaneous negotiations could go on, replied Litvinov, with the government and with bankers and businessmen on debts and loans, to be concluded
at the same time but without establishing any connection between the two.

This approach is impossible, Hamilton "hotly" replied: recognition of
debts must be a precondition of negotiations. "He had in mind mainly the
losses of American bankers," Litvinov observed dryly. Of course, Hamilton,
the banker, would insist on bankers' rights. He represented banking interests,
and every reader knows how a banker abhors a defaulted debt or mortgage.
Call in the bailiffs was the instinctive reaction, though that was not possible
in the Soviet Union. The bailiffs had been tried, but the Red Army blocked
their way. It was frustrating though, for a principle was a principle and recognition of the debt was as important as its actual repayment. On this point,
most bankers everywhere were unrelenting. Little had changed since Genoa.

"I said to him," Litvinov recorded, "that a business agreement was possible
even with bankers, but that if they insisted on recognition by us of their
principles, then we will never agree with them on anything."

That was Hamilton: Vauclain was more disposed to do business, and naturally he was more interested in locomotives, which is why he had come to
Moscow. "Along the way he talked about the possibility of taking orders for
locomotives on the basis of long-term credits."[58] And *there* was the difference
between the banker and the businessman, whether in the United States or in
Europe. Hamilton's principles would not fill Vauclain's order book.

The Clash of Comrades
Narkomindel'cheskii and Kominternovskii

How could the Soviet government get around the perennial obstacles to better relations with the West? When the Politburo approved a public feeler to Washington, Litvinov objected that the resulting resolution did not correspond to his recommendations. More than that, Litvinov expressed his irritation, indirectly to be sure, that the Politburo had approved the resolution in his absence. Litvinov reminded his colleagues that he had only recommended an informal, *secret* approach in Europe through one of the U.S. embassies. "This on no account meant that the NKID really expects any results from such a démarche. On the contrary," Litvinov reported: "we believe that no appeal by us now to the American government will lead us out of the existing dead end."[59] What is apparent in reading the NKID correspondence with the Politburo is that there was real, open debate on foreign policy, and that Litvinov, for one, was willing to challenge Politburo decisions. In the 1930s, during the Stalinist purges, Litvinov took up his concerns with Stalin privately in his office. Open disagreement would be too dangerous, and more's the pity, because the debates of the 1920s illustrate beyond a doubt the clash of Comrades Narkomindel'cheskii and Kominternovskii and the slow, often interrupted ascendency of realpolitik and Machtverhältnisse in Soviet foreign policy making, impeded only by party politics.

The Sokolnikov Mission to the United States

The Politburo duly altered its resolution to reflect Litvinov's concerns, and an informal, secret approach in Europe was approved. In the spring of 1926 the debate continued on a next step to get negotiations started with the U.S. government. For the time being Litvinov's low-profile approach was left in abeyance, and the Politburo approved the dispatch to the United States of G. Ia. Sokolnikov, the former commissar for finance, who had run afoul of Stalin after calling for his removal as *gensek* at the party congress in December 1925. Instead, Sokolnikov was sacked as *narkom*, though he remained useful for other tasks.

There was some discussion about how long Sokolnikov should stay in the United States and what he should do there, but it was finally determined that he would look for important contracts with American firms and credits to finance them. He would also explore the possibility of political negotiations with the U.S. government. It sounded like an ambitious initiative, and a commission was set up under Litvinov and Sokolnikov to develop "preparatory materials" for the mission.[60]

There remained the question of a U.S. visa for Sokolnikov. The NKID directed Rakovskii to approach Vauclain, the locomotive man, then in Paris, to obtain his assistance in supporting the visa request. Rakovskii denied rumors that Sokolnikov was going to Washington for negotiations with the U.S. government; he was only going for business. No one in Moscow wanted to provoke the hyper-sensitive State Department.

As the last planning documents were being completed at the end of June 1926, Prigarin, the New York Amtorg boss, informed Moscow that the State Department had refused the visa to Sokolnikov. Prigarin attempted to discover why but could only report an article in the *New York Times* to the effect that the Coolidge administration had referenced the December 1923 Hughes declaration that there was no need to send "anyone" to the United States until the Soviet government accepted American preconditions on debts, restitution or compensation, and propaganda.[61]

Kellogg later wrote privately to his ambassador in London that he had denied the visa "on the ground that Sokolnikov was on the Executive Committee of the Third International which is still carrying on their propaganda in the United States." There is "considerable propaganda in this country already looking towards inducing us to change our attitude," he advised; "a number of [our] businessmen" were involved. Vauclain had asked that the visa be issued, and Rakovskii had been in touch with "New York business interests to use their influence with me."[62] In fact, Sokolnikov was only briefly on the executive committee of the Comintern in 1924, but most high-level Bolsheviks had been associated with the Comintern at one time or another. If Comintern associations were the criteria for denying U.S. visas, few Soviet diplomats would ever have obtained them.

In 1926 Sokolnikov was vice chair of Gosplan, the Soviet state planning office. If the Coolidge administration had wanted to improve relations with the Soviet Union, Sokolnikov would have been an excellent interlocutor. The State Department continued to spurn Soviet overtures on "doctrinal" grounds, as Litvinov had put it, and any pretext would do. In a further act of hostility, the State Department blocked American banks from participating in German trade credits for Soviet commerce. It was still principles and reprisals: "That regime," as a State Department letter put it, "has repudiated Russia's obligations to the United States and to American nationals."[63]

The NKID was well informed, for American businessmen were quite open about the obstacles to trade. "First of all, before getting into the Russian business," according to Amtorg boss Prigarin, "each manufacturer, each banker considers it his duty to inquire at the Department of Commerce and the Department of State, can I go to the USSR. He trusts completely these institutions. Naturally, they return from there extremely discouraged." The most enthusiastic businessmen come back from their visits "in a completely different mood." It's the "propaganda," say American officials. "While the Soviet government does not give sufficient guarantees that it will stop the propaganda, the American government does not consider it possible to enter into any relations with the Soviet government." And then there was the issue of the "old debts." Still, in Prigarin's opinion, the lobbying from business circles meant that the situation was "not without hope." If we send representatives to the United States, "not tied in any way with the Comintern," progress might be made. The Americans insist that the debts must be paid, although, according to one intermediary with ties to Kellogg and Hoover, the U.S. government might be willing to delay the first payments for ten years.[64]

Visas were another battlefield in Litvinov's "silent conflict," not only with Washington, but with all the European powers. In 1924 the NKID denied visas as a reprisal against states that did not recognize the Soviet Union. In 1926 Litvinov noted that the Soviet government was more generous in issuing visas to Americans than the State Department was to Soviet citizens. Americans coming to the Soviet Union on business were in general never refused a visa.[65] But in the 1920s the Soviet Union was the needy partner, not the United States. In an act of pure "doctrinal" spite, the State Department declined a transit visa to Aleksandra Mikhailovna Kollontai, who was taking up her post in Mexico as Soviet *polpred*. The State Department press release justified the refusal of the visa because Kollontai was "a member of the Russian Communist Party, a member of the Third Congress of the Communist International, and a member of the Soviet Diplomatic Service" and therefore "actively associated with the International Communist subversive movement."[66] In fact, Kollontai was a Bolshevik feminist, unconventional in her ideas. Her face appears on a Soviet propaganda poster in 1930, celebrating Soviet women's liberation. The Third Comintern Congress took place in 1921, but the State Department was unforgiving, even the most casual association with the Comintern would do as a pretext to deny a visa.

The NKID also knew how to refuse a visa in the "silent conflict," especially when it came to "Sovietophobe" western journalists. The *Chicago Tribune* was well known to the NKID as a virulent, incorrigible enemy of the Soviet Union. When one of their journalists asked for a visa, it was refused with delight. F. A. Rotshtein, the head of the NKID press bureau, advised the Paris embassy that some "thugs" from the *Tribune* had bribed a Turkish journalist, the first "swallow" from the Middle East to arrive in Moscow. We treated the Turk "like a bishop," and he returned the favor by writing "a series of nasty articles against us" at the *Tribune*'s behest. Rotshtein had spoken with other American journalists in Moscow, and they all said that the *Chicago Tribune* was "the dirtiest newspaper in America." But Rotshtein instructed Paris to tell the *Tribune* reporter that if he "gradually disarmed during a period of three months, then I will let him in."[67] Well, Rothstein at least retained a sense of humor, which is more than one could have said about the State Department.

Soviet agents tried every imaginable approach to break down opposition to better relations. In the United States B. E. Skvirskii, the unofficial Soviet representative in Washington, was no exception. He was acutely aware of press hostility. "In regard to the perfidy of some American journalists, I do not see how we can fight them," Skvirskii reported: "In the majority of cases they conduct themselves in a friendly manner when in Moscow and only show their true colors after they leave the country." So Skvirskii did his best to show a friendly face in Washington, inviting them to tea and *pechen'e*, biscuits, every Thursday afternoon. It was not much, said Skvirskii, but one has to show some trust; otherwise we will never have better relations with the press.[68]

The Soviet government thus persisted in attempting to start negotiations with the United States, in spite of all the rebuffs. Litvinov returned to his original idea to establish contact with the United States through one of the American embassies in Europe. The fireman Krasin was once again called to service, even though he was seriously ill. "At the end of the elections in about a month's time," Litvinov wrote to Krasin in London, "we will probably have to discuss some new appeal to the American government, taking advantage of the favorable opinion which has developed there during the last year." Litvinov reckoned that Ambassador A. B. Houghton would be the best channel to use to communicate with Washington. "If he is not more friendly to us, he is at least less hostile than other American ambassadors in Europe." His opinions carry some weight in Washington and he is even tipped to succeed Kellogg. So get in touch with Houghton and "ask his advice about the best approach to the solution of Soviet-American problems."[69] Two days later Kellogg sent a private letter to Houghton which indicated, inter alia, that business pressure was increasing for recognition. Kellogg repeated the same demands as before, referencing previous statements by Hughes, and noting that the American Federation of Labor still opposed recognition. He also pointed out that American trade with the Soviet Union was higher than that of any other country, and so, he implied, recognition was unnecessary. As for British recognition, it "has simply opened another source for propaganda with diplomatic immunity." Without revealing his mind one way or another, Kellogg anticipated a possible Soviet initiative and asked Houghton for his views on how to proceed.[70]

A severe decline in the price of American cotton seemed to give a lift to better American-Soviet relations. On 9 October 1926, the same day Litvinov wrote to Krasin, Prigarin met with Commerce Department officials in

Washington. A commerce official asked if the Soviet Union would be interested in buying a million bales of cotton based on payment over three years. Such a purchase could help ease the U.S. "cotton crisis." Moreover, this same official even suggested that the Soviet government approve a concession for American manufacturers to develop the Soviet cotton industry equal to 2 to 3 million spindles. Readers will be immediately struck by the irony of Hoover's Commerce Department appealing to the Soviet Union to help the United States out of difficulty in cotton markets. One can easily imagine the reaction of the State Department had roles been reversed, but the shrewd, acquisitive "Yankee trader" could drop his "social antipathies," it seemed, when it came to enough dollars.

Prigarin said that he could not comment on the U.S. proposal. The Commerce official replied "categorically" that American ambassadors in Europe had been instructed to discuss this question with their Soviet counterparts, if the latter broached the subject.[71] The collapse of U.S. cotton prices, Prigarin reported, had produced alarm (bol'shaia trevoga) in banking and manufacturing circles. President Coolidge had named a special commission to study the problem. Some of the big producers and manufacturers believed that a good solution might be the sale on long-term credit of a million and a half cotton bales to the USSR. Senators and other politicians in the southern states would be bound to support the deal. So Prigarin asked for instructions, advising that he had been invited to Washington to talk about "negotiations for the settlement of mutual relations."[72]

On 21 October Prigarin was again in Washington at the Commerce Department, but the discussion was not just about cotton; it was also about more general questions. Economic relations suffered because of the absence of political relations. "I put the question," Prigarin reported, "what is the way out of the existing situation?" The director of the international division replied that the Soviet government "should take the first step," approaching an American ambassador in Europe, in London, for example, "with concrete suggestions." Prigarin insisted on obtaining confirmation from someone at the State Department, and two hours later R. F. Kelley met him with E. C. Ropes, head of the Slav division at Commerce. Kelley, a good Bolo hater, immediately forgot about the cotton and raised the issues of compensation for private property holders and "propaganda." Prigarin responded that he had no authorization to discuss these matters, but he assumed they would be the subject of negotiations.

I will get back to you in a few days, Kelley replied. Leaving the State Department, Ropes said he thought there would be a favorable reply. Prigarin had the impression that Commerce Secretary Hoover now favored recognition and was particularly interested in the sale of cotton to the USSR.[73]

It happens that Kelley also left a record of this meeting and it differs like night and day from Prigarin's.

> Mr. Prigarin . . . stated that he had received telegraphic instructions from his government to inform the American Government that the Soviet Government was "ready to pay the old debts" and that it desired us to indicate the place and time for negotiations to settle this matter. Prigarin added that there would be no difficulties involved in coming to an agreement with regard to the question of confiscated American property, his government being prepared to come to arrangement with various individual claimants. Likewise, he stated there would be no difficulty with regard to the matter of propaganda.[74]

Who knows which version is correct, Prigarin's or Kelley's. If Chicherin or Litvinov had seen the American record, they would have thrown up their hands in despair. This was exactly the problem, which so irked Chicherin, of unofficial Soviet agents exceeding, and by a long way, their instructions.

Nevertheless, acting on Prigarin's cables, the Politburo quickly approved negotiations for the purchase of American cotton. In Moscow, an improvement of relations finally seemed possible. But Litvinov warned against moving too quickly. The cotton *krach* could be a powerful "trump" to obtain not only commercial credits but also "a more important card." If we go forward too quickly, we might get the credits but not the other "card," that is, diplomatic recognition. We can afford to wait a few months. Let the pressure build; the cotton and the credits will still be there when we need them.[75] Does this strategy sound like advice from Marx or from Machiavelli?

Litvinov then wrote to Stalin, asking for authorization to instruct Krasin to get in touch with Houghton and broach the question of how we might break the "deadlock" in Soviet-American relations. With the conclusion of the American elections, the time could be right to take the initiative. And he reiterated that it was going to take some time to make the cotton deal. Someone with a higher political profile than Prigarin would need to conduct the negotiations. The crisis in over-production was not going to end, said Litvinov, nor the price of cotton rise in the next few months. The Politburo duly gave its consent for the contacts between Krasin and Houghton.[76]

Litvinov was skeptical that any progress could be made with the U.S. government.

> We cannot refuse to negotiate with America on the basis of recognition of the Kerenskii war debt and American government agreement to examine our counter-claims regarding the intervention. This also means that the American government must not insist on the recognition by us of the tsarist debts or the principle of compensation for the nationalized property of American citizens.

The *Instantsiia*, advised Litvinov, meaning Stalin, was little inclined to enter into negotiations even on this basis. So do not force discussions and do not commit yourself to anything beyond your instructions. It would be useful nevertheless to establish contact with Houghton without making any proposals, and discussing our basis for negotiation only if Houghton raises the subject. Litvinov also instructed Krasin to broach the visa issue, especially in view of the Sokolnikov incident. And Litvinov warned Krasin that Houghton could open the question of propaganda. You can give any assurances you like about the Soviet government and its agents, but not of course about the Comintern or the American Communist Party, for which we take no responsibility.[77]

In the meantime, on 27 October, Houghton informed the State Department that a go-between had contacted him to discover if he would agree to meet Krasin. A Soviet approach was to be expected, Houghton said; it only remained to decide if it should be received. Why not meet him and see what he has to say, was Houghton's advice. Kellogg finally replied on 4 November, not objecting to a meeting where Houghton simply "listened" to what Krasin had to say. Then Kellogg reviewed the U.S. government position on Soviet recognition, which had not changed. It was the same position on recognition of debts and compensation that Litvinov had anticipated in his instructions to Krasin. But there was more at stake, according to Kellogg:

> The question of recognition . . . is not merely a question of money compensation but a question of principle. While we acknowledge the right of the people of every foreign country to maintain any form of government which they voluntarily choose . . . we cannot recognize a regime whose very foundation principle is ultimately to bring about the overthrow of every foreign government by revolution and in the meantime to carry on in foreign countries activities calculated to promote the realization of this aim. It is perfectly idle for the Soviet government to claim that these activities are carried on by an organization with which it has no connection. We know the organic connection between the Soviet government and the Communist International. . . .The Bolshevik leaders regard the establishment of peaceful relations with other nations as merely a temporary expedient pending the successful culmination of their efforts to subvert the governments of such nations. It is obvious that the establishment of normal friendly relations with a regime cherishing such purposes . . . is impossible.[78]

Sir Robert Vansittart, then the head of the American Department at the Foreign Office, nicely summed up the State Department position: they are *all*, "especially Mr. Kellogg . . . obsessed with the Bolshevik bogey."[79] As if Vansittart's Foreign Office colleagues, or the Die-Hards, were not.

Figure 7.2. Leonid B. Krasin, reported seriously ill, ca. 1925–1926. Photographer: Georg Pahl. *Bundesarchiv, Bild* 102-03445.

Nevertheless, Kellogg instructed Houghton to listen but not take the initiative, and Litvinov did the same with Krasin. Would the two interlocutors have anything at all to say to one another? Houghton indicated to the go-between that he would receive and Krasin replied through the same channel that he would send a note asking to see Houghton. For the time being, however, as Houghton informed the State Department, Krasin was ill and "in the hands of his physicians."[80] *Hélas*, Krasin's doctors could not save his life, and he died of leukemia on 24 November 1926, a week after he should have written to Houghton. The Soviet fireman, *par excellence*, the "Red merchant" and industrialist, was no more. No one took his place to see Houghton, and so yet another initiative to improve Soviet-American relations, however doubtful, failed to materialize.

From New York, Prigarin returned to the charge in December, asking for directives on the two big questions that always came up when talking to Americans. Will the USSR pay debts to the U.S. government, and if yes, how much and over what time period? And would we pay compensation, or not, to private individuals who had lost holdings in Russia because of the revolution? G. L. Piatakov, who was to take Sokolnikov's place as a special agent in the United States, forwarded these questions to the NKID and NKVT, the foreign trade commissariat, for answers. "I am afraid," wrote Piatakov, "that my visit to America without concrete directives in answer to Prigarin's questions could have negative rather positive consequences."[81]

Litvinov was irritated by Piatakov's query, for these were just the kind of questions which the NKID had sought to avoid ever since Genoa. The Soviet government, Litvinov wrote to the Politburo, had pushed too aggressively for a rapprochement, repeating to various and sundry intermediaries our position on relations with the United States. Unfortunately, these intermediaries had not always conveyed the position correctly to the State Department, exaggerating our willingness to make concessions and exaggerating the economic advantages of agreement. To neutralize the "negative impact" of these impressions, Litvinov suggested that for the time being the Soviet government should exercise restraint in pursuing an American rapprochement and take a harder line on American demands for recognition. Some of these demands we would never meet, but Americans appear to have "the illusion" that they would be acceptable to us. "This illusion must in decisive fashion be dispelled [*unichtozhat*']."

Just to underline his irritation, Litvinov added a point about the Comintern, since the subject always seemed to turn up like a bad kopek in conversations with American intermediaries. Their usual line was that something *had* to be done about the Comintern; otherwise, progress could not be made on other issues. Litvinov responded that the West would just have to get used to the Comintern; the subject was not up for discussion. "We are ready to give any guarantee of non-interference of the Soviet government and its diplomatic agents in American domestic affairs." "*But*," he added, "in no case can we say or give any promises whatsoever in the name of the Comintern and the American Communist Party or about the exclusion of VKP members from election as delegates of the Comintern."[82] Hence, if Litvinov was a realist, he could also tell which way the wind was blowing in the Politburo, and the Comintern was not an issue where the NKID could give ground in the West. Ironically, Soviet trade policy began to resemble the American position: we will continue to trade on terms that benefit us, and efforts to obtain American recognition are for now put on hold.

Notes

1. Litvinov to Berzin, no. 0167, secret, 28 Feb. 1925, AVPRF, f. 069, o. 9, p. 20, d. 3, ll. 5–8; and Litvinov to Rakovskii, no. 0340, secret, 9 May 1925, ibid., ll. 22–25.

2. Rakovskii to Chicherin, no. 11, very secret, nd (but July 1925), AVPRF, f. 069, o. 9, p. 20, d. 4, l. 136; and Rakovskii to Litvinov, no. 15, very secret, 19 Sept. 1925, ibid., ll. 185–89.

3. Litvinov to Berzin, no. 0167, as cited above in n. 1; and Litvinov to Arkadii Pavlovich Rozengol'ts, Soviet chargé d'affaires in London, no. 0836, secret, 12 Dec. 1925, AVPRF, f. 069, o. 9, p. 20, d. 3, ll. 54–56.

4. Litvinov to Dmitrii Vasil'evich Bogomolov, first counselor in London, no. 0482, secret, 28 Aug. 1925, AVPRF, f. 069, o. 9, p. 20, d. 3, ll. 35–36; Litvinov to Rozengol'ts, no. 0672, 24 Oct. 1925, ibid., ll. 45–48; Litvinov to Rozengol'ts, no. 0817, secret, 5 Dec. 1925, ibid., ll. 52–53; and Pierre de Margerie, French ambassador in Berlin, nos. 1602–3, 3 Oct. 1925, MAÉ Grand-Bretagne/64, ff. 101–2.

5. "Secretary of State, Zinovieff Letter," Gregory, 20 Apr. 1925, N2894/29/38, FO 371 11010; minutes by Mounsey, 10 Dec. 1925; and Tyrrell, 14 Dec. 1925, N6982/102/38, FO 371 11016; and Berzin to Litvinov, not numbered, very secret, 5 Nov. 1924, RGASPI, f. 359, o. 1, d. 6, ll. 281–87.

6. Mounsey's minute, 17 Dec. 1925, N6951/102/38, FO 371 11016; and note by Miles W. Lampson (Paris), 29 Oct. 1925, N6054/102/38, ibid.

7. Litvinov to Rozengol'ts, no. 0800, secret, 28 Nov. 1925, AVPRF, f. 069, o. 9, p. 20, d. 3, ll. 50–51; and Peters, no. 35, 13 Jan. 1926, N317/23/38, FO 371 11778.

8. Citrine to Chicherin, very private and confidential, translation from English, 6 Feb. 1926, AVPRF, f. 069, o. 10, p. 25, d. 12, ll. 10–12; excerpt from Maiskii to Litvinov, 6 Feb. 1926, ibid., ll. 16–17; and Maiskii to Chicherin, 6 Feb. 1926, ibid., ll. 14–15.

9. Chicherin to Politburo, cc. NKID *kollegiia*, no. 303/ChS, 13 Feb. 1926, AVPRF, f. 069, o. 10, p. 25, d. 12, ll. 6–8.

10. Litvinov to NKID *kollegiia*, no. 2624, 15 Feb. 1926, AVPRF, f. 069, o. 10, p. 25, d. 12, ll. 2–4; and Litvinov to Chicherin, secret, 8 Feb. 1926, AVPRF, f. 069, o. 10, p. 24, d. 1, l. 2.

11. Litvinov to Maiskii, no. 2641, secret, 20 Feb. 1926, AVPRF, f. 069, o. 10, p. 25, d. 13, ll. 9–10.

12. Maiskii to Litvinov, secret, 27 Feb. 1926, AVPRF, f. 069, o. 10, p. 24, d. 4, ll. 63–69; and Chicherin to Citrine, 28 Feb. 1926, DVP, IX, pp. 142–43.

13. Maiskii to Litvinov, 12 March 1926, AVPRF, f. 069, o. 10, p. 24, d. 4, ll. 84–95.

14. Maiskii to Litvinov, secret, 6 March 1926, AVPRF, f. 069, o. 10, p. 24, d. 4, ll. 75–83.

15. Litvinov to Rozengol'ts, no. 2831, secret, 30 April 1926, AVPRF, f. 069, o. 10, p. 24, d. 3, ll. 27–28.

16. Gabriel Gorodetsky, "The Formulation of Soviet Foreign Policy: Ideology and *Realpolitik*," in Gordetsky, *Soviet Foreign Policy*, pp. 30–44.

17. Excerpt from Politburo protocol, no. 21, 22 April 1926, *Politbiuro i Komintern*, pp. 357–58.

18. Politburo protocol, no. 23 (special no. 17), 4 May 1926, *Politbiuro i Komintern*, pp. 360–62.

19. Pierre Broué, *Histoire de l'Internationale communiste, 1919–1943* (Paris, 1997), pp. 415–20.

20. Litvinov to Rozengol'ts, no. 2842, secret, 8 May 1926, AVPRF, f. 069, o. 10, p. 24, d. 3, ll. 29–31; Rozengol'ts to Litvinov, secret, 22 May 1926, AVPRF, f. 069, o. 10, p. 24, d. 4, ll. 142–53; and Note by N. M. Butler, 10 June 1926, N2675/387/38, FO 371 11786.

21. Extract from Cabinet, 40 (26), 16 June 1926, N2844/1687/38, FO 371 11795; and Rozengol'ts to Chicherin, no. 16, very secret, 5 July 1926, AVPRF, f. 069, o. 10, p. 24, d. 7, ll. 243–49.

22. Fleuriau, no. 286, 15 June 1926, MAÉ Grande-Bretagne/64, ff. 149–50; Crewe (Paris), no. 1901, 13 Oct. 1926, N4595/418/38, FO 371 11788; and Saint-Aulaire (Fleuriau's predecessor in London), nos. 617–20, 1 Nov. 1924, MAÉ Grande-Bretagne/64, ff. 25–28.

23. Note by N. M. Butler, 10 June 1926, as cited above in n. 20.

24. Rozengol'ts to Litvinov, no. 115/s, very secret, 13 April 1926, AVPRF, f. 069, o. 10, p. 23, d. 7, ll. 65–66.

25. Rozengol'ts to Litvinov, no. 8, very secret, 24 April 1926, AVPRF, f. 069, o. 10, p. 24, d. 7, ll. 115–25.

26. Rozengol'ts to Litvinov, no. 9, secret, 22 May 1926, AVPRF, f. 069, o. 10, p. 24, d. 7, ll. 135–46; and Litvinov to Rozengol'ts, no. 2909, secret, 1 June 1926, AVPRF, f. 069, o. 10, p. 24, d. 3, ll. 36–37.

27. Herbette, no. 251, 17 June 1926, MAÉ Grande-Bretagne/64, fol. 152.

28. Note by N. M. Butler, 10 June 1926, as cited above in n. 20; and A. Iu. Vatlin, Komintern: Pervye desiat' let (Moscow, 1993), pp. 60–71.

29. Broué, Internationale, p. 454; and Philip Leigh-Smith's minute, 29 April 1927, N1930/190/38, FO 371 12588.

30. Peters, no. 3, confidential, 1 Jan. 1926, N121/53/38, FO 371 11779; Thomas H. Preston (British consul general in Leningrad) to Peters, no. 1, confidential, and enclosure, 2 Jan. 1926, N313/53/38, ibid.

31. Maxse's minute, 9 March 1926, N1066/53/38, FO 371 11779; minutes by A. D. F. Gascoigne, Northern Department, 27 July 1926, N3499/53/38, ibid., and 25 Jan. 1927, N310/190/38, FO 371 12588; Hodgson, no. 29 July 1926, and Gregory's minute, 1 Aug. 1926, N3549/53/38, FO 371 11779.

32. Chicherin to Rozengol'ts, no. 11, 18 June 1926, AVPRF, f. 069, o. 10, p. 24, d. 1, l. 35; and Chicherin to Rozengol'ts, no. 12, 25 June 1926, AVPRF, f. 069, o. 10, p. 24, d. 2, l. 6.

33. Fleuriau, no. 305, 26 June 1926, MAÉ Grande-Bretagne/64, ff. 238–39.

34. Hodgson, no. 769, 21 Oct. 1926, N4881/387/38, FO 371 11787; and Chamberlain's minute, ibid.

35. "Record of conversation with Chamberlain, 13/VII-26," Rozengol'ts, AVPRF, f. 069, o. 10, p. 24, d. 7, ll. 237–42; and Chamberlain to Hodgson, no. 535, 13 July 1926, DBFP, 1a, II, pp. 147–50.

36. Chicherin to Bogomolov, no. 1, 23 July 1926, AVPRF, f. 069, o. 10, p. 24, d. 2, l. 13; Litvinov to Rozengol'ts, no. 2926, secret, nd (but July or August 1926), AVPRF, f. 069, o. 10, p. 24, d. 3, ll. 38–39; and Chicherin to Rozengol'ts, no. 14, 2 July 1926, AVPRF, f. 069, o. 10, p. 24, d. 2, l. 10.

37. Dufour-Feronce, no. A.2117, very secret, 16 Sept. 1926, AzDAP, B, II, 2, pp. 274–77.

38. Gascoigne's minute, 14 Aug. 1926, N3752/7/38, FO 371 11777; untitled unsigned memorandum, nd, N105/7/38, FO 371 11776; minute by C. W. Orde, Northern Department, 29 March 1926, N1377/7/38, ibid; and Chamberlain's minute, 31 March 1926, ibid.

39. Litvinov to Krasin, no. 2992, secret, 25 Sept. 1926, AVPRF, f. 069, o. 10, p. 24, d. 3, ll. 48–51.

40. Chicherin to Krasin, very urgent, 8 Oct. 1926, AVPRF, f. 069, o. 10, p. 24, d. 2, ll. 15–16.

41. Krasin to Litvinov, report no 2, very secret, 14 Oct. 1926, AVPRF, f. 069, o. 10, p. 24, d. 5, ll. 12–5 (published in DVP, IX, pp. 499–506); and Chamberlain to Hodgson, no 752, 11 Oct. 1926, DBFP, 1a, II, pp. 431–34.

42. Litvinov to Krasin, no. 3021, secret, 16 Oct. 1926, AVPRF, f. 069, o. 10, p. 24, d. 3, ll. 55–56.

43. Krasin to Litvinov, report no. 3, very secret, 23 Oct. 1926, AVPRF, f. 069, o. 10, p. 24, d. 5, ll. 38–26 (published in DVP, IX, pp. 512–22).

44. Khromov, Krasin, pp. 121–22.

45. "Russia," Gregory, 24 Oct. 1926, N4818/387/38, FO 371 11787.

46. "Memorandum," by T. H. Preston for Tyrrell, 13 Nov. 1926, N5135/245/38, FO 371 11785.

47. Excerpt from Litvinov to Krasin, no. 3068, secret, 6 Nov. 1926, AVPRF, f. 069, o. 10, p. 24, d. 5, l. 49.

48. Chicherin to Stalin, no. 24/ChS, 11 Jan. 1925, Moskva-Vashington, I, pp. 165–66; Chicherin to Politburo, no. 30/ChS, 12 Jan. 1925, ibid., p. 166; Politburo resolution, no. P45/I-D/s, rigorously secret, 15 Jan. 1925, ibid., p. 167; Chicherin's draft on Hughes, 15 Jan. 1925, ibid., pp. 168–71.

49. Krasin (Paris) to Stalin, no. 5558, secret, immediate, 26 June 1925, Moskva-Vashington, I, pp. 176–77; Politburo resolution, no. P69/opr-2/s, rigorously secret, 26 June 1925, ibid., p. 178; Lapinskii, NKID, to Stalin, no. 884/ChS, very secret, 7 June 1925, ibid., pp. 173–76; and Chicherin to Politburo, very secret, 9 July 1925, ibid., p. 180.

50. Politburo resolution, no. P71/1-A-s, rigorously secret, 16 July 1925, Moskva-Vashington, I, p. 181; Chicherin to Politburo, no. 1094/ChS, secret, 4 Aug. 1925, ibid., pp. 184–85; Chicherin to Karakhan, no. 80, 20 July 1925, Perepiska I. V. Stalina i G. V. Chicherina, pp. 576–78; Litvinov to Politburo, no. 0563, secret, 26 Sept. 1925, Moskva-Vashington, I, pp. 190–93; and Politburo resolution, no. P81/1-V/s, rigorously secret, 1 Oct. 1925, ibid., p. 193.

51. "Mr. Secretary," Robert F. Kelley, 25 Nov. 1925, 711.61/118½, NA RG59, M-333, reel 2; and Litvinov to Politburo, no. 0563, secret, 26 Sept. 1925, Moskva-Vashington, I, pp. 190–93.

52. Kellogg to Skinner, consul general in Paris, 19 May 1925, FRUS, 1925, II, p. 703.

53. Poole to Hughes, 2 Jan. 1923, 711.61/66, NA RG59, M-333, reel 2.

54. Trotskii to Central Committee and NKID, 4 Sept. 1925, SAO, Gody nepriznaniia, 1918–1926, pp. 444–50; and Litvinov to Trotskii, secret, 9 Sept. 1925, ibid., p. 450.

55. J. G. Schurman, U.S. ambassador in Berlin, no. 166, 30 Sept. 1925, 711.61/104, NA RG59, M-333, reel 2; and Kellogg to Schurman, no. 179, 30 Sept. 1925, ibid.

56. Litvinov to Stalin, no. 2642, especially secret, 20 Feb. 1926, Moskva-Vashington, I, pp. 202–6; and Goodrich (Indianapolis) to Litvinov, 11 Jan. 1926, ibid., pp. 207–13.

57. Prigarin to L. B. Kamenev, commissar for trade, secret, 5 March 1926, SAO, Gody nepriznaniia, 1918–1926, pp. 484–89.

58. Litvinov's record of conversation, 2–6 May 1926, SAO, Gody nepriznaniia, 1918–1926, pp. 513–15.

59. Litvinov to Politburo, no. 2669, secret, 3 March 1926, Moskva-Vashington, I, pp. 214–15.

60. Politburo resolution, no. P28/opr.7/s, rigorously secret, 25 May 1926, Moskva-Vashington, I, p. 223; Politburo resolution, no. P28/1-E/s, rigorously secret, 27 May 1926, ibid., p. 224; four "protocols," May–June 1926, ibid., pp. 225–37; and various NKID planning documents, May–July 1926, SAO, Gody nepriznaniia, 1918–1926, pp. 522–33.

61. Prigarin (New York), no. 4720, 25 June 1926, Moskva-Vashington, I, pp. 237–38.

62. Kellogg to Alanson B. Houghton, personal and confidential, 11 Oct. 1926, 861.01/1163A, NA RG59, M. 316, reel 75; and report by B. S. Stomoniakov to Politburo, secret, 12 July 1926, SAO, Gody nepriznaniia, 1918–1926, pp. 531–33.

63. Leland Harrison, Assistant Secretary of State, to New York Trust Company, 15 July 1926, 861.51/2056, NA RG59, M-316, reel 123.

64. Prigarin to L. B. Kamenev, secret, personal, 5 Aug. 1926, SAO, Gody nepriznaniia, 1918–1926, pp. 543–46.

65. Litvinov to Moscow Soviet, 10 Dec. 1924, SAO, Gody nepriznaniia, 1918–1926, pp. 415–16; and Litvinov to Iu. V. Lomonovsov, Soviet trade representative in the United States, 9 March 1926, ibid., pp. 490–91.

66. Press release, Department of State, 4 Nov. 1926, *FRUS, 1926*, II, p. 911.

67. Zh. (Jean) L. Arens (Paris) to Rakovskii, 29 March 1926, SAO, *Gody nepriznaniia, 1918–1926*, p. 496; and Rotshtein to Arens, secret, 16 April 1926, ibid., p. 499.

68. B. E. Skvirskii to Chicherin, 18 June 1926, SAO, *Gody nepriznaniia, 1918–1926*, pp. 537–38.

69. Litvinov to Krasin, secret, 9 Oct. 1926, SAO, *Gody nepriznaniia, 1918–1926*, pp. 553–54.

70. Kellogg to Houghton, personal and confidential, 11 Oct. 1926, 861.01/1163A, NA RG59, M. 316, reel 75.

71. Prigarin to Anastas I. Mikoyan, commissar for trade, nos. 7120–21, very secret, 14 October 1926, *Moskva-Vashington*, I, p. 253.

72. Prigarin to Mikoian, no. 7279, rigorously secret, 16 Oct. 1926, *Moskva-Vashington*, I, p. 254; and Prigarin to Mikoian, no. 7252, rigorously secret, 20 Oct. 1926, ibid., p. 255.

73. Prigarin to Mikoian, nos. 7310–12, rigorously secret, very confidential, 22 Oct. 1926, *Moskva-Vashington*, I, pp. 256–58.

74. "Conversation . . . Alexis V. Prigarin, E. C. Ropes . . . ," strictly confidential, Kelley, 21 Oct. 1926, 861.01/1182½, NA RG59, M-316, reel 75.

75. Politburo resolution, no. P65/1-s, rigorously secret, 29 Oct. 1926, *Moskva-Vashington*, I, p. 263; and Litvinov to NKID *kollegiia*, cc. Mikoian, no. 3061, secret, 2 Nov. 1926, ibid., pp. 264–65.

76. Litvinov to Stalin, no. 3069, secret, 6 Nov. 1926, *Moskva-Vashington*, I, pp. 265–67; and Politburo resolution, no. P67/2-A/s, rigorously secret, 11 Nov. 1926, ibid., p. 268.

77. Litvinov to Krasin, secret, 13 Nov. 1926, SAO, *Gody nepriznaniia, 1918–1926*, pp. 557–58.

78. Kellogg to Houghton, no. 212, strictly personal and confidential for the ambassador, 4 Nov. 1926, 861.01/1175, NA RG59, M-316, reel 75.

79. Vansittart's minute, 22 Feb. 1927, N628/209/38, FO 371 12589.

80. Houghton to Kellogg, personal and confidential, 11 Nov. 1926, 861.01/1409, NA RG59, M-316, reel 75.

81. Piatakov to Litvinov and Mikoian, no. 1351, very secret, 23 Dec. 1926, *Moskva-Vashington*, I, pp. 277–78.

82. Litvinov to Politburo, no. 2220, secret, 27 Dec. 1926; and instructions for Piatakov approved by the Politburo, 30 Dec. 1926, *Moskva-Vashington*, I, pp. 279–82.

CHAPTER EIGHT

~

"The Blind and the Lame"

Rapallo Reaffirmed, 1925–1927

While relations with Britain continued to deteriorate, relations improved with Germany, but not at first. We left the story of German-Soviet relations in the summer of 1925. Soviet-German trade negotiations were skating in circles because of German discussions about mutual security with France and Britain. Germany wanted to keep to a middle course between East and West, maneuvering one against the other to gain advantage. Stresemann's idea was to weaken relations between France and Britain and to avoid excessive intimacy with Moscow, but not to the point of encouraging a Franco-Polish-Soviet rapprochement, which remained a German *cauchemar*. Krestinskii, still the ambassador in Berlin, was a strong proponent of the Rapallo axis.[1]

Nikolai Nikolaevich Krestinskii

Krestinskii played an important role in Soviet foreign policy during most of the inter-war years, and he therefore merits introduction. He was born in 1883 into a family of teachers in Mogilev. Taking after his parents, Nikolai Nikolaevich was a brilliant student, winning a gold medal at the end of his studies at *gimnaziia* in 1901. Two years later he joined the Russian Social Democratic Party, soon siding with the Bolsheviks. Eventually he completed a degree in law at the University of St. Petersburg. He had close ties to Lenin, was a member of the original Politburo, and was *narkom* of finances until 1921 when he was sacked for oppositional sympathies. Shortly thereafter, Krestinskii was sent to Berlin as Soviet *polpred*. It was then the most important Soviet diplomatic posting abroad. Multi-lingual and pragmatic like

Figure 8.1. Nikolai N. Krestinskii, 1929. Photographer: Georg Pahl. *Bundesarchiv, Bild* **102-08858.**

Litvinov, he was the right person for the job of dealing with the bourgeois Weimar Republic. In surviving photographs, the younger Krestinskii appears a gentle man, round faced, balding, sometimes with a thick, dark Vandyke moustache and beard. He was said to have a prodigious memory. "Better ask Krestinskii," Lenin would say when in need of some forgotten but important information. His shortcoming, according to Lenin, was his lack of interest in "politics." This would have suited Stalin, but Molotov noted in his memoirs that Krestinskii was a Trotskyist, which was a ticket to the executioner's cellar during the Great Purges. He lost his position as a party secretary in 1921 for being too soft on the then "Workers' Opposition."

Krestinskii sided with Trotskii during the conflict with Stalin, though not so openly as Rakovskii. In 1930 Krestinskii returned to Moscow as first deputy commissar at the NKID, where he reinforced Litvinov's pragmatism in dealing with the West. The French ambassador in Berlin, a hard-line anti-Bolshevik, had mixed emotions about Krestinskii's return to Moscow. He moved skillfully around Berlin business circles, a talent vital to Soviet trade policy, but which irritated certain officials at the Auswärtiges Amt, who disliked him intensely. Krestinskii avoided the public limelight, said the French ambassador, and knew how to keep out of trouble, unlike other Soviet diplomats elsewhere.[2]

Years later Krestinskii was unable to keep out of trouble in Moscow. Like most of the Old Bolsheviks, he fell victim to the Stalinist purges and was one of the accused in the last show trial of "the right Trotskyist bloc" in 1938. A man of courage and integrity, he was the only one publicly to plead not guilty, for which he was apparently beaten or blackmailed into grudging submission. As with Rakovskii, the Quai d'Orsay recognized his role in improving relations with France and instructed the French ambassador in Moscow, Robert Coulondre, to intervene on his behalf. Not his finest moment, Coulondre responded that it would do no good. Krestinskii was shot on 15 March 1938.[3]

Rapallo Reaffirmed, Union of "the Blind and the Lame"

In 1925 these incomprehensible events were 13 years in the future. During the summer of that year, Soviet diplomats had other matters to worry about. In spite of the usual holiday period, German-Soviet relations continued to be strained. Chicherin appeared resigned to a "logic of things [which would] pull Germany in a western orientation."[4] There was one problem after another to disturb bilateral relations. After the repeated public indiscretions of Zinoviev and Stalin, there was a serious row over the alleged activities of a German diplomat in Moscow, Gustav Hilger, who ran afoul of the OGPU by accident rather than by any violation of his diplomatic status. Stresemann was so riled that he threatened to recall Ambassador Rantzau and leave only a chargé d'affaires in the Moscow embassy. Tell Chicherin, Stresemann cabled to Rantzau, that Soviet policy is "beginning to drive me crazy."[5]

In Berlin Krestinskii was worried by the resulting "cold" relations with government officials and the German press, and he proposed a way out. If Germany cannot count on us, Krestinskii warned, they will conclude "with the Entente" and join the League. The Politburo was sufficiently alarmed to instruct the NKID to accept Krestinskii's proposals and "liquidate" the conflict over Hilger "immediately." The real stake in this latest Soviet-German row was not Hilger at all, but an OGPU agent arrested in Germany and sentenced to death. He was eventually swapped for two unlucky German students who had met up with Hilger by chance on a train to Moscow and had his visiting card.[6] The incident was not of great importance—well, except perhaps for the condemned OGPU agent and the German students taken as hostages to trade—but it illustrated the fragility of Rapallo.

The conflict over Hilger was not the only problem. In Moscow, trade negotiations were stalled. "The Germans are leading us around by the nose,"

Figure 8.2. From left to right, members of the NKID *kollegiia*, Maksim M. Litvinov, Georgii V. Chicherin, Lev. M. Karakhan, and Iakov Stanislavovich Ganetskii, ca. 1923. *Rodina*, Moscow.

complained the chief Soviet negotiator, Ia. S. Ganetskii: "We put pressure on them to conclude, we expose their delaying tactics, but we do not obtain the desired result." They raise fresh demands on questions which we thought were settled. We complained to Rantzau that proposals we made more than a month ago remain unanswered.

The German ambassador offered polite excuses. "You know," Rantzau replied, "that at home there is a cabinet crisis brewing and that it makes matters more difficult." Soviet negotiators heard "from reliable sources" that the German foreign ministry "did not intend to hurry with the signature of the trade agreement. The Soviet Union needed the signature more than Germany." German negotiators calculated that by stalling they could obtain further concessions. And Stresemann did not want to stir up the Reichstag again "with the Russian red banner." A highly irritated Ganetskii proposed to threaten his German counterparts with a suspension of negotiations. "Only thus can we show the Germans that we are not more interested in the agreement than they are." A suspension would put Germany in a difficult position in its negotiations with "the Entente," according to Ganetskii; it was the only way to influence German negotiators.[7]

The Politburo did not approve of a rupture of negotiations, but Ganetskii's impatience seemed to produce some movement because the German delegation agreed to terms during the night of 4 August 1925. Still, negotiations dragged on, for agreeing did not mean signing. It was all a question of timing as Ganetskii reported: the Germans would not sign until it was "advantageous" in relation to negotiations in Geneva with the French and British.[8] A correct surmise, but there were further hitches to work out. The Politburo of course understood German strategy, for it too had to be mindful of relations with France and Britain. Both sides wanted to use the new trade agreement as leverage in London and Paris.

In the meantime discussions continued over the German entry into the League of Nations. Tempers were frayed but each side still tried to reassure the other. We are committed to Rapallo, Stresemann told Rantzau, no matter what the result of the negotiations with the British and French. Soviet public doubts about our intentions will in the long run be harmful in Germany. We would ask the NKID at least to wait and see before worrying about Rapallo.[9] Krestinskii played his usual role reassuring the Germans, this time Schubert. It was early June 1925. The ambiance was better in Moscow, he said; government opinion believes that relations can be strengthened. Schubert responded by saying that Germany did not intend to become an instrument of Anglo-French policy. Chicherin is too pessimistic about Germany and its entry into the League. Whatever changes occur will not be as drastic as he seems to fear. Schubert reminded Krestinskii that Chicherin had not offered "a recipe" that would permit Germany to free the Rhineland from Allied occupation. This was an issue which Stresemann had to take up with the British and French, and where Krestinskii admitted Moscow could not help.[10]

The NKID still hoped to obtain German agreement not to enter the League of Nations without Soviet agreement. There was another important meeting between Chicherin and Rantzau at the beginning of July which went over the same ground as before. The NKID worried about Germany being dragged into the wake of British policy. Germany was trying to weaken Anglo-French ties, Rantzau replied.[11] These conversations were remarkably frank in airing out anxieties and concerns on both sides.

Another meeting occurred between Litvinov and Rantzau at the end of August.

We are not trying to put you in a situation of choosing "for or against Russia," Litvinov said.

Though it seems that way to us, Rantzau replied.

Litvinov continued that the Soviet government could live with Germany in the League, if an agreement on Soviet-German "neutrality" could be concluded.[12]

The NKID continued to worry about German policy. Litvinov and Chicherin spent a lot of time in Berlin that summer and autumn of 1925 nurturing Rapallo. It was Chicherin's turn in the autumn when he made the rounds with German leaders. Returning to a constant preoccupation, he warned Chancellor Hans Luther about "the danger of being dragged into the orbit of England."

You are trying to outsmart England, Chicherin quipped, but England will finish by outsmarting you!

Hah! Luther swore, that will be hard to do.[13]

Poland: A Delicate Question

Chicherin also met Stresemann who reassured him that Germany would not enter into the League unconditionally and would not make any anti-Soviet side deals with Britain. Chamberlain himself, added Stresemann, did not support such a policy. German entry into the League also raised the issue of Poland and notably its western frontiers with Germany. Imposed by the Versailles Treaty, these frontiers provided a Polish corridor separating East Prussia from the rest of Germany. If Germany entered the League, would it be obliged to accept western Polish frontiers? It was not the first time that Stresemann or Rantzau had broached the question of Polish frontiers with Soviet diplomats.

In December 1924 Rantzau had asked Chicherin what the Soviet position on Poland would be under various eventualities. For Chicherin this was like touching a hot stove, and he veered away from anything but vague replies. Rantzau said that reducing Poland to its ethnic frontiers was "obviously" an objective "for the future, but not a task for today." Chicherin wanted to know whether Germany, in the eventuality of entering the League, would support Poland in a conflict against the USSR. Rantzau asked if there was any truth to rumors that the USSR was negotiating with Poland at German expense. In August 1925 Rantzau discretely raised the Polish question with Litvinov during their discussion of a possible Soviet-German agreement on neutrality. He warned Stresemann that Chicherin was looking for a French-Polish "card" to play just in case, but he did not have it yet.[14] For the Soviet side Poland might be a stake in German-Soviet relations, or a trump to secure better relations with France and to keep Germany from straying too far from Rapallo.

Figure 8.3. Georgii V. Chicherin and Nikolai N. Krestinskii, arriving at the Auswärtiges Amt, the German foreign ministry, Berlin, September 1925. Photographer: Georg Pahl. *Bundesarchiv, Bild* 102-12859.

For Stresemann, too, Poland was a delicate question, especially in October 1925 as he was preparing to depart for Locarno to conclude security agreements with France and Britain. Rantzau's too-candid talk about Poland made Stresemann nervous, and he told Chicherin that anything his ambassador might have said on that subject should not be taken seriously. They were only "minor inconsequential remarks."[15] The Polish issue however was never far from the German or Soviet mind.

Do you love me or not? Each side worried, though Soviet-German relations were never about love. In August 1925, in a conversation with Litvinov, Stresemann "spoke in an irritated tone about our constant reproaches" that Germany was changing sides. There was no new orientation, Stresemann insisted, according to Litvinov's account.

> Germany wants fully to maintain prior friendly relations with the USSR. We are threatening Germany with a Polish rapprochement, but after all we ourselves need it in the continuing period of peace; Germany also needs it. He [Stresemann] reiterated that German feelings toward the USSR and Poland were not changing. . . . If we ourselves do not want a military conflict, then why should the USSR and Germany not establish peaceful relations with Poland?

"In fact, we are not preparing for a conflict with Poland," Litvinov replied.

> But it's impossible to swear that a conflict will not arise in spite of our peaceful intentions. This eventuality, as it were, does not pose a problem now, but we would prefer that the USSR and Germany did not tie their hands. Unfortunately, Germany is going down the path of limiting its freedom of action in the West as well as in the East. Given the circumstances, we are talking about those possible steps which we will be obliged to take in the defense of our interests.

"You should not interpret this as a threat," Litvinov assured Stresemann. Of course it was, but not a threat on which the USSR could make good since neither Poland nor France were interested in a Soviet rapprochement.[16]

What Shall We Do?

When Chicherin asked for Litvinov's view of Rapallo, the *zamnarkom* responded that it was less important for its details than for its "spirit . . . its ideological superstructure, not expressed in words, but erected by mutual agreement." The treaty's lack of structure meant it could be abrogated or changed by either side. Let's not force the issues, especially over the German entry into the League of Nations, Litvinov continued. If Stresemann is willing to offer us guarantees in some form or other, or a trade agreement, "we must welcome and accept. We should through negotiations attempt to obtain the broadening and elaboration of the declaration and its transformation into a separate agreement without any ultimatum." Let's not move too quickly; let's not put the question to the Politburo yet. We can make counter-proposals if the German decision to enter the League becomes final. Chicherin pursued these same lines when he met Stresemann in Berlin, and they became in effect Soviet policy.[17]

In the meantime, the German-Soviet trade agreement had still not been signed. In Moscow people were impatient: if Germany concluded with France and Britain at Locarno before signature of the trade agreement, the Germans could lose interest in it and resume stalling, which they had been doing "almost all year."[18] Litvinov reported that discussions with the German delegation had concluded, but there remained one last question to settle. In these negotiations there was *always* a last question to settle, in the event a tax issue, but this time it was the Soviet delegation that needed instructions. The Politburo responded immediately, giving the necessary approval, and the treaty was signed, finally, on 12 October, to strengthen the German hand at Locarno.[19] It was nice timing for Stresemann.

The Locarno Accords were concluded on 16 October and signed in London on 3 December 1925. Chicherin and Litvinov had done their best to mitigate the impact of Locarno on Rapallo, but they still feared that Germany could be turned against the USSR through the League of Nations. In the days following the signature of the Locarno Accords, Litvinov was morose: "It would be naïve to believe," he wrote to Krestinskii,

> that nothing has happened in Europe, and that our relations with Germany have not suffered any damage. We have to recognize that the Rapallo Treaty . . . has lost at least 75 percent of its meaning for us. If it is true that Germany had still "not finally crossed into the Entente camp," then all the same we have to recognize that Germany has made a sharp turn in direction, and that for us it only remains to see how far it will go along this new path.

In Berlin Rapallo's *raison d'être* was antagonism between Germany and the Entente and Germany's need for an ally. Now, said Litvinov, in so many words, the game has changed.[20]

The game had indeed changed, as German diplomats in Berlin, such as Erich Wallroth, aptly noted: German-Soviet relations were like those between "the blind and the lame," each seeking through their association some slight amelioration of their afflictions. If Russia should be restored to sight, it would no longer have need of Germany; and likewise if Germany regained its strength, we would have no further need of Russia. The USSR was still floundering in "doctrinaire blindness," but we have regained some of our strength through the Dawes Plan, Locarno, and entry into the League of Nations. Each increase of strength has alarmed our blind ally, and further increases will have a similar effect. "The Rapallo alliance," concluded Wallroth, "has undoubtedly had considerable value for Germany. But this value must not be overestimated in the present, much less in the future."[21]

Rapallo was reaffirmed after two years of tensions and uncertainty but in a new environment where Locarno had blurred the previous clear lines of conflict in Europe. Fresh German-Soviet negotiations followed for commercial credits and a political accord to reinforce the October 1925 trade agreement. With Germany, as Trotskii put it, "one had to hit the iron while it was hot."[22]

Litvinov summed up the advantages of a potential political agreement. There were negatives of course: discounting the value for Paris of a Franco-Soviet agreement, which unbeknownst to Litvinov, the Quai d'Orsay had already rejected. The same calculation applied to discussions with Poland. In January 1925 Litvinov had acknowledged that a rapprochement with Poland prior to a German agreement would put paid to Rapallo. And anyway who knew how the Polish negotiations would turn out? Success seemed remote. With Germany in the League, it could not assist the USSR in the event of war with Poland. On the other hand, "a bird in the hand is better than two in the bush," as Litvinov put it, getting over his discouragement with Locarno: we have to tell Germany our policy remains unchanged. A political agreement, in fact a non-aggression pact, would neutralize Germany's entry into the League and its flirt with Britain. It would strengthen the Soviet international position and weaken the significance of Locarno. There was one sticking point: Litvinov wanted to obtain a change in the German proposed draft of a non-aggression pact which held that if one of the concluding parties provoked an attack upon itself, the other was not bound to neutrality. What if Britain bombarded our ports or Poland seized Kiev or Smolensk? Would Germany be able to claim we had provoked aggression?[23]

Litvinov was not above putting pressure on his German interlocutors. We want stronger guarantees, he told Rantzau in April 1926, "in order to take this into account in our relations with other countries. The less we have guarantees from Germany, the more we will have to look for them in our relations with third countries."[24] Here again was the application of Litvinov's realpolitik without any references to Marx and Engels.

Defining neutrality became a sticking point and the cause of much discussion with German negotiators until the signature of a neutrality pact in Ber-

Figure 8.4. Austen Chamberlain, Aristide Briand, Gustav Stresemann, Carl von Schubert, Geneva, 1926, *Agence Meurisse. Bibliothèque nationale de France.*

lin on 24 April 1926. According to a French journalist, Stresemann declared that Germany had won the race with France for a treaty with the USSR. In a conversation with Berthelot in Paris, the German ambassador denied that Stresemann had said any such thing. He might have though. Berthelot would have been unconcerned, for the French were not racing to get to Moscow ahead of the Germans—far from it.[25]

The NKID might have worried less about relations with Germany in spite of all the publicity over Locarno and Low's "Good Fairies." Although there was dissent within the German government about the value of relations with the USSR, Schubert considered that Germany still had to hew to a middle course between East and West. After Locarno and entry into the League, we have veered a little too far to the West; we need now to straighten our course by tacking back to the East. Moscow had trumps to play; Poland was one. France was another, or so it appeared at times in Berlin. Economics too weighed in the balance. "Our entire industry," Schubert noted, "is hypnotized by Russia." Business groups would not understand our abandoning that market, especially with the French appearing to warm to Moscow.[26] Appearances of warming Franco-Soviet relations were false, though Litvinov could have laid off the heavy hand. The Germans were coming around on their own.

The NKID's New *Bête Noire*

There were still problems over minor incidents: the arrest of a German diplomatic courier and continued public indiscretions by Soviet officials. Would they ever learn? This time it was Stalin's crony K. E. Voroshilov, but he was not inciting German communists; instead he was quoted in *Izvestiia* saying that the German army, "by hook or by crook," had become a formidable force. In high dudgeon, Ambassador Rantzau went to see Chicherin to complain that Voroshilov was tipping the Entente to "the secret rearmament of Germany," evidently "one of the most sensitive issues between the defeated and Versailles powers." This incident is worse than all the others, Rantzau insisted. Chicherin wrote to Molotov to ask that the problem be "liquidated" as soon as possible before the gaffe became more widely known. A simple, discreet correction published in the press would do. Chicherin must have recorded the ambassador's words with a certain relish; he titled his letter to the Politburo "Scandal with Germany."[27]

Trotskii endorsed Chicherin's position, although at this point Stalin would not have appreciated his advice no matter how useful. In any case, Voroshilov's office said there would be no change in the record of his remarks. It was the usual anarchy inside the Soviet government when it came to foreign policy. Chicherin reminded Voroshilov that the Politburo had "several times" indicated that all statements by "authoritative comrades" should be vetted by the NKID before being published.[28]

If Chicherin intended to needle Voroshilov, he definitely succeeded. The commissar for war responded in writing that the Germans were scarcely above launching public attacks against the USSR. Chicherin should have gone to my defense, Voroshilov wrote: there is not one word in the *narkom*'s record of conversation about how he had parried Rantzau's complaints.

Obviously not, since Chicherin's intention was not to defend Voroshilov, but to silence him and other gaffe-prone comrades, and to secure NKID control over Soviet foreign policy. Readers can only imagine how Chicherin must have relished meeting with stenographers to dictate his reports of discussions with Rantzau. Voroshilov understood the point but balked: I circulated my comments to Stalin and others, he noted, "who did not offer the slightest comment." If the idea was to pull rank on the NKID, it only provoked Chicherin to write again to suggest that Voroshilov was not on top of all his facts, and to emphasize again that "*narkoms* of the USSR do not make denunciations of the Entente." They kept their mouths shut and submitted remarks on foreign policy to the NKID for vetting to avoid diplomatic gaffes.[29]

Poland as Joe Btfsplk's Rain Cloud

Soviet-German relations impacted on relations with other European states, and gaffes were common. The German press for example reported that the Soviet government was negotiating an agreement to recognize Poland's western borders with Germany. At the time the NKID was indeed talking to the Polish government about better relations, for it could not hope to improve relations with Paris without Warsaw. But having resecured Rapallo, the NKID had to proceed carefully with France—the bird in the hand, in effect, being worth more than two in the bush. Hence, when Rantzau queried Chicherin about the reports of a Soviet guarantee of Poland's western borders, the latter dismissed them. The rumors are "so absurd," Chicherin replied, that a *démenti* would be superfluous.

I don't believe them myself, Rantzau rejoined, but I have to ask. He guessed that such rumors were being deliberately circulated by elements wanting to push Germany into a western orientation. Rantzau admitted that the Soviet-Polish discussions alarmed him since in Berlin a Soviet-Polish agreement would devalue Rapallo. For Germany the value of "friendship with the USSR" was that Poland would have to keep an eye cocked in the East, calming its hostility to Germany. In so many words left unsaid, if the USSR did not like Locarno, Germany did not like the prospect of a Soviet-Polish accord and for similar reasons. Chicherin responded honestly: one of the main tenets of Soviet foreign policy was "the preservation of peace," and because of Poland's geographical position in Europe, it was an important factor in that regard. So the USSR wanted to consolidate peaceful relations with Warsaw: "it was to the highest degree important." But even more important, Chicherin added, was the strengthening of Soviet relations with Germany. Not in an interview for the press, but in a secret record of meeting forwarded to Stalin, Chicherin underlined the importance of Rapallo, but also of improved relations with Poland and thus with France to prevent Germany from straying too far westward.[30] Rantzau was right about Chicherin's intentions. Each side knew the other very well indeed.

For Germany Poland was a source of constant irritation. It was the dark rain cloud over Al Capp's cartoon character Joe Btfsplk's head which never went away and always brought misfortune. According to Schubert, Germany considered virtually any development favoring Poland to be undesirable.

We were forced to agree to an arbitration treaty with Poland as a quid pro quo for the Locarno agreements, Schubert told the Soviet chargé d'affaires in Berlin, but arbitration was constrained to the narrowest possible compass. What was good for the German goose however was *not* good for the Soviet gander: the German-Polish arbitration treaty should not be interpreted, Schubert said, as a Soviet license to conclude a non-aggression pact with Warsaw. This would put us in a bind, for Britain would pressure Germany to make further concessions to Poland.[31] Like Litvinov, Schubert was worrying for nothing. There was no chance of a Soviet-Polish rapprochement.

Rapallo: "A Necessary Evil"

Poland was not the only problem between Berlin and Moscow. In early December 1926 the *Manchester Guardian* published two sensational articles constituting an exposé on German-Soviet cooperation in military research and development. The information was also published in the German and French press. In Moscow the press reports prompted speculation about who originated the articles and why. Soviet military intelligence held that the articles were known to the German foreign ministry, which wanted to shift press attention away from itself to Moscow and loosen its Russian ties.[32]

The press reports infuriated Chicherin who was in Berlin. He rounded on the OGPU, "spreading rumors" that "Germany is ready to change its policy toward us."

"I consider this to be absolute rubbish. The OGPU is falling for disinformation. I know here the material in question. It is all rubbish. We must not become victims of disinformation."

And then Chicherin had this to say on an old theme: "Anti-German articles in *Pravda* are very harmful. The greatest offense would be to allow to be snatched from our hands the essential trump, which is friendship with Germany."[33]

Here was a new episode in the NKID's struggle to exert and maintain control over Soviet foreign policy, where attempts to destabilize it could come from almost anywhere in Moscow, not just the Comintern. Litvinov therefore challenged the reports from Soviet military intelligence, wanting to know its sources of information before drawing any definite conclusions. The revelations could, for example, be an attempt to undermine Stresemann in his continuing negotiations with France and Britain.

Litvinov also wrote to N. I. Bukharin, the new Comintern boss, about the *Manchester Guardian* revelations, since European socialists were using them to attack the Comintern. "It would seem to me to be timely to develop a general line for all communist party organs in the said polemic. This line, of course, should be harmonized with NKID tactics, and I would therefore ask you to communicate those directives which the IKKI will give to communist parties. Do you deem it necessary to submit the question to the Politburo?"[34] Litvinov's letter was polite, knowing that Bukharin was then Stalin's right-hand man. Trotskii, Zinoviev, and Kamenev were marginalized, relegated to an increasingly powerless opposition. Bukharin had taken Zinoviev's place as Comrade Loose Cannon in charge of the Comintern, and Litvinov did not want him firing off public blasts at Berlin. So he broke his own rules and proposed NKID-Comintern coordination. All in the cause of coherent policy, Litvinov would certainly have explained.

In the meantime deputy commissar for war I. S. Unshlikht responded to Litvinov with a lengthy report on military intelligence regarding German-Soviet relations. Stresemann was looking for a rapprochement with France without irritating Britain in order to hasten the end of the French occupation of the Rhineland, subordinating his eastern policy to these ends. He viewed the value of relations with the USSR as an asset in his policy of "maneuver" (*lavirovanie*) and in trade, but his interest in the Soviet counterweight "each day" took less account of Soviet interests. Exposure of Soviet ties with the Reichswehr was also part of Stresemann's strategy to weaken his eastern orientation and as a possible anti-communist card to play in London.[35]

All well and good was Litvinov's brief reply:

> Who does not know that the political interest of Germany in the USSR has diminished and that it [Germany] uses its closeness with the USSR for other objectives. But then we also approached Germany not for love or friendship, but to use it. Approaching now England or France, Germany also has in mind to use them for its purposes. Diplomacy, political coalitions, alliances do not have any other goal except for the use of these relations for definite purposes.

Nor was Litvinov persuaded that Stresemann was behind the exposure of Soviet-German military contacts.[36] Intelligence reports had to be assessed with a critical eye. Here again was Litvinov, the realist, without any reference to Marxist doctrine.

Not surprisingly, Litvinov had his counterparts in Berlin. Herbert von Dirksen, deputy chief of the Eastern Department in the Auswärtiges Amt, gave a similar lesson to colleagues in Berlin several months later. Germany could not pursue a policy oriented either to the East or the West; it could only steer a course between them. Echoing Litvinov and his chief Wallroth, Dirksen then wrote that German policy was not based on any sympathy for the Soviet government, but on the recognition of parallel political and economic interests. The USSR is "the necessary evil, on which, given our awareness of those parallel interests, we must calculate." The USSR would sell us out, Dirksen noted, "for the slightest advantage," and we would turn to an anti-Russian policy if it produced advantages for Germany. *Niebelungentreue*, absolute loyalty, did not figure in international relations.[37] It was

Figure 8.5. Gustav Stresemann and Carl von Schubert, Geneva, 1927.
Agence Meurisse. Bibliothèque nationale de France.

the age-old game of realpolitik. Everybody played the game and everybody knew it, not least Stresemann and Schubert.

In spite of the brief lesson on the purposes of diplomacy given by Litvinov, Unshlikht was not fully convinced and asked for a Politburo discussion of Soviet relations with the Reichswehr. The commissariat for war had become increasingly uncomfortable with those relations and wanted to restrict them, especially after their exposure in the western press. There were also hearings in the German Reichstag where the war minister, Otto Gessler, revealed details of Soviet-German military cooperation beginning in 1922 when Soviet Russia, inter alia, supplied ammunition to the Reichswehr. Krestinskii cabled the news to Moscow, adding that German "communists were extremely embarrassed and alarmed by these stories."[38]

Litvinov warned Rantzau that further revelations could have damaging consequences for Soviet-German relations. Rantzau agreed, underlining to Berlin how the loss of ties to Moscow would weaken German policy in the West.[39] Krestinskii called on Schubert to reinforce Litvinov's concerns: the unwanted publicity not only violated secret bilateral relations, but also suggested a change in German policy which would make impossible such agreements in the future. Schubert was evasive in reply saying only that Gessler could not refuse to testify in secret sessions of a Reichstag committee. Krestinskii informed Moscow that the revelations did not signal a radical change in policy but only the wish to "liquidate" secret relations with the USSR and were "a logical consequence of entry into the League of Nations." They also cut the ground from underneath social democrats wanting to attack the government.[40] There was further testimony in the Reichstag toward the end of February. The German social democratic newspaper *Vorwärts* ran stories on the revelations, not missing a chance to attack the communists. *Vorwärts* got one thing right, Krestinskii noted sarcastically, when it reported that German communists were defending Soviet transactions with the Reichswehr: "Moscow, in the interests of its consolidation and the world revolution, had to arm itself by any means and to this end even enter into accord with [the war minister] Gessler."[41]

In late February 1927 the Politburo determined that future military cooperation with Germany would be limited to "legal forms." "All secret joint undertakings with the Reichswehr" were to be halted; a plant to produce poison gas was the notable example. This information was conveyed "very politely" to the German military attaché in Moscow. Gessler's revelations ruled out future "secret" joint projects. The German position was similar; cooperation should be kept to a modest scale.[42]

It was nevertheless not bad publicity that killed Soviet-Reichswehr military-industrial enterprises; these were already moribund when the stories broke in the *Manchester Guardian*. In April 1926, even as the Treaty of Berlin was being signed, Deputy Commissar for War Unshlikht submitted a pessimistic report to the Politburo on future military cooperation with the Reichswehr. His conclusion was that future development of Soviet military technology and industry in cooperation with the Reichswehr was "completely impossible." The Reichswehr ministry either was not interested or did not have the money to pursue such cooperation. We should continue to maintain relations with the Reichswehr, Unshlikht concluded, but not count on any "practical results." And Unshlikht added that "it would be necessary to observe all the necessary caution" in continuing these relations. The Politburo agreed.[43]

In the spring of 1927 when the Reichswehr invited Soviet staff officers to participate in German maneuvers, Litvinov responded cautiously, seeing pros and cons. He agreed in the end, reasoning that the Soviet presence would counter western public impressions of Soviet isolation.[44] Rapallo thus had well defined limits and value for both sides, but it survived even the hardest blows from Berlin and Moscow.

Delay the "Divorce" as Long as Possible

In the meantime, Litvinov continued to fight on another front, this one against his habitual *bête noire*, the Comintern. In January 1927, Bukharin made a speech in Moscow in which he attacked a German industrialist and by implication the German government. It caused a sensation in the Berlin press, and once again Rantzau complained to Litvinov. It seemed he was always complaining to the NKID about Soviet expressions of hostility toward Germany. Was the Soviet government serious about Rapallo, or was it just a show?

Litvinov reacted, complaining directly to Stalin. Bukharin had attacked the only government in Europe with which the Soviet Union had tolerable relations. Litvinov was blunt: these public statements would not facilitate the maintenance of "friendly relations" with Berlin. Even worse, Bukharin had made claims that were "simply untrue," based on "false citations." And then Litvinov gave examples. The German ambassador, he continued, came to see me to complain. Litvinov made excuses, the usual lines. Bukharin was not a member of the government and was speaking on his own initiative. Not that Litvinov thought Soviet-German cooperation would last forever. From a historical perspective, he commented, this was not to be expected. On the other hand, why hasten the process? Our purpose must be to delay the divorce for as long as possible.

One can see the problem with Bukharin, the head of the Comintern, a Bolshevik and member of the Politburo, making speeches on foreign policy intended perhaps for a domestic audience, but leaking into the foreign press. It was a no-win situation, as Litvinov observed: either "our enemies" in the West say that the Soviet government directs the Comintern, or they say the Soviet government is under the "influence and control of the Comintern." He reminded Stalin that the Politburo had already approved a resolution requiring speeches or articles on foreign policy by "authoritative comrades" to be vetted by the NKID before they were delivered, and in any case before publication. It was a sensible idea in principle certainly, but not so much in practice in the heat of politics in Moscow.[45]

Rantzau reckoned that political and economic tensions were behind Bukharin's speech. Germany is the only source of foreign financial and political support, and there are fears that this support will be lost. The NKID understands that this is unlikely, but others in Moscow think that Locarno will eventually lead Germany into the British orbit. And Britain, noted Rantzau, is perceived as being the main threat to Soviet security.[46]

Rantzau again followed up at the NKID, two days after Litvinov had written to Stalin. Litvinov gave his usual lines dismissing the importance of Bukharin who was not a member of the government and noting that his views did not reflect those of the government.

This is just "a fairy story," Rantzau replied: I demand that the Soviet government restrain Bukharin as it did Zinoviev!

"Perhaps it has already happened," Litvinov replied glibly, being unable simply to read the letter he had written to Stalin. One of the NKID desk officers assured Rantzau that the government had already acted to contain Bukharin.[47]

Stalin had the same problem with Bukharin that he had with Zinoviev. As his main ally of the moment, Stalin had to be careful. Hit Bukharin too hard at the wrong moment and he could turn to the opposition of Trotskii, Zinoviev, and Kamenev. Like the latter two, Bukharin contemplated such a move toward Trotskii when it was too late. So Stalin went easy on his favorites and temporary allies, but rarely for long. Internal political considerations thus trumped Soviet foreign policy priorities. This is a phenomenon that was not unique to the Soviet Union.

Litvinov certainly knew all of this. When Rantzau complained again a few months later about the latest Comintern anti-German rant, Litvinov gave a stock-in-trade reply: the NKID cannot act against the Comintern executive. This was true if put in that particular way, but Litvinov did not add that he was trying to get a straitjacket on the Comintern.

No one believed, Rantzau replied, that the IKKI, that is Bukharin, was independent of the Soviet government and beyond its ability to control.

I had hoped, Litvinov replied piously, that Germany would recognize the existing situation here: the Soviet government cannot act against the Comintern.

"If the government here is powerless to prevent such disloyalty, for I cannot express it in any other way," Rantzau countered sharply, "then German-Russian relations must unavoidably suffer serious damage."

According to Rantzau, Litvinov reacted with a "pained expression" to these remarks, reinforced by a reference to the Petrov fiasco in 1923 when the Soviet military attaché, a former French naval officer, had been accused of smuggling guns into Germany. "Pained expressions" were a practiced routine by Litvinov and Chicherin when it came to Rantzau's complaints. The ambassador knew NKID's vulnerabilities, and Litvinov finally promised to forward Rantzau's latest observations to the government, which meant Stalin.[48] The German and Soviet advocates of Rapallo had to possess the patience of saints, reinforced by a strong conviction in their respective national interests, in order to hold to their course.

The Auswärtiges Amt saw the Soviet Union as caught between policies of economic "consolidation" and communist "expansion." Germany had an interest in weaning the Soviet government away from "world revolution." "Consolidation" was at the base of the German Rapallo: draw the poison from the revolutionary, boisterous tendencies of the Soviet government and bring it closer to the West. It was not clear which way the USSR would go, and so Stresemann and Rantzau repeatedly reminded the NKID of their desired outcome.[49] The usual grievances came up again in June 1927.

Chicherin is due in Berlin, Stresemann informed the German cabinet. I am afraid, he joked, that Chicherin will want to play his usual role as our "special adviser." Instead, Stresemann turned the tables.

The Soviet association with the Comintern is a big problem, Stresemann told Chicherin. I protested recently against a Comintern canard that Germany was secretly preparing to join an imperialist war against Russia. "Lies of this kind" put out by the Moscow press, Stresemann said, are a "great danger" to Soviet foreign policy. We deny them repeatedly, and still they turn up in the Soviet press. The German government is concerned that its denials make no impression in Moscow, and that the "lies," in spite of everything, seem to gain credibility.

I agree that these circumstances endanger Soviet policy, Chicherin replied. The Comintern is "a very complicated organization." There is no way to get it out of Moscow. I have constantly struggled against Comintern outbursts and I will continue to do so when I return home.[50] As readers will see, Chicherin was as good as his word. But who knew whether Comrade Narkomindel'cheskii or Comrade Kominternovskii would get the upper hand?

Notes

1. Chicherin's report to the Politburo on Soviet-German relations, 1 July 1925, *Moskva-Berlin*, I, pp. 556–60.

2. Margerie, nos. 673–75, 23 July 1930, MAÉ URSS/1260, ff. 60–62.

3. Yvon Delbos, French foreign minister, to Robert Coulondre, French ambassador in Moscow, no. 139, 4 March 1938, MAÉ, *Bureau du chiffre, télégrammes, Moscou, départ, 1938–1 octobre 1939*; Coulondre's reply, nos. 239–45, 6 March 1938, *Documents diplomatiques français, 2e série*, 19 vols. (Paris, 1963–1986), VIII, pp. 637–38; Resis, *Molotov Remembers*, pp. 120, 148; and Jacobson, *Soviet Union*, pp. 128–29.

4. Chicherin to Karakhan, no. 76, secret, 23 June 1925, *Perepiska I. V. Stalina i G. V. Chicherina*, pp. 541–43.

5. Stresemann to Rantzau, no. 172, urgent, 29 June 1925, AzDAP, A, XIII, pp. 455–57.

6. Krestinskii to Chicherin, no. 701, 28 July 1925, *Moskva-Berlin*, I, pp. 581–86; Politburo resolution, no. P73/1-A/s, rigorously secret, 30 July 1925, ibid., p. 586; 504, n. 8; 574, n. 1; 914, n. 3; and Carr, *Socialism in One Country*, III, pp. 275–78.

7. Ganetskii to Politburo, no. 330/s, very secret, 21 July 1925, *Moskva-Berlin*, I, pp. 574–75.

8. Ganetskii to Politburo, no. 338/s, very secret, very urgent, 28 July 1925, *Moskva-Berlin*, I, pp. 578–80; Ganetskii to Politburo, very secret, 4 Aug. 1925, ibid., pp. 595–96; and Ganetskii to Politburo, no. 361/s, very secret, 22 Aug. 1925, ibid., pp. 600–602.

9. Stresemann to Rantzau, no. 54, urgent, 23 May 1925, AzDAP, A, XIII, pp. 142–44.

10. Schubert's note, no. 79, very secret, 2 June 1925, AzDAP, A, XIII, pp. 198–206.

11. Chicherin's report to the Politburo, 1 July 1925, *Moskva-Berlin*, I, pp. 556–60; and Rantzau, no. 186, very secret, 3 July 1925, AzDAP, A, XIII, pp. 517–19.

12. Litvinov's *dnevnik*, record of conversation with Rantzau, 25 Aug. 1925, *Moskva-Berlin*, I, pp. 603–7; and Rantzau, no. 34, very secret, 27 Aug. 1925, *AzDAP*, A, XIV, pp. 100–102.

13. Chicherin (Berlin) to Litvinov, no. 6, 2 Oct. 1925, *Moskva-Berlin*, I, pp. 636–37.

14. "Record of conversation of G. V. Chicherin with Rantzau . . . ," no. 1525/ChS, rigorously secret, 19 Dec. 1924, *Moskva-Berlin*, I, pp. 454–60; Rantzau, no. 34, very secret, 27 Aug. 1925, *AzDAP*, A, XIV, pp. 100–102; and Rantzau, no. 94, urgent, very secret, ibid., pp 241–42.

15. Chicherin (Berlin) to Litvinov, no. 7, 4 Oct. 1925, *Moskva-Berlin*, I, pp. 637–41; and Stresemann's notes, no. 109, 30 Sept. 1925; and no 110, 2 Oct. 1925, *AzDAP*, A, XIV, pp. 284–91, 292–96.

16. Litvinov to NKID *kollegiia*, no. 0452, secret, 20 Aug. 1925, AVPRF, f. 082, o. 8, p. 18, d. 2, ll. 84–85.

17. Litvinov (Berlin) to Chicherin, not numbered, secret, 21 Sept. 1925, AVPRF, f. 082, o. 8, p. 18, d. 2, ll. 107–8; and Stresemann's note, no. 109, 30 Sept. 1925, as cited above in n. 15.

18. Krasin to A. I. Rykov, chairman, Sovnarkom, no. 10021, very secret, most immediate, 6 Oct. 1925, *Moskva-Berlin*, I, p. 644.

19. Litvinov to Stalin, no. 0604, secret, immediate, 7 Oct. 1925, *Moskva-Berlin*, I, pp. 645–46; and Politburo resolution, no. P83/opr.2/s, rigorously secret, 7 Oct. 1925, ibid., p 645.

20. Litvinov to Krestinskii, no. 0664, secret, 21 Oct. 1925, AVPRF, f. 082, o. 8, p. 18, d. 2, ll. 129–32.

21. Wallroth's memorandum, 26 May 1926, *AzDAP*, B, II, 2, pp. 480–89.

22. Trotskii, then member of VSNKh presidium, to Secretariat, TsK VKP(b), no. 9/s, very secret, 18 Jan. 1926, *Moskva-Berlin*, I, p. 679.

23. Litvinov to Krestinskii, no. 0030, secret, 14 Jan. 1925, AVPRF, f. 082, o. 8, p. 18, d. 2, ll. 5–6; Litvinov to Krestinskii, no. 2553, secret, 23 Jan. 1926, AVPRF, f. 082, o. 9, p. 22, d. 2, ll. 11–14; and Litvinov to NKID *kollegiia*, Krestinskii, no 2667, especially secret, 3 March 1926, *Moskva-Berlin*, I, pp. 796–98.

24. Litvinov's *dnevnik*, "Meeting with Rantzau," 13 April 1926, AVPRF, f. 082, o. 9, p. 22, d. 2, ll. 26–28.

25. Leopold von Hoesch, German ambassador in Paris, no. 372, very confidential, 24 April 1926, *AzDAP*, B, II, 1, pp. 409–11.

26. Schubert to Hoesch, 26 Jan. 1926, *AzDAP*, B, II, 1, pp. 120–26.

27. Chicherin to Molotov, no. 418/ChS, 5 March 1926, *Moskva-Berlin*, I, pp. 799–800; and "Record of conversation . . . with Rantzau . . . ," 5 March 1926, ibid., pp. 800–801.

28. Trotskii to Molotov, no. 41/s, very secret, 6 March 1926, *Moskva-Berlin*, I, p. 816; and Chicherin to Voroshilov, no. 424/ChS, 6 March 1926, ibid., p. 817.

29. Voroshilov to Molotov, cc. to Politburo and NKID *kollegiia*, no. 7326, very secret, 7 March 1926, *Moskva-Berlin*, I, pp. 819–20; and Chicherin to Molotov, no. 436, very secret, 8 March 1926, ibid., p. 821.

30. "Record of conversation . . . with Rantzau on 13 March . . . ," 14 March 1926, *Moskva-Berlin*, I, pp. 833–35.

31. Schubert's memorandum, secret, 28 Aug. 1926, *AzDAP*, B, II, 2, pp. 238–40.

32. Rozengol'ts (London) to NKID, no. 9859, very secret, 7 Dec. 1926; and Davtian (Paris) to NKID, no. 9863, very secret, 7 Dec. 1926, *Moskva-Berlin*, I, p. 945; and I. S. Unshlikht, head of military intelligence and deputy commissar for war, to Politburo, cc. Voroshilov and Litvinov, no. 75/k, very secret, 10 Dec. 1926, ibid., pp. 963–65.

33. Chicherin to Litvinov, no. 4, secret, 8–9 Dec. 1926, *Moskva-Berlin*, I, pp. 962–63.

34. Litvinov to Unshikht, no. 3187, secret, 16 Dec. 1926, *Moskva-Berlin*, I, pp. 966–67; and Litvinov to Bukharin, cc. Stalin, no. 3237, secret, 30 Dec. 1926, ibid., pp. 967–68.

35. Unshlikht to Litvinov, cc. Stalin, Voroshilov, no. 78, very secret, 31 Dec. 1926, *Moskva-Berlin*, I, pp. 968–79.

36. Litvinov to Unshlikht, cc. Stalin and Voroshilov, no. 3018, secret, 6 Jan. 1927, *Moskva-Berlin*, II, pp. 5–6.

37. Memorandum by Dirksen, very secret, 19 Sept. 1927, *AzDAP*, B, VI, pp. 465–68.

38. Krestinskii to NKID, no. 1292, very secret, 16 Feb. 1927, *Moskva-Berlin*, II, p. 15.

39. Rantzau, no. 261, very secret, 18 Feb. 1927, *AzDAP*, B, IV, pp. 347–48.

40. Krestinskii to NKID, nos. 1394–95, very secret, decipher immediately, 19 Feb. 1927, *Moskva-Berlin*, II, pp. 25–26.

41. Krestinskii to NKID, nos. 1506, 1509–10, very secret, immediate, 23 Feb. 1927, *Moskva-Berlin*, II, pp. 27–28.

42. Unshlikht to Stalin, no. 014, very secret, 4 March 1927, *Moskva-Berlin*, II, p. 36; and Dirksen's memoranda, very secret, 24 Jan. and 9 Feb. 1927, *AzDAP*, B, IV, pp. 139–42, 256–57.

43. Unshlikht to Politburo, no. 178/ss, very secret, 5 April 1926, *Moskva-Berlin*, I, pp. 886–91.

44. Litvinov to Molotov, no. 3419, secret, 10 June 1927, *Moskva-Berlin*, II, pp. 54–55.

45. Litvinov to Stalin, no. 3064, secret, 21 Jan. 1927, AVPRF, f. 082, o. 10, p. 27, d. 2, l. 2 (published in *Moskva-Berlin*, II, pp. 9–11); Litvinov to Chicherin, no. 3112, secret, 5 Feb. 1927, AVPRF, f. 05 o. 6, p. 21, d. 89, ll. 13–15; and Litvinov to Brodovskii (Berlin), no. 3330, secret, 7 May 1927, AVPRF, f. 082, o. 10, p. 27, d. 2, ll. 10–11.

46. Rantzau, no. 101, very secret, 19 Jan. 1927, *AzDAP*, B, IV, pp. 99–101.

47. Rantzau, no. 124, secret, 23 Jan. 1927, *AzDAP*, B, IV, pp. 138–39.

48. Rantzau, no. 631, secret, 5 May 1927, *AzDAP*, B, V, pp. 258–60.

49. Wallroth's memorandum, strictly secret, 20 April 1927, *AzDAP*, B, V, pp. 210–13; and Dirksen's memorandum, very secret, 3 June 1927, ibid., pp. 454–58.

50. Excerpt from Cabinet Protocol, 30 May 1927, *AzDAP*, B, V, pp. 418–21; and Stresemann's memorandum, Baden-Baden, 7 June 1927, ibid., pp. 465–73.

~

CHAPTER NINE

Red Scare, War Scare

China and the Rupture of Anglo-Soviet Relations, 1925–1927

Having resecured its footing in Berlin, however precariously, the Politburo could deal more confidently with the British government. At the end of 1926, Anglo-Soviet relations were bad and getting worse. In December Rozengol'ts went to see Gregory. There was not much new to report to Moscow, unless it was that the attitude in the Foreign Office was "even cooler to us." Gregory, who was personally cordial, remarked that British foreign policy toward the Soviet Union had become "very much dependent on the internal party situation."[1] Chicherin, who was still in Germany, asked Moscow about a meeting with Chamberlain. Not unless there is a direct invitation, Stalin replied.[2]

China: "Everything Has Become Complicated"

When Rozengol'ts said that Anglo-Soviet relations had worsened since the summer of 1926, he was understating the case. At the very time in December when he visited Gregory, Foreign Office officials were discussing their options on Soviet policy. Chamberlain still tried to keep a lid on tensions, but his officials, some of them anyway, had lost patience. Events in China were going badly. Readers will remember that we last left Chinese developments in mid-1925. Sun Yat-sen had died in March, and the Politburo had increased its stakes in China, backing Sun's successor, General Chiang Kai-shek, who was consolidating his control in south China. Money, arms, and personnel were committed.

On 30 May 1925 a police shooting into a crowd in Shanghai set off a massive nationalist, anti-foreign movement across China. Most Chinese who thought about such matters wanted to abolish the unequal treaties, close down the treaty ports, and retake control of their country. The movement was popular, anarchistic, violent, disorganized. It needed revolutionary leaders and cadres. Stalin was willing to commit assets in China, but without being carried away by "fantasies," and keeping feet planted firmly on reality's ground. But Soviet priorities were shifting from West to East. The biggest loser in China stood to be Britain with its important commercial interests. A greater Soviet commitment in China would anger the British government, but Anglo-Soviet relations were bad and getting worse.

How much worse could they get by raising the ante in China? On 12 June 1925 Stalin cabled to Karakhan to say that money had been allocated for the Shanghai strike movement. "Don't worry, we are faithfully supporting the revolutionary movement of workers." It was 50,000 rubles, and collections were to be undertaken to support Chinese strike action.[3]

Soviet activities in China were by no means limited to Comintern agents. Chicherin was a member of the Politburo "Chinese Commission" and was involved in eastern policy and planning. In the summer of 1925 he seemed rather casual about increasing dangers in the West. Events in China were exciting anti-communist, "interventionist" opinion in Europe, increasing the danger of an anti-Soviet "united front." Like Stalin, Chicherin explained to Karakhan, still *polpred* in Beijing, that there were limits to what the USSR could do. "In the discussion of the Chinese question one has always to keep in mind that our type of government has to operate primarily by political, party, organizational methods and through agitation." Military means could play a supporting role: "they sometimes proved necessary, but are not a primary [strategy]." When Karakhan wanted to go further, Chicherin cautioned him: it was not a question of "all or nothing."

"You can do something, and there are results, if the business is politically well conceived." We cannot, Chicherin continued, throw resources to the four winds, any more than we can sit on our hands and do nothing. "With us there is nevertheless a duality, for we cannot forget . . . [that] on the one hand, we are pursuing a definite line, but on the other we are observing caution." So when Krasin's counselor in the Paris embassy said something in public in support of the Chinese revolution, we recalled him. "Now everything has become complicated since the question of Chinese events and the connections between them and the USSR have become the center of attention of the capitalist press and the British government." So be careful, Chicherin wrote to Karakhan, about what you say in public.[4]

Karakhan was of course not a foolish ideologue. "I completely agree," he replied to Stalin, "that we must stay on solid ground and that it would be dangerous to engage in fantasy, although I have to say, that here in China the ground is so hot that it is very easy to lose sight of reality." And Karakhan agreed that 10 or 20 million was out of the question, but what about half a million for cavalry and rifles for the northern warlord Feng Yuxiang?[5]

In spite of Stalin's desire not to lose sight of reality, the May 30th movement appears to have led the Politburo to approve important new resources to support its China policy: some 5 million rubles, inter alia, for logistical support of Soviet activities and cadres in China, and for the organization and supply of "international" units in Mongolia to support the warlord Feng and to arm the Canton military forces. From 12,000 rubles in early 1923, to half a million, to 5 million in June 1925, one can see the deepening Soviet commitment in China. It was a relatively modest investment in so populous and large a country as China, but important money for the Politburo. There was also advice to be given to Chinese workers, shopkeepers, and intellectuals, "to refrain from killing and beating foreigners, from rude nationalist outbursts, like putting up signs saying 'Englishmen, Japanese and dogs forbidden entry into Chinese public places' . . . so as not to give foreign instigators reasons to talk about a Boxer-like movement and not to facilitate . . . armed intervention by the imperialists." This advice, added the Politburo resolution, should come first of all from the Chinese Communist Party.[6]

Stalin cabled Karakhan to warn of imperialist efforts to divide the nationalist movement and turn the conservative Beijing government against Canton and the Guomintang. You have to warn Canton to be careful, said Stalin, and not fall into a trap. The imperialist states will try to derail the revolutionary movement. "Do not succumb to foreign provocation and do not take their bait." Canton should become the center of the nationalist movement, drawing in the Beijing government and warlord Feng. The Manchurian warlord Zhang, "a very dangerous weapon in the hands of the imperialists," has to be isolated. This sounded like the power politics and the maneuvering of Ioffe or Karakhan among the warlords, and it was not bad advice on the face of it. But Stalin did not once mention the Chinese Communist Party. Paradoxically he thought to protect the revolutionary movement without reference to the real revolutionaries. Karakhan agreed with Stalin's ideas, though he mentioned, almost inadvertently, that the Chinese Communist Party should work inside the Guomintang.[7]

As 1925 unfolded the Politburo increased its commitment of arms and matériel to Canton and to warlord Feng's army. It also continued to back the Guomintang. Chiang Kai-shek became commander in chief of the Guomintang National Revolutionary Army. Readers will remember that the Guomintang and Chinese Communist Party had formed an alliance, and that Chinese communists held posts inside the Guomintang. This was the "bloc within" policy. Chicherin favored the widest possible union of Chinese national forces, but he worried that the Chinese communists were getting too aggressive inside the Guomintang. They might prompt a right-left split in the Guomintang which could harm future development of the nationalist movement. The right wing of the Guomintang could betray the movement, becoming a "screen" for "imperialist agents." Hence, Chicherin's watchword was "unity."[8]

This meant working with Chiang Kai-shek who proved to be the Trojan horse of the nationalist revolutionary movement. He saw cooperation with the USSR as a temporary expedient, and he had close ties with Chinese bankers, compradors, and landowners who feared the mass revolutionary movement. But few people in Moscow seemed to have much of an idea about what was going on in China. Chicherin complained about it, saying decision making had been delegated to the ad hoc Chinese commission, which meant it was out of NKID hands, although he participated in Politburo discussions and planning. Rumors circulated about worst-case scenarios in China, from, it seemed, Soviet intelligence sources. These "panicky phantasmagorical" reports appeared overly pessimistic to Chicherin, generated by short-term, local political or military setbacks. So he asked Karakhan for detailed information about Chinese developments.[9]

So did Stalin, who was impatient for more intelligence. "The general political situation in China seems to us not fully clear," Stalin observed. What is going on? The situation in north and central China appeared to be going against the revolutionary movement; what are the chances of uniting the country under a single government?[10] Many questions and not enough answers, Stalin must have thought, especially with Trotskii ready to attack if things went wrong in China, as they could well do.

The Chinese situation was dangerous, and in spite of Stalin's earlier caution, the Politburo became more deeply involved, trying to direct and channel a chaotic revolutionary movement far beyond Soviet borders. It was not just that China was in the midst of violent social and political upheaval; it was still a semi-colony, with its most important cities occupied by foreign troops guarding western and Japanese concessions. As the USSR thrust more deeply into the Chinese revolution, the NKID was marginalized in Politburo decision making. Chicherin worried about the management of Soviet policy, over which he no longer had an important influence, and in particular he worried about the creation of an anti-Soviet bloc in China. Trotskii, not yet excluded from power, wondered whether the USSR should make concessions to Japan in Manchuria and to France in Canton to prevent the formation of a "united imperialist front." In the north it would be a kind of Manchurian Brest-Litovsk to neutralize the warlord Zhang by making concessions to Japan. Chicherin himself was skeptical about any success with France, their

Far Eastern policy lacking "consistency." He was more interested in exploiting the "deep and irreconcilable antagonism between the United States and Japan," both of which were expanding powers in the Pacific basin and bound to clash. Chicherin even raised the prospect of an eventual war between them. In the short term, however, he thought Japan had to be neutralized.[11] In fact, during the spring and summer of 1926 Chicherin pressed for, and the Politburo endorsed, new policy directives for an improvement of relations with Japan.[12] These new directives do not seem to have gone beyond generalities, being difficult to transform into concrete policies. The situation was so volatile that relations with Japan appeared to get lost in the effort to keep up with fast-moving events in China.

Even routine logistical questions caused problems. In early 1926 warlord Feng's army needed ammunition, but the Soviet government was short of foreign exchange to pay for it. The Politburo wanted Karakhan to find the necessary ammunition from stocks already available in China. We have to cut back on expenditures abroad, Chicherin advised. "In fact, we just don't have the foreign exchange to make big expenditures." Temporarily broke in effect, the Politburo thought the Guomintang should start paying half the costs of military supplies.[13] Moscow was trying to pursue a champagne policy on beer money. The Politburo nevertheless agreed to send 10 million cartridges to Feng on credit and on condition "of total secrecy."[14]

On 20 March 1926, a week after Chicherin informed Karakhan of Soviet budgetary difficulties, Chiang Kai-shek staged a minor coup d'état in Canton, sacking certain political commissars and solidifying his control over the army and Guomintang.

What happened? Moscow wanted to know. One report said there was a shift within the Guomintang to the right, reflecting powerful comprador interests who wanted communists and left-wing elements out of the party and who wanted to come to terms with the imperialist powers in China, putting an end to the national strike movement. There was a common interest between comprador and British traders in Hong Kong: the strikes were harming business. The Comintern wanted more information and reckoned that it needed to "clarify" the situation between the Guomintang and the Chinese Communist Party.[15]

It was a little late asking for clarity, but certainly it would have helped in dealing with Chiang. A further report offered more details on what had happened on 20 March but came to the same conclusions, that the compradors with foreign backing were in conflict with the workers' and peasants' movements. The Politburo decided nevertheless that its policy line should be maintained: unity of the nationalist movement and continuation of the "bloc within" the Guomintang.[16]

In the meantime the NKID had trouble with Soviet officials and workers in Manchuria responsible for the administration of the Chinese Eastern Railroad (CER), a rail line built across northern Manchuria during the reign of Tsar Nicolas II as a shortcut from the Trans-Siberian to Vladivostok. The railroad was still controlled by Soviet officials who treated local Chinese authorities in cavalier fashion. There were tensions between Soviet and Chinese workers because of Russian "chauvinism." The situation was serious enough to draw the attention of the Politburo during the winter of 1926. Local CER authorities were directed to sack the worst offenders and to remind employees that they were on Chinese territory and to adopt themselves to the Soviet policy of friendship with the Chinese people. The Soviet chief administrator was himself dismissed.[17]

The problem persisted, for Chicherin complained that the Soviet government was getting into danger in Manchuria, running up against the warlord Zhang, who was probing Soviet weakness along the CER, a rich prize if he could seize it. The Soviet railroad administration needed the support of local Chinese "progressive" elements, but behaved so badly toward them, excluding them from any serious role in the running of the railway, that Soviet authorities found themselves isolated against the dangerous Zhang. For Chinese progressives, as Chicherin put it, "the veil had fallen away from their eyes," and they had seen "the imperialist essence of our policies." Chicherin was disgusted with Soviet conduct, and not just in Manchuria: our old "imperialist" instincts were running everywhere across our "Eastern" policy. He mentioned Mongolia, Persia, and Turkey, but his main concern was China. Nowhere was the behavior of Soviet officials worse than in Manchuria, putting at risk "the whole of our Chinese policies." On the one hand, Chicherin complained to Karakhan, we make speeches "about solidarity with oppressed peoples, but on the other in practice we pursue a line in the spirit of tsarist satraps." This was strong language. "Our China policy in general cannot have any success when we on the CER demonstrate before all the Chinese people imperialist practices and methods of intimidation, pressure, and disregard for the Chinese."[18] So it was not just that Chicherin's proverbial Soviet goat had no wool or milk, which was indeed a problem, but it was also true that some Soviet officials retained the very same Orientalist attitudes toward the Chinese that the West maintained toward the USSR.

The Politburo had a bull by the horns; the only question was, could it hold on without being gored? At the end of May 1926 the Politburo reiterated its support for the "bloc within" policy. Support for the Chinese Communist Party (CCP) would be increased, and Chinese communists would continue to work within the Guomintang to "isolate" its right wing.[19] No policy was more likely to encourage the right and notably Chiang to turn on their communist allies. If Stalin wanted to avoid fantasies and maintain limits in Soviet China policy, his caution seemed to have gone by the boards in a classic case of mission over-extension, provoked by domestic politics and perhaps an irrepressible Bolshevism in the Politburo.

In London: Die-Hards Triumphant

If events in China were not going smoothly for the USSR, they were not going well for the British either. The strike movement continued, wreaking havoc on British trade, and during the summer of 1926 Chiang launched, with Soviet advisers, guns, and money, the "northern expedition," ultimately to take Beijing and reunite the country. In September 1926 there was a clash between British gunboats and Chinese soldiers at the Yangzi River town of Wanxian about 2,400 kilometers upstream from Shanghai, where a large number of Chinese civilians and soldiers were killed after a British naval bombardment. The number of casualties was far higher than the Shanghai fusillade that touched off the May 30th movement, and a government White Paper was issued to explain what had happened. In a way, it hardly mattered, for the Foreign Office always had a ready explanation for its problems: Bolshevik propaganda remained the British "bull's eye."

Gregory recalled an exchange with Rakovskii or Krasin, he could not remember who. "You regard the mere fact of our existence as propaganda," said his Soviet interlocutor. "And indeed he was right," observed Gregory.

Chamberlain objected to this comment, as well he might have done, since it contradicted his relatively conciliatory message to Krasin at their last meeting in October 1926. Gregory offered an apologetic explanation which Chamberlain accepted. But Gregory's thought was not different from the comments often heard in the State Department or the Quai d'Orsay. It was nothing new. According to Gregory, the Bolsheviks "are very curious unfathomable characters, not wholly impervious to personal pressure, provided it is kindly."

> Clearly it is not going to do more than keep them in order up to a certain point, and it is certainly not going to settle anything. But nothing is going to settle this problem but itself and that is going to take still a long time—as it is after all an experiment, though a pretty nasty one at that, which has got to work itself out.

Tyrrell, the permanent undersecretary, was not nearly as detached as Gregory, who was ostensibly attempting to respect Chamberlain's line. "I think we should clear our minds on the subject of Russia," Tyrrell wrote, and face the fact that we are virtually at war with Russia, in spite of Russia discarding the time-honored practice of force and substituting for it the far more insidious weapon of peaceful penetration on the one hand in the internal affairs of other countries, and, on the other, the stirring up of revolution everywhere in order to prevent us from carrying on trade, and thereby undermining the commercial prosperity on which our national life depends.

It was two issues that galled: the coal strike and the "successful efforts in destroying our trade with China." Tyrrell did not recommend an immediate rupture of relations. He wanted to maintain "our present attitude of watchful vigilance . . . to catch the Soviets in a case of flagrant delicto, which will enable us to clear them out of this country." And then, thinking like a good Tory, Tyrrell added, "We should endeavour to force the Labour party either to associate itself with our policy or frankly come into the open on the side of the people who are determined upon our destruction." Tyrrell minuted that his comments and those of Gregory had been "seen and approved by the prime minister."[20]

Chamberlain was at the time in Paris, which is why Tyrrell forwarded his notes to Baldwin. In fact, Tyrrell had spent the weekend at the prime minister's residence at Chequers, meeting with Baldwin. "I told the PM," Tyrrell informed Chamberlain, "that the Russian interference in our coal strike and Russian proceedings in China might justify us in assuming that we are virtually at war with that country." Although Tyrrell was thus informing Chamberlain that he had been to see Baldwin, it was after the fact and gave the appearance, mistaken perhaps, of going around him to break out of the Foreign Secretary's more cautious approach to Moscow.[21] In January 1927 Rozengol'ts advised Litvinov that according to various reliable sources, Tyrrell *and* Gregory had been working "behind Chamberlain's back." The Foreign Secretary was known for his "mental limitations" and was in fact following *their* policy.[22] It may have been that Tyrrell's early December discussions with Baldwin forced Chamberlain's hand, but there is no indication in the Foreign Office files of Chamberlain's "mental limitations." Quite the contrary, he seemed to hold his officials well in hand.

Undoubtedly encouraged by Tyrrell, Gregory reverted to an old Foreign Office theme. "The Russians are Orientals," he wrote in a long memorandum, "and it is among Orientals that their propaganda is most successful."

The success that they are having is largely due to the propagated conviction that Great Britain is too weak to take any action against them, and has no alternative but to sit down impotently under their provocation. A sudden reversal of our attitude, if properly stage-managed, might act as a bombshell throughout China, Persia, Afghanistan and along the Indian border: the Oriental being traditionally reported to understand only a display of strength.

Gregory went on a long rant, noting that Britain might be well advised to break with the USSR, not only on the merits, but to send a clear message to "the East." An ironic comment indeed, since it resembled those which Chicherin often made when he talked about the Soviet goat without milk or wool unable to support Soviet "eastern" policy. Paradoxically, the Soviet and British constituencies were often the same. Gregory went on at length about Soviet "propaganda" but not about Soviet cartridges and rifles for warlord Feng and the Guomintang. Was he briefed? It may have been that British intelligence was unaware of the extent of the Soviet investment in China. And Gregory thought the USSR might do another U-turn in reaction to a new British ultimatum, making concessions that would be hard to refuse.[23] On this point he need not have worried. Krasin was dead, and the Politburo was in no mood to "go hat in hand" to London.

The Cabinet resumed debate on its Soviet policy in January 1927 based on a policy memorandum submitted by Chamberlain, presenting the pros and cons of a diplomatic rupture with Moscow. There were the usual issues of impact on British interests in Asia and on trade relations. A good part of his paper concerned domestic political issues, notably the position of the Labour Party. Tory policy was intended to divide Labour between "moderates" and "extremists." Between these two groups, according to Chamberlain, it was a fight to the finish: if the moderates were defeated, the party would pass into "Red hands." His view was that the government should not pursue a policy likely to unite Labour with the Liberals against it.[24]

In spite of Tyrrell's initiative, Chamberlain still tried to hold the line against a rupture, but he was up against formidable Die-Hard opposition. "I am increasingly concerned about China," Jix wrote to Chamberlain. This was because the British position in China continued to deteriorate. Two days earlier, British authorities had been forced to evacuate their concession in Hankou, at the fork of the Han and Yangzi rivers in central China, under pressure from large crowds throwing bricks and stones at British sailors. "Situation very grave last night," reported the British consul general. "I had to ask for Chinese troops to control the crowd. Our forces are quite inadequate and have had to be withdrawn: if they were landed they would have to fire and that would be signal for a general uprising against foreigners."[25]

"I read in the French papers," Jix wrote from France, "of attacks on British sailors *unresisted* of evacuating B[ritish] women from our concessions & reembarkation of our sailors because if they stayed on shore in *our* [emphasis in the original] concession they would be compelled to fire."

"Why not?" he asked. In retaliation, Jix suggested a blockade of Canton. And he had another proposal: "to quite definitely tell the Chinese officials at Hankow [sic] that unless they clear the mob away from the concession within 2 hrs we shall fire." Jix was in favor of "uphold[ing] the B[ritish] position by arms."

As I said in the Cabinet when we last discussed China I do not accept the FO theory that China will get rid of her Bolshevic [sic] advisors as soon as she gets her freedom.

Au contraire I believe that the Chinese leaders are Bolshie in heart and that unless we are vy forceful we may find the Bolshie led Cantonese in command of the whole of China.[26]

Chamberlain would not go so far and wished to avoid the use of force in China except as a last resort. He had to hold back not only his excited colleagues in London, but also British authorities in China. They were ugly, archetypical colonialists whose imperialism was mixed with racism toward the Chinese. Hong Kong authorities were spending large sums on propaganda, $155,000, according to one Colonial Office report, fueling the English-language press in North China, which even by Foreign Office reckoning was "extremist," treating all Chinese nationalists "as Reds." Even Tyrrell noted the "anti-nigger feeling" of "the average Englishman" in East Asia. "It is obvious," Mounsey commented, "that the attitude of the British communities and press in China continues to do us incalculable harm."[27] It was a poisonous brew which could provoke what Consul General Goffe called a "general uprising." But "what a dangerous thing it is to give way in China!" was often the European view. As the British minister in Beijing put it,

I always get back to the same old axiom which I am convinced is as true to-day as it always has been: the Chinese is a bully by nature, though a reasonable bully if properly handled. To do that you must meet him with reason in one hand and ample force in the other, and you must put both hands together on the table and show that you mean to use them if necessary. Then [emphasis in the original], and only then—do you get to business and a basis of mutual respect without which nothing in China of a permanent nature is possible.[28]

Ironic of course that the British should talk of the Chinese as "bullies" since the British had been bullying the Chinese for more than 80 years.

In spite of Jix's indignation, Chamberlain kept his sangfroid: "I agree on the latest available information . . . that the authorities on the spot appear to have acted not only with great restraint but wisely; but I do not conceal from myself the heavy blow which British prestige has suffered, &

I am frankly shocked when the Foreign Office talks Chinese & begins to ask how we can 'save face.'"[29]

Nevertheless, the British cabinet decided to reestablish its "face" against the Soviet Union. On 17 January 1927, the Cabinet authorized Chamberlain to instruct Hodgson in Moscow to prepare for a rupture of relations and to destroy his ciphers and secret documents.[30] Rozengol'ts of course could feel the heat rising and wrote to Litvinov that a rupture of relations was possible but that it was too soon to tell what would happen. Litvinov agreed: "Much will depend on the future development of events in China." He did not think that all relations would be broken off; diplomatic relations might rupture, but trade relations would continue. "Needless to say," he added, "a purely diplomatic break should be avoided at all costs." Special attention therefore had to be devoted to relations with the TUC and Labour leadership. Rozengol'ts, Maiskii, and Bogomolov had an impressive range of contacts with British politicians, trade unionists, businessmen, and journalists, and they exploited their contacts to avert a rupture of relations. Preparing for the worst, Litvinov nevertheless directed Rozengol'ts to transfer new business contracts from Britain to Germany.[31]

Rozengol'ts still thought the dangers of a rupture or of war were exaggerated in Moscow, even as he reported increasing Die-Hard pressures on the Baldwin cabinet. He had another meeting with Gregory in mid-January. The usually cordial Gregory was reserved and complained about China, mentioning the Soviet agent Borodin.

Who? Rozengol'ts replied. I don't know his nationality, "maybe he is Russian, but in any case he does not have any relations with the Soviet government."

Gregory must have been incredulous, but Rozengol'ts had to write to Litvinov. The British seemed to be greatly interested in Borodin, he noted, in something of an understatement; "I personally do not know Borodin and also do not have any information about him." It's a pity Litvinov's reply remains unrevealed in Russian archives because Litvinov certainly knew of Borodin. In any case, Rozengol'ts remarked that the Soviet interest in China was motivated by the belief that the Chinese people should be "independent," and not by the desire to make an enemy of Britain. Now there's a fine distinction, Gregory would have thought.[32]

As for Maiskii, he was relatively optimistic about future relations with London, as indeed he continued to be after his appointment as *polpred* in 1932. A reader might think he was simply naïve, but his untiring persistence facilitated the formation of the Grand Alliance in 1941. "You seem to look at things too pessimistically," he wrote to Rotshtein in the NKID press bureau. "I do not at all believe that in the spring we will have to pack our bags."[33]

Maiskii also wrote directly to Stalin, and he was not very happy. "Even though we have made the greatest revolution in the world," Maiskii wrote,

> among our workers, diplomatic as well as commercial, there remains and lives deep inside them some trace of that feeling of inferiority in relation to Europe which in former times was so deeply ingrained in us . . . which in the language of the everyman of that time manifested itself in the common expression, "How can we! What can we do! You cannot sell pigs in a pastry shop."

So we hang our heads, Maiskii went on, fall over ourselves to conform to western traditions and habits that have long outlived their time and are deeply hostile to the Soviet government. We imitate details of etiquette, clothing styles, manners of expression accepted "in good bourgeois society." In order to avoid "scandal" we have to wear a tuxedo or a smoking jacket, Maiskii wrote, but it would be far better to have our own distinctive diplomatic uniforms.[34] We need to be ourselves, was Maiskii's main point, and be proud of our accomplishments as revolutionaries. This was an idea that would have appealed to Stalin, though a new diplomatic uniform would not alone change deeply ingrained Russian mentalities.

Sisyphus-Narkomindel'cheskii

Nor would new clothes and new attitudes swing the balance in London. Litvinov had his doubts about the prospects. He informed Chicherin, who was in Germany, that relations with London were still at an impasse, neither they nor the British being willing to make new proposals.[35] Like Chamberlain, he tried to restrain what he now frequently called "the orators" in Moscow. They were uncontrolled in their criticism of Britain, accusing it of seeking to encircle the Soviet Union and to push Poland into a new war in Eastern Europe. It was the period of the so-called war scare in the Soviet Union.

In London, Maiskii dismissed these war fears. When Rozengol'ts asked for detailed intelligence on British intrigues in Eastern Europe, Litvinov replied emphatically that he did not have any (*u nas net i nikogda ne bylo*) unless it was "disinformation" from Orlov's Berlin factory. In fact, he appeared to be reading Foreign Office correspondence which indicated that Britain was *not* pushing Poland toward war with the Soviet Union.[36]

There were other intelligence reports about a possible assassination attempt on Chicherin, who was ailing and in Germany for medical care. Litvinov wrote to him to say that there was no substance to these rumors, at least as far as the NKID could determine, though of course he should remain vigilant.[37] Rumors of war in Eastern Europe or over China were rife in 1927, causing everyone to be on edge.

It was not long before Litvinov's irritation found its way into his correspondence. By "orators," Litvinov had in mind Bukharin, among others. Since Zinoviev had fallen out with Stalin, Bukharin had become Comintern boss and the new NKID *bête noire*. As Hodgson put it, Zinoviev had "retired into obscurity," and "Bukharin has taken his place as the throatiest among our local bullfrogs."[38] If only he would keep his mouth shut, Hodgson or Litvinov might have said. This was of course impossible, for the struggle for power in Moscow was open and brutal, and foreign policy figured among the points at issue. As in the West, so it was in the Soviet Union that domestic politics trumped foreign policy.

In early 1927 in a meeting with French ambassador Herbette, Litvinov said he disapproved of press attacks on Chamberlain in particular, for he was aware of the Foreign Secretary's "moderation." "I repeat this to journalists," Litvinov said to Herbette, "but I have not succeeded in changing the current. It is the force of inertia." This is not the first time, added Herbette, "that I have seen Litvinov fight against prejudices or abuses. And in spite of the ironic doubts which he readily manifests about the results of his efforts, his persistent energy often obtains results."[39]

Several ambassadors came to see Litvinov, alarmed about the rumors of war that were circulating based, inter alia, on speeches by Voroshilov and Bukharin. Litvinov replied that the public had exaggerated "the orators' words," and he dismissed any serious possibilities of war in Europe. Not yet anyway, Litvinov added; the speeches were only intended to warn of "the current volatile political situation." "Preparations for war," Litvinov added, "can be made with feverish speed, and the circumstances are somewhat reminiscent of the pre-war situation in 1914." But still he did not anticipate war "in the months or years ahead." No government in Europe wanted war, though he made qualified exceptions for Mussolini and Piłsudski. Apparently many rank-and-file communists did not take the war scare too seriously either, considering it to be "a tool of social agitation," which undoubtedly it was.[40]

Voroshilov was Stalin's civil war crony, then commissar for war, and Bukharin a real "orator" and Stalin's *exécuteur de basses oeuvres* against Trotskii. Neither was particularly good at his job. Voroshilov survived the purges of the 1930s to prove himself incompetent during the wars against Finland in 1939–1940 and against Nazi Germany in 1941. "Mentally limited and submissive" was how Trotskii described him.[41] As for Bukharin, one historian asserts that he was trying to rehabilitate the Comintern as an effective defender of Soviet security. Litvinov and Chicherin would have gasped at such a preposterous idea. Bukharin's principal biographer has sought to rehabilitate him, but not entirely successfully.[42] Bukharin was vicious in his attacks on Trotskii, only to discover, too late, that Stalin was the real menace. He was executed in 1938 during the purges after pleading in vain with Stalin for his life. He was not, of course, the only one: Ganetskii, Kamenev, Karakhan, Krestinskii, Rakovskii, Rozengol'ts, and Zinoviev were all dead men walking.

In early 1927 the NKID approached several Moscow papers in order "to restrain their zeal" against Britain. These efforts had some success, Rotshtein reported to Chicherin, "but as you know, in the case of *Izvestiia*, they consider it beneath their dignity to receive directives from me. . . . Maksim Maksimovich succeeded in fixing the problem, though with great difficulty."[43] Clearly, the western conviction that the Soviet press was entirely directed from one source at the top was erroneous, at least in the 1920s.

Litvinov's complaint to Stalin about Bukharin's seemingly careless public statements had no effect, for the French ambassador Herbette called at the NKID six weeks later to object to yet another speech by Bukharin in which he alluded to various French leaders as "warmongers" (*vinovniki voiny*). Litvinov must have been sick of making excuses for his colleagues: "We consider all the bourgeois statesmen of that period to be warmongers," he blithely informed Herbette, even mentioning the names of some tsarist diplomats.[44] Still, it was not astute to make negative comments about the French, when, as we shall see, Rakovskii was trying to negotiate a debt settlement in Paris. Chicherin reckoned that the right hand of the Soviet press did not know what the left was doing. Of course, it was not just the press where one hand did not know what the other was doing.

"I came to this conclusion long ago," Litvinov replied to Chicherin, liking to compare the NKID to Sisyphus, a Greek who betrayed the secrets of the Gods and was condemned to push forever a large rock to the top of a mountain only to see it fall back each time. "The further we go, the worse it gets," Litvinov concluded. "I have the feeling that we are flying headlong into a catastrophe and that the NKID is powerless to prevent or even delay it."[45]

As for Bukharin, one wonders whether he was swept away by the sound of his own words or by the headiness of the power he derived from being Stalin's temporary right arm and ideologue. "We do what we can, but we are swimming against the current," Litvinov said. "We write, we protest, Bukharin repents, but . . . tomorrow he will do the same thing."[46] Obviously it was a bad time for Litvinov for he continued to vent his spleen to Chicherin about the "orators" and the press: they put "spokes in [our] wheel, and not for the first time." In spite of his complaint to Stalin, Litvinov foresaw no change: "As it has been, so unfortunately, probably, it will continue to be and for a long time."[47]

Litvinov's complaints finally provoked Stalin's anger. At a plenum of the party Central Committee in early February Litvinov offered further comments on the need to maintain good relations with Germany, following up on what he had written to Deputy Commissar for War Unshlikht in January.[48] "If Germany pulls away from us," Litvinov said, "it will draw closer to someone else, exchanging one friendship for another, and if we begin to draw away, then we will fall into a vacuum, into complete isolation." We have not exactly rushed, Litvinov added sarcastically, to throw ourselves into the arms of England or France. There was of course nothing new in these views. On this issue Litvinov and Chicherin spoke as one: Rapallo was a way to prevent Soviet isolation and the formation of a new anti-Soviet bloc.[49]

On a bit of paper Stalin scribbled a note to Politburo colleagues during the plenum asking if he should reply. Molotov, the Politburo secretary, did not think it worth more than an "ironic" comment, but A. I. Rykov, chairman of the Sovnarkom, the council of commissars, replied that he should make, "if possible, a cautious declaration."[50] Even before the plenum someone in the NKID had sent to the Politburo secretariat a résumé of Litvinov's views which he had offered during a meeting of NKID department heads in mid-January, including his remark about a looming "catastrophe" in Soviet foreign policy.[51]

Stalin told Litvinov at the plenum that the Politburo did not agree with certain points bearing on England, Germany, and the East. Litvinov replied in writing that he had not had much to say about the East except that it would constitute an exposed flank in the event of a "clash" in the west. Then Litvinov summarized his views on various European issues, most notably repeating what he had already written to his ambassadors that there was no immediate danger of a European war, though Mussolini might be thinking about one. There is no reliable information, he added, to suggest "that England is pushing Poland toward war with us." If British and Polish hostility is growing, it comes in part "from own declarations and the conduct of our press." Litvinov's observations were hardly likely to please Stalin, but the *zamnarkom* did not stop there.

> In the course of the last two years [in fact, over more than three years], we have lived through three serious crises [the Curzon ultimatum, the "Zinoviev letter", and the British general strike] when a rupture of relations with England lay on a knife's edge. Repeated threats of a rupture create a dangerous atmosphere for war and also cut across our material and financial interests. An agreement

with the Conservative government is possible, but we must discuss and take measures to soften the superfluous rough edges of our relations.

These comments could only further provoke Stalin, but in for a penny, in for a pound. The times are dangerous, Litvinov must have thought, and here is an opportunity to lay out the case to the Politburo for a change in policy.

Poland was also on Litvinov's mind. He feared a military threat from Piłsudski, but only if France went along. Poland would not risk war even if it had British support without French consent. A "political agreement" with France was therefore "especially important" and was "entirely possible in the event of a debts settlement." As for Germany, its resurgence in international affairs and its bilateral agreements with France weakened its interest in relations with the USSR. It could eventually move away from us, but only in the long term. For the present its interest in relations with the USSR has not diminished. Litvinov then repeated what he and Chicherin had been saying for years: "Germany is our sole economic and political point of support in Europe to which we must hold dear." In a final line likely to intensify Stalin's annoyance, Litvinov pressed the Politburo to indicate which of the NKID's assumptions, as he had laid them out, were "mistaken."[52]

To challenge Stalin and the Politburo to explain themselves on crucial foreign policy issues while the conflict with Trotskii and the opposition was still hot must have been too much for the *gensek*. Although he hated correspondence, Stalin drafted himself in red ink a typed five-page "rigorously secret" letter to the Politburo in which he attempted to demolish Litvinov's main points, even suggesting that his views did not entirely represent those of other colleagues in the NKID and stating flatly that they were not shared by the Politburo.

On the most important question Stalin rejected the idea that any agreement with Britain was possible: "The main enemy of the USSR . . . is the English finance bourgeoisie and its Conservative government . . . [which] is waging an elaborate policy of encirclement of the USSR not only in the east (China, Afghanistan, Persia, Turkey), but also in the west (borderlands, etc.)." Litvinov says that England is not our main enemy and is not pursuing a policy of encirclement of the USSR. If relations are strained, the "guilty parties first of all are our party press and our party orators and if there were not this noise (extremism of the press and orators), then we would have now a security pact with England." This is not of course what Litvinov or Chicherin had said, but Stalin's rebuttal was about politics and polemics. Rigorous argument was not required; bluster would do.

Stalin went on, turning to Soviet policy in China, about which Litvinov had in fact said little. It was easy to extrapolate from what Litvinov did say, or to guess what he might have said if he had chosen to pursue the subject. Stalin would not have failed to notice the overlap with his nemesis Trotskii's criticisms of Soviet policy. So the *gensek* hammered away at Litvinov, ignoring the advice of Molotov and Rykov to be careful. "One of the most important reasons for the present strain in relations between the USSR and England is our revolutionary policy in China . . . our eastern policy represents one of the axes of our foreign policy." For Litvinov, Stalin said, it is merely the Soviet press which has exacerbated the strain in Anglo-Soviet relations—this was again distorting Litvinov's view. Litvinov saw more harm than good in Soviet eastern policy, Stalin continued, and therefore he thought that it should be curtailed. Here Stalin was certainly correct. In the opinion of the Politburo, "our policy in the east and first of all in China is the most important means of strengthening and reinforcing the international position of the USSR and that without such a policy the USSR could not serve as the center of the world liberation movement." According to Litvinov, Stalin added, our China policy will "lead us to catastrophe." Stalin might have regretted these imprudent lines only six weeks later when Litvinov's "catastrophe" did in fact come to pass. But this is getting a little ahead of the story.

Having blithely disposed of Litvinov's worries about Soviet eastern policy, Stalin turned to Germany, noting that the Politburo supported trade relations with Germany and that there was no reason to doubt their continuation. According to Litvinov, Stalin said, the strengthening of Germany's international position would lead it away from the USSR. Unfortunately, Litvinov had a tendency "to put in one sack all the bourgeois governments and saw no difference between Germany and other great powers." This too misrepresented Litvinov's views. If the Politburo supported good Soviet-German economic relations, all the better, Litvinov must have thought. But was it true while Voroshilov and Bukharin publically criticized the German government? Stalin paid no attention to Litvinov's observation that Rapallo would not last forever and that therefore the USSR could not burn its bridges elsewhere. As readers will know, the *zamnarkom* would prove right once again.

Then Stalin commented on the more general issue of Soviet foreign policy. As the USSR grew stronger, he wrote, its relations with the "bourgeois governments" would become more strained. We should harbor no illusions about establishing "good" and "friendly" relations with them. Who then was putting all the "bourgeois governments" in "one sack", Litvinov might have retorted. When this situation came to pass, Stalin added sarcastically, neither the "moderate tone of our press nor the combinations of 'wise, experienced' diplomats" would avert it. Litvinov held that we can and should establish good relations with "all the bourgeois governments" and that if such relations were not established, "then the guilty would be ourselves, because of our ineptitude and our lack of respectability." That of course was not what Litvinov was saying.

> Litvinov forgets that a socialist government can and must pursue a socialist foreign policy, that a socialist policy does not correspond and cannot correspond with the imperialist policy of the so-called great powers, though of course this circumstance did not exclude but supposes the necessity of exploiting the contradictions between these powers for the decomposition of the imperialist camp and the strengthening of the international position of the USSR.

As an example Stalin brought up the case of Japan and the Soviet policy of preventing a united front of the colonial powers in China. This is an ironic reference, since it was a policy proposed by Trotskii, but it had been little developed beyond discussions in Moscow and had no effect on great power divisions.[53] Their own rivalries and mutual suspicions divided them more than any policy pursued by the Politburo. Of course Chicherin and Litvinov understood the importance of preventing a new capitalist bloc. Stalin was only falling back on Lenin's old saws—and bluster. Everyone played the game of divide and rule and had done so since ancient times.

Litvinov's report to the central committee plenum, Stalin concluded, did not reflect the views of the Politburo "on a series of the most important questions of international politics." The trouble was not differences of opinion inside the Politburo but between the Politburo and Litvinov, and not the absence of directives but Litvinov's lack of respect for them. "Comrade Litvinov . . . has an inclination, to say the least, to alter these directives," Stalin concluded:

> I think that there is no need for new Politburo directives for the Narkomindel. There are more directives than necessary. It's not a question of new directives but rather categorically to impress upon Comrade Litvinov the need to carry out precisely the directives of the Politburo.[54]

What is one to make of this extraordinary exchange between Litvinov and Stalin? Was the ideologue Stalin hitting out at the pragmatic, too independent Litvinov? Is this proof that Stalin merely sought to exploit conflicts between the capitalist powers to enhance the position of the USSR? Had Litvinov's stubborn audacity flushed out the real Stalin? Or was the *vozhd'* in fact thinking about Trotskii, ready to attack, and keeping the Politburo in line, or rallying it, at a decisive moment in the conflict with the opposition and the revolution in China? All Politburo members signed and approved

Stalin's memorandum which does not say much for their abilities to think critically. But they were afraid, and Litvinov's critique could have potential political consequences. The *zamnarkom* had to be disciplined. On the face of it, there were no differences between Litvinov and the Politburo on German policy, if Stalin represented the Politburo position correctly. There is reason to doubt that he did in view of the anti-German tirades of Voroshilov and Bukharin. In 1927 the big questions were China and Britain, and as Stalin noted correctly, the two issues were linked. But Stalin vigorously defended the Politburo's China policy because Trotskii and the opposition were attacking it and therefore attacking him. Trotskii too warned of a catastrophe in China if there was no change in policy.[55] The *gensek*'s reply was thus political. Reduced to essentials, Soviet politics trumped Soviet foreign policy.

It was the usual chaos in Soviet foreign policy created by the struggle for power between Stalin and his rivals. Readers may now more easily understand Litvinov's despair over the NKID's inability to set Soviet policy on well-spiked rails. "The further we go, the worse it gets," Litvinov had written to Chicherin only a month before, warning of "catastrophe." But Litvinov did not flinch in the fight, and his written reply to Stalin lays out his views plainly and sensibly. Stalin replied like a disingenuous politician, no doubt thinking of Trotskii and the opposition and not about foreign policy on its merits. His lines may cheer historians of the Cold War. One can imagine the late Adam Ulam impatiently trying to get out of his tomb to tell us, "I told you so," though it is not as simple as that. There was no contention in Soviet foreign policy making, said Ulam, and no independent-minded Soviet diplomats, save Krasin. Here is indisputable proof to the contrary. Behind the apparent clash of Comrade Narkomindel'cheskii and Comrade Kominternovskii, in this case Comrades Litvinov and Stalin, lay another, more decisive conflict between the *gensek* and Trotskii where any argument, however lame, would do in the fight. In the brief blowup between Stalin and Litvinov, Trotskii was the real preoccupation. Stalin's attack on Litvinov was political bravado, the more so since, as readers will see, Rapallo continued and the Soviet government would soon make extraordinary efforts to obtain agreement with France. Litvinov proved right and Stalin wrong on almost every point of the compass, which the latter tacitly admitted by endorsing the *zamnarkom*'s policies.

There was however a point where Stalin did not err: he correctly recognized the irreconcilability between the capitalist West and the USSR which could only be bridged on expedient bases. But our narrative still has a long way to run, and readers will have to be patient until issues are clarified at the end. As we shall see, Litvinov, like his mythical hero Sisyphus, did not relent in trying to turn Soviet policy toward what he considered more practical objectives.

"Anti-Bolshevik Psychosis" in London

While Litvinov and Stalin faced off in Moscow, Chamberlain had troubles of his own with the three Die-Hard horsemen, Birkenhead, Churchill, and Jix, charging at the Bolsh bogey. The ever-perceptive cartoonist David Low portrayed a scarecrow sitting on the front bench in the House of Commons next to Churchill and Baldwin and other Die-Hards. He called it "anti-Russian hysteria."[56] Ironically, Litvinov and Chamberlain had more in common than one might normally expect between a former gunrunner and a British patrician. Each had his burden to bear: Litvinov his "orators," and Chamberlain his Die-Hards. Both were pragmatists. How interesting too were Litvinov's perceptions of the state of Europe and the direction of German foreign policy. It would only be five years before Litvinov shifted from protecting Soviet relations *with* Germany to seeking alliances *against* Germany, supported by Stalin himself.

Litvinov had nothing per se against *Izvestiia*, which published on 5 February an NKID communiqué on the situation in China, hoping that the troubles at Hankou would be settled peaceably. It pursued all the usual lines, spiced with Litvinov's pungent sarcasm, and playing to the TUC and Labour leadership. Chamberlain got the point. "This impudent production," he minuted, "is not an overture to the British Govt but an appeal over its head to the (non-'Conservative') opposition."[57]

Chamberlain wished that he had had to hand Litvinov's "impudent" communiqué when he received Rozengol'ts on 14 February. The conversation was little different from previous meetings. Chamberlain raised the propaganda issue. When Rozengol'ts asked what propaganda, Chamberlain referred to various Soviet press commentaries and published speeches by Soviet leaders. "Relations between our two countries are bad," Chamberlain said; "the situation is dangerous." Rozengol'ts repeated Soviet willingness to resolve outstanding issues. But then it was a question of who would take the first step. "After you, Alphonse. No, you first, my dear Gaston" was the by now the habitual exchange.

"I would be extraordinarily happy to reach agreement with you," said Chamberlain, "if you really came with acceptable proposals, but at the same time I consider it undesirable to start negotiations in the absence of any confidence in a positive outcome." For that, Chamberlain explained, the Soviet government had to make satisfactory assurances about a cessation of anti-British propaganda, understand that there could be no government loan or guarantee of a loan, and recognize its debts.

Rozengol'ts reported that while Chamberlain was polite, his courtesy was strained. Anglo-Soviet relations, the *polpred* predicted, would not survive the

Figure 9.1. David Low cartoon, LSE7475, "The Embarrassing Mascot," *The Star*, 8 February 1927. British Cartoon Archive.

term of the Conservative government. An "anti-Bolshevik psychosis" had taken over the Conservative Party; even Chamberlain showed symptoms of it. A rupture could prove advantageous, increasing British prestige in the colonies and in China. "In addition, of course, the Russian question now plays an important role in the internal political machinations of the Conservative Party." The Tories are already preparing to use "the Russian question" in their next electoral campaign. Many people were talking about it openly, even Gregory.[58] Litvinov assured Rozengol'ts that in Moscow, everyone was maintaining "complete calm," although we do not deny the risk of a rupture. He wondered when the Conservatives would play their electoral trump, the "Red scarecrow," as he called it.[59] Perhaps Litvinov had seen Low's cartoons.

On 23 February the Foreign Office sent a note to the Soviet government complaining about the usual topics and singling out for objection comments by "orators" Bukharin and Voroshilov, among others. Negative speeches and published articles in the Soviet press figured heavily in the British note. Gregory, for one, wondered whether the British démarche was a good idea "except on domestic grounds." But the note went out all the same, beefed up in Cabinet to threaten a rupture of diplomatic relations.[60]

In Moscow Herbette reported that the British note had caused "more surprise than emotion." But if there was no emotion, he added, there was plenty of irritation: the British note was left with the concierge at the Soviet embassy in London and was published before being received in Moscow. The Soviet government responded badly to threats and insults, but Litvinov passed the usual conciliatory message to Herbette: "We are always ready to come to agreement with England," but not on British terms, he might have added, as Chamberlain of course knew. Like the NKID, Herbette thought the British démarche was driven by domestic politics. "The Conservative government has neither reduced unemployment nor achieved success in China. In this situation it can scarcely enter a new electoral battle, even on an anti-Bolshevik platform as in 1924." Litvinov told Herbette that he would do all he could to avoid a rupture, as in fact he had written to Rozengol'ts. This was an admirable characteristic in Litvinov: his messages were normally the same whether to other comrades or to his western interlocutors. Herbette urged Litvinov to produce a moderate reply, but as the ambassador noted, "the USSR also has its domestic politics." He hoped there would be no all-out confrontation, for it would not only be between Britain and the Soviet Union, but between two "social conceptions" and two systems of government in Europe and Asia. It was not conservatism and colonialism, he added perceptively, which would win out in the end.[61]

Litvinov reacted much as Herbette described, not liking British "rudeness," especially directed at Chicherin, or their threats. He thought the British note was more a concession to the Die-Hards than preparation for an immediate rupture of relations. "But one has to recognize that the thin layer of ice holding up Anglo-Soviet relations has melted even more." He informed Rozengol'ts that the Soviet reply would be handed over that day (26 February) to the British counselor in Moscow, William Peters. We have to react quickly, for "our public opinion," meaning *Instantsiia* and the Moscow press, are impatient for a riposte. This was putting it mildly given the very recent exchange between Stalin and Litvinov. We will follow the British example, Litvinov advised, and leave our reply with the porter at Peters' flat if our clerk does not find him in.[62] The NKID, and especially Stalin, did not believe in asymmetrical diplomacy; it was tit for tat, slight for slight.

The Soviet response was not as restrained as Herbette might have wished. Litvinov liked nothing better than exposing British hypocrisy and double standards, especially with Stalin looking over his shoulder. If Chamberlain could cite nasty lines from Bukharin and Voroshilov, Litvinov had no trouble citing equally offensive comments from the Die-Hard trio of Birkenhead, Churchill, and Jix. And they were not the only ones. "There exist no [Anglo-Soviet] agreements," Litvinov observed facetiously, "which should limit the freedom of speech and of the press." We know of course that in his secret correspondence Litvinov deplored the statements of Soviet "orators," but the Foreign Office had offered up such inviting targets that he could not resist shooting at them, nor would Stalin have expected anything less. Litvinov also hit another raw nerve when he pointed out that the so-called ubiquitous Comintern "agents" could not explain "each and every difficulty of the British Empire in pretty well every corner of the globe." Still, at the end of his note, Litvinov indicated the usual Soviet willingness to settle outstanding issues with the British government.[63]

According to Ambassador Fleuriau in London, Chamberlain seemed pushed by "an irresistible pressure toward rupture with the Soviets." Moscow has got to understand, Chamberlain insisted that the present state of Anglo-Soviet relations cannot continue. These relations are nothing but "troubles and insults." "But Briand knows," said Chamberlain, "I am a good European which is why I have been so patient."[64]

Fleuriau also spoke with an unnamed Foreign Office informant, Gregory perhaps, who indicated that officials were against sending the British note, but that Die-Hard pressure had overwhelmed their resistance. Chamberlain was under pressure from the Conservative Party. Elections were anticipated in the winter of 1928–1929. Labour was already gearing up. The Tories want the adoption of a clear platform, as in 1924, "against the Soviets." "I have the impression," wrote Fleuriau, "that Sir Austen Chamberlain could be dragged under the current." Baldwin and other ministers have supported him until now because of a fear "of adventures." "But they are assailed with criticism and reproaches of which the press gives only a very weak echo." Party members accuse them of "pusillanimity and irresolution"; they want action in defense of British interests abroad. Events in China, Fleuriau concluded, would ultimately determine the fate of Anglo-Soviet relations.[65]

A little-known British cabinet minister in the 1920s, much better known in the 1930s, explained the position to a German journalist in March 1927. According to Sir Samuel Hoare, Secretary of State for Air, "public opinion" was near the boiling point. "The Russians," said Hoare, were "maliciously" seeking to destroy British interests in China. Everything which British lives and capital have built up there is threatened, but Russia has been warned and will suffer the consequences if it does not cease and desist.

The German then raised the issue of trade with the Soviet Union, and Hoare replied that whereas the China trade was worth fighting and dying for, in true imperial fashion, British trade with the Bolsh was not worth a farthing. "We don't bother a hang about trade with Russia," snarled Hoare:

> Even before the war trade with Russia was nearly laughable. We only hope that the German-Russian relations will not develop into a friendship, because although we find ourselves opposed to the Bolsheviks, we are well disposed to Germany. We have tried time and again to get onto a good footing with the Russians but have been repeatedly swindled economically and politically by them.

"Swindled," you say? Litvinov or Chicherin would have laughed at that line, but Hoare went on, confiding to the German, as if to a fellow he vaguely knew at his London club. In the Near East and Far East and in our other spheres of influence, Hoare said, we are always colliding with the Russian. "Whether there is a tsar, a president or a Bolshevik swindler at their head, it is all the same." Had Chicherin heard of Hoare's rant, he might have responded cynically, for who were the greatest "swindlers" if not Albion perfide. Even the French would agree on that.

When Hoare asked his German interlocutor what his government would do in the event of an Anglo-Soviet rupture, the latter replied with a shrug: "Nothing at all; Germany would be neutral and its businessmen would seek the business which London would not then be able to obtain."Although Hoare bristled at this comment, it must have rankled, as it would have rankled in some business circles in London. But the German went on to needle Hoare even more: "You know, the banker always lends his money to the one who will give him the greatest security and the highest rate of interest whoever he may be."[66]

All the big questions of European international relations were linked together: trade, imperial rivalries, China, Anglo-Soviet/Russian-German relations. Only the French issues were left unmentioned in this conversation. What really infuriated Hoare and the British elite was the threat to their China position. English blood and trade mattered: this was something which the NKID may not have fully grasped.

German diplomats were in a nice position in the 1920s; everyone confided in them, from London and Paris to Moscow. Like nosy medieval priests, they knew everybody's secrets and most intimate obsessions.

Not as well informed as the Germans, Litvinov calculated that the British cabinet had decided against a rupture of relations because it provided no immediate advantages and would deprive the Tories of a "very valuable trump" in the run-up to Parliamentary elections. The British note thus relieved pressure for a rupture provided no "new extraordinary events" occurred. "On our side we must take measures both through the GPU [the Soviet secret police] and our press to avoid giving unnecessary new nourishment (*pishchi*) to the anti-Soviet campaign." In the new fight picked by London, Litvinov reckoned that Moscow had won the first round. A few days later he was not so sure: the exchange of notes had been badly received by the British papers; Chamberlain would therefore be forced to take a harder line.[67] What after all did Litvinov expect? In any case, the days were gone when a Soviet fireman like the late Krasin would be sent to London to appease Tory Die-Hards.

Oddly enough, some Foreign Office clerks perceived a flicker of light in the darkness. Peters, the British counselor in Moscow, noticed that the Soviet papers were free of their "usual volubility." This was because the Politburo in a closed session on 3 March had forbidden *Pravda* and *Izvestiia* to publish *anything* on Soviet activities in China or anything on India or other British colonies without special permission of the Central Committee. Maybe Stalin was going to rein in Comrade Kominternovskii after all, accepting Litvinov's recommendation to quiet down the press, only ten days after the *gensek*'s eruption in the Politburo. Peters would not have known about the Politburo directives, but he mentioned a political cartoon in *Pravda* on 1 March of "Bukharin muzzled as Sir Austen would like to see him," the inspiration for which must have come from Litvinov. The cartoon on the front page shows Bukharin at a podium with a gag over his mouth. In parentheses underneath the cartoon it says, "Illustration attached to the British note [of 23 February]." This was a subtle message from Litvinov to Chamberlain, and original too, if only the Foreign Office would pick up the cue. "Completely muzzled" was how one Foreign Office clerk described the Moscow press.[68] There was also a public message from Stalin who told a meeting of workers on the same day *Pravda* published its gagged Bukharin that there was no immediate danger of war and little likelihood of a rupture of Anglo-Soviet relations. Stalin saw the need to calm the troubled waters—perhaps to prevent hoarding in the rural districts around Moscow.[69]

Some Foreign Office clerks did pick up the cue, thinking there was an opening in the conciliatory conclusion of Litvinov's note, an "olive branch" one clerk called it. During a meeting in Paris, Briand had given Chamberlain a cable from Herbette, indicating that Litvinov was open to a resumption of discussions. Litvinov heard about the exchange through the Soviet embassy in Berlin. When all of this led to minutes in the Foreign Office, Chamberlain squelched a response. "Briand tossed it [Herbette's cable] across the table to me as possibly interesting & I remarked that it was the old story. I do not expect another direct advance (tho' such a thing is possible) & in any case must wait for it before deciding how to answer it."[70]

Indeed it *was* "the old story," as readers might surmise from Litvinov's dispatches, because he also did not consider the time right to resume negotiations. Both sides still declined to take the initiative, since both calculated that formal negotiations would produce no results. The positions of Litvinov and Chamberlain were identical, as indeed Litvinov sometimes noted.[71]

As March unfolded, Litvinov speculated that Prime Minister Baldwin might call a snap election, running "on an anti-Soviet platform," and that the Conservatives could be returned to power. One should nevertheless admire Litvinov's pertinacity, for he still hoped to calm Anglo-Soviet relations. He had in mind to name a formal replacement for the late Krasin, though he admitted his plan was based on a lot of "ifs."

If I can "restrain our press from intemperate attacks against England . . . which set one's teeth on edge . . . if our press and our orators take a less hostile tone," and *if* the situation in China did not provoke "new anti-Soviet eruptions," then *maybe* the nomination of a new *polpred* "could serve as a further step toward some calming of relations."[72] Stalin's February outburst did not change Litvinov's policy one iota.

Dénouement in China

All these "ifs" were beyond Litvinov's power to secure, not only in Moscow but more importantly in China, where Chiang's northern expedition, with Soviet support, made spectacular progress. It was not just a military advance but a rallying of the Chinese masses which frightened the right Guomintang, its landowners and compradors, and it frightened and angered the British.

The Red genie, Revolution, was out of his lamp *again*. Property, money, and "civilization" were again in danger. God damn the Bolsh! They have got a new revolution going in China.

In early March, Manchurian warlord Zhang, who had taken control in Beijing, sent one of his generals to see the British ambassador to sound him out about a major offensive against the Bolsheviks. Zhang would drive them out of China, and the British, French, and Poles would make for Moscow from the west. Sir Miles Lampson, the British minister, thought the idea was "insanity," but, he added, "it does not do to tell [Zhang Zuolin] that he is an ass;—he is apt to resent it."

Zhang's "eagerness to declare war on the USSR . . . is very remarkable," commented one Foreign Office clerk: "One would have thought he already had enough on his hands." No doubt he would fish for "the usual . . . financial assistance or a few old men of war." But Zhang was not as stupid as he sounded; his main idea was to launch an attack against the Soviet presence in Manchuria to seize the CER, and he was looking for western support. Chamberlain minuted that he "would have nothing to do with it."[73]

At the end of March, British and other foreign naval forces bombarded Nanjing on the Yangzi not far inland from Shanghai in response to the seizure of the city and its foreign concessions by nationalist troops. It was a humiliating experience for the foreign powers, who had imposed their will on China for 80 years, heaping scorn upon the Chinese, to be run out of Nanjing and Hankou by "Chink" mobs. China was a tinderbox in flames. And it was easy to blame the USSR: "Russian advice, example, organization, equipment and money have formed the electric current which has vitalized a very helpless man [China]. The Cantonese owe everything to the Russians."[74]

Shanghai, the hub of foreign privilege in China, was still in turmoil. Japanese and British troops were barely able to protect the foreign settlements. Chiang's troops began to arrive in Shanghai during the last week of March. In Moscow the Politburo still advocated unity, while Chiang plotted a *coup de force* to wipe out the mass movement and the Chinese Communist Party. At a closed Politburo session on 3 March directives were approved encouraging worker and peasant involvement in the Chinese Communist Party *and* the Guomintang. The latter was to be transformed into an "elective" organization and the right Guomintang was to be "ousted."[75] The Politburo was not oblivious to the danger of Chiang and wondered if he should be attacked *in the Soviet press*. The right Guomintang would oppose agrarian reform, and therefore immediate "practical" measures needed to be taken to demonstrate to the peasant masses that communists and the left wing of the Guomintang were defending their interests.[76] But who was going to strike first, Chiang or Stalin?

On 30 March Bukharin presented a report to the IKKI recognizing the danger of Chiang as a sword of the right Guomintang. But he was not Kerenskii, said Bukharin, that is, an outright enemy. In spite of himself he was "leading a revolutionary war," and there were communists inside the Guomintang which provided security for the revolutionary movement in spite of Chiang and the right. It could be, Bukharin admitted, that Chiang and his allies, fearing the growing strength of the mass movement, would strike at it. Then we would have to pass to the attack, but before that ultimate eventuality there were potential "intermediate steps." It was premature to turn on Chiang Kai-shek.[77]

Bukharin could not have been more wrong. Chiang and his landlords and compradors did not think it premature to strike first. We'll see, they must have thought to themselves, who is going to oust whom. The day after Bukharin's report, the Politburo received alarming news from Shanghai: Chiang had begun a coup (*povorot*) and had ordered the dissolution of the Shanghai revolutionary government. The Chinese Communist Central Committee wanted to know what to do. Should we make concessions to Chiang to preserve unity?

Here is the Politburo reply:

1/ We are leading a campaign among the masses against the coup; 2/ in the meantime do not take open military action; 3/ do not surrender your arms, as a last resort hide them; 4/ expose the policies of the right, rally the masses; 5/ in the army conduct agitation for the National and Shanghai governments against personal dictatorship and the bloc with the imperialists; 6/ keep us informed daily.[78]

These instructions were not much help to the Chinese communists and Soviet advisers as Chiang stole a march on Moscow. On 12 April 1927 he turned openly against his communist allies in Shanghai and Canton and began to slaughter them. In Shanghai, local communists, following Politburo directives, organized a peaceful demonstration of 100,000 workers to protest Chiang's actions; his troops gunned down the demonstrators with machine guns.[79] Bukharin's analysis on 30 March and the Politburo instructions on the following day were disconnected from Chinese realities and costly in blood. Just the "catastrophe" Litvinov had foreseen.

In the Foreign Office clerks contemplated international action in China against the nationalist movement and against the Soviet Union, if only it were possible. It was tempting to send in a division or two of Gurkhas and Sikhs and a fleet of gunboats, but not possible, the Foreign Office concluded. Everyone hesitated, and with good reason: it was "a far more risky game in China than it would be anywhere else in the world," as one senior Foreign Office official observed. The French might play, but would the Americans or Japanese? "It is right & even necessary to try to work with the USA, but is a heartbreaking task," remarked Chamberlain. And then no one knew "whom and where to strike."[80]

Officials were only beginning to grasp what was happening on the spot. "Over 100 Reds have been killed" in Canton, according to a preliminary report; 1,500 had been arrested. There was cautious optimism: "The attack on the Communists is indirectly a great score for us. We should let it work its own way out."

"Remarkable," commented another clerk. "But will it satisfy the Governor of Hongkong?"

"Vy. Doubtful," came the droll reply.[81]

The governor general and local military commanders were keen to jump into the fray, and it was all the Foreign Office could do to hold them back.

"The Govr. of Hongkong & his band of fire eaters," noted Undersecretary Wellesley, "seem to me quite incapable of seeing an inch beyond their noses."

"The Governor makes me tired," replied Chamberlain.[82]

The tide had turned against the "Reds" and their Soviet advisers in China. Litvinov could see that Soviet "prestige" had been damaged, and he looked for escape routes. He thought he saw one in negotiations with the British Midland Bank for a large line of credit for contracts with British companies.[83]

Trade or the expansion of trade could avert a rupture, he hoped, but not this time. The Die-Hards were determined on a break. Their blood was up. Millions in trade with the Soviet Union could not slake the thirst for vengeance.

In the meantime, on 6 April, Chinese police in Beijing, on warlord Zhang's orders and apparently with British complicity, raided the Soviet embassy, looking for compromising documents. Zhang also arrested Soviet diplomatic couriers.[84] It was more bad news. The Beijing raid had produced a "deep impression" in Moscow, Litvinov wrote to Rozengol'ts: there is too much superfluous paper being kept in our embassies. He authorized Rozengol'ts to take the necessary measures to prepare for a rupture of relations. In a further speculation about British elections, Litvinov interpreted Die-Hard polemics as little more than pre-electoral campaigning. "In the best of cases," he supposed, "the Conservatives would be returned to power with a smaller majority."[85] In fact, it was not just pre-electoral politics driving the Die-Hards; it was thirst for Bolsh humiliation and for blood. Although Litvinov did not mention it to Rozengol'ts, there were Chinese communists taking refuge in the Beijing embassy. They were led away and soon executed. It was a blow to Soviet credibility and prestige, keenly felt in the Politburo.[86] In late February Stalin had declared that Soviet policy in China was "the most important means of strengthening and reinforcing the international position of the USSR." Readers can judge for themselves whether he was right or not. Litvinov apparently did not comment, but Trotskii was quick to go on the attack though it did him no good.[87] After all, it was not just Stalin's neck on the line but that of the Politburo, all of whose members had endorsed his letter of 23 February. That was certainly Stalin's intention—to lock them into his policies and prevent their defection if events turned out badly.

The bloodletting in China went on throughout 1927. One source estimates that more than half a million communists, workers, and peasants were slaughtered by Chiang and his warlord allies.[88] Incredibly, the Politburo did not seem to learn any prudence from the catastrophes of the spring and summer. At the end of November 1927, Heinz Neumann, a 25-year German communist and Comintern agent, arrived in Canton. The city was controlled by a local warlord, but Chiang's reign of terror had not entirely annihilated the strong communist network there. Neumann was a bright newcomer, said to be a revolutionary prodigy and a favorite of Stalin, but at 25 years old, he had only a subaltern's experience in leading men in battle. All the same, on 29 November he sent a cable directly to the Politburo in Moscow, saying in effect that the city was ripe for revolt: "We have decided to take a firm line in Canton toward the preparation of an uprising and the establishment of Soviets. We are organizing a general strike, have begun setting up Red Guard units under the command of revolutionary unions." No date, Neumann advised, had been set for rising, but he asked for immediate instructions from Moscow.[89]

That same day the Soviet consul in Canton, B. A. Pokhvalinskii, wrote to Karakhan, then back in Moscow, to warn him: "The policy of an immediate uprising is a mistake because the party does not have the power for the seizure and organization of power in Canton." It would only lead to "a pointless massacre." The consul asked that immediate instructions be sent to Neumann.[90]

In the meantime, Neumann returned to the charge, providing detailed intelligence on available forces of modest size, 2,000 men with derisory arms in one of the biggest cities in China and the trigger-happy British governor of Hong Kong not far away. The local provincial party committee was unanimously in favor of the rising for the beginning of the following week. Slogans included "Rice for the workers," "Land for the peasants and soldiers," "Down with militarist war," "Confiscation of bourgeois apartments for the workers," and other banalities. No wonder the Soviet consul in Canton warned against a rising. It was pure folly. Nevertheless, the OGPU head of foreign intelligence, M. A. Trilisser, forwarded Neumann's cables to Stalin, Bukharin, Voroshilov, and Karakhan, among others. Trilisser added a last cable just received from Neumann to the effect that if he did not hear otherwise, a rising would begin three days later, on Monday, 12 December.[91]

Trilisser offered no comment on Neumann's recommendations; the date of his note to Stalin and the others is 9 December. The Politburo had little time to react. Did Karakhan respond, or Chicherin or Litvinov? The available evidence gives no indication. Litvinov appears to have been consulted on Chinese affairs only infrequently. Chicherin was often ill and out of the country. Trilisser forwarded his note to Karakhan and not to Chicherin or Litvinov. Were they informed? On the following day, 10 December, the Politburo gave its consent for the rising without meeting. Members were polled by telephone. Stalin signed the Politburo protocol. The cable for Neumann encouraged him "to act confidently and decisively."[92]

As Soviet consul Pokhvalinskii had foreseen, the uprising was a fiasco, and a mass slaughter of communists, workers, and peasants ensued. An estimated 25,000 people were killed, including five clerks of the Soviet consulate general in Canton. Once again, the NKID had lost control of Soviet foreign policy, this time in China, gradually from mid-1925 onward. In fact, Chicherin told Karakhan in late July 1926 that the conduct of China policy had passed from the NKID to the Politburo Chinese Commission. "No questions in the PB occupy its time so often and for so long, as the Chinese. I am only a technical adviser," Chicherin noted. "The door is open to various influences and also intrigues." He had warned Karakhan that there were intrigues being mounted against him in the Politburo. Chicherin was not sure who was behind them: "Helping things along is that in the plenum a secret resolution was put forward accusing the opposition of opportunism, and it proposed to recall you."[93] Karakhan was indeed recalled during the autumn of 1926, on the pretext at least that he had given a press interview without authorization. The real reason was that Stalin thought that Karakhan had "outlived his usefulness" in Beijing.

"He was and *has remained* the ambassador of the first stage of the Chinese revolution and is entirely useless as a leader in the current new situation, both the Chinese and the international."[94] Stalin had thus come a long way from wanting to avoid "fantasies" and remain cautious in China. Comrade Kominternovskii had gotten the upper hand again.

In the meantime, Stalin must have remembered that Karakhan had followed his directives, and he was appointed *zamnarkom* in the NKID and Politburo contact for China questions. If he attempted to discourage the uprising in Canton, it was in vain. Neumann and Pokhvalinskii survived the ensuing slaughter. According to one account, Neumann was one of the first to flee and was safely back in Moscow early in the new year.[95] He did not however survive Stalin's bloody purges ten years later; neither did Pokhvalinskii or Trilisser. They too were dead men walking.

As the massacre in Canton unfolded, there was jubilation in the Foreign Office. Consul General Brenan reported from Canton that local forces had control of the city:

> Order is being restored. Summary executions took place all over the city . . . and streets are littered with hundreds of corpses. Three Russians have been executed and ten others have been arrested [and] will be executed. . . . Government have issued proclamation calling upon population to denounce all communists for extermination. . . . City has been badly looted and large sections burned. . . . No attempt to molest foreigners.

Foreign Office officials could scarcely hide their relief. "Our prayers for a Russian Downfall in China," noted one clerk, "have been answered beyond our wildest expectations." And added another, "The absence of anti-foreign manifestations is a welcome new feature."[96] The slaughter of Communists and unlucky Russians was appropriate retribution for challenging British commercial interests in China.

After it was over, the IKKI recommended that demonstrations be organized in front of the British, Japanese, and American consulates in defense of the Chinese revolution and the USSR.[97] It was a pointless gesture, approved by Bukharin, which could not bring back the dead whose lives had been wasted, nor could it advance the revolution in China, set back by 20 years. The demonstrations underlined the fatuity of Politburo policy but were undoubtedly a political diversion.

Trotskii was not fooled: he accused Stalin of looking for a victory in Canton to divert attention from his expulsion and that of the Left Opposition from the party in November–December 1927. Stalin would use any tool in the shed against his adversaries, even if the price was a coherent, careful foreign policy. Stalin did not want to be outflanked on his left. Hence, Soviet prudence in 1925, avoiding "fantasies," gave way to recklessness in 1927—"insane adventurism culminating in gross tragedy," said one western historian.[98] Litvinov would have agreed, if he had dared; the Canton uprising was the penultimate result of the "catastrophe" which he had foreseen in early 1927.

Diplomatic Rupture with Moscow, Spring 1927

In London Chamberlain too lost control of policy. In the spring of 1927 he still held out against a diplomatic rupture with Moscow. It was made certain by a Home Office raid on the Soviet trade agency Arcos and the Soviet trade mission on 13 May 1927. According to French ambassador Fleuriau, who reported on the raid, Joynson-Hicks did not inform the Foreign Office of his intentions. Maiskii was shocked and reckoned, his habitual optimism departed, that it was a step toward rupture. What kind of rupture, trade and/or diplomatic, remained to be seen, according to Litvinov, though he did not have long to wait for an answer. The Politburo reacted immediately to the London raid, ordering various public protests and directing, inter alia, that all superfluous secret documents be immediately destroyed in all Soviet diplomatic establishments.[99] Moreover, Litvinov worried that the British might still be reading Soviet cables, and he warned Rozengol'ts to be careful.[100]

The Cabinet report on the Arcos raid made a great deal of the relationship between Borodin and the Soviet government, citing cables between Rozengol'ts and Litvinov concerning him, but without mentioning earlier correspondence in which Rozengol'ts asked Litvinov for information on

Borodin, not knowing who he was. Litvinov gave his usual line to Hodgson that Borodin had no relationship with the Soviet government, though he did with the Comintern and the Politburo which issued his orders. In 1923 Borodin had traveled to China in the company of the then new Soviet *polpred* Karakhan.[101] The Cabinet paper made Litvinov out to be a liar, though in fact technically speaking Borodin did not report to the Soviet government. Litvinov would *never* answer for anyone who worked for the Comintern, as the Foreign Office well knew. It was a mere technical distinction, but strictly maintained by the NKID.

The Die-Hards thought the Arco raid was a great triumph, but some Foreign Office officials had their doubts. "I do not see that any of the facts disclosed," noted Palairet, then head of the Northern Department, "can be taken as incriminating either the Soviet diplomatic mission or the Soviet government. Obviously the Trade delegation are [sic] extremely discredited and we can at once denounce the Trade Agreement, but unless further proof of the complicity of Rozengolz [sic] and the Soviet government is forthcoming, it seems to me that we have very flimsy reasons for breaking off diplomatic relations."[102]

"Flimsy" was good enough, and on 23 May the British cabinet decided upon the rupture of relations and the denunciation of the 1921 trade agreement, though trade should be allowed to continue "as in the USA." This latter concession was made to mute criticism from British firms doing business in the Soviet Union, though the Politburo was not interested in trade on such terms. Current business only would continue. The Tories habitually underestimated Soviet determination to resist western pressures. In a public statement, Litvinov compared the Tory performance in the House of Commons to "a good American super-film . . . absolutely laughable." The rupture was not the result of the raid; the raid was the pretext to justify the rupture. The Soviet assessment of the evidence found during the raid coincided with the judgment of the head of the Northern Department. And given the "Zinoviev letter," added Litvinov, the legitimacy of Tory claims was to be doubted. As though he wanted to needle, Litvinov repeated his assertions concerning Borodin. "By a technical quibble," one Foreign Office clerk acknowledged, "the disclaimer about Borodin may possibly be literally accurate."[103] The triumph of the Die-Hards was complete, though some months later Chamberlain told Litvinov that he had gone along "unwillingly" with the rupture of relations.[104] Ironically, both the Die-Hards and Comrade Kominternovskii, who were birds of a feather, had gotten the upper hand.

The German government was uneasy about the rupture. They did not want to be caught in the middle of an Anglo-Soviet conflict. Don't worry, Chamberlain assured Stresemann; we're not going to war with the USSR.[105]

Even in the Foreign Office there were doubts about the rupture, though it was mostly among the clerks. "It is interesting to note," Palairet minuted, "that the Russians expect us to attack them in Afghanistan—which is exactly where we expect them to attack us. I submit that we ought to be very careful lest this mutual distrust of each other may lead to the disaster (for disaster it must be, if it involves war with Russia) which both parties really wish to avoid."[106]

In Moscow Ambassador Herbette expressed similar fears. "A policy of encirclement and rupture . . . against the USSR" would not in the least limit unrest in other countries, though it might increase the danger of war in Europe. Since war in Europe would lead directly or indirectly to revolutionary unrest, encirclement might bring about the precise result it was intended to prevent. And while Fleuriau opined that the rupture with Moscow was "essentially an act of internal politics," Herbette suggested that anti-communism was a pretext to pursue a traditional British anti-Russian policy. It was *not*, said Herbette, in French security interests to pursue a similar policy. Geography, as Herbette suggested, had to make France more cautious, not having the Channel as a barrier against invasion. In Paris Briand regretted that Britain "had been obliged for internal reasons to break relations with Moscow." He would have preferred more consultation and cooperation between Paris and London, possibly in the form of a joint démarche to the Soviet government, though short of rupture. Of course this might have been just talk after the fact.[107] As readers will see, Briand's policy toward the Soviet Union was similar to Chamberlain's and indeed to Litvinov's in that all three had to resist their respective ideologues. Of the three, however, Briand may have been the more *rusé*, and he had to be because France was in greater need of strong allies. How fortunate, Briand would later say, that we did not follow Britain and break off relations with Moscow.[108]

Notes

1. Rozengol'ts to Litvinov, report no. 2, very secret, 10 Dec. 1926, AVPRF, f. 069, o. 10, p. 24, d. 7, ll. 348–56.

2. Litvinov to Chicherin (Frankfurt), no. 3236, secret, 30 Dec. 1926, AVPRF, f. 05, o. 6, p. 21, d. 90, l. 1.

3. Stalin to Karakhan, 12 June 1925, *Perepiska I. V. Stalina i G. V. Chicherina*, p. 539; and excerpt from Politburo protocol, no. 66, 11 June 1925, *VKP(b), Komintern v Kitae*, I, p. 573.

4. Chicherin to Karakhan, no. 76, secret, 23 June 1925, *Perepiska I. V. Stalina i G. V. Chicherina*, pp. 541–43; and Chicherin to Karakhan, no. 78, 7 July 1925, ibid., pp. 560–62.

5. Karakhan to Stalin, 23 June 1925, *Perepiska I. V. Stalina i G. V. Chicherina*, pp. 550–53.

6. Excerpt from Politburo protocol, no. 66, 11 June 1925, and attached recommendations from the Chinese Commission, 11 June 1925, *VKP(b), Komintern v Kitae*, I, pp. 573–74; and excerpt from Politburo protocol, no 68, signed Stalin, 25 June 1925, ibid., pp. 575–77.

7. Stalin to Karakhan, 29 June 1925, *Perepiska I. V. Stalina i G. V. Chicherina*, pp. 554–55; Stalin to Karakhan, immediate, not later than the middle of June 1925, ibid., p. 540; Karakhan to Stalin, very secret, immediate, 1 July 1925, ibid., pp. 556–57.

8. Chicherin to Karakhan, no. 1, 1 Jan. 1926, *Perepiska I. V. Stalina i G. V. Chicherina*, pp. 586–88.

9. Chicherin to Karakhan, no. 2, 15 Jan. 1926, *Perepiska I. V. Stalina i G. V. Chicherina*, pp. 589–91; and Chicherin to Karakhan, no. 3, 26 Jan. 1926, ibid., pp. 597–99.

10. Stalin to Karakhan et al., 10 Feb. 1926, *Perepiska I. V. Stalina i G. V. Chicherina*, pp. 601–2.

11. Chicherin to Viktor L. Kopp, Soviet *polpred* in Tokyo, cc. Karakhan et al., very secret, 23 March 1926, *Perepiska I. V. Stalina i G. V. Chicherina*, pp. 615–19.

12. Chicherin to Politburo et al., 7 May 1926 and 7 Aug. 1926; and Politburo resolution on Japan, no. P48/3-G-s, rigorously secret, 19 Aug. 1926, *Moskva-Tokio: Politika i diplomatiia Kremlia, 1921–1931* (Moscow, 2007), II, pp. 29–30, 43–44, 49–50.

13. Chicherin to Karakhan, no. 9, personal, very secret, 5 March 1926, *Perepiska I. V. Stalina i G. V. Chicherina*, pp. 606–7; and Chicherin to Karakhan, no. 11, 12 March 1926, ibid., pp. 607–8.

14. Excerpt from Politburo protocol, no. 13 (special no. 9), signed Molotov, 4 March 1926, *VKP(b), Komintern v Kitae*, II, pt. 1, p. 135.

15. Report on "events of 20 March 1926 in Canton," very secret, I. Ia. Razgon, deputy head of Soviet adviser group in South China, 25 April 1926, *VKP(b), Komintern v Kitae*, II, pt. 1, pp. 190–92; and IKKI, Far East secretariat, protocol no. 3, 27 April 1926, ibid., pp. 194–95.

16. Report on "events of 20 March 1926 in Canton," V. P. Rogachev, deputy head of Soviet adviser group in South China, 28 April 1926, *VKP(b), Komintern v Kitae*, II, pt. 1, pp. 198–201; and excerpt from Politburo protocol, no. 22 (special no. 16), 29 April 1926, ibid., pp. 201–2.

17. Excerpts from Politburo protocol, no. 10, signed by Stalin, 11 Feb. 1926; no. 13, signed Molotov, 4 March 1926; no. 16, signed Stalin, 18 March 1926, *VKP(b), Komintern v Kitae*, II, pt. 1, pp. 59–61, 134, 137–38.

18. Chicherin to Karakhan, no. 12, 16 March 1926, *Perepiska I. V. Stalina i G. V. Chicherina*, pp. 609–13.

19. Excerpt from Politburo protocol, no. 27 (special no. 21), 20 May 1926, *VKP(b), Komintern v Kitae*, II, pt. 1, pp. 227–28.

20. Memoranda by Godfrey Locker-Lampson, Parliamentary undersecretary of state, 2 Dec. 1926; by Gregory, 3 and 14 Dec. 1926; by Tyrrell, 4 Dec. 1926; and Chamberlain's minutes, 13–14 Dec. 1926, N5425/387/38, FO 371 11787.

21. Tyrrell to Chamberlain, private, 6 Dec. 1926, AC53/566, U.Birm., A. Chamberlain Papers.

22. Rozengol'ts to Litvinov, no. 59/s, very secret, 28 Jan. 1927, AVPRF, f. 069, o. 11, p. 30, d. 2, ll. 4–8.

23. "Russia: Memorandum by Mr. Gregory," confidential, 10 Dec. 1926, N5670G/387/38, FO 371 11787.

24. "Diplomatic Relations with the Soviet Government," C.P. 25 (27), by Chamberlain, secret, 24 Jan. 1927, Cab 24/183, ff. 203–4.

25. Sir Herbert Goffe, British consul general, Hankou, no. 2, 3 Jan. 1927, F67/67/10, FO 371 12430; Goffe, no. 5, 5 Jan. 1927, F92/67/10, ibid.

26. Joynson-Hicks (Meudon) to Chamberlain, 7 Jan. 1927, AC54/298, U.Birm., A. Chamberlain Papers.

27. Minute by C. J. Norton, Far Eastern Department, 21 Oct. 1926, and Colonial Office correspondence, F4349/307/10, FO 371 11679; Mounsey's memorandum and Tyrrell's minute, 20 Feb. 1927, F1715/48/10, FO 371 12430.

28. Minute by Mounsey, then head, Far Eastern Department, quoting Roger Cambon, from the French embassy, 9 Jan. 1927, F175/67/10, FO 371 12430; and Sir Miles Lampson to Chamberlain, private, 16 April 1927, AC54/317, U.Birm., A. Chamberlain Papers.

29. Chamberlain's minute, 10 Jan. 1927, F176/67/10, FO 371 12430.

30. Cabinet extract 2 (27), 17 Jan. 1927, N229/209/38, FO 371 12589.

31. Rozengol'ts to Litvinov, no. 7/s, very secret, 7 Jan. 1927, AVPRF, f. 069, o. 11, p. 30, d. 3, ll. 3–11; and Litvinov to Rozengol'ts, no. 3045, secret, 15 Jan. 1927, AVPRF, f. 69, o. 11, p. 30, d. 1, l. 3.

32. Rozengol'ts' *dnevnik*, no. 46/s, 21 Jan. 1927, AVPRF, f. 069, o. 11, p. 30, d. 3, ll. 38–21; Rozengol'ts to Litvinov, no. 52/s, very secret, 21 Jan. 1927, AVPRF, f. 069, o. 11, p. 30, d. 2, ll. 1–3; Rozengol'ts to Litvinov, no. 62/s, secret, 28 Jan. 1927, AVPRF, f. 05, o. 7, p. 22, d. 5, ll. 194–95; and untitled memorandum, Gregory, 14 Jan. 1927, F438/28/10, FO 371 12419.

33. Maiskii to Rotshtein, no. 48, secret, 21 Jan. 1927, AVPRF, f. 069, o. 11, p. 31, d. 23, ll. 25–23.

34. Maiskii to Stalin, no. 57, secret, 28 Jan. 1927, AVPRF, f. 05, o. 7, p. 22, d. 5, ll. 203–5.

35. Litvinov to Chicherin (Baden-Baden), no. 3026, secret, 8 Jan. 1927, AVPRF, f. 05 o. 6, p. 21, d. 89, l. 5.

36. Maiskii to Rotshtein, no. 48, as cited above in n. 33; and Litvinov to Rozengol'ts, no. 3091, secret, 29 Jan. 1927, AVPRF, f. 069, o. 11, p. 30, d. 1, l. 4.

37. Litvinov to Chicherin, no. 3020, secret, 6 Jan. 1927, AVPRF, f. 05, o. 6, p. 21, d. 89, ll. 1–3.

38. Hodgson, unnumbered dispatch, 17 Jan. 1927, N275/190/38, FO 371 12588.

39. Herbette, no. 59, 26 Jan. 1927, MAÉ Grande-Bretagne/65, fol. 1.

40. "Meeting with [Peter] Schou [Danish minister in Moscow]," Litvinov, 26 Jan. 1927, AVPRF, f. 05, o. 7a, p. 32, d. 27, l. 17; and Anna Di Biagio, "Moscow: The Comintern and the War Scare, 1926–28," in Silvio Pons and Andrea Romano (eds.), *Russia in the Age of War, 1914–1945* (Milano, 2000), pp. 83–102.

41. Trotskii, *Stalin* (New York, 1967), p. 418.

42. Di Biagio, "Moscow: The Comintern and the War Scare," pp. 98–99; and Stephen F. Cohen, *Bukharin and the Bolshevik Revolution: A Political Biography, 1888–1938* (New York, 1975).

43. Rotshtein to Chicherin, no. 14032, secret, 15 Jan. 1927, AVPRF, f. 05, o. 6, p. 21, d. 89, l. 6.

44. Litvinov to Stalin, no. 3064, secret, 21 Jan. 1927, AVPRF, f. 082, o. 10, p. 27, d. 2, l. 2 (published in *Moskva-Berlin*, II, pp. 9–11); and "Meeting with Herbette," Litvinov, 16 March 1927, AVPRF, f. 05, o. 7a, p. 32, d. 27, ll. 26–27.

45. Litvinov to Chicherin, no. 3044, secret, 15 Jan. 1927, AVPRF, f. 05, o. 6, p. 21, d. 89, ll. 7–9.

46. Litvinov to Chicherin, no. 3076, secret, 26 Jan. 1927, AVPRF, f. 05, o. 6, p. 21, d. 89, ll. 10–11.

47. Litvinov to Chicherin, no. 3090, secret, 29 Jan. 1927, AVPRF, f. 05, o. 6, p. 21, d. 89, l. 12.

48. See chapter 8, n. 36.

49. Untitled, undated, unsigned summary, personal communication from Sergei V. Kudryashov, editor, *VESTNIK AP RF*, Moscow.

50. "Members of Politburo," nd, personal communication from S. V. Kudryashov, editor, *VESTNIK AP RF*, Moscow.

51. Untitled, undated (but Jan. 1927), unsigned report, personal communication from S. V. Kudryashov, editor, *VESTNIK AP RF*, Moscow.

52. Litvinov to Stalin, ccs. to members of the Politburo, Stomoniakov, Rakovskii, Rotshtein, Krestinskii, no. 3130, very secret, 15 Feb. 1927, personal communication from S. V. Kudryashov, editor, *VESTNIK AP RF*, Moscow.

53. See above n. 11; and Chicherin to Kopp, very secret, 23 March 1926, *Perepiska I. V. Stalina i G. V. Chicherina*, pp. 615–19.

54. "To the Politburo," rigorously secret, make no copies, upon reading return immediately, Stalin, signed by members of the Politburo, 23 Feb. 1927, personal communication from S. V. Kudryashov, editor, *VESTNIK AP RF*, Moscow.

55. Harold R. Isaacs, *The Tragedy of the Chinese Revolution* (New York, 1966), pp. 160–63.

56. "The Embarrassing Mascot," *The Star*, 8 Feb. 1927, British Cartoon Archive.

57. Hodgson, no. 89, 5 Feb. 1927; and Chamberlain's minute, 15 Feb. 1927, N617/209/38, FO 371 12589.

58. Rozengol'ts to Litvinov, no. 96/s, very secret, 18 Feb. 1927, AVPRF, f. 069, o. 11, p. 30, d. 2, ll. 11–31.

59. Litvinov to Rozengol'ts, no. 3138, secret, 19 Feb. 1927, AVPRF, f. 05, o. 7, p. 23, d. 9, ll. 82–83.

60. Draft note, confidential, nd; Gregory's minute, 15 Jan. 1927, N341G/209/38, FO 371 12589; and Cabinet meeting of 23 Feb. 1927, Cab 23/54.

61. Herbette, nos. 73–74, 25 Feb. 1927, MAÉ Grande-Bretagne/65, ff. 26–27.

62. Litvinov to Rozengol'ts, no. 3151, secret, 26 Feb. 1927, AVPRF, f. 05, o. 7, p. 23, d. 9, l. 74.

63. Peters, no. 145, 3 March 1927, enclosing Litvinov's reply, N1079/109/38, FO 371 12590.

64. Fleuriau, no. 105, 24 Feb. 1927, MAÉ Grande-Bretagne/65, fol. 23.

65. Fleuriau, no. 86, very confidential, 26 Feb. 1927, MAÉ Grande-Bretagne/65, ff. 31–32.

66. Memorandum by André Rostin, London correspondent for *Industrie-und Handelszeitung*, 31 March 1927, E158.652–57, AA, *Büro Staatssekretär, Akten betreffend politische Anglegenheiten der UdSSR, Band* 16, 4562H/R.29265.

67. Litvinov to Rozengol'ts, no. 3168, secret, 5 March 1927, AVPRF, f. 069, o. 11, p. 30, d. 1, ll. 9–10; and Litvinov to Rozengol'ts, no. 3181, secret, 11 March 1927, ibid., ll. 12–13.

68. Peters, no. 147, 4 March 1927; Gascoigne's minute, 10 March 1927, N1100/209/38, FO 371 12590; and excerpts from Politburo protocol, no. 89 (special no. 67), 3 March 1927, *VKP(b), Komintern v Kitae*, II, pt. 2, pp. 632–34.

69. Vatlin, *Komintern*, pp. 72–73; Gascoigne's minute, 11 Feb. 1927, N585/190/38, FO 371 12588; and the text of Stalin's speech enclosed in Peters, no. 167, 11 March 1927, N1321/209/38, FO 371 12590.

70. Litvinov to Rozengol'ts, no. 3196, secret, 19 March 1927, AVPRF, f. 05, o. 7, p. 23, d. 9, ll. 59–60; and minutes by C. M. Palairet, head, Northern Department; Gregory, 14 March 1927; and Chamberlain, 15 March 1927, N1167/209/38, FO 371 12590.

71. Litvinov to Rozengol'ts, no. 3138, secret, 19 Feb. 1927, AVPRF, f. 05, o. 7, p. 23, d. 9, ll. 82–83.

72. Litvinov to Rozengol'ts, no. 3223, secret, 26 March 1927, AVPRF, f. 05, o. 7, p. 23, d. 9, ll. 54–55.

73. Miles Lampson, British minister in Peking, to Walford Selby, Geneva, 9 March 1927, F2301/28/10, FO 371 12420; Chamberlain's minute, 9 March 1927, ibid.; and minute by Strang (?), 23 March 1927, F2631/28/10, ibid.

74. Ashton-Gwatkin's minute, Far Eastern Department, 25 Jan. 1927, F678/87/10, FO 371 12439.

75. Excerpts from Politburo protocol, no. 89 (special no. 67), 3 March 1927, VKP(b), Komintern v Kitae, II, pt. 2, pp. 632–34.

76. Excerpts from Politburo protocol, no. 90 (special no. 68), 10 March 1927; and no. 92 (special no. 70), 24 March 1927, VKP(b), Komintern v Kitae, II, pt. 2, pp. 643–45, 648–49.

77. Bukharin's report to the presidium of the IKKI, very secret, 30 March 1927, VKP(b), Komintern v Kitae, II, pt. 2, pp. 651–57.

78. Excerpt from Politburo protocol, no. 93 (special no. 71), 31 March 1927, VKP(b), Komintern v Kitae, II, pt. 2, pp. 658–59.

79. Broué, Internationale, p. 438.

80. Mounsey's minutes, 7 April 1927, F3288/2/10, FO 371 12404, and F3818/1530/10, FO 371 12478; Chamberlain's minute, 23 April 1927, F3934/1530/10, FO 371 12479; and Ashton-Gwatkin's minute, 22 April 1927, F3937/1530/10, ibid.

81. J. F. Brenan, British consul general in Canton, no. 26R, 17 April 1927, F3784/2/10, FO 371 12404; Mounsey's minute, 20 April 1927, ibid.; and minutes by Strang, 19 April 1927, and Mounsey, 20 April 1927, F3737/2/10, ibid.

82. Minutes by Wellesley, 21 April 1927, and Chamberlain, 21 April 1927, F3818/1530/10, FO 371 12478.

83. Litvinov to Chicherin (San Rafael), no. 3297, secret, 22 April 1927, AVPRF, f. 05, o. 6 p. 21, d. 89, ll. 25–27; Litvinov to Rozengol'ts, no. 3243, secret, 2 April 1927, AVPRF, f. 05, o. 7, p. 23, d. 9, ll. 50–51; and Litvinov to Stalin, no. 3238, secret, 30 March 1927, AVPRF, f. 069, o. 11, p. 31, d. 15, l. 4.

84. Lampson, no. 479, 22 March 1927, F2631/28/10, FO 371 12420.

85. Litvinov to Rozengol'ts, no. 3298, secret, 22 April 1927, AVPRF, f. 05, o. 7, p. 23, d. 9, ll. 42–43; and Litvinov to Chicherin, no. 3312, secret, 30 April 1927, AVPRF, f. 05, o. 6, p. 21, d. 89, l. 28.

86. Excerpt from Politburo protocol, no. 94 (special no. 72), 7 April 1927, VKP(b), Komintern v Kitae, II, pt. 2, pp. 661–62.

87. Trotskii, Problems of the Chinese Revolution (Ann Arbor, 1967), pp.17–121.

88. Broué, Internationale, p. 440.

89. Neumann to Politburo, especially secret, 29 Nov. 1927, VKP(b), Komintern v Kitae, III, pt. 1, pp. 164–65.

90. Boris Aleksandrovich Pokhvalinskii to Karakhan, especially secret, 29 Nov. 1927, VKP(b), Komintern v Kitae, III, pt. 1, pp. 165–66; Mikhail Alekseev, Sovetskaia voennaia razvedka v Kitae i khronika "kitaiskoi smuty" (1922–1929) (Moscow, 2010), pp. 220–21.

91. Trilisser's report, very secret, 9 Dec. 1927, VKP(b), Komintern v Kitae, III, pt. 1, pp. 188–89.

92. Excerpt from Politburo protocol, no. 139 (special no. 116), 6–17 Dec. 1927, VKP(b), Komintern v Kitae, III, pt. 1, p. 191.

93. Chicherin to Karakhan, no 19, personal, very secret, 25 June 1926, Perepiska I. V. Stalina i G. V. Chicherina, pp. 691–92.

94. Stalin to Molotov, 23 Sept. 1926, Lih et al., Stalin's Letters, pp. 129–30.

95. Isaacs, Tragedy, p. 291.

96. Brenan, no. 66, 14 Dec. 1927, and minutes by Ashton-Gwatkin and Mounsey, 15 Dec. 1927, F9240/2/10, FO 371 12411.

97. IKKI to TsK, 23 Dec. 1927, VKP(b), Komintern v Kitae, III, pt. 1, p. 194.

98. Isaacs, Tragedy, p. 282; and Boris Souvarine, Stalin: A Critical Survey of Bolshevism (New York, 1939), p. 471.

99. Fleuriau, no. 195, 14 May 1927, MAÉ Grande-Bretagne/65, ff. 88–88bis; Maiskii to Rotshtein, secret, 13 May 1927, AVPRF, f. 069, o. 11, p. 30, d. 6, ll. 110–13; Litvinov to Rozengol'ts, no. 3367, secret, 21 May 1927, AVPRF, f. 069, o. 11, p. 30, d. 1, ll. 25–26; and Politburo protocol, no. 102, 13 May 1927, Politbiuro Osoboi papki, pp. 148–50.

100. Litvinov to Rozengol'ts, no. 3243, secret, 2 April 1927, AVPRF, f. 05, o. 7, p. 23, d. 9, ll. 50–51.

101. Hodgson to Chamberlain, no. 114, confidential, 11 Feb. 1927, F1716/28/10, FO 371 12420; and Perepiska I. V. Stalina i G. V. Chicherina, p. 71, n. 6.

102. Palairet's minute, 19 May 1927, N2289/2187/38, FO 371 12602.

103. Politburo protocol, no. 105, 26 May 1927, Politbiuro Osoboi papki, pp. 150–52; Peters, no. 347, 26 May 1926, N2574/209/38, FO 371 12592; and C. W. Orde's minute, 26 May 1927, N2411/209/38, FO 371 12591.

104. Litvinov's dnevnik, "Conversation with Chamberlain in Geneva, 5 December [1927]," secret, AVPRF, f. 05, o. 7a, p. 32, p. 32, d. 27, ll. 114–18.

105. Cabinet Protocol, Berlin, 15 March 1927, AzDAP, B, IV, pp. 559–67.

106. Palairet's minute, 13 July 1927, N3342/309/38, FO 371 12595.

107. Herbette, nos. 289–94, 21 May 1927, MAÉ Grande-Bretagne/65, ff. 107–12; Fleuriau, no. 208, 25 May 1927, ibid., ff. 149–50; and "The Minister," Ralph F. Wigram, first secretary, British embassy in Paris, 7 June 1927, N2761/209/38, FO 371 12592.

108. Unsigned memorandum, Berlin, 11 April 1929, AzDAP, B, XI, pp. 377–81.

CHAPTER TEN

~

"Colossal Misfortune"

Hostile Coexistence in Paris, 1925–1927

Having resecured Rapallo with Germany, more or less, the NKID turned to Paris to counterbalance hostility in London, exacerbated by events in China. It was undoubtedly naïve to think that the USSR could wedge itself between France and Britain, but it was necessary to try if for no other reason than to discourage Germany from straying too far from Rapallo. Franco-Soviet relations had gotten off to a bad start with communist demonstrations in Paris and little interest in the Quai d'Orsay for pursuing negotiations.

In spite of the pessimism in Moscow, there was a turn for the better in the autumn of 1925. General good feelings about the Locarno Accords seemed to rub off on Franco-Soviet relations. The Soviet government kept up the pressure for a settlement, and Chicherin publicly challenged the French to cease their "dilatory tactics" and negotiate.[1] Rakovskii went to Paris, replacing Krasin who then returned to his old stand in London. Litvinov instructed Rakovskii to try to take advantage of the favorable circumstances to move forward. In November 1925 it was agreed to start formal political and economic negotiations. Berthelot was friendly with Rakovskii and blamed the failure of the Krasin proposals on the finance ministry. If finance takes over the debt negotiations, said Berthelot, it will be "a colossal misfortune . . . for we are dealing above all with a political question." Briand was also friendly and worried about American domination, "unconscious economic imperialism," he called it. Through its economic power, the United States was penetrating deeply into the whole economic life of Europe. First the Americans lend money, then they demand trade rights, then rights to buy into individual business enterprises,

Figure 10.1. Khristian G. Rakovskii, Paris, ca. 1925, *Agence Meurisse*. *Bibliothèque nationale de France*.

and then into the whole economic and financial life of European states. Rakovskii easily agreed, as readers might even now.[2]

Unlike Krasin, Rakovskii had a more positive view of Monzie. This was just as well since they would soon be facing each other across the negotiating table. And he did not think there was any point to continue paying "allowances" to the French press. While Rakovskii made his first rounds, the Locarno Accords were concluded and the Painlevé government collapsed on 22 November. Let's not take Locarno too tragically, Rakovskii advised, it would only demonstrate our weakness. And let's be careful not to put a foot wrong on the boggy ground of French politics. According to Paris police, he meant what he said. A notice was circulated in the *polpredstvo*: "To all comrades," anyone caught in contact with French communists will immediately be sent home.[3]

Chicherin visited Paris in November and December 1925 and had discussions with Briand and Berthelot among others. The conversations were friendly and wide ranging. Are you serious about a debts settlement? asked Berthelot. If we were not serious, replied Chicherin, we would not begin discussions, since failure would only make relations worse. And he repeated

Figure 10.2. Philippe Berthelot, Georgii V. Chicherin, Khristian G. Rakovskii, during a meeting at the Quai d'Orsay, Paris, December 1925. *Agence Meurisse. Bibliothèque nationale de France.*

a joke he had heard from a French interlocutor, which had its serious side: "We recognize our debts, but we do not pay; you do not recognize your debts, but you are ready to pay." In effect, the French were not paying their debts, though they had paid one to the United States in 1920, with sequestered Brest-Litovsk gold. Chicherin concluded that if discussions had previously gone wrong, the fault lay on the French side. Berthelot had to admit, negotiations with Krasin had not been well handled.[4] "Given that very intense struggle between personal conceit and interests, which is so characteristic of French political life, one needs to be extraordinarily careful," observed Rakovskii. Chicherin was not sure of French intentions.[5] The Quai d'Orsay agreed however to begin formal negotiations to settle outstanding differences. Talks were set to begin in February.

In January 1926 on the eve of the Franco-Soviet conference, the Soviet chargé d'affaires in Paris, Davtian, had breakfast with Rollin and Edgar Roels of *Le Temps*. "France was going through an extraordinarily difficult crisis," Roels said, "which is a crisis of the system. Parliament has moved into a dead end and there appears no way out of it." Davtian elaborated: "In the large mass of the population at every level there exists discontent with parliament and parliamentary democracy." The French Communist Party offered no solutions for it is still weak, and on the other side the fascists "do not represent a real force sufficient to launch a coup d'état." Davtian did not see a way out of the parliamentary crisis, though one was coming

Figure 10.3. Georgii V. Chicherin, Khristian G. Rakovskii, Soviet embassy, rue de Grenelle, Paris, December 1925. *Agence Meurisse. Bibliothèque nationale de France.*

for the short term, in the form of a new Poincaré government.[6] But this is getting a little ahead of the story.

Despite Rakovskii's recommendation against press subsidies, the Soviet government continued to pay. "You have no doubt observed," Davtian wrote to Litvinov, "that the line of the big newspaper is still unsatisfactory." While *Le Temps* had stopped its "rude attacks," it was not taking an "active" line toward the Soviet Union. Roels and Rollin explained that "objective conditions" were not conducive to a more favorable position. Nevertheless, Davtian recommended paying, in view of the upcoming negotiations in Paris. "All past debts" to *Le Temps*, he reported, had been settled, and new contacts made. "It is impossible to work in Paris without being able to provide our point of view regularly and systematically to the wider press," and for this one has to pay.[7]

The Franco-Soviet conference began in February 1926. As preparations were made for the conference, Herbette sent good advice to Paris. Most western information on the Soviet Union, he said, is false or tendentious. "The Soviet regime is depicted as a sort of irrational organisation of rogues . . . , the government is portrayed as . . . incompetent, as . . . corrupt, and as hopelessly divided. Perhaps this system of denigration has for a time served certain electoral, financial, or diplomatic interests." But it could also be counter-productive: "French diplomacy cannot retain its freedom of action if the French public is continually excited against Russia by spurious reports or by erroneous analysis, since the French government will be inhibited in its relations with the USSR by domestic political campaigns."[8]

Herbette urged Paris to reach a settlement with Moscow. "If others reproach us later for having allowed a new war and a new invasion to be prepared because we could not find the necessary solutions to settle the Russian debt and because we did not anticipate inevitable future changes in Eastern Europe, what responsibility will we bear?"[9] These were prophetic words, but in 1939 when it mattered most, they were long forgotten, undoubtedly even by Herbette.

On the day after the opening of formal negotiations in February 1926, *Izvestiia* reiterated a point Chicherin had made to Berthelot in December: accept the Soviet Union "as we are," just as we must accept France as it is. Like Herbette a few months earlier, *Izvestiia* asked the French government not to load negotiations with demands which a much weaker Soviet government had rejected in previous years.[10] The Soviet Union could not fund a debts settlement without credits in return. Soviet officials applied the Roman law *do ut des*, "I give, that you may give." The French understood the concept and had their own expression, *donnant, donnant*; the question was, would they apply it? Apparently not. Ambassador Fleuriau told Gregory in March that trade credits for the Soviet government were "totally out of the question," and that "negotiations would come to nothing."

Why conduct negotiations at all if they were not expected to succeed? Gregory did not ask but must have wondered. Because Herriot had promised them at the time of recognition, Fleuriau replied, anticipating the question.[11] A few weeks later Briand confirmed the position to the British ambassador in Paris: "no result" was in fact expected from the negotiations. "The difference of principle between the two parties renders agreement impossible."[12] The French passed the same message to Rakovskii, but diplomatically. "There is no need to hurry," said Berthelot, Monzie, and others. According to Rakovskii, "Berthelot said that we need to prepare public opinion." In the meantime, France had other "more serious political problems" to solve with Britain and the United States.[13]

Under the circumstances, the Paris negotiations were hard going. The focus was on finding a settlement for tsarist bonds, some 9 billion francs held by French citizens, in exchange for trade credits. By July 1926 some progress had been made. The Soviet government was willing to pay 60 million gold francs a year for up to 62 years in exchange for $250 million in credits over three years. French negotiators were enthusiastic about Soviet annuities, but not about French credits. The principle of *donnant, donnant* was not to be applied. Monzie told Davtian that he was "far ahead" of his delegation and that he had constantly to bargain for even the smallest concessions. "He asked me to pass on," the Soviet chargé d'affaires Davtian wrote in his journal, "that if we want a successful outcome of the work of the conference, we have to help him."[14] This sounds like a good cop, bad cop routine. One can only imagine Litvinov's derisive reaction to Monzie's message.

Let's wait until autumn, Berthelot told Rakovskii. The French were still stalling. Political instability continued to plague the government with ministries changing every few months, then every few weeks, then in July a new Herriot cabinet lasted only two days. Part of the reason for political instability was financial instability. The franc was falling on foreign exchange markets, and then it began to plummet. The French treasury is empty, observed Rakovskii, and "rats are dancing inside." The empty treasury meant trade credits were impossible, though Rakovskii did not seem to make the connection. At the same time Die-Hards in London were gnashing their teeth about Soviet support for British miners and Chinese revolutionaries. The French anti-communist press, sympathetic to the Die-Hards, was quick to lend them support. Chicherin noted the French right turn and thought it better to accept slow negotiations than no negotiations at all.[15]

Because of the political instability in Paris, Rakovskii tried to force the pace and to persuade Monzie to sign a protocol marking the progress of negotiations—60 million francs per annum for 60 years against $225 million in credits over three years. If we can't put on paper now points of agreement, Rakovskii argued, then in the autumn we may lose any gains. A dramatic meeting occurred on 18 July of French and Soviet delegates, recorded by a secret chronicler of the Franco-Soviet conference, S. B. Chlenov, secretary general of the Soviet delegation. The meeting took place the day after yet another government fell. Chlenov waited outside a conference room at the Quai d'Orsay while Monzie and several French officials argued and shouted at each other over the draft of a joint protocol. When Chlenov was finally invited to join the meeting, everyone looked glum, he noted, and Monzie "embarrassed and dejected."

We can't do anything, they said; "with the fall of the cabinet, everything has changed . . . we have to wait until a new government is formed. Otherwise the delegation will be disavowed."

Monzie later told Chlenov there had been a revolt (bunt) in the delegation: "It was physically impossible in two days to force 20 members of the delegation." If the civil servants could not agree, neither could the ministers, who were only passers-by in the negotiations. Monzie complained to Chlenov that Rakovskii was putting too much pressure on and this could force him to resign.

"Chlenov, give us 75 million," Monzie pleaded, "and we can conclude a deal."

All the same, 60 million was not bad, Chlenov must have thought, and he said 75 million would never fly.

When it came to credits, Monzie said there was no way the government would agree to $225 million.

No way his government would accept less, Chlenov replied.

The exchange sounded a little like those between Lloyd George and Chicherin at Genoa. After which the conversation turned to speculation on the next finance minister. If it's Poincaré, well, you know Poincaré, said Monzie.[16] Berthelot later told Eric Phipps, the British chargé in Paris, "confidentially" that he "had put his foot down" to stop any exchange of letters "giving away the French position far too much." Rakovskii had protested "in somewhat violent terms to Berthelot in private conversation," but to no avail. In reading Rakovskii's account of the meeting with Berthelot, Litvinov may have thought the former Soviet nemesis was up to his old tricks.[17]

On 23 July, after a week of uncertainty, another Soviet *bête noire*, Poincaré, formed a government. He took the finance portfolio, in view of the financial crisis, but this gave finance officials a stronger hand in Franco-Soviet negotiations, the "colossal misfortune" Berthelot had earlier feared. Monzie warned Soviet officials that the British were doing "everything possible" to break up the conference. They are furious with Moscow, he said, over events in China. Hundreds of British companies had gone bankrupt. It would be just like Monzie to blame the British, when the main obstacles to agreement were French. Whoever was to blame, the NKID *kollegiia* recommended a speedy signature of a protocol on debts and credits.[18]

Apparently Litvinov did not yet understand that the Quai d'Orsay never intended to conclude an agreement with Moscow. In late August, a worried Herbette went to see Litvinov who made a record of their discussion: "Becoming more intimate, his voice trembling, and almost with tears in his eyes," Herbette said he was concerned about the Soviet international position to the extent that he almost did not sleep at night.

Don't worry about it, a deadpanned Litvinov replied.[19]

The situation was nevertheless worrisome. In October 1926 Poincaré took control over the Soviet negotiations. Until that time, discussions had focused on a settlement of bondholders' claims and trade credits. Just as Litvinov had anticipated and just like Genoa, Poincaré loaded on more demands, sending instructions to Briand that state-to-state war debts and the claims of dispossessed industrialists also had to be settled before there could be an agreement. The French government knew, however, that to raise either of these issues would block a settlement since Soviet officials would press counter-claims with respect to war debts and would refuse to indemnify French industrialists or others, except through individual business arrangements or concessions.[20] As usual, the NKID was well informed: Berthelot was said to be pessimistic about the success of negotiations, and Poincaré had demanded the last word on financial issues. In mid-October Monzie admitted to Rakovskii that the Quai d'Orsay had wanted to put off a debts agreement until after the summer holidays to avoid irritating the British and American governments.[21] Monzie privately felt that it was time to conclude, a position which Rakovskii also held. Time was working against us, not for us, Rakovskii thought: our relations with Britain are worsening, and if we fail to obtain a debt settlement, it could form the platform upon which to build an anti-Soviet front. Monzie tried to obtain approval for a letter to Rakovskii defining differences rather than points of agreement—unlike the previous summer's efforts—but even this Poincaré vetoed. The French were stonewalling, and this prompted a Soviet review of whether to continue negotiations.[22]

At the end of 1926 a Politburo commission, including Litvinov, was set up to examine the putative agreement. It was highly critical and recommended virtually starting negotiations over again. Litvinov instructed Rakovskii to stall, a tactic borrowed from the French, while the Politburo commission deliberated. From Soviet intelligence sources reading Herbette's correspondence, Litvinov knew Herbette was saying that the Soviet government was desperate for an agreement, and that Monzie, who favored a delay, was possibly trying "to blackmail us." If so, fine, said Litvinov: "This is exactly what we need." He went further:

> The commission's conclusions would have delighted us a year or two ago, for it is doubtful whether anyone of us would have thought that the receiving of trade credits for five to seven years could justify the payment of a percentage of the old debts over a period of 50 to 60 years. Personally I always considered and still consider that any linkage of recognition of any kind whatever of the old debts with commercial credits, even with a rotational extension of these credits over an extended period, is for us unprofitable. The resolution of these questions is found exclusively on the political level. We are confronted by the question of whether we are forced by the political situation to make those material sacrifices which the agreement requires of us.

Litvinov was now convinced, quite correctly, that the French would not come to terms, and that therefore there was no risk in maintaining previous policy, however unfavorable economically.[23]

The larger political questions remained: Would economic sacrifices secure for the Soviet Union the disruption of an anti-Soviet bloc? Would it end Soviet political isolation? Would it lessen the possibility of war? But none of these questions had been discussed with the French, Litvinov pointed out, so we have agreed to large economic sacrifices which in no way guarantee any political advantage, though it was for this reason that economic concessions were contemplated. I am afraid, Litvinov said, that even a debts settlement will not satisfy the French, and they will raise other demands such as the claims of dispossessed property owners. And if we do not want to proceed with the political questions, we ought to break off negotiations on a debts settlement. This could be done by asking for credits, which the French will not offer. Even on purely economic grounds a debts settlement was a pig in a poke: 60 million a year and *maybe* western confidence in us will grow, *maybe* we can obtain guaranteed loans and credits, and *maybe* we can obtain better interest rates. But who knows for certain?[24] Here again was the quintessential Litvinov, making calculations based on realpolitik, according to Machiavelli, not Marx.

On 13 January 1927 the Politburo approved new guidelines for the Soviet delegation in Paris which maintained the demand for $225 million in credits over three years, among other unpalatable or impossible items for the French government. If Litvinov had it in mind to make unacceptable demands in Paris, the Politburo certainly gave him the authority to do so.[25]

As readers will remember, the political situation was worsening week by week in Britain where the Die-Hards were looking for a pretext to break off diplomatic relations. The *polpredstvo* in London could only watch with growing disquiet as the situation deteriorated, and Rozengol'ts urged the NKID to conclude an agreement with France as quickly as possible in order to lessen the danger of a rupture with Britain.[26] After backing and filling, the Soviet government decided to offer the French a non-aggression pact. Rakovskii raised the issue in Paris in March 1927. We need to settle the debts first, Briand replied.[27]

This was a polite evasion. France should be in no hurry to continue negotiations, advised Quai d'Orsay officials, in order to signal that it was the Soviet Union, not France, who really needed a deal. If the Soviet government needed credit as badly as most experts appeared to believe, Soviet creditors should form a united front to impose their minimum terms. Then the Soviet Union might be persuaded to lower its demands. It was always thus in western-Soviet negotiations: who was the needier interlocutor and how much more could thus be extracted in concessions. And the French had other reasons for refusing to conclude. The Quai d'Orsay was concerned not to offend the British or Polish governments, which would take a dim view of overly close Franco-Soviet relations. Comintern support for the revolutionary movement in China continued to aggravate French right-wing opinion.[28]

There was one meeting of the French and Soviet delegations in March, the last as it turned out. The British chargé in Paris, Phipps, went to the Quai d'Orsay to discover what was going on. Berthelot told him that "Poincaré . . . would have the last word to say in the matter of the negotiations" and that "if anything, there is even less hope now than there was some months ago of a successful issue."[29] Eirik Labonne, Monzie's right arm, later confirmed the position. "Nothing could be obtained from the Russians," he said, which was hardly the case, but then he was in the presence of Quai d'Orsay colleagues and could only sing the team song. In April Briand informed Herbette that any political agreement with the Soviet government that affected the main lines of French foreign policy was out of the question.[30]

Briand's instructions should be no surprise: in April 1927 Britain and France were hotbeds of anti-communist agitation in the press and in government circles. In February François Coty, the right-wing perfume mogul and owner of the influential anti-communist daily Le Figaro, had lunch with Chamberlain in London to discuss the organization of an anti-Soviet front. Chamberlain was open-minded, and Coty launched a trial balloon in Le Figaro. Even Briand thought the concept might have merit.[31] Events started to go against the revolution in China, and this gave further encouragement to the right. In April Albert Sarraut, the interior minister, trumpeted the alarm against communist subversion in a widely publicized speech. "Le communisme, voilà l'ennemi!" he declared. In May the Chamber of Deputies debated the lifting of Parliamentary immunity of communist deputies so they could be prosecuted for subversive activities. In May, too, the word "elections" began to turn up in the press and in Soviet and French calculations concerning the debt negotiations. Plus ça change, plus c'est la meme chose: as in 1924, a settlement would help the left in national elections in 1928; worsening relations with Moscow would help the right. On 29 May a political cartoon appeared in the Paris daily L'Oeuvre which depicted Poincaré discussing with interior minister Sarraut the celebrated 1919 poster of a bloodthirsty Bolshevik clenching a knife in his teeth. "Hm, do you think it will work again?" read the caption. Poincaré must have thought it would, because earlier in May his officials had raised the problem of elections as an impediment, among others, to a Franco-Soviet agreement. Rakovskii also heard of it.[32]

In the spring of 1927 Chicherin planned a trip to France for health reasons, and it was decided that he should stop in Paris for political talks with Briand and Poincaré, among others. Finance official Jean-Jacques Bizot asked rhetorically, what if Chicherin agrees to all our demands? Answer: we will put two more obstacles in the way (read: war debts and the indemnification of private property). Litvinov had already guessed as much: if Poincaré insists on these demands, negotiations will fail. Chicherin went to Paris anyway;

the Soviet government still sought agreement, with the Politburo issuing new instructions for Rakovskii. Litvinov advised that the Politburo was more interested in the conclusion of a "political pact" with France and "even" to some form of repayment of the old debts.[33] The Politburo instructions were detailed and focused on debts and the essential quid pro quo of credits. Had Berthelot seen the instructions he would have shaken his head in disbelief. Moscow was the needy interlocutor, for the British government broke off diplomatic relations with the USSR while Chicherin was in Paris.

Incredible Negotiations and Tumult in Paris

Believe it or not, in spite of everything, Monzie and Rakovskii, incorrigible to the end, continued to negotiate. Rumors circulated that an agreement was near, which the French finance ministry formally denied.[34] In fact, it was almost true. In May Rakovskii published an interview saying so, which infuriated Poincaré. Rakovskii is trying to win over French bondholders, Poincaré complained. He called in the owner of the anti-Red, right-wing daily Le Matin, Maurice Bunau-Varilla, to ask him to rebut Rakovskii's claims. "A comedy which has lasted long enough," duly ran Matin's leader a few days later under Stéphane Lauzanne's byline.[35] Bunau-Varilla stood far to the right: after the fall of France in 1940, he collaborated with the Nazis, as did his associate Lauzanne. Fortunately for Bunau-Varilla he died just before the liberation of Paris in August 1944; not so fortunately for Lauzanne, he got 20 years for collaboration with the enemy.

The French right, with notable exceptions, never did understand who were the real enemies of France. But this is getting ahead of our narrative. In the spring of 1927, there was still movement forward in negotiations in Paris, and Labonne thought an "agreement . . . virtually concluded on the question of debts." Monzie and a majority of his colleagues agreed to submit a draft agreement for a debts settlement to the Soviet delegation. Only the finance delegates dissented. Once again the French could put nothing on paper. Quai d'Orsay officials reported that the finance ministry "was doing everything possible . . . to drag things out." Negotiations were going to be "dampened down."[36]

Chicherin met Poincaré on 24 May. Negotiations are very unlikely to succeed, advised the premier; we think it best to drag out negotiations or informally suspend them. Poincaré complained about Rakovskii's press statements since bondholders might conclude that a failure of negotiations was the French government's fault. Then Poincaré launched into a "rude, prolonged diatribe against the revolutionary communist policies of the Soviet government, against its interference in the internal affairs of other countries.

. . . He said that public opinion in France is becoming more irritable, that the French will never tolerate the interference of a foreign government in its affairs. . . . The situation has not gone as far as in England, but it could come to that." Herriot, Painlevé, and others all confirmed the seriousness of the situation. Anti-communist agitation was pre-electoral campaigning, said one politician; and it is bound to get worse. The situation is far more serious than two years ago, said the *Le Temps* journalist and Soviet go-between Rollin: "Be careful and don't give your enemies a pretext to attack you." Chicherin even met some French communists and weighed into them for their imprudent politics. Stop claiming to represent the authority of the Soviet government, Chicherin demanded.[37]

Berthelot also gave an account to Phipps of his meeting with Chicherin and Rakovskii. It was never good for Moscow to be in a position of weakness vis-à-vis "the Entente," as this report demonstrated. Berthelot was in high spirits according to Phipps: "Chicherin seemed desperately anxious, as indeed he has been for some time past, to conclude some political arrangement with France in the shape of a treaty of non-aggression . . . but Berthelot held out no hopes in this respect." The negotiations had come to an impasse, "owing to the fact that the French government firmly declined to provide the Soviets with . . . credits." Berthelot smirked that Chicherin looked "profoundly depressed."[38] As well he might have been, though with the French it was not wise to show it, and the Politburo held to its formula of credits in exchange for payments on the tsarist debt. A few days earlier Briand had commented to Chamberlain that "all negotiations with the Soviet authorities were, in fact, *des duperies.*" Then he proceeded to brag about how the French had outsmarted their Soviet counterparts in negotiations. A fortnight later Briand held a similar conversation with Stresemann: "It's bad to negotiate with the Russians. Their policy is that of Penelope; they take back in the night everything they have given in the day."[39] Readers should laugh at this comment; Chicherin had used a similar image, the "distant princess," to describe the French. Who was deceiving whom? Let's just say pot called kettle black, as was so often the case in western-Soviet relations.

American Interlude in Paris

Berthelot was smug about Soviet distress in the aftermath of the British diplomatic rupture, but Chicherin soon had another card up his sleeve which he played in the coming months, to counter the setback in London. Soon after Chicherin returned home, he received among other Americans a newly elected senator, Gerald Nye, by no means the first to visit Moscow, who must have immediately picked up his spirits. "The Anglo-Soviet rupture,"

Nye said, "not only does not harm Soviet-American relations, but will propel them forward." Chicherin had long favored better relations with the United States, and so Nye's words were music to his ears.

More music soon arrived from New York from S. G. Bron, the Amtorg boss, who reported that he had been talking to Charles Mitchell, the president of National City Bank, about the usual subjects of a debts settlement favorable to U.S. banks and stockholders, trade credits, and recognition.[40] It is ironic that Chicherin would take an interest in Mitchell, who is the caricature of a super-wealthy, grasping speculator of the 1920s. He was "Sunshine Charley," pockets stuffed with money, who in the early 1930s ran afoul of the New York federal attorney's office for tax evasion. Mitchell claimed to be speaking "with the knowledge of Washington," which of course heightened Chicherin's interest. The Bolsh and the banker should talk. Chicherin at once wrote to the Politburo, saying he knew nothing about the conversations with Mitchell and asking for Bron's cables. Are we talking about an agreement with American banks or the American government? Chicherin wanted to know. "Any agreement with America at the present time would take precedence . . . over any other possible international acts." Mitchell would be traveling to Paris and Berlin: he is willing to meet with us; we should talk to him, Chicherin recommended. Having read Bron's cables, Chicherin returned to the charge in dithyrambic phrases. Even a hardened Bolshevik could have his illusions. An agreement with the Americans, Chicherin opined, would "paralyze the consequences of the Anglo-Soviet rupture." It "represents for us such colossal importance, that I would recommend not to put it at risk by being too insistent in advancing demands for credits."[41] That was going very far indeed. Left unsaid by Chicherin, but certainly in his mind: with an American agreement, we could send Poincaré and France to the devil, or render them apoplectic with envy.

Trade Commissar A. I. Mikoian recalled to the Politburo the Soviet strategy with regard to the United States. "Even before the rupture with England, we had taken measures to extend our trade with America, having in view to use this channel of economic relations to attract American credit resources for the financing of foreign trade." We calculated, Mikoian went on, that the involvement of U.S. banks in our business would eventually push the U.S. government to extend recognition. This strategy had met with some success since business with the United States had increased considerably. After the rupture with Britain we had to increase our efforts to counter Tory policy "aimed at the organization of a credit-economic blockade of the USSR." American investors were looking for new profitable markets, and after the rupture with Britain, the NKVT increased its efforts to attract American investment. Mikoian's report to the Politburo was long on information but short on recommendations, proposing that Rakovskii and Piatakov, who had been named *torgpred* in Paris, should meet with Mitchell.[42]

Chicherin was of course in favor of talking to Mitchell, emphasizing again the importance of obtaining an American agreement. It would represent "a complete turnaround" in the Soviet international position. But Chicherin rounded on Mikoian who could only make one recommendation:

> Let comrades Piatakov and Rakovskii speak with Mitchell. This is the typical maneuver of the Soviet bureaucracy: talk, talk, and never arrive at anything. The Americans will not put up with this. Mitchell made definite proposals, and if he makes them to comrades Rakovskii and Piatakov, then he makes them in order to obtain a clear and definite reply. If at the meeting with him, comrades Rakovskii and Piatakov will only talk themselves out, then as a result Mitchell will say that with these people it is impossible to do business and the entire position will be lost.

So we need, said Chicherin, to develop as quickly as possible, a definite answer to Mitchell's proposals. Otherwise nothing will come of a meeting in Paris.[43]

Bron too returned to the charge with a message from Kellogg passed through "oil friends," for Bron had been talking with the president of Vacuum Oil. The message would have made a Bolshevik laugh:

> If your Bolshevik friends can say that it is not communism which is the basis and object of dispute between the USSR and England and that the difficulty to conclude with the French is tied to the desire of France to receive from them [payment of debts], when [the French] do not want to pay [their debts to] America itself, and that with us they are ready to negotiate, then I do not see special difficulties in settling our mutual relations since, and tell your Bolshevik friends, I do not see any conflicting interests between America and Russia.

And to hammer home his point, Mitchell showed Bron a copy of Kellogg's letter acknowledging receipt of their previous record of conversation. Bron asked for instructions. There was nothing of course in Kellogg's brief letter about his alleged comment to "oil friends," reported secondhand by Bron.[44]

Mikoian forwarded to the Politburo Bron's report of Kellogg's comments, and the latter, accepting Chicherin's advice, organized a committee to prepare instructions for Rakovskii and Piatakov. Everybody was excited. There was another report from Washington from Skvirskii saying that businessman Averell Harriman was pushing National City Bank to get involved in Russian business, but Mitchell said that the old bank debts had to be settled before there could be any question of business credits. Harriman's objective and that of other American businessmen was to free up credit for contracts in the USSR.[45]

The Politburo commission met quickly and made recommendations. Open negotiations in the name of the Soviet government would be "inopportune" obviously because of the continuing negotiations in Paris. The standard Soviet formula was advanced, de facto discharge of debts against important commercial credits. The Politburo added to the agenda government-to-government debts which Mitchell had not raised. Sokolnikov, the former commissar for finance, was to join Rakovskii and Piatakov in Paris to meet Mitchell. In an additional sign of Soviet intentions, the Politburo gave Bron authority to issue visas for American businessmen on an accelerated 48-hour basis.[46]

Chicherin and Mikoian were right; if they could pull off negotiations with the United States, it would be a bombshell, leaving the British and French out in the cold and looking foolish. But as in all western-Soviet negotiations, it was a long way between the cup and the lip. Could a deal be pulled off? The instructions for Soviet delegates were vague in spite of Chicherin's complaints, but at least the Politburo had moved quickly.

This was a serious initiative. Rakovskii, back in Paris, indicated in a long report that Boris Said of Standard Oil as well as Harriman were involved in the Mitchell initiative. It could be big business. Rakovskii went over the pros and cons and details of various debts and claims at stake in negotiations. He explained that Soviet credit in the United States was very expensive at 24 percent per annum and that a debts settlement which led to the end of the credit "blockade" against Soviet business would alone save the Soviet government $15 million per annum, more than enough, he did not say, to cover annual annuities to discharge a debts agreement, both private and public.[47] The Soviet government always sought to obtain more than it would have to give, and so the Politburo established an opening bargaining position of $1.5 to $2 million per annum to extinguish the debts to the National City Bank—which it is true was more than Bron had originally projected. The Bolsheviks did not like kulaks, but they bargained like them. For $2 million a year, the Politburo wanted a loan of $50 million over not less than five years and the satisfaction of unspecified Soviet claims against American banks. Both Mikoian and Chicherin insisted on the "colossal" importance of relations with the United States, but the Politburo was only willing to pay peanuts, $1.5 to $2 million a year, to achieve a settlement, even though Rakovskii noted that Soviet traders would save $15 million a year on lower interest rates. At the same time the Politburo set up a "permanent American commission" which could not have pleased Chicherin though he was to be a member of it.[48] It was another raid on NKID authority over foreign policy. Paradoxically, the Politburo seemed serious about its relations with the United States, in spite of its meager opening offer to settle the old bank debts. Of course, it was better to bid low and move up than to bid higher and refuse to budge.

The trouble was, as Litvinov signaled to Stalin, noting pointedly that he had not been at the relevant Politburo meeting, that a settlement of American bankers' claims would create a precedent which would be used by the French and Germans to make similar claims and could provoke a serious conflict with Germany. Such negotiations would also complicate Rakovskii's negotiations in Paris, Litvinov not having written them off, though Poincaré already had.[49]

On the same day Chicherin returned to the charge, because Litvinov's objections could scuttle the negotiations with Mitchell. He suggested that an agreement with the American banks could be drawn up in narrow terms so as to avoid any problems with Germany. Litvinov did not agree, Chicherin noted, and so he asked for Mikoian's opinion.[50] There was also bad news from Skvirskii in Washington. On the vital issue of credit for Soviet business in the United States, Mitchell was vague, saying only that after a debts settlement, the "usual short credit" would be available. "Long-term credit was tied to policy and dependent on the State Department."[51] If this was true, there would be no breakthrough in Soviet-American relations.

A few days later Mitchell arrived in Paris and met the Soviet trio of Rakovskii, Piatakov, and Sokolnikov on 9 and 10 September. This was a high-level Soviet delegation, sent by the Politburo, and it meant business. There are both American and Soviet records of the meetings, and they largely agree. The main sticking point was not the details of a debts settlement, but the issue of credit, the American quid pro quo for the Soviet settlement offer. The Soviet delegation zeroed in on this point:

> Almost the entire conversation spun around the possibility of the extension to us of this or that form of credit; the Americans at the beginning declared firmly that on this point there was no question. In the end they entered into a discussion of possible forms of long-term commercial credits for our orders in America. Mitchell insisted on the impossibility of banks in the present conditions taking on themselves the conduct of operations for long-term credits, but when we raised the possibility of providing concrete guarantees [i.e., collateral], Mitchell said that this changed things, since for the banks it lowered the risk.

Mitchell wanted to know what the Soviet delegates had in mind for collateral; the Soviet delegates replied that they would discuss this point if the Americans agreed in principle to the credits. At the second meeting on 10 September there was much discussion of the amount of debt owed to National City Bank and how to calculate it, but inevitably the discussion returned to the question of credit. The Soviet delegation made clear that there could be no deal without credits; Mitchell replied that he was not prepared to discuss "the question of credits" but would talk about the easing of short-term credit operations. As for collateral, Mitchell demanded 100 percent of the value of the credits placed in gold in the United States. So if the Politburo had started off with a hard position, Mitchell was even less forthcoming, and by a long way, than the Soviet delegation. In view of the impasse, the two sides agreed to meet again on 23 September.[52]

Even Chicherin was discouraged by the news from Paris. Mitchell's proposals, he informed Rakovskii, "produced a very negative impression" in the Politburo where they were discussed on 15 September.

> Everything leads us to believe that comrade Bron got carried away and that in reality in the given business there is absolutely nothing that could lead to interesting results for us, and for agreement with Mitchell there is no basis. His proposals are so ridiculous that while being read out, there was constant laughter.

So at the next meeting with Mitchell, the delegation should stick to the original Politburo instructions of 1 September offering $1.5 to $2 million and asking for $50 million in long-term credit. Chicherin emphasized that Mitchell's proposals "do not present any advantages for us; according to the proposals we only pay. If we began to pay him what he demands from us, then what do we receive for it in return?" Mitchell gave the usual reply that we would be able to create an "atmosphere of good faith," the usual line "we have heard a million times." Chicherin informed Rakovskii that after the Politburo discussion, we concluded that the only thing to do was to "get out of this business" as decently as possible.[53] This was a point which Litvinov reemphasized in a note to Stalin in order to prevent Mitchell from reporting to the State Department that any negotiations with us would be a waste of time. He therefore proposed a polite counter-proposal for Mitchell which was unlikely to be accepted, but would at least demonstrate a Soviet willingness to explore new ways of reaching agreement.[54] There was more discussion and uncertainty in Moscow about whether Mitchell might go further on the issue of credits. But the meeting on 23 September put an end to the conversations. As was to be expected, Mitchell accused the Soviet delegation of wasting his time.

The State Department reaction to the failure of the talks in Paris was as Litvinov had foreseen. Kelley, still the Bolos hater, informed Kellogg that according to National City Bank, "the Bolsheviks apparently were not prepared to make any substantial concessions of any sort."[55] Not only was this statement untrue, but it was also pot calling kettle black, at least as the Soviet side saw the problem, for Mitchell made no concessions on the one issue that mattered for the Soviet government, credits for trade. As Mitchell's colleague, Garrard Winston, informed Kellogg, "at no time did we seriously consider a clean credit for Russia."[56]

When Mitchell returned to Washington, he met with a State Department official to complain. Russia, he said, "should be surrounded with a band of iron until the disease works itself out." According to the State Department record, "Mitchell is violently opposed to the extension of any credits to Russia, believing that business should be carried on, if at all, entirely on a cash basis."[57] Of course, "Sunshine Charley" might have sung a different song if he had obtained a settlement for his bank, perhaps bragging about how he had outsmarted the Bolos and got his money without offering credit in return. Chicherin thus correctly concluded that negotiations were pointless and should be concluded as decently as possible. Litvinov was correct also; the only way to get positive results was to negotiate directly with the U.S. government. This attempt would have to wait until 1933.

There was one other aspect of these talks which brings us back to the Franco-Soviet negotiations. Prior to the last meeting with Mitchell, Rakovskii wrote to Chicherin that Poincaré had apparently received information on the negotiations, and very likely his supporters would put the "maximum pressure" on Mitchell to break off discussions.[58] On the American side, there was similar information. "I believe," Winston wrote to Kellogg,

> that the French government decoded the messages between the Soviet representatives in Paris, conducting these negotiations, and Moscow. It was even reported that the French Government had dictagraphs in the rooms in which we met. I am not certain of this . . . [but] I was told that the French Government was anxious that no settlement be arrived at with us and gave this information for private dissemination with the expectation that it would help to kill all negotiations.[59]

Anti-communist Frenzy in Paris

We left the narrative of Franco-Soviet negotiations at the end of May when Chicherin was in Paris and met a hostile and negative Poincaré. During the summer the anti-communist press campaign built in intensity, as it had in Britain. Communist deputies André Marty and Marcel Cachin, among others, were arrested for anti-military propaganda. The right-wing press loudly approved.[60] Poincaré gave written instructions to Monzie not to acknowledge fresh concessions from Rakovskii and to press the new demands on war debts and compensation for nationalized property.

It is the more astonishing then that Monzie and the Quai d'Orsay civil servant, Labonne, secretly attempted to go *in exactly the opposite direction.* On 22 June Labonne met Chlenov and explained Poincaré's position. Then Labonne asked if the Soviet government wanted to sign a debts settlement or to break off negotiations.

Would credits be included in the agreement? Chlenov asked.

Labonne replied that the formula of a debts settlement in exchange for credits came from the French delegation, and in particular from him, "and that the ministry of foreign affairs did not have the habit of going back on its word. Hence, if the Soviet side wanted an agreement on these terms, it could be done." Chlenov did not openly express his doubts about the integrity of the Quai d'Orsay, and the two agreed that their bosses, Rakovskii and Monzie, should meet.[61]

Labonne saw Rakovskii a few days later. French opinion was shifting to the right. Elections were coming, and Poincaré wanted to take from the left its "only trump" in foreign policy. To deliver the finishing stroke, Poincaré had to prevent an agreement with the USSR. A debts agreement could change events, but without it, the future boded ill for the left.

"Franco-Soviet relations now hung only by a string," said Labonne; though a complete rupture was unlikely, relations would be kept to an "unimportant minimum."[62]

In July Rakovskii met often with Monzie, sometimes long into the night. Monzie confirmed Labonne's assessment.

What about Herriot? asked Rakovskii.

"Spineless," replied Monzie, who was not his friend.

When will you have a proposal? asked Rakovskii.

It's coming, Monzie promised.

The finance ministry chronicler of the negotiations, Monsieur Bizot, accused Monzie of "clandestine démarches" with the Soviet ambassador, which was true. We could find ourselves, Bizot complained, faced with a *fait accompli.* Also true, this was *exactly* Monzie's strategy. Finance strategy was to keep talking to Labonne in order to "moderate Monzie."[63] Hah! If Bizot pinned his hopes on Labonne, he had bought a lemon!

On 23 July Rakovskii saw Poincaré to hear a *reprise* of the May meeting with Chicherin. Poincaré said there would be no credits for the Soviet Union until there were better political relations, and this could not occur until there was an end to Comintern support for the French communists. It was yet another demand because Poincaré could not be sure he had killed the negotiations.

And for good reason: later that same day Monzie and Labonne proposed to Rakovskii $60 million in credits over five years, a long way from the $225 million demanded by the Soviet government, but still an offer flying in the face of Poincaré. According to a Quai d'Orsay note, Monzie told Rakovskii that this was the maximum French concession, that the French government's acceptance even of this proposal was "highly problematic," and that "it would be very desirable for the USSR to give immediately its formal approval [to the proposal], failing which we fear a rapid rupture of Franco-Soviet relations."

The offer is derisory, Rakovskii replied.

The $60 million could be expanded later, said Monzie, but not now: any allusion to such intentions in "the present mood of hostility" in France would provoke a "storm of protest."

Would the credits be tied to war debts and expropriated property? asked Rakovskii.

"Monzie and Labonne declared that they will take on themselves the elimination of such links." Little wonder the French negotiators declined to put their proposals to Rakovskii on paper. These would have to come from the Soviet side. Monzie hoped, so Labonne informed Herbette, that when Rakovskii returned from consultations in Moscow in August, he could give unambiguous approval to the French credit proposal, which was the only way to overcome opposition in Paris. Briand may also have hoped, since he knew about Monzie's offer and did nothing to prevent it. But someone in the Quai d'Orsay, trying to stop Monzie, sent the proposal to Poincaré. We have not yet heard the reaction, Labonne told Herbette: "If it should be as negative as the mood of the *bureaux* of the rue de Rivoli [i.e., the finance ministry], we will be in desperate straits."[64]

Rakovskii duly left for Moscow. While he was away, Labonne lobbied other Soviet officials. He repeated his arguments that a rapid agreement was essential before it ran up against the elections. Right and left were girding for battle, and the right intended to make the "struggle against communism" its main platform, just as the Tories were doing in Britain. But if the Soviet government accepted Monzie's proposals now, Poincaré would be hard put to reject them; otherwise he could be demolished in the elections.[65] Labonne was not the only *intrigant*. Victor Dalbiez, deputy head of the French delegation, went behind his boss Monzie's back to Poincaré with a proposal to scuttle the talks. We don't want to offend the British, he said, and we have no credits to offer the Russians.

We need to be careful, cautioned Bizot, that the French government does not get the blame for the failure of negotiations. Fresh demands should be enough to cause a breakdown.[66] It was an electoral issue; Poincaré did not want to lose the holders of tsarist bonds. Ironically, this sounded like the NKID and the Foreign Office always trying to appear positive about negotiations when in fact neither side really was.

The Soviet government took Monzie's proposals seriously. The Politburo quickly organized a commission to consider the new offer, which Chicherin supposed came from the French government. He was also willing to make other concessions, proposing a circular to all Soviet diplomatic and commercial posts stressing the importance of non-interference in the domestic politics of other countries.[67]

Rakovskii returned to Paris on 17 August. He was preparing for negotiations with Mitchell, but he immediately saw Monzie and Labonne, who wanted to know if the Soviet government had accepted their proposals. Rakovskii explained the new Soviet position: 60 million gold francs per annum to pay off the tsarist debt and $120 million in credits, double what Monzie had proposed, but down from the original $225 million. Monzie and Labonne replied that the $60 million was "the maximum of the maximum," that even this offer would be difficult to promote, and that Poincaré "dreams of only one thing, in what manner he can break up the conference." Monzie and Labonne calculated on relying on the Quai d'Orsay and in particular on Briand, and on the threat of Monzie's resignation, to advance their position. Don't put these new proposals in writing, Labonne warned; it would provide Poincaré with a pretext to scuttle negotiations. Rakovskii did not think the French offer was final but rather that Labonne was simply maneuvering to promote his own proposal.[68] How wrong he was.

It was not clear to Moscow at that moment, but the negotiations were doomed. Rakovskii unwisely signed a Trotskyist opposition declaration in Moscow on 10 August stating that the Soviet government should encourage desertion among western armies waging war on the USSR.[69] This was the same day that Rakovskii met with the Politburo commission to discuss instructions for the meeting with Mitchell. Soviet politicians were good at juggling government business with their party infighting.

The day after his return to Paris, Rakovskii went to see the political director of the Quai d'Orsay, Jean de Beaumarchais. Rakovskii said he had further propositions to make to the French government, but Beaumarchais replied frigidly, wanting instead to discuss Rakovskii's endorsement of military desertion. The French government, he warned, would lodge a protest in Moscow. To this observation, "Rakovskii affected great astonishment," recorded Beaumarchais, saying that his signature on the opposition statement of 10 August had nothing to do with France. After Rakovskii outlined the new Soviet proposals, including a non-aggression pact, Beaumarchais commented that the Soviet government would do better to call a halt to communist propaganda in France. À la guerre, comme à la guerre, replied Rakovskii, in wartime all governments use such tactics. A reasonable reply, and true, but no one was going to listen to reason in the anti-communist frenzy which erupted in Paris in that August of 1927.[70]

Rakovskii's meeting with Beaumarchais was a mistake, Labonne thought. The Soviet proposals "were immediately transmitted to the other side of the water [i.e., the Seine, to the rue de Rivoli]. You can imagine the effect." I told Rakovskii without any beating around the bush that his action could scuttle negotiations. We've been sabotaged by Poincaré and his officials, Labonne said; the council of ministers was worked up and indignant. Politics had "devoured" the negotiations. To Chlenov, Labonne said that Rakovskii's meeting with Beaumarchais had put him in a bind because the finance ministry had rounded on Monzie for offering credits without its authorization.[71] Incredibly, Monzie was still optimistic. Rakovskii wants to see me, Monzie told Labonne. Would he accept our July proposals? "If he agrees, is not my position extraordinary? To fear a yes from my interlocutor."[72]

This should have been the least of Monzie's worries. On 21 August, on instructions from Paris, Herbette met Chicherin to lodge a formal complaint about Rakovskii's signature on the opposition declaration. Chicherin tried to dismiss it as unimportant: France was not targeted or even mentioned in the opposition declaration. The conversation drifted into the usual subjects of the Comintern, propaganda, and money for the French Communist Party. Herbette made some suggestions about how to reply to the French protest.[73]

Chicherin was vexed and complained to Stalin: Rakovskii's signature on a document, "not having anything at all to do with diplomacy and even being the opposite of such, compels us to draw attention to this general fact, before which the Narkomindel is powerless without the active intervention of the decision-making bodies of the party."

> Ambassadors of the USSR must take into account their situation as ambassadors. They do not always do this and it puts the USSR in a difficult position. A diplomat is a diplomat; he is involved in all sorts of relationships, the neglect of which can cause the most serious damage to the political and economic interests of the USSR.

The NKID kollegiia therefore asked the Politburo to establish the principle that ambassadors must keep in mind their diplomatic status in all public statements, even of a party nature.[74]

That did not solve the problem at hand, and the NKID issued a statement on 26 August disapproving of Rakovskii's signature on the opposition declaration. It was not good enough for Poincaré who wanted to rub it in.

The Quai d'Orsay therefore returned to the charge, demanding a "formal disavowal" and linking Rakovskii's signature with similar statements published in an unimportant communist newspaper called *La Caserne*, with which the Soviet ambassador had no relations whatever. Obviously the French government was trying to pick a fight. On 29 August Herbette demanded another urgent meeting with Chicherin to deliver the message. "Herbette made an extraordinarily long declaration, partly based on a telegram or telegrams from Briand and partly on commentaries of Herbette himself." They then went back and forth on the usual issues which Chicherin reported to Stalin in a long letter. At the end of the conversation they agreed that the Soviet government "considered inadmissible" (*nedopustimyi*) Rakovskii's unfortunate signature.[75] Herbette used the word "disavow" in his cable to Paris, which is not the word Chicherin used, but the Quai d'Orsay in a cable drafted by Berthelot accepted the Soviet declaration and said it would be published in the Paris press.[76]

"Expel Rakovskii!"

This was far from the end of Rakovskii's gaffe. The drama's last act played out in September. On 23 August there were violent street demonstrations in Paris after the execution in the United States of anarchists Sacco and Vanzetti on what appeared to be trumped-up murder convictions. At the same time *Le Matin* started publishing alleged incriminating Soviet documents—which Scotland Yard reckoned were forgeries—on a new subversive campaign in French colonies.[77] The Paris papers also got wind of the opposition declaration in Moscow. The French right pounced on poor Rakovskii like starving predators. On 4 September a right-wing press campaign opened up which aimed at his expulsion and the breaking of diplomatic relations with the USSR. The "comrade-ambassador" has been caught dead to rights meddling in French affairs: throw him out, said the right-wing press, and shut down the "Red embassy" on the rue de Grenelle.[78] *Le Matin* was again in the van of the attacks. "I hear," Phipps wrote to London, "that the 'Matin' campaign for the recall of Monsieur Rakowsky is inspired by the Minister of the Interior, Monsieur Albert Sarraut, who preaches to a willing listener on this point to Monsieur Bunau-Varilla."[79] If Phipps' information was correct, Sarraut was working against Briand who opposed a rupture of relations with Moscow. Readers should be reminded of the late Krasin's comment on French politicians: "One . . . has to take into account the rivalries between these gentlemen and their willingness to kick the legs out from under one another." Sarraut was not the only culprit. "Berthelot told me in confidence," advised Phipps, "that he had evidence that the violent campaign in the

French Press . . . was being paid for by oil mogul, Sir Henri Deterding." The fee was £10,000, according to Rakovskii, which was not beer money.[80] Deterding was the British equivalent of the slippery, grasping American banker Mitchell. His Royal Dutch Shell had lost its oil concessions in the Caucasus, and if Deterding could not get them back, he would retaliate against Moscow where he could. In Paris a report from the *Sûreté générale* surmised that the anti-Rakovskii campaign was being "encouraged or perhaps even being subsidized by England."[81] It was a gang-up on poor Rakovskii; nothing personal, mind you, but rather aimed at the USSR.

At the end of August Briand thought that the NKID's disapproval of Rakovskii's gaffe had closed the matter. But after Briand left for League of Nations meetings in Geneva, the French cabinet went behind his back to ask for Rakovskii's recall. Briand heard about it through the press and threatened to resign. "It is impossible for me to believe," said Briand, "that the foreign relations of France can be influenced by press campaigns and decided under such pressure." Poincaré tried to conciliate Briand on the matter of the press leak, but on the main issue, Rakovskii's recall, he was adamant. Berthelot admitted to Phipps that the French government was on "distinctly weak ground" to insist on Rakovskii's recall, but Briand did not resign and Poincaré got his way.[82] And all the while Rakovskii and his colleagues were trying to obtain a settlement with Mitchell of National City Bank.

Monzie, who was on holiday, read about the press rumors of Rakovskii's recall and publicly disagreed with Poincaré, endorsing Rakovskii and implicitly threatening to publish "the possibilities of an agreement which in principle had been achieved."[83] Publicity of this nature was exactly what finance officials preferred to avoid, but which now erupted. Press communiqués on the state of negotiations began to fly back and forth: Litvinov said the two sides were close to agreement on debts; the French falsely denied it. Rakovskii confronted Monzie at his apartment, accusing him of deceit. The ensuing loud argument drew curious neighbors around Monzie's door. I was trying to head off Poincaré, Monzie protested, which caused a row with finance officials, including Bizot.[84]

And still Labonne angled for a deal. He met several times with Chlenov in mid-September, urging the Soviet delegation to accept the 60 and 60 formula. Rakovskii's gaffe was not serious, said Labonne; it was only a pretext to launch a campaign against the USSR. If it had not been this pretext, it would have been another. Now no one in France was interested in the conference, debts, or credits. Poincaré wanted to put the negotiations to sleep; Chlenov called it the "policy of the night light," *politika nochnoi lampochki*. The recall of Rakovskii was not personal; no one had anything against him. Labonne said that the recall idea was "very popular in the cabinet and even

in the Quai d'Orsay." Poincaré wanted to downgrade Franco-Soviet relations, recall Rakovskii, and recall Herbette, leaving only chargés d'affaires
in Paris and Moscow. "Everything was subordinated to considerations of
electoral politics; the campaign had already begun and pre-election passions
were rising . . . the war against communism is the main platform." Readers
should be reminded of Rozengol'ts' and Litvinov's analyses of British electoral politics, for the situation in France was identical. Labonne thought the
dynamics might still be changed if the Soviet government sweetened its offers by paying the first annuity of 60 million gold francs. The gesture would
cause a sensation on the Bourse. The atmosphere would be transformed and
the press campaign stopped dead in its tracks. If you make the gesture, said
Labonne, you can count on six votes against five in the cabinet, though he
did not include two other likely hostile votes.[85]

The NKID paid attention. The sound of "ringing metal" might have a
calming effect on the press campaign, or it might not, said Litvinov; we
ought not to risk such a sum. But he agreed to put 30 million francs in escrow in a French bank, to be made payable on condition of an agreement on
credits.[86] Incredibly, Bizot knew it was Labonne's idea, and he was not happy.
"It was to put a knife to the throat of the government." Developments are
shaping up, wrote Bizot, into a "moral disaster." "The Soviets will publish
that they are negotiating credits. . . . We are going to find ourselves faced
immediately with this refusal [to continue negotiations]."[87]

Only the delicacy of the situation and the need to avoid a scandal must
have saved the mutinous Labonne's job. The expulsion of Rakovskii offered
a better way out, and on 25 September the French government officially
requested his recall. As Bizot put it trenchantly, "If Rakovskii is recalled =
the business will be settled."[88] By the way, readers should not worry about
Labonne; he kept his job at the Quai d'Orsay. In 1940 he became the last
ambassador of the Third Republic to Moscow, as France collapsed under the
guns of the Wehrmacht. True to the end, Labonne tried to salvage something from the wreckage of Franco-Soviet relations even then. Too late, was
the Soviet reply.

Apart from French electoral politics and the anti-communist campaign,
the finance ministry would not endorse, organize, or guarantee trade credits
to the Soviet Union under any circumstances, *even if finance officials considered Soviet offers for a debt settlement to be acceptable.* Moreover, the mere
discussion of "'credits' . . . could not fail to have a definitely considerable
[favorable] influence on the domestic and international situation of the
USSR." And just to make sure that Monzie did not "dig up" another *fait accompli,* he was forbidden to make any further written communications to the
head of the Soviet delegation.[89]

Rakovskii's Fate

This left the question of whether Rakovskii would remain in Paris or not. The maneuvering over his recall went on throughout September and into October. It became a drama. Poincaré wanted Rakovskii out of Paris. The NKID resisted. Chicherin and Litvinov knew, as did Poincaré, that Rakovskii's recall would kill Franco-Soviet negotiations. But at the beginning of September, things looked to be calming down. On 2 September Herbette, who still advocated a moderate course, noted that Rakovskii's signature was not so bad. It was no different in fact than placards displayed at the French front inviting German soldiers to pass to the French side.[90] On 4 September Herbette informed Chicherin that the Rakovskii incident was closed and that his position had been "saved." Chicherin made clear to Herbette that the NKID had not "disavowed" Rakovskii but had only disapproved of his signature on the opposition declaration. Herbette took note. Inevitably, the subject of the Comintern came up. "Is it possible in Paris, not to understand," asked Chicherin,

> that there are things which are impossible for the Comintern IKKI? We cannot forbid the Comintern to meet, to write, to support its members. Our historical position is tied to our role as a communist government, and that position binds us. I mentioned that the most powerful person, and even the pope is a captive not only of the Italian government but even more so of his own program and the organization which he represents. In Nibelungen, Wotan, king of the Gods, is more bound than anyone else. In the end you have to stop making completely unrealistic demands and requests.

Readers may wonder whether Chicherin's fictional Wotan was Stalin. Herbette laughed at Chicherin's image but repeated that the Comintern should not send money to the French Communist Party.[91] The conversation turned to other subjects, as it always did when the Comintern came up for discussion. In his cable to Paris, Herbette said that he had taken it upon himself to say to Chicherin that if he had failed to make the statement of 29 August, Rakovskii could not have remained in Paris.[92] This comment does not appear in Chicherin's record, which indicated that the two parted on good terms.

The main thing for Chicherin was that Rakovskii's position had been saved, as indeed Briand thought it had also. But whether it had or not remained to be seen, and the news from Paris continued to grow worse. Chicherin did not like the fact that the Quai d'Orsay had published an incomplete version of his comments on the Rakovskii gaffe, and he did not think the French communiqué could be left unanswered, for this might give the impression that the NKID did not support its ambassador in Paris. But he feared that a Soviet response would only make matters worse, causing an even "bigger scandal and . . . even more negative consequences." Rakovskii recommended not getting "into a polemic with the Quai d'Orsay"; Piatakov, still in Paris, recommended challenging the French. Chicherin concluded that the NKID could not remain silent and that some kind of low-key response correcting French "distortions" should be published in Moscow.[93]

While the Politburo debated what to do, Rakovskii complained, saying the right-wing press was exploiting the alleged NKID "disavowal" of its ambassador. It's a "strange situation," and not a word out of Moscow. "I understand," Rakovskii wrote, "the present tangled and delicate situation, but an escape from it you must find there, and not here."[94]

Litvinov also thought Rakovskii's gaffe had been settled, but he was wrong. Chicherin was irritated by Rakovskii's cable: "Either we suffer the rogue pronouncements of the Quai d'Orsay . . . or get into polemics with it; we have to do one or the other in indirect, covert form." Chicherin's irritation with Rakovskii was unfair since the Soviet government faced a dilemma. The NKID still wanted to salvage *something* from the negotiations in Paris, but the situation was deteriorating by the day, as Chicherin advised Stalin: on 10 September the Havas news agency reported that the French cabinet had decided that "in the best interests of Franco-Soviet relations," Rakovskii should go. "Poincaré has for a long time been sharpening his teeth on Rakovskii," Chicherin observed, "and this latest step is likely a reflection of his wishes and efforts." In the final analysis, if the French government made a formal request for Rakovskii's recall, we will have to comply.[95]

Tempers were rising. Litvinov wrote to Chicherin that he had not done anything on the Rakovskii file since Chicherin was handling it, but he complained, "You have sent a number of letters to the Politburo, not once putting the question to a discussion in the *Kollegiia*." Here was an example of a clash between the commissar and his deputy. "Of course there is no need for two people to do the same thing," Litvinov continued, but I remind you that at the last meeting of the *kollegiia*, I expressed my "bewilderment regarding the concealment from our press and from our public opinion of the new phase in which our relations with France have entered." The NKID, Litvinov concluded, could comment on the right-wing press campaign without entering into a polemic directly with Briand. In other words, we need to respond.[96]

"I remind you [Vam]," Chicherin replied sharply,

that already a week ago I officially put the question [to the Politburo] about informing our readers of the affair concerning Comrade Rakovskii; thereupon I sent a draft of such an informative communiqué and thereupon I wrote several times officially on that very same subject. You [vy] had copies of all these letters. Only now do we have the objective possibility of publicizing the right-wing press campaign without a polemic with Briand, while a few days ago publication [osvedomlenie] would have been linked necessarily to a polemic against Briand.

The difference being that the NKID now knew of the rift, such as it was, between Poincaré and Briand.[97]

On orders of the Politburo, Chicherin summoned Herbette on 12 September. This time there would be no allegorical references to Wotan. Chicherin laid hip and thigh into Herbette, passing in review recent Franco-Soviet relations, the "hooligan right-wing press campaign," British influences and that of the oilman Deterding against the USSR. If Berthelot knew about Deterding's financing of the Paris press campaign, so did Chicherin, who continued his long monologue about the "communiqués, counter-communiqués, denials" over Rakovskii and especially about the "disloyal characterization of [his] declaration to Herbette" concerning the so-called disavowal of Rakovskii. In reply, Herbette took responsibility for the use of the word "disavowal," thinking, so he said to Chicherin, that it would put an end to the controversy. He also confirmed that Briand had considered the affair closed. But then the situation had deteriorated again. Herbette said he had not received any instructions but that he had been reading the Paris papers. And here the ambassador broached the subject of the recall of Rakovskii.

The Soviet government wants to keep Rakovskii in Paris, Chicherin said; "like a good soldier," he is willing to remain at his post.

"I very much like Rakovskii," Herbette responded. "I respect his work . . . would be sorry if Rakovskii were forced to leave Paris." But if he is not recalled, the issue of a diplomatic rupture could arise.

"It would be a serious blow for our relations," replied Chicherin.

The call for soldiers to desert, Herbette said, made a bad impression among people not normally hostile to the USSR. He reiterated that the Quai d'Orsay communiqué was intended to end the affair.

The articles and communiqués in the French press have produced a very bad impression in Moscow; they could compel us, Chicherin remarked, to publish the exchange of notes.

"I would not recommend this," retorted Herbette, "it could be very dangerous." Very few people were thinking about a rupture with the USSR, he continued, but "others are thinking about a platform for the elections; they want to return to the situation in 1919 [i.e., the Red Scare of that year]; and meanwhile the left finds itself in a difficult situation." Rakovskii's signature "would not improve the situation of the left parties in the elections; it threatened them with a loss of votes." Herbette appeared to imply, Chicherin reported, that the left could sacrifice Rakovskii in order to improve their situation during the upcoming elections.

What would you recommend that I put in a cable to Paris? Herbette asked.

Inform them of the distortion of my words about the "disavowal" of Rakovskii, Chicherin replied.

Herbette laughed. If I do that, I will get a return cable from Paris telling me to pack my bags. The ambassador added that for the time being the Quai d'Orsay was "leaving him in peace," not sending him instructions. Let's let sleeping dogs lie, he appeared to imply.[98]

Herbette's report to Paris of his meeting at the NKID was somewhat different than Chicherin's. He maintained the myth of the "disavowal," saying only that Chicherin, not he, had hoped the statement would put an end to the controversy. Herbette obviously did not want to pack his bags, though he did correctly report that Chicherin would greatly regret Rakovskii's recall and that his gaffe was merely a pretext in Paris to justify a rupture of relations. At the end Herbette offered his opinion that a rupture was not in French interests, but that the Quai d'Orsay should lay down its conditions for the continuation of relations with Moscow.[99]

For whatever reasons, Herbette had doctored Chicherin's words on Rakovskii's gaffe and refused to own up to it afterward, deceiving the Quai d'Orsay and threatening Chicherin with dangerous consequences if the NKID published the deception in the press. On 13 September, the day following Chicherin's meeting with Herbette, Izvestiia published the first Soviet comments on the Paris press campaign, taking up many of Chicherin's points to Herbette but not saying anything about the ambassador's doctoring of the NKID position. Several other Moscow papers also published comments on the following day, a summary of which Herbette sent to Paris. The articles underlined the Soviet wish to improve relations with France.[100]

At the same time Herbette was still without instructions from Paris, a sign perhaps of Briand's clandestine resistance to Poincaré. On his own initiative, Herbette began to lobby the Soviet government to recall Rakovskii "voluntarily" without a formal demand from the Quai d'Orsay. He first broached the subject with the NKID press boss Rotshtein on 14 September.[101]

Chicherin had a series of subsequent meetings with Herbette where the same issues were rehashed. "In tragic phrases," Chicherin commented sarcastically, Herbette claimed he had done his best in the cause of Franco-Soviet relations and that his "conscience was clear." What is the French policy Chicherin wanted to know, complete rupture or the nochnaia lampochka? Herbette avoided a reply. He repeated his idea that the Soviet government should recall Rakovskii voluntarily, but that he had no instructions on this point and that if Rakovskii considered that he could remain in Paris, then he, Herbette, had nothing against it.

This was *not* what Herbette was saying to Paris. Chicherin continued to be galled by Herbette's distortion of his statement on Rakovskii's gaffe. At this point the Soviet press was responding daily to the press campaign in Paris, but it did not reveal Herbette's legerdemain. Chicherin put his finger on the issue which Poincaré wanted to pass over, the fate of the French bondholders. If you don't want our money, the 60 million, Chicherin told Herbette, well and good, we will keep it at home. In reporting this conversation to Paris, Herbette continued to recommend against a rupture of relations with Moscow, but not against Rakovskii's recall.[102]

Herbette had been reading the Paris papers and was not sure of the ultimate outcome of Rakovskii's gaffe. On 16 September, Herbette asked the Quai d'Orsay for advanced instructions in anticipation of a rupture, in order to protect French citizens and property in the USSR. The Quai d'Orsay responded that there was no plan to break off relations with Moscow, but that Rakovskii did not seem to be the appropriate Soviet representative to continue negotiations in Paris.[103]

These instructions prompted Herbette to return to the NKID on 18 September to see Chicherin to convey this information. "With a very gloomy face," Chicherin reported (again, sarcastically), Herbette regretted the necessity of passing to "a very difficult and unpleasant moment in the conversation," that of the French government's desire for Rakovskii's recall. Herbette then repeated the information that he had received from Paris. The bait to encourage Soviet compliance was the French willingness to discuss the non-aggression pact proposed by Rakovskii. Even on this question, however, the French government was playing false, for it intended to load such negotiations, if ever they occurred, with so many impossible demands on the Comintern, propaganda, and so on, that Moscow could never accept them.[104]

On 20 September Berthelot conveyed the same message to Rakovskii in Paris. There was no hope that the French government would modify its position, said Berthelot; you should consider the general interests of your mission and not try to hang on, putting at risk what you have accomplished to improve Franco-Soviet relations.[105] This line, already advanced by Herbette, was badly received in Moscow. Neither Chicherin nor Litvinov was prepared to recommend recall to the Politburo.

While Chicherin equivocated for want of information—although he had a good deal from Labonne via Chlenov in Paris—Litvinov was more decisive. If the French want Rakovskii out of Paris, he wrote to Stalin, let them take the responsibility and make the formal request for his recall. Litvinov was nothing if not consistent; he did not share Chicherin's patience with the French.[106]

And there was a further wrinkle: Ambassador Rantzau went to see Chicherin in some alarm, having heard the stories of possible negotiations for a Franco-Soviet non-aggression pact. Prospects of a Franco-Soviet accord which might include Soviet recognition of Poland's western frontiers always aroused intense German anxieties. Chicherin reassured Rantzau that Soviet policy toward Germany remained unchanged, and he wrote to Stalin to recommend caution. "We have to maneuver and tack with the greatest caution and attention between underwater reefs surrounding us on all sides."[107] Rantzau need not have worried. The French were not half so clever. Poincaré did not have the slightest intention of negotiating anything with Moscow, whatever Briand might have been thinking. The non-aggression pact was just a mirage to get Rakovskii out of Paris and so to scuttle the debt negotiations.

Chicherin wrote to Rakovskii asking for more information. "In the present scrape, some things are not clear to me." Briand seems to be pursuing a "zigzag" policy. And the biggest zigzags are coming from Herbette who appears to have changed his position. "What kind of fly," Chicherin asked, "has bitten Herbette's butt?" And what about the elections? "Herbette told me that your continuation in Paris could be expensive for the Radicals during the elections, costing them seats in the Chamber of Deputies." Litvinov sent a similar note to Rakovskii. He also asked about Herbette, who

> is playing a strange role in which not only does he fail to fulfill the directives from Paris . . . but in his own name he is making the stupidest of proposals to Paris, pouring oil on the fire. We know, from a very reliable source [Litvinov's code for intercepted documents or cables], that he is proposing to Briand . . . a formal demand for your recall. . . . Aside from that, his tone has become absolutely insulting.

Would you know, asked Litvinov, what has come over Herbette?[108]

Herbette had "obviously" turned his jacket, replied Rakovskii; he is in contact with "French reactionaries" and wants "to curry favor with Poincaré."[109] In the meantime Rakovskii reported on his meeting with Berthelot, and Herbette informed Chicherin of it on the following day, 21 September. Litvinov was incensed that this information had been leaked all over the French press, and not by us, Litvinov later said pointedly to Herbette. You can drop the act about the "delicacy" of the situation and not leaking information to the press. This remark came during a very tough exchange between Litvinov and Herbette on 28 September. Herbette retorted that the French government, especially Poincaré, did not like the fact that Rakovskii had appealed to French bondholders over the head of the government. The offer of 30 million in escrow on the first year's debt repayment was beyond French patience, although the original idea came from Labonne. Herbette had immediately protested to Chicherin when he heard about it. This remained the vulnerable point of Poincaré's policy because the bondholders were to be sacrificed to his electoral politics.

"France is not China," Herbette exclaimed, "where Borodin could pursue such a policy." Comparing Rakovskii to Borodin was theatrical. Litvinov let the ambassador go on for a while and then he pulled the string, asking pointedly who had informed Paris of Rakovskii's signature on the opposition declaration.

"Herbette, very confused and turning red, muttered that he, of course, communicated to his government all that he considered worthy of its attention." In fact, of course, he had done more than that, pouncing immediately on Rakovskii's gaffe and proposing that the Quai d'Orsay "take advantage" of the situation, though without rupture or recall.[110] Litvinov suggested to Herbette that the Quai d'Orsay could have put a stop to the press campaign at any time. Instead, all sorts of declarations, both true and invented, coming from ministers' mouths, were published, throwing "oil on the fire." We held our fire as long as we could, Litvinov continued, until it looked like the French government intended to break off relations. And it was impossible not to note that the press campaign started at the same time a debts agreement appeared to be coming together. Litvinov repeated that if the French government wanted Rakovskii to be recalled, it should take the responsibility by making a formal demand. At the end of the conversation, which went on for two hours according to Herbette, Litvinov asked if the French government was going to call off the campaign against Rakovskii or at least bring it back within the "bounds of decency."

Can you remember, Litvinov asked Herbette, any case where an ambassador has been so villainously treated . . . called a bastard (kanal'ia, canaille) or portrayed in a caricature as a pile of "horse shit"?

I am willing to use my influence to calm the press campaign, Herbette replied, provided that you use your influence to obtain Rakovskii's recall.

"I replied indignantly," wrote Litvinov, "that such a promise I could not give him."

"At the end," Litvinov recorded,

Herbette tried to indulge in a lyrical outpouring about the difficulties of his position, of his sleepless nights, of his boring life, and so on, but I let all of this fall on deaf ears. He left very agitated, knowing, that we by no means consider him a friend and that we no longer retain our previous trust in him.

I have outlined in such detail the conversation because of the inclination of diplomatic representatives, and especially Herbette, to attribute to their interlocutor their own thoughts and suggestions and to distort conversations.[111]

This observation hit Herbette between the eyes. Since the beginning of the Rakovskii controversy, the ambassador had done just that, notably in reporting that Chicherin had "disavowed" his ambassador in Paris. According to Herbette's report, Litvinov had opined that the French government should calm the press in Paris. "I responded to him," wrote Herbette, "that before telegraphing his words to Paris, I was obliged to wait for the settling of the Rakovskii *affaire*."[112] Litvinov must have known of Herbette's distortions in reading his communications to Paris, supplied by Soviet intelligence. The British were not the only ones who could pry.

Litvinov reported to Stalin that Rakovskii's optimism about a Franco-Soviet settlement was "somewhat exaggerated." There was still the blockage on credits and the likely presentation of new demands. Herbette's statement "should be attributed to his usual attempts at intimidation."

"France cannot now bring itself to a complete rupture," Litvinov wrote to Stalin. "It is possible however that there will be new dirty tricks." As for Rakovskii's recall, Litvinov recommended trying to stall, getting the French government to put off a decision for a month or two.[113]

The conflict over Rakovskii dragged on for another fortnight. Chicherin and especially Litvinov were furious with the French government, and with Herbette, and they intended to make Rakovskii's recall as hard as possible. On 25 and 30 September the Quai d'Orsay sent cables to Herbette asking for, and then insisting on, the recall of Rakovskii. On 1 October Herbette read to Litvinov, Chicherin being ill, the French government's declaration asking for Rakovskii's recall. When asked for a copy of the declaration, Herbette refused to hand it over, though he held out the mirage of continued negotiations if Rakovskii were recalled.[114] On 3 October a United Press dispatch indicated erroneously that Chicherin had agreed to the recall. Litvinov recommended a complete denial.

Three days later Litvinov signed a formal letter to Herbette refusing to accept the ambassador's verbal request for Rakovskii's recall.[115] Obviously the *zamnarkom* was not going to make things easy for Herbette.

An NKID bureau chief handed over a written reply to Herbette at 8 p.m. on 4 October. The ambassador had apparently expected a verbal reply and was "somewhat agitated" when handed Litvinov's letter. "As he read the letter," according to the desk chief's report, "Herbette's emotion visibly increased, and his face went from pale to almost white." Clearly the NKID clerk enjoyed writing this report, and he continued,

After having finished his reading, he rose suddenly from his place, and in a hoarse voice noted, "*Chto zhe eto?* What is this, mistrust of the ambassador?" . . . Then Herbette began again to repeat that he personally had made every effort so that the incident was not inflated and extended, and that Briand and the French government also were against a deepening of the conflict and against a rupture. "But such things . . ." (there Herbette shook the envelope and did not finish his sentence).[116]

Litvinov wanted to deliver a message to Herbette, which clearly he had understood, that the NKID no longer trusted him. In diplomacy there are always ways to make a statement without uttering a single word.

The French government and Herbette returned to the charge on 6 October with a formal request for recall. Herbette asked for an immediate meeting, and in his bed an ailing Chicherin received him at 11:00 in the evening. The ambassador delivered the written demand for recall. Chicherin asked after the health of Herbette and his wife and they discussed Chicherin's "injured foot." Not a long conversation, unlike the dramatic meeting with Litvinov on 28 September, and the ambassador took his leave.[117] Chicherin recognized that the Soviet government had no choice but to recall Rakovskii, though he was in no hurry to reply to Herbette. Litvinov disagreed, reversing himself and arguing that dragging things out now would only make matters worse. "We should," Litvinov recommended to Stalin, "retreat, returning fire, and not simply surrender the position."[118] In the end the Politburo followed Litvinov's advice. The crisis ended quietly when in mid-October Rakovskii left Paris unceremoniously by car early on a Sunday morning. The French right-wing press gloated over its victory. Deceiving the Quai d'Orsay, Herbette concluded smugly that in Litvinov's view the USSR preferred to have France as a "friend" than as an adversary.[119] In the run-up to 1939, this assessment would certainly be true, but Herbette was not thinking that far ahead. In the meantime, he had burned his bridges at the NKID.

As the crisis wound down, Chicherin wrote to Rakovskii to explain the NKID's position. We were thrown off, he admitted, by Herbette's statement on 4 September that you had been "saved." "In reviewing authentic materials [*podlinnye materialy*; this being an oblique reference to Herbette's intercepted correspondence], I see that the demand for your recall runs like a red thread beginning on 20 August [the date when the first cable from Paris arrived in Moscow]."[120] There were "zigzags" in French policy, said Chicherin, but the main objective remained unchanged. Rakovskii reckoned that the USSR had suffered a defeat. Chicherin did not think so since once the formal request for recall was made the NKID had no choice but to comply.[121]

The last act of this crisis took place in Moscow after Bukharin, still Sta-lin's henchman, criticized Rakovskii in the party Central Committee for the prolonged Soviet silence at the beginning of September in response to the press campaign in Paris. No doubt this was part of the renewed campaign against Trotskii that would lead to his expulsion from the Communist Party in November 1927. In response, Chicherin prepared a long report passing day by day over the events of the crisis. He reported on the distortion of his words concerning the "disavowal" of Rakovskii, but passed over in silence his critical meeting with Herbette on 12 September when the ambassador refused to inform Paris of his doctoring of Chicherin's declaration. Obviously the *narkom* preferred not to reveal his failure to expose Herbette's legerde-main and blackmail. The period from 12 to 17 September, Chicherin re-ported, was critical, and Franco-Soviet relations hung in the balance. On 17 September the French cabinet decided against rupture, but there remained the question of how far the Soviet government should go in defending Ra-kovskii. We could have refused to recall him, but this would have risked a French rupture, playing into the hands of "world reaction." We could not go that far on a "question of personnel."[122]

It is interesting that Herriot made brief notes of the cabinet meetings of 17 and 30 September, when Poincaré himself referred to the conflict between the "Anglo-Saxon oil trusts" and the Soviet government, the implication being that since Chicherin's declaration settled the matter concerning Rakovskii, France should not rupture its relations with Moscow to please the oil trusts. The French cabinet was unaware of Herbette's doctoring of Chicherin's declaration. Ironically, Herriot wrote that the cabinet "greatly appreciated Herbette's dispatches," which, Litvinov observed, tended "to at-tribute to [his] interlocutor [the ambassador's] own thoughts and suggestions and to distort conversations."[123]

Valerian Savel'evich Dovgalevskii

Meanwhile, the Politburo had to find a replacement for Rakovskii. They settled on Valerian S. Dovgalevskii, who was recalled from the Soviet embassy in Tokyo. Born in 1885, he was of Ukrainian Jewish descent. He followed the usual patterns of his generation, getting involved in the revolutionary movement and going into exile in Western Europe in 1908 after running afoul of the tsarist police. Dovgalevskii was an Old Bolshevik who lived in Belgium, Switzerland, and France before the war and studied in Toulouse where he obtained a degree in electrical engineering. When the revolution broke out in Petrograd, he was living in Paris, managing

Figure 10.4. Valerian Savel'evich Dovgalevskii, ca. 1920s. AVPRF, f. 779, d. 1671,
l.f. Maiskii, I. M.

an electrical supply store on the Boulevard Pereire in the 17th arrondisse-
ment. Like many others of his generation, he returned to Russia, fought in
the Red Army during the civil war, and later became commissar for post
and communications. Dovgalevskii was not a high-ranking Bolshevik, and
unlike Rakovskii he kept out of party politics after a flirt with the opposition in the early 1920s. In 1924 he was sent to Stockholm as ambassador
and there was appreciated for his discretion and business-like competence.
According to Swedish authorities, he was missed in Stockholm . . . well, insofar as any Soviet representative could be.[124] As readers will learn, Dovgalevskii played an important role in the reestablishment of Anglo-Soviet
relations in 1929. In the early 1930s he was the Soviet negotiator with
Berthelot and later Herriot who brought about a Franco-Soviet rapprochement. In 1934 Dovgalevskii died of a heart attack at age 49; his ashes were
carried to the Kremlin wall for inhumation, by no less than Stalin, Molotov, Litvinov, and other notables of the Soviet state. Dovgalevskii proved
a good replacement for Rakovskii, for he got along well with Briand and
Berthelot. His diplomatic skills were almost at once put to the test.

Anticlimax

At the end of 1927 Franco-Soviet relations were in a shambles, and as if they were not bad enough, there was another open row in the new year. Parliamentary elections had not yet been held, and there was still some talk of resuming Franco-Soviet negotiations. Poincaré must have thought a final *coup de grâce* was necessary. On 2 March 1928 he directed Briand to support an action in the United States by the *Banque de France* to seize Soviet gold being shipped there as collateral for orders with American manufacturers.[125]

In 1918 the Soviet government had confiscated 52 million francs in gold ingots and coin deposited in the Russian state bank in Petrograd.[126] Fourteen thousand three hundred fifty-five kilograms of gold weighed heavily on the *Banque de France* and offered a suitable and symbolic pretext for Poincaré to attempt to seize the "stolen" specie being shipped to New York. The French government was in a poor position to talk about stolen gold since in collusion with Britain it had appropriated the Brest-Litovsk gold confiscated from Germany, which ought to have been returned or credited to Soviet Russia. Understandably, Moscow took umbrage.

It is "the beginning of economic war," accused Chicherin. Herbette denied it, but Chicherin was not persuaded. The act was politically inspired, he said.[127] The State Department investigated and found that the French government had not touched previous Soviet gold sent *to* France, which seemed to prove Chicherin right. Dovgalevskii went to the Quai d'Orsay to lodge a protest, but Berthelot blamed it on the finance ministry. "Read Poincaré," Dovgalevskii reported to Moscow.[128]

The consequences of the finance ministry's action were predictable. It made angry headlines in the Moscow press. According to the American embassy in Berlin, a Soviet official said that his government would probably suspend further negotiations with the French, just what Poincaré wanted. Briand put it politely when he told Dovgalevskii that Poincaré was too busy to "catch" a little time for Soviet affairs.[129] A Quai d'Orsay official explained the strategy to the American ambassador in Paris: the French government never intended to respond to Rakovskii's proposals "until after the elections." And then the French government would only say that the last Soviet proposals were unsatisfactory, though the Soviet government could advance others if it "cared to make them."[130] Dovgalevskii protested French action to Berthelot, who promised "to think matters over." He eventually did, which may surprise readers, raising questions about the wisdom of French policy.[131] But Poincaré turned a deaf ear, having elections to win that spring. Afterward, the suit brought by the *Banque de France* was forgotten—except perhaps by the bank—and it failed in the American courts in March 1929.[132]

As if to symbolize the deterioration in relations with Moscow, Herbette, who for nearly three years had promoted a Franco-Soviet rapprochement, turned his jacket in the late summer of 1927 and began to rail against Soviet perfidy, propaganda, and money for French communists. In December 1927 Litvinov complained to Briand in Geneva about Herbette's "changed" attitude toward the USSR, but Briand defended his ambassador and Litvinov did not insist.[133]

Herbette lingered on in Moscow until 1931 in an increasingly bitter relationship with the NKID. How bad relations had become was typified by a dangerous row between Herbette and Chicherin in April 1928 in the aftermath of the *Banque de France* uproar in the United States. In more pot calling kettle black, Herbette criticized the Moscow press for its harsh treatment of France, forgetting the dirty campaign against Rakovskii, and then accused the USSR of making military preparations against its neighbors. Chicherin tried to keep his composure but failed. It was too much even for him. "I expressed my indignation. . . . France is armed to the teeth," and we are only providing for our own defense. Herbette accused the Soviet Union of planning aggression; Chicherin replied that the Soviet government planned only to defend itself. "But if you don't like it," Chicherin added, "may I refer you to what the Spartan Leonidas said to the Persians [at Thermopylae] when they demanded his arms. 'Come take them,' he said."

"I was struck," Herbette commented sanctimoniously, "by the intensity of [Chicherin's] anger."[134] Chicherin seldom lost his composure with foreign diplomats, but it was more than he could stand listening to a French ambassador complain about the Soviet press after all the filth slung at the USSR from the venal Paris papers. It must have been the more exasperating since the NKID had invested heavily in "allowances" to avert the anti-Soviet campaigns. Soviet patience with France was at an end. Litvinov later made it known in Berlin that the NKID deeply distrusted Herbette, who "was unfriendly to the Soviets." He "varied his instructions according to his personal inclination and was not in any way to be relied upon."[135]

Relations between France and the Soviet Union did not improve until 1932 when Herriot was again premier and his government ratified a Franco-Soviet non-aggression pact, which Rakovskii had first proposed in 1925. As in Britain, anti-communism and electoral politics took precedence over securing a rapprochement with the Soviet Union. But "so long as the Anglo-French Entente remains solid," Berthelot observed, the French government did not need to fear a rupture with Moscow or closer German-Soviet relations.[136] And of course the bondholders, about whom the French government professed so much concern, were sacrificed without remorse by Poincaré and finance ministry officials. Apart from electoral politics, it was important to deny any gain in prestige or creditworthiness to the USSR. Basically the first and second Poincaré governments pursued the same, hard anti-Soviet line.

In late October, Herriot, as minister of education, met his Soviet counterpart, A. V. Lunarcharskii, in Paris after the dust of the Rakovskii affair had settled. They passed in review the major points of the crisis. Rakovskii's signature on the opposition declaration had been blown out of all proportion, said Herriot; it was a trifling matter and of no danger to France. But the Soviet side had to move away from its assumptions about a European war against it. Then minor irritants would lose their capacity for harm. And Rakovskii had been too careless, said Herriot; "he had to understand that in Europe he was surrounded by enemies and that he had to be ten times more careful than any other ambassador." The Soviet Union should be more concerned about keeping "the democratic parties" in power. The victory of the right "would undoubtedly mean the danger of war." The victory of the "democratic" parties gave the Soviet Union more room to maneuver. And yet the French Communist Party and the Soviet Communist Party itself could not tell a friend from a foe and were often more critical of socialists than of the right-wing parties. Rank-and-file members of the democratic parties ask me, said Herriot, if there was any point in making concessions to the communists.[137]

In December Litvinov met Briand in Geneva, and they talked over recent events. If only Rakovskii had gone on a three-month leave, Briand said, as I had suggested, events would have turned out better.

Could Rakovskii have returned to Paris? Litvinov asked.

I have "no doubt," Briand replied.

There is no danger now of a diplomatic rupture, he went on, and if there were, I would resign in protest. Briand said negotiations could resume when a new Soviet ambassador arrived in Paris. He appears to have wanted a renewal of negotiations, which is why Poincaré provoked a fresh crisis of Soviet gold in the United States.[138]

There was much to be said in Herriot's and Briand's observations, but it was easy for them to act as though they were somewhat disinterested observers. Most French politicians and civil servants of the inter-war years were hostile to the USSR, as were their counterparts in London and Washington. Soviet diplomats however had to shrug off their setbacks, for who knew, tomorrow could bring fresh possibilities. As Litvinov noted, the Soviet government did not seek relationships in the West for love or friendship but in the interests of the USSR.

One cannot blame the Politburo for the fiasco in Paris. Failure of Franco-Soviet negotiations was the result *desired* by Poincaré to assure the electoral success of the *Bloc national*. The rocambolesque efforts of Monzie and Labonne to wrest an agreement from Poincaré's tightly clenched fists had no chance. Monzie's 60 and 60 formula was too puny for Rakovskii to recommend to Moscow, and the Soviet government would never again make such generous offers in the West. One need only read again Litvinov's January 1927 critique of the debt and credit proposals to understand the importance of Soviet concessions.[139] France missed a golden opportunity not only in the short term to settle the defaulted tsarist bonds, but in the longer term to prepare the way for better political relations with Moscow in the face of an inevitable German resurgence. Herriot and Herbette were not the only ones to anticipate a renewed German menace; in Moscow Litvinov could see that Rapallo, such as it was, would not last forever. The USSR needed to keep its options open, but France, Britain, and the United States had lessons to teach to communists: play by the rules of capitalism, renounce the October Revolution, or we will punish you. And they did, too. Poincaré was not the only one to pursue hard-line policies or to exploit the Red Scare to win elections.

The Soviet failure to achieve success in the West helped to legitimize Stalin's subsequent policies. The so-called war scare of 1927 seemed all too plausible after the rupture of relations with Britain and the near rupture with France. When the Soviet government failed to obtain trade credits and loans in the West to rebuild and develop its economy, Stalin resorted to "socialism in one country" and the Five Year Plans to bring about rapid industrialization. The late Krasin had anticipated just such an eventuality. We will modernize by ourselves, if we must. And so they did, at a price many reckoned far too high.

Notes

1. Pierre de Margerie, French ambassador in Berlin, no. 120s, 6 Oct. 1926, encloses the text of a Chicherin interview in the *Berliner Tageblatt*, MAÉ Russie/141, ff. 140–45.

2. Excerpt from Rakovskii's *dnevnik*, no. 113/D, very secret, nd (end of Oct. 1925), AVPRF, f. 0136, p. 105, d. 104, ll. 305–11; and Litvinov to Rakovskii, no. 0748, secret, 14 Nov. 1925, AVPRF, f. 04, o. 42, p. 264, d. 53713, ll. 2–4.

3. Rakovskii to Litvinov, no. 1, 19 Nov. 1925, AVPRF, f. 0136, p. 105, d. 104, ll. 315–17; Rakovskii to NKID, no. 0326, very secret, 23 Nov. 1925, ibid., ll. 330–35; and "Ambassade de l'URSS, un ordre de Rakowsky," A. 9.584, *Préfecture de police*, 21 Nov. 1925, AN F7 13495.

4. Untitled memorandum, E. Rowe-Dutton, Treasury official, 27 Nov. 1921, T 160 777/ F815/2; and "Paris discussions of comrades Chicherin and Rakovskii," very secret, 23 Nov. 1925, AVPRF, f. 0136, p. 105, d. 104, ll. 339–50.

5. Rakovskii's journal, no. 0321, very secret, 17 Nov. 1925, AVPRF, f. 0136, p. 105, d. 104, ll. 327–19; and Rakovskii's journal, no. 2, late Nov. 1925, ibid., ll. 362–51.

6. Excerpt from Davtian's journal, very secret, meeting with Roels and Rollin on 13 January 1926, AVPRF, f. 05, o. 6, p. 13, d. 47, l. 65; and Davtian to Litvinov, letter no. 19, very secret, 18 Jan. 1926, ibid., ll. 60–63.

7. Davtian to Litvinov, no. 121/D, personal and very secret, 18 Jan. 1926, AVPRF, f. 05, o. 6, p. 13, d. 47, l. 71; and Davtian to Litvinov, letter no. 22, very secret, 25 Jan. 1926, ibid., ll. 91–93.

8. Herbette, no. 20, 28 Jan. 1926, MAÉ Russie/1168, ff. 328–30.

9. Herbette to Eirik Labonne, secretary general of the French delegation to the Franco-Soviet conference, 24 March 1926, *Fondation nationale des sciences politiques*, Paris [hereinafter FNSP] Papiers Anatole de Monzie/1. The papers in this collection are not the originals but are old, faded copies, some of which are partially illegible.

10. "La reconstruction des 'Ponts coupés,'" *Izvestiia*, 26 Feb. 1926, MF B32012.

11. Gregory's record of meeting with Fleuriau, 27 March 1926, N1460/418/38, FO 371 11787.

12. Crewe, no. 669, 13 April 1926, N1642/418/38, FO 271 11787.

13. Rakovskii to Litvinov, no. 4, 27 Feb. 1926, AVPRF, f. 05, o. 6, p. 13, d. 47, ll. 101–7.

14. Davtian's *dnevnik*, no. 9, very secret, 9 June 1926, AVPRF, f. 05, o. 6, p. 14, d. 52.

15. Extract from Rakovskii's *dnevnik*, no. 6, 16 July 1926, AVPRF, f. 04, o. 42, p. 266, d. 53773, l. 46; and Chicherin to Rakovskii, no. 14, 18 June 1926, AVPRF, f. 04, o. 42, p. 262, d. 53772, ll. 145–46.

16. Excerpt from Arens' *dnevnik* (Paris), no. 12, 25 June 1926, AVPRF, f. 04, o. 42, p. 262, d. 53772, l. 159; excerpt from Rakovskii's *dnevnik*, no. 0358, very secret, July 1926, AVPRF, f. 0136, p. 113, d. 215, ll. 337–38; excerpt from Rakovskii's *dnevnik*, no. 7, "Meetings with Caillaux, Briand, de Monzie, and Berthelot," very secret, 15–18 July 1926, ibid., ll. 357–71; untitled memorandum, Chlenov, very secret, 18 July 1926, 18h.00, AVPRF, f. 04, o. 42, p. 266, d. 53775, ll. 25–27; "Projet de procès-verbal préparé par M. Rakowsky et discuté avec M. de Monzie," 17 July 1926, FNSP Papiers Monzie/1 (there are various drafts of the protocol in AVPRF, f. 04, o. 42, p. 266, d. 53775).

17. Phipps to Gregory, confidential, 22 March 1927, N1388/47/38, FO 371 12584; and excerpt from Rakovskii's *dnevnik*, no. 0358, very secret, July 1926, AVPRF, f. 0136, p. 113, d. 215, ll. 337–38.

18. Arens' *dnevnik*, no. 12, 26 July 1926, AVPRF, f. 05, o. 6, p. 14, d. 52, ll. 37–40; Rakovskii to Stalin, no. 1099/ChS, 24 July 1926, AVPRF, f. 04, o. 42, p. 266, d. 53775, l. 23; and extract from NKID *kollegiia*, protocol no. 79, 24 July 1926, AVPRF, f. 04, o. 42, p. 266, d. 53773, l. 158.

19. Litvinov's *dnevnik*, 31 Aug. 1926, AVPRF, f. 0136, p. 112, d. 214, ll. 68–70.

20. "Note pour M. Berthelot," Jacques Seydoux, *directeur adjoint des Affaires politiques*, 25 Oct. 1926, MAÉ Russie/488; Poincaré to Briand, no. 11904, 6 Nov. 1926, ibid.; Briand to Poincaré, no. 3040, 9 Nov. 1926, MF B32013; Poincaré to Monzie, no. 12097, 13 Nov. 1926, ibid.; "Section financière, 9ᵉ séance," 2 Mar. 1926, MF B32014; and Herbette, nos. 255–56, 7 Mar. 1926, MAÉ Russie/487.

21. Litvinov to Rakovskii, no. 3086, secret, 18 Nov. 1926, AVPRF, f. 04, o. 42, p. 266, d. 53774, ll. 14–16; "Conversation with de Monzie, 16 October," very secret, Rakovskii, 16 Oct. 1926, ibid., l. 26; and Rakovskii's *dnevnik*, no. 3, very secret, 12 Nov. 1926, AVPRF, f. 0136, p. 113, d. 215, ll. 435–40.

22. Excerpt from Rakovskii's letter to Litvinov, no. 4, 16 Nov. 1926, AVPRF, f. 04, o. 42, p. 266, d. 53774, ll. 59–61; Poincaré to Briand, no. 12672, 30 Nov. 1926, FNSP Papiers de Monzie/1; and Labonne to Herbette, 9 Dec. 1926, ibid.

23. Litvinov to Rakovskii, no. 3086, secret, 18 Nov. 1926, AVPRF, f. 04, o. 42, p. 266, d. 53774, ll. 14–16; Litvinov to Rakovskii, no. 3150, secret, 4 Dec. 1926, AVPRF, f. 0136, p. 112, d. 212, l. 94; Litvinov to Rakovskii, no. 3195, secret, 18 Dec. 1926, ibid., l. 95; and Litvinov to Rakovskii, no. 3234, secret, 29 Dec. 1926, AVPRF, f. 0136, p. 112, d. 213, ll. 64–65.

24. Litvinov to Stalin, no. 3014, 4 Jan. 1927, AVPRF, f. 0136, p. 117, d. 303, ll. 1–3; Litvinov to Rakovskii, no. 3022, secret, 8 Jan. 1927, AVPRF, f. 04, o. 42, p. 269, d. 53821, ll. 5–7; and Litvinov to Rakovskii, no. 3042, secret, 15 Jan. 1927, AVPRF, f. 0136, p. 117, d. 304, ll. 4–6.

25. Excerpt from Politburo protocol, no. 78, 13 Jan. 1927, *Politbiuro Osoboi papki*, pp. 130–32.

26. Rozengol'ts to Litvinov, no. 52/s, very secret, 21 Jan. 1927, AVPRF, f. 069, o. 11, p. 30, d. 2, ll. 1–3; and Rozengol'ts to Litvinov, no. 155/s, very secret, 25 March 1927, ibid., ll. 90–98.

27. Excerpt from Rakovskii to Litvinov, no. 6, very secret, 24 March 1927, AVPRF, f. 04, o. 42, p. 269, d. 53821, l. 25.

28. "Note pour le secrétaire général," Alexis Léger, *directeur politique*, 17 Feb. 1927, MAÉ Russie/359, ff. 126–27; and "Note de M. [Charles] Corbin [*sous-directeur, Europe*]," 26 Feb. 1927, MAÉ Russie/489.

29. Phipps to Gregory, confidential, 22 March 1927, N1388/47/38, FO 371 12584.

30. Phipps, no. 788, 4 April 1927, N1567/47/38, FO 371 12584; and Briand to Herbette, nos. 237–39, 10 April 1927, MAÉ Russie/359, ff. 134–36.

31. Selby, FO, London to Phipps, British chargé d'affaires in Paris, 21 Feb. 1927, FO 800 260, ff. 238–48; Phipps to Selby, 7 March 1927, ibid., ff. 281–82; and various papers in F5018/2/10, FO 371 12406.

32. Gustave Téry, "Agiter afin de s'en servir," *L'Oeuvre*, 1 May 1927; Jean Pilot, "Distinction nécessaire," *L'Oeuvre*, 27 May 1927; J.-J. Bizot's personal notes, 7 May 1927, MF B32013; Rakovskii to Litvinov, 7 May 1927, *DVP*, X, pp. 188–91; and Rakovskii to Litvinov, no. 14, 13 May, very secret, 13 May 1927, AVPRF, f. 04, o. 42, p. 269, d. 53821, ll. 52–55.

33. Bizot's untitled, handwritten notes, 13 May 1927, MF B32013; Litvinov to Rakovskii, no. 3286, secret, 16 April 1927, AVPRF, f. 0136, p. 117, d. 304, l. 12; Litvinov to Chicherin (San Rafael), no. 3297, secret, 22 April 1927, AVPRF, f. 05, o. 6, p. 21, d. 89, ll. 25–27; and excerpt from Politburo protocol, no. 99, 30 April 1927, *Politbiuro Osoboi papki*, pp. 139–42.

34. Untitled note, 11 April 1927, FNSP Papiers de Monzie/2.

35. "Une interview de M. Rakowski, la question des dettes russes et les ouvertures de nouveaux crédits," *Paris-Soir*, 4 May 1927, MF B32013; untitled note, Bizot, 6 May 1927, ibid.; Poincaré to Briand, no. 4833bis, 6 May 1927, ibid.; and Stéphane Lauzanne, "Une comédie qui a assez duré, c'est celle des négociations franco-soviétiques," *Le Matin*, 9 May 1927.

36. "Rapport au Président du conseil, Ministre des Finances," no. 5338, Moret, approved by Poincaré, 19 May 1927, MF B32013; and "Négociations franco-soviétiques," *sous-direction d'Europe*, ns, 20 May 1927, MAÉ Russie/489.

37. "From a conversation with Poincaré on 24 May 1927," very secret, Chicherin, AVPRF, f. 04, o. 42, p. 269, d. 53821, ll. 65–69; "Discussions with [Alfred] Margaine, [Victor] Dalbiez, and [Henri] Rollin," very secret, Rakovskii, 24 May 1927, AVPRF, f. 0136, p. 117, d. 305, ll. 55–57; "From Chicherin's conversations with Painlevé and Herriot 25 May 1927," ibid., ll. 68–71; and "Conversations with various people on 24–26 May," very secret, Chicherin, ibid., ll. 72–76.

38. Crewe, no. 104, 26 May 1927, N2425/47/38, FO 371 12584.

39. Conversation with Briand, 28 May 1927, N2447/47/38, FO 371 12584; and Carley and Debo, "Always in Need of Credit," pp. 332–33.

40. Bron to Mikoian, nos. 3916–17, 3914, rigorously secret, immediate, 20 July 1927, *Moskva-Vashington*, I, pp. 342–43.

41. Chicherin to Mikoian and Politburo, no. 432/ChS, 21 July 1927; and no. 439/ChS, 22 July 1927, *Moskva-Vashington*, I, p. 344–45.

42. Mikoian to Politburo, cc. Chicherin, no. PB/060, very secret, 27 July 1927, *Moskva-Vashington*, I, pp. 349–55.

43. Chicherin to Politburo, no. 477/ChS, very secret, 27 July 1927, *Moskva-Vashington*, I, pp. 356–57.

44. Bron to Chicherin and Mikoian, no. 4251, rigorously secret, immediate, 5 Aug. 1927, *Moskva-Vashington*, I, pp. 357–58; J. H. Hayes to Kellogg, 27 July 1927, 861.51/2151, NA RG59, M-316, reel 123; and Kellogg to Hayes, 3 Aug. 1927, ibid.

45. Mikoian to Politburo, no. PB/064, very secret, by courier, 8 Aug. 1927, *Moskva-Vashington*, I, pp. 360–61; Chicherin to Stalin, no. 523/ChS, 8 Aug. 1927, ibid., pp. 361–62; and Skvirskii to NKID, no. 687, especially secret, 10 Aug. 1927, ibid., pp. 362–63.

46. Protocol of Politburo Commission on Mitchell proposals, very secret, 10 Aug. 1927, *Moskva-Vashington*, I, pp. 363–64; Politburo resolution, no. P120/10-s, rigorously secret, special file, 18 Aug. 1927, ibid., p. 364; and Politburo resolution, no. P120/10-v-s, rigorously secret, 18 Aug. 1927, ibid., p. 365.

47. Rakovskii to Chicherin, no. 0258, secret, 23 Aug. 1927, *Moskva-Vashington*, I, pp. 383–87.

48. Politburo resolutions, nos. P122/4a-s and P122/4b-s, rigorously secret, 1 Sept. 1927, ibid., p. 391.

49. Litvinov to Stalin, no. 3470, secret, 5 Sept. 1927, *Moskva-Vashington*, I, pp. 392–93.

50. Chicherin to Mikoian, cc. Stalin, Molotov, et al., no. 692/ChS, 5 Sept. 1927, *Moskva-Vashington*, I, pp. 393–94.

51. Skvirskii to NKID, no. 7476, especially secret, 5 Sept. 1927, *Moskva-Vashington*, I, p. 396.

52. Rakovskii, Piatakov, Sokolnikov to NKID, nos. 7646–47, especially secret, immediate, 9 Sept. 1927; nos. 7676, 7678–80, especially secret, immediate, 10 Sept. 1927, *Moskva-Vashington*, I, pp. 397–401; and Kelley to Kellogg, and enclosures, 18 Oct. 1927, 861.51/2162 3/4, NA RG59, M-316, reel 123.

53. Chicherin to Rakovskii, no. 38, 16 Sept. 1927, *Moskva-Vashington*, I, pp. 406–7.

54. Litvinov to Stalin, no. 3493, 19 Sept. 1927, *Moskva-Vashington*, I, pp. 416–17.

55. Kelley to Kellogg, 11 Oct. 1927, 861.51/2162, NA RG59, M-316, reel 123.

56. Winston to Kellogg, 24 Oct. 1924, 861.51/2162 1/2, NA RG59, M-316, reel 123.

57. William R. Castle, Assistant Secretary of State, to Kelley, 21 Oct. 1927, 861.51/2163 1/2, NA RG59, M-316, reel 123.

58. Rakovskii and Sokolnikov to Politburo, secret, 17 Sept. 1927, *Moskva-Vashington*, I, pp. 410–14.

59. Winston to Kellogg, 24 Oct. 1924, 861.51/2162 1/2, NA RG59, M-316, reel 123.

60. E.g., "L'arrestation du député Marty," *Journal des débats*, 15 Aug. 1927.

61. "Record of a conversation of Chlenov with Labonne 22 June 1927," Chlenov, 2 July 1927, AVPRF, f. 04, o. 42, p. 262, d. 53821, ll. 71–72.

62. "*Dnevnik*," 26 June 1927, AVPRF, f. 0136, p. 117, d. 306, ll. 169–72.

63. "Reçu la visite de M. Labonne," Bizot, 19 July 1927, MF B32013.

64. Untitled MAÉ note, ns, *vu par M. Berthelot*, 20 July 1927, MAÉ Russie/490; Rakovskii to Chicherin, no. 26, very secret, 22 July 1927, AVPRF, f. 0136, p. 117, d. 306, ll. 200–209; Rakovskii to Chicherin, no. 27, very secret, 23 July 1927, ibid., ll. 196–99; Rakovskii to Chicherin, 24 July 1927, DVP, X, pp. 343–44; Labonne to Herbette, 3 Aug. 1927, FNSP Papiers de Monzie/II.

65. Evgenii A. Preobrazhenskii, member of the Soviet delegation in Paris, to Chicherin, no. 2, 5 Aug. 1927, AVPRF, f. 04, o. 42, p. 269, d. 53821, ll. 115–21; and Preobrazhenskii to Chicherin, no. 0249, 12 Aug. 1927, ibid., ll. 129–34.

66. Carley and Debo, "Always in Need of Credit," pp. 335–36.

67. Chicherin to Stalin, no. 476/ChS, very secret, immediate, 27 July 1927, AVPRF, f. 0136, p. 117, d. 303, l. 5; Chicherin to Stalin, no. 500/ChS, 4 Aug. 1927, AVPRF, f. 04, o. 42, p. 269, d. 53822, l. 11; Chicherin to Stalin, no. 522/ChS, 8 Aug. 1927, ibid., l. 12; and Chicherin to Stalin, no. 548/ChS, 15 Aug. 1927, ibid., l. 13.

68. Rakovskii to Narkomindel, 19 Aug. 1927, DVP, X, pp. 365–66; Rakovskii to Chicherin, no. 28, very secret, 20 Aug. 1927, AVPRF, f. 0136, p. 117, d. 306, ll. 210–17; Rakovskii to Chicherin, no. 29, very secret, 23 Aug. 1927, ibid., ll. 218–24; cf., Labonne's retrospective account, "Négociations franco-soviétiques depuis le mois de juillet 1927," 29 Sept. 1927, MAÉ Russie/490/MF B32013.

69. Reported by Herbette, nos. 462 and 466, 10 Aug. 1927, MAÉ Russie/359, ff. 172–73.

70. "Visite de M. Rakowsky," Beaumarchais, 19 Aug. 1927, MF B32013/MAÉ Russie/359, ff. 192–93; and Rakovskii to Chicherin, no. 28, very secret, 20 Aug. 1927, AVPRF, f. 0136, p. 117, d. 306, ll. 210–17.

71. Labonne to Monzie, 28 Aug. 1927, FNSP Papiers de Monzie/II; and Rakovskii to Chicherin, no. 30, very secret, 24 Aug. 1927, AVPRF, f. 0136, p. 117, d. 306, ll. 227–28.

72. Monzie to Labonne, 29 Aug. 1927, FNSP Papiers de Monzie/II.

73. Chicherin to Stalin, no. 582/ChS, 21 Aug. 1927, AVPRF, f. 04, o. 42, p. 269, d. 53825, ll. 1–3; and Herbette, nos. 495–97, 21 Aug. 1927, MAÉ Russie/359, ff. 194–96.

74. Chicherin to Stalin, no. 591/ChS, 22 Aug. 1927, AVPRF, f. 0136, p. 117, d. 303, l. 24.

75. Chicherin to Stalin, no. 661/ChS, 29 Aug. 1927, AVPRF, f. 04, o. 42, p. 269, d. 53825, ll. 7–10; and Herbette, nos. 526–27, 29 Aug. 1927, MAÉ Russie/359, ff. 226–27.

76. Briand (draft by Berthelot) to Herbette, no. 424, 2 Sept. 1927, MAÉ Russie/360, fol. 1.

77. Phipps to Chamberlain, no. 1801, 22 Aug. 1927, N3986/47/38, FO 371 12584; and Gascoigne's minute, 24 Aug. 1927, ibid.

78. See, e.g., L'Écho de Paris, Le Figaro, Le Journal des débats, Le Matin, Le Temps, Sept.–Oct. 1927.

79. Phipps to Chamberlain, no. 1893, 5 Sept. 1927, N4218/47/38, FO 371 12584.

80. Phipps to Tyrrell, 14 Sept. 1927, N4376/47/38, FO 371 12584; and Rakovskii to Litvinov, no. 34, very secret, 30 Sept. 1927, AVPRF, f. 04, p. 42, p. 269, d. 53824, ll. 91–113.

81. Unsigned note, no. 6392 (appears to be from the Sûreté générale), 15 Sept. 1927, MAÉ Russie/360, ff. 58–60.

82. Briand (Geneva) to Poincaré, nos. 15–18, 10 Sept. 1927, MAÉ Russie/360, ff. 31–34; Poincaré to Briand, no. 12, 10 Sept. 1927, ibid., fol. 38; Poincaré to Briand, no. 18, 12 Sept. 1927, ibid., fol. 45; and Phipps to Chamberlain, no. 190, 14 Sept. 1927, N4376/47/38, FO 371 12584.

83. "M. de Monzie nous dit . . . ," L'Avenir, 12 Sept. 1927 (MAÉ Russie/360, fol. 48).

84. Rakovskii to Litvinov, no. 33, very secret, 24 Sept. 1927, AVPRF, f. 0136, p. 117, d. 306, ll. 235–40; and "Tel. de M. de Monzie," Bizot, 23 Sept. 1927, MF B32013.

85. "Record of conversation of Chlenov with Labonne, [Charles] Alphand, and [Gaston] Bergery, 9.IX.27g.," secret, Chlenov, AVPRF, f. 04, o. 42, p. 269, d. 53824, ll. 24–27; "Record of conversation of Chlenov with Labonne and Alphand on 14 and 15 September (in all four conversations)," secret, Chlenov, AVPRF, f. 04, o. 42, p. 269, d. 53821, ll. 156–58; Chlenov to Chicherin, no. 0286, secret, nd, ibid., l. 159; and "Record of conversation of Chlenov with Labonne on 20 September 1927," secret, Chlenov, ibid., ll. 161–64.

86. Litvinov to Stalin, no. 3495, secret, 20 Sept. 1927, AVPRF, f. 04, o. 42, p. 269, d. 53825, ll. 36–39.

87. Untitled, handwritten note by Bizot, concerning a meeting with Labonne, 21 Sept. 1927, MF B32013; "Téléph. Labonne," Bizot, 22 Sept. 1927, ibid.; and "Tél. Labonne," Bizot, 24 Sept. 1927, ibid.

88. Untitled note by Bizot (embellished with a drawing of the proverbial Bolshevik with a knife in his teeth), 26 Sept. 1927, MF B32013; and Briand to Herbette, nos. 472–76, 25 Sept. 1927, ibid.

89. "Note pour le Président du Conseil," Moret, approved by Poincaré, 24 Sept. 1927, MF B32013; "Note pour le Président du Conseil, Ministre des Finances," Moret, 29 Sept. 1927, ibid.; "Note pour Monsieur le Président du Conseil," no. 9719, Moret, approved by Poincaré, 6 Oct. 1927, ibid., "M. Moret," *Cabinet du ministre*, signature illegible, 11 Oct. 1927, ibid.

90. Herbette, no. 535, 2 Sept. 1927, MAÉ Russie/360, ff. 3–5.

91. "Résumé of a conversation with Herbette, 4 September 1927," no. 634/ChS, AVPRF, f. 04, o. 42, p. 269, d. 53824, ll. 13–17.

92. Herbette, no. 539, 4 Sept. 1927, MAÉ Russie/360, fol. 8.

93. Chicherin to Stalin, no.690/ChS, most immediate, 5 Sept. 1927, AVPRF, f. 04, o. 42, p. 269, d. 53825, ll. 17–18; and no. 704/ChS, 6 Sept. 1927, ibid., ll. 19–20.

94. Rakovskii to Litvinov, unnumbered cable, 10 Sept. 1927, AVPRF, f. 04, o. 42, p. 269, d. 53824, l. 28.

95. Excerpt from Litvinov to Brodovskii (Berlin), no. 3480, 10 Sept. 1927, AVPRF, f. 04, o. 42, p. 269, d. 53824, l. 30; and Chicherin to Stalin, no. 723/ChS, very secret, 10 Sept. 1927, AVPRF, f. 04, o. 42, p. 269, d. 53825, l. 23.

96. Litvinov to Chicherin, no. 3482, secret, 12 Sept. 1927, AVPRF, f. 042, o. 42, p. 269, d. 53824, l. 34.

97. Chicherin to Litvinov, no. 228, secret, 12 September 1927, AVPRF, f. 042, o. 42, p. 269, d. 53824, l. 32.

98. "Résumé of a conversation with Herbette 12 Sept. 1927," no. 732/ChS, very secret, AVPRF, f. 04, o. 42, p. 269, d. 53824, ll. 35–37; and Chicherin to Stalin, no. 731/ChS, 12 Sept. 1927, AVPRF, f. 04, o. 42, p. 269, d. 53825, l. 26.

99. Herbette, no. 559, 12 Sept. 1927, MAÉ Russie/360, fol. 42; and no. 560, 13 Sept. 1927, ibid., ff. 49–51.

100. Herbette, nos. 563–64, 13 Sept. 1927; no. 566, 14 Sept. 1927, MAÉ Russie/360, ff. 52, 55–56.

101. "Conversation with Herbette," no. 14428, secret, Rotshtein, 14 Sept. 1927, AVPRF, f. 04, o. 42, p. 269, d. 53824, ll. 43–44.

102. "Résumé of a conversation with Herbette, 15 September 1927," no. 747/ChS, AVPRF, f. 04, o. 42, p. 269, d. 53824, ll. 49–51; Chicherin to Rakovskii, no. 37, 15 Sept. 1927, ibid., l. 48; and Herbette, nos. 568–72, 16 Sept. 1927, MAÉ Russie/360, ff. 61–65.

103. Herbette, nos. 574–76, 16 Sept. 1927, MAÉ Russie/360, ff. 68–70; and Briand (draft by Berthelot) to Herbette, nos. 445–48, 17 Sept. 1927, ibid., ff. 76–78.

104. "Conversation with Herbette, 18 Sept. 1927," no. 765/ChS, AVPRF, f. 04, o. 42, p. 269, 53824, ll. 53–59; and Note, Europe, ns, 27 Sept. 1927, MAÉ Russie/360, ff. 146–50.

105. Berthelot to Briand (Geneva), nos. 27–33; Herbette, nos. 450–56, 20 Sept. 1927, MAÉ Russie/360, ff. 90–93.

106. Chicherin to Stalin, no. 781/ChS, very secret, 20 Sept. 1920, AVPRF, f. 04, o. 42, p. 269, d. 53825, ll. 32–34; and Litvinov to Stalin, no. 3495, secret, 20 Sept. 1927, ibid., ll. 36–39.

107. Chicherin to Stalin, no. 780/ChS, very secret, 20 Sept. 1927, AVPRF, f. 04, o. 42, p. 269, d. 53825, ll. 30–31; and "Résumé of a conversation with Rantzau 20 Sept. 1927," no. 779/

ChS, very secret, AVPRF, f. 04, o. 42, p. 269, d. 53824, ll. 63–66 (published in *Moskva-Berlin*, II, pp. 70–76).

108. Chicherin to Rakovskii, no. 44, very secret, 23 Sept. 1927, AVPRF, f. 04, o. 42, p. 269, d. 53821, l. 174; and Litvinov to Rakovskii, no. 3499, secret, 24 Sept. 1927, AVPRF, f. 0136, p. 117, d. 304, ll. 30–33.

109. Rakovskii to Litvinov, no. 34, very secret, 30 Sept. 1927, AVPRF, f. 04, p. 42, p. 269, d. 538–24, ll. 91–113.

110. Herbette, nos. 462 and 466, 10 Aug. 1927; nos. 484–90, 17 Aug. 1927, MAÉ Russie/359, ff. 172–73, 183–89.

111. Litvinov's *dnevnik*, "Conversation with Herbette," 28 Sept. 1927, AVPRF, f. 04, o. 42, p. 269, d. 53824, ll. 81–87.

112. Herbette, nos. 621–22, 28 Sept. 1927, MAÉ Russie/360, ff. 151–52; and especially Herbette's, no. 587, 28 Sept. 1927, ibid., ff. 153–55.

113. Litvinov to Stalin, no. 3508, secret, 29 Sept. 1927, AVPRF, f. 04, o. 42, p. 269, d. 53825, l. 40.

114. Briand to Herbette, nos. 472–76, 25 Sept. 1927; no. 481, 30 Sept. 1927, MAÉ Russie/360, ff. 141–43, 168; Litvinov's *dnevnik*, "Conversation with Herbette," 1 Oct. 1927, AVPRF, f. 04, o. 42, p. 269, d. 53824, l. 118.

115. Chicherin to Litvinov, no. 297, 3 Oct. 1927, AVPRF, f. 04, o. 42, p. 269, d. 53824, l. 127; Litvinov to Stalin, no. 3513, secret, 4 Oct. 1927, AVPRF, f. 04, o. 42, p. 269, d. 53825, l. 41; and Litvinov to Herbette, no. G/432, 4 Oct. 1927, AVPRF, f. 04, o. 42, p. 269, d. 53824, l. 136.

116. "Visit of Herbette," no. 25100/R, secret, by S. B. Kagan, bureau chief, Anglo-Latin section, 4 Oct. 1927, AVPRF, o. 04, o. 42, p. 269, d. 53824, l. 137.

117. Briand to Herbette, nos. 493–98, 6 Oct. 1927, MAÉ Russie/361, ff. 35–36; and Chicherin to Stalin, no. 862/ChS, 7 Oct. 1927, AVPRF, f. 04, o. 42, p. 269, d. 53825, ll. 42–44.

118. Chicherin to Stalin, no. 866/ChS, 8 Oct. 1927, AVPRF, f. 4, o. 42, p. 269, d. 53825, ll. 47–48; and Litvinov to Stalin, nos. 3533 and 3535, secret, 10 Oct. 1927, ibid., ll. 67–68, 69.

119. Herbette, nos. 724–31, 13 Oct. 1927, MAÉ Russie/361, ff. 73–80.

120. Briand to Herbette, no. 396, 19 Aug. 1927, MAÉ Russie/359, fol. 190.

121. Chicherin to Rakovskii, no. 51, personal, very secret, 7 Oct. 1927, AVPRF, f. 04, o. 42, p. 269, d. 53824, ll. 147–48.

122. "To members of the TsK and TsKK," secret, Chicherin, 23 Oct. 1927, AVPRF, f. 04, o. 42, p. 269, d. 53824, ll. 230–35.

123. *Conseils du 17 et 30 septembre 1927*, Herriot's notes, MAÉ Papiers Herriot/12, ff. 209–10; and Litvinov's *dnevnik*, 28 Sept. 1927, AVPRF, f. 04, o. 42, p. 269, d. 53824, ll. 81–87.

124. "Note, au sujet de M. Dovgalevski," *sous-direction d'Europe*, 22 Oct. 1927, MAÉ Russie/1116, ff. 164–67; Armand Bernard, French minister in Stockholm, no. 283, *très confidentiel*, 26 Oct. 1927, ibid., ff. 171–72 ; and Bernard, no. 84, *confidentiel*, 18 Dec. 1927, ibid., ff. 199–201.

125. Poincaré to Briand, no. 58/50, 2 March 1928, MAÉ Russie/483, fol. 37.

126. "Note remise au service russe le 13 avril 1928 par M. Favre-Gilly du secrétariat général de la Banque de France," MAÉ Russie/483, ff. 176–79.

127. Chicherin to Dovgalevskii, 12 March 1928, *DVP*, XI, pp. 155–56; and Herbette, nos. 292–98, 11 March 1928, MAÉ Russie/483, ff. 47–53.

128. Castle to Alphonse Gaulin, U.S. consul general in Paris, no. 2682, 17 March 1928, 861.51/2194, NA RG59, M-316, reel 123; Gaulin, no. 812, 12 April 1928, 851.61/2211, ibid.; and "Record of a conversation . . . with . . . Berthelot," Dovgalevskii, 13 March 1928, *DVP*, XI, pp. 156–58.

129. Herbette, nos. 309–11, 16 March 1928, MAÉ Russie/483, ff. 69–72; Schurman (Berlin), no. 3352, confidential, 27 March 1928, 851.51-Germany/2, NA RG59, M-316, reel 124; and "Record of a conversation . . . with . . . Briand," Dovgalevskii, 29 Feb. 1928, DVP, XI, pp. 127–30.

130. Herrick (Paris), no. 8507, 13 Apr. 1928, 861.51/2209, NA RG59, M-316, reel 123.

131. "Record of a conversation . . . with . . . Berthelot," Dovgalevskii, 21 March 1928, DVP, XI, pp. 184–86; and Berthelot's minute on MAÉ note, ns, 11 May 1928, MAÉ Russie/483, fol. 198.

132. Paul Claudel, French ambassador in Washington, no. 137, 23 March 1929, MAÉ Russie/483, ff. 217–18, 220.

133. G. A. B. Clauzel (Geneva, from Briand), nos. 29–31, 6 Dec. 1927, MAÉ Russie/361, ff. 140–43.

134. "Stormy scene with Herbette, 8 April 1928," no. 343/ChS, 8 April 1928, AVPRF, f. 0136, p. 124, d. 407, ll. 86–89; and Herbette, nos. 428–39, 8 April 1928, MAÉ Russie/362, ff. 37–48.

135. J. B. Schurman, U.S. ambassador in Berlin, no. 4799, strictly confidential, 14 Aug. 1929, 861.002/104, NA RG59, M-316, reel 69.

136. Phipps, British chargé d'affaires in Paris, no. 118, 13 June 1927, N2852/47/38, FO 371 12584.

137. "Conversation of comrade A. V. Lunarcharskii with Herriot on 21 October 1927," very secret, AVPRF, f. 04, o. 42, p. 269, d. 53824, ll. 216–24.

138. Litvinov to Chicherin, cc. Stalin, secret, 4 Dec. 1927, AVPRF, f. 05, o. 6, p. 21, d. 89, ll. 49–53.

139. Litvinov to Stalin, no. 3014, 4 Jan. 1927, AVPRF, f. 0136, p. 117, d. 303, ll. 1–3.

~

CHAPTER ELEVEN

"These Are Times of Quick Suspicions"

Sullen Coexistence, 1927–1930

In Europe the last years of the 1920s were still the "Roaring Twenties," and outside government circles, the leisure classes seemed little preoccupied with foreign affairs. According to the French, the twenties were the *années folles*, the wild years. The nightclub scene in European capitals was hot, licentious, vibrant. American jazz and jazz musicians were popular. Those who had money dressed to the nines; exotic women in feathers and furs, and men in their tuxedos, swigged champagne and danced to big band music. Paris was where you had to be, if you could afford it. Pablo Picasso, Georges Braque, George Grosz were at the height of their artistic powers. The literary scene was bohemian and fashionable. Henry Miller and a contingent of talented American writers made Paris home. Hidden by the glamour and the jazz, however, were other darker currents, created by the aftershocks of the Great War, riling still-traumatized ex-soldiers and the working classes. British miners, the under-classes, the unemployed had little time and no money for buying Picassos or taking in the nightlife of Paris. Their venues were the local café or pub, and their indulgences, cigarettes, cheap wine, and draft beer. Vengeance, violence, and anti-Semitism fermented, nourishing new political movements, which in the coming decade would transform Europe into an unstable, smoldering volcano, ready to explode.

In the late 1920s another volcano shuddered in the Soviet Union fed by unresolved and seemingly insoluble economic and social problems. In the aftermath of the foreign intervention and civil war, the Soviet government commenced the enormous task of rebuilding. It was not easy when everything was in ruins and society was reduced to a primeval state of desperate poverty and survival of the fittest. By early 1928 a semblance of economic and social normalcy had been reestablished. Industrial production was at or near pre-war levels, but Soviet factories did not make essential manufactured goods, like machine tools, automobiles, tractors, fertilizers. Products available for peasant consumption were priced high. Unemployment in the cities was widespread, and grain production was hampered by millions of inefficient smallholdings held by peasant freeholders barely able to feed their families. Limited grain surpluses fed Soviet cities or were exported to obtain foreign exchange to finance trade in the West. A developing class of relatively prosperous, kulak farmers, arising out of the NEP, the mixed Soviet economy, produced most of the grain surpluses. If prices were too low—as they were bound to be, to make bread affordable in the cities—the kulaks stored their surpluses or did not sow their fields. This led to scarcity and higher prices in the cities. Most people were discontented: kulaks because grain prices were too low and the cost of consumer goods too high, while workers and the unemployed in the cities suffered because bread and meat, for those who could afford it, were too dear.

The kulaks could hold the Soviet government to ransom and in a larger sense threaten the October Revolution. Should backward, primitive rural Russia, and its kulak elite, such as it was, be allowed to dictate the pace of industrialization and modernization? No one was content, not the underpaid or unemployed workers in the cities, not the majority of peasant freeholders or farm laborers who lived in poverty, nor even the kulaks, impatient with the constraints and taxes imposed on them by Soviet authorities. Acute tensions between city and countryside were reflected in the Communist Party where everyone saw the dangers and felt the popular anger. No one seemed to have a solution for the crisis. Few Bolsheviks ever liked the NEP, but what other options were there? Trotskii promoted industrialization; Bukharin and his group, economic growth by allowing the kulaks to stimulate Soviet development at a much slower pace. In the meantime industrial and agricultural reconstruction was hobbled in a hostile capitalist world. Soviet security and the future of socialism were at stake, and everyone knew it. We're not going to be "an agrarian colony for any country," Stalin said, and no Bolshevik would have disagreed with him.[1]

How did these Soviet domestic issues affect Soviet foreign policy? In one way, they strengthened the NKID's innate pragmatism. No matter how you saw the resolution of the problems of Soviet development, one objective remained unchanged. The USSR had to trade and obtain credit to trade in the West to build up its industrial infrastructure. It was the only way to satisfy both town and countryside. Credit always funded international commerce, but in the case of the USSR it was even more important because the Soviet government was cash poor; it did not have the necessary foreign currency reserves to buy everything it needed, and it needed almost everything. No matter who won the political and economic debates in Moscow, trade and credit would remain important, even essential for Soviet reconstruction and development. This meant establishing and maintaining correct, if not good relations with the capitalist West in order to facilitate Soviet foreign commerce. Western governments understood this, and at the beginning of the 1920s they discouraged credit for trade or tried to force it onto a cash-and-carry basis to exhaust Soviet foreign exchange and gold reserves. When interventionist bayonets failed, the West resorted to the splintery wooden spoon to break the Bolshevik revolution. In a sense western bankers became allies of the kulaks who held the Soviet government to ransom in the same way Soviet businessmen and western industrialists came to share the common interest of doing business together.

The Soviet volcano of popular discontents smoked and heaved underneath the struggle for power between Stalin and his rivals. The issues were important, but power was important too. So issues also became objects for Stalin, to be manipulated, muddied, and abused in the maneuvering for dominance and control in the Politburo and in the Communist Party bureaucracy. At the lower levels of the political conflict, intimidation and hooliganism were commonplace. At Communist Party meetings, after Stalin gained the upper hand, opposition speakers were left agape, whistled down and humiliated, among them the greatest figures of the October Revolution and civil war period. When they tried to meet clandestinely, Stalinist ruffians rousted them. Trotskii, Zinoviev, Kamenev, and others were expelled from the party in November 1927. Their supporters, confused, frightened, isolated, began to make their peace with Stalin, so they thought, abasing themselves in public recantations of their previous political ideas. Stalin would brook no opposition.

Ioffe, the former *polpred* in Beijing and Trotskii's friend and loyal supporter, did not join in the recantations. Sick and discouraged, he shot himself on 16 November 1927. Lev Davidovich delivered the eulogy; it was his last public speech in the USSR. "He glowed with a soft and even light," Trotskii said, "which warmed the heart." Ten thousand people were said to have come out to the funeral; it was a public, political demonstration, the last, as it turned out, of the Left Opposition.[2]

In the end there was only one group left in the Politburo, the so-called right deviation of Bukharin, Tomskii, and Rykov, capable of challenging Stalin. They feared a Stalinist turn toward forced collectivization and industrialization. In 1928 Bukharin, the *gensek*'s former henchman, became a target himself only months after the expulsion of Trotskii, Zinoviev, and

Kamenev. In March 1927 *Pravda* ran a cartoon of Bukharin with a gag in his mouth; a year later Stalin was looking for a beam with which to silence him. Bukharin's political destruction marked the end of any serious opposition to Stalin's dictatorship.

Ironically, Stalin's consolidation of power freed him to support the NKID's more pragmatic foreign policy, unencumbered by the need to appease temporary political allies in Moscow, although he appeared to retain the Comintern as a defensive screen on his left, adopting a new ultra-revolutionary line, the so-called third period, where collaboration between communists and western socialists was spurned. No one was going to outflank Stalin on his left.

As for the seemingly insoluble problems of Soviet development, Stalin took the great fist of Russian in the guise of Soviet police power and smashed the roadblocks of the 1920s with forced collectivization and the First Five Year Plan for all-out industrialization. Stalin accused Trotskii of being the enemy of the kulaks and a "super-industrializer," but in the end it was the old story of pot calling kettle black, although this time it was a party affair. The volcano continued to shudder. Peasants and workers were angry and discontented, but so what? The police were there for that.

Stalin was in a hurry, and he did not boggle at the means to get where he wanted to go. The USSR must industrialize, he said in 1931, in a speech explaining his policies.

> To slacken the tempos would be to fall behind. And the backward get beaten. We don't want to be beaten. . . . The history of old Russia consisted, among other things, in her being ceaselessly beaten for her backwardness. She was beaten by the Mongol khans. She was beaten by the Turkish beys. She was beaten by the Swedish feudal rulers . . . by the Polish-Lithuanian lords. She was beaten by the Anglo-French capitalists . . . [and] by Japanese barons. Everyone gave her a beating for her backwardness. . . . They beat her because it was profitable and could be done with impunity.

"Such is the law of the exploiters: beat the backward and the weak," Stalin said. "We have fallen behind the advanced countries by 50 to 100 years. We must close that gap in ten years. Either we do this or we'll be crushed." Stalin called it "the wolf's law of capitalism." He liked the allegorical image of the wolf, and he drew from Russian parables about them. "If you live among wolves," Stalin would say in 1938, "you must behave like a wolf."[3] And Stalin did, too, though there was never a rogue wolf like him. It is the law of the strongest, Litvinov might have corrected, and it is the usual conduct of states. He knew that a buildup of industrial power would command the respect of the western powers and strengthen Soviet security. Stalin's drive to modernize provoked desperate suffering and huge popular discontents, but it also attracted support, especially among the younger urban generation coming to maturity in the 1920s. So if the volcano of popular anger shuddered and vented beneath Stalin's feet, he appears to have maintained enough popular support to stand the cauldron's heat.

Meanwhile, the NKID continued to pursue its policies of accommodation with the West, though not with great success. After elections in the spring of 1928 Soviet relations with France settled down under a dim night lamp of hostility, the *nochnaia lampochka*, sought by Poincaré and typified by Herbette's clashes with the NKID. In London there were no official relations with the USSR, and there the night lamp burned even dimmer. When a British acquaintance wrote to Litvinov about his son's wish to see the Soviet countryside, Litvinov discouraged him. "These are times of quick suspicions," he wrote, "especially as regards the English."[4] Such Anglo-Soviet exchanges as there were took place through insulting press comments from one side or the other. Unlike France which traded very little with the USSR, British manufacturers did important business with Moscow and suffered from the rupture of diplomatic relations, the more so since American competitors picked up their contracts.

Renewal of Anglo-Soviet Relations

Even in 1926 the Foreign Office was not blind to the inconveniences of a rupture of diplomatic relations. "There is no point in slamming a door," Gregory observed, "which has only got to be opened again quite soon."

> If there was any reason to believe that the present regime would fall as a result of a rupture of relations, there might be some sense in such action. But we know that this would not happen, and we should only find ourselves six months hence in an embarrassed position, conducting our routine business with the Soviets in a neutral capital and wondering how on earth to resume direct relations.

The worst of it, Gregory concluded, was that "we should undoubtedly lose money. Quite a considerable number of Russian orders have been placed in this country and many of them on a credit basis and a break would undoubtedly involve certain firms in a substantial loss."[5]

This was exactly the problem which confronted the British government, foreseen by Gregory early on, but by others also. Briand thought the diplomatic break with Moscow "a great mistake." The Czechoslovak foreign minister, Edvard Beneš, termed the Tory rupture a "fiasco." The Conservative government might in due course be replaced by a Labour cabinet or Labour-Liberal coalition, one of whose first decisions would be to resume relations with Moscow.[6]

In the Foreign Office no one much cared what Beneš thought, or perhaps even Briand, but Gregory might have been more influential, if he had not been dismissed from the Foreign Office in 1928 because of his involvement in amateurish currency speculations. Gregory's disgrace did not make his foresight in 1926 less pertinent, for as he had predicted, business pressure mounted to resume relations with the USSR. At the beginning of 1929 the Conservative government still opposed a renewal of diplomatic relations, though the Cabinet noted there was increasing support for it in the House of Commons.[7] One can find the usual dismissive comments about the Soviet Union in the Foreign Office files. Over a diplomatic lunch, the Swedish minister in London opined that Soviet days were numbered: "'catastrophe' was imminent."

"I should dearly like to believe," recorded the Parliamentary undersecretary Godfrey Locker-Lampson, "in the imminence of a catastrophe involving the overthrow of the present rulers of Russia and a return to sanity; but I greatly doubt it."

So did Chamberlain.[8]

The Tory government could afford to be glib about the Soviet Union especially because the Chinese revolutionary movement—which had threatened to boot Britain and the other foreign powers out of their concessions and treaty ports—had suffered a near death blow from Chiang Kai-shek. This would-be hangman of the revolution betrayed his Soviet quartermasters and slaughtered all the Chinese communists, trade unionists, and rebellious peasants on whom his bravos could lay their hands.

We last left the story of Soviet involvement in China in December 1927 when the Politburo without discussion authorized an uprising in Canton which led to a massacre of some 25,000 people. Understandably, there was a policy review in Moscow about the Canton fiasco which put blame everywhere but where it belonged, on the shoulders of Stalin, who had signed the directive authorizing the uprising. After the catastrophe, Stalin appears to have learned a lesson. In February 1928 the Comintern IKKI directed that the Chinese Communist Party leadership should "absolutely" not embark upon any "ill-prepared, premature uprisings."[9] This advice was closing the doors after the cows were out of the barn, but it was better late than never. Moreover, the Politburo, which had discussed the China question at practically every meeting in 1927, began to discuss it less and less and to delegate authority on China issues to the Comintern IKKI and its various commissions. The Politburo Chinese Commission likewise appears to have stopped meeting after March 1928.[10] If there were new defeats in China, Stalin could not be blamed. The Politburo still provided very secret communications support from the Harbin consulate in Manchuria, and it sent funds to the Chinese Communist Party on a modest scale.[11] The supply of arms, relatively lavish before Chiang's betrayal in 1927, was halted.

In the NKID, control over Soviet "eastern" policy, in China and elsewhere, remained a problem. Readers will remember that the NKID had lost control over China policy in 1925–1926. After the Canton fiasco, it took time before the NKID could reassert its authority. Chicherin was ill off and on. Would he continue as *narkom*, or would he be replaced? No one knew except perhaps Stalin, and he was not saying. In spite of the uncertainties, Litvinov took the bull by the horns while Chicherin was again in Germany for medical treatment. In January 1929 Litvinov complained to Stalin about the unsatisfactory situation in the NKID.

On several recent occasions, Litvinov noted, you have asked me questions about our eastern policy and then expressed "amazement" because of the insufficiency of my responses. I wrote to the Politburo several times in 1928 about the unusual situation in the NKID where some members of the *kollegiia* were insufficiently informed about eastern policy. The Politburo did not respond to my complaints, and the absence of response seemed to sanction this peculiar situation.

Litvinov expressed *his* "amazement" to Stalin at the continuing blockage which seemed to come from Deputy Commissar Karakhan, who was not circulating his correspondence on eastern policy.[12] The cat was out of the bag: would-be rivals for the succession to Chicherin's position, Litvinov and Karakhan, Stalin's "opportunists," were not getting along. The Turkish foreign minister, Tevfik Rüstü, had heard and passed on what he knew to the British ambassador in Ankara: "Russia's foreign policy was entirely in the hands of Litvinov and Karakhan, Litvinov taking Europe and America, and Karakhan Asia, each of them pursuing an independent policy." Litvinov obviously sought to put right this irregular situation, which would not facilitate an improvement in Anglo-Soviet relations, as the British ambassador, Sir George Clerk, rightly noted.[13]

Restoration of diplomatic relations with Britain was a high priority. The defeat of the revolution in China had reduced to a low boil the level of Tory anger toward Moscow. After the rupture of diplomatic relations in 1927, there was after all nothing more the British government could do short of covert operations or open war. This latter option was out of the question. The settling of jangled Tory nerves allowed cooler heads to think about practical matters like trade. Even in 1928 British manufacturers lobbied the

Conservative government. In February 1929 a consortium of British firms, the Anglo-Russian Committee, led by Ernest Remnant, a wealthy land speculator and editor of the literary magazine *English Review*, made public a planned trip to Moscow to discuss business opportunities. Remnant had traveled to Paris several times in 1928 to discuss his ideas with Ambassador Dovgalevskii. The Foreign Office, which was cool to the project and refused to endorse it, took the usual bemused attitude toward businessmen whose family connections were not sufficiently illustrous. As one Foreign Office clerk noted, such gentlemen were "afflicted with an excessive & irrational optimism." It is a "misguided & ill-timed venture," opined Locker-Lampson. Chamberlain refused to receive Remnant, "the organiser whoever he is." It was "purely an affair of traders . . . , it has no political meaning or interest."[14]

The Soviet government took a different view. Litvinov knew how to entertain businessmen with visions of lucrative contracts. One for lumber, at below-market prices, seems to have provoked British business interest and been an additional impetus for the Moscow trip.[15] Elections were expected in the spring of 1929, and the parties were looking for issues to exploit. The French embassy in London followed these developments closely. According to Ambassador Fleuriau, the Labour Party sought to exploit the Remnant mission to demonstrate the usefulness of regular Anglo-Soviet relations. The Soviet government had the same objective in mind. If political relations improve, trade relations would also. The Politburo ordered that a realistic program of purchases from British firms be developed to attract their interest, but of course potential orders were made conditional on a renewal of diplomatic relations. A special train was laid on to pick up the British delegation of 85 delegates at the Soviet frontier. Receptions, opera, and a gala night were also organized. The hook was heavily baited.[16] Unlike Chamberlain, Litvinov met with Remnant and two of his colleagues, welcoming them, but also warning that they should not have unrealistic expectations. They could discuss future possibilities for business, but no contracts would be signed until "the removal of existing obstacles" to better trade relations.[17] That meant the renewal of diplomatic relations.

The Soviet objective, according to Herbette, was to generate a British movement of opinion that would bring down the Tory government in the upcoming elections. Herbette saw "danger" in the movement, financing "communist agitation" and threatening "European peace." Public opinion should be informed.[18] There he goes again, Litvinov would have thought had he read the ambassador's report. Maybe he did. Coincidentally, a report by the well-connected *Times* correspondent Vladimir Poliakoff (or Augur), inspired perhaps by the Foreign Office News Department, smeared Remnant and his colleagues as Soviet agents. Poliakoff's obvious intent was to discredit the Anglo-Russian Committee.[19]

These speculations and intrigues were cut short when Prime Minister Baldwin dissolved Parliament and called elections for 30 May. Both the Labour and Liberal parties campaigned on the renewal of diplomatic relations with the USSR. The Tories took a beating, losing 152 seats, while Labour picked up 136. Not quite enough to form a majority government, Labour was again dependent on the Liberals who held the balance of power in the House of Commons. MacDonald came back as prime minister, and Arthur Henderson was named Foreign Secretary. Labour had promised to reestablish relations with Moscow, and they now had to do so with a minority government dependent on uncertain Liberal support.

A week after the elections, on 5 June, Litvinov advised Stalin of what to expect. Nothing would happen for about a month before the new government met the House of Commons. MacDonald had promised to reestablish relations with the USSR, but acting by electoral obligation, he would not be in a hurry. We could also expect, Litvinov warned, unofficial contacts from the Labour Party. There would be no shortage of "go-between volunteers" wanting "to play a role" in negotiations. This situation should be avoided: we would designate official representatives to meet unofficial individuals acting without responsibility. We could be committed to a position, but they would not be. Litvinov nevertheless recommended that the Soviet government should prepare its position on issues likely to be raised: "so-called propaganda and English claims." We should demand the reestablishment of diplomatic relations without any preconditions or prior discussions. Under no circumstances should we be lured into negotiations on debts before the renewal of diplomatic relations. "I would recommend now, without any commissions being created, limiting ourselves to decisions in the spirit of my suggestions." Litvinov's message was clear: the NKID is where foreign policy recommendations should originate, not in Politburo commissions.

The Politburo approved of Litvinov's recommendations on the following day, 6 June.[20] Litvinov sent similar instructions to his ambassadors in the event they heard from Labour intermediaries. "Don't show any excess of nervous impatience, but quietly wait on events." It looked like go-betweens would contact Dovgalevskii in Paris, and special instructions were sent to him. "We need to avoid discussion of any concrete questions with unofficial go-betweens."[21]

In the Foreign Office officials raised questions about how to proceed and about what advantages, particularly economic, might be gained from recognition. Remnant's group had returned from the USSR with big promises of trade, too big to be believed. It was the late Krasin's policy of using trade prospects as bait to encourage diplomatic recognition. The Anglo-Russian Committee thought that a debts settlement might be obtained as a condition of recognition, but this was precisely the strategy that Litvinov was determined to thwart. The only hope of a settlement was the quid pro quo of "a British loan," long-term credit to finance Soviet trade and economic development. This remained the main obstacle to agreement since, according to the Foreign Office, it was "inconceivable that . . . English banks . . . would be prepared or would be in a position to accord such enormous credits to a country which has steadfastly refused to honour its old debts." Apart from debts was the issue of "propaganda," and there too Litvinov held to the line of strict separation between the Soviet government and the Comintern.[22] Prospects did not seem good for the new MacDonald cabinet to obtain satisfaction on either debts or "propaganda."

The anticipated go-betweens were not slow to present themselves. Old standby W. P. Coates, of "Hands off Russia," telephoned Dovgalevskii in Paris to say that he would have "an important visit." The following day, W. N. Ewer, chief foreign correspondent of the *Daily Herald*, arrived at the Soviet embassy on the rue de Grenelle. "His goal," reported Dovgalevskii, "is to inform us." Readers will remember that Litvinov did not have a high opinion of Ewer, a purveyor of disinformation, but this time he was well briefed on the Labour government's position.

Are you acting on anyone's instructions? Dovgalevskii asked.

No, Ewer replied. Not only am I not acting on instructions, but the government "does not suspect and must not suspect" that I am here.

Then Ewer proceeded to inform Dovgalevskii of what the Labour government was doing or intended to do. It would propose the reestablishment of relations at the level of ambassador, not chargé d'affaires. It was consulting the dominions and intended to pass a message through the Norwegian embassy in Moscow inviting a Soviet representative to come to London to discuss the renewal of relations. All this was true, and not disinformation.

Dovgalevskii asked what would be the subject of discussion in London.

Propaganda, replied Ewer, and debts.

What did the Labour government hope to obtain from us regarding propaganda? Dovgalevskii asked.

The government had not yet made up its mind, replied Ewer, but it probably would ask that the Comintern stop sending money to the British Communist Party. These decisions were the result of compromises inside the new cabinet with right-wing members and MacDonald. Ewer "and his friends" were concerned about how the Soviet government would react to an invitation to send a representative to London, and they wanted some indication of what Moscow would do.

Dovgalevskii replied that he had no instructions and could say nothing about Soviet policy, though he expressed his surprise at the proposed British démarche since Labour and the Liberals had both campaigned for a prompt renewal of Anglo-Soviet diplomatic relations. Dovgalevskii's "surprise" must have been feigned, since he would have known even then the value of party promises in western elections.

When will the Soviet government determine its policy? Ewer wanted to know.

Moscow could hardly make policy decisions based on information from a private individual, Dovgalevskii replied. He informed Moscow that Ewer had probably received his information from a Cabinet member. He claimed to be acting on his own initiative, Dovgalevskii reported, but it might well be some form of government sounding. My comments to Ewer would get back to whoever had sent him. Perhaps Ewer wanted to encourage the Labour government, and us also, to pursue a private channel before making a public statement. Dovgalevskii made no definite response to Ewer, but he asked for instructions.[23]

The Politburo opposed any preliminary discussions with Ewer or anyone else. Karakhan, in the absence of Litvinov, who was on holiday, instructed Dovgalevskii to make no response to Ewer. *Izvestiia* published an editorial stating the Soviet position. It was to be hoped that Ewer and "his friends" would see the editorial and make profitable use of it.[24]

Ewer departed; other go-betweens presented themselves. Ben Tillet, trade union leader and newly elected MP, and E. Frank Wise, also freshly elected Labour MP, both turned up in Paris. Tillet met A. F. Neiman, the counselor at the Soviet embassy, to complain about nasty Soviet press comments on the new MacDonald government, which, he pointed out, was committed to renewing relations with Moscow. The attacks put MacDonald in a bind, embarrassed him, and "made it impossible to approach you." Cut us some slack was Tillet's message: "For friends of the Soviet Union, the attacks in the press rendered more difficult all their activities." Like Ewer, Tillet was well versed on Labour government policy. When Neiman asked him if he came in some official capacity, Tillet replied that he had come on his own initiative and had no instructions.[25]

This was not the case with Wise, who cabled Litvinov, then in Germany, to ask to meet him. Readers will remember that Wise had been Lloyd George's go-between at Genoa in 1922. Wise and Litvinov were old acquaintances. Litvinov reckoned that he could not refuse to see Wise if he had instructions from the British government. He did, and traveled from Paris to the German resort where Litvinov was staying.

"Wise said the following to me," Litvinov reported to Moscow: "Henderson had instructed him to explain to me his position. . . . The English government is trying as quickly as possible to reestablish friendly relations."

Very well briefed, Wise passed through the various steps necessary to achieve this objective, consulting the Dominions and sending a note to the Soviet government inviting it to send a representative to London to discuss "procedures" for the reestablishment of relations and namely the settlement of "disputed questions," that is, debts and "propaganda." The government would then make a report to Parliament. Wise read from notes, Litvinov reported; he said that he came on a "more or less official mission about which supposedly only Henderson and his private secretary were informed, but perhaps also MacDonald." The government's position was "shaky." It had to take into account public opinion and the mood of Parliament. The majority of the Labour caucus was indifferent or even hostile to the Soviet Union, especially trade unionists, who resented Soviet financial support of the left "minority," by which Wise may have meant British communists. All this, Wise laid out, according to Litvinov, in order to indicate how "awkward" it would be if, as a result of "unacceptable" Soviet demands, diplomatic relations were not reestablished.

Litvinov did not take well to Wise's approach, drawing attention to editorials in *Izvestiia* which spelled out the Soviet position, to wit, that the Soviet government would not undertake negotiations to settle outstanding questions as a condition of recognition. That was out. We never agreed to such terms prior to 1924 when we were weak, Litvinov said; we would certainly not agree to it now when we are much stronger. It was also clear that the "Zinoviev letter" and the Arcos raid of 1927, used as a pretext for rupture, still riled Litvinov. We don't take any responsibility for the 1927 rupture, and we have nothing over which to "repent." During the electoral campaign the Labour Party had promised, if elected, to reestablish immediately and unconditionally diplomatic relations with the USSR. You have only to do what you promised, Litvinov said. The Liberal Party had also made similar campaign statements. Only the Conservative Party, though not all Tory MPs, objected. If MacDonald wants to take into account Tory opinion, that is his privilege, but then there will be no discussion about the reestablishment of diplomatic relations.

If Wise could threaten failure of Labour policy, Litvinov reciprocated by indicating that the Soviet government could live with the status quo, without diplomatic relations. To hell with MacDonald, Litvinov went on, flinging defiance in Wise's face. But Wise returned to the charge: if the Soviet government refused to send a representative to London, it would allow the government "to wash its hands" of recognition and to live with the status quo. No party in Parliament would reproach the government for failing to reestablish relations with Moscow, not even the Anglo-Russian committee. Litvinov repeated his position: if Wise feared the consequences of the Soviet response to his approach, then he should persuade Henderson *not* to send the intended British note to the Soviet government.

Then Wise dropped his hard line: Henderson could not retreat from the note. Let's work up together an acceptable draft for London.

"I cannot agree to a joint drafting of the note," replied Litvinov, "inasmuch as I am in principle against the basic point of negotiations in London." Then Litvinov also softened a little and suggested that the Foreign Office should simply give notice to the Soviet government of its decision to reestablish relations. The intended British note, he warned Moscow, speaks only of discussions about "procedures," but everyone will understand what this means since the Soviet government never refuses to discuss outstanding claims. Moreover, if we send a plenipotentiary to London to discuss a mutually acceptable formula, agreement will be difficult if dependent on Conservative support. So if Henderson insists on prior negotiations, he is essentially taking over Chamberlain's policy. Litvinov suggested that if Wise wanted some prior agreement on an exchange of notes, he should obtain plenipotentiary powers from Henderson and then enter into negotiations with Moscow through the Soviet embassy in Berlin. Wise did not like this idea and, after a final exchange of views, took his leave, saying he would brief Henderson.

I doubt, Litvinov advised, that Wise would succeed in changing Henderson's intention to invite a Soviet representative to London; maybe he would obtain some cosmetic changes. In any case, we are faced with a trap. If we accept Henderson's proposal, it could go as Wise suggests. If we refuse to go, MacDonald will try to portray us as "saboteurs." We did not refuse to talk to Chamberlain in Geneva; but we won't talk to a Labour government in London. "I have the impression that what MacDonald really fears is the Conservatives and Liberals tripping him up. . . . He is such a frightful coward that he will be happy to have a reason to delay recognition . . . putting the blame on us." Given the circumstances, Litvinov recommended against any "sharp reply" to London: we should respond that we are at once ready to resume diplomatic relations and to name diplomatic representatives, and ready to enter into negotiations to settle outstanding differences. We could also agree to send a special representative to London to discuss "international issues," but not right away, not until after the recessing of Parliament, for otherwise the Tories could make trouble. I am not expecting to see Wise again, Litvinov advised Moscow, since I am going to Austria and did not give him my forwarding address.[26]

There is no record in the Foreign Office files about Wise, but Henderson did not receive in time his report of conversation with Litvinov.[27] Thus, on 15 July the Foreign Office invited the Soviet government to send a representative to London "in order to discuss with the Foreign Secretary the most expeditious procedure for reaching as rapidly as possible a friendly and mutually satisfactory settlement of the outstanding questions between the two countries including those relating to propaganda and debts." On 23 July Karakhan responded favorably but indicated a willingness to talk about procedures only, not about the substance of disputed issues until after diplomatic relations had been reestablished. Dovgalevskii would go to London to negotiate with Henderson.[28] The Soviet message was not subtle, and the Foreign Office of course understood. Litvinov had no intention of walking into a Foreign Office trap.

Dovgalevskii arrived in London on 28 July and met Henderson the following day. Prior to the meeting he received Wise and Coates. Wise in particular was clearly worried that there might be an impasse in the negotiations and thus that the minority government could be imperiled. I "sensed" in his words, Dovgalevskii reported, a plea for help. According to the Soviet record, Henderson reiterated what Wise had said, to wit, that the government did not have a majority in the Commons, that a Conservative "onslaught" could be expected. When it came down to it, according to Dovgalevskii, Henderson was asking for help, in particular on the issue of "propaganda." The Cabinet saw the danger of "reefs" everywhere which could sink the government. Let's take advantage of the three months before Parliament reconvenes to make progress on the settlement of outstanding questions. It would improve the atmosphere in the autumn. The British record says only that recognition could not take place until a report to Parliament after its resumption of business at the end of October. Dovgalevskii cabled Moscow for instructions and returned to see Henderson on 31 July without the "help" which the Foreign Secretary wanted. The Soviet government refused any substantive discussions before the reestablishment of diplomatic relations. Just to underline Soviet insistence on reciprocity, the NKID emphasized that it would be unable to proceed further until it had consulted a plenary session of the Central Committee at an as yet undetermined date. According to Dovgalevskii, Henderson was "irritated" by the Soviet reply. This was perhaps an understatement, especially since the ambassador intended to return to Paris on the following day, having nothing further to discuss with the Foreign Secretary. Dovgalevskii's report is much more revealing than that of the Foreign Office, indicating that Henderson "rather heatedly" objected to the Soviet sine qua non of formal recognition before any discussion of substantive issues.

Dovgalevskii was slow to send his reports to Moscow, prompting a sharp NKID rejoinder. The ambassador pleaded problems with encryption, a "stupid" chauffeur in London who got lost, and rough seas in the Channel to explain why he was late getting back to Paris.[29]

The Politburo was quick to respond to Henderson in *Izvestiia* on 2 August: "The pseudo-Labour government broke off negotiations with the USSR. Henderson is a pupil of Chamberlain." Readers will be amused to know that the Foreign Office translator softened *Izvestiia*'s blow in translating the same headline as "Labourites following in the footsteps of the Conservatives"![30] Nevertheless, the Foreign Office understood Dovgalevskii's point, as one official, H. J. Seymour, put it: "The resumption of relations must precede the discussion of outstanding questions, & not form part of a settlement." "Propaganda" remained an important issue, though one clerk thought there was improvement in Soviet comprehension of the problem: "There are strong indications that the Soviet Government, or at any rate the Foreign Commissariat, are becoming embarrassed by the activities of the Komintern & that the Politbureau intends to restrict the Komintern's activities." Henderson told Seymour that "the hitch in the negotiations" was due to the necessity to seek Parliamentary approval before an exchange of ambassadors.[31] This was the trap into which the Labour government had fallen, according to Litvinov. As Krestinskii explained it to Stresemann in Berlin, Henderson had made a "tactical error" in proposing preliminary negotiations. The Soviet government could simply have refused the invitation to London and waited on developments. "We wanted to help Henderson escape from the 'awkward situation' in which he had put himself." So we sent Dovgalevskii to London to discuss "procedural" issues in the hope that Henderson "would take the escape exit which we gave him out of his self-created dead end." Unfortunately, Henderson did not see the escape route, or wanted "stubbornly" to stick to his original position. Either way, on this question we will not make concessions.[32] Soviet diplomats later learned that MacDonald did not take the July impasse too tragically. Hearing the news, "he apparently expressed his complete satisfaction and said 'That's good, now we can give a sufficient rejoinder to our leftists.'" Henderson did not agree "and considered the renewal of negotiations with the USSR to be necessary."[33]

The king was not happy about the meetings with Dovgalevskii, advising the Foreign Office that he was loath to see a Soviet representative above the rank of chargé d'affaires in London. "It would be repugnant to His Majesty to shake hands with any representative of the Govt who . . . connived at and approved of the brutal murder of the King's First Cousins." He meant the tsar Nicholas II and his family. The permanent undersecretary, Sir Ronald Lindsay, met the king's private secretary to set him straight; ambassadors it was going to be, for otherwise the government's policy would be "shattered." Of course the king had to yield, though according to his private secretary, His Majesty "would derive small comfort" from Lindsay's explanations.[34]

In August Litvinov returned from his holiday to find the talks between Henderson and Dovgalevskii still stalled, and he immediately set about to get them moving again. Henderson did also, sending Wise to Moscow for further unofficial, secret discussions with Litvinov. The impasse, according to Litvinov, appeared to stem from a misunderstanding perhaps created by Dovgalevskii's insufficient understanding of English and the absence of a translator. I don't see anything in the instructions for Dovgalevskii or in the Politburo resolutions, Litvinov wrote to Politburo secretary Molotov, that prevented Dovgalevskii from discussing "procedures" with Henderson. Litvinov did not like the situation but in no case wanted to get dragged into substantive negotiations before an exchange of ambassadors. So he proposed a reply to London reiterating the previous Soviet position on recognition, but indicating a willingness to discuss matters of procedure for negotiations that would follow recognition. "We need again to get into contact with Henderson," Litvinov recommended, "and this possibility we achieve by the dispatch of a plenipotentiary for discussion of procedures. Henderson cannot reject our suggestion, and will himself be glad of the reestablishment of contact." If he tries to lay on new demands, we can reject them, though with less haste than before. There is always the chance that Henderson "has not said his last word and that if we hold strongly to our line, we may obtain concessions."[35]

On 21 August Litvinov received Wise in Moscow, who came direct after seeing Henderson, a point he did not attempt to hide. Obviously the idea was to agree to a resumption of discussions before making it public to avoid any further embarrassments. He produced a memorandum spelling out a process for resumption of discussions which had the approval of Hugh Dalton, the Parliamentary undersecretary in the Foreign Office. Whether Litvinov liked "semi-official emissaries" or not, he reckoned Wise to be a reliable intermediary. In June he "had in my presence sent a telegram to Henderson asking him to delay the note to Moscow before his return to London." Afraid that the Tories had got wind of Wise's mission, Henderson went ahead to avoid embarrassing Parliamentary questions. Wise explained what Litvinov already knew, that MacDonald could not count on Liberal votes in the House and therefore had to proceed carefully for fear of being defeated on a confidence motion. According to Wise, Henderson hoped for some negotiations before the reconvening of Parliament which could facilitate getting a resolution through the House of Commons with Liberal support.

Wise is trying to bargain with us, Litvinov noted; he's probing. "The MacDonald government is trying by every means to retain power and greatly

fears again being defeated on the Russian question, thanks to a surprise betrayal by the Liberals." Litvinov thought these fears were exaggerated, but
they were playing a role in the negotiations. Henderson wants concessions
which would calm Parliament and "demonstrate the diplomatic ability of
the MacDonald government." There thus remained only the question of
how a further exchange of notes might be handled.[36] In a subsequent note to
Molotov, Litvinov pointed out the dangers of "unofficial" communications
sent through Wise. "At the same time, I am ready to guarantee 100 percent
that the English government will in no case in its official communications
make any reference to my discussions with Wise."[37] On this point Litvinov
was dead right because even Foreign Office officials appear to have been
unaware of Wise's role.

Litvinov met Wise again on 23 and 30 August where they went over the
various issues that divided the two governments. The Soviet position remained no substantive negotiations until after the exchange of ambassadors;
prior discussions could only be about procedures. There was also the issue of
how a resumption of negotiations would be made public and who would take
the initiative. Henderson had an "irritable" personality, according to Wise,
already annoyed with Soviet public statements about the negotiations. It
was not certain how he would take to Soviet propositions. Henderson might
still have wanted to finesse substantive discussions, but Litvinov would not
budge. In any case, the Foreign Secretary wanted assurances that if he extended a second invitation, it would be promptly accepted. He was already
expecting awkward questions from his left at an upcoming party meeting. It
was not just the Tories who worried the government. The idea was to avoid
a further failure of negotiations in London and more polemics in the press.[38]

These informal discussions led Henderson to make a statement in Geneva
on 4 September which explained that the resumption of diplomatic relations
could not take place until a report was made to Parliament; in the meantime
negotiations could take place "in arranging the procedure and programme
for the subsequent negotiations," leading, Henderson stated, to a successful
settlement of "outstanding questions." On 5 September the Politburo authorized Litvinov to respond positively, agreeing to send Dovgalevskii back to
London for further negotiations.[39] The unofficial Wise-Litvinov discussions,
of which there appears to be no record in the Foreign Office files, had led
out of the impasse.

Stalin was pleased with the outcome, though not with Litvinov, who had
in fact engineered the result. "It's not Henderson who is dangerous," Stalin
growled to Molotov, "since we have pushed him to the wall, but Litvinov,
who believes Wise and other bastards more than the logic of things. Especially dangerous are 'our' Paris 'advisers' [inter alia Ewer and Ben Tillet], who

recommended that we send Henderson a 'sympathetic' answer. These people are Henderson's agents, who inform the *British* government and *dis*inform us."

> Remember we are waging a struggle (negotiations with enemies is also struggle), not with England alone, but with the whole capitalist world, since the MacDonald government is the vanguard of the capitalist in the work of "humiliating" and "bridling" the Soviet government with "new," *more* "diplomatic," *more* disguised, and thus *more* "effective" methods. The MacDonald government *wants to show* the whole capitalist world that it can take more from us . . . than Mussolini, Poincaré, and Baldwin, that it can be a greater Shylock than the capitalist Shylock himself. And it wants this because only in this way can it win the trust of its own bourgeoisie. . . . We really would be worthless if we couldn't manage to reply to these arrogant bastards briefly and to the point: "*You won't get a friggin' thing from us.*"[40]

Stalin was in some ways right about MacDonald, who did need to gain the confidence of the British elite, or at least keep the Liberals and Conservatives from turning Labour out of office. He was also right about British and western attitudes toward the USSR: they did mean to "humiliate" the USSR, forcing it to eat sour porridge with a splintery wooden spoon. Stalin considered Litvinov to be an "opportunist," but as such it was his policy that had succeeded in getting Henderson to make his 4 September statement.[41] As in February 1927 Stalin again blustered at Litvinov, while at the same time he endorsed his policy recommendations.

On 23 September Dovgalevskii returned to London. Two days later he met with Henderson for a series of meetings in order to reach agreement on an agenda for future negotiations. There were disagreements over the appearance of the word "propaganda," which was at the top of the British list of questions to be settled. Another objectionable word, according to Dovgalevskii, was "debts." He preferred "claims and counter-claims." There were also disagreements over the order of priority of the questions to be settled. "Propaganda" disappeared from the common list, but Henderson insisted on the word "debts." Of course, the issue of propaganda did not disappear from the British agenda; it was to be covered by mutual pledges to be issued at the time of the exchange of ambassadors. A protocol was signed on 3 October, finalizing the agreement.

Dovgalevskii's account of the meetings with Henderson is much more revealing than the British records. "Both Henderson and I maintained a strictly official tone" in the negotiations, Dovgalevskii reported, but Henderson often tried to slip into "a more habitual for him artificial benevolent form of communication."

"I always cut short these attempts," Dovgalevskii said, and when this or that approach did not work, Henderson, "visibly not knowing how to conduct himself in an argument, seemed close to a complete loss of composure." It was only because of the presence of translators that Henderson could obtain time to regain his composure. According to Dovgalevskii, the Foreign Secretary appeared to try to control the agenda by presenting various papers and drafts, "palming them off" on Dovgalevskii, who defended himself by asking for time to study them. Henderson stressed the importance, especially from a Parliamentary point of view, of "debts and propaganda." Dovgalevskii returned to the charge with his own ideas and proposals, for which he gained acceptance, thus wresting the initiative from Henderson who could not conceal his "undisguised annoyance." He and his officials "did not stop complaining about the one-sided nature of the concessions being made by them, stressing my alleged undue stubbornness and unwillingness to give away anything whatever from our side."

Unreported by the Foreign Office papers, Wise, Ewer, and Coates were in the corridors. Wise acted as Henderson's barrister, according to Dovgalevskii, seeing me after each meeting: "He came to persuade me in a friendly way about the correctness or inevitability of this or that importunity of Henderson . . . demonstrating that he was informed in the most detailed way of about everything which took place between Henderson and me." Ewer was not so well informed and "for the most part limited himself to expressions of agreement and gestures of sympathy for this or that argument advanced by our side. In contradistinction to Wise, he did not take upon himself the task of amplifying Henderson, but obviously rather sought to understand our intentions and wishes." Dovgalevskii also met Coates who like Ewer expressed his "sympathy" for us but did not press too hard for information.[42]

It had taken three months to conclude and sign a one-page document, mainly owing to the mistrust and susceptibilities of both sides, and the Labour government's minority position in the House of Commons. On 5 November the government made its report to Parliament and obtained approval from the House of Commons for the renewal of diplomatic relations, the vote taken being 324 for, 199 against.[43]

Sir Edmond Ovey was named British ambassador in Moscow, and the former commissar for finance, Sokolnikov, *polpred* in London. Relations seemed thus to be headed in the right direction, sufficient to worry Ambassador Herbette, who fretted that the British and Soviet governments might conclude a debts agreement, leaving French bondholders out in the cold. It was just like the French to cast a jealous eye on the British renewal of relations with Moscow, when their own Soviet relations were so bad.

Herbette raised the subject in a conversation with Litvinov in September. He attributed the blame for the failure of the 1927 negotiations to the Soviet government—which readers will know was a preposterous claim—and wondered whether Moscow might take some initiative to improve relations. Litvinov replied sarcastically, as he often did with Herbette, that the Soviet government was still waiting for a reply to Rakovskii's August 1927 proposals.[44] Herbette knew very well from Labonne that Poincaré had sacrificed French bondholders to the greater good of his electoral success, rejecting what the finance ministry considered to be acceptable Soviet offers. The French had only themselves to blame for their discomfort at the prospect of better Anglo-Soviet relations.

Litvinov Takes Over

While Chicherin remained in Germany, Litvinov became acting *narkom* if not in name. He enjoyed Stalin's confidence, despite the *gensek's* occasional grumbling. Like Chicherin, Litvinov was particularly sensitive to matters riling foreign governments and their diplomats in Moscow. Among these, "propaganda" was at the top of his list.

In March 1929 he complained to Stalin of rough Soviet press treatment of a Polish diplomat. Measures should be taken, Litvinov recommended, to ensure that the press respected NKID guidelines on Soviet foreign policy and foreign governments and diplomats.[45] For Chicherin too, the management of the Soviet press was essential to prevent needless quarrels with foreign governments.

The public attacks went too far and were a constant source of complaints. After the renewal of Anglo-Soviet relations, Litvinov wrote again to Stalin to complain about Comintern and Profintern radio broadcasts in French and German, and he mentioned other examples. We are accused "from all sides" of interfering in the internal affairs of other countries, and the broadcasts add new force to these accusations. We could of course reply that the station in question is not governmental, "but in reality this changes nothing." Making available a powerful radio station to international revolutionary organizations would "undoubtedly give cause to the British government to protest." Stories about Soviet life and culture could be produced in foreign languages; revolutionary appeals should be broadcast in Russian, "but without harsh attacks against heads of governments with whom we have normal relations." We should forbid, Litvinov added, "broadcasts in foreign languages which could be interpreted as revolutionary or as interference in the affairs of other governments."[46] On this too Chicherin and Litvinov were in perfect agreement.

Litvinov also wrote to Stalin about financial support of foreign communist parties. Herbette, the NKID *bête noire*, protested against Soviet factory collections for the Paris communist daily *L'Humanité*, or rather the Soviet government's exchange of rubles for French francs. This was support for "propaganda," according to Herbette, and interference in French internal affairs. I gave the usual reply, Litvinov advised Stalin, "but I think that we must now take measures so that there are no communications either in our press, or even in *L'Humanité*, about the transfer or receipt of currency from the USSR." Naturally *L'Humanité* "can publish that workers in the Union collected such and such sums . . . but not that they were actually transferred or received in France." Rather cynical, readers might think, but Litvinov could not stop the payments to *L'Humanité*, nor could he propose to stop them. At least let's not publicize them was his recommendation to Stalin.[47]

A few months later Litvinov followed up along the same cynical lines with Dovgalevskii, who had "exaggerated" when denying Moscow's financial support of the French Communist Party. Since the Soviet government and the Comintern were two entirely separate organizations, how could Ambassador Dovgalevskii know anything about Comintern relations with the French Communist Party? "We cannot know," Litvinov advised.[48]

In his subtle and not so subtle ways Litvinov tried to explain to foreign diplomats that he was doing what he could about "propaganda." In May 1929 the Norwegian minister in Moscow, then representing British affairs, observed to Litvinov that publishing a manifesto in Moscow to support a Soviet republic of India would not help in renewing diplomatic relations with London.

"You are right," replied Litvinov. "The Comintern is of no advantage to us"[49]

In a conversation with a Japanese diplomat in Geneva that same month, Litvinov had similar things to say: Soviet propaganda did not produce the hoped-for results and sometimes was simply "ridiculous."

"Personally, I think," said Litvinov, "that it would be wise to lower the tone of the propaganda in order to reestablish mutual confidence and economic relations between foreign powers and the Union."

Why not simply get rid of it, was the unspoken question to which Litvinov then replied: there were "insurmountable difficulties" in the way, "for the propaganda is the most important symbol of the Union."[50]

In September Herbette raised the same subject, as he so often did. "Moscow is bigger than the Soviet government," replied Litvinov, a formula which Herbette took to mean that the "government's authority did not extend to everything that happened here."[51]

With western ambassadors Litvinov could not do otherwise than maintain the distinction between the Soviet government and the Comintern and communist parties. In secret he took a different line, often writing to Stalin to ask that Comintern agencies be disciplined and that press commentary on foreign policy be subject to NKID vetting. On this issue too Chicherin and Litvinov were in harmony.

In a conversation with Litvinov, Ambassador Ovey pointed out that there was no British propaganda in Russia.

"In Russia," Litvinov replied, "such propaganda would be impossible." It's up to you, he told Ovey, "to take similar measures," if you so wish, regarding the British Communist Party. "You can hang them or burn them alive if you catch them," he said.

Ovey thought Litvinov was being "grimly humorous," and perhaps he was, but he was also being serious in his way, for clearly he had lost patience with the Comintern and its associated activities.[52]

Not satisfied apparently with this sally, Litvinov launched another two months later. It's "hopeless," he said to Ovey. "Why don't you take the thing? You are a free country. We do not want it here. Do arrange for it to hold its sessions in London."[53]

Stalin was only too aware of Litvinov's position, receiving regular complaints from him over the years about the Comintern and its "orators," whose ill-judged statements irritated the West for nothing and undermined Soviet foreign policy. In 1929 Stalin nevertheless supported tough press comments on the MacDonald government. "It helps Communists of the world," he wrote to Molotov, "to educate workers of all nations (England above all). . . . Litvinov does not see and is not interested in [the revolutionary aspect of policy]. But the Politburo should take all this into account."[54]

Litvinov did not appear to be intimidated by Stalin, at least not then, and he pressed for an end to Soviet propaganda excesses. When Henderson insisted on the release from prison of two former Russian employees of the British embassy in Moscow, Litvinov intervened. "All the same, we should not," he wrote to Stalin, "irritate England over trifles." Only one person remained incarcerated, and Litvinov recommended that he be released before the new British ambassador raised the issue. It would be "best of all to remove the reason for a conversation."[55] While Stalin puffed himself up in his letters to Molotov and called Litvinov an "opportunist," he nevertheless listened to him, which was remarkable in view of his intolerance of political opposition. The Politburo adopted Litvinov's policy toward Britain, and on his advice freed the former British embassy employee. Stalin may have liked to blow off steam about "capitalist Shylocks," but Litvinov did not.

The *"Nochnaia Lampochka"* Still Burned Low in Paris

Litvinov was not so accommodating with the French. Relations with France remained strained through the end of the 1920s leading to an open confrontation in the autumn of 1930.[56] Apart from the French attempt in March 1928 to seize Soviet gold on deposit in the United States and the confrontation between Chicherin and Herbette in April 1928, there was the daily grind of bad relations. Briand and Berthelot treated Dovgalevskii correctly, even cordially. But in April 1928 Dovgalevskii reported hearing that Poincaré had "invited" French banks to decline all "direct or indirect" business in the USSR and to refuse to support French firms seeking Soviet contracts.[57] In October 1928 Dovgalevskii observed that Poincaré's hostility toward the USSR remained unchanged and that the Soviet government would have to continue a "waiting policy." We are trying, Dovgalevskii said, to avoid any incidents which could provoke new anti-communist campaigns.[58]

The corrupt French press drew Litvinov's special ire. "We have had very sad experiences with French journalists, whose unscrupulousness surpasses anything we know about foreign journalists." Their bylines are almost always for sale to the highest bidder, Litvinov noted in 1928, and since most of those bidders are hostile to us—and can pay more freely than we can, he might have added—almost no positive articles are published. Visits by French journalists are thus of no use, if not harmful to us, and we uniformly deny visas to them. The Quai d'Orsay retaliated by refusing visas to Soviet journalists, but Litvinov reckoned the price worth paying.[59]

In Moscow Herbette's relations with the NKID worsened, if that was possible. After one irritating conversation with Herbette in March 1928 Litvinov commented that the ambassador would be more comfortable as a private detective or as an intelligence operative than as a diplomat. In June 1928 the ambassador complained to Chicherin about a 1,000-ruble donation to striking textile workers in France. A trifle, Chicherin thought, but it was further evidence of Herbette's habit of seizing upon any pretext for a protest.[60]

Chicherin and Litvinov did not hide their scorn for Herbette, often complaining to Rantzau, who gleefully reported to Berlin on his French competitor's fall from grace. Chicherin described Herbette as a former journalist who still behaved like one, not able to get rid of his reporter's pushiness or get his stories straight. A "perfidious slanderer," he was the source of rumors about this or that Soviet policy. Either the USSR was planning for war to compensate for a difficult domestic political situation, or, according to Herbette, there were secret clauses to the Rapallo Treaty. Litvinov denied that there were and did not care a pin whether Herbette believed him or not. The

French ambassador, according to another NKID official, played "an evil role as a 'hater and well-poisoner [sic],' dangerous to all." Motivated by "personal animosity," according to Rantzau, Herbette could cause a "moment of danger to peace," spreading rumors about war, though he was not the only ambassador to do so.[61]

Herbette came up in a conversation in January 1929 between Dovgalevskii and Briand and Berthelot. The ambassador wondered what kind of reports Herbette was submitting to Paris. Briand knew where the *polpred* was going and defended Herbette, saying he had no biases against the USSR, which was a polite lie.

You know, he is a journalist, said Briand; he attentively reads the Soviet press and, because of a journalist's old habits, is constantly on the lookout for his daily "story."

And naturally, rejoined Berthelot, the single reader of these articles is of necessity me, each day, sometimes twice a day, implying that it was not his favorite activity.

Everyone laughed, reported Dovgalevskii, Berthelot recalling that he had responded once to a report from Herbette, citing Pascal, "your assumptions are correct, but your conclusions are false."[62]

The three of them had a good laugh, but in Moscow, it was no laughing matter. At the end of December 1929 Herbette demanded to see Litvinov to lodge a protest about an alleged Soviet military buildup on Romanian frontiers.

"I told Herbette," recorded Litvinov, "that I did not intend to accept any such communication . . . and when Herbette pushed the note off on me, I returned [the paper] without even looking at it." Readers might be reminded of the pantomime between Gregory and Rakovskii over the "Zinoviev letter" in 1924.

> Herbette then, in spite of my protests, began to read this note, but I immediately got up from my chair and said that I did not intend to listen to him. Herbette replied that he had instructions from his government which he was obliged to fulfill. I noted that the instructions from his government did not oblige me to accept the note and that Herbette could thus inform his government that he attempted to hand me the note but that I refused to accept it. Getting up to leave, Herbette left the note on the table. I wanted to return it to him but he refused to accept it, and consequently in his presence I tore up the note and threw it in the wastebasket.[63]

Litvinov was so incensed by this incident that he wrote to Stalin on the same day. "His behavior today," wrote Litvinov, "exceeds any insolence which Herbette has permitted himself in recent years." His conduct is unacceptable and justifies his recall. The French government might decide not to replace him, leaving only a chargé d'affaires, but so what?[64]

Here was a chance for Stalin to show his contempt for the French, as he had done with Henderson and the Labour government, but he chose not to, and Herbette stayed at his post for another year. Stalin, it seems, could act with more self-possession than he sometimes did when erupting with his amanuensis Molotov.

On the last day of 1929, perhaps still under the influence of his last clash with Litvinov, Herbette wrote to Paris that the Soviet Union would never abandon its hostile policies toward France—unconsciously he really meant toward himself—and therefore the only French option was to take stronger measures to discourage Soviet aggressiveness.[65] Had Litvinov read this preposterous dispatch, he would certainly have thought, there he goes again.

The French ambassador had little shame. Two months later, and going on leave, Herbette put aside his usual hostility to ask Litvinov, somewhat sheepishly, if he could send home personal items acquired in Moscow without paying export duties. Herbette and his wife had a reputation for being cheap, and here was proof of it. Litvinov recorded sarcastically that the customs authorities had agreed, fearing yet another anti-communist press campaign in Paris. As for the "so-called" Soviet military preparations on the Romanian frontier, Litvinov asked Dovgalevskii, the next time he saw Briand, to tell him that these rumors had French origins, namely Herbette.[66]

Dead End in Soviet-American Relations

While the NKID was relatively indifferent to relations with France, it was otherwise with the United States. We left Soviet-American relations in the autumn of 1927 after the collapse of the Paris discussions with National City Bank. Charles Mitchell, the bank president, left France at the end of September in high dudgeon. Back in Washington, he boasted that he had never intended to offer long-term credits to the Soviet government, and that the State Department should take a hard line against the USSR. Naturally, no one in Moscow was informed of Mitchell's rants back home, and there was still some discussion of trying for a settlement. Chicherin for one was interested: an agreement with National City Bank would cost only a few million in exchange for long-term credits; it was the key to opening up Wall Street for Soviet trade. Let's continue to negotiate with Mr. Mitchell in New York, Chicherin recommended. A Soviet-American rapprochement should be based on better trade relations.[67]

"'Choose' America is not a new principle," added Sokolnikov on his return from Paris. "On the contrary, it is the realization of this line which we have pursued with regard to America since the first weeks of the October Revolution." Let's get on with it, recommended Sokolnikov; the longer we wait, the harder it will become to reach agreement. The benefits to Soviet trade in terms of lower interest rates and even the extension of long-term credits were worth far more than the beer money necessary to settle the National City Bank claims.[68]

Litvinov on the other hand took a more nuanced position which appears to have swayed the Politburo. We parted company with Mitchell, Litvinov observed, because he asked too much for the debt and offered too little on credit. I do not deny that it would be advantageous to settle with National City Bank, but after it there would be other creditors who also had claims to make against us which were by no means small change. Unlike Chicherin, Litvinov did not think that a settlement with Mitchell was "the key to a change in our relations with America." If ever the USSR is going to get on better terms with the United States, it ought to "take the bull by the horns" and negotiate directly with the U.S. government over state-to-state debts. Negotiations would be easier than haggling with bankers over millions about which the State Department would not break off negotiations. If we can achieve such a settlement, "the private creditors will temper their appetites, and agreement with them will cost us much less." This approach was the only way, according to Litvinov, to resolve the problems in Soviet-American relations, though maybe not right away since the present moment was unfavorable for such negotiations. Eventually "it seems to me that it will be impossible to avoid going down this path, if we really want to obtain any results at all."[69]

With Chicherin and Sokolnikov in favor of a deal with Mitchell, and Litvinov against, the Politburo stuck to its original position against a resumption of negotiations.[70] Given Mitchell's posturing in the State Department about getting his money back without offering credit in exchange, readers will have to agree that Litvinov and the Politburo were right and Chicherin and Sokolnikov wrong. The latter were still implausibly naïve about the underlying hostility in the United States and in Europe toward the Soviet Union. As if to underline this point, the Tass deputy bureau chief in New York reported to Moscow a not-for-publication comment by Secretary of State Kellogg that it was "entirely useless" to raise the "Russian question . . . since 'in the given situation' it is impossible to speak of recognition."[71]

The Politburo asked Litvinov to prepare a more detailed proposal for an agreement with the United States. Basically it came to settling the so-called Kerenskii debt, in the same way that other governments had settled war debts with the United States. But Litvinov was in no hurry to start negotiations; better to wait awhile. Chicherin must have been stung by his defeat in the Politburo on the Mitchell negotiations for he responded aggressively to Litvinov that a government-to-government settlement was not possible and that the best way to proceed was through settlement of private debts like that with National City Bank. Bron, still in New York at Amtorg, also returned to the charge with news that National City Bank wanted to renew negotiations where they had been left off in Paris. In a sorry piece of self-interested pleading, Mitchell's colleague, Garrard Winston, told Bron that a settlement with National City Bank was the best way "to settle our problems with America."[72] Chicherin appears to have persuaded the Politburo to refer Litvinov's recommendations to the American Commission, where he had a seat and Litvinov did not. But Chicherin was unable to advance his ideas, and the American Commission devoted most of its time to the calculation of Soviet debts in the United States. Following Litvinov's recommendations, the Politburo moved cautiously on American relations and rejected a proposal to send a high-ranking official to the United States on an exploratory mission.[73]

Chicherin was not quite ready to give up on a new approach to the United States. In July 1928 he returned to the subject of National City Bank, openly criticizing the Politburo's position on the negotiations with Mitchell. He insisted again that the best way to improve relations with the United States was through settlements with private claimants which would facilitate government-to-government negotiations.[74] The differences between Chicherin and Litvinov were still a question of tactics: Chicherin wanted to settle with private firms first and move on to government-to-government negotiations; Litvinov wanted to do the reverse, thinking it would be an easier, less costly approach. In Moscow cost was always a factor in discussing debts settlements, and so Litvinov's approach was more appealing to the Politburo.

Although Soviet trade with the United States improved, there were setbacks. The Equitable Trust Company in New York stopped a Soviet line of credit in the summer of 1928 based on adverse press reports on a bad Soviet harvest and other negative economic news. Exports were down, and thus also was the ability to pay credit obligations. It was the usual exaggerations: according to one British journalist, "in the next six months a catastrophe should be expected." As Bron put it, whenever there was some setback in the USSR, the American banks always hesitated on future contracts and credit lines. To deal with the lack of foreign exchange, the Politburo directed that exports should be increased, museum valuables sold, and gold and platinum extraction increased to the maximum.[75]

In order to counter adverse western media propaganda, the Soviet government was keen to encourage Americans to visit the USSR, but not just any Americans. When the University of Chicago proposed to send a group of professors and students to study in the USSR, Litvinov equivocated. He did not object if the visitors came for a short time, but if for a longer stay, the project was bound to turn sour. The visitors would observe and complain about "the imperfections and dark sides of our life"; they would naturally gravitate to foreign journalists and diplomats, accepting as given their "gossip and slander." When they left the Soviet Union, they would take with them these prejudices, painting "our life in very black tones." Better to let the professors and students stay home and focus on American business circles in order to encourage trade. The professors and students would not produce one extra ruble's worth of credit, but leaving the USSR with negative attitudes, they could adversely influence businessmen.[76] The Politburo nevertheless invited the students—the professors were not mentioned in the Politburo resolution—and directed that Soviet agencies be "friendly" and offer all necessary assistance. Litvinov was instructed "to undertake the necessary measures" to assist arriving Americans, and there-fore to hold his tongue.[77] The Politburo often followed Litvinov's recom-mendations, but not always.

At the beginning of 1929 the National City Bank claims also returned to the fore. The reader might be surprised by this development because Litvinov's position had carried in the Politburo, but, as was often the case in negotiations with the West, local Soviet representatives exceeded their instructions. In this case it was New York Amtorg boss, Bron, and A. L. Sheinman, former Gosbank head, sent to New York to promote U.S. busi-ness and credit with the USSR.

On 1 February 1929 Sheinman reported that he and a Gosbank agent had entered into discussions with Mitchell, the same "Sunshine Charley" who had gone to Paris in September 1927 to negotiate with Rakovskii, Sokol-nikov, and Piatakov. Sheinman reported that they had "agreed" with Mitch-ell on negotiations and that, based on a "preliminary exchange of opinions, we came away with the impression that the given directive from Moscow could be a basis for agreement."

Wait a minute, Stalin wondered, as he read Sheinman's report, "what kind of directive?" Worse was to come as Stalin read on. We agreed with Mitchell, Sheinman reported, that starting to work with National City Bank "could serve as the basis for maximizing big questions and big business."[78]

What kind of *duraki*, idiots, do we have in New York, Stalin must have wondered, who would swallow Mitchell's bogus promises? Clearly alarmed, Stalin directed that a cable be sent to Sheinman instructing him not to conclude with Mitchell and to stick to a sounding of his ideas. No less than Rykov, titular head of the Soviet government, immediately complied: a renewal of negotiations with Mitchell was "inexpedient" since the failure to achieve an agreement could have negative effects. Do not discuss claims; stick to current trade credits. If Mitchell makes new proposals, say only that you will forward them to Moscow.[79]

At the same time, Bron reported that he had heard from a reliable source that the incoming president Hoover would continue to "stand on Hughes' position" regarding recognition. Readers will remember that the former Secretary of State Hughes was intransigent toward the Soviet government and demanded its prior acceptance without discussion of all U.S. demands on recognition of debts and private property, in effect demanding the renunciation of the Russian Revolution.[80]

In view of Hoover's position there was not much point in departing from Litvinov's policy and negotiating with Mitchell. But Sheinman cabled again: an agreement with National City Bank would be "a step forward." Mitchell acknowledged the possibility of "secured credits" in exchange for an agreement on debts. Rykov's instructions forbid the conclusion of any agreement with Mitchell, and so Sheinman asked for new instructions. In the meantime, he disregarded Rykov and discussed details of a settlement with the bank directors.[81] Clearly Sheinman was headed for trouble, but instead of calling him to order, Piatakov, as deputy head of the Supreme Economic Council (VSHKh), recommended that yet another special committee be convoked to reexamine the question.

Too many cooks are going to spoil this broth, Stalin must have thought. The Politburo canceled previous instructions to Sheinman and directed Bukharin, still Stalin's right arm but not for long, to study the file and make recommendations. The upshot was that the Politburo ordered the formation of yet another commission on American affairs.[82] This step did not solve the immediate problem: either there was a willful disregard of Moscow's instructions or total confusion in New York, because the Gosbank representative there recommended a settlement with National City Bank, even proposing terms of agreement. Enough was enough; the Politburo commission on American affairs ordered a halt to all New York discussions.[83]

Readers might think that a Politburo directive would have put an end to the negotiations, but not just yet. Confusion continued. On 28 March the Politburo approved a visa for National City Bank directors, Ferdinand Schwedtmann and John Link, to visit Moscow, the purpose of their visit not being specified in the resolution. The following week the Politburo reproached Piatakov for allowing the discussions with Mitchell and ordered that in the future all matters concerning debt compensation pass first by the Politburo and that Soviet departments follow its resolutions to the letter.[84] All well and good, matters were being clarified, but what was to be said to Schwedtmann when he arrived in Moscow? No one seemed to know.

On 23 April, Schwedtmann met with Piatakov in Moscow. I have come to discuss a settlement of our claims, Schwedtmann said.

"We are not ready to discuss this question," replied Piatakov. "We gave special instructions about this to our representatives in New York." They should have informed you. We agreed to your trip to Moscow, we agreed to provide relevant information, but we did not agree to any negotiations on the claims of National City Bank.

It was not an issue of giving me permission to visit Moscow, Schwedtmann retorted, but rather about an invitation, twice given, to come to negotiate a settlement!

Piatakov expressed his astonishment. There must be some misunderstanding, he replied.

We would like to work in the USSR, continued Schwedtmann, but not without a settlement of claims. Based on the statements made in New York by all Soviet officials, we assumed that an agreement was possible. Schwedtmann was polite, thanked Piatakov for his candidness, which he added would allow him to stop wasting his time in Moscow, and immediately returned home.

The Politburo did not want to offend American businessmen, nor National City Bank, so Piatakov immediately reported to Stalin. He also wrote to New York for clarification of Schwedtmann's claims.[85] It was Sheinman's fault, Bron replied: he had proposed the Moscow visit early on before receiving instructions, though he had stressed that even without an agreement, such a trip would be useful. It was on this basis that the bank had decided to send Schwedtmann to Moscow.[86]

Since the Politburo had approved Schwedtmann's visa, all the blame could not be put on poor Sheinman. On instructions, Piatakov told Schwedtmann that it was nevertheless Sheinman's fault. He had acted beyond his authority and had been sacked. On the general question of negotiations over the bank's claims, the Politburo considered that the establishment of diplomatic relations with the United States was a prior condition.[87] This was Litvinov's policy, the same then being applied to the resumption of relations with Britain.

Piatakov saw Schwedtmann again after he had met with other Soviet officials, and he did his best to deliver the bad news without offense. Piatakov apologized for the unauthorized conduct of Soviet officials and repeated that Sheinman had been sacked. He reiterated that the Soviet government considered it unrealistic to conduct negotiations with private claimants prior to a "general agreement" with the U.S. government. The quid pro quo of a settlement with National City Bank was a loan, which would be impossible without "normal" relations with the United States. Better no negotiations than failed negotiations. At the end of their conversation, according to Piatakov, Schwedtmann was conciliatory. I understand the Soviet position, he said, but I draw your attention to the importance of an agreement with us, and I hope that eventually it can be obtained.[88] Litvinov's policy had thus been confirmed, though not without confusion and muddle in Moscow and New York.

Because Schwedtmann did not return to the United States until midsummer, John Link, a National City Bank director, went to see a Gosbank official in New York to ask what the devil had happened in Moscow. The poor Gosbank representative was at a loss to explain and asked Link what he knew, which was not much. "Everyone was gracious, but categorically refused to discuss business." Schwedtmann was "very annoyed," according to Link, and did not know how he would explain the fiasco to Mitchell when he returned home. A journey to Moscow was not cheap and would rest heavy upon the bank's ledger. "Obviously Mitchell was very angry: 'he, apparently, had never heard of such a thing' and that 'it all looked like some kind of operetta.'"

"Of course I myself," said the Gosbank agent, "had some difficulty in providing an explanation, and I avoided responding to all direct questions." Everything was in Sheinman's hands. He was supposed to return to Moscow to be present when Schwedtmann arrived, but he fell sick in Berlin and did not return, and so no one knew in Moscow what exactly had been said during the New York discussions. "All this," concluded the Gosbank agent, "was an extremely regrettable business, caused by an unfortunate combination of circumstances."[89] Well, it was certainly a muddled file at a time when the Soviet government was trying to increase trade with the United States.

There was also the strange case of Sheinman himself who had held important positions in the Soviet government, not least as head of Gosbank and *zamnarkom* of finance. On arriving in Berlin at the end of March, he informed the Soviet government that he did not wish to return to the Soviet Union. In April of course he was sacked, as Schwedtmann was informed, but instead of sending the OGPU after him, accommodations were made, in exchange for access to secret funds, and he ended up for a time as the director of the Intourist Office in London in the late 1930s.

Soviet trade with the United States continued to develop in spite of the absence of diplomatic relations and the bungled negotiations with National City Bank. From Washington the Soviet unofficial representative Skvirskii sent detailed reports to Moscow on political and economic developments. He had contacts with various American politicians and lobbyists who favored Soviet recognition, but they could make no headway. The American Federation of Labor (AFL) continued to oppose recognition, and the

Republicans, ironically, used such opposition as a convenient excuse for taking no initiative toward Moscow.[90] In October 1929 the NKID received information from Washington that Hoover had not changed his position on recognition. Bankers and industrialists, who told Soviet agents that they favored recognition, were not putting pressure on Washington. Hoover held to his early views of the USSR as an "economic void" where nothing could happen as long as "capitalist individualism" was not reestablished. In spite of Soviet economic growth, Hoover still counted on the "economic collapse of the USSR in the not distant future." This expectation was not just Hoover's: in April 1929 State Department assistant secretary William R. Castle had quipped to his new boss, Henry L. Stimson, "We have waited almost 10 years for the Soviets to be overturned in Russia."[91] It was ironic that Hoover expected an imminent Soviet "economic collapse" when it was the American economy which was about to fail. On Black Thursday, 24 October 1929, share prices on the New York Stock Exchange began to fall. The following week there were other black days as the slide continued. It marked the onset of the Great Depression which soon spread to Europe.

On 27 October, Litvinov forwarded Skvirskii's most recent report to Mikoian, Stalin, and others. Litvinov was in high dudgeon because increased trade with the United States was not leading to a "political rapprochement." It was the old Soviet strategy to obtain western diplomatic recognition. It had worked in Britain, but not in the United States. Litvinov worried that British Tories might notice: if they could reverse the minority Labour government, Anglo-Soviet relations would remain broken. German industrialists were also angry to see so much business going to the United States. We need to inform our trade organizations, said Litvinov, that when placing orders, they consider only our economic interests and not "chase after political mirages." But he added a proviso: "Our political interests imperatively demand that, at least, given equal economic benefits, the preference in the distribution of orders is always to be given to those countries with which we have normal diplomatic relations."[92]

Litvinov's preoccupations became moot in the coming months. At first sight the U.S. stock market collapse seemed to give an advantage to the USSR. Lower interest rates and lower product prices were anticipated since American manufacturers needed orders. Soviet trade agencies thought they had gained the upper hand in contract negotiations, and big orders could be used as leverage to obtain diplomatic recognition.[93]

It was still the late Krasin's policy, but Great Depression or not, it did not work. Anti-communism remained intense, however desirable trade might be with the USSR. Amtorg was a favorite target. In early 1930 police visited the Amtorg New York offices, wanting to know why they worked on Sundays.

On another occasion detectives came to investigate a tip that communists worked in the Amtorg offices, which could hardly have been a revelation. The police visits were a minor irritant and were quickly forgotten in the welter of anti-Soviet press and political attacks. The AFL also remained hostile. Rumors circulated, still ironically, that the USSR would go bankrupt in the next six months. One of the authors of these rumors was none other than National City Bank. We'll teach you Bolos a lesson, Mitchell and his colleagues must have thought, if you don't settle your debts with us. Instead of business improving, the banks obstructed Soviet trade. In May 1930 the *New York Daily News* published counterfeit documents linking Amtorg with the Comintern. Amtorg New York issued an immediate denial and threatened to sue. The *New York Times* published the Amtorg communiqué, and there were related stories in the press about the bogus Zinoviev letter and Orlov forgeries against U.S. Senators Borah and Norris. At the same time two congressional committees prepared to investigate communist "propaganda" and links with Amtorg.[94] If you worked in Soviet trade organizations in the United States, you could never let down your guard. An improvement in American-Soviet relations would have to wait until the election of Franklin D. Roosevelt as U.S. president.

Notes

1. Maxse's minute, citing Stalin, 14 Sept. 1926, N121/53/38, FO 371 11779.

2. Iurii Fel'shteinskii and Georgii Cherniavskii, *Lev Trotskii*, 4 vols. (Moscow, 2013), III, pp. 284-88; and Nadezhda A. Joffe, *Back in Time: My Life, My Fate, My Epoch*, trans. Frederic S. Choate (Oak Park, Mich., 1995), pp. 65–66.

3. Service, *Stalin*, pp. 272–73; Silvio Pons, *Stalin and the Inevitable War, 1936–1941* (London, 2002), pp. 219–20.

4. Litvinov to Charles Roden Buxton, London (in English), 29 April 1928, AVPRF, f. 05, o. 8, p. 42, d. 71, l. 178.

5. "Russia," Gregory, 12 June 1926, N2868/1687/38, FO 371 11795.

6. Report by Stresemann on meeting with Briand, Geneva, 14 June 1927, AzDAP, B, V, pp. 513–18; and "Politique russe de l'Angleterre," ns, but Joseph Paul-Boncour, Genève, 12 June 1927, MAÉ Grande-Bretagne/66, fol. 36.

7. Extract from Cabinet conclusions, 21 Jan. 1929, N436/18/38, FO 371 14029.

8. "Mr. Oliphant," Locker-Lampson, 15 Feb. 1929; and Chamberlain's minute, 15 Feb. 1929, N1102/55/38, FO 371 14038.

9. IKKI to the Chinese Communist Party Central Committee, very secret, 4 Feb. 1928, *VKP(b)*, *Komintern v Kitae*, III, pt. 1, pp. 290–91.

10. *VKP(b)*, *Komintern v Kitae*, III, pt. 1, pp. 35–36.

11. Excerpt from Politburo protocol, no. 15 (special no. 14), 15 March 1928, *VKP(b)*, *Komintern v Kitae*, III, pt. 1, pp. 349–50; and I. A. Piatnitskii, IKKI, to Stalin, very secret, 11 June 1928, ibid., pp. 431–33.

12. Litvinov to Stalin, no. L/3061, secret, 24 Jan. 1929, AVPRF, f. 05, o. 9, p. 43, d. 1, l. 12.

13. Sir George Clerk, British ambassador in Ankara, no. 443, 11 Nov. 1929, N5149/280/38, FO 371 14041.

14. Minutes by S. Harcourt-Smith, 6 Feb. 1929, N720/18/38, FO 371 14029; Locker Lampson, 11 March 1929, N1483/18/38, ibid.; and Chamberlain, 11 March 1929, ibid.

15. Fleuriau, no. 59, 8 Feb. 1929, MAÉ Grande-Bretagne/67, ff. 16–17.

16. Briand to Herbette, no. 137, 22 Feb. 1929, MAÉ Grande-Bretagne/67, fol. 19; Herbette, nos. 223–24, 12 March 1929, ibid., ff. 24–25; Fleuriau, no. 154, 26 March 1929, ibid., fol. 34; and excerpt from Politburo protocol, no. 70, 25 March 1929, Politbiuro Osoboi papki, pp. 182–84.

17. Litvinov's dnevnik, "Meeting with members of the British delegation . . . ," secret, nd (late March–early April 1929), AVPRF, f. 05, o. 9, p. 43, d. 3, ll. 90–91.

18. Herbette, nos. 287–90, confidential, 5 April 1929, MAÉ Grande-Bretagne/67, ff. 54–57.

19. Leeper to Collier, 8 April 1929, covering Poliakoff's memorandum, 5 April 1929, N1902/18/38, FO 371 14029.

20. Litvinov to Stalin, no. L/3310, secret, 5 June 1929, AVPRF, f. 04, o. 4, p. 41, d. 564, ll. 2 (r/v); and excerpt from Politburo protocol, no. 83, 6 June 1929, Politbiuro Osoboi papki, pp. 190–91.

21. Litvinov to D. V. Bogomolov (Warsaw), no. 194, secret, 7 June 1929, AVPRF, f. 069, o. 13, p. 37, d. 3, l. 2.

22. "Report on the Visit of the Anglo-Russian Trade Delegation to the USSR," nd, N2975/18/38, FO 371 14030; and untitled note for the prime minister, H. J. Seymour, head, Northern Department, 26 June 1929, N3061/18/38, ibid.

23. Dovgalevskii to NKID, no. 0581/s, very secret, 28 June 1929, AVPRF, f. 04, o. 4, p. 41, d. 564, l. 4 (r/v); and Dovgalevskii to Karakhan, no. 0582/s, very secret, 28 June 1929, AVPRF, f. 069, o. 13, p. 37, d. 3, l. 12.

24. Excerpt from Politburo protocol, no. 87, 4 July 1929, Politbiuro Osoboi papki, p. 191; and Karakhan to Dovgalevskii, no. 4426, 6 July 1929, AVPRF, f. 069, o. 13, p. 37, d. 3, l. 14.

25. "Record of conversation of A. F. Neiman with Ben Tillet, 13 July 1929," no. 0650/s, secret, 18 July 1928, AVPRF, f. 04, o. 4, p. 41, d. 565, ll. 1–3.

26. Litvinov to Karakhan, 14 July 1929, AVPRF, f. 04, o. 4, p. 41, d. 563, ll. 13–20.

27. Litvinov to Molotov, cc. Politburo members, no. L/3342, secret, 21 Aug. 1929, AVPRF, f. 04, o. 4, p. 41, d. 563, ll. 50–54.

28. Henderson to F. O. Lindley (Oslo), no. 29, 15 July 1929, N3263/18/38, FO 371 14030; Karakhan to Alfred Danielson, Norwegian chargé d'affaires in Moscow, 23 July 1929, AVPRF, f. 04, o. 4, p. 41, d. 563, l. 75; and Lindley, no. 25, 24 July 1929, N3416/18/38, FO 371 14031.

29. Dovgalevskii to Karakhan, no. 0681/s, very secret, 2 Aug. 1929, AVPRF, f. 04, o. 4, p. 41, d. 563, ll. 36–37; no. 0682/s, very secret, 8 Aug. 1929, ibid., ll. 40–41; "Conversation of V. S. Dovgalevskii with . . . Henderson, 29 July 1929," no. 683/s, very secret, ibid., ll. 42–44; "Record of conversation between Mr. A. Henderson and M. Dovgalevsky [on 29 July]," 1 Aug. 1929, N3619/18/38, FO 371 14031; and "Record of conversation between Mr. A. Henderson and M. Dovgalevsky [on 31 July]," 1 Aug. 1929, N3620/18/38, ibid.

30. Politbiuro Osoboi papki, p. 192, n. 1; Izvestiia, 2 Aug. 1929, DVP, XII, pp. 429–30; and Memorandum, A. Cave, 7 Aug. 1929, N3649/18/38, FO 371 14031.

31. Minutes by Seymour, 1 Aug. 1929, N3556/18/38; by Harcourt-Smith, 25 July 1929, N3539/18/38; and by Seymour, 2 Aug. 1929, N3556/18/38, FO 371 14031.

32. "Excerpt from a record of conversation of comrade Krestinskii with Stresemann," no. 831/s, 3 Aug. 1929, AVPRF, f. 04, o. 4, p. 41, d. 563, l. 32.

33. Excerpt from the dnevnik of Bogomolov, then chargé d'affaires in London, no. 3, 31 Dec. 1929, AVPRF, f. 069, o. 13, p. 37, d. 3, l. 86.

34. Arthur Lord Stamfordham to Lindsay, 8 Aug. 1929, and "Sect. of State," Lindsay, 10 Aug. 1929, N3715/18/38, FO 371 14031.

35. Litvinov to Molotov, cc. Politburo members, no. L/3341, secret, 20 Aug. 1929, AVPRF, f. 04, o. 4, p. 41, d. 563, ll. 46–48.

36. Litvinov to Molotov, cc. Politburo members, no. L/3342, secret, 21 Aug. 1929, AVPRF, f. 04, o. 4, p. 41, d. 563, ll. 50–54.

37. Litvinov to Molotov, cc. Politburo members, no. L/3344, secret, 22 Aug. 1929, AVPRF, f. 04, o. 4, p. 41, d. 563, l. 54.

38. Litvinov to Molotov, cc. Politburo members, no. L/3348, secret, 24 Aug. 1929, AVPRF, f. 04, o. 4, p. 41, d. 563, ll. 56–58; excerpt from Litvinov's *dnevnik*, "Meeting with Wise, 30.VIII-29g.," secret, ibid., ll. 59–60; and excerpt from Litvinov to Dovgalevskii, no. 1529, secret, 7 Sept. 1929, AVPRF, f. 069, o. 13, p. 37, d. 3, l. 45.

39. Henderson's statement, 4 Sept. 1929; Litvinov's reply, 6 Sept. 1929, N4038/18/38, FO 371 14031; and excerpt from Politburo protocol, no. 96, 5 Sept. 1929, *Politbiuro Osoboi papki*, pp. 193–94.

40. Stalin to Molotov, 9 Sept. 1929, *Stalin's Letters*, pp. 177–79.

41. Stalin to Molotov, 1 Sept. 1929, *Stalin's Letters*, p. 176.

42. Dovgalevskii to Litvinov, no. 0864/s, secret, 1 Oct. 1929, AVPRF, f. 069, o. 13, p. 37, d. 3, ll. 59 61.

43. "Conversations with Soviet Representative and Protocol," C.P. 267 (29), secret, 4 Oct. 1929, N4293/18/38, FO 371 14032 (published in *DBFP*, 2nd, VII, pp. 20–38); and Fleuriau, no. 494, 8 Nov. 1929, MAÉ Grande-Bretagne/68, fol. 76.

44. Litvinov's *dnevnik*, "Meeting with Herbette," 17 Sept. 1929, AVPRF, f. 0136, p. 131, d. 487, ll. 22–24; and Herbette, no. 152bis, 17 Sept. 1929, MAÉ Grande-Bretagne/68, ff. 14–20.

45. Litvinov to Stalin, no. L/3164, secret, 5 March 1929, AVPRF, f. 05, o. 9, p. 43, d. 1, ll. 43–44.

46. Litvinov to Stalin, no. L/3545, very secret, 1 Dec. 1929, AVPRF, f. 05, o. 9, p. 43, d. 1, ll. 176–77.

47. Litvinov to Stalin, no. L/3580, very secret, 18 Dec. 1929, AVPRF, f. 05, o. 9, p. 43, d. 1, l. 190.

48. Litvinov to Dovgalevskii, no. L/3338, 7 Feb. 1930, AVPRF, f. 0136, p. 139, d. 584, ll. 3–2.

49. Lindley, no. 207, confidential, 10 June 1929, N2840/55/38, FO 371 14039.

50. Record of conversation in French between Litvinov, Lunarcharskii, and Japanese diplomat Yotaro Sugimura (Geneva), 28 May 1929, N2646/55/38, FO 371 14039.

51. Herbette, no. 152bis, 17 Sept. 1929, MAÉ Grande-Bretagne/68, ff. 14–20.

52. Ovey to Henderson, no. 9, confidential, 16 Dec. 1929, N6121/18/38, FO 371 14036 (published in *DBFP*, 2nd, VII, pp. 56–57).

53. Ovey to Henderson, no. 138, 25 Feb. 1930, N1404/75/38, PRO FO 371 14860.

54. Stalin to Molotov, 9 Aug. 1929, *Stalin's Letters*, pp. 174–75.

55. Litvinov to Stalin, no. L/3257, secret, 20 Nov. 1929, AVPRF, f. 05, o. 9, p. 43, d. 1, l. 171.

56. M. J. Carley, "Five Kopecks for Five Kopecks: Franco-Soviet Trade Relations, 1928–1939," *Cahiers du monde russe et soviétique*, vol. 33, no. 1 (Jan.–March 1992), pp. 23–58.

57. Dovgalevskii to Chicherin, no. 0377/s, very secret, 12 April 1928, AVPRF, f. 0136, p. 124, d. 408, ll. 91–94.

58. Dovgalevskii to Litvinov, no. 0966/s, very secret, 26 Oct. 1928, AVPRF, f. 0136, p. 124, d. 408, ll.164–67; and no. 0964/s, very secret, 26 Oct. 1928, ibid., ll. 162–63.

59. Litvinov to A. V. Lunacharskii, commissar for education, no. L/2753, secret, 21 May 1928, AVPRF, f. 05, o. 8, d. 66, p. 41, l. 68.

60. Litvinov's *dnevnik*, "Record of conversation with Herbette," 28 March 1928, AVPRF, f. 0136, p. 124, d. 407, ll. 67–68; and Chicherin to Dovgalevskii, secret, 1 June 1928, AVPRF, f. 0136, p. 124, d. 405, l. 14.

61. Rantzau, no. 225, 6 March 1928, AzDAP, B, VIII, pp. 285–87; no. 388, 16 April 1928, ibid., pp. 494–96; and no. 424, 26 April 1928, ibid., pp. 541–42. Soviet official B. S. Stomoniakov to Rantzau (Rantzau, no. 639, 12 June 1928, AzDAP, B, IX, pp. 165–66); and Rantzau, no. 489, 12 May 1928, AzDAP, B, IX, pp. 29–30.

62. "Conversation with Briand and Berthelot," no. 071/s, very secret, Dovgalevskii, 25 Jan. 1929, AVPRF, f. 0136, p. 131, d. 488, ll. 14–18.

63. Litvinov's *dnevnik*, "Meeting with Herbette," secret, 21 Dec. 1929, AVPRF, f. 05, o. 9, p. 43, d. 3, l. 164.

64. Litvinov to Stalin, no. L/3586, very secret, 21 Dec. 1929, AVPRF, f. 05, o. 9, p. 43, d. 1, l. 194.

65. Herbette, no. 781bis, 31 Dec. 1929, MAÉ Russie/362, ff. 249–59.

66. Litvinov's *dnevnik*, "Meeting with Herbette," secret, 26 Feb. 1930, AVPRF, f. 0136, p. 139, d. 585, l. 17; and Litvinov to Dovgalevskii, no. L/3455, secret, 27 March 1930, AVPRF, f. 0136, p. 139, d. 584, l. 6.

67. Chicherin to Stalin, cc. to Politburo and others, nos. 886/ChS, 10 Oct. 1927, 898/ChS, very secret, 12 Oct. 1927, *Moskva-Vashington*, I, pp. 436–40.

68. Sokolnikov to Politburo, no. 14088/s, secret, 12 Oct. 1927, *Moskva-Vashington*, I, pp. 440–42.

69. Litvinov to Stalin, secret, 12 Oct. 1927, SAO, *Gody nepriznaniia, 1927–1933*, pp. 61–62.

70. Politburo resolution, no. P129/8-s, rigorously secret, 13 Oct. 1927, *Moskva-Vashington*, I, p. 442.

71. Deputy bureau chief, Tass, New York, to Ia. G. Dolestkii, director, Tass, Moscow, 22 Oct. 1927, *Moskva-Vashington*, I, pp. 443–44.

72. Litvinov to Stalin, no 3620, secret, 14 Nov. 1927, Chicherin to V. V. Osinskii, head of Politburo American Commission, cc. Stalin and others, no. 1050/ChS, very secret, 28 Nov. 1927; and Bron to Mikoian, no. 569, 2 Dec. 1927, *Moskva-Vashington*, I, pp. 454–57, 472–77.

73. Politburo resolutions, no. P136/3-s, rigorously secret, 17 Nov. 1927, no. P138/4-s, rigorously secret, 30 Nov. 1927, *Moskva-Vashington*, I, pp. 463 and 475.

74. Chicherin to Politburo, no. 627/ChS, 23 July 1928, *Moskva-Vashington*, I, pp. 680–82.

75. M. G. Gurevich, Amtorg, to Mikoian, and others, no. MG/251/s, 8 Aug. 1928, *Moskva-Vashington*, I, pp. 684–88; Bron to Mikoian, no. 540, secret, most immediate, 9 Aug. 1928, ibid., pp. 689–90; and Politburo resolution, no. P38/4-s, very secret, special file, 16 Aug. 1928, ibid., pp. 697–98.

76. Litvinov to Molotov, cc. to Politburo members, no. L/2861, secret, 23 Aug. 1928, *Moskva-Vashington*, I, pp. 700–702.

77. Politburo resolutions, no. P39/14-s, rigorously secret, 25 Aug. 1928; no. P43/11-s, rigorously secret, 20 Sept. 1928, *Moskva-Vashington*, I, p. 703.

78. Sheinman to Rykov, very secret, 1 Feb. 1929; and Stalin's marginal note, nd, *Moskva-Vashington*, II, pp. 18–20.

79. Politburo resolution, no. P63/19-s, rigorously secret, 7 Feb. 1929; and Rykov to Sheinman, cc. Bron, no 3026, very secret, 8 Feb. 1929, *Moskva-Vashington*, II, pp. 21–22.

80. Bron to Stalin, nos. 2953–54, rigorously secret, 11 Feb. 1929, *Moskva-Vashington*, II, pp. 22–23.

81. Sheinman to Rykov, Piatakov, no. 2930, rigorously secret, 13 Feb. 1929, *Moskva-Vashington*, II, p. 23; Sheinman to Mikoian, no. 2951–52, rigorously secret, 14 Feb. 1929, ibid.,

p. 24; and Sheinman to Rykov, Bron, nos. 3069, 3071, 3076, rigorously secret, 19 Feb. 1929, ibid., p. 26.

82. Piatakov to Rykov, Stalin, no. 1735/s, very secret, 20 Feb. 1929, Moskva-Vashington, II, p. 26; Politburo resolution, no. P66/5-rs, rigorously secret, 25 Feb. 1929, ibid., pp. 28–29; Bukharin's notes for the Politburo, no. 10764/s, very secret, 27 Feb. 1929, ibid., pp. 29–32; and Politburo protocol, no. P67/15-s, rigorously secret, 7 March 1929, ibid., pp. 33–34.

83. V. S. Korobkov to Piatakov, nos. 3745–48, 3752, rigorously secret, 16 March 1929, Moskva-Vashington, II, pp. 35–37; and Protocol of Politburo commission on American affairs, very secret, 20 March 1929, ibid., pp. 39–41.

84. Politburo protocols, no. P70/5-s, rigorously secret, 28 March 1929, and no. P71/17-s, rigorously secret, 4 April 1929, Moskva-Vashington, II, p. 43.

85. Piatakov to Stalin, cc. Mikoian, no. 180/p-s, very secret, immediate, 23 April 1929, Moskva-Vashington, II, pp. 49–50.

86. Bron and Korobkov to Piatakov, no. 4535, rigorously secret, immediate, 24 April 1929, Moskva-Vashington, II, p. 51.

87. Politburo resolution, no. P76/1-rs, rigorously secret, 24 April 1929, Moskva-Vashington, II, pp. 51–52.

88. Piatakov to Stalin, Rykov, Mikoian, no. 183/p-s, very secret, 25 April 1929, Moskva-Vashington, II, pp. 57–61.

89. A. I. Fainberg, deputy director, Gosbank, New York, to Piatakov, 21 May 1929, Moskva-Vashington, II, pp. 75–76.

90. Bron to Stalin, no. 2953–54, rigorously secret, 11 Feb. 1929, Moskva-Vashington, II, pp. 22–23.

91. Castle to Stimson, April 1929, 861.51/2280, NA RG59, M-316, reel 123.

92. Litvinov to Mikoian, Stalin, and others, no. L/3461, secret, 27 Oct. 1929, enclosing the excerpt of Skvirskii's undated report, Moskva-Vashington, II, pp. 102–104.

93. S. A. Lozovskii, Profintern head, to Politburo, no. 1/59/8, secret, 28 Dec. 1929, Moskva-Vashington, II, pp. 178–79.

94. Skvirskii to Litvinov, 19 March 1930, SAO, Gody nepriznaniia, 1927–1933, pp. 257–62; P. A. Bogdanov, Amtorg head, New York, to Mikoian, no. 4983, rigorously secret, 18 March 1930, Moskva-Vashington, II, p. 219; nos. 6782, 6786–87, rigorously secret, 2 May 1930, ibid., pp. 227–28; nos. 6828–29, rigorously secret, 3 May 1930, ibid., p. 229; Skvirskii to NKID, no. 995, very secret, 6 May 1929, ibid., p. 230; and Skvirskii to Litvinov, 14 May 1930, SAO, Gody nepriznaniia, 1927–1933, pp. 276–81.

CHAPTER TWELVE

~

"Always a Trump in Our Game"

Rapallo Sustained, 1927–1930

If the NKID was unable to make headway in Washington or Paris, it also continued to have difficulties in Berlin. We last left the narrative of Soviet-German relations in June 1927. The Rapallo policy had been reestablished, for better or for worse, with misgivings on both sides. Chicherin and Krestinskii nurtured the German relationship, maintaining close contacts with the

Figure 12.1. From left to right, Carl von Schubert (standing), Gustav Stresemann, Georgii V. Chicherin, Käthe Stresemann, Nikolai N. Krestinskii. Behind standing are officials of the Auswärtiges Amt, December 1926. Photographer: Georg Pahl. *Bundesarchiv, Bild* 102-08486.

Auswärtiges Amt and with politicians, bankers, and businessmen. They did not have an easy time of it. There was always something going wrong. In June 1927 it was a spate of executions of "White Guards" in reprisal for the assassination in Warsaw of the Soviet *polpred* P. L. Voikov. The reaction in Berlin was predictable: there was a "panic" among business and banking groups and yet another anti-Soviet campaign in the German papers.[1] In September 1927 Rantzau worried about a Franco-Soviet rapprochement—though this was the farthest thought from Poincaré's mind. Chicherin reassured Rantzau that Soviet policy remained unchanged. The German ambassador was always quick to worry about a Soviet endorsement of Poland's western frontiers as part of a deal with France. Two weeks later, it was a potential rupture of Franco-Soviet relations that worried Rantzau, for fear that the French and British governments might then gang up on Germany to abandon Rapallo.[2]

Who Is Max Hoelz?

The German ambassador was easily worried, and sometimes with good reason. How, for example, was the diplomatic corps going to deal with the celebration of the tenth anniversary of the revolution in November 1927? Would the Soviet government invite diplomats to a reception where speakers condemned capitalism? This time it was Litvinov who gave a reassuring, typically evasive reply.[3] The reassurances proved unpersuasive, for in connection with the ten year anniversary it was announced that Voroshilov would give the Order of the Red Banner to a number of German revolutionaries. Most notable among them was one Max Hoelz, the "Red Robin Hood," then incarcerated in a German prison, serving a life sentence for various acts of revolutionary violence. Not a reason for a diplomatic scandal, the reader might think, but it angered the German government, and Chicherin too. Hoelz was a well-known figure in Germany and the subject of a popular movement to free him from prison. It therefore looked like the Soviet government was meddling in German domestic affairs once again.

Chicherin complained to Stalin and to everyone in the Politburo. The announced gesture, Chicherin wrote, had provoked an "entirely inevitable reaction from Germany." The German chargé d'affaires has already visited, and I expect to see the ambassador in the next few days.

So what is it to be? Chicherin asked. "Are we trying to improve or worsen our international position?"

> Given the extreme shakiness of our position in France, when our relations with Germany are, obviously, our most important support and when the German government, in spite of tendentious stories, until now has maintained entirely

correct relations with us, why must we by our own hands push Germany into the camp of our enemies? There is not the slightest doubt that the results will be very serious and that this incident will be exploited to the fullest extent possible by enemies not only in Germany but also in other countries.

What really galled the Germans, Chicherin noted, was that Commissar for War Voroshilov was going to hand out the medals. Lenin had established the principle of separation between the government and the Comintern; this gives us "the possibility of strengthening our international position." The proposed event would go against this "basic principle of our international relations."[4]

As Chicherin expected, Rantzau soon came to complain, for two hours and not for the last time either, about Voroshilov distributing medals to German revolutionaries.

It's "a scandal," Rantzau exclaimed: you've handed my enemies in Germany "a poison weapon" with which to attack me.

The award was made out of the blue, Chicherin replied, without the knowledge of the Politburo. It was a decision of the military authorities.

You always complain about Germany being drawn into a western policy of encirclement, Rantzau continued, but I have to tell you that "Russia itself is driving us into this circle." In his report of the meeting, Rantzau noted that Chicherin did not try to put a good face on the situation.[5] Obviously not, since he had already anticipated the German protest and agreed with it, though he did not say so openly to Rantzau. Chicherin must have relished the dictation of his report of conversation; he used it to defend Rapallo and attack Voroshilov. It was only nine months after Litvinov's defense of Rapallo in February of that year.

This incident was far from over. Stresemann himself called in Krestinskii to protest. What would the Soviet response be if, say, the German government were to award Trotskii with one of their highest military awards? This was a good question and would have got Stalin's attention. It was all Stresemann could do to prevent a new *cause célèbre* from being taken up in the Berlin press. Poor Krestinskii bowed his head in penitence according to Stresemann's report.[6]

In Chicherin's report of Stresemann's protest, the reference to Trotskii disappeared. Why not give a medal "to a criminal for his crimes"? Chicherin obviously wanted to make a point without going too far. Only a few days before, on 12 November, Trotskii had been expelled from the Communist Party.

Litvinov, who happened to be in Berlin at the end of November, tried to smooth things over: the medal for Hoelz was given for action against "the Entente," not against the German government.

Stresemann was dubious: "I don't understand the Soviet explanation."

The war commissariat, Litvinov confirmed, had approved the decoration on its own responsibility. As he so often did in such situations, of which there were many, Litvinov tried to make light of the issue. Hoelz had not been the only one to be awarded a medal: German Marxist Clara Zetkin, Jacques Sadoul from France, and others were on the list.

Zetkin, retorted Stresemann, is not "an assassin"! Even President Hindenburg is angry!

The Soviet government eventually announced that the medal was given not for Hoelz's politics but for his *faits d'armes* against the Entente.[7] The incident might seem laughable in hindsight, though neither Rantzau nor Chicherin considered it a laughing matter. How could Voroshilov have been so insensitive to the impact of his *beau geste*? Or was it a sign of opposition or indifference to Rapallo?

True, Voroshilov was not known for his great intellect. A few months later, apparently not the least bit repentant, Voroshilov accepted honorary membership in the Berlin communist pioneer organization, which again aroused German discontent. There was always something; it was the usual fiasco. Voroshilov is an *enfant terrible*, Chicherin would say a few months later, no doubt tired of defending him.[8] Soviet attempts at making light of the situation were not persuasive in Berlin. Herr Wallroth, among the Rapallo pessimists at the Auswärtiges Amt, commented that with all its political and economic troubles, the USSR was "a ball which no longer bounces." The desired evolution toward "consolidation" was not developing.[9]

The same old problem bedeviled the Soviet government: how to remain a revolutionary state, celebrating its accomplishments, in a hostile capitalist world? More to the point, how could coherence and discipline be maintained in Soviet foreign relations in the midst of Stalin's zigzag maneuvering against his political adversaries? With the capitalist West ready to pounce on any Soviet gaffe, it was not an easy thing to do.

As for Hoelz, he benefitted from a Reichstag amnesty in 1928 and was set free. In 1929 he visited the USSR for the first time, eventually moving there after Nazi death threats. He was eccentric and undisciplined, just the type of fellow not appreciated by Stalin. The People's Commissariat for Foreign Affairs (NKVD) allegedly murdered him in 1933. In any case, he was too outspoken to have survived the coming Stalinist purges.

Other Business: Trade Negotiations

Rantzau continued to complain about the Hoelz affair until the end of 1927, but inevitably other more important business came up to occupy the attention of the German and Soviet governments. Basically, it was economics: the German economy was suffering and the Soviet government was embarking on the First Five Year Plan. It would be a drive for all-out industrialization, a concept, as the Norwegian minister in Moscow pointed out, that Stalin had taken over, inter alia, from his nemesis Trotskii.[10] In order to nourish Soviet industrialization, Mikoian and Chicherin wanted a new trade agreement with the German government to follow on the end of the trade credits approved in 1926. Given the anticipated lengthy negotiations, it was time to get a move on. On 22 December 1927 the Politburo authorized the new talks.[11]

The German government was also ready to move forward. It wanted improvements in the previous trade agreement which had not produced sufficient economic advantages, or rather had benefited the USSR more than Germany. The Politburo, as always, was looking for a loan or long-term trade credits. Discussions began in Berlin in February 1928 but progressed slowly for two reasons, government instability in Berlin and hostile German public opinion. Reichstag elections were expected in the spring, and no one wanted to tie the hands of a new government or raise questions which might end up as election issues. The German press was always ready to pounce on "the Russian question" for a new anti-communist campaign. The Soviet delegation reported the difficulties to Moscow, explaining that because of the 1927 negotiations with France, German banks had got the idea of tying new credits to a debts settlement, thus emulating French, British, and American policy. On the Soviet side there was also a debate about whether to offer prior concessions to improve the atmosphere for credit negotiations.[12] This latter approach had never been popular in the Politburo, and there was no interest in opening the old question of debts with Germany, especially since this problem had been settled by the Rapallo Treaty in which both sides renounced claims on the other.

The Shakhty Affair

The trade negotiations might have proceeded in spite of the usual difficulties if events in the northern Caucasus, far from Berlin, had not interfered. Local OGPU authorities reported in late February on an alleged conspiracy to sabotage the coal-mining industry in the Shakhty region of the northern Caucasus. On 1 March the Politburo ordered an investigation into charges against local engineers and technicians.[13] There was no reason why this investigation should have impacted trade negotiations in Berlin except that six German engineers were among those suspected of industrial espionage and sabotage.

On the same day, no doubt wanting to avoid complications in Berlin, the Politburo ordered the negotiations in Berlin to be broken off within seven to ten days. In the interim the delegation could try to settle secondary questions, but larger issues would have to be left to subsequent discussions. Litvinov authorized Krestinskii to say that the main reasons for the Soviet decision to end negotiations were the negative German press campaign and the attempt to raise the pre-Rapallo debt claims. The real reason however was the prospective arrest of German nationals in the northern Caucasus. Krestinskii, apparently unaware of what was going on, expressed his bewilderment at the orders from Moscow. The directives were "unexpected and not understood," he replied, for negotiations had been going well. The German delegation had never raised the pre-Rapallo debts. We have written to ask for a review of the Politburo decision.[14] Krestinskii and his NKVT colleague, I. O. Shleifer, proposed new concessions to Germany, obviously not understanding what was afoot in Moscow. In reaction, on 9 March, Stalin and Mikoian obtained the Politburo's reiteration of its decision to halt negotiations.[15]

In the meantime Chicherin summoned Rantzau at 11 p.m. on the night of 6 March to inform him of what was happening. He said that a number of engineers, mostly Soviet citizens, but among them, six German nationals, working for the German company *Allgemeine Elektricitäts-Gesellschaft* (AEG), had just been arrested for industrial sabotage.

We are both going to have to work hard to prevent this "very sad affair," Chicherin told Rantzau, from damaging German-Soviet relations.

"How long have you known?" Rantzau asked.

"Since last night," Chicherin replied, but I have no details.

This "could not come at a worse time," Rantzau responded.

Apparently Chicherin agreed. According to the ambassador, the *narkom* was clearly pained by what had happened and hoped "to avoid threatening complications." Here we go again, Chicherin must have thought, having written to Stalin only three months before to complain about the Hoelz affair. Rantzau said that the German government would do all in its power to protect its citizens.[16]

On 8 March the Politburo approved the organization of a commission, including Stalin, Rykov, and Molotov, that would make recommendations on how to handle the Shakhty investigation. The Politburo directed local authorities "not to touch" British nationals suspected of involvement, although close surveillance of British companies in the USSR was ordered.[17]

Litvinov was in Berlin on his way to Geneva when the Shakhty story broke. On 13 March he cabled that the arrests had provoked widespread indignation. Everybody is talking about them, including "exasperated" industrialists. "I foresee the most serious consequences for our relations not only with Germany but also with the American industrial world." Litvinov recommended the immediate creation of an "authoritative commission" to investigate and deal expeditiously with the allegations against the Germans.[18]

Unbeknownst to Litvinov, the Politburo had already set up the special commission. On 15 March orders were issued to make haste in the examination of the individual case files to determine which should be pursued and which should be set aside because of insufficient evidence. In the latter cases—yes, of course one wonders if there was any real evidence—the arrested engineers were to be freed. A prosecutor was also named and ordered to move quickly to familiarize himself with the case.[19]

In Berlin Stresemann called in Krestinskii on 14 March to advise that because of the arrests the trade negotiations would have to be broken off. German banking and industrial groups, he said, were up in arms. German companies were threatening to pull their employees out of the Soviet Union. Krestinskii reported to Moscow that he had defended the Politburo's actions, saying that the charges of industrial sabotage were serious and had to be investigated. If the charges against the German nationals proved groundless, all the better. In the meantime it would be regrettable "for both countries" to break off negotiations. Stresemann replied that he was willing to delay an announcement of the rupture of negotiations for a couple of days, but beyond that he could not go.[20]

This report might confuse readers since two weeks before, the *Politburo* had ordered Krestinskii to break off the negotiations. Chicherin recognized the flimflam and was not above using it on Rantzau in Moscow. The German government, he said, was shooting itself in the foot by breaking off negotiations, since their successful conclusion would have benefits for Germany. It began to sound like the usual game of pot calling kettle black. Krestinskii noticed, remarking to Chicherin that *we* had wanted the rupture.

I don't have anything against this "official version," Krestinskii remarked sarcastically, "but I am afraid that we may take [it] seriously." The rupture of negotiations, he added pointedly, is "more harmful to us than to them."[21]

This was all too much for Stalin, who hated correspondence but hated criticism and insubordination even more. Obviously irate, he dashed off a sharp rejoinder to Krestinskii. "Your letter to me I have read, Comrade Krestinskii," he wrote. "I do not agree on any of the questions which you raised." Even before the arrests in the Northern Caucasus, the Germans had nothing to offer in negotiations; they came to us "with empty hands" because of government instability. The arrests were simply a pretext to break off discussions, to hide behind, in order to blame us for the rupture of negotiations. "At the same time, they demonstrated their readiness once again to injure us and to bargain for something with our adversaries."

And you, Comrade Krestinskii (and Shleifer), you sabotaged a decision of the party TsK on the [delegation's] immediate return to Moscow, you helped the Germans to undermine us and consequently to throw the Russian delegation shamefully out of Berlin. That's the thing . . . you and Shleifer flagrantly violated the Bolshevik tradition of our party, haggling with the Politburo for an entire week and thus delaying the departure of the delegation until the moment when it was thrown out of Berlin.

And then Stalin berated Krestinskii over his discussions with Stresemann about the arrested German engineers. "Is it so difficult to understand that the Germans interfered flagrantly in our internal affairs, and you, instead of breaking with the Germans, you continue to be nice to them." The German press is even talking about "your disagreements with Moscow."

"You could not," concluded Stalin, "have done any worse" (*Dal'she idti nekuda*).[22] So much for Rapallo in Stalin's mind; it was Chicherin, Litvinov, and Krestinskii who fought to keep it alive. On the other hand, Stalin was moving toward all-out industrialization and against Bukharin. He wanted to discourage any foot dragging on industrialization. It was more politics over policy, and it risked backfiring because of the German threat to pull out of the USSR. Had Krestinskii dared, he would have pointed all this out to Stalin. The Politburo, he might have added, broke off the Berlin negotiations in anticipation of the Shakhty arrests, knowing full well that they could not continue with German engineers in a Soviet jail. Instead, like other former oppositionists, Krestinskii threw in the towel and recanted his previous dissident activities. Here were echoes of Stalin's February 1927 letter to the Politburo attacking Litvinov.

The Politburo considered the Shakhty indictments a serious matter requiring a full investigation, but if it would not "touch" British nationals at a time when there were no diplomatic relations with Britain, why arrest German nationals in the midst of important trade negotiations? If Rantzau had known about the no-arrest order of British citizens, he might well have asked Chicherin, why us? In July 1928 Chicherin offered arguments in terms of realpolitik to end the Shakhty affair, which the Politburo then accepted.[23] Why not have done so earlier on and avoided the interruption of important negotiations for new trade credits? As it was, three of the German engineers were quickly released. The arrests were a needless provocation, assuming the engineers were innocent.

Were they? The German cabinet supposed that the engineers had been framed. Soviet "legal practices," Rantzau pointed out politely to Chicherin, would be "impossible anywhere else." It was, after all, so easy to offend in the USSR.[24]

Still in Berlin doubts remained. When Rantzau sent his private secretary to Berlin to report, Stresemann asked him, "Are they guilty?" Rantzau was sure they were not, but not so sure about "carelessness" in the installation of German turbines in Soviet plants. Stresemann agreed. And who knew if the engineers had not been provoked into making derisory comments about the USSR?[25]

While Litvinov warned the Politburo of the dangers of the Shakhty affair, he took the opposite line in Berlin. When Stresemann asked him in April what he thought about the situation, Litvinov "laughed . . . and said these incidents must not be taken too seriously." Stresemann replied indignantly. Litvinov was putting it on, and he tried to change the subject. In Moscow Rantzau heard from the Lithuanian minister that the NKID took the matter more seriously than Litvinov admitted to Stresemann. "The Foreign Commissariat has done everything in its power and was fully aware of the seriousness of the situation, but it simply could not prevail against the chauvinistic elements who were now making policy."[26] The Shakhty affair was not really about "chauvinism" but about Stalin's domestic political agenda, which came before NKID concerns.

Rapallo: A "Necessary Evil"

The Shakhty arrests and trial only briefly disturbed the Rapallo policy. The trial ended in early July, and the three accused German engineers were released. This eased the way for a resumption of trade negotiations. Even in June, before the end of the trial, plans went ahead for reciprocal visits of German and Soviet officers to upcoming army maneuvers.[27] On 6 July, the day the Shakhty trial concluded, Chicherin wrote to Mikoian about planning for a resumption of negotiations. Chicherin however was not for rolling over to the Germans and disagreed with Krestinskii about any gratuitous concessions to Germany.

Business is business. Let's not be in a rush, Chicherin advised the Politburo. A new cabinet had been formed in Berlin, and it was not clear what its intentions were regarding future negotiations.[28] These were among Chicherin's last activities as *narkom* before he went on leave, falling ill yet again and returning to Germany for medical treatment.

Meanwhile, German relations with Britain and France in the last half of 1928 became strained over reparations and security issues. A conference in Lugano, Switzerland, in December 1928 produced no results. It was the last time that the "Good Fairies," the Locarno-Nobel trio of Briand, Chamberlain, and Stresemann, would meet as ministers.

Figure 12.2. Gustav Stresemann, Austen Chamberlain, Aristide Briand during an impromptu discussion in the lobby of the *Hôtel Splendide*, Lugano, Switzerland, December 1928. Photographer: Erich Salomon. *Berlinische Galerie*, Berlin, Art Resource, NY.

Given the German strategy of balancing between East and West, Berlin tilted once more toward Moscow despite the Shakhty affair. In August the German government took the initiative to propose a renewal of trade negotiations. Litvinov recommended acceptance of the German proposal, with negotiations to take place in Moscow away from the negative influences of German press and business elements.[29]

The Soviet government pursued the same strategy as Germany: when relations were bad in the West, the Rapallo policy rose in value. So both sides, still "the blind and the lame," had an interest during the autumn of 1928 in concluding a new trade agreement which was signed on 21 December 1928, not coincidentally at the time of the unsuccessful Lugano Conference.

The chief negotiator, B. S. Stomoniakov, complained to Stalin that the Politburo had been in too much of a hurry to come to terms. It was always thus; one could never be more impatient than the other side to conclude an agreement for fear of prompting attempts to obtain last-minute concessions. Stomoniakov was so disgusted that he asked to be assigned to another job.[30] This led Litvinov to intervene to defend what was essentially his policy. Citing an OGPU "secret document," Litvinov contended that the German government was discussing whether to delay conclusion of the Soviet trade agreement as a concession to France and Britain, unhappy with the renewal of German-Soviet negotiations. The OGPU information was correct. According to Litvinov, the policy of making small Soviet concessions (*ustupochki*) to lock up the agreement was justified and had been successful. The Politburo took Litvinov's side in the argument, reprimanded Stomoniakov, and ordered him to continue to work at the NKID.[31] Obstinately, Stomoniakov returned to the charge, but his riposte did not change the outcome or the position of the Politburo. Disagreement over policy, if not public, was still allowed in 1928. Stomoniakov remained at the NKID, and Krestinskii continued as *polpred* in Berlin in spite of Stalin's rebuke. Such tolerance of dissent, secret though it might have been, was not going to last. Stomoniakov and Shleifer, like so many of their colleagues, were dead men walking.

Trotskii's Fate

In January 1929, perhaps thinking to exploit lingering holiday goodwill after the conclusion of the new trade agreement, Litvinov put a delicate question to the new German ambassador in Moscow. This was Herbert von Dirksen, who had replaced Rantzau, dead in September 1928 of a galloping cancer. The subject of conversation was Trotskii, who had been expelled from the Communist Party in November 1927, and exiled to Alma Ata, a long way from Moscow, in January 1928. Stalin was not yet an absolute dictator who could freely dispose of his colleagues' lives, and Trotskii remained a big problem. What was to be done with him? Stalin could not suffer his presence even in Central Asia and wanted him out of the USSR. But where could Trotskii be sent? The Turkish government agreed to accept him, but Trotskii had balked. He wanted to go to a western country, and so Litvinov sought to prevail upon the Soviet Union's "closest friend" to accept him.

Dirksen thought Litvinov had lost his reason: this was not how to treat a "friend." If Trotskii was a problem in Central Asia, what did Stalin think he would become free of Soviet control? He would speak in public; he would write; he would command an audience. In short, he would make a lot of trouble, and not just for Stalin.

The Soviet government, Litvinov replied, is more comfortable with Trotskii out of the USSR than in. Can we have a prompt reply?

Dirksen must have also been a bit confused, for he recommended accepting the Soviet request. The German cabinet discussed it and concluded that Trotskii in Germany would create many unwanted problems. To avoid aggravating Soviet susceptibilities, the German government preferred to evade a direct refusal but would resort to one if pressed.[32] Dirksen so informed Litvinov, who said he understood the reasoning.

Does this mean, Litvinov asked, according to Dirksen's account, that the German government is in fact rejecting our request? I ask because "there are people in the [Soviet] government who have little sense of nuance and [I will] have to make the situation clear and uncomplicated for them."[33]

Every now and again Litvinov made such comments which turn up in foreign reports. Readers may regret that Litvinov's record of this conversation is not available because a comparison with Dirksen's account might well be entertaining and revealing.

Stresemann did not want Trotskii in Germany on any account. "Nothing shows more clearly the weak state of Soviet Russian relations," he commented, "than the fact that they [Soviet authorities] no longer dared to keep Trotskii within the borders of Russia." He would also make trouble for us. "I don't place too high a value on our relations with Soviet Russia. But they are always a trump in our game." Economics were also important, not less than politics. If Trotskii succeeds "in reducing Russia to total chaos, we will also suffer."[34] Ironically, it was not Trotskii who was about to "reduce Russia to total chaos"; it was Stalin.

Other Issues, Other Gaffes

So Trotskii, now a pariah, went to Turkey, never to return to the USSR, and the NKID moved on to other issues. The new German-Soviet trade agreement did not include the provision of credits which the Soviet government still hoped to obtain in Germany as elsewhere. Foreign trade was needed to feed the Five Year Plan. In April 1929 just as the British trade delegation arrived in Moscow, Mikoian laid out the approach which Stomoniakov, still responsible for negotiations, was to take with the Germans. He had preliminary discussions with the German embassy in Moscow, though they produced no results in 1929.

Rapallo remained what it had always been, an unstable agreement between partners in a loveless relationship. And Bolsheviks still had trouble keeping their mouths shut or controlling their impulses. Voroshilov replaced Zinoviev and Bukharin as the German and NKID *bête noire*. A new gaffe occurred on 1 May 1929 when Voroshilov made a speech in Red Square celebrating May Day. The new ambassador, Dirksen, fit seamlessly into his predecessor's role, protesting against the indiscreet, anti-German comments of Soviet officials. Would Voroshilov ever learn? Apparently not; in the excitement of the May Day holiday, he appeared to get carried away. Forgetting Rapallo, and not for the first time, he launched into an attack on the

German government which he compared to the fallen "tsarist regime." The Berlin police chief had banned May Day demonstrations in the capital. In spite of police barricades, Voroshilov said, German workers should celebrate May Day and demonstrate against the "capitalist world."

The German ambassador was quick to respond. He told Karakhan, who was acting in the absence of Litvinov, that Voroshilov had made an "official speech at an official parade in the presence of the entire diplomatic corps." Even worse, it was broadcast on radio "to the entire world." This was going too far, as Dirksen pointed out.

Well, yes, broadcast worldwide, one can understand German irritation, but it is harder to understand why the Soviet gaffes continued. To modify a familiar American axiom, you could take the Bolsh out of the revolution, but not the revolution out of the Bolsh. One group of May Day parade marchers, as Dirksen remarked, carried a papier-mâché battleship onboard which were unflattering caricatures of German government ministers, again observed by the entire diplomatic corps. The ambassador protested. One can imagine Stalin and other Politburo comrades doubled over with laughter as they read Karakhan's report of German complaints, but Dirksen was serious and lodged a formal protest. Karakhan avoided comment on Voroshilov's speech with the excuse that he had not heard it. Then he added that the Soviet government had not wished to interfere in May Day demonstrations, which might, at the limits, have been true in 1929, but would not be much longer. The ambassador was not mollified. Dirksen, Karakhan reported, was in an unusually sour mood.[35]

So was Stresemann, who summoned Krestinskii to complain. The ambassador lamely defended Voroshilov, a true "friend" of Germany, though this was gilding the lily.

"He was probably attacking the Social Democrats rather than the German government," Krestinskii added weakly, the Berlin police chief being a Social Democrat.

Stresemann was not satisfied; the caricatures of German leaders also rankled.

Germany was not singled out, Krestinskii replied.

The diplomatic corps was present, Stresemann rejoined.[36]

These refrains were all too familiar, as though over-rehearsed excerpts from a parable too often repeated. It was yet another Soviet gaffe, to be repeated a week later in Leningrad in a raucous demonstration in front of the German consulate general. As usual, the May incidents did not have lasting effects. Dirksen recommended against making too much of them since Voroshilov had been cooperating recently with the war ministry in Berlin, and Karakhan promised that Soviet authorities would prevent similar incidents in the future. Let's not overplay matters in the German press, Dirksen advised. Why give unnecessary pleasure to the western powers?[37]

A few weeks later the ambassador brought up the Comintern with Litvinov. It was the usual observations about its negative effect on Soviet-German relations. Dirksen reverted to Voroshilov's May Day speech, which still rankled, and he asked Litvinov to intervene to prevent further Moscow encouragement of German communists. According to Dirksen, Litvinov issued his habitual regrets; according to Litvinov's account, his habitual disclaimer on the Comintern. "I noted," said Litvinov in his own account, "that even if I could and wanted to influence . . . party organizations, I could not, in any case, speak about this with the German ambassador, or give him any promises, since I would be giving an official character to a conversation on a subject which I consider inappropriate for diplomatic discussions." Dirksen took this statement to mean that while Litvinov was not prepared to comment on any intervention he might undertake, he would do what he could.[38]

The NKID had its own grievances to air out with the German government, and these had to do with the arrest and trial of the document forger Orlov in the spring of 1929. Readers will remember that the trial turned into the butt of jokes because of revelations about Orlov's relationship with U.S. and various European intelligence services.[39] It was no laughing matter however in Moscow. "Russian public opinion would not understand," warned the Soviet chargé d'affaires in Berlin, "if these counterfeiters got off lightly." Litvinov worried that the Orlov affair could go sour and disturb Soviet-German relations. It might because of revelations that Orlov was in the pay of the German interior ministry.[40] The OGPU would have liked to lay their hands on Orlov for all the trouble counterfeiters had caused to Soviet relations with the West. In Moscow he would certainly have been shot instead of let off by German authorities with four months of time served.

The "Zinoviev letter" also came up in conversations between Krestinskii and Schubert. The NKID suspected that Orlov had been involved in its fabrication and was looking for evidence. Would the German government mind asking the Foreign Office for a facsimile copy of it? We want to prove the "letter" is a fake, Krestinskii said, dropping the hint that such proofs would come in handy during the impending British Parliamentary elections.[41] Hah! Krestinskii hoped to turn the tables on the Tories during the election campaign, but Schubert was having nothing to do with that idea. One can see why the "Zinoviev letter" still irritated Litvinov when the subject came up in July in his conversation with Henderson's go-between Wise.

The Orlov trial, like the Shakhty affair, could not long distract Moscow and Berlin from their habitual problems and complaints. The usual troubles continued. German communist leaders came to Leningrad to celebrate

"World Peace Day" on 1 August. According to Dirksen, these activities were not to promote world peace but to ignite world revolution. He vented his spleen, this time with Stomoniakov, the NKID department head, who was "clearly pained," and not for the first time. Stomoniakov gave the usual reply that the Soviet government could not control the Comintern, and Dirksen the usual skeptical rejoinder.[42]

Stomoniakov would have much rather talked about new trade credits, but negotiations on that topic remained stalled. Moreover, a new "international settlement bank" had been established in Berlin, which aroused Politburo suspicions. Ever on the alert for signs of western collective action against it, the Politburo asked Litvinov for an opinion. Although leery of the new bank, he did not think an anti-Soviet bloc was likely. It's too difficult, Litvinov advised, for the capitalist states, and especially their banks, to overcome rivalries and agree to work against the Soviet Union.[43]

Let's get on with credit negotiations, Litvinov recommended, though nothing came of them in 1929. According to one Soviet report in August, the German government itself was "sabotaging" or at least delaying negotiations until the conclusion of a new reparations agreement being discussed in The Hague, at a conference presided over by the American industrialist Owen D. Young.[44] So trade credits, which the Soviet Union needed more than Germany, according to Krestinskii, were on hold.

Rapallo continued to operate with its usual level of mutual dissatisfaction and dysfunctionality. Litvinov brought to Stalin's attention in early 1930 a recurring complaint not only from the German embassy but also from the other diplomatic missions: "In their words, the German embassy here is literally cut off from communication with the outside world." Even at the NKID communications are limited to official meetings: no one wants to talk "unofficially." Communications are conducted through couriers.

The tailor, doing work for the embassy, refuses to come to us, said a German diplomat; with the barber "it is the same tactics." Outside of Moscow, "the situation is even worse."

"Our consul in Kiev writes in a despairing letter . . . that he is subjected to an official blockade." Those few people with whom he had contact in the past "have now cut off all relations with him." Litvinov limited his note to Stalin to reporting the facts: "I am not making any recommendations; however I cannot remain silent in the existing situation." In a subsequent letter, Litvinov complained again about the situation concerning German and other embassies and consulates. Even in matters of families where a spouse was of a foreign nationality, there were problems with the OGPU. There are also issues about sham marriages. Can we not take a more relaxed approach? Litvinov asked. "The NKID believes that the Union will lose nothing if in the course of a year a few Soviet citizens succeed in going abroad with the help of sham marriages." Quite apart from German complaints, Litvinov continued, foreign marriages could turn into a big problem, with thousands of foreign specialists and workers in the Soviet Union. Soviet-foreign marriages were becoming frequent.[45]

It was ironic that Litvinov should raise this issue since his own spouse was British. But Litvinov was not quite finished about the matter of foreign access to diplomatic missions and consulates. The OGPU often arrested people coming out of the consulates right under the noses of foreign diplomats, Litvinov informed Stalin; they complain to the NKID, and we give the usual reply that people were not arrested for visiting the consulate but for "other crimes."

"Our arguments, however, have proven to be insufficiently convincing for foreign diplomats, who apparently find it bizarre that all their countrymen visiting them turn out to be criminals straightaway after their call at the consulate." If the OGPU is worried, they would certainly know that spies will find more clandestine ways to communicate with their consulates. "This OGPU practice needlessly provokes constant complaints not only from the German but also from other missions." Can the Politburo instruct the OGPU to stop the arrests?[46]

That was not the only bee in Litvinov's bonnet in that spring of 1930. The Soviet Union was in turmoil not only because of collectivization and the First Five Year Plan, but also because of an anti-religious campaign which proved to be another source of complaint from the German and foreign missions. Litvinov was not as categorical as he had been about the OGPU arrests of foreign nationals, but he asked Stalin to moderate the campaign. Not across the board, mind you; even Litvinov had no patience with Roman Catholic priests peddling "religious propaganda" and getting their cues from Poland and the Vatican. He recommended that a special commission be established to examine arrest files and release those people less compromised. In so doing, Litvinov noted, we can undermine hostile foreign press campaigns in Germany, Britain, and the United States and mitigate anti-Soviet hostility in "influential political and financial circles."[47] With diplomatic relations reestablished with Britain, Litvinov also wanted to get Rapallo safely back on the rails.

A few months earlier British Ambassador Ovey had reported rumors that Litvinov was not likely to keep his job as acting commissar, as he did "not see quite eye to eye with the all-powerful Stalin." But Litvinov's letters do not sound like those of someone afraid of losing his job. They give the impression of an acting commissar taking charge of Soviet foreign policy. "My colleagues tell me," Ovey added, "that Litvinov is usually ready, as far as lies in

Figure 12.3.   Gustav Stresemann, Geneva, ca. 1926.
Agence Meurisse. Bibliothèque nationale de France.

his power, to meet their wishes in respect of cases of injustice brought before him, but that his power does not extend very far."[48] This assessment is borne out by Litvinov's letters to Stalin.

The Parliamentary undersecretary, Hugh Dalton, also heard of Litvinov's possible sacking. Such rumors often circulated in the West, but they proved to be unfounded for another ten years. Dalton reckoned that Litvinov was "realistic enough to desire to end the isolation of the Soviet government from the important world of Central Europe."[49]

This was true too even as the guard was changing in Berlin. On 3 October 1929 Stresemann died suddenly of a stroke. He was only 51 years old. Julius Curtius, a conservative German nationalist and colleague of Stresemann, took over as foreign minister. In Moscow Dirksen assured Litvinov that despite the usual anti-communist agitation, the German government remained "strongly" committed to the "Rapallo and Berlin treaties." Curtius would turn his mind to German-Soviet relations, said the ambassador, after dealing with reparations and security issues.

In February 1930, Dirksen aired out the usual list of complaints with Litvinov. The eccentric German communist Max Hoelz was receiving honors in Leningrad, as were "Red veterans," other German communist militiamen, who were being feted in Moscow by none other than Voroshilov. You complain about the German government receiving anti-Bolshevik politicians in Berlin, Dirksen observed, but you don't see any problem with receiving German communists, whom the German government considers to be "criminals."

Litvinov listened politely to Dirksen's complaints and then responded with some of his own, focusing on yet another hostile German press campaign against the Soviet Union. It was all well and good for Curtius to have other priorities, but the anti-Soviet campaign continued with open throttle. When Curtius finally turned his mind to Soviet files, Litvinov added, he would say to us that he had to consider hostile German opinion. What the German government needed to do was to take a more proactive role in advancing German-Soviet relations.[50] Well, yes, but it was not the first time that Soviet and western diplomats called the other's kettle black. While Litvinov replied sharply to Dirksen, he nevertheless wrote to Stalin to deal with German grievances.

In Berlin Krestinskii was relatively positive about Soviet-German relations, more so than Litvinov. Ambassadors normally hope for the best, at least at the beginning of their postings, and even after his long stint in the Berlin embassy Krestinskii remained committed to Rapallo. He sought a public statement from the German government affirming its commitment to Rapallo in order to calm the anti-Soviet press campaign. On 31 March Curtius replied that for the time being the government considered it "inexpedient" to do so.[51] In early April Krestinskii tried again with Curtius, reprising Litvinov's February conversation with Dirksen. Curtius was well prepared for the meeting, with files on various difficulties, the usual ones, between Germany and the Soviet Union. Each time Krestinskii responded to one problem, Curtius pulled a new paper from his files to air another. There were complaints about espionage, the "Red Veterans," and propaganda among German sailors in Soviet ports. Krestinskii emphasized the usual differences between the Soviet government and Soviet trade unions. Curtius was not ready to be fobbed off with that old canard.

"Excuse me," Curtius rejoined,

> but in your country everything is so closely related to each other—government, party organization, and trade unions. At the head of everything stands Mr. Stalin. This is a man who is able himself with a decisiveness, which astonishes us all, to turn the political wheel so abruptly, as he is doing in regard to collectivization and religious questions; this man must be all powerful.

So, Curtius asked, why can't Stalin resolve the little problems troubling German-Soviet relations?

Even Stalin, Krestinskii replied, with all his authority could not go against the internationalist solidarity of the working classes. Curtius would have been skeptical. Krestinskii said in so many words that Stalin could not ignore Soviet domestic politics, especially attacks on his left from critics, like Trotskii, who accused him of betraying the October Revolution.

After hearing everything, Curtius concluded that Krestinskii had told him nothing new. Anyway, the German government was not ready to make immediate decisions on big issues like trade and credits. Curtius wants concessions to take to the German cabinet, Krestinskii reported, in order to give concessions which we want.[52] It was the traditional principle of *donnant, donnant,* I give so that you may give. The Politburo ruled out any negotiations on Curtius' "little questions" until the German government had considered the big issues of German-Soviet relations.[53] Discussions continued nevertheless and relations improved again. In April 1931 the Soviet government finally obtained new trade credits worth 300 million marks, and in June of that year the Treaty of Berlin was renewed. Rapallo, of "the blind and the lame," would live on for yet a while.

Notes

1. "Record of conversation . . . with German Chancellor Wilhelm Marx," no. 267/ChS, 22 June 1927, *Moskva-Berlin,* II, pp. 61–62; and Krestinskii to Chicherin, no. 642, secret, 11 July 1927, ibid., pp. 66–69.

2. "Résumé of conversation . . . with . . . Rantzau," no. 858/ChS, very secret, 6 Oct. 1927, *Moskva-Berlin,* II, pp. 81–83.

3. Excerpt from Litvinov's *dnevnik,* Meeting with Rantzau, 20 Oct. 1927, *Moskva-Berlin,* II, pp. 84–87.

4. Chicherin to Stalin and Politburo members, no. 1008/ChS, 14 Nov. 1927, *Moskva-Berlin,* II, p. 94.

5. Rantzau, no. 1285, very secret, urgent, for Stresemann, *AzDAP,* B, VII, pp. 262–63.

6. Stresemann to Rantzau, no. 781, very secret, 20 Nov. 1927, *AzDAP,* B, VII, pp. 281–82.

7. Schubert's memorandum on a conversation with Litvinov, Krestinskii, and Stresemann, 25 Nov. 1927, *AzDAP,* B, VII, pp. 348–49; Schubert's memorandum, 28 Nov. 1927, ibid., pp. 372–73; "Record of conversation . . . with . . . Rantzau . . . ," no. 1042/ChS, very secret, 25 Nov. 1927, *Moskva-Berlin,* II, pp. 95–98; and "Record of conversation . . . with . . . Rantzau . . . ," no. 1053/ChS, very secret, 29 Nov. 1927, ibid., pp. 99–101.

8. Gerhard Koepke (Berlin) to Rantzau, no. 99, 6 March 1928, *AzDAP,* B, VIII, p. 300; and Rantzau, no. 372, 9 April 1928, AA, *Büro Staatssekretär, Band* 21. E159.582–83, 4562H/R.29271.

9. Wallroth's memorandum, 20 Nov. 1927, *AzDAP,* B, VII, pp. 286–92.

10. Lindley, no. 108, 26 March 1929, forwarding Urbye's report of 27 Feb. 1929, N1811/55/38, FO 371 14038.

11. Chicherin/Mikoian to Politburo, no. 1078/ChS, secret, 14 Dec. 1927, *Moskva-Berlin*, II, pp. 116–18; and Politburo resolution, no. P1 /2-s, rigorously secret, special file, 22 Dec. 1927, ibid., p. 118.

12. I. O. Shleifer, Soviet trade delegate in Berlin, to Mikoian, nos. 16 and 18/Shg, secret, 20 Feb. 1928, *Moskva-Berlin*, II, pp. 144–53.

13. Excerpt from Politburo resolution, no. 12, 1 March 1928, V. N. Khaustov et al., *Lubianka: Stalin i VChK-GPU-OGPU-NKVD, ianvar' 1922–dekabr' 1936* (Moscow, 2003), p. 147.

14. Excerpt from Politburo protocol, no. 12, and text of proposals on German negotiations, 1 March 1928, *Politbiuro Osoboi papki*, pp. 160–62; Litvinov to Krestinskii, no. 1033, especially secret, immediate, 1 March 1928, *Moskva-Berlin*, II, p. 185; and Krestinskii to Litvinov, no. 1496, especially secret, immediate, 2 March 1928.

15. Politburo resolution, no. P 15/opr. 1/s, rigorously secret, special file, 9 March 1928, *Moskva-Berlin*, II, p. 187.

16. Rantzau, no. 233, 6 March 1928, *AzDAP*, B, VIII, pp. 300–301. Cf., *Politbiuro Osoboi papki*, p. 163, n. 1.

17. Excerpt from Politburo resolution, no. 14, 8 March 1928, *Lubianka, 1922–1936*, pp. 147–48.

18. Litvinov to Stalin and Chicherin, especially secret, highest priority, 13 March 1928, *Lubianka, 1922–1936*, p. 152.

19. Politburo resolution, no. 15, 15 March 1928, *Lubianka, 1922–1936*, p. 152.

20. Krestinskii to NKID, 14 March 1928, *DVP*, XI, pp. 161–62; and Stresemann to Rantzau, no. 125, 14 March 1928, *AzDAP*, B, VIII, pp. 332–34.

21. Chicherin to Krestinskii, 16 March 1928, *DVP*, XI, pp. 164–65; and Krestinskii to Chicherin, no. 237/s, secret, 19 March 1928, *Moskva-Berlin*, II, pp. 191–94.

22. Stalin to Krestinskii, very secret, 21 March 1928, *Moskva-Berlin*, II, p. 195. Krestinskii referred to a letter to Stalin on 17 March, but it has not been published (Krestinskii to Chicherin, no. 237/s, as cited above in n. 21).

23. Chicherin to Politburo, no. 611/ChS, very urgent, very secret, 18 July 1928, *Lubianka, 1922–1936*, pp. 175–77.

24. Rantzau, no. 275, 16 March 1928, *AzDAP*, B, VIII, pp. 359–60.

25. Andor Hencke's memorandum, 28 April 1928, *AzDAP*, B, VIII, pp. 546–48; and "Conversation with [Hermann] Buecher," Herbert von Dirksen, 4 May 1928, *AzDAP*, B, IX, pp. 12–15.

26. Record of conversation between Stresemann and Litvinov, by Dirksen, 10 April 1928, *AzDAP*, B, VIII, pp. 470–73; and Rantzau, no. 531, 22 May 1928, *AzDAP*, B, IX, pp. 58–61.

27. Orgburo resolution, no. OB/48/3g.s., rigorously secret, special file, 2 July 1928, *Moskva-Berlin*, II, pp. 197–98.

28. Chicherin to Mikoian, no. 574/ChS, secret, 6 July 1928, *Moskva-Berlin*, II, pp. 198–99; Chicherin to Politburo, no. 593/ChS, very secret, 14 July 1928, ibid., p. 199.

29. Litvinov to Molotov, no. 2059, secret, 23 Aug. 1928, *Moskva-Berlin*, II, pp. 213–15.

30. Stomoniakov to Stalin, no. T53, very secret, personal, 21 Dec. 1928, *Moskva-Berlin*, II, pp. 294–96.

31. Litvinov to Politburo, no. L/3198, secret, 27 Dec. 1928, *Moskva-Berlin*, II, pp. 303–305; and Politburo resolution, no. P 56/2-s, rigorously secret, 27 Dec. 1928, ibid., p. 305.

32. Dirksen, no. 97, 29 Jan. 1929, *AzDAP*, B, XI, pp. 74–76.

33. Schubert to Dirksen, no. 61, urgent, very secret, for ambassador personally, 6 Feb. 1929, *AzDAP*, B, XI, pp. 101–3.

34. Stresemann to Paul Loebe, Reichstag president, 19 March 1929, AzDAP, B, XI, p. 199, n. 19.

35. "Record of conversation . . . with Dirksen . . . ," Karakhan, 3 May 1929, Moskva-Berlin, II, pp. 330–32; and Dirksen, no. 311, 3 May 1929, AzDAP, B, XI, pp. 487–89.

36. Memorandum by Stresemann, conversation with Krestinskii, 6 May 1929, AzDAP, B, XI, pp. 502–3.

37. Dirksen, no. 334, 10 May 1929, AzDAP, B, XI, 521–23; and Dirksen, no. 335, 10 May 1929, E160.086–87, AA, Büro Staatssekretär, Akten betreffend politische Beziehungen UdSSR zu Deutschland, Band 23.

38. Dirksen, no. 414, 10 June 1929, AzDAP, B, XII, pp. 41–42; and excerpt from Litvinov's dnevnik, "Meeting with Dirksen, 10.VI, [1929]," secret, AVPRF, f. 05, o. 9, p. 43, d. 3, ll. 104–5.

39. See chapter 2, this volume.

40. Dirksen, no. 189, 11 March 1929, AzDAP, B, XI, pp. 264–65, and p. 264, n. 1.

41. Schubert's memoranda, 27 April 1929, AzDAP, B, XI, pp. 452–54; and 11 May 1929, ibid., pp. 523–24.

42. Dirksen, no. 559, 30 July 1929, AzDAP, B, XII, p. 282, n. 3.

43. Litvinov (Germany) to Stomoniakov, secret, 4 July 1929, Moskva-Berlin, II, pp. 341–44.

44. Ian E. Rudzutak, secretary, TsK, to Politburo, no. 14526/s, very secret, 9 Aug 1929, Moskva-Berlin, II, pp. 348–51.

45. Litvinov to Stalin, no. L/3312, secret, 26 Jan. 1930, Moskva-Berlin, II, pp. 357–58.

46. Litvinov to Stalin, no. L/3512, secret, 13 April 1930, Moskva-Berlin, II, pp. 385–87.

47. Litvinov to Stalin, no. L/3514, secret, 23 April 1930, Moskva-Berlin, II, pp. 387–89.

48. Ovey, no. 20, 20 Dec. 1929, N6228/55/38, FO 371 14040.

49. Dalton's minute, 19 Nov. 1929, N5149/280/38, FO 371 14041.

50. Excerpt from Litvinov's dnevnik, "Meeting with Dirksen," secret, 20 Feb. 1930, Moskva-Berlin, II, pp. 358–63.

51. Krestinskii to NKID, 31 March 1930, DVP, XIII, pp. 182–83.

52. Krestinskii to Litvinov, no. 12/k, secret, 11 April 1930, Moskva-Berlin, II, pp. 373–84; and Krestinskii's aide-mémoire, 11 April 1930, DVP, XIII, pp. 202–7.

53. Excerpt from Politburo protocol, no. 124, 25 April 1930; and no. 126, 15 May 1930, Politbiuro Osoboi papki, pp. 222–24.

CHAPTER THIRTEEN

~

Conclusion

Sorting It Out

Changing of the Guard: Exit Comrade Chicherin

By the end of the 1920s Stalin had established his control over the Soviet Union. His rivals, from Trotskii to Bukharin, were defeated, powerless men. Bukharin, Tomskii, and Rykov were the last opposition group in the Politburo to be toppled from their posts, Bukharin in November 1929. In fact, Bukharin was defeated long before. Like a cat with mice, Stalin played with his victims before dispatching them. The Norwegian minister in Moscow, who represented British interests in the USSR, Andreas Urbye, had some interesting things to say about the Bolshevik transition of power. "A change," he observed, "was rapidly taking place."

> The old guard, composed of life-long revolutionaries imbued with fanatical ideals and thoroughly conversant with the life and thought of Western Europe, was fast disappearing under persecution and the strain of an insane manner of living. Many had already gone; others, such as Chicherin, would never be fit for work again. It was doubtful that Litvinoff [sic] could last much longer. There were few or no idealists amongst them and they were strangers to Western civilization. They were frankly out for power and would stick at nothing to retain it.

The British minister, commenting on Urbye's remarks, looked on the bright side of things. Those who wanted to keep power in the USSR, he quipped, might lose interest in the Comintern and "confine their attention to the misgovernment of their own countrymen."[1]

"Out for power" was a good way to describe Stalin and his cronies. Urbye was wrong about Litvinov, however, if correct that Chicherin could not resume his duties as *narkom*. He had effectively stopped work in July 1928, returning to Germany for medical care in September of that year. Twelve months later Chicherin was still in Berlin, and Krestinskii raised concerns about it with Moscow.

Chicherin is seriously ill, Krestinskii reported, and recognizes that he cannot resume his duties as commissar. He also understands that he ought to return to the USSR and reconcile himself to life as a simple pensioner.

> But Georgii Vasil'evich lives with some antediluvian ideas about our reality. All our sanatoria and rest homes, even the very best, appear to him bug infested, in which patients are poisoned with rotten fish, grain for pigs, potatoes, and cabbage. It seems to him that life in the USSR as a pensioner, this is some kind of slow death in very hard domestic conditions. Therefore he prefers to avoid anything which would compromise his present position on endless holiday as *narkom* so as not to return to the USSR. . . . To return, this means to self-destruct.

Krestinskii felt bound, as the one closest to Chicherin over the last few years, to report his situation to Moscow. In December 1929 the Politburo took up the matter and decided that, with all due care, Chicherin should return to the USSR.[2]

Figure 13.1. Georgii V. Chicherin, ca. 1925.
Agence Meurisse. Bibliothèque nationale de France.

"Mr. [Bruce] Lockhart of Moscow," as Ramsay MacDonald called him, remembered Chicherin from his last months in Berlin. A sad man, stricken with diabetes, who as Lockhart put it only wanted "to be left in peace." When he was young, Chicherin confided to a German acquaintance that "he had had to choose between music and Socialism." He had chosen socialism and put music out of his life, though in fact not really, for Mozart remained his passion. Now "his diabetes was under control," according to Bruce Lockhart, "but his nerves were shattered."[3] "I am mostly in a bad state," he wrote to the American journalist Louis Fischer, "with some life coming back for a short time usually late in the evening."[4]

With no wife or children, and without his NKID stenographers and comrades, who were his family, Chicherin must have been very lonely indeed. In January 1930 Karakhan went to Berlin to accompany the *narkom* home. In July he was officially relieved of his duties.

Chicherin's "Testament"

At the beginning of that month Chicherin left in the NKID archives a very secret, handwritten "sort of testament" intended for his successor, if it was not Litvinov. In it Chicherin vented his spleen, leaving to his imagined successor a guide to all the troubles, large and small, he would face. He started with Litvinov, who acted as a lone rider, disregarding his authority. Whenever Chicherin complained, Litvinov "always responded" that they met three times a week in the *kollegiia*, and that there, Chicherin could ask him any questions he liked. Or he could write letters on particular issues, Litvinov said; "no further contact is necessary." On western issues, Chicherin went on,

> I was nothing, an ordinary member of the *kollegiia*, and as I struggled, attempted to influence policy, there was perpetual tension. Of course, the participation of Comrade Litvinov in the Politburo, on western affairs, increased his role. I brought Karakhan to the Politburo to participate in the discussion of eastern matters to weaken Litvinov's exclusive role. I myself was politically so helpless that my appearance in the Politburo in support of any particular position was more often than not the basis for taking the opposite decision. I don't understand: if they did not have confidence in me, why did they not want to make use of me in some other work. Too late now, I am like a toy, broken by a careless child.

If Chicherin was bitter about Litvinov, he praised Karakhan, "a subtle, brilliant, talented political person." Anyone in Litvinov's camp was an intriguer, constantly going behind the *narkom*'s back, pursuing dual policies. "A good business meant it had to be stopped." In Krestinskii there was "a narrow bureaucratic" personality, but in Litvinov it was "an aversion to any vision." How ironic that Litvinov had attacked Karakhan for the same insubordination of which Chicherin accused Litvinov.

In his "testament" Chicherin never mentioned Stalin by name, but at one point he turned his ire against him. Since 1929, he wrote, "the gates have opened for every sort of demagoguery and hooliganism."

> Now we don't need to work; we need to "struggle against the right deviation" [i.e., against Bukharin], so there are a sea of squabbles, intrigues, denunciations. It is a frightful impairment of the state apparatus especially felt by us, where business cannot wait. . . . The demagoguery in our "public organizations" has become completely intolerable. If you do not stamp out this demagoguery, then in the NKID (*u vas*) all will be lost.

Party cells consider the NKID's Turkish policy to be evidence of the "right opportunist deviation." "And you," Chicherin wrote to his imagined successor, "will have to endure all of this."

If Chicherin was angry with Litvinov, there were many points upon which they entirely agreed, like it or not. "One of the most important questions," Chicherin advised, "is NKID control over the press."

> No foreign policy can be conducted when, under the influence of anonymous backdoor pressure, newspapers indulge in all sorts of rot. Prior to 1928 everything in *Izvestiia* and *Pravda* which had anything to do with foreign policy was sent to me in proofs or read to me over the telephone. I could reject or revise. Sometimes I directly saved the situation, especially when some idiot from a brother communist party pushed through a bit of dreadful nonsense.

Obviously Chicherin did not intercept all the "nonsense" that was published in Moscow. Readers will remember his letters of protest to Stalin: he had the devil of a time controlling various NKID *bêtes noires*. On this point, Chicherin and Litvinov were entirely of one mind.

It was a joke in the NKID, Chicherin wrote on, that the number-one "internal enemy" was the Comintern. Before 1929, although troubles with it were endless, matters settled down and we overcame "a million torments." Since 1929 matters have worsened, becoming "completely intolerable," wrote Chicherin. "It is the death of foreign policy." He mentioned problems with Germany and in particular the scandal over Max Hoelz. He got the "Red Banner" for "crimes against a friendly German government." It was too much. "Rantzau was in complete despair ('it's the end of my policy')." "Especially harmful and dangerous," Chicherin added, "were Comintern speeches by our leading comrades and any detection of contacts between [Soviet] officials and [foreign] communist parties."

The second "internal enemy," Chicherin observed, was the GPU, with which the NKID was involved in endless disputes. In the last few years the GPU bosses had been "backhanded, cunning, always trying to thwart, to cheat us." It was a many-headed "hydra," acting with impunity, arresting foreign nationals and causing "a million international incidents." The GPU communicated with the NKID as though it were a "class enemy"; it was beyond redemption, "exceeding all limits." Again, there was full agreement between Chicherin and Litvinov whether Georgi Vasil'evich wanted to admit it or not.

There was also a third "internal enemy," the NKVT operating in Asia. Persia shields Baku, he wrote, and Turkey the Caucasus. Here Chicherin was returning to old themes. Could the NKVT keep in mind these political considerations when trading with southern neighbors?

"No! Our 'hucksters' [torgashi] skin mercilessly [chto est' mochi] the Turkish and Persian peoples." They short-weighted bulk deliveries and in general "cheated and robbed" clients. Chicherin's criticisms were redolent of those he made about "Russian" behavior on the Chinese Eastern Railway in Manchuria. Our so-called "mixed" companies, "permeated with hucksterism and an imperialist mentality toward the Persians, were the main instruments of our attempts at the economic enslavement of Persia, and they did a great service to England."[5]

And on and on Chicherin went, in one last, great cry of indignation, no doubt inflamed by illness and the realization that he had done all he could do as narkom. His "testament" underlined the tensions and chaos of Soviet foreign policy making in the 1920s, so richly illustrated in the NKID files. Chicherin spent his last years out of the public eye, "ill and half mad," according to one American diplomat, living "a hermit's existence." He died in July 1936, on the eve of Stalin's bloody purges.[6] The gensek appears to have made no objection to the construction of a tall stone obelisk over Chicherin's grave in Novodevichii Cemetery in Moscow. It still stands out to passers-by.

In July 1930 Stalin named Litvinov—a cat with nine lives, it seems—as Chicherin's successor. Apparently, Stalin did not mind having an "opportunist" in the NKID, or receiving Litvinov's challenging mail, as long as it was not public or political. In fact, like the late Krasin, Litvinov abhorred Soviet party politics. When State Secretary Schubert once asked him what he thought about the political situation in Moscow, Litvinov responded that he knew nothing about it. "Fortunately, I do not have the slightest thing to do with the party in Russia." The late Ambassador Rantzau had observed that Litvinov was "a clear and absolute practitioner of realpolitik."[7] Stalin agreed, if one is to judge from his letters to Molotov. Litvinov's indifference to party politics and his close attention to the interests of the Soviet state would have reassured the intolerant, ever vigilant Stalin. His appointment as *narkom* was an indication of Stalin's foreign policy priorities. Had Litvinov converted "the boss"? Not really, for no one had that kind of influence on Stalin, in whose scheme of things party politics still took precedence over foreign policy.

Looking Back

The 13 years since the October Revolution must have seemed like a long time to those comrades who survived them. Lenin had been dead for six years, and that too must have seemed to them like a lifetime. In 1917 no one could have imagined that Lenin would die young, that Trotskii would be exiled, and that Koba, or Stalin, would hold unchallenged power in the Kremlin. How could anyone have foreseen the political destruction and humiliation of the most prominent leaders of the October Revolution and the closest to Lenin himself?

Looking back on what happened, readers may wonder how the Bolsheviks even survived the early months of 1918. No theories of Marx and Engels could have prepared them for the insoluble problems they faced after taking power. To be sure, in their public statements and debates the Bolsheviks still sought their bearings in Marxist theories about imperialism, dialectics, and the inevitability of capitalist self-destruction. For proof of the latter of course one had only to read the newspapers about the frightful, pointless bloodshed of the Great War.

When the Bolsheviks took hold of the levers of power of the Russian state, they found that the controls did not work and that Marxist ideas were not a good guide for making them work. They faced war in the west and south against the German army and its allies. Russian forces had wasted away. The Germans could march on Petrograd and Moscow, and there were only ragtag Red militias to stop them. Unemployment was widespread; coal and food supplies in the cities were scarce; inflation galloped. Chaos, violence, and anarchy reigned.

Before dealing with troubles at home, however, the Bolsheviks had to get Russia out of the war. In the beginning, they kept to their Marxist compass, encouraging the German proletariat to rise up and join their world socialist revolution. When that did not work, the Bolsheviks negotiated at Brest-Litovsk with the very generals and bourgeois politicians they so utterly despised. The German negotiators had armies that followed orders; the new

Soviet government did not. Brest-Litovsk was the Bolsheviks' first lesson in reality and in the practice of realpolitik. Lenin was a hard task maker, a revolutionary theorist who recognized reality when he saw it. He could be a windbag at times and crude in his directives to colleagues, but he knew how to abandon ideas that did not work and pick up those that did.

Nowhere was realpolitik and common sense more necessary than in Soviet relations with the outside world. After concluding peace at Brest-Litovsk, such as it was, the Soviet government had to face the western Allies, who were just as dangerous as Germany. They clapped an ironclad blockade around the new Soviet state. The British and French sent what troops they dared to Soviet Russia and they shot at Reds on sight. They talked of erecting a long line of gallows from which to hang the Bolsh, and they armed and en-couraged former tsarist generals to overthrow Soviet authority. It was ironic that Germans and Allies, who were freely killing each other on the Western Front, made temporary common cause against Soviet Russia.

Bolshevik strategy was to fight Allied forces when necessary, but talk to them when possible. The Soviet formula was to offer economic and political concessions and trade time and space in order to *survive* and build up Soviet strength. The strategy did not fit into any neat Marxist theories, except per-haps the one about exploiting capitalist "contradictions," but that idea, divide and rule, was as old as states and politics and not Marxist at all. It was a near-run thing, but the Soviet strategy worked, Marxist or not, thanks, inter alia, to the transient power of Bolshevik propaganda and thanks also to British and especially French soldiers and sailors who refused to fight against Soviet Russia.

When intervention failed, when the civil war, nourished by western soldiers, arms, and money, petered out, when the world revolution did not take root beyond the borders of Russia, the Bolsheviks had again to adjust to new realities. Chicherin, Litvinov, Krasin, Rakovskii, and their colleagues went west to parley with their once and present enemies. The fat bankers, businessmen, generals, and warmongers portrayed in Bolshevik propaganda posters were now to be wooed, appeased, and engaged. Marx could not help much in those practical endeavors, though Machiavelli did. Lenin admired his ideas but hesitated to say so openly. Realpolitik was more useful as a tool of foreign policy, as it turned out, than *The Communist Manifesto*.

Lenin made more compromises, supporting the New Economic Policy, the mixed economy of private and state ownership. To make that policy work, or any other, Soviet Russia had to trade with the West, obtain credit in order to buy goods and machines to restart the devastated Soviet economy, run new industries, and modernize agriculture. As Krasin liked to say in the West, we have common interests; you need the business and so do we. "Give Russia a chance to keep its word," he argued, jingling bags of Soviet gold.

Soviet traders signed contracts with western industrialists who needed to fill their order books, but to obtain credit to finance trade they had a harder time with the bankers. Most would not deal with the Soviet state until it had accepted responsibility for the tsar's debts. The Bolsheviks replied that the tsar's debts were not *their* debts, and they would respect to the letter any contracts which they signed. They did too, but this did not satisfy most bankers who regarded the USSR as a defiant, defaulted debtor. How would Krasin and his colleagues get around the impasse? Western industrialists needed credit to fill their order books as much as the Soviet traders needed it to sign contracts. Factory owners and Bolshevik traders appeared to be natural allies. By the end of the 1920s Moscow had made headway even with the bankers, especially in Germany, but only a little elsewhere.

Meanwhile, to facilitate trade and assure the bankers, the Soviet government sought diplomatic recognition in the West. They succeeded first with Germany and then turned to Britain, France, and the United States, among others. No state was too unimportant to woo. But formidable obstacles lay in the way: "Die-Hards" in Britain, the *Bloc national* in France, and Republican administrations in the United States hated the Bolsheviks and opposed diplomatic recognition. Anti-communist ideologues fought against pragmatists promoting recognition and trade.

The NKID also faced formidable problems at home. The Comintern was one problem that seemed unsolvable. It was "internal enemy" number one, according to Chicherin. Litvinov and his colleagues often told western diplomats that it was impossible to get rid of the Comintern. How could Bolsheviks who had only just emerged victorious from a momentous struggle against the capitalist West so easily give up revolutionary principles embodied in the Comintern? The principled Comrade Kominternovskii confronted the practical Comrade Narkomindel'cheskii. Or so it seemed.

There was more to this classic confrontation between foreign policy pragmatists and revolutionary ideologues. Bolshevik party politics, and not simple revolutionary principles, were a *third* factor complicating coherence in Soviet foreign policy. During the struggle for power between Stalin and his rivals, politics often trumped policy. Zinoviev and Bukharin, who one after the other led the Comintern, were Stalin's transient allies. "Orators," Litvinov called them, whose imprudent public utterances were a constant source of trouble for the NKID in dealing with the West. Could Stalin rein in the Comintern without endangering his political alliances, first with Zinoviev and then with Bukharin? Could he risk attacks from his nemesis Trotskii for betraying the world revolution? It appears that he could not. Not at first anyway, not until he had beaten Trotskii and no longer needed Zinoviev or Bukharin as allies and could expel them, one after the other, from the Politburo. Stalin was a ruthless opportunist in his political struggles for power, maneuvering this way and that to gain advantage. Foreign policy became a tool in his kit, left to temporary allies to aggrandize themselves, or used as a screen to deflect attacks by Trotskii and his allies.

Finally recognizing the danger, and echoing Trotskii, Bukharin accused Stalin of being "an unprincipled intriguer who subordinates everything to the preservation of his power. He changes theories depending on whom he wants to get rid of at the moment." Even Lenin in his last days of lucidity remarked that Stalin was "devoid of the most elementary honesty." He's "a Genghis Khan," Bukharin lamented in 1928, a little late, like Lenin, to notice the problem.

Stalin "has succeeded," said Bukharin, "in expelling the Communist International from the Kremlin."[8] The *gensek* also succeeded, Bukharin might have added, in inserting the Kremlin into the Comintern in order to control it, though not necessarily to help the NKID. Litvinov was still on his own. The Comintern appears to have become a shield for Stalin to parry thrusts from the left and to strike at rivals on the right. In 1928–1929 the new Comintern hard line predicted an end of "capitalist stabilization" and opposed collaboration between communists and parliamentary socialists, identified as "social fascists." This so-called third period may be explained as much by politics as by ideology, if indeed ideology was a factor at all. Chicherin railed against the new line in his "testament"; in Paris Herriot also noticed early on and complained to his Soviet interlocutors. As one Russian historian proposes, the debates over Comintern strategy were only a battle on the flanks of the main struggle against Bukharin and his allies, but in 1928 it was "the decisive flank."[9] Was the conflict over the Comintern just a sideshow employed in Stalin's last great campaign against his rivals? What was the true indicator of Stalin's intent in foreign policy: the Comintern's "third period" or his appointment of the pragmatic Litvinov as *narkom*? Or was the "third period" simply irrelevant? as Litvinov might have proposed. Whatever the answer, Comintern rhetoric had no influence on NKID foreign policy, except as an impediment, though it nicely covered Stalin's flanks, left and right. No one was going to stick on the *gensek* the charge of betraying the world revolution. It was only after he had consolidated his power at the end of the 1920s and gained more freedom of action that Stalin could better deal with foreign policy issues on their merits.

In the meantime, everything was turned on its head. Bukharin, the "orator" by Litvinov's lights, became the "right deviationist" in domestic politics who resisted the new Comintern line.[10] While Stalin, the prudent realist, clenched his fists and smashed everything in his way, pursuing radical policies of collectivization and industrialization at home and giving the Comintern an ultra-revolutionary line.

Chicherin and Litvinov fought hard battles to defend the NKID's pre-rogatives. The personal differences between them were mere sibling rivalries compared with the incursions against NKID authority from elsewhere in Moscow. The Comintern was less a problem than the Politburo, where Lit-vinov and Chicherin were only invited as technical advisers and where any-thing could happen in discussions on foreign policy. Even though Chicherin was *narkom*, a government minister, he did not have a permanent seat in the Politburo. He was relegated, at times, and Litvinov too, to the role of a permanent undersecretary who offered advice which might or might not be accepted. The Comintern boss, Zinoviev, then Bukharin, sat in the Polit-buro, but not Chicherin.

The fiascos in Germany, Britain, and China were examples of where the NKID lost control of foreign policy. Rapallo was hard to defend in the com-missariat for war and against the oratorical extravagances of another NKID *bête noire*, Stalin's ally and crony Voroshilov.

Let's not go to the Politburo, Litvinov would sometimes say, until we are better prepared. And no wonder. Foreign policy was like raw meat thrown into the Politburo arena to be fought over and wrenched away from the NKID.

China was a case in point. The Politburo set up a Chinese Commission to make policy recommendations. Chicherin sat on the commission but was only one of several members, and by no means *primus inter pares*. The NKID was out of the loop. Readers will remember that Chicherin complained to Karakhan about his helplessness in directing Soviet policy in China. Stalin said that the Politburo should not become deluded by Chinese "fantasies," but in an obvious case of a mission gone out of control, he himself appeared to hide behind them as a strategy for consolidating his power. Chicherin and Litvinov could do nothing about it.

China was part of a bigger question in the Politburo about foreign policy priorities, the western or eastern orientation. At the beginning, western policy, notably in Germany and Britain, held sway. Rapallo succeeded, more or less, but a rapprochement with Britain did not. Lloyd George, the cagey, conniving pragmatist, resigned, and Curzon, the cold hater of the Bolsh, became freer to pursue an anti-Soviet line, resulting in the Foreign Office ultimatum in May 1923. After the electoral defeat of the minority Labour government in October 1924, the Conservatives pursued a policy of controlled hostility toward Mos-cow. Outraged by events in China, the Die-Hards wanted to go further, but at first they could not carry the Cabinet with them. The Foreign Office objective was to force the Soviet Union to come "hat in hand" to London. This policy did not work: instead of obtaining Soviet submission, the Foreign Office pro-voked Soviet defiance. The western line gave way to the eastern in China.

Soviet policy incoherence was greatest in regard to Berlin. Rapallo was the centerpiece of Soviet western diplomacy. Germany was the only European state with which the Soviet Union had tolerable economic and political relations. In early 1923 there were what amounted to German-Soviet staff talks; six months later the Politburo encouraged a German revolution. The Rapallo honeymoon lasted scarcely a year. Chicherin and Litvinov often complained to Stalin about the tempestuous, apparently thoughtless public utterances or actions of Zinoviev, Bukharin, and Voroshilov, all of whom sat in the Politburo.

We are a government now, Chicherin once reminded Stalin; we are not simply presiding over a meeting of comrades. It's no longer 1919, we can't conduct foreign policy based on "proclamations." Comrades must think before they speak. Or were their oratorical flourishes prompted by the constituencies they represented—or by politics?

Bukharin "repents" his gaffes and promises to do better, Litvinov remarked in 1927, only to return to his old ways. For Litvinov, 1927 was the nadir. Here was Sisyphus-Narkomindel'cheskii struggling against what seemed to be the incoherent, dangerous behavior of the Politburo. The situation is hopeless, Litvinov told Chicherin. But Sisyphus never abandons his rock, and neither did Litvinov. When Stalin challenged him in February 1927, Litvinov did not flinch.

There were also occasional fiascos in Soviet policy toward the United States, either because local agents promised concessions they could not deliver or because they did not or could not follow the sometimes imprecise instructions from Moscow. The negotiations with National City Bank are a good example of the chaos and confusion that sometimes reigned in Soviet foreign policy. It was of course State Department hostility which forced the Politburo to pursue roundabout ways to break down U.S. government animosity. In the 1920s these methods never worked, though Soviet-American trade gradually increased.

If muddled instructions sometimes caused confusion in Soviet foreign policy, party politics appear to have been the main cause of the chaos. If Trotskii said Stalin's China policy was wrong, for example, Stalin would have to demonstrate that it was right, even when it was horribly wrong. These public debates were couched in Marxist theory about "capitalist stabilization," "imperialist contradictions," or a "new era of revolutions and wars."

Some historians say Soviet foreign policy changed according to changes in leadership doctrine.[11] In fact, NKID policy never changed through all these public gesticulations. It was *always* about improved relations with the West, at first to eliminate the danger of a new military intervention or blockade, but always to facilitate trade and the acquisition of commercial credits to reinforce Soviet reconstruction and industrialization.

International relations are *never* about love, Litvinov lectured his colleagues; they are *always* about interests. This is quite all right, he added, for it is the normal conduct of states.

Whether it was during the NEP period, the transition to socialism in one country, collectivization and the First Five Year Plan, NKID policy remained consistent and unchanged. Shortly before his death, Krasin dismissed the public statements of Trotskii and Zinoviev as foolish and irrelevant. They were "only camouflage for what were really personal bids for power and position." This goes for Stalin's public statements too, Krasin might have added, for no one was better than the *gensek* at party maneuvers and deception.

Litvinov commented that the "war scare" was a western exaggeration of the exaggerated statements of "orators" Bukharin and Voroshilov. There was no immediate danger of war in Europe. He was saying in his discreet way that western diplomats should learn to distinguish between Soviet public and secret discourse. Few ever could, but it was a hard thing to do. To a doubtful western diplomat, a smiling Litvinov might have quipped, "Well, if you prefer, I can speak the language of the Moscow press."

The salient characteristic of the secret language of the NKID, or NKVT for that matter, is the absence of doctrinal debate. Even Politburo resolutions on foreign policy are free of it.[12] NKID discussions were couched in terms of Soviet national interests and the traditional calculations of trade and realpolitik. If any theorist guided the NKID it was certainly Machiavelli, discretely admired by Lenin, and not Marx and Engels. Or perhaps it was the spirit of Talleyrand, the versatile French foreign minister of many coats, to whom Litvinov was sometimes compared.[13] The disconnection between the *secret* discourse of the NKID and the *public* discourse of Soviet politicians struggling for power is remarkable. Chicherin once said to Rantzau that even Zinoviev, the NKID *bête noire*, was "quite a different man" in private. This confidential remark is revealed in one of Rantzau's reports, though not in Chicherin's, where Zinoviev is the Comintern arsonist.[14] In Soviet politics perhaps more than elsewhere role-playing was essential. Language on stage was different from language backstage. "Speaking Bolshevik" is what one historian calls the public discourse, but "Bolshevik" was not the private, secret language of the NKID.[15]

Rantzau often said the Soviet government could not pursue antithetical policies at the same time. Chicherin and Litvinov agreed and said so to Stalin, often using the German ambassador as a battering ram. This "dual policy," as some historians call it, seems less intentional and doctrinal than inadvertent and improvised.[16] It was the result of circumstances and the need to function in a hostile capitalist world in the midst of an internal struggle for power where foreign policy was often an important political stake. Let me sort out the oppositionists, Stalin might have said to Chicherin in a rare moment of candidness, and then we can deal with our foreign policy issues without distractions. Of course Stalin was not going to confide in Chicherin and sometimes rudely dismissed his arguments, and Litvinov's, in support of common sense.

In view of the inaccessibility of the Russian archives until the 1990s, it was understandable that western historians would focus on public Soviet discussions of foreign policy and therefore on doctrinal disputes. It was all there was, apart from Chicherin's, or more often Litvinov's, sarcastic comments to foreign diplomats, duly recorded in their reports home. Readers may only imagine what these two said in private, which was *not* recorded in documents now found in the archives in Moscow or elsewhere. Chicherin's "testament" gives us an idea.

It is ironic that a focus on Soviet public debates appears to have diverted some historians away from similar debates in the West. There, the secret language of the foreign ministry was much the same as the public language of politics, whether in France, Britain, or the United States. If pragmatists in the Soviet Union had a difficult time, so did pragmatists in the West. The Quai d'Orsay, Foreign Office, and State Department were pullulating hives of anti-communist animosity. Litvinov called it "social antipathy," the "silent conflict," or the "Red scarecrow"; the *polpred* in London, Rozengol'ts, spoke of an "anti-Bolshevik psychosis." Cartoonist Low ridiculed the Tories' "anti-Russian hysteria." White crows in the West like the French politician Herriot resisted the storm as best they could. There were few of them on the branch in France, and fewer still in London or Washington. The Die-Hards dismissed them as "arch-Bolsheviks," naïve amateurs, or "boring," "somewhat dubious" traders of the second rank. The anti-communists were good haters and earnestly hoped for, indeed counted on the imminent collapse of the Soviet state, even at the end of the 1920s, even as "Black Tuesday" approached on Wall Street.

The street corner, or more discreetly the private club, was a good place to hear such chatter over cigars and brandy. "Stand to your glasses," might have been the common toast. "Let's drink to the end of the Bolsh. Here's to them that's dead already; here's to the next to die!"[17]

Anti-communism had a very public face in the Red Scare. The western image of the bloodthirsty Bolshevik clenching a knife between his teeth was omnipresent after 1919. It was propaganda used by the political right to rally support against the left and to win elections. The Soviet Union was not the only place where domestic politics trumped foreign policy. In

Figure 13.2. David Low cartoon, LSE7322, "The Empire Is Saved.—Official," *The Star,* **17 October 1925. British Cartoon Archive.**

France Poincaré sacrificed the interests of more than a million bondholders to pursue an anti-communist electoral campaign in 1927–1928 against the *Cartel* of Socialists and Radicals. In Britain, Tories used the forged "so-called Zinoviev letter" to defeat Labour in the 1924 Parliamentary elections. Cartoonist Low was unrelenting and derided Tory anti-communism as a small, mangy dog surrounded by ranks of police, among other images. "Communism," he mocked, "will abolish baths, umbrellas, motor cars, sausage rolls." In the United States, too, anti-communism was an election issue. Politicians who supported Soviet diplomatic recognition held their tongues until after elections in order to avoid handing an issue to their opponents. In the right-wing press in Europe and the United States anti-communism flourished. For the document forger Orlov, it was the best of times. If the Soviet government was suspicious of western hostility, it had reason to be without any reference to Marxist ideas. Even Soviet paranoia, Litvinov might have joked, was sometimes justified.

As other historians have observed, western anti-communism was reinforced by racism and anti-Semitism. It was a poisonous brew. The western states were colonial powers. Their dark-eyed subjects evoked fear and suspicion, and even more so when aroused to believe in national liberation by Comintern revolutionaries. Hatred of the Bolsheviks was reinforced by the perception of them as "Orientals," "anarchists," "apostate Jews."[18] Soviet policy in China only aggravated these sentiments. President Wilson considered radical Jews on the East Side of New York to be the worst of the worst.

What was it about Gotham's East Side? Wilson, the segregationist, promoted "self-determination" as long as it was not inconvenient and did not apply to American "Negroes." This was the western "dual policy": vaunt democracy and "self-determination of peoples" while maintaining colonial empires and the unequal treaties in China, enforced by gunboats and colored troops commanded by white officers ready to shoot.

Western epigones of the Cold War overlooked their own "dual policy" and drew distinctions between the West and the USSR. "Many people in the Western governments came to hate the Soviet leaders for what they *did*," according to Kennan, an American defender of Cold War policy; "the communists, on the other hand, hated the Western governments for what they *were* [emphasis in the original]."[19] Meet Mr. Pot calling Comrade Kettle black, the very same characters whom readers have encountered many times in the pages of this book. The elites of the West hated the Bolsheviks "for what they were" from the first day they took power, for ideological reasons just as powerful as the Marxist ideas that motivated Soviet leaders.

As for Stalin, he appeared to learn from his mistakes—well, some of them. Soviet China policy was downgraded. After Stalin sacked Bukharin, a member of the Politburo no longer served as general secretary of the Comintern. Litvinov gradually reasserted the prerogatives of the NKID, often writing to Stalin to bridle Comintern or OGPU excesses which needlessly provoked the West. Stalin knew very well what kind of a *narkom* he was getting when he named Litvinov to succeed Chicherin. But there were limits. The Comintern would remain active and vociferous, though Litvinov considered it "hopeless" and had his ideas about how to get rid of it. Stalin would not go that far, for party politics could still trump foreign policy, and he liked to keep his options open. Foreign ambassadors still called at the NKID to complain about the Comintern, and Litvinov continued to offer his stock-in-trade rejoinders. Nevertheless, Stalin appeared more disposed to support a coherent foreign policy, for the overt domestic political battles in which it was a stake were over.

This was a timely development, for the priorities of Soviet foreign policy were about to change. In September 1930 the Nazi Party in Germany made big electoral gains. Henceforth, the Nazis would be a major political force. In January 1933 Adolf Hitler became chancellor of Germany and quickly dispensed with Weimar democracy. Even though Litvinov had launched the Rapallo initiative in the autumn of 1921, he never reckoned it would last forever. Under Hitler, it didn't. Rapallo vanished, as if by prestidigitation, under an avalanche of Nazi anti-Soviet propaganda.

How would the Soviet Union react to events in Germany? Could it adjust to the radical change in European politics created by Hitler's rise to power?

Could France and Britain? To do so, the western powers and the Soviet Union would have to put the "silent conflict" of the 1920s behind them. Could they? It was the old question in the West: who's enemy number one, *Boche* or *Bolcho*? Readers of course now know the easy answer, but hindsight is always 20/20. "Aftermindedness," one historian called it: "It is very hard to remember that events now long in the past were once in the future."[20] In 1933 what became clear to Litvinov and to white crows in the West was not so clear to dominant elites in Paris, London, and Washington. Only time would tell if Stalin and his Anglo-French counterparts would recognize a deadly common enemy, before it was too late, and band together to crush him. Unfortunately, the "silent conflict" was not a good foundation upon which to build a Grand Alliance against Nazi Germany. But that is another story.

Notes

1. F. O. Lindley, no. 312, confidential, 9 Aug. 1929, N3670/18/38, FO 371 14031.

2. Krestinskii to Molotov, Litvinov, et al., no. 3365, personal, secret, 7 Sept. 1929, AVPRF, f. 05, o. 9, p. 43, d. 1, ll. 130–32; and excerpt from Politburo protocol, no. 108, 3 Dec. 1929, *Politbiuro Osoboi papki*, p. 206.

3. R. H. Bruce Lockhart, *Retreat from Glory* (Toronto, 1934), pp. 263, 357–58.

4. Fischer, *Soviets*, p. vi.

5. "Absolutely confidential, very personal, unconditionally secret," nd (but beginning of July 1930), in Chicherin's hand, *Istochnik*, no. 6 (1995), pp. 99–116.

6. George F. Kennan, *Memoirs, 1925–1950* (Boston, 1967), pp. 63–64; and O'Connor, *Chicherin*, p. 162.

7. Memorandum by Schubert, secret, 5 Aug. 1926, AzDAP, B, II, 2, pp. 102–4; and Rantzau to Schubert, no. 809, very secret, 18 July 1928, AA, *Büro Staatssekretär, Band 21*, 4562H/R.29271, E.159.705–6.

8. Cohen, *Bukharin*, pp. 286, 291; Souvarine, *Stalin*, pp. 483–85; and Trotskii, *Stalin*, p. 375.

9. Vatlin, *Komintern*, p. 110.

10. Cohen, *Bukharin*, pp. 291–94.

11. E.g., Jacobson, *Soviet Union*, passim.

12. E.g., *Politbiuro Osoboi papki*, passim.

13. A. M. Kollontai, *Diplomaticheskie dnevniki, 1922–1940*, 2 vols. (Moscow, 2002), entry of 7 May 1939, II, p. 435.

14. Rantzau, no. 237, 29 March 1924, AzDAP, A, IX, pp. 620–22.

15. Stephen Kotkin, *Magnetic Mountain: Stalinism as a Civilization* (Berkeley, Calif., 1995).

16. Jacobson, *Soviet Union*, pp. 44–46 and passim.

17. Cf., Bennett, *Zinoviev Letter*, p. 55, n. 64.

18. Foglesong, *American Mission*, pp. 58–59.

19. Kennan, *Russia and the West*, p. 181.

20. Citing Frederick William Maitland, A. J. P. Taylor, *The Origins of the Second World War* (Harmondsworth, 1964), p. 282; and Stephen A. Schuker, "The End of Versailles," in Gordon Martel (ed.), *The Origins of the Second World War Reconsidered*, 2nd ed. (London, 1999), pp. 38–56.

~

Selected Bibliography

Archival Collections

France
Archives nationales, Paris
Bibliothèque nationale, Paris
Ministère des Affaires étrangères, Paris
Ministère des Finances, Paris
Service historique de l'armée de terre, Château de Vincennes

Great Britain
National Archives of the United Kingdom, Kew
India Office archives, London

Russian Federation
Arkhiv vneshnei politiki Rossiiskoi Federatsii, Moscow
Rossiiskii gosudarstvennyi arkhiv sotsial'no-politicheskoi istorii, Moscow

United States
National Archives, Washington, D.C.

Published Archival Collections

Akten zur deutschen auswärtigen Politik 1918–1945, series A (1918–1925), 14 vols.; series B (1925–1933), 21 vols. Baden-Baden and Frankfurt, 1966–1993.
Documents on British Foreign Policy, 1919–1939, 1st series, 27 vols.; 1a series, 7 vols.; 2nd series, 21 vols. London, 1947–.

Dokumenty vneshnei politiki SSSR. 24 vols. Moscow, 1958–.

Lubianka: Stalin i VchK-GPU-OGPU-NKVD, ianvar' 1922–dekabr' 1936: dokumenty. Moscow, 2003.

Moskva-Berlin: Politika i diplomatiia Kremlia, 1920–1941, 3 vols. Moscow, 2011.

Moskva-Rim: Politika i diplomatiia Kremlia, 1920–1939. Moscow, 2002.

Moskva-Tokio: Politika i diplomatiia Kremlia, 1921–1931, 2 vols. Moscow, 2007.

Moskva-Vashington: Politika i diplomatiia Kremlia, 1921–1941, 3 vols. Moscow, 2009.

Perepiska I. V. Stalina i G. V. Chicherina s Polpredom SSSR v Kitae A. M. Karakhanom, 1923–1926gg. Moscow, 2008.

Politbiuro TsK, RKP(b)-VKP(b) i Evropa: Resheniia 'osoboi papki,' 1923–1939. Moscow, 2001.

Politbiuro TsK, RKP(b)-VKP(b) i Komintern, 1919–1943, dokumenty. Moscow, 2004.

Rossiia i SShA: Ekonomicheskie otnosheniia, 1917–1933. Moscow, 1997.

Russkaia voennaia emigratsiia, 20-x–40-x godov, 6 vols. Moscow, 1998–.

Sovetsko-Amerikanskie otnosheniia: Gody nepriznaniia, 1918–1926, dokumenty. Moscow, 2002.

Sovetsko-Amerikanskie otnosheniia: Gody nepriznaniia, 1927–1933, dokumenty. Moscow, 2002.

VChK-OGPU v gody Novoi Ekonomicheskoi Politiki, 1921–1928. Moscow, 2006.

VKP(b), Komintern i Kitai, 1920–1943, dokumenty, 8 vols. Moscow, 1994–2007.

Books and Articles

Alekseev, Mikhail. *Sovetskaia voennaia razvedka v Kitae i khronika "kitaiskoi smuty" (1922–1929)*. Moscow, 2010.

Andrew, Christopher. *Secret Service: The Making of the British Intelligence Community*. London, 1987.

Barbusse, Henri. *Le feu*. Paris, 1917.

Bennett, Gill. *"A Most Extraordinary and Mysterious Business": The Zinoviev Letter of 1924*. London, 1999.

Borzecki, Jerzy. *The Soviet-Polish Peace of 1921 and the Creation of Interwar Europe*. New Haven, 2008.

Broué, Pierre. *Histoire de l'Internationale communiste, 1919–1943*. Paris, 1997.

Carley, Michael Jabara. "The Politics of Anti-Bolshevism: The French Government and the Russo-Polish War, December 1919–May 1920." *Historical Journal*, vol. 19, no. 1 (March 1976), pp. 163–89.

———. "The Origins of the French Intervention in the Russian Civil War, January–May 1918: A Reappraisal." *Journal of Modern History*, vol. 48, no. 3 (Sept. 1976), pp. 413–39.

———. "Anti-Bolshevism in French Foreign Policy: The Crisis in Poland in 1920." *International History Review*, vol. 2, no. 3 (July 1980), pp. 410–31.

———. *Revolution and Intervention: The French Government and the Russian Civil War, 1917–1919*. Montréal, 1983.

———. "Allied Intervention and the Russian Civil War, 1917–1922." *International History Review*, vol. 11, no. 4 (Nov. 1989), pp. 689–700.

———. "From Revolution to Dissolution: The Quai d'Orsay, the Banque Russo-Asiatique, and the Chinese Eastern Railway, 1917–1926." *International History Review*, vol. 12, no. 4 (Nov. 1990), pp. 721–61.

———. "Five Kopecks for Five Kopecks: Franco-Soviet Trade Relations, 1928–1939." *Cahiers du monde russe et soviétique*, vol. 33, no. 1 (Jan.–March 1992), pp. 23–58.

———. "Down a Blind-Alley: Anglo-Franco-Soviet Relations, 1920–1939." *Canadian Journal of History*, vol. 29, no. 1 (avril 1994), pp. 147–72.

———. "Prelude to Defeat: Franco-Soviet Relations, 1919–1939." *Historical Reflections*, vol. 22, no. 1 (Winter 1996), pp. 159–88.

———. "Episodes from the Early Cold War: Franco-Soviet Relations, 1917–1927." *Europe-Asia Studies*, vol. 52, no. 7 (Nov. 2000), pp. 1275–1305.

———. "Behind Stalin's Moustache: Pragmatism in Early Soviet Foreign Policy, 1917–1941." *Diplomacy & Statecraft*, vol. 12, no. 3 (Sept. 2001), pp. 159–74.

———. "A Soviet Eye on France from the rue de Grenelle, 1924–1940." *Diplomacy & Statecraft*, vol. 17, no. 2 (June 2006), pp. 295–346.

Carley, Michael Jabara, and Richard Kent Debo. "Always in Need of Credit: The USSR and Franco-German Economic Co-operation, 1926–1929." *French Historical Studies* (Purdue University), vol. 20, no. 3 (Summer 1997), pp. 315–56.

Carr, E. H. *The Bolshevik Revolution, 1917–1923*, 3 vols. Baltimore, 1966.

———. *The Interregnum, 1923–1924*. Harmondsworth, 1969.

———. *Socialism in One Country, 1924–1926*, 3 vols. Harmondsworth, 1970–1972.

Chicherin, Georgii V. *Stat'i i rechi*. Moscow, 1961.

———. "'Diktatura Iazykocheshushchikh nad Rabotaiushchimi': *Posledniaia sluzhebnaia zapiska G. V. Chicherina*." *Istochnik*, no. 6 (1995), pp. 99–116.

Cohen, Stephen F. *Bukharin and the Bolshevik Revolution: A Political Biography, 1888–1938*. New York, 1975.

Conte, Francis. *Christian Rakovski (1873–1941)*. Boulder, Co., 1989.

D'Agostino, Anthony. *The Rise of the Global Powers: International Politics in the Era of the World Wars*. Cambridge, 2012.

Davis, Donald E., and Eugene P. Trani. *The First Cold War: The Legacy of Woodrow Wilson in U.S.-Soviet Relations*. Columbia, Mo., 2002.

Debo, Richard Kent. *Revolution and Survival: The Foreign Policy of Soviet Russia, 1917–1918*. Toronto, 1979.

———. *Survival and Consolidation: The Foreign Policy of Soviet Russia, 1918–1921*. Montréal, 1992.

———. "G. V. Chicherin: A Historical Perspective." In Gabriel Gorodetsky (ed.), *Soviet Foreign Policy, 1917–1991: A Retrospective*. London, 1994, pp. 21–30.

Dessberg, Frédéric. *Le triangle impossible: Les relations franco-soviétiques et le facteur polonais dans les questions de sécurité en Europe (1924–1935)*. Brussels, 2009.

Deutscher, Isaac. *Stalin: A Political Biography*. New York, 1960.

———. *Trotsky*, 3 vols. New York, 1965.

Fel'shtinskii, Iurii, and Georgii Cherniavskii. *Lev Trotskii*, 4 vols. Moscow, 2013.

Fink, Carole. *The Genoa Conference: European Diplomacy, 1921–1922*. Chapel Hill, 1984.

Fischer, Fritz. *Germany's Aims in the First World War*. New York, 1967.

Fischer, Louis. *The Soviets in World Affairs: A History of the Relations between the Soviet Union and the Rest of the World, 1917–1929*, abridged edition. New York, 1951.

Foglesong, David S. *America's Secret War against Bolshevism: U.S. Intervention in the Russian Civil War, 1917–1920*. Chapel Hill, 1995.

———. *The American Mission and the "Evil Empire": The Crusade for a "Free Russia" since 1881*. Cambridge, 2007.

Gardner, Lloyd C. *Safe for Democracy: The Anglo-American Response to Revolution, 1913–1923*. New York, 1984.

Gatzke, Hans W. *Stresemann and the Rearmament of Germany.* New York, 1969.

Golovko, V. A., M. G. Stanchev, and G. I. Cherniavskii. *Mezhdu Moskvoi i Zapadom: Diplomaticheskaia deiatel'nost' Kh. G. Rakvoskogo.* Kharkov, 1994.

Gorlov, Sergei. *Sovershenno sekretno, Moskva–Berlin, 1920–1933: Voenno-politcheskie otnosheniia mezhdu SSSR i Germaniei.* Moscow, 1999.

Gorodetsky, Gabriel. *The Precarious Truce: Anglo-Soviet Relations, 1924–1927.* Cambridge, 1977.

——— (ed.). *Soviet Foreign Policy, 1917–1991: A Retrospective.* London, 1994.

Haslam, Jonathan. "Litvinov, Stalin and the Road Not Taken." In Gabriel Gorodetsky (ed.), *Soviet Foreign Policy, 1917–1991: A Retrospective.* London, 1994, pp. 55–62.

Heywood, Andrew. *Modernising Lenin's Russia: Economic Reconstruction, Foreign Trade and the Railways.* Cambridge, 1999.

Hogenhuis-Seliverstoff, Anne. *Les Relations franco-soviétiques, 1917–1924.* Paris, 1981.

Isaacs, Harold R. *The Tragedy of the Chinese Revolution.* Stanford, 1961.

Jacobson, Jon. *Locarno Diplomacy: Germany and the West, 1925–1929.* Princeton, 1972.

———. *When the Soviet Union Entered World Politics.* Berkeley, 1994.

———. "On the Historiography of Soviet Foreign Relations in the 1920s." *International History Review,* vol. 18, no. 2 (May 1996), pp. 336–57.

Jeanneney, Jean-Noël. *L'Argent caché.* Paris, 1981.

Jeffrey, Keith. *The Secret History of MI6.* New York, 2010.

Joffe, Nadezhda A. *Back in Time: My Life, My Fate, My Epoch.* Translated by Frederic S. Choate. Oak Park, Mich., 1995.

Kartunova, A. I. (ed.). *V. K. Bliukher v Kitae 1924–1927gg. Novye dokumenty glavnogo voennogo sovetnika.* Moscow, 2003.

Kennan, George F. *Russia and the West under Lenin and Stalin.* New York, 1960.

Khlevniuk, Oleg V. *Master of the House: Stalin and his Inner Circle.* New Haven, 2009.

Khromov, Semen S. *Leonid Krasin: Neisvestnye stranitsy biografii, 1920–1926gg.* Moscow, 2001.

Kochan, Lionel. *Russia and the Weimar Republic.* Cambridge, 1954.

Lenin, V. I. *On the Foreign Policy of the Soviet State.* Moscow, 1967.

Lewin, Moshe. *Lenin's Last Struggle.* New York, 1970.

Lih, Lars T., et al. (eds.). *Stalin's Letters to Molotov.* New Haven, 1995.

Lockhart, R. H. Bruce. *British Agent.* New York, 1933.

———. *Retreat from Glory.* Glasgow, 1934.

Marks, Sally. *The Illusion of Peace: International Relations in Europe, 1918–1933,* 2nd edition. Houndmills, 2003.

Mayer, Arno J. *Politics and Diplomacy of Peacemaking: Containment and Counter Revolution at Versailles, 1918–1919.* New York, 1967.

McFadden, David W. *Alternative Paths: Soviets and Americans, 1917–1920.* New York, 1993.

Neilson, Keith. "Stalin's Moustache: The Soviet Union and the Coming of the War." *Diplomacy & Statecraft,* vol. 12, no. 2 (June 2001), pp. 197–208.

———. *Britain, Soviet Russia and the Collapse of the Versailles Order, 1919–1939.* Cambridge, 2006.

Nekrich, Aleksandr M. *Pariahs, Partners, Predators: German-Soviet Relations, 1922–1941.* New York, 1997.

O'Connor, Timothy Edward. *Diplomacy and Revolution: G. V. Chicherin and Soviet Foreign Affairs, 1918–1930.* Ames, Iowa, 1988.

———. *The Engineer of Revolution: L. B. Krasin and the Bolsheviks, 1870–1926.* Boulder, Co., 1992.

Oudin, Bernard. *Aristide Briand. La paix: une idée neuve en Europe*. Paris, 1987.

Phillips, Hugh D. *Between the Revolution and the West: A Political Biography of Maxim M. Litvinov*. Boulder, Co., 1992.

Pons, Silvio, and Andrea Romano (eds.). *Russia in the Age of War, 1914–1945*. Milano, 2000.

Resis, Albert (ed.). *Molotov Remembers: Inside Kremlin Politics, Conversations with Felix Chuev*. Chicago, 1993.

Roberts, Geoffrey. "Stalin, the Pact with Nazi Germany, and the Origins of Postwar Soviet Diplomatic Historiography." *Journal of Cold War Studies*, vol. 4, no. 4 (Fall 2004), pp. 93–103.

Service, Robert. *Lenin: A Biography*. Cambridge, MA, 2000.

——. *Stalin: A Biography*. Cambridge, MA, 2004.

Sevost'ianov, G. N. *Moskva-Vashington: Na puti k priznaniiu, 1918–1933*. Moscow, 2004.

Sheinis, Z. *Maksim Maksimovich Litvinov. Revoliutsioner, diplomat, chelovek*. Moscow, 1989.

Shishkin, V. A. *Sovetskoe gosudarstvo i strany Zapada v 1917–1923gg*. Leningrad, 1969.

——. *V. I. Lenin i vneshne-ekonomicheskaia politika sovetskogo gosudarstva (1917–1923gg.)*. Leningrad, 1977.

——. *Tsena priznaniia: SSSR i strany Zapada v poiskax kompromissa (1924–1929gg.)*. St. Petersburg, 1991.

——. *Stanovlenie vneshnei politiki poslerevoliutsionnoi Rossii (1917–1930 gody) i kapitalisticheskii mir*. St. Petersburg, 2002.

Souvarine, Boris. *Stalin*. New York, 1939.

Steiner, Zara. *The Lights That Failed: European International History, 1919–1933*. New York, 2005.

Trotskii, L. D. *Stalin*. New York, 1967.

——. *Problems of the Chinese Revolution*. Ann Arbor, 1967.

——. *My Life*. New York, 1970.

Tucker, Robert C. *Stalin as Revolutionary, 1879–1929*. New York, 1974.

Ulam, Adam B. *Stalin: The Man and His Era*. New York, 1973.

Uldricks, Teddy J. "Russia and Europe: Diplomacy, Revolution, and Economic Development in the 1920s." *International History Review*, vol. 1, no. 1 (Jan. 1979), pp. 55–83.

Ullman, Richard H. *Anglo-Soviet Relations, 1917–1921*, 3 vols. Princeton, NJ, 1961–1972.

Vatlin, Aleksandr Iu. *Komintern: Pervye desiat' let*. Moscow, 1993.

Wheeler-Bennett, John W. *Brest-Litovsk: The Forgotten Peace, March 1918*. London, 1963.

White, Christine A. *British and American Commercial Relations with Soviet Russia, 1918–1924*. Chapel Hill, 1992.

White, Stephen. *The Origins of Détente: The Genoa Conference and Soviet-Western Relations, 1921–1922*. Cambridge, 1985.

Williams, Andrew J. *Trading with the Bolsheviks: The Politics of East-West Trade, 1920–1939*. Manchester, 1992.

Wilson, Joan Hoff. *Ideology and Economics: U.S. Relations with the Soviet Union, 1918–1933*. Columbia, Mo., 1974.

Wohl, Robert. *French Communism in the Making, 1914–1924*. Stanford, 1966.

Young, Robert J. *Power and Pleasure: Louis Barthou and the Third French Republic*. Montréal, 1991.

——. *An American by Degrees: The Extraordinary Lives of French Ambassador Jules Jusserand*. Montréal, 2009.

Index

biography of, 187–88; "Briand knows," 283; on China, 193, 270–71, 287, 288–89; and "Die-Hards," 191, 205, 216, 261, 280; and Krasin, 218–19; and Labour/TUC, 210–11, 214, 269; and Litvinov, 272, 280, 286, 293; Low's representations of, *157, 158*; meeting with Chicherin, 207–8, 210, 216, 261; meeting with Herriot, 144; one of "Good Fairies," 157, 395; and Rakovskii, 108, 191; "steady, don't let us get jumpy," 186–87; "we're not going to war with USSR," 293

Chamberlain, Joseph, 187
Chamberlain, Neville, 187
Chanak crisis, 65
Cheka, Soviet Russia, 150
Chiang Kai-shek, 261, 265, 266, 267, 286, 287, 290, 354, 355; *coup de force* in Shanghai, 287–88; Trojan Horse of revolution, 264
Chicago Tribune, 227–28
Chicherin, Georgii V., xii, 34, 35, 40, 48, *61*, 71, 87, 109, 117, 143, 147, 154, 161, 185, 200, 213, 222, 230, *242, 245,* 272, 278, 282, 284, 290, 319, 355, 371, *387,* 409, *410,* 415, 423; on "allowances" for French press, 174–75; Barthou's appreciation of, 56–57, 58; on Berthelot, 170; biography of, 30–33; on British trade unionists, 208–9, 211, 212; on CER, 266, 413; on China, 191, 194–95, 196, 198, 201, 262, 264, 266, 291, 418; and Citrine, 208–9; on Comintern, 46, 181, 195, 258, 274, 326, 412–13, 416; complaint to Politburo, 164, 214; and Curzon, 49; death of (1936), 413; on debts, 302–3; "eastern policy," 106–7, 266; and "English gold," 106–7, 184; Foreign Office views of, 33, 192, 194–95; and France, 83, 98, 134–35, 142, 162, 264–65, 302–3, 305, 313, 321, 326–27, 331, 333, 334, 335, 337–38; and French Communist Party, 312; and French "distant princess," 172, 312; and Genoa Conference, 51–52, 54, 56–58, 61–62, 306; and Germany, 81–82, 96–97, 145–46, 150–52, 159, 241, 243, 244, 246, 250, 251, 258, 275, 276, 331, 387,

388, 391, 394, 395; and Great Britain, 54, 65–66, 85–86, 103, 106–7, 110, 114–15, 201, 206, 208–9, 210, 215, 217, 218; on Great Russian imperialism, 266, 413; and Herriot, 76, 134; on Hoelz affair, 388–89, 390, 412; and Japan, 265; and Karakhan, *185, 242,* 411; and Krasin, 85–86, 141–42; and Krestinskii, 411; "lamb" and "wolf," 209, 219; and Litvinov, 41, 111, 327–28, 374–75, 411–12, 413, 418; on MacDonald, 115; and meeting with Chamberlain, 207–8, 210, 261; and meeting with Poincaré, 310, 311–12; and Monzie, 77–78, 134, 166, 167; and National City Bank, 313–18, 373, 374–75; on OGPU, 252, 413; on Poland, 244, 251; and Rakovskii, 106–7, 111, 321, 322–23, 326, 328 29, 333; relations with Brockdorff-Rantzau, 148; relations with Herbette, 326, 328–30, 334, 338, 371; and Shakhty affair, 392, 394; on Soviet press, 274, 268, 412; and Stalin, 32, 81–82, 152–53, 412, 417, 419, 421; "testament," 411–13; and Turkey, 65; and United States, 88, 89–90, 221, 223, 265, 313, 315; visits to Paris, 302–3, 310–12; and Voroshilov, 250, 419; "what . . . fly has bitten Herbette's butt," 331; and Zinoviev, 96–97, 146, 148, 149, 419, 420; and "Zinoviev letter," 123, 129, 130
Childs, Sir Wyndham, 50
China, 37, 51, 65, 105, 133, 182, 184, 188, 190, 192, 193, 194, 196, 197, 199, 200, 201, 205, 207, 218, 219, 261, 265, 267, 268, 269–70, 273, 276–77, 278, 279, 281, 282, 284, 286, 289, 301, 307, 309, 310, 354–55, 418, 419, 423; Boxer rebellion, 189; "Christ will win out," 188; "despatch . . . a Division," 186; "the enemy has come in like a flood," 188; "gigantic powder box," 189; "helpless man," 287; "our prayers . . . have been answered," 291–92; semi-colony, 37, 105, 264; "sudden bolt to Bolshevism," 189; "unequal treaties," 182, 186, 190, 262
Chinese Communist Party, 105, 198, 199, 201, 263, 264, 287, 355; "bloc within," 263, 265, 266

~

About the Author

Michael Jabara Carley holds a doctorate from Queen's University in Kingston, Ontario, and is professor of history at the *Université de Montréal*. He has published widely in twentieth-century international politics, notably Soviet relations with the West and the origins of World War II. Based on extensive research in U.S., British, French, and Soviet archives, his histories are narrated in an engaging style that brings watershed moments to life. He is the author of *1939: The Alliance That Never Was and the Coming of World War II* (Ivan R. Dee, 1999), which has also been published in French, Russian, and Italian editions.